MILITARY Living's

TEMPORARY Military Lodging

AROUND THE WORLD

by

William "Roy" Crawford, Sr., Ph.D.
Chief Executive Officer, Military Marketing Services, Inc.
and Military Living Publications

and

L. Ann Crawford
Executive Vice President, Military Marketing Services, Inc.
and Publisher, Military Living Publications

and

R.J. Crawford - President, Military Marketing Services, Inc.
and Military Living Publications

Editor - Deborah K. Harder

Graphic Designer - Lynn Olinger Amri

Military Living Publications
P.O. Box 2347
Falls Church, Virginia 22042-0347
TEL: 703-237-0203 - Fax: 703-237-2233
E-mail: militaryliving@aol.com
www.militaryliving.com

NOTICE

The information in this book has been compiled and edited either from the activity/installation listed, its superior headquarters, or from other sources that may or may not be noted by the authors. Information about the facilities listed, including addresses, contact phone numbers and rate structures, could change. This directory/book should be used as a guide to the listed facilities with this understanding. Please forward any corrections or additions to: **Military Living Publications, P.O. Box 2347, Falls Church, Virginia 22042-0347. TEL: 703-237-0203, FAX: 703-237-2233, E-mail: militaryliving@aol.com.**

This directory is published by Military Marketing Services, Inc., T/A Military Living Publications, a private business in no way connected with the U.S. Federal or any other government. This book is copyrighted by L. Ann and William Roy Crawford, Sr. Opinions expressed by the publisher and authors of this book are their own and are not to be considered an official expression by any government agency or official.

The information and statements contained in this directory have been compiled from sources believed to be reliable and to represent the best current opinion (at press time) on the subject. No warranty, guarantee, or representation is made by Military Marketing Services, Inc., or Military Living Publications as to the absolute correctness or sufficiency of any representation contained in this or other publications and we can assume no responsibility.

Library of Congress Cataloging-in-Publication Data

Crawford, Ann Caddell.
    Temporary military lodging around the world /by L. Ann Crawford and William "Roy"
Crawford, Sr. ; editor J.J. Caddell.
      p. cm.
    Includes index.
    ISBN 0-914862-90-1
    1. United States--Armed Forces--Barracks and quarters--Directories. 2. Military bases,
American--Directories. I. Crawford, William Roy, 1932- II. Caddell, J.J. III. Title.

UC403 .C72 2000
355.7'1'0973--dc21   00-060573

ISBN 0-914862-90-1

INTRODUCTION

This book will pay for itself many times over. All you have to do is use it! There are places to stay on military installations for as little as $5 to $8 per night. The most common charges we found quoted were in the $35-$50 price range for a family of five sharing one unit in a transient lodging facility, or $41-$56 for a Navy Lodge unit, most of which have sleeping space for five, wall-to-wall carpeting, color TV, kitchenette with all utensils, and more. Since our last edition, inflation has caused some military lodging prices to increase; however, they have not increased to the same extent or at the same rate as prices in the civilian sector. In some large cities, the commercial cost of lodging has risen to $250 per night, or more. Clearly, *Temporary Military Lodging Around the World* can greatly reduce the high cost of travel experienced by military families.

Before the first edition of this book was published in 1971, there was a big "catch" involved in getting to use temporary lodging facilities. The problem was finding out which installation had what. Military Living Publications has solved that problem by doing the leg work for you. Just glance through the hundreds of listings that follow and you will find out why this book is indispensable if you want to "travel on less per day . . . the military way!"

HOW TO USE THIS DIRECTORY

Each listing has similar information, listed in the following order:

Official Name of Installation (AL01R2)
Complete installation mailing address, including street number or building number, street name, city or installation, state and zip codes. Overseas or foreign installation addresses may include unit/organization name, unit designation, APO/FPO region and numbers and/or complete foreign country addresses including city, country and postal codes.
Scheduled to close month/day/year (if applicable).

Location Identifier: Example: (AL03R2). The first two-character set (letters) is U.S. state/possession or foreign country abbreviations used in Military Living's books. The next two-character set is random numbers (00-99) assigned to a specific geographic location (military installation). The fifth character, the letter R, is our symbol for region. The sixth character indicates one of nine precise geographic regions.

TELEPHONE NUMBER INFORMATION: C- This is the commercial telephone service for the installation's main or information/operator assistance number. The designation "C" has also been used for other commercial numbers in this directory, including the number to be called for temporary military lodging reservations. Within the North American Area Code System, the first three digits are the area code. For foreign country locations, we have provided full telephone numbers for dialing from the U.S. and in-country. The first two to three digits, after direct dial long distance (011), are the Country Code, the next one to four digits are the city code, if used (consult your local directory or operator for specific dialing instructions). The next three digits are the area telephone exchange/switch number. For foreign countries, the exchange number can be either fewer or more digits than in the U.S. system. The last four digits are usually the information or operator assistance number or the individual telephone line number. In the United Kingdom (UK), dialing instructions are given from the telephone exchange serving the installation. These numbers are different for each location in the UK from which you are dialing.

Consult the local directory or operator for specific dialing instructions. The extensive increase in the use of telephones over the past few years as the result of cell telephones, computer modems and fax service has required many changes in the numbering plans of all telephone systems worldwide. New area and country codes have been created to meet the overall new demands for telephone services around the world. Also, to meet this expanded need for telephone service, new switch numbers have been created along with new city codes for foreign countries. In many U.S. metropolitan areas, because of new and overlapping area codes, it is often now necessary to dial the ten-digit number. Lastly, many line numbers have been changed and new ones added. **We see these changes continuing to meet the needs of the ever-expanding demand for telephone services worldwide.**

DSN- This is the Department of Defense, worldwide, Defense Switched Network. We have, at the request of our readers, included the DSN prefix (area voice codes) with most numbers in each listing. (For example, the area code/DSN prefix for CONUS is 312. This prefix is not used when calling from one point within CONUS to another; it is used only when dialing from outside CONUS.) In most cases, the DSN number given is for information/operator assistance.

FAX: Fax numbers are listed for reservations when available.

E-mail: The e-mail address of the Reservation Information office is listed when available.

WEB: The web site address when available.

LOCATOR: The telephone number for installation civilian and/or military (employees/residents) locator service.

MEDICAL: The telephone number for emergency medical or ambulance services.

SECURITY POLICE: The telephone number for emergency police protection or consultation.

LOCATION: Here you will find specific driving instructions to the temporary military lodging location from local major cities, interstate/country highways and routes. More than one routing may be provided. USMRA: Coordinates in Military Living's *United States Military Road Atlas* which are given for each CONUS and U.S. Possession location. EUSMRA: Coordinates in Military Living's *European United States Military Road Atlas* are given when available. **NMC:** is the nearest major city. Distance in miles or kilometers as appropriate in use in the country and directions from the temporary military lodging (TML) location to the nearest major city are provided.

RESERVATION INFORMATION: We have listed the complete address for contacting the temporary military lodging office via mail. The building number, street address, etc., are listed to provide you the physical location of the lodging office. The C- and/or DSN- telephone numbers and fax numbers along with the e-mail address of the temporary military lodging office are given when provided to us. **We have "bolded" (darkened) reservation numbers for the convenience of our readers - this should help, particularly when making expensive overseas calls.** Hours of operation of the temporary military lodging office, main desk, or contact office are listed. Check in/check out points and times are given. Use of TML by government civilian employees on duty and leave (vacation), where appropriate is specified. Other helpful general temporary military lodging information is detailed. E-mail addresses, when available, are listed at the end of each lodging office text. Anything unusual or unique about each lodging facility is listed here.

TML: (Temporary Military Lodging) Each category of TML, i.e., Guest House, Hotel, Army/Navy/Air Force/Marine Corps Lodge, and so on, is listed separately in most cases. The category of occupancy, i.e., all ranks, specific grades, officer, enlisted, male, female, is given. Occupancy by leave or duty status is given. Reservation requirements and some contact telephone numbers are listed. The accommodations (bedroom, two bedroom, three bedroom, separate bedroom, suite), and number of each category of accommodation is given last in parentheses. Appointments, services and supporting facilities such as kitchens, utensils, television, air conditioning, maid service, cribs, cots, washer/dryer, ice, vending machines, handicapped facilities, etc., are given where they were provided to us. Where there is a charge for services it is noted, otherwise it is free. Whether the structure is older or modern, its condition, and if renovations or improvements have taken place since 1995 are specified. The per day rates are listed for each category of occupant. Please note that rates can change often. Priorities and restrictions on occupancy are listed. **NOTE:** Pets are not allowed in temporary lodging facilities unless otherwise noted, but for the convenience of our readers we have noted where kennel facilities are available. Also, all facilities are open to men and women unless otherwise noted.

DV/VIP: (Distinguished Visitor/Very Important Person) The contact office or person, building, room and telephone number for DV/VIP lodging and other support is given where available. The grade/status for DV/VIPs at the installation is specified. The use of DV/VIP facilities/services by retirees and lower grades is indicated.

TML AVAILABILITY: The best and most difficult times for TML are listed as reported. If possible, call, fax or write regarding availability before you travel or take your chances on space-available use.

POINTS OF INTEREST: Points of interest for visitors are indicated and are bolded near the bottom of the installation listing. Some listings carry military information of interest to visitors such as famous units stationed, or on post/base military museums.

Please review Appendix A, General Abbreviations, Appendix C, Billeting Regulations and Policies. Also see Appendix B, Temporary Military Lodging Questions and Answers about TML Regulations that supplement the basic TML listings and Appendix D, Telephone Information.

NEW CATEGORIES OF INFORMATION: In an effort to give the traveler more elements of essential travel information we have included the following categories of information in recent editions.

AMENITIES: Supporting features such as Meeting/Conference Rooms, Snack Vending Machines and Soft Drink Machines, Ice Machines, Exercise Equipment and Rooms, TV or Game Rooms and etc.

CREDIT CARDS ACCEPTED: The credit/debit cards accepted by each installation are listed.

TRANSPORTATION: Local on and off the installation transportation means and contacts are listed.

DINING OPPORTUNITIES: Dining facilities within walking distance and within a short drive.

NEW OR DIFFERENT INFORMATION: If you find new or different information please send this information to Military Living Publications to receive a valuable reward.

Military Living Publications
ATTN: Editor - TML or Ann/Roy Sr.
P.O. Box 2347
Falls Church, VA 22042-0347

BASE CLOSURES

The following installations no longer offered temporary lodging as of 2001 due to closure or downsizing: McClellan Air Force Base, CA (30 June); Letterkenny Army Depot, PA (1 September); Bad Kreuznach Community, DE (July).

The 1995 Defense Base Closure and Realignment Commission's Report was accepted by Congress and became Public Law on 28 September 1995.

The 1995 law, along with previous directed closures and realignments in the basic law in 1988, 1990, 1991 and 1993, complete the base closure and realignments which have been approved by Congress. These directed closures have been noted at the beginning of each listing affected with the DoD estimated date of final closure. Most bases have already closed and consequently have been deleted from this edition.

It should also be noted that final closure dates will be established for each installation. These dates could change as the DoD completes the final closure plans and as funding becomes available to effect the closures. Support facilities on the affected bases will normally decrease gradually; therefore, it is best to check with each military installation scheduled for closure or realignment before you go. Some bases scheduled for closure or realignment do not have temporary lodging and, consequently, are not listed in this book. There are very few (less than five) installations remaining for closure under the Defense Base Closure and Realignment Laws.

We have noted in the title of each listing scheduled for closure, the planned closure of the temporary lodging facility.

Lastly, it should be noted that the 1995 Defense Base Closure and Realignment Law along with previous base closure laws only apply to domestic United States Bases and United States Bases located in U.S. possessions. The Secretary of Defense, acting within his authority, can close bases located in foreign countries. Under this authority, in late 2000, the Department of Defense announced the closure of bases in the Kitzingen Community, Germany.

Some Words About Our Changing World

The military is undergoing sweeping changes which have made this book both challenging and interesting to publish. Some installations are closing, and others are realigning. We have included the dates of expected closure as provided to us at the beginning of each listing. Installations which will close prior to March 2001 have been excluded from this book. The information in this book is as accurate as we can make it. The information in this book has been provided by billeting facilities worldwide. However, as with all directories, there are changes occurring daily that cause inaccuracies. Military Living Publications has always relied on its readers to write or call when information has become outdated. It is the secret of our success. Please do not hesitate to let us know when information is incorrect, or if we have missed a lodging opportunity for your fellow travelers. Enjoy.

PHOTO CREDITS

COVER PHOTO CREDITS

Marines' Memorial Club, San Francisco, CA
Photo courtesy of the Marines' Memorial Club

Cape Henry Inn, Fort Story, VA
Military Living Photo Archives

Fourth Cliff Recreation Area, Humarock, MA
Photo courtesy of Fourth Cliff Recreation Area

Seward Resort, AK
Photo courtesy of Seward Resort, AK

Navy Lodge Welcomes You!
Photo courtesy of the Navy Lodge Program

Wainwright Hall, Fort Myer, VA
Photo courtesy of Fort Myer Marketing

The Inn at Schofield Barracks, HI
Photo courtesy of Schofield Barracks, HI

The Mologne House Hotel, WRAMC, Washington, D.C.
Photo courtesy of the Mologne House Hotel

The Hale Koa Hotel, Honolulu, HI
Photo courtesy of the Hale Koa Hotel

TEXT PHOTO CREDITS

Fort Tuthill Recreation Area, AZ
Military Living Photo Archives

March Air Reserve Base, CA
Military Living Photo Archives

North Island Naval Air Station, CA
Military Living Photo Archives

Mayport Naval Station, FL
Military Living Photo Archives

Key West Naval Air Station, FL
Military Living Photo Archives

Shades of Green on Walt Disney World®, FL
Military Living Photo Archives

The Inn at Schofield Barracks , HI
Military Living Photo Archives

Waianae Army Recreation Center, HI
Photo Courtesy of Karen Donovan

Staten Island Navy Lodge, NY
Military Living Photo Archives

Short Stay Recreation Area, SC
Military Living Photo Archives

The Cape Henry Inn, Fort Story, VA
Military Living Photo Archives

Knadle Hall at Fort Belvoir, VA
Photo Courtesy of Fort Belvoir

La Fondation Furtado Heine, Nice, France
Photo Courtesy of La Fondation Furtado Heine

The Franklin House at Mannheim, Germany
Military Living Photo Archives

Royal Fleet Club, United Kingdom
Photo Courtesy of the Royal Fleet Club

CENTRAL RESERVATION SYSTEMS

The United States Army, the United States Navy and the United States Air Force have central reservation systems for temporary military lodging, operating through 1-800 toll-free telephone numbers. At press time, the United States Marine Corps and the United States Coast Guard had not established central reservation services for temporary military lodging. The following information is provided for these central reservations systems:

ARMY LODGING RESERVATIONS
1-800-GO-ARMY-1 (1-800-462-7691)

United States Army Lodging Reservations: The Army Central Reservation Center (ACRC), located at Redstone Arsenal, Alabama, is an ongoing Army "Quality of Life" initiative of the Business Programs Directorate of the U.S. Army Community and Family Support Center. The ACRC also includes the *Lodging Success Program*, which gives official duty travelers the opportunity to make reservations at conveniently located, high-quality, economically priced commercial hotels in Atlanta, GA; Hampton/Newport News, VA; Miami, FL; National Capital Region (Washington, D.C. area); San Antonio, TX; and San Juan, PR. The ACRC may be used by active duty military personnel and DoD civilians on official TDY/TAD travel orders to Army installations, soldiers and their families on permanent change of station (PCS) orders to Army installations and Army Reservists on official travel to Army facilities.

This is how the ACRC operates: When you call the toll-free number **1-800-GO-ARMY-1 (1-800-462-7691)** you will hear three choices:

Dial 1 to make reservations for on-post lodging in a temporary duty or permanent change of station status or to make *Lodging Success Program* reservations for official travel. ACRC agents are on duty Monday through Friday during normal business hours.

Dial 2 to make official duty group reservations or meeting reservations.

Dial 3 for Customer Service.

Once you make your choice, you will be connected to a reservations agent ready to help you book your room. (**Leisure and Space-A lodging reservations, including reservations for Armed Forces Recreation Centers and MWR Recreational lodging, are no longer handled by ACRC. For leisure and Space-A lodging please refer to the individual listings in this book and contact the facilities directly.**)

Official travelers from outside the CONUS can use ACRC by dialing DSN-312-897-2790. Reservations may also be faxed to C-205-876-6870 or DSN-312-746-6870. Patrons for overseas locations must dial direct (please see each listing in this book for dialing numbers from CONUS/overseas). Some individual Army Lodging locations in CONUS have toll-free, 1-800 or 1-888 numbers which are contained in each listing in *Temporary Military Lodging Around the World.*

NAVY LODGING RESERVATIONS

BACHELOR QUARTERS CENTRAL RESERVATION SYSTEM (BQCRS)

TOLL-FREE RESERVATION SERVICE 1-800-576-9327 (SATO)
(For Official Navy Funded Travel Only)

The Navy provides a Navy-wide Bachelor Quarters Central Reservation System (BQCRS) system for convenient, one-stop travel services for personnel traveling on Navy-funded travel orders only. Navy Bachelor Quarters at each base are connected on line through the BQCRS. All Navy military and many Navy civilian personnel on official temporary duty travel are required to make lodging reservations through BQCRS when they make transportation arrangements through their local travel offices. Personnel who are traveling on Navy-funded orders via personally owned vehicles or those who require reservations for lodging only should call the Scheduled Airline Ticket Office **(SATO) at 1-800-576-9327.**

Personnel on leave, vacation or leisure time travel (Not on Navy-funded orders in connection with PCS, TAD/TDY) or other uniformed services not on Navy travel orders must call each Navy BEQ/BOQ directly for information and reservations. Please see the reservations telephone and fax numbers in each Navy listing in *Temporary Military Lodging Around The World*. Most lodging for personnel on leave and retirees is on a space-A basis only.

NAVY LODGE PROGRAM

(Operated by Navy Exchange Command (NEXCOM))

FOR TOLL-FREE RESERVATIONS: 1-800-NAVY INN (1-800-628-9466)

Reservations and all other information such as rates and hours of operation can be obtained by calling 1-800 NAVY-INN (1-800-628-9466). Only the Navy Lodges located in Guantanamo Bay, Naples, Atsugi, Sasebo, Yokosuka, and Rota can be reached via the toll-free numbers. All other Navy Lodges that are located in foreign countries must be called directly for reservations (except personnel on PCS orders). Complete telephone dialing instructions from CONUS are in each Navy Lodge listing. Call 1-800-NAVY INN (1-800-628-9466) for rates, hours of operation and other information. Although the Navy Lodge at the Miramar Marine Corps Air Station has been renamed "Miramar Inn" and is now a Marine Corps Community Services facility, reservations may still be made through the Navy Lodge 1-800 number. Reservations for The Inn at Schofield Barracks, HI (an Army facility) also may be made through the Navy Lodge 1-800 number.

Navy Lodges worldwide now offer free local telephone calls for all guests, while all continental United States Navy Lodges feature daily in-room coffee service. Navy Lodge guests in all locations except El Centro Naval Air Facility, CA; Fallon Naval Air Station, NV; and Guantanamo Bay Naval Station, Cuba receive a complimentary morning newspaper. At press time there were 43 Navy Lodges operating worldwide.

To make Navy Lodge reservations from within foreign countries, call: from Japan 00531-11-3313; from Spain 900-931123; from United Kingdom 0500-893652 and from Italy 800-87-0740.

AIR FORCE CONUS LODGING RESERVATIONS

TOLL-FREE AIR FORCE RESERVATION SERVICE: 1-888-AF LODGE (1-888-235-6343)

The United States Air Force operates a toll-free central reservation service at 1-888-AF LODGE (1-888-235-6343) for facilities in the continental United States, plus Elmendorf Air Force Base and Eielson Air Force Base in Alaska and Hickam Air Force Base in Hawaii for both official travelers and Space-A travelers. After you dial the toll-free number, you will hear a recorded prompt asking you to dial the first three letters of the name of the desired base. For example, if you are calling to make lodging reservations at Nellis Air force Base, Nevada you punch in "NEL," and you'll be connected to the lodging office at Nellis Air Force Base where there will be a further recorded prompt. In some cases you will receive a recorded prompt to make a choice between two different bases or two different lodging facilities on the same base.

Check the listings for individual bases in *Temporary Military Lodging Around The World* for overseas Air Force lodging commercial and defense telephone and fax numbers. Many Temporary Lodging Facilities worldwide have e-mail addresses which can be used to make reservations and request information. All e-mail addresses which we have are listed in the text of each listing contained in this book.

United States Marine Corps and United States Coast Guard Lodging Reservations

As of press time, there were no central reservation systems for the United States Marine Corps or the United States Coast Guard. Reservations for lodging facilities operated by these Uniformed Services must be coordinated directly with each lodging facility or billeting office. One exception is that reservations for the Miramar Inn (formerly a Navy Lodge) at Miramar Marine Corps Air Station, CA can be made through the Navy Lodge toll-free reservations number at 1-800-NAVY INN (1-800-628-9466). Postal mail and e-mail addresses when available along with commercial and defense telephone and fax numbers, are published in each lodging listing in this book.

CONTENTS

UNITED STATES

FLORIDA

GEORGIA

HAWAII

UTAH

VIRGINIA

WASHINGTON

UNITED STATES

ALABAMA

Dauphin Island Coast Guard Recreational Facility (AL07R2)
100 Agassiz Street
P.O. Box 436
Dauphin Island, AL 36528-0436

MAIN INSTALLATION TELEPHONE NUMBERS: C-251-861-7113. Locator 861-7113; Medical 861-3422; Security Police 861-5523.

LOCATION: On Gulf of Mexico approximately 40 miles south of Mobile. Take I-10 east or west to Highway 193 south (exit 17); south approximately 25 miles to Dauphin Island. Left (east) at dead end to east end of island. Follow signs to complex. *USMRA: Page 36 (B-10)*. **NMC:** Mobile, 40 miles north. **NMI:** Mobile Coast Guard Group (Brookley), 40 miles north.

RESERVATION INFORMATION: C-251-861-7113, Fax: C-251-861-6313. Hours: 0900-1700 Mon-Thurs and Sat, 0900-1800 Fri and Sun. E-mail: uscgrecreationfac@zebra.net. Telephone reservations required, with advance credit card payment. Up to 90 days in advance for active CG; up to 60 days, all other.

TLF Three-bedroom cottages, private bath (13). Kitchenette, refrigerator, microwave, utensils, A/C, CATV, ice machine, washer/dryer, crib, cots. Seven day maximum stay for cottages during summer. Handicap accessible units. Rates: Off Season (1 Oct-31 Mar): weekend (Fri-Sun) $100-$120; weekly (Sun-Fri) $140-$160; weekly (Sun-Sun or Fri-Fri) $240-$280. Summer: (1 Apr-30 Sept): weekend (Fri-Sun) $100-$120; weekly (Sun-Fri) $230-$250; weekly (Fri-Fri or Sun-Sun) $330-$370.

AMENITIES: Mini Mart, Snack and Soft Drink Vending Machines. Arcade, bicycles, outdoor recreation courts and paddle boats.

TML AVAILABILITY: Best, Oct-Apr.

CREDIT CARDS ACCEPTED: Visa and MasterCard.

TRANSPORTATION: None available.

DINING OPPORTUNITIES: Blue Herron, Seafood Galley Restaurant and Island Club are within walking distance.

Gulf beaches, visits to historic Fort Gaines and Mobile, serious bird watching, wading for flounder and crab at night, or deep sea fishing are all a part of the simple, unhurried relaxation that is Dauphin Island.

Fort Rucker (AL02R2)
Commander, USAAVNC
ACS, Attn: ATZQ-DCF-FS
Fort Rucker, AL 36362-5000

MAIN INSTALLATION TELEPHONE NUMBERS: C-334-255-1030, DSN-312-558-1030. Locator 255-1030; Medical 255-7900; Security Police 255-2222.

LOCATION: Eighty miles southeast of Montgomery, midway between the capital city and the Florida Gulf Coast, and seven miles south of Ozark, on US-231 to southwest on Al-249. Clearly marked. *USMRA: Page 36 (F,G-8)*. **NMC:** Dothan, 26 miles southeast.

RESERVATION INFORMATION: Bldg 308, 6th Avenue, Fort Rucker, AL 36362-5000. **C-334-598-5216, DSN-312-558-2626,** Fax: C-334-598-1242, 24 hours daily. All travelers report to billeting. Check in between 1400-1800 hours, check out 1100 hours. Reservations 90 days in advance for PCS, 60 days for TDY, 21 days for Active Duty, others seven days. ***Winner of Lodging Operation of the Year Award.***

VOQ/VEQ Bldg 308. TDY facility. Standard Room, with or without kitchen; Efficiency Suite; Family Suite. Rates: $22-$31.

Army Lodging Bldg 124. Two double beds, sofabed, private bath. Kitchen, A/C, TV, housekeeping service, washer/dryer. Maximum five per unit. Rates (subject to change): Official $28, Unofficial $38.

Cottages Lake Cottage (7). Amenities, housekeeping service. Maximum five per unit. Rates (subject to change): Official $31, Unofficial $41.

DV/VIP Attn: Protocol, Bldg 114 (Post HQ), **C-334-255-1134, DSN-312-558-1134.** O7/GS-15+. Family Suite, maximum four per unit. Amenities, housekeeping service. Rates (subject to change): Official $31, Unofficial $41.

TML AVAILABILITY: Best, Oct-Apr. Limited, May-Sep.

CREDIT CARDS ACCEPTED: Visa, MasterCard and American Express can be used to secure/confirm room.

TRANSPORTATION: Off base shuttle/bus.

DINING OPPORTUNITIES: Burger King; O Club, C-334-598-2426; and NCO Club, C-334-598-2491 are within walking distance. Larry's Real Pit BBQ, C-334-598-3772; and McLin Kitchenette, C-334-598-2774 are within driving distance.

"Dixie's Heartland" is sprinkled with fine freshwater fishing. Landmark Park has sixty acres of shady nature trails and boardwalks, picnic sites and historic restorations. Waterworld in Dothan is good family entertainment.

Gunter Annex, Maxwell Air Force Base (AL04R2)
42 MSS/DPF
50 LeMay Plaza South
Maxwell AFB, AL 36114-5000

MAIN INSTALLATION TELEPHONE NUMBERS: C-334-416-4611/1110, DSN-312-596-1110. Locator 270-4000; Medical 416-5816; Security Police 416-4250.

LOCATION: From I-65 north or south take exit 173 northeast onto Northern Blvd (AL-152) 6.1 miles to intersection with US-231. Take south exit onto Federal Drive, then south 1.5 miles to Main Gate on left (southeast) side of street. From I-85 east or west, take exit 6 north onto Eastern Blvd (US-231 north). Continue north 4 miles, exit south onto Federal Drive, then southwest 1.5 miles to Main Gate on left (south) side of street. *USMRA: Page 36 (E,F-6)*. **NMC:** Montgomery, two miles southwest.

RESERVATION INFORMATION: University Inn, Bldg 826, 100 S. Turner Blvd, Gunter Annex, AL 36114-3011. **C-1-888-AFLODGE (1-888-235-6343), C-334-416-3360/5501, DSN-312-596-3360,** Fax: C-334-416-3945, DSN-312-596-3945. WEB: www.au.af.mil/42abw/42svs/lodgingreservations.html Duty can make reservations any time; others Space-A 24 hours in advance. Check in 1400 hours at Lodging Office, check out 1200 hours.

VAQ Bldgs 1016, 1017. Separate bedroom, semi-private bath (247); bedroom, private bath (250); chief suites, private bath (6). Refrigerator, A/C, TV, housekeeping service, laundry facility. DAV facilities, modern structure. Rates: $10; suites $15.

VOQ Bldgs 872-874, 1014, 1015. Suites with private bath (37); rooms, semi-private bath (enlisted use this facility) (69); rooms, private bath (40). Refrigerator, A/C, TV, housekeeping service, laundry facility, cribs, cots, DAV facilities, older buildings. Check out 1200 hours. Handicap accessible. Rates: $13.50; suites $20.50.

TLF Bldg 1503. Refrigerator A/C, TV, housekeeping service, laundry facility. Rates: $13.50.

DV/VIP Bldgs 872-874. O6+. Separate bedroom, private bath, kitchenette (17). Rates: $20.50.

TML AVAILABILITY: Good, except for enlisted quarters (SNCOA expansion).

CREDIT CARDS ACCEPTED: Visa and MasterCard.

TRANSPORTATION: Off base shuttle/bus, C-334-265-0892; Car Rental, C-1-800-736-8222; Off base taxi, C-334-263-7137.

DINING OPPORTUNITIES: Choices Chinese Restaurant, C-334-262-0888; and Subway, C-334-265-0305 are within driving distance.

Visit Oak Park's W.A. Gayle Planetarium, the Montgomery Zoo and the state capitol building where Jefferson Davis took the oath of office as President of the Confederate States of America.

Maxwell Air Force Base (AL03R2)
42nd MSS/DPF
50 LeMay Plaza South
Maxwell AFB, AL 36112-5000

MAIN INSTALLATION TELEPHONE NUMBERS: C-334-953-1110, DSN-312-493-1110. Locator 953-5027; Medical 953-7861; Security Police 953-7222.

LOCATION: Take I-85 south to I-65 north to Herron Street (exit 172) west to right (north) on Dickerson Street two blocks to left (west) on Bell Street approximately 0.9 mile and follow signs to Bell Street Gate Visitor Center on right (north side of street). *USMRA: Page 36 (E-6)*. **NMC:** Montgomery, 1.5 miles southeast.

RESERVATION INFORMATION: Bldg 157, 351 West Drive, Maxwell AFB, AL 36112-6024. **C-1-888-AFLODGE (1-888-235-6343), C-334-953-2055/2401/2430, DSN-312-493-2055/2401/2430,** Fax: C-334-953-5696, DSN-312-493-5696, 24 hours daily. WEB: www.au.af.mil/42abw/42svs/lodgingreservations.html Directions: Go through Main Gate on Mitchell to Ash Street. Turn right on Ash to Poplar. Turn left on Poplar and stay right at junction of Poplar and West Drive. Lodging office is located on corner of West Drive and East Hickory (Bldg 157). Duty can make reservations any time; others Space-A 24 hours in advance. Check in at 1400 hours, check out 1100 hours.

TLF Bldgs 46-49. One-bedroom apartments, private bath (30). Kitchen, utensils, A/C, TV, housekeeping service, laundry facility, cribs. Modern structure. Rates: All ranks $24.50 per day. Maximum five persons per unit.

VAQ Bldg 695-697, 1014, 1015. Chief suites, private bath (11); single rooms, shared bath (56). Rates: suites $17; single rooms $10 per room.

VOQ Bldgs 157, 679, 680, 872-874, 1416-1419, 1422, 1428-1434, 1468, 1470. Bedroom, semi-private bath (563); bedroom, private bath, kitchenette (78); suites with kitchenette, private bath (97); bedroom, private bath (103). Kitchen, A/C, TV, housekeeping service, laundry facility, cribs, cots. Modern and older structures. Rates: $13.50/$21.50 per night.

DVQ Suites. Bldgs 117, 121, 142, 143. Separate bedrooms, private bath. Refrigerator, microwave, wet bar, A/C, TV, housekeeping service, laundry facility. Rates: $16.

DV/VIP Protocol Office, Bldg 119, **C-334-953-2095.** O7+. Suites (16).

AMENITIES: Ice, Snack and Soft Drink Vending Machine.

TML AVAILABILITY: Extremely limited, year-round.

CREDIT CARDS ACCEPTED: Visa and MasterCard.

TRANSPORTATION: Off base shuttle/bus, C-334-265-0892; Car Rental, C-1-800-736-8222; On base taxi, C-334-953-5038, DSN-312-493-5038; Off base taxi, C-334-263-7137.

DINING OPPORTUNITIES: O Club, C-334-264-6423; E Club, C-334-262-8364; AAFES Food Court, C-334-834-5948; and Burger King, C-334-265-3913 are within walking distance. Many restaurants are within driving distance.

While here be sure to visit the Civil Rights Memorial, Montgomery Zoo, W.A. Gayle Planetarium, Executive Mansion, State Capitol Archives and History Museum, the first White House of the Confederacy, and the Rosa Parks Museum.

Redstone Arsenal (AL06R2)
US Army Aviation and Missile Command
Attn: AMSAM-RA-CF-BF
Redstone Arsenal, AL 35898-5350

MAIN INSTALLATION TELEPHONE NUMBERS: C-256-876-2151, DSN-312-746-2151. Locator 259-876-2151; Medical 256-955-8888 ext 2; Security Police 259-876-2222.

LOCATION: From I-565 east west take exit 14 south onto Rideout Road for 0.4 miles to gate 9. Or, from I-565 in city of Huntsville, exit south onto US-231 (Memorial Drive) for 4.5 miles to right (west) on Martin Road to Main Gate (Gate 1). Uniformed personnel may take I-565 to US-231 (Memorial Drive) south 1 mile to Drake exit west. Go west on Drake which becomes Goss Road to Gate 8. *USMRA: Page 36 (E-1)*. **NMC:** Huntsville, adjacent.

RESERVATION INFORMATION: Attn: AMSAM-RA-CF-LF, Bldg 244, Goss Road, Redstone Arsenal, AL 35898-5350. **C-256-876-5713/8028, DSN-312-746-5713/8028,** Fax: C-256-876-2929, DSN-312-746-2929, 24 hours daily. E-mail: ghouse@mwr.redstone.army.mil Check in 1400 at facility, check out 1100 hours.

TML The Trail Blazer, Bldg 244. C-256-837-4130. Motel type bedrooms, private bath, microwave, refrigerator, rollaway, cribs (22), four units with kitchenette. Community kitchen with utensils and cooking facilities, coin operated washers/dryers, ice machine, soft drink/snack vending. **The 1400 Area** (24) *two-bedroom apartment units designated for large families and families with pets.* Rates: $37.50.

VOQ Bldgs 55, 60, 62. Official duty only. Cottage units, three bedroom, two full baths, living room, dining room, kitchen, sunroom. Furnished. Cottage rates: $41-$51 per night. Bldg. 111, 131,133,135 are newly renovated. Suite units (66). Suite rates: $46-$56 per night; Mini suite rates: $41-$51 per night. One bedroom units (54) with study, living room, dining room and full kitchen. Rates: $35.50 per night.

DVQ Bldgs 56, 58. Field grade and General Officers. Decorated and fully equipped three-bedroom cottages. Rates: $46-$58. Official duty can make reservations, others Space-A.

DV/VIP Contact lodging office. **C-256-876-5713/8028, DSN-312-746-5713/8028.** O6+. Retirees and lower ranks Space-A.

TML AVAILABILITY: Very good.

CREDIT CARDS ACCEPTED: Visa, MasterCard and American Express.

TRANSPORTATION: On base shuttle/bus, C-256-876-2261; Off base shuttle/bus, C-256-532-7433; On base taxi, C-256-876-2261/62; Off base taxi: A-1 United Deluxe, C-256-536-3600; AAA Cab, C-256-536-9444; Rocket City Cab, C-256-534-4524.

DINING OPPORTUNITIES: Golf Course Snack Bar, C-256-883-7977; Spakman Center Cafeteria, C-256-876-8894; Suldatenstube, C-256-830-CLUB(2582); Officers' and Civilian Club; and AAFES Dining Court are within driving distance.

Visit the Alabama Space and Rocket Center, I-565 West of Huntsville.

ALASKA

Clear Air Force Station (AK18R5)
13 SWS, 200A Street, Room 1019
P.O. Box 40013
Clear AFS, AK 99704-0013

MAIN INSTALLATION TELEPHONE NUMBERS: C-907-585-1110, DSN-317-585-1110. Locator 585-1110; Medical 585-6414; Security 585-6313.

LOCATION: From Fairbanks, 80 miles southwest on Fairbanks/Anchorage Highway (AK-3). Located on east side of highway. **NMC:** Fairbanks, 80 miles northeast.

RESERVATION INFORMATION: 13 SWS/CSV, Bldg 200, Clear AFS, AK 99704-0013. **C-907-585-6224, DSN-317-585-6224,** 0800-1700 hours Mon-Fri. Check in at billeting, check out 1200 hours. Reservations required. Government civilian employee billeting.

TLQ Bldg 202. Official duty. Bedroom, private bath (6); bedroom, shared bath (2). Kitchen, refrigerator, limited utensils, TV in room and lounge, housekeeping service, laundry facility. Barracks, renovated. Reservations required.

TLQ Bldg 3. C-907-585-6425/6487, DSN-317-585-6576, 0730-1630 hours. Official duty, retired, guests, dependents. After hours report to Combined club, Bldg 209 or call C-907-585-6557. Check out 1100 hours. Bedrooms, shared bath (6); separate bedroom, private bath (6); DV Suite (1). Community kitchen, limited utensils, TV in room and lounge, housekeeping service, laundry facility, ice machine. Wood frame building. Reservations required.

AMENITIES: Exercise Room, Snack Vending Machine and Soft Drink Machine.

AVAILABILITY: Extremely limited, May-Sep.

CREDIT CARDS ACCEPTED: Visa and MasterCard.

DINING OPPORTUNITIES: Northern Lights Inn, C-907-585-6519 within walking distance. Clear Sky Lodge, C-907-582-2251 and Dew Drop, C-907-582-2856 are within driving distance.

This facility is in the heart of Alaska, near Denali (Mount McKinley) National Park and has wonderful fishing, hunting and many other outdoor activities. The last weekend of July is the Bluegrass Festival in the nearby town of Anderson.

Eielson Air Force Base (AK15R5)
3125 Wabash Avenue, Suite 1
Eielson AFB, AK 99702-1720

MAIN INSTALLATION TELEPHONE NUMBERS: C-907-377-1110, DSN-317-377-1110. Locator 377-1841; Medical 377-2296; Security Police 377-5130.

LOCATION: On east side of Richardson Highway (AK-2) at mile post 341. AFB is clearly marked. *USMRA: Page 128 (F,G-4)*. **NMC:** Fairbanks, 26 miles northwest.

RESERVATION INFORMATION: Gold Rush Inn, Bldg 2270, Central Avenue, Eielson AFB, AK 99702-1870. **C-907-377-1844, DSN-317-377-1844,** Fax: C-907-377-2559, 24 hours daily. Check in at billeting, check out 1100 hours. Duty can make reservations any time; others Space-A 24 hours in advance. Government civilian employee billeting.

TLF Bldg 3305. Separate bedrooms, private bath (40). Kitchen, microwave, complete utensils, TV/VCR, housekeeping service, laundry facilities, cribs. Modern structure. Handicap accessible. Rates: $35 per room. Maximum five per room.

VOQ/VAQ Bldgs 2270-2272. One-bedroom, private bath. Refrigerator, microwave, TV/VCR in room and lounge, housekeeping service, laundry facilities, cribs, ice machine. New three story structures. Handicap accessible. Rates: VOQ (207) $18.50; VAQ (179) $17.00 per person.

DV/VIP Protocol Office, 354 FW/CCP, Bldg 3112, Room 5, **C-907-377-7686.** E9, O6+. Rates: $25. Retirees Space-A.

TML AVAILABILITY: Good, Sep-Apr. Space-A extremely limited, May-Aug.

CREDIT CARDS ACCEPTED: Visa and MasterCard.

TRANSPORTATION: On base shuttle/bus; On base taxi, C-907-459-1011.

DINING OPPORTUNITIES: Some restaurants available within driving distance.

Enjoy Denali National Park, historical Fairbanks, hunting, fishing and skiing in season. All outdoor activities are available both on and off base.

Elmendorf Air Force Base (AK09R5)
3 MSS/DPF
1890 36th Street
Elmendorf AFB, AK 99506-2760

MAIN INSTALLATION TELEPHONE NUMBERS: C-907-552-1110, DSN-317-552-1110. Locator 552-4860; Medical 552-5555/6; Security Police 552-3421.

LOCATION: Off Glenn Highway (AK-1) adjacent to north Anchorage. Take Boniface Parkway Exit. Take either Elmendorf Access Road or North Post Road. The base is adjacent to Fort Richardson. *USMRA: Page 128 (F-5), page 131 (B,C,D,E-1)*. **NMC:** Anchorage, two miles southeast.

RESERVATION INFORMATION: North Star Inn, Bldg 7153, Fighter Drive, Elmendorf AFB, AK 99506-3565. **C-907-552-2454 ext 1118, DSN-317-552-2454 ext 1118,** Fax: C-907-552-8276, DSN-317-552-8276, 24 hours daily. Duty can make reservations any time; Space-A can make reservations 24 hours in advance. Check in at facility, check out 1000 hours.

TLF Bldgs 3000, 7000. TDY or official duty. Bldg 3000: One-bedroom, sofa rollaway bed, private bath (100). Full kitchen, refrigerator, microwave, TV, housekeeping service, laundry facility. Bldg 7000: Three-bedroom, private bath. Full kitchen, refrigerator, microwave, TV, housekeeping service, laundry facility. Older structures. Rates: $35 per unit.

VAQ TDY or official duty. E1-E3 shared bedroom and bath (258 rooms, 464 beds); E4+ single room, shared bath (15). Lounge, reading room. Rates: single $21; double $42.

VOQ TDY or official duty. Bedroom, private bath (166); bedroom, private bath, kitchenette (20). Rates: $22.50 per room.

DV/VIP Protocol Office. Reservations for O6+, **C-907-552-3210, DSN-317-552-3210.** VAQ. DV suites (9). Lounge, reading room. Rates: $34.

AMENITIES: Meeting/Conference Room.

TML AVAILABILITY: Fairly good. Best, Nov-Jan. Extremely limited, May-Sep.

CREDIT CARDS ACCEPTED: Visa and MasterCard.

TRANSPORTATION: On base shuttle (no shuttle on weekends); Car Rental.

DINING OPPORTUNITIES: Bowling Alley, Dining Hall and NCO Club are within walking distance.

Alaska's largest city boasts many cultural events, museums, sporting events (the Anchorage Bowl is a world class ski resort) and restaurants in a spectacular setting. Outdoor activities abound.

Fort Greely (AK10R5)
Army Community Services
Unit 45807
Fort Greely, AK 96508-5000
Scheduled to close 2001.

MAIN INSTALLATION TELEPHONE NUMBERS: C-907-873-4113, DSN-317-873-4113. Locator 873-3255; Medical 873-4498; Security Police 873-1111.

LOCATION: West of AK-4 six miles south of junction of AK-2 and AK-4. Five miles south of Delta Junction. *USMRA: Page 128 (F,G-4).* **NMC:** Fairbanks, 105 miles northwest.

RESERVATION INFORMATION: Bldg 663, First Street, P.O. Box 1023, Delta Junction, AK 99737-5000. **C-907-873-3285, DSN-317-873-3285,** Fax: C-907-873-3003, DSN-317-873-3003, 0730-1530 hours Mon through Fri. After hours, call 907-873-3889. E-mail: rebecca.wells@wainwright.army.mil TDY or PCS may make reservations 120 days in advance; unofficial, seven days. Check in 1300 hours, check out 1100 hours. Government civilian employee billeting.

VOQ Bldg 801. Double bed, sitting room, kitchenette, private bath (12); single bed, kitchenette, private bath (4); DVQ has queen-size bed, sitting room, full kitchen, microwave, mini-bar, private bath (2). CATV, phone, housekeeping service (Mon-Fri), laundry facility, cribs, cots. Rates: $28 first occupant for single bed, $44 first occupant for double bed; DVQ $49 first occupant. Each additional person $4. *Pets allowed,* $10 per pet/per day, limit 2 pets. Contractor rate, $86.

TML AVAILABILITY: Good. Best, Apr-May and Sep-Dec. Difficult, Jan-Feb and Jul-Aug.

CREDIT CARDS ACCEPTED: Visa, MasterCard, American Express and Discover.

TRANSPORTATION: Off base shuttle/bus, C-907-873-4650; Off base taxi, C-907-895-5175.

DINING OPPORTUNITIES: Caribou Corner, C-907-873-7622; and Diamond Willow Combined Club, C-907-873-3105 are within walking distance. Alaska Steakhouse, C-850-895-5175; Buffalo Center Diner, C-850-895-5089; and Trophy Lodge, C-850-895-4685 are within driving distance.

Hunting, fishing, all summer and winter sports are part of living in Alaska. A visit to nearby Delta Junction and Fairbanks, farther north, will give a visitor a taste of life on "the last frontier."

Fort Richardson (AK03R5)
Attn: APVR-RPA-CFA (RELO)
600 Richardson Drive, #6625
Fort Richardson, AK 99505-6625

MAIN INSTALLATION TELEPHONE NUMBERS: C-907-384-1110, DSN-317-384-1110. Locator 384-0306; Medical 552-5555; Security Police 384-0823.

LOCATION: Main gate is on east side of Glenn Highway (AK-1), eight miles south of Eagle River. *USMRA: Page 128 (F-5), page 131 (E-1).* **NMC:** Anchorage, eight miles southwest.

RESERVATION INFORMATION: Bldg 602, Room 128, 2nd Street and Richardson Drive, P.O. Box 5-625, Fort Richardson, AK 99505-5625. **C-907-384-0421/36, DSN-317-384-0421/36,** Fax: C-907-384-0470, 24 hours daily. E-mail: rayHM@richardsonemh2.army.mil Reservation 120 days in advance for official PCS, TDY or ADT, three days in advance for Space-A (May-Aug), seven days in advance (Sep-Apr). Check out 1100 hours. Reservations check in after 1500 hours. Government civilian employee billeting in VOQ/DV.

VOQ Bldgs 55, 57, 58, 1107, 1113, 1114. Separate bedroom, private bath (96). Refrigerator, microwave, CATV, housekeeping service, laundry facility, cribs, cots, ice machine. Older structure, renovated. Rates: Summer (May 1-Sep. 30) $58-$63, each additional person $4, Winter call for current rates. Pets are allowed.

DV/VIP Attn: APVR-CS-P, Protocol Office, Bldg 1, Room 111, **C-907-384-2067. The Igloo.** Bldg 53. **C-907-384-1586.** O5+. Separate bedroom suites, private bath (14); bedroom, kitchen, private bath apartments (2). Refrigerator, limited utensils, CATV, housekeeping service, laundry facility, cribs, cots, ice machine. Older structure, renovated. Rates: Summer apartments $67, suites $65, Winter call for current rates. Pets are allowed.

TML AVAILABILITY: Good, Oct-Apr. Difficult, other times.

CREDIT CARDS ACCEPTED: Visa, MasterCard, American Express and Discover.

TRANSPORTATION: Off base shuttle/bus, C-907-343-6543; Car Rental, C-907-753-2178; Off base taxi, C-907-563-5353, C-907-276-1234, C-907-245-2222.

DINING OPPORTUNITIES: AAFES Exchange, C-907-428-1221, Phillips International Inn, C-907-338-7606 are within driving distance.

Visit the Fish and Wildlife Museum in Bldg 600. The Earthquake Park in Anchorage commemorates the violence of the far North, while towering mountains, wildlife parks, the Cook Inlet and great downhill skiing welcome visitors nearby.

Fort Wainwright (AK07R5)
1060 Gaffney Road, #6600
Fort Wainwright, AK 99703-6600

MAIN INSTALLATION TELEPHONE NUMBERS: C-907-353-6113/7500, DSN-317-353-6113/7500. Locator 353-1110; Medical 353-5143/5172; Security Police 353-7535.

LOCATION: From Fairbanks, take Airport Way (AK-3) east which changes to Gaffney Road and leads to the Main Gate of the post. *USMRA: Page 128 (F-4).* **NMC:** Fairbanks, adjacent.

RESERVATION INFORMATION: Murphy Hall, Bldg 1045, Gaffney Road, P.O. Box 35086, Fort Wainwright, AK 99703-0086. **C-907-384-3241, DSN-317-384-3241,** Fax: C-907-353-7409, 24 hours daily. WEB: www.usarak.army.mil/framwr/transient_housing.htm. Check in at billeting 1500 hours, check out 1100 hours. Duty TDY and PCS can make reservations 120 days in advance. Visitors can make reservations up to 7 days in advance, based on availability, between 31

August until 30 April, and up to 3 days in advance with a 5 day booking limit, also based on space availability, between 1 May to 31 August.

VEQ/VOQ Bldg 4056. Suites (12), Singles (15) with private bath. Refrigerator, microwave, TV/VCR, housekeeping service, laundry facility, cribs, rollaways, soft drink/snack vending, ice machine. Older structure. Rates: sponsor, two/three bedroom $44, singles $28; suites $40, each additional person $4. Rates change during summer months. *Pets allowed in building 4056* with $100 dollar refundable deposit and $10 per pet daily fee. Smoking on second floor only.

VEQ/VOQ Bldg 4063. Two-bedroom, private bath (4); single bedroom, private bath (4); Suite, private bath (11), one handicap accessible. Refrigerator, microwave, TV/VCR, housekeeping service, laundry facility, cribs, rollaways, soft drink/snack vending, ice machine. Rates: sponsor, two/three bedroom $44, single $28; suite $40, each additional person $4. Rates change during summer months. No Smoking.

VEQ/VOQ Bldgs 4064. Two-bedroom, private bath (8); Suite, private bath (8). Refrigerator, microwave, TV/VCR, housekeeping service, laundry facility, cribs, rollaways, soft drink/snack vending, ice machine. Rates: sponsor, two/three bedroom $44, suites $40, each additional person $4. Rates change during summer months. No Smoking.

VEQ/VOQ Bldg 4062. Suites, private bath (16). Refrigerator, microwave, TV/VCR, housekeeping service, laundry facility, cribs, rollaways, soft drink/snack vending, ice machine. Rates: sponsor, suites $40, each additional person $4. Rates change during summer months. No Smoking.

VEQ/VOQ Bldg 1045. Suites, private bath (21), one handicap accessible. Refrigerator, microwave, TV/VCR, housekeeping service, laundry facility, cribs, rollaways, soft drink/snack vending, ice machine. Rates: sponsor, suites $40, each additional person $4. Rates change during summer months. No Smoking.

VEQ/VOQ Bldg 1063. Suite, private bath (19). Refrigerator, microwave, TV/VCR, housekeeping service, laundry facility, cribs, rollaways, soft drink/snack vending, ice machine. Rates: sponsor, suites $40 each additional person $4. No Smoking.

DV/VIP Bldg 1045. Protocol **C-907-353-6671/2/8/9 or 907-653-6503.** O6+. Bedroom deluxe suite (4). Refrigerator, microwave, TV/VCR, housekeeping service, laundry facility, cribs, rollaways, ice machine. Rates: DVQ apartment with kitchenette $49; DVQ suite $46, each additional person $4. Rates change during summer months.

AMENITIES: Snack Vending and Ice Machine, Laundry Facilities.

TML AVAILABILITY: Difficult, year round.

CREDIT CARDS ACCEPTED: Visa, MasterCard, American Express and Discover.

TRANSPORTATION: Off base shuttle/bus; Off base Car Rental; Off base taxi. PCS call Replacement at C-907-353-CARE(2273).

DINING OPPORTUNITIES: All Ranks Dining Facilities; Off base dining.

In summer Fairbanks hosts Midnight Sun baseball games, in winter (Feb-Mar) the North American Championship Sled Dog Race (and others), University of Alaska Eskimo Olympics. New shopping malls belie the wilderness nearby.

Kodiak Coast Guard Integrated Support Command (AK08R5)
P.O. Box 195014
Kodiak, AK 99619-5014

MAIN INSTALLATION TELEPHONE NUMBERS: C-907-487-5267, DSN-317-487-5267. Locator 487-5267; Medical 487-5757; Security Police 487-5555.

LOCATION: From Kodiak City, take Chiniak Highway southwest for seven miles. Base is on left (southeast) side. *USMRA: Page 128 (E-7).* **NMC:** Kodiak, seven miles northeast.

RESERVATION INFORMATION: Guesthouse, Bldg N-30, P.O. Box 195030, Kodiak CGISC, AK 99619-5030. **C-907-487-5446,** Fax: C-907-487-5075, 24 hours daily. Directions: From Main Gate proceed to Albatross Avenue, turn left two blocks; three story building on the right. Check in at facility 1400 hours, check out 1200 hours.

Guesthouse Bldg N30, 205 Albatross Avenue. Basic rooms with either full bed and pull out hide-a-bed chair or two twin beds (38). Family suites. Two bedroom with two twin beds in one and a queen bed in the other (5). Living room suite. Two rooms, one with queen-size bed and the other as a sitting room (1). Handicap accessible rooms on first floor with fold down shower seat and hearing impaired fire alarms (2). All rooms have private baths. On each floor, community kitchen with utensils, TV lounge and guest laundry room. All rooms have CATV and refrigerator. Housekeeping services are available Monday through Friday. Rates: Basic rooms $65; Family Suites and Living Room Suite $90; Joining Rooms $95.00. This is a first come, first serve hotel. No smoking, no pets.

BEQ C-907-487-5260. Rooms (10), 19 beds. Rates: no charge.

DV/VIP Guesthouse. **C-907-487-5446.** E9, O5/GS15+, official duty. Suites (3), two interconnecting by bath. Community kitchen, freezer, CATV, housekeeping service, laundry facility, cribs, ice machine, playground, pool. Older structure, three floors. Rates: $70. Reservations accepted, others Space-A.

AMENITIES: Gym, playroom, pool, mini mart.

TML AVAILABILITY: Good, Oct-Apr. Difficult, May-Sep.

CREDIT CARDS ACCEPTED: Visa, MasterCard and American Express.

TRANSPORTATION: Car Rentals: Avis, C-907-487-2264; Budget, C-907-487-2220; Kodiak Car Rental, C-907-486-4900; Rent-A-Heap, C-907-487-4001; Off base taxis: AAA Ace Mecca, C-907-486-3211; A&B Taxicabs, C-907-486-4343.

DINING OPPORTUNITIES: MWR Pizza Parlor and Family Fun Center and All Hands Dining Facility are within driving distance.

Kodiak is known for its big bears (the biggest in the world), which are tourist attractions in themselves, great scenery, wonderful king crab and salmon, which are not so threatening, and more tasty. Movie theater, bowling alley and beach with gazebo are all within 3/4 of a mile to the Guesthouse.

Seward Air Force Camp (AK05R5)
P.O. Box 915
Seward, AK 99664-5000

MAIN INSTALLATION TELEPHONE NUMBERS: C-907-552-1110, DSN-317-552-1110. Locator 552-1110; Medical 911; Security Police 911.

LOCATION: Off base. From Anchorage south on AK-1 to AK-9 south to mile post 2.1 of the Seward Highway. Camp is on right (west) side of AK-

9 on Resurrection Bay. Follow signs. *USMRA: Page 128 (F-6)*. **NMC:** Anchorage, 124 miles north.

RESERVATION INFORMATION: P.O. Box 915, Seward, AK 99664-5000. C-907-224-5425, C-1-800-501-5642 (18 May-4 Sep); C-907-552-5526 (1 Feb-14 May); DSN-317-552-5526, 0600-2200 hours.

(TML) Active Duty, retired, reserve, DoD, NAF and contract civilians. One-bedroom Duplex Cabin (12), sofabed, furnished. Kitchen, laundry facility, picnic area, playground. Recently renovated. Non-smoking. Rates: $110. No pets in cabins or unattended, short leash only.

TML AVAILABILITY: Open season 2001 is May 18-Sep 4.

CREDIT CARDS ACCEPTED: Visa and MasterCard.

TRANSPORTATION: Off base shuttle, Seward Trolley; Car Rental; Off base taxi, Glacier Taxi and PJ's Taxi.

DINING OPPORTUNITIES: Snack bar on campgrounds.

Heavily wooded on a scenic 16-acre site. Within a ten-minute walk to mountains, ocean or town center. Multiple glaciers can be viewed from the campground. A haven for saltwater fisherman!

Seward Resort (AK06R5)
P.O. Box 329
Seward, AK 99664-5000

MAIN INSTALLATION TELEPHONE NUMBERS: Recording: C-1-800-770-1858. Reservations: C-907-224-2654/2659/5559. Locator 224-5559; Medical 911; Security Police 911.

LOCATION: Off post. Located in Seward 120 miles south of Anchorage, near Resurrection Bay. Take Seward Highway (AK-1) south to Seward. Follow signs. *USMRA: Page 128 (F-6)*. **NMC:** Anchorage, 120 miles north. **NMI:** Fort Richardson, 133 miles north.

RESERVATION INFORMATION: Recording: **C-1-800-770-1858** or Reservations: **C-907-224-2654/2659/5559**, Fax: C-907-224-5573, DSN-317-384-0248. Reservations desk is open 24 hours during summer, Memorial Day-Labor Day and 7:00am-11:00pm all other days. WEB: www.usarak.army.mil/framwr/seward.htm Reservations can be made 364 days in advance.

ELIGIBILITY: Open to all Active Duty and retired military, National Guard, Reserves, DoD/NAF civilians, their families, guests, and other DoD federal government employees.

(TML) Two Deluxe Townhouses, private bath, sleeps six, one-bedroom, sleeper sofa, loft with two single beds, furnished, kitchen, CATV/VCR, and fireplace. Rates: Summer $159-$199 per night; Winter $100 per night. Standard Townhouses (10), private bath, sleeps six, one-bedroom, sleeper sofa, loft with two single beds, furnished, kitchen, and CATV/VCR. Rates: Summer $129-$169 per night; Winter $75 per night. Motel rooms, bedroom with two double beds, full private bath (56), refrigerator, microwave, table and chairs, CATV/VCR. Romantic log cabin for two persons (1), with log queen-size bed, private bath, TV/VCR, kitchenette, hot tub, porch swing, and gas grill on wrap around deck. Rates: Summer $120-$160 per night; Winter $125 per night. Coin operated laundry facilities, full service Bar/Lounge during summer located in Seabolt Hall with a large rock fireplace, big screen TV, pool table, shuffleboard and snack machines. No pets allowed in townhouses, motel rooms and log cabin. See *Military Living's Military RV, Camping and Outdoor Recreation Around the World* for Seward Resort RV and Camping information.

AMENITIES: Charter fishing (four large 42' fishing boats) for individuals and groups in Resurrection Bay and Prince William Sound. Wildlife Glacier Cruises (53' boat) to Holgate Glacier. Discounted tickets and tours from local operators to include Fly-in fishing, Alaska SeaLife

Center tickets, sea kayaking, Kenai River fishing, horseback riding, Alaska tour packages for Denali, Talkeentna and St. Elias National Park, etc. Full service bar with a variety of beer, wines, and spirits, open every day in summer from Memorial Day to Labor Day and special weekends in fall, winter, and spring. Annual New Year's Eve Party. Family BBQ's every Saturday in summer. Meeting/Conference room for rent for groups, weddings, parties, etc. Game room, picnic tables, children's playground. Mountain bike, fishing equipment, day packs, hip boots for rent. Two fish houses for do-it-yourself filleting and vacuum packing, walk-in freezers for fish storing (free for Seward Resort guests only). Also, see the Seward Resort concierge for discount travel and tour ticket information.

TML AVAILABILITY: Open year round.

CREDIT CARDS ACCEPTED: Visa, MasterCard, American Express and Discover. A credit card is needed to make reservations.

TRANSPORTATION: Off resort shuttle/bus to military boat docks, Seward Trolley; Off base Car Rental and Off base taxi.

DINING OPPORTUNITIES: Several local eating establishments with a wide variety of foods and prices in and out of town.

Lots to do in this beautiful area! Great hiking trails in Chugach National Forest, Caines Head State Recreational Area and Kenai Fjords National Park. Sea kayaking, deep sea Charter Fishing, Glacier Cruises, Kenai and Russian River Fishing, fly-in to a remote lake and fish or hike out. Summer dog sled tours.

ARIZONA

Davis-Monthan Air Force Base (AZ01R4)
355 MSS/DPF
3500 S Craycroft Road
Davis-Monthan AFB, AZ 85707-0001

MAIN INSTALLATION TELEPHONE NUMBERS: C-520-228-3900/1110, DSN-312-228-3900/1110. Locator 228-3347; Medical 228-3233; Security Police 228-4444.

LOCATION: From the east on I-10, exit 270 north onto Kolb Road, north 6 miles to Golf Links Road, left (west) to Craycroft Road, left (south) to Main Gate. From the west on I-10, exit 264 north onto Alvernon Way; turn left (north) following road to the Main Gate. (Alvernon Way turns into Golf Links Road at intersection with Ajo Way.) *USMRA: Page 108 (F-9)*. **NMC:** Tucson, in city limits.

RESERVATION INFORMATION: Inn on Davis-Monthan, Bldg 2350, 3375 S. Tenth Street, Davis-Monthan AFB, AZ 85707-4237. **C-1-888-AFLODGE (1-888-235-6343), C-520-228-3230/3309, DSN-312-228-3230/3309,** Fax: C-520-228-3312, DSN-312-228-3312, 24 hours daily. E-mail: lodging@dm.af.mil Directions: South on Craycroft (Main Gate) approximately 0.5 miles on the left (east side) of the street. Check in at lodging after 1400 hours, check out 1100 hours. Government civilian employee lodging.

(TLF) Various buildings. One-bedroom units (25) and two-bedroom units (25) contain full kitchen with utensils, coffee, A/C, CATV, housekeeping service, laundry facility, separate living room with sleeper sofa, cribs, cots. Modern structure. Rates: $28.00. Duty can make reservations any time; Space-A can make reservations 24 hours in advance.

(VAQ) Bldg 3501. E1-E4. Single-bedroom units, common bath, sleeps one (61 rooms). Refrigerator, coffee, A/C, CATV, housekeeping service, laundry facility, ice, vending machines. Modern structure. Rate: $20.50. Duty can make reservations any time; Space-A can make reservations 24 hours in advance.

(**VOQ**) Bldgs 2350, 2550, 4065. Officers all ranks, E5-E9. Single-bedroom units contain private bath with toiletries (144), shared kitchen. Two-room suites contain separate bedroom, private bath with toiletries (22), kitchenette. Two-bedroom units contain private bath with toiletries (4), kitchenette. Chief/SNCO suites contain separate bedroom, private bath with toiletries (4), kitchen. Refrigerator, microwave, coffee, A/C, CATV, housekeeping service, laundry facility, ice machine. Modern structure. Rates: $24.00. Duty can make reservations any time; Space-A can make reservations 24 hours in advance.

(**DV/VIP**) 355th WG Protocol. **C-520-228-3600.** O6+. Bldg 4065. Two-bedroom suites, private bath, toiletries (10); One-bedroom deluxe suites (two special for general/flag officers). Refrigerator, microwave, stocked bar, complete utensils, coffee, A/C, CATV, housekeeping service, ice machine. Modern structure. Rates: $28.00. Duty can make reservations any time; Space-A can make reservations 24 hours in advance. Protocol may cancel reservations for non-Active Duty if Active Duty requires space.

AMENITIES: Available at front desk.

TML AVAILABILITY: Difficult. Best, Dec-Feb.

CREDIT CARDS ACCEPTED: Visa and proprietary MasterCard.

TRANSPORTATION: Off base shuttle/bus (24 hour notice), C-520-889-1000; Car Rental, C-520-571-0886; On base taxi, C-520-228-3391, DSN-312-228-3391; Off base taxi, C-520-624-6611.

DINING OPPORTUNITIES: Burger King, C-520-745-2878; E Club, C-520-228-3100; O Club, C-520-228-3301; and Bowling Center, C-520-228-3461 are within walking distance. Applebee's, C-520-750-9780; Olive Garden, C-520-790-5787; and Red Lobster, C-520-519-1002 are within driving distance.

Visit Old Tucson, Reid Park and Zoo, Arizona-Sonora Desert and Pima Air Museum. Nearby Mt Lemmon is the site of local snow sports in winter.

Fort Huachuca (AZ02R4)
Army Community Service
Attn: ATZS-HRF-A, Bldg 50010
Fort Huachuca, AZ 85613-6000

MAIN INSTALLATION TELEPHONE NUMBERS: C-520-538-7111, DSN-312-879-7111. Locator 538-7111; Medical 533-9200; Security Police 533-2181.

LOCATION: From I-10 take exit 302 south onto AZ-90 south approximately 28 miles to Sierra Vista and Main Gate to fort on right (west) side of road. *USMRA: Page 108 (F,G-9,10).* NMI: Davis-Montham AFB, 75 miles northwest. **NMC:** Tucson, 75 miles northwest.

RESERVATION INFORMATION: Bldg 43083, Grierson Service Road, P.O. Box 12775, Fort Huachuca, AZ 85670-2775. **C-520-533-2222, DSN-312-821-2222,** Fax: C-520-458-0459, 24 hours daily. Check in 1400 hours, check out 1100 hours. Military and government civilian employee lodging.

(**Army Lodging**) Bldgs 42017, 52054. Bedroom, one or two double beds, private bath (21); separate bedroom, double bed, private bath (6); two-bedroom, double beds, private bath (3); three-bedroom, double beds, private bath (3). Community kitchen, refrigerator, A/C, TV, housekeeping service, laundry facility, cribs. Modern structure. Rates: Official $41, Unofficial $46 per unit. Maximum eight persons in Bldg 42017, five persons in Bldg 52054. Duty can make reservations; others Space-A can make reservations up to eight days in advance. Pets allowed first night only. Must be boarded by second day. On-post kennels usually available. *Pet rooms available.*

(**VOQ/VEQ**) Bldgs 43083-43086. Bedroom, private bath or semi-private bath (210). Kitchen and refrigerator in most units, A/C, TV, housekeeping service, laundry facility. Modern structure.

Rates: Official $41, Unofficial $46, $5 for spouse. Active Duty can make reservations.

(**DVQ**) Bldg 22104. O4+, official duty. Separate bedroom suites, private bath (4); two-bedroom, private bath (2). Kitchen, A/C, TV, housekeeping service, laundry facility, cribs. Older structure. Rates: Official $50, Unofficial $55, each additional person $5. Duty can make reservations.

TML AVAILABILITY: Best, Dec. Difficult, other times

CREDIT CARDS ACCEPTED: Visa, MasterCard, American Express and Discover.

TRANSPORTATION: Off base shuttle/bus: ABC Cab Co. C-520-458-8429; AA Cab Co. C-520-378-2100; Transportation Express Shuttle C-520-459-7778; Car Rental: Avis, C-1-800-831-2847; Alamo Rent a car 1-800-327-9633; Enterprise, C-520-458-2425; Hertz, C-1-800-654-3131; Ideal, C-520-458-4808; Serria Toyota, 520-458-8880; Monty's Motors, C-520-458-2665; Kugel Air Flight Services, C-520-458-9496.

DINING OPPORTUNITIES: Anthony's Pizza, C-520-459-2370; Burger King, C-520-459-1430; Jeannie's Diner, C-520-533-5759; PX food court and Popeye's Chicken are within walking distance. Cafeteria, C-520-458-8358; La Hacienda, Pepperoni's Dining, C-520-533-3002; and The Ozone, C-520-533-0861 are within driving distance.

Visit historic Bisbee, the Karchner Caverns and Tombstone, the "Town too tough to die." The ITR office on post is the information office on local activities. Hunting and fishing are good. How about a picnic on Reservoir Hill with a view of 100 miles!

Fort Tuthill Recreation Area (AZ11R4)
Luke Rec Area
HC 30, Box 5
Flagstaff, AZ 86001-8701

MAIN INSTALLATION TELEPHONE NUMBERS: C-1-800-552-6268, C-928-774-8893, DSN-312-896-3401.

LOCATION: Located at an elevation of 7,000 feet at the base of the San Francisco Peaks. Four miles south of Flagstaff. Take I-17 north to exit 337 (Airport/Sedona). Enter park area at Fort Tuthill (adjoins Coconino County fairgrounds.) Take first road to left. *USMRA: Page 108 (E-4).* **NMC:** Flagstaff, four miles north. NMI: Luke AFB, 138 miles southwest.

RESERVATION INFORMATION: C-1-800-552-6268, DSN-312-896-3401, Fax: C-623-856-7990, 24 hours daily. Reservations required, confirm with credit card or mail deposit. Active Duty may make reservations up to a year in advance, others up to six months in advance.

Fort Tuthill Recreation Lodging at Fort Tuthill features southwestern decor.

Cancellations must be received at least 48 hours in advance of arrival to avoid penalty fees. Check in at front desk after 1500 hours, check out 1100 hours.

(TML) Chalet (1), three-bedroom, furnished; A-Frame Chalet (11), two-bedroom, furnished; Cabins (11), studio, furnished; Hotel (20 rooms), two double beds, sleeps four (8); queen-size bed, sleeps two (8); queen-size bed, handicap accessible, sleeps two; queen-size bed (2), kitchenette, sleeps two. Refrigerator, utensils, TV in room and lodge, housekeeping service, washer/dryer, cribs, cots. Rates: $80-$155 daily (Chalets); $55 daily (Cabins); $40-$45 daily (Hotel). **See** *Military Living's RV, Camping and Outdoor Recreation Around the World* **for additional information.**

AMENITIES: Meeting/Conference Room. Ice, Snack and Soft Drink Vending Machine.

TML AVAILABILITY: Good, Oct-Apr.

CREDIT CARDS ACCEPTED: Visa and MasterCard.

TRANSPORTATION: Off base taxi.

DINING OPPORTUNITIES: Restaurants within driving distance.

Gila Bend Air Force Auxiliary Field (AZ16R4)
3096 First Street
Gila Bend AFAF, AZ 85337-5000

MAIN INSTALLATION TELEPHONE NUMBERS: C-928-683-6200, DSN-312-896-5200. Locator 683-6200; Medical 683-6200; Security Police 683-6200.

LOCATION: From I-10 34 miles west of Phoenix, take exit 112 (Yuma/Gila Bend); south on AZ-85 through Gila Bend; right (west) at Gila Bend AFAF/Ajo sign, approximately three-and-a-half miles to the AFAF. Also take I-8 east or west, exit 116 north to left (west) at Gila Bend AAF/Ajo sign and 3.5 miles to base. *USMRA: Page 108 (C-7,8)*. **NMC:** Phoenix, 69 miles northeast.

RESERVATION INFORMATION: Desert Hideaway Inn, Bldg 4300, HC01, Box 22, Gila Bend AFAF, AZ 85337-5000. **C-928-683-2911, DSN-312-896-2911,** Fax: C-928-683-6188, DSN-312-896-5188, 0700-2000 hours Mon-Fri (depending on occupancy). After hours check in at Security Bldg 300. Check out 1100 hours.

(VAQ) Bldg 4300. Private bedroom, private bath (50); semi-private bath (5). A/C, refrigerator, microwave, CATV, laundry facility. Rates: $10 per room. Duty can make reservations; others Space-A.

(VOQ) Bldgs 2358 A-D. Two-bedroom, semi-private bath (4). A/C, fully equipped kitchen, CATV in living room. Rates: $13.50 per room. Duty can make reservations; others Space-A.

AMENITIES: Exercise Room.

TML AVAILABILITY: Very good. Difficult, Oct-Jan.

CREDIT CARDS ACCEPTED: Visa and MasterCard.

TRANSPORTATION: None available.

DINING OPPORTUNITIES: Exit West Cafe, C-928-683-6458; and Space Age, C-928-683-2761 are within driving distance.

Trips to the Organ Pipe National Monument and Rocky Point Mexico are favorite activities in this area.

NEW ADDITION !
CAMP NAVAJO (AZ08R4)-As we go to press, we've just heard that lodging facilities are available at Camp Navajo Training Site. Call C-928-773-3238, DSN-312-853-3238 for details.

Luke Air Force Base (AZ03R4)
56FW/PA
7282 North 137th Avenue
Luke AFB, AZ 85309-1520

MAIN INSTALLATION TELEPHONE NUMBERS: C-623-856-1110, DSN-312-896-1110. Locator 856-6405; Medical 856-7506; Security Police 856-6349.

LOCATION: From Phoenix, west on I-10 to Litchfield Road, exit 128, north on Litchfield Road approximately five miles. Also, from Phoenix, north on I-17 to Glendale Avenue exit 205 west on Glendale Avenue to intersection of Glendale Avenue and Litchfield Road approximately 10 miles. *USMRA: Page 108 (D-6,7)*. **NMC:** Phoenix, 20 miles east.

RESERVATION INFORMATION: Fighter Country Inn, 7012 N. Bong Lane, Luke AFB, AZ 85309-1534. **C-1-888-AFLODGE (1-888-235-6343), C-623-935-2641/856-3941, DSN-312-896-3941,** Fax: C-623-856-3332, DSN-312-896-3332, 24 hours daily. E-mail: 56svs.reservations@ luke.af.mil Check in at lodging office 1400 hours, check out 1100 hours.

(TLF) Four buildings. Bedroom, private bath (40). Kitchen, utensils, A/C, CATV/VCR, housekeeping service, laundry facility. Older structure. Rates: $23.50 per night. Duty can make reservations any time; Space-A can make reservations 24 hours in advance.

(VAQ) Two buildings. One- to two-bedroom, private bath (74); Chief Suites (3). Kitchen, utensils, A/C, CATV/VCR, housekeeping service, laundry facility. Older structure. Rates: Maximum $15 per per night. Duty can make reservations any time; Space-A can make reservations 24 hours in advance.

(VOQ) Five buildings. Bedroom, private bath (182). Kitchen, refrigerator, A/C, CATV/VCR, housekeeping service, laundry facility. Modern structure. Rates: $13.50 per person per night. Duty can make reservations any time; Space-A can make reservations 24 hours in advance.

(DV/VIP) Protocol Officer, 56th FW, **C-623-856-5840.** O6+. In VOQ, suites, private bath (13), O7+. Two-bedroom house, private bath (2). Kitchen, utensils, A/C, CATV/VCR, housekeeping service, washer/dryer. Rates: DV Suite $20.50, DV House $22.50. Duty can make reservations any time; Space-A can make reservations 24 hours in advance.

TML AVAILABILITY: Best, Oct-Apr. Difficult, other times.

CREDIT CARDS ACCEPTED: Visa and MasterCard.

TRANSPORTATION: On base shuttle/bus.

DINING OPPORTUNITIES: Bowling Alley Snack Bar, Burger King, McDonald's, NCO Club and O Club are within driving distance.

See Phoenix State Capitol Building murals, the Desert Botanical Garden in Papago Park. Pioneer Arizona, a living history museum, and the Phoenix Zoo are worth a visit. Also, the Grand Canyon is 90 miles away.

Yuma Army Proving Ground (AZ05R4)
Army Community Service
STEYP-MWR-FSD, Bldg 309
Yuma, AZ 85365-9111

MAIN INSTALLATION TELEPHONE NUMBERS: C-928-328-2151, DSN-312-899-2151. Locator 328-2151; Medical 328-2911; Security Police 328-2720.

LOCATION: Northeast of I-8, turn right (north) on US-95 which bisects the post. Southwest of I-10 turn left (south) on US-95. US-95 bisects Army Proving Ground. *USMRA: Page 108 (A-6,7,8; B-7,8)*. **NMC:** Yuma, 27 miles southwest.

RESERVATION INFORMATION: Attn: STEYP-EH-H, Bldg 506A, Yuma, AZ 85365-9124. **C-928-328-2129, DSN-312-899-2129,** 0630-1700 hours Mon-Fri. Check in 1400 hours, after hours Bldg 611, check out 1100 hours. Government civilian employee billeting.

VEQ Bldg 506A. Official duty only. Two-man rooms. TV/VCR, coffee maker, microwave, laundry facility, ice machine, housekeeping service (Mon-Fri). Rates: $12.50 per person.

VOQ Bldg 1004. Official duty only. Suites, private bath (15). Refrigerator, microwave, coffee maker, A/C, TV/VCR in room and lounge, housekeeping service, laundry facility, ice machine. Modern structure. Rates: sponsor $31, each additional person $4. All categories can make reservations. No smoking.

Army Lodging Bldg 538. Bedroom, private bath (10). Kitchen, utensils, A/C, TV in room and lounge, housekeeping service, laundry facility, cribs, cots, ice machine. Modern structure. Handicap accessible (1). Rates: sponsor $27, each additional person $3. Maximum four per room. Reservations advised. No smoking, no pets.

DV/VIP Bldg 944 A/B, **C-928-328-6600,** O6/GS15+, official duty. Suites, private bath (2). Kitchen, refrigerator, coffee maker, honor bar, living room, dining room, A/C, TV/VCR, housekeeping service, laundry facility, cribs, cots, ice machine, beverages. Older structure. Rates: sponsor $36, each additional person $4.

TML AVAILABILITY: Good, Apr-Dec. Difficult, Jan-Mar.

CREDIT CARDS ACCEPTED: Visa and MasterCard.

TRANSPORTATION: Car Rental and Off base taxi. No base transportation.

DINING OPPORTUNITIES: Cactus Cafe, C-928-328-2333/2533; Coyote Lanes, C-928-328-2308; and SGT Pepperoni's, C-928-328-3663, are within walking distance.

Visit the Century House Museum for local history, Fort Yuma and the St. Thomas Mission, Yuma Territorial Prison and Museum, and the Quechan Indian Museum in Old Fort Yuma to get a taste of this pre-old west town.

Yuma Marine Corps Air Station (AZ04R4)
Marine Corps Community Services
Box 99119
Yuma MCAS, AZ 85369-9119

MAIN INSTALLATION TELEPHONE NUMBERS: C-928-269-2011, DSN-312-269-2011. Locator 269-2011; Medical 269-2772; Security Police 269-2361.

LOCATION: From I-8 take exit 3 onto Avenue 3E south for 1 mile to base on right, adjacent to Yuma IAP. *USMRA: Page 108 (A-8).* **NMC:** Yuma, three miles northwest.

RESERVATION INFORMATION: Bldg 1088, Box 99119, Yuma, AZ 85369-9119. **C-928-269-2262, DSN-312-269-2262,** Fax:C-928-269-6639, 24 hours daily. Directions: From Main Gate go one block to Bldg 1088 on south side. Check in 1500 hours, check out 1100 hours.

TLF Dos Rios Inn, "The Marine Corps' Premiere Southwest Facility," Bldg 1088. C-928-269-2262, DSN-312-269-2262. Rooms (36). Double queen with kitchenette (24); king (12); handicap with kitchenette (2). Refrigerator, microwave, coffee maker, A/C, CATV, housekeeping service, cribs, high chairs, guest laundry, snack and ice machine. New structure. Rates: $36-$40. Reservations up to three months in advance.

TML AVAILABILITY: Extremely limited, recommend calling for reservations.

CREDIT CARDS ACCEPTED: Visa, MasterCard, American Express and Discover.

TRANSPORTATION: Car Rental: Enterprise, C-928-269-1495; Off base taxi, C-928-782-0111.

DINING OPPORTUNITIES: MCCS Combined Clubs C-928-269-2406; Godfathers Pizza C-928-341-0150; Burger King, C-928-341-0490; La Flor Mexican Food C-928-269-5183; and Subway, C-928-269-3466 are all on base.

Located within miles of the Colorado River, fishing, hunting, golf, shopping and the festivities in Mexico.

ARKANSAS

Camp Joseph T. Robinson (AR07R2)
ATTN: TAG-AR-PR
Building 6000
North Little Rock, AR 72199-9600

MAIN INSTALLATION TELEPHONE NUMBERS: C-501-212-5100, DSN-312-962-5100. Locator 212-5100; Medical 212-5262; Police 212-5280.

LOCATION: From east or west on I-40, take Burns Park exit 150 to Military Drive, follow signs north to camp (two miles). *USMRA: Page 76 (D-5).* **NMC:** North Little Rock, 2 miles south.

RESERVATION INFORMATION: Lodging Office, Bldg 5130, Phillips Armory, Arkansas Avenue. **C-888-366-3205, C-501-212-5100/5274/5275,**

DSN-312-962-5100/5274/5275, Fax: C-501-212-5271, 0700-1530 hours, Sun-Thu; 0700-2000 hours Fri; and 0700-1630 hours Sat. Check in anytime. After hours check in at security office, Bldg 7200. Check out 1000.

(TML) 155 units. One and two person rooms; VIP rooms with private bath, towel service, coffee maker. One and two person rooms have amenities that vary. All rooms have CATV, laundry facilities, housekeeping service. Rates: One and two person rooms $7-$11; VIP rooms $13-$17.

AMENITIES: Lounge.

TML AVAILABILITY: Difficult, Oct and drill weekends.

CREDIT CARDS ACCEPTED: Visa, MasterCard and American Express.

TRANSPORTATION: Off base buses and taxi service.

DINING OPPORTUNITIES: Cafeteria on camp, C-501-212-4646; The Rock Restaurant C-501-758-8468; The Rock Lounge C-501-758-5076.

Plenty to see and do in the State Capital with Burns Park, Wild River Country, Quapaw District, Little Rock Zoo, Arkansas Arts Center, Governor's Mansion, Old Mill, Pinnacle Mountain, War Memorial Park and Arkansas Travelers baseball all nearby.

Fort Chaffee Maneuver Training Center (AR04R2)
Bldg 1370, Fort Smith Blvd
Fort Chaffee, AR 72905-5000

MAIN INSTALLATION TELEPHONE NUMBERS: C-479-484-3170, DSN-312-962-3170. Locator 484-2666; Security Police 484-2666 (2911 from rooms).

LOCATION: From I-40 take the I-540 exit 7 southwest in Fort Smith. From I-540 exit 8 onto AR-22 southeast (Rogers Avenue) and continue through the town of Barling to Fort Chaffee, one mile east of Barling. *USMRA: Page 76 (A,B-4,5)*. **NMC:** Fort Smith, six miles north.

RESERVATION INFORMATION: Bldg 1370, Fort Smith Blvd, Fort Chaffee, AR 72905-5000. **C-479-484-2252, DSN-312-962-2252,** Fax: C-479-484-2259, 0700-1530 hours Mon-Fri, 0700-1530 hours Sat. Reservations accepted two weeks in advance. Check in at facility, after hours check in at police department, Bldg 2100. Closed on Federal holidays. All ranks, State and Federal employees and Retirees.

(BEQ/BOQ) Various buildings. Bedrooms, private/shared baths; suites, private bath. Refrigerator, A/C, TV, housekeeping service, free laundry facility. Rates $10-$23.75. No pets.

(DVQ) Cottages (9). Kitchen (2). Refrigerator, A/C, TV, phone, housekeeping service, washer/dryer. Rates: single $15.75; double $23.75. No Pets.

TML AVAILABILITY: Difficult, summer.

CREDIT CARDS ACCEPTED: Visa, MasterCard, American Express, Discover, Diners and Carte Blanche.

TRANSPORTATION: Car Rental, C-479-646-7823; Off base taxi, C-479-783-1118.

DINING OPPORTUNITIES: Hitching Post Restaurant, C-479-452-3645 is within walking distance. Many restaurants including Hardee's, C-479-452-4192; McDonald's, C-479-452-5500; and Olive Garden, C-479-478-7008 are within driving distance.

Historic Fort Smith, on the Arkansas River, five miles. Gateway to the Ozarks. Fayetteville-University of Arkansas is an opportunity for sporting events. Wildlife management area, excellent hunting and fishing.

Little Rock Air Force Base (AR02R2)
314 MSS/DPF
1024 Cannon Circle
Little Rock AFB, AR 72099-5288

MAIN INSTALLATION TELEPHONE NUMBERS: C-501-987-1110, DSN-312-731-1110. Locator 987-6025; Medical 987-8811; Security Police 987-3221.

LOCATION: From I-40 take exit 155 north on US-67/167 to Jacksonville, take exit 11 west to Vandenberg Blvd Follow signs to Main Gate west of US-67/167. *USMRA: Page 76 (D,E-5)*. **NMC:** Little Rock, 18 miles southwest.

RESERVATION INFORMATION: Bldg 1024, Cannon Circle, P.O. Box 1192, Little Rock AFB, AR 72078-1192. **C-1-888-AFLODGE (1-888-235-6343), C-501-987-6651 DSN-312-731-6651,** Fax: C-501-987-7769/6200, 24 hours daily. E-mail: 314svs/svml@littlerock.af.mil WEB: www.little-rock.af.mil Duty personnel can make reservations at any time; Space-A can make reservations 24 hours in advance. Directions: Vandenberg Drive to Arnold Drive. Turn left onto Arnold. Go to first traffic light, turn left onto Cannon Circle, then left at second street. Check in at billeting 1400 hours, check out 1100 hours.

(VAQ) Bldgs 746, 850, 880. Official duty. No TLF. Spaces available (144). Refrigerator, microwave, A/C, CATV/VCR, housekeeping service, laundry facility, ice machine. Modern structure, remodeled. Rates: $18-$23. Limited rooms for children/family. No pets.

(VOQ) Bldgs 882, 884, 1020, 1024, 1036. Official duty. Spaces available (193). No TLF. Refrigerator. A/C, CATV/VCR, housekeeping service, laundry facility, ice machine. Modern structurre, remodeled. Rates: $21.50-$30.50. Limited rooms for children/family. No pets.

(DV/VIP) Bldg 1036 and 1024, 314 AW/CCP. **C-501-987-6828/8475 or DSN-312-731-6828/8475.** O6+, Active/Retiree. TDY to base only. Rates: $30.50. No pets.

AMENITIES: Exercise Room. Ice, Snack and Soft Drink Vending Machines.

TML AVAILABILITY: Limited, Jan-Nov. Very Good, Dec.

CREDIT CARDS ACCEPTED: Visa and MasterCard.

TRANSPORTATION: Car Rental, C-501-791-7300; On base taxi, C-501-987-6086/6087, DSN-312-731-6086/6087; Off base taxi (Active Duty or TDY personnel only), C-501-988-4425.

DINING OPPORTUNITIES: Airlifter Combined Dining, C-501-987-1111; and J.R. Rockers, C-501-987-5555 are within walking distance. AAFES Snack Bar, Burger King and Popeye's are within driving distance.

See War Memorial Park, Burns Park, and Governor's Mansion.

Pine Bluff Arsenal (AR03R2)
10020 Kambrick Circle
Pine Bluff, AR 71602-9500

MAIN INSTALLATION TELEPHONE NUMBERS: C-870-540-3000, DSN-312-966-3000. Locator 540-3000; Medical 540-3409; Security Police 540-3506.

LOCATION: Southeast of Little Rock, take US-65 south to exit 32, then east to AR-256 to Main Gate. Off US-65 northwest of Pine Bluff. Take AR-256, cross AR-365 into the Main Gate of arsenal. *USMRA: Page 76 (E-6)*. **NMC:** Pine Bluff, eight miles southeast. NMI: Little Rock Air Force Base, 32 miles northwest.

RESERVATION INFORMATION: SIOPB-PAL-AMSSB-OPB-PAL, Bldg 15-330, Sibert Road, Pine Bluff Arsenal, AR 71602-9500. **C-870-540-3008, DSN-312-966-3008,** Fax: C-870-540-3582, DSN-312-966-3582, 0630-1600 hours Mon-Thu. Other hours OC, C-870-540-2700. Directions:

SAFETY, SECURITY AND SAVINGS
Await you at U.S. Military Installations.

Learn the Secrets of Military Travel with Military Living's R&R Travel News®.

Features

✻ A six time yearly, by subscription, 16 page military travel newsletter.

✻ Military Installations offer YOU more SAFETY, big dollar savings, and old-fashioned military camaraderie and a ton of fun.

✻ Keep your good military memories alive and growing. Travel to places where you feel at home - U.S. Military Installations.

✻ Be among the first to know about NEW military travel opportunities at worldwide U.S. Military Installations!

✻ Learn how to hitch-hike around the world FREE on U.S. Military aircraft. Space-A is fun and can save YOU thousands of $$$$'s.

✻ Our R&R subscribers are circling the globe flying SPACE-A on military aircraft, staying in military lodging, taking trips and tours with ITT/ITR travel offices and having fun at military RV/camping and outdoor recreation areas. Together, these subscribers have a powerful clearinghouse of information by sharing their travel "finds" with each other via Military Living's R&R Travel News®.

How to Subscribe

Call our Toll-Free Order Line 1-888-685-0203 or 703-237-0203 and order with your credit card.

Fax: 703-237-2233 (Please include credit card number and expiration date and a phone number where we may reach you with any questions.)

Online: Go to www.militaryliving.com and click on the order form button on the left side of the first page and order through our secure server with your credit card.

Write: Military Living, PO Box 2347, Falls Church, VA 22042-0347. Send check, money order or credit card information VISA, Mastercard, American Express, Discover (Please include credit card number and expiration date plus phone number and billing address if different than your shipping address). We do not bill, in order to keep the prices of our publications as low as possible.

MILITARY PUBLICATIONS *Living*™

www.militaryliving.com

Free Gift with 5-Year Subscription

Look below under subscription rates to see how YOU can receive a free gift of Military Living's Military Space-A Air Basic Training and Reader Trip Reports! (A $17.45 mail order value!)

Subscription Rates

1 year - $23 (6 issues)
2 years - $34   SAVE 26%*
3 years - $46   SAVE 33%*
5 years - $69   SAVE 40%* & FREE GIFT

5 Year Subscription - Includes a FREE copy of Military Living's Military Travel Guide U.S.A., your step-by-step guide to free travel on Military Aircraft. Sorry, no substitutions on this special one-time offer, which expires 31 December 2003. Thirty issues for $69 - less than $2.25 per issue business class mail delivery and YOUR free Military Travel Guide U.S.A!
*Off 1 year Rate

SAVE TIME AND MONEY

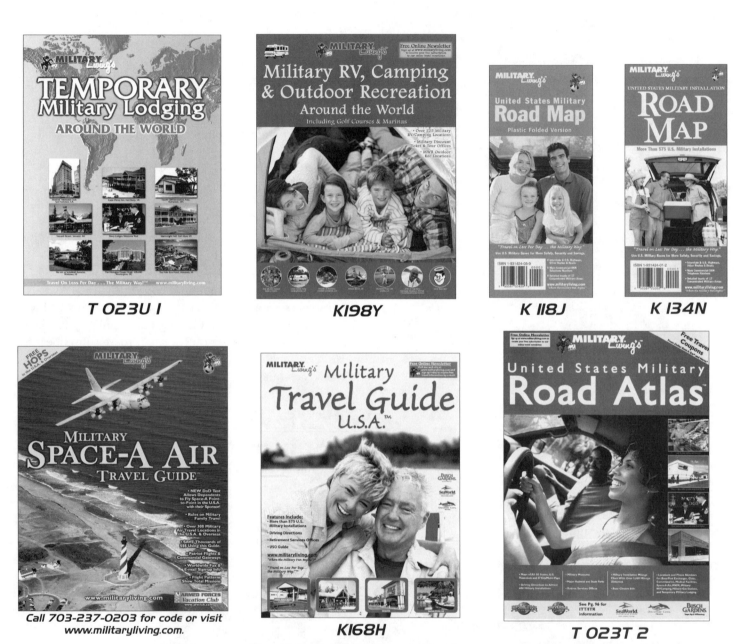

T O23U I

KI98Y

K II8J

K I34N

Call 703-237-0203 for code or visit
www.militaryliving.com.

KI68H

T O23T 2

YOU BUY AT EXCHANGE PRICES AND SAVE!

Standard shipping and handling is included, unless you select to have your purchased
items delivered to you by Priority Mail at an additional charge*.

TWO WAYS TO BUY FROM YOUR ONLINE MILITARY EXCHANGE
1. Call 1-800-527-2345 (U.S.A.) and give the operator your catalog item code (above).
2. Log on to AAFES.com and order using the Exchange Online Ordering System.

*subject to change

From Main Gate go half a block to stop sign, make a left. Travel north about one mile to the billeting office—the first office to the right, past the health clinic. Check in at billeting, check out 1200 hours. Government civilian employee billeting.

TML TQ and BOQ. Bldgs 16-220, 15-330, 15-350. Bedroom, private bath (6); separate bedroom, private bath (14); two-bedroom, private bath (1). Community kitchen, refrigerator, microwave, utensils, A/C, CATV, housekeeping service, laundry facility, iron/ironing board. Older structure. Rates: VEQ $20; BOQ $31; DV/VIP $35; additional adults $1, children under 12 free. Duty can make reservations; others Space-A.

AMENITIES: Exercise Room, Meeting/Conference Room, Business Center, Ice, Soft Drink and Snack Vending Machine, Internet/E-mail access for all customers.

TML AVAILABILITY: Extremely limited.

CREDIT CARDS ACCEPTED: Visa, MasterCard and American Express.

TRANSPORTATION: On base taxi, ext 3595.

DINING OPPORTUNITIES: Danny's Inc, C-870-534-1632; Pizza Hut, C-870-535-4451; and Sonic's, C-870-247-1500 are within driving distance.

Great hunting and fishing. Also a nine hole golf course, a recreation center with excellent exercise equipment, a swimming pool and small PX.

CALIFORNIA

Barstow Marine Corps Logistics Base (CA13R4)
Family Service Center
Box 110100
Barstow MCLB, CA 92311-5001

MAIN INSTALLATION TELEPHONE NUMBERS: C-760-577-6211, DSN-312-282-6611/6612. Locator 577-6211; Medical 577-6591; Security Police 577-6666.

LOCATION: On I-40, one and a half miles east of Barstow. Take I-15 northeast from San Bernardino, or west from Las Vegas, NV exit East Main Street east to I-40 east, exit to Josep L. Boll Avenue and Main Gate. Signs mark direction to MCLB. *USMRA: Page 111 (G-12,13).* **NMC:** San Bernardino, 75 miles southwest.

RESERVATION INFORMATION: Food and Hospitality Branch, Bldg 171, Barstow MCLB, CA 92311-5047. **C-760-577-6418, DSN-312-282-6418,** Fax: C-760-577-6110, 0800-1600 hours. Other hours BDO, Bldg 15, C-760-577-6961. Duty can make reservations; other Space-A. Check in 1400 hours at billeting, check out 1100 hours.

TLF **Oasis Lodge.** Bldg 114. Bedroom, private bath (2); two-bedroom, private bath (2). Half a mile from Main Gate. Rates: $25.

DV/VIP Commanding General, Bldg 15, **C-760-577-6555, DSN-312-282-6555,** Fax: C-760-577-6058. VIP: Bldg 8. 05+. Three-bedroom, two private baths (1). Kitchen, utensils, A/C, TV, housekeeping service, laundry facility. Older structure. Rates: $40 per unit.

TML AVAILABILITY: Good, Aug-Apr. Difficult, other times.

CREDIT CARDS ACCEPTED: (normal duty hours only) Visa, MasterCard, Discover and American Express (government card only).

TRANSPORTATION: Car Rentals: Avis, C-760-256-8614; Enterprise, C-760-256-0761.

DINING OPPORTUNITIES: Family Restaurant is within walking distance.

Visit Calico Ghost Town, eight miles east. Lake Delores is 13 miles east for water recreation. Southern California is within easy reach and Las Vegas is not too far east.

Beale Air Force Base (CA47R4)
9th MSS/DPF
17800 13th Street, Suite 400
Beale AFB, CA 95903-1525

MAIN INSTALLATION TELEPHONE NUMBERS: C-530-634-3000, DSN-312-368-3000/1110. Locator 634-2960; Medical 634-4849; Security Police 634-2131.

LOCATION: From CA-70 north or south, take Feather River Blvd exit east (south of Marysville), follow to North Beale Road, take right (east), (follow signs to Beale), continue for 7 miles until road dead ends at Main Gate of AFB. *USMRA: Page 110 (C,D-5,6).* **NMC:** Sacramento, 35 miles southwest.

RESERVATION INFORMATION: Gold Country Inn, 9 SVS/SVML, Bldg 24112, A Street, Beale AFB, CA 95903-1615. **C-1-888-AFLODGE (1-888-235-6343),** C-530-634-2953/2954, DSN-312-368-2953/2954, Fax: C-530-634-3674, DSN-312-368-3674, 24 hours daily. WEB: www.beale.af.mil/units/sptg/svs/frntpg.htm Check in at lodging, check out 1100 hours. Government civilian employee billeting. Space-A reservations confirmed 24 hours prior.

TLF Bldgs 5109-5116. Two-bedroom, private bath (3); three-bedroom, private bath (6); four-bedroom, private bath (8). Kitchen, microwave, complete utensils, A/C, TV in lounge, housekeeping service, laundry facility, cribs, cots. Older structure. Rates: $21.50.

VAQ Bldg 2156. Bedroom, semi-private bath, (50); SNCO suites, private bath (3). Refrigerator, microwave, A/C, TV in room and lounge, housekeeping service, laundry facility, cribs, cots, ice machine. Older structure, remodeled. Rates: bedroom $13; suite $13.50.

VOQ Bldgs 2350-2360. Bedroom, private bath (47). Kitchen, microwave, limited utensils, A/C, TV in room and lounge, housekeeping service, laundry facility, cribs, cots. Older structure. Rates: $13.50.

DV/VIP Protocol Office, **C-530-634-2120.** O6+, Retirees. Reservations required.

TML AVAILABILITY: Good, Sep-May. Difficult, other times.

CREDIT CARDS ACCEPTED: Visa and MasterCard.

TRANSPORTATION: On base shuttle/bus.

DINING OPPORTUNITIES: Bowling Center, C-530-634-2299; Burger King, C-530-788-2624; and Tri-Club, C-530-634-4948 are within driving distance.

In the center of historic California gold rush country, east of Marysville and north of Sacramento. Outdoor sports are popular.

Big Bear Recreation Facility (CA05R2)
Miramar Marine Corps Air Station
San Diego, CA 92145-2008

MAIN INSTALLATION TELEPHONE NUMBERS: C-858-577-4126/4141. Medical 911; Security Police 911.

LOCATION: Off base. Located at Big Bear Lake. From I-10 at Redlands, take CA-30 north to CA-330. Go north on CA-330 to CA-18 at Running

Springs. Take CA-18 east to Big Bear. At Big Bear Dam, turn right. This is still CA-18 but also called Big Bear Blvd Take Big Bear Blvd, past the Village, to Moonridge Road. Turn right and go to right on Elm Street, right on Switzerland Drive, take an immediate left. Facility is about 0.25 miles down the dirt road. *Note: Don't be tempted to take a shortcut through Snow Summit Ski Area as the road is gated during winter months.* USMRA: Page 111 (G-13). NMI: March ARB, approximately 30 miles southwest. **NMC:** San Bernardino, 50 miles southwest.

RESERVATION INFORMATION: C-858-577-4126/4141. Reservations required. Reservations accepted Mon-Fri ONLY. Priorities apply-Active Duty personnel stationed at Miramar MCAS and all other USMC bases may make reservations beginning the first business day of the month for the following calendar month. Active Duty stationed at all other Military bases may make reservations beginning the second business day of the month for the following calendar month. Retirees, Reservists and DoD employees may make reservations beginning the fourth business day of the month for the following calendar month. There ia a limit of one cabin per sponsor per month. Additional cabin reservations may be made following the fourth business day of the month depending on availability. An authorized patron is required present in the cabin during the entire stay.

TML Chalets (8). One-bedroom, living room, loft (two double beds), sleeps a maximum of six persons including infants. Kitchen, microwave, utensils, fireplace, TV/VCR. Personal items and towels not provided. Rates: $45-$75 daily.

TML AVAILABILITY: Good, May-Oct.

CREDIT CARDS ACCEPTED: Visa, MasterCard and Discover.

TRANSPORTATION: Car Rental: Enterprise, C-909-866-1156.

DINING OPPORTUNITIES: Alpine High Country Cafe, C-909-866-1959; Boo Bear's Den, C-909-866-2167; La Montana Restaurant, C-909-866-2602 and several fast food restaurants are within driving distance.

Camp Pendleton Marine Corps Base (CA30R4)
ACS, Military Human Resources
Box 555019
Camp Pendleton MCB, CA 92055-5019

MAIN INSTALLATION TELEPHONE NUMBERS: C-760-725-4111, DSN-312-365-4111. Locator 725-4111; Medical 725-6308; Security Police 911.

LOCATION: From north or south of Oceanside, take I-5 which is adjacent to Camp Pendleton along the Pacific Ocean. From I-5 north or south take the "Camp Pendleton Only" off ramp from I-5 at Oceanside to Vandegrift Blvd USMRA: Page 111 (F-14,15). **NMC:** Oceanside, adjacent to base southeast.

RESERVATION INFORMATION: Bldg 1341, Box 555013, Camp Pendleton MCB, CA 92055-5013. **C-760-430-4701, DSN-312-365-3451/3718,** Fax: C-760-725-3221, DSN-312-365-3221, 24 hours daily. Directions: Check in for Bldgs 1341, 1342, 1751, go through Main Gate, 12 miles to Mainside; turn right at Mainside Bowling Alley/Theater, three blocks to Bldg 1341; check in for Bldg 210440, go through Main Gate, take first left at light, follow signs to Sharkey's O Club, check in at lobby, check out 1200 hours. Government civilian employee billeting.

BEQ Camp Pendleton Naval Hospital. C-619-725-1383. E1-E4. Bedroom, sleeps three, iron/ironing board. Check in after 1200 hours, check out 1100 hours.

CBQ **Marine Manor.** TAD/TDY, Reservists on A.T. or drill may reserve up to 90 days in advance. Space-A: PCS, and leave/non-duty, Retirees may not reserve in advance. Availability: Best in winter and on holiday weekends. Difficult on reserve weekends. Facilities: Bldg 1341: no children, no females, singles only. 20 single room, shared bath. CATV, refrigerator, microwave, iron/ironing board, laundry facilities. Rates: $25 for one person, $30 for two people.

CBQ **Harborsite Inn,** Bldg 210440. Reservations: same as Marine Manor. 144 units total, many with Ocean or Harbor views, Sharkey's O Club on premises, small conference space, laundry facilities on each floor. Beach, shops within walking distance. No children. 124 shared units with private bath, irons/ironing board, shared living room with CATV/VCR, refrigerator. Single occupancy only, no females. Rates: $22 per night. 16 private room, private bath for females and couples, CATV, refrigerator, microwave. Rates: $22 for one person, $27 for two people. Eight suites for E9, O6+. Limited availability for suites.

TML MWR Guesthouse. **Ward Lodge.** Bldg 1310, fifteen miles from Main Gate. C-760-725-5304/5194, Fax: C-760-725-5609. Check in at facility. Bedroom with two queen beds, private bath (64). Fully equipped kitchen (36 units), A/C, CATV/VCR, hairdryer, iron/ironing board, coffee maker, voicemail, movie rentals, housekeeping service, coin laundry facility, ice machines, facilities for DAVs, swimming pool. Modern structure. Rates: $45 with kitchen, $35 without kitchen. Reservations accepted one year in advance.

DV/VIP Attn: Joint Protocol Officer, Bldg 1160, **C-760-725-5780/5080.** Bldg 1342, 1751. O6+. DVQ/VIP: Two-bedroom, 1.5 baths (3); kitchen, living room, dining room, den. DVQ bedroom, queen-size bed, private bath, (2); living room, refrigerator, utensils, service bar. Microwave, coffee maker, CATV, AM/FM radio, base phone, laundry facility. Older structure. Rates: TAD/TDY $20-$30, others $27-$52, each additional person $5. Maximum six per suite. Handicap accessible (1). TAD/TDY can make reservations, others Space-A. General/Flag rank have priority.

AMENITIES: Exercise Room, Meeting/Conference Room, Mini Mart, Snack Vending Machine and Soft Drink Machine.

TML AVAILABILITY: Fairly good, Oct-Mar. Difficult, other times.

CREDIT CARDS ACCEPTED: Visa, MasterCard and American Express.

TRANSPORTATION: On base shuttle/bus: North County Transit; Off base shuttle/bus, C-619-295-1900; Car Rental: Enterprise, C-760-385-5149.

DINING OPPORTUNITIES: Fast food, military dining facilities, E Club and O Club are within walking distance. Oceanside Harbor restaurants, Hometown Buffet and a variety of local Mexican and American restaurants are within driving distance.

Beaches, all forms of water recreation, Mission San Luis Rey and 72 golf courses are within easy reach of Camp Pendleton.

Camp Roberts (CA98R4)
California Army National Guard Training Site
Headquarters, Building 109
Camp Roberts, CA 93451-5000

MAIN INSTALLATION TELEPHONE NUMBERS: C-805-238-3100, DSN-312-949-8210, Locator 238-8390; Medical 911, Security Police 911.

LOCATION: On US-101, halfway between Los Angeles and San Francisco, 14 miles north of Paso Robles. Use Camp Roberts exit west. USMRA: Page 111 (C-10). **NMC:** Paso Robles, 14 miles south.

RESERVATION INFORMATION: Bldg 6038, Camp Roberts, CA 93451-5000. **C-805-238-8312, DSN-312-949-8312,** Fax: C-805-238-8384, 0800-1630 hours Mon-Fri.

BEQ/BOQ Rates: $14.50 Official, $15.50 Unofficial. No pets allowed.

TML AVAILABILITY: Best during week.

CREDIT CARDS ACCEPTED: Visa, MasterCard, American Express and Discover.

TRANSPORTATION: None on post.

DINING OPPORTUNITIES: Consolidated Mess, C-805-238-8237 and Snack Bar, C-805-238-8120. Various restaurants within driving distance in Paso Robles.

A short drive to the Hearst Castle and the Pacific Ocean, hunting, fishing, military museum, Mission San Miguel Arcangel, Fort Hunter Liggett and Mission San Antonio nearby. Military RV and camping on training site.

Camp San Luis Obispo (CA83R4)
CANG, Western Mobilization and Training Complex
Highway 1, HQ Bldg 738
San Luis Obispo, CA 93403-4360

MAIN INSTALLATION TELEPHONE NUMBERS: C-805-594-6500/01, DSN-312-630-6500/01. Medical 911; Security Police 911.

LOCATION: From US-101 north or south to San Luis Obispo, then northwest on CA-1 (Cabrillo Highway) for approximately 5 miles toward Morro Bay to Camp San Luis Obispo on southwest side of CA-1. *USMRA: Page 111 (C-11).* **NMC:** San Luis Obispo, 5 miles southeast.

RESERVATION INFORMATION: Bldg 738, San Joaquin Avenue, P.O. Box 4360, San Luis Obispo, CA 93403-4360. **C-805-594-6500, DSN-312-630-6500,** 0800-1630 hours Mon-Sun. Check in 1100-1630 hours, check out 1200 hours. Government civilian employee billeting.

BEQ/BOQ Transient housing. Rooms, apartments, cottages. Bedroom, community bath (101); bedroom, hall bath (39); two-bedroom, private bath (8); three-bedroom, private bath (3); various bedroom/bath combinations (4). Refrigerator, kitchen (some units), limited utensils, TV, housekeeping service. Older structure, redecorated. Rates: BEQ sponsor: official $13.50, unofficial $16.00; BOQ sponsor: official $15.50, unofficial $16; Family rates: $48 per night, up to five people, each additional person $16. Maximum varies per unit. Duty can make reservations, Space-A tentative reservations up to one month in advance. No pets.

DV/VIP O6+. Rates: $13.50-$18.75. Retirees and lower ranks Space-A.

AMENITIES: Exercise Room, Meeting/Conference Room, Snack and Soft Drink Vending Machine.

TML AVAILABILITY: Fairly good. Best, Sept-Mar. Difficult, other times.

CREDIT CARDS ACCEPTED: Visa, MasterCard and American Express.

TRANSPORTATION: Off base shuttle/bus, C-805-541-CARS (2277); Car Rental, C-805-543-8843; Off base taxi, C-805-543-1234.

DINING OPPORTUNITIES: Firestone Grill, C-805-783-1001; McClintocks, C-805-541-0686; and Tortilla Flats, C-805-544-7575 are within driving distance.

There is a small aircraft museum on post. Don't miss local state beaches. Visit local wineries, Hearst Castle, San Luis Obispo Mission Plaza and Farmers Market. There is a golf course across from the main post.

Visit Military Living online at
www.militaryliving.com

China Lake Naval Air Weapons Station (CA34R4)
Commanding Officer NAWS, Code 8J0000D
1 Administration Circle
China Lake, CA 93555-6100

MAIN INSTALLATION TELEPHONE NUMBERS: C-760-939-9011, DSN-312-437-9011. Locator 939-9011; Medical 911; Security Police 939-3323.

LOCATION: From north or south on US-395 or CA-14, go east on CA-178 to Ridgecrest to the Main Gate at the corner of Inyokern Road and China Lake Blvd. *USMRA: Page 111 (G-10,11,12; H-11).* **NMC:** Los Angeles, 130 miles south.

RESERVATION INFORMATION: China Lake Inn, Bldg 1395, China Lake NAWS, CA 93555-6100. **C-760-939-3146/2383, DSN-312-437-3146/2383,** Fax: C-760-939-2789, 24 hours daily. E-mail: ChinaLakeInn@navair.navy.mil Duty personnel can make reservations, others Space-A. Check in after 1500 hours, check out 1200 hours. Government civilian employee billeting.

BEQ/BOQ Bldg 1395. E1-E4. Shared bedroom, private bath (8), E5-O4 private room, private bath (16). Rates: $5 per person shared, $10 single. Bldgs 00496 (Pinnacles), 00499 (Portals). E7-E9 and Officers. Bedroom, private bath, living room, kitchenette (24). Rates: $15, extra person $6. Bldgs 02243 (Panamint), 02244 (Summit). E7-E9 and Officers. Bedroom, private bath, living room, full kitchen (23). Rates: $20, extra person $6. All facilities refrigerator, microwave, A/C, CATV/VCR, phone, housekeeping service, laundry facilities. No children, no pets.

TML Transient Family Housing. Thirteen units. Three-bedroom, private bath. Full kitchen, refrigerator, microwave, A/C, TV/VCR, phone, housekeeping service, washer/dryer in unit. Rates: $30-$35. No pets.

DV/VIP Protocol Office, **C-760-939-3039/2338, DSN-312-437-3039/2338.** Bldg 02243 (Panamint). O6-010/GS15+. Suites, private bath (4). Living Room, full kitchen, refrigerator, microwave, A/C, CATV/VCR, phone, housekeeping service, laundry facilities. Older structure. Rates: $25, extra person $6. No children, no pets.

CREDIT CARDS ACCEPTED: Visa, MasterCard, American Express and Discover.

TML AVAILABILITY: Good.

TRANSPORTATION: On base Taxi, C-760-939-2208. Car Rental: Avis, C-760-446-5556; Enterprise, C-760-384-2816. Off base taxi, C-760-371-4222.

DINING OPPORTUNITIES: MaryAnne's Kitchen, C-760-939-2739 is within walking distance. Denny's, C-760-375-5572; Kentucky Fried Chicken, C-760-375-4551; and McDonald's, C-760-446-8876 are within driving distance.

Four wheelers enjoy hundreds of trails nearby, while popular mountain areas (Mammoth, June and the Greenhorn Mountains) draw other enthusiasts year round. Visit Red Rock Canyon and Fossil Falls.

Coronado Naval Amphibious Base (CA38R4)
3420 Guadalcanal Road
P.O. Box 357033
San Diego, CA 92135-7033

MAIN INSTALLATION TELEPHONE NUMBERS: C-619-437-2011, DSN-312-577-2011. Locator 437-2011; Medical 437-2376; Security Police 545-7423.

LOCATION: From San Diego, take I-5 south to CA-75 across Coronado-San Diego Bay Bridge ($1 toll for non-carpool, free to motorcycles and carpools). Left (south) on Orange Avenue which becomes Silver Strand Blvd) for 2.2 miles. Pass Hotel del Coronado and watch for signs to base. Left (northeast) turn at fourth light after hotel. *USMRA: Page 118 (C,D-7,8)*. **NMC:** San Diego, five miles north. **NMI:** North Island Naval Air Station, three miles northwest.

RESERVATION INFORMATION: Bldg 504, Tulagi Street, San Diego, CA 92155-5000. BOQ: **C-619-437-3860, DSN-312-577-3860,** Fax: C-619-437-3475; BEQ: Bldg 302, **C-619-437-3494, DSN-312-577-3494,** Fax: C-619-437-2556, 24 hours daily. Check in at billeting 1500 hours, check out 1200 hours. For group reservations call BEQ, C-619-437-3496, DSN-312-577-3496; BOQ, C-619-437-3859, DSN-312-577-3859.

(BEQ) Bldg 303. E1-E4 common bath (80). Refrigerator, CATV, phone, clock radio, housekeeping service, laundry facility. Handicap accessible. Rates: $7 per person. Duty can make reservations; others Space-A after 1500 hours.

(BOQ) Bldg 504. Officers all ranks, E5-E9. Bedroom units, private bath (354); separate bedroom, private bath (30). Refrigerator, CATV, phone, clock radio, housekeeping service, laundry facility, ice machine. Modern structure. Handicap accessible. Rates: sponsor $13, each additional person $2. Duty can make reservations; others Space-A 24 hours in advance.

(DV/VIP) Bldg 504, **C-619-437-3860.** O6+/civilian equivalent. Separate bedroom suites, private bath (20). Refrigerator, CATV, phone, clock radio, housekeeping service, laundry facility, ice machine. Modern structure. Rates: sponsor $31, each additional person $2. Duty can make reservations; others Space-A 24 hours in advance.

AMENITIES: Exercise Room. Ice, Snack and Soft Drink Vending Machine.

TML AVAILABILITY: Good most of the year.

CREDIT CARDS ACCEPTED: Visa, MasterCard and American Express.

TRANSPORTATION: Off base shuttle/bus; Car Rental; Off base taxi.

DINING OPPORTUNITIES: Cafe Coronado, C-619-437-2160; Club Coronado, C-619-437-3040; Galley, C-619-437-2046; and McDonald's, C-619-435-7036 are within walking distance. Bricantine Restaurant, C-619-435-4166; The Chart House, C-619-435-0155; and Miguel's, C-619-437-4237 are within driving distance.

Coronado Bay and the Pacific Ocean offer all water sports; Seaport Village and Sea World are good family fun. There are a multitude of attractions in San Diego.

Edwards Air Force Base (CA48R4)
95 SPTG/SVML
36 North Wolfe Avenue
Edwards AFB, CA 93524-6745

MAIN INSTALLATION TELEPHONE NUMBERS: C-661-277-1110, DSN-312-527-1110. Locator 277-2777; Medical 277-4427; Security Police 277-3340.

LOCATION: From north or south on CA-14, to Rosamond (11 miles north of Lancaster). Exit east onto Rosamond Blvd, then east approximately 16 miles to Edwards AFB. Also, from east or west on CA-58, exit at Mojave south onto CA-14, then approximately 12 miles south to Rosamond, then east on Rosamond Avenue approximately 16 miles to air base. *USMRA: Page 111 (F,G-12)*. **NMC:** Los Angeles, 90 miles southwest. **NMI:** China Lake Naval Air Weapons Station, 40 miles north.

RESERVATION INFORMATION: High Desert Inn, 95 SPTG/SVML, Bldg 5602, 115 Methusa Avenue, Edwards AFB, CA 93524-6745. **C-1-888-AFLODGE (1-888-235-6343), C-661-277-4101/3394 or C-661-275-**

7666, DSN-312-527-4101/3394 or 312-525-7666, Fax: C-661-277-2517, DSN-312-527-2517, 24 hours daily. Duty can make reservations anytime, Space-A can make reservations two weeks in advance. Check in 1400 hours, check out 1100 hours.

(VAQ) Bldgs 5604, 5605. Bldg 5604: Rooms, shared bath (52), private bath (2). Bldg 5605: suites (26), private bath (2). A/C, TV, housekeeping service, laundry facility. Older structure, newly furnished. Rates: $19 per room.

(DVAQ/DVOQ) Bldgs 5601-5603. VOQ: Bldg 5601, Suites (16). Bldg 5602, Suites (22), private bath (1), handicap accessible (2). VAQ: Bldg 5603, Suites (26), private baths (2). Fully furnished, A/C, TV, housekeeping service, laundry facility. Older structure, newly furnished. Rates: DVOQ $26 per room; DVAQ $19 per room.

(TLF) Bldgs 7022-7031. One-bedroom suite/family quarters, private bath (50). Queen and twin size beds, sleeper couch and sleeper chair in living room. A/C, kitchen, microwave, TV, housekeeping service, laundry facility. Rates: $30 per night.

(DV/VIP) Protocol, Attn: AFFTC/CCP, Bldg 1, **C-805-277-3326.** O6+ Bldg 5601. One-bedroom suite, private bath (10). A/C, TV, housekeeping service, laundry facility. Older structure, newly furnished. Rates: $26 per room.

AMENITIES: Exercise Room and Ice machine in each VOQ/VAQ building.

TML AVAILABILITY: Good, all year.

CREDIT CARDS ACCEPTED: Visa and MasterCard.

TRANSPORTATION: On base taxi (for official use only, TDY on orders, limited hours), Car Rental.

DINING OPPORTUNITIES: Club Muroc Dining Room, Muroc Lake Golf Course Snack Bar, Oasis Pizza Pub w/delivery, Cactus Cafe, High Desert Bowling Center Snack Bar. AAFES facilities include: Popeye's Chicken, Burger King, Taco Bell, Robin Hood, Pizza Hut Express and Anthony's Pizza.

Los Angeles, 90 miles southwest, many southern California attractions are nearby.

El Centro Naval Air Facility (CA09R4)
Naval Air Facility Command
Attn: Public Affairs
El Centro NAF, CA 92243-5001

MAIN INSTALLATION TELEPHONE NUMBERS: C-760-339-2524, DSN-312-958-4935/4918. Locator 339-2555; Medical 339-2675/2666; Security Police 339-2525.

LOCATION: From east or west on I-8, two miles west of El Centro, to Forrester Road ((S-30) exit, north 1.5 miles to Evan Hewes Highway (S-80) left (west) for 4 miles, right on Bennet Road to Main Gate. *USMRA: Page 111 (H-15,16)*. **NMC:** El Centro, seven miles east.

RESERVATION INFORMATION: Bldg 401, El Centro NAF, CA 92243-5001. **C-760-312-6000/6020, DSN-312-958-4918,** Fax: C-760-337-4936, DSN-312-958-4936, 24 hours daily. Duty may make reservations; others Space-A. Check in at billeting, check out 1100 hours. Government civilian employees on orders billeted. *Earned a five-star rating for Excellence in Bachelor Housing.*

(BEQ) Bldg 4001. Bedroom, two beds, shared bath (48); suites, private bath E7+ (6); single bed, shared bath (24). Refrigerator, CATV, A/C, housekeeping services, TV lounge, arcade games, non-smoking lounge. New structure. Rates: $14.

(BOQ) Bldg 270. Bedroom, two beds, private bath (36); separate bedrooms, private bath (2). Refrigerator, limited utensils,

A/C, TV in room and lounge, housekeeping service. Older structure, remodeled. Rates: $14 per room. Also TVQ rooms ($14). Inquire.

 Navy Lodge. Bldg 388, 3rd Street, El Centro NAF, CA 92243-5000. **C-1-800-NAVY-INN.** Lodge number is C-760-339-2342, Fax: C-760-352-4914. Directions: Two blocks from Main Gate at Bldg 201, Navy Exchange. Check in Mon, Tues, Wed, Fri 1500-1700 hours, Thu 1900 hours, Sat 1400 hours. After main store hours check in at Bldg 200, Mini Mart until 2100 hours. After hours check in can be prearranged. Check out 1200 hours. Two-bedroom trailers, one queen-size bed, one double bed, private bath (5). Full kitchenette, microwave, coffee maker, utensils, A/C, CATV/VCR, housekeeping service, free washer/dryer in each unit, cribs, picnic grounds, playground, mini mart. Handicap accessible (1). Rates: $44 per unit. All categories may make reservations. No pets.

(DV/VIP) Bldgs 270, 4001. O6+. Bedroom suite, private bath (2). Refrigerator, limited utensils, A/C, TV in room and lounge, housekeeping service. Older structure, remodeled. Rates: $22.

(DV/VIP) Guesthouse. Bldg 3358. Officers. Bedroom, private bath, sleeps four. Kitchen, refrigerator, A/C, TV, housekeeping service. Rates: $48 per night.

AMENITIES: Exercise Room, Meeting/Conference Room, Mini Mart. Ice, Snack and Soft Drink Vending Machine.

TML AVAILABILITY: Fair. Difficult, Sep-Jun.

CREDIT CARDS ACCEPTED: Visa, MasterCard, Discover and American Express. The Navy Lodge accepts Visa, MasterCard, American Express and Discover.

TRANSPORTATION: Car Rental, C-760-353-3600.

DINING OPPORTUNITIES: Mirage Club (All Hands); and Sports Alley are within walking distance. Carrow's, C-760-353-8206; Denny's, C-760-352-2576; and Sizzler, C-760-353-3780 are within driving distance.

Hunting, fishing, golfing, tennis, hiking and camping are all available. This is the winter home (Jan-Mar) of the "Blue Angels."

Fallbrook Naval Ordnance Detachment (CA18R4)
Building 40, Sparrow Road
Fallbrook, CA 92028-5000

MAIN INSTALLATION TELEPHONE NUMBERS: C-760-731-3573, DSN-312-873-3573.

LOCATION: From I-15 north or south at exit 11 to S-13 west for 5 miles to entrance of detachment. *USMRA: Page 111 (G-15).* **NMC:** Temecula, eleven miles northeast.

RESERVATION INFORMATION: BEQ Office, Bldg 40, Sparrow Road, Fallbrook, CA 92028-5000. **C-760-731-3573, DSN-312-873-3573,** Fax: 760-731-3804, 0730-1700 hours Mon-Fri.

(BEQ) Rooms (32). Active Duty and reservists, on orders. Refrigerators, A/C, TV. Rates: no charge. *Earned a five-star rating for Excellence in Bachelor Housing.*

AMENITIES: Snack and Soft Drink Vending Machine.

TML AVAILABILITY: Extremely Limited.

TRANSPORTATION: Local buses, Taxis.

DINING OPPORTUNITIES: Club Restaurant within walking distance, local restaurants within driving distance.

Located on the east side of the very large Camp Pendleton Marine Corps Base.

Fort Hunter Liggett (CA37R4)
Attn: AFRC-FMH-CDR
P.O. Box 7000
Fort Hunter Liggett, CA 93928-7000

MAIN INSTALLATION TELEPHONE NUMBERS: C-831-386-3000, DSN-312-686-3000. Locator 386-2030; Medical 386-2513; Security Police 386-2513.

LOCATION: From US-101 north or south, exit approximately one mile northwest of King City onto G-14 (Jolon Road), then south approximately 19 miles to Main Gate. *USMRA: Page 111 (C-10).* **NMC:** King City, approximately 20 miles north.

RESERVATION INFORMATION: Gibb Hall, Commander Attn: AFRC-FMH-PWH, Bldg 229, P.O. Box 631, Jolon, CA 93928-0631. **C-831-386-2511/2108, DSN-312-686-2511,** Fax: C-831-386-2209, DSN-312-686-2209, 0800-1630 hours daily. Duty can make reservations; others Space-A. Check in 1200 hours, after hours check in at police station. Check out 1000 hours. Government civilian employee billeting. DV/VIP-C-831-386-2605.

(Lodge) Guest Lodge. Bldg 128. Separate bedrooms, private bath (50). Shared kitchen with adjoining room, refrigerator, A/C, CATV, housekeeping service. Modern structure. Rates: $28.50 per night, each additional person $5.

AMENITIES: Snack and Soft Drink Vending Machine.

TML AVAILABILITY: Good, most of the year.

CREDIT CARDS ACCEPTED: Visa, MasterCard and American Express.

TRANSPORTATION: None.

DINING OPPORTUNITIES: Hacienda Restaurant, C-831-386-2446; and Snack Bar, C-831-385-6038 are within walking distance.

Famous for the yearly return of the swallows—just like Capistrano. Nearby is Mission San Antonio de Padua. Hunting and fishing available on post in season.

Fort Irwin National Training Center (CA01R4)
Army Community Service
P.O. Box 105090
Fort Irwin, CA 92310-5090

MAIN INSTALLATION TELEPHONE NUMBERS: C-760-380-4111, DSN-312-470-4111. Locator 380-3369; Medical 380-3114/3115; Security Police 380-4444.

LOCATION: From east or west on I-15, exit onto CA-58 at Barstow (approximately 2.5 miles northeast of junction with I-40). Go west on CA-58 approximately 2.6 miles to intersection with Irwin Road. Go north on Irwin Road, which becomes Fort Irwin Road, approximately 36 miles to fort. Watch for signs. *USMRA: Page 111 (G,H-11,12).* **NMC:** San Bernardino, 70 miles southwest.

RESERVATION INFORMATION: Landmark Inn. 39 Inner Loop Road, P.O. Box 11097, Fort Irwin, CA 92310-5090. **C-760-386-4040, DSN-312-470-4040,** Fax: C-760-386-4041, 24 hours daily. Directions: go through Main Gate and turn left on Inner Loop Road. DV/VIP-C-760-380-4224. Very limited.

(Army Lodging) Landmark Inn. This is a civilian run hotel with Duty facilities. Single room with queen bed (18); double room with queen bed (127); suites with queen bed and sofa bed (18). All units have private bath, refrigerator, microwave, A/C, hair dryer, CATV, cribs, cots, housekeeping service, laundry facilities.

Handicap accessible (9). Coffee in lobby. Rates: single $64; double queen $64; suites $79, based on double occupancy.

AMENITIES: Ice, Soft Drink and Snack Vending Machine.

TML AVAILABILITY: Good, winter. Difficult, summer.

CREDIT CARDS ACCEPTED: Visa, MasterCard, American Express, Discover and Diners.

TRANSPORTATION: Off base shuttle, On base/Off base Car Rental, On base Taxi.

DINING OPPORTUNITIES: Bowling Center, C-760-380-4249; and PX Food Court, C-760-380-2060 are within walking distance. Other food establishments within driving distance.

Visit NASA's Goldstone Deep Space Tracking Station for a group tour. Rainbow Basin has many interesting fossils (not collectable!) and Park Moabi Marina in a quiet cove off the Colorado River are of interest to visitors.

Fort MacArthur (CA46R4)
Fort MacArthur Inn
2400 South Pacific Avenue, Bldg 37
San Pedro, CA 90731-2960

MAIN INSTALLATION TELEPHONE NUMBERS: C-310-363-8296, DSN-312-833-8296. Locator 363-1876; Medical 363-8301; Security Police 363-8385.

LOCATION: From I-110 (Harbor Freeway) go south toward San Pedro. Keep left to Gaffney Street, continue south approximately 1.5 miles to 19th Street, then left (east) to Pacific Avenue and right (south) approximately 0.25 miles to Main Gate on left (east) side of street. *USMRA: Page 117 (C-7)*. **NMC:** Los Angeles, in city limits. **NMI:** Los Angeles AFB, 18 miles north.

RESERVATION INFORMATION: Fort MacArthur Inn, Bldg 37, 2400 South Pacific Avenue, San Pedro, CA 90731-2960. **C-1-888-AFLODGE (1-888-235-6343), C-310-363-8296, DSN-312-833-8296,** 0600-2000 hours Mon-Sun, 0600-1800 hours on holidays. Duty can make reservations any time; Space-A can make reservations 24 hours in advance. Check in 1400 hours, check out 1100 hours.

(TLF) Bldg 40. Separate bedrooms, private bath (22). Sofabed, single bed. Kitchen, utensils, CATV, housekeeping service, laundry facility, cribs, cots, ice machine. Older structure. Renovated 1992. Rates: $30 per night. Maximum three to five per room.

(VOQ) Bldg 36. Bedroom, private bath (27). Microwave, complete utensils, CATV, housekeeping service, laundry facility, cribs, cots, ice machine. Older structure. Rates: $19.

(DV/VIP) Cottages, Bldgs 14-17. Reservations through Protocol, **C-310-363-5147.** O6+. Two-bedroom units, private bath (2); bedroom, private bath (2). Kitchen, utensils, TV, housekeeping service, laundry facility, cribs, cots. Older structure, renovated. Rates: sponsor $38.50. Maximum four per cottage.

TML AVAILABILITY: Best, Nov-Apr. Difficult, other times.

CREDIT CARDS ACCEPTED: Visa and MasterCard.

TRANSPORTATION: On base shuttle/bus.

DINING OPPORTUNITIES: Numerous restaurants available within driving distance.

Only 18 miles from Los Angeles. Many things to see and do!

Fort Mason Officers' Club (CA45R4)
Bay and Franklin Streets, Bldg 1
San Francisco, CA 94123-5000
This facility closed December 2002.

MAIN INSTALLATION TELEPHONE NUMBERS: C-415-441-7700. Locator 441-7700; Medical 911; Security Police 911.

LOCATION: Entrance on Bay and Franklin Streets, three blocks north of US-101 (Lombard Street). *USMRA: Page 119 (C-5)*. **NMC:** San Francisco, in city limits.

RESERVATION INFORMATION: Bldg 1, Bay and Franklin Streets, San Francisco, CA 94123-5000. **C-415-441-7700,** Fax: C-415-441-2680, 0900-1700 hours Tue-Sat. Reservations accepted up to six months in advance. Check in 1400 hours, check out 1100 hours.

(TML) Guest Quarters. Club Members, Officers, Active and Retirees. Suites, private bath (2); bedroom, private bath (3). Refrigerator, CATV, phone, housekeeping service, ice machine, continental breakfast, morning paper and other amenities. Lunch and dinner available on scheduled days. Older Victorian structure, remodeled 1990. Rates: Single or double bedroom, Mon-Thu $65, Fri-Sun and Holidays $75; Single or double suite, Mon-Thu $85, Fri-Sun and Holidays $100; each additional guest $15, deposit required.

TML AVAILABILITY: Difficult, all year.

CREDIT CARDS ACCEPTED: Visa, MasterCard and American Express.

TRANSPORTATION: Car rental, Off base taxi, local buses.

DINING OPPORTUNITIES: Numerous fine restaurants are within driving distance in San Francisco.

Fort Mason is located on a National Park. It offers a magnificent view of Alcatraz Island and San Francisco Bay. Close to North Beach, Fisherman's Wharf and Chinatown. Convenient location, good public transportation.

Lake Tahoe Coast Guard Recreation Facilities (CA24R4)
Lake Tahoe Coast Guard Group
Tahoe City, CA 96145-5000

MAIN INSTALLATION TELEPHONE NUMBERS: C-530-583-7438 (0700-1500 hours Mon-Fri), Police for recreational facilities 911.

LOCATION: Take I-80 to CA-89 (N Lake Blvd), south through Tahoe City, north on CA-28 to Lake Forest Blvd, right to USCG Station Lake Tahoe. *USMRA: Page 110 (E-6)*. **NMC:** Reno NV, 45 miles northeast. **NMI:** Beale AFB, Marysville, 80 miles northwest.

RESERVATION INFORMATION: Required, by written application only, with payment in full by check or money order, 45-60 days in advance. Write or call for application. Address: A-Frame Coordinator, Coast Guard Station Lake Tahoe, 2500 Lake Forest Road, P.O. Box 882, Tahoe City, CA 96145-0882. **C-530-583-7438** (Leave name, phone number and address.) Check in 1600-2000 hours with caretaker, check out 1100 hours.

(TML) Two-bedroom apartment, sleeps nine (2). One-bedroom apartment, sleeps seven (2). All units have private bath, kitchen, microwave, heat, CATV. Rates: two bedroom, $30-$45 daily; one bedroom $15-$30 (minimum rates, depending on rank of sponsor and number of persons). No pets.

TML AVAILABILITY: Year round.

CREDIT CARDS ACCEPTED: None.

TRANSPORTATION: Bus and airlines in Reno.

DINING OPPORTUNITIES: Many restaurants and fast food establishments in Reno and Tahoe City.

There is much to do and see in nearby Reno and Carson City. Many recreational activities are available on Lake Tahoe and surrounding Sierra Mountains.

Lake Tahoe Condominiums (CA49R4)
Alameda Coast Guard Integrated Support Command
Alameda, CA 94501-5100

MAIN INSTALLATION TELEPHONE NUMBERS: C-510-437-5395; Security Police 911.

LOCATION: Off post. Located at Lake Tahoe. **To Lake Forest Glen (North Shore Condo):** Take I-80 to CA-89 (to Tahoe City). CA-89 becomes CA-28 (North Lake Blvd). Go through Tahoe City, turn right on Lake Forest Road. Turn left on Bristlecone. **To Tahoe Keys (South Shore Condo):** Take I-80 to US-50 toward Placerville to South Shore Lake Tahoe. Follow US-50 toward Nevada state line. Turn left on Tahoe Keys Blvd *USMRA: Page 110 (E-6)*. NMI: McClellan AFB, Sacramento, CA, 110 miles southwest. **NMC:** Carson City, NV, 30 miles southeast.

RESERVATION INFORMATION: USCG (MWR), Alameda, CA 94501-5000. **C-501-437-3541.** E-mail: TahoeCondos@aol.com WEB: www.uscg.mil/mlcpac/iscalameda/forms/TahoeRequest.html Reservations accepted up to six months in advance for Active Duty; up to three months in advance for retired/reserve. Check in 1300 hours, check out 1100 hours. Military member must fax ID card before reservations will be confirmed (will be shredded after verification).

ELIGIBILITY: Active Duty- six months advance reservations. Reservists/Retirees- three months advance reservations.

TML **Tahoe Keys Condo (South Shore):** Two-level. Sleeps six to eight. Three bedrooms, two baths, full kitchen with dishes and utensils, fireplace, stereo, TV/VCR, washer/dryer, sun deck, two parking spaces. Also, indoor and outdoor pool, tennis courts, private beach, boat launch, sauna, tennis, volleyball and nearby playground. Guests must supply linens. Rates: $80 per night (Sun-Thu, min 2 nights), $90 per night (Sun-Thu, one night only), $105 per night (Fri and Sat nights), $125 per night (All holidays and nights preceeding holidays), $600 (Weekly rate, not including holidays), $150 refundable key/cleaning deposit. Check in 1300 hours. Check out 1100 hours. No pets.

TML **Lake Forest Glen Condo (North Shore):** Two-level. Sleeps ten. Three bedroom, two and one-half baths, full kitchen with dishes and utensils, fireplace, grill, jacuzzi/sauna, patio deck, stereo, TV/VCR, washer/dryer, beach, boat launch and picnic area. Also, two outdoor pools, jacuzzi, sauna and tennis courts. Guests must supply linens. Rates: $80 per night (Sun-Thu, min 2 nights), $90 per night (Sun-Thu, one night only), $105 per night (Fri and Sat nights), $125 per night (All holidays and nights preceeding holidays), $600 (Weekly rate, not including holidays), $150 refundable key/cleaning deposit. Check in 1300 hours. Check out 1100 hours. No pets.

TML AVAILABILITY: Busy, year round.

CREDIT CARDS ACCEPTED: Visa, MasterCard and Discover.

TRANSPORTATION: Off base taxi.

DINING OPPORTUNITIES: Some restaurants are within driving distance.

See *Military Living's Military RV, Camping and Outdoor Recreation Around the World* for additional information.

Lemoore Naval Air Station (CA06R4)
Family Service Center
Bldg 737, Code 13000
Lemoore NAS, CA 93246-5001

MAIN INSTALLATION TELEPHONE NUMBERS: C-559-998-5791, DSN-312-949-1110. Locator 998-0100; Medical 998-4435; Security Police 998-4749.

LOCATION: In south central part of state. From north or south on I-5, exit onto CA-198 east for approximately 24 miles to Main Gate on north (left) side of highway. Or, from north or south on CA-99, exit onto CA-198 west for approximately 27 miles to Main Gate on right (north) side of CA-198. *USMRA: Page 111 (D-10)*. **NMC:** Fresno, 40 miles north.

RESERVATION INFORMATION: CBH Division, Code 44, Avenger Avenue, NAS Lemoore, CA 93246-5001. BOQ: Bldg 821, **C-559-997-7000/7001, DSN-312-949-7000,** Fax: C-559-998-2542, 24 hours daily. Directions: Take immediate right after Main Gate and go about 1/2 mile until the lodging office registration sign. Handicap accessible units. *Earned a five-star rating for Excellence in Bachelor Housing.*

BEQ E1-E6. Check in/out 1200 hours at billeting office. Double and single rooms (44). Refrigerator, microwave, A/C, CATV/VCR, coffee maker, hair dryer, housekeeping service, cribs, cots, free laundry facility, sauna, jacuzzi, game room. Modern structure. Rates: $7 per person for double, $12 per person for single. Duty can make reservations, Retirees and DAVs Space-A.

BOQ Officers all ranks and E7+. Check in/out 1200 hours at front desk of facility. Rooms, private bath (76). Refrigerator, microwave, A/C, CATV/VCR, coffee maker, hair dryer, housekeeping service, free laundry facility, jacuzzi. Modern structure. Rates: $12-$30. Retirees, DAVs, Reservists Space-A, others can make reservations.

NAVY LODGE Navy Lodge. Bldg 919, Tracker Road, Lemoore NAS, CA 93245-5000. **C-1-800-NAVY-INN.** Lodge number is C-559-998-5829, Fax: C-559-998-6149, 24 hours daily. Directions: Enter front gate, turn right on Avenger then a left on Tracker. Check in 1500-1800 hours, check out 1200 hours. Efficiency rooms, private bath, two queen-size beds (56), one queen-size bed and one sofa (12). Kitchen, complete utensils, A/C, CATV/VCR, video rental, HBO, housekeeping service, coin laundry facility, iron/ironing board. Handicap accessible (4). Rates: $51. Maximum five per room. All categories may make reservations. Military member may sponsor guest. Non-smoking rooms available. No pets.

DV/VIP Commanding Officer, **C-559-998-3344.** O6+, Retirees or official visitors.

AMENITIES: Exercise Room, Meeting/Conference Room. Ice, Snack and Soft Drink Vending Machine.

TML AVAILABILITY: Good all year.

CREDIT CARDS ACCEPTED: Visa and MasterCard. The Navy Lodge accepts Visa, MasterCard, American Express, Discover and Diners.

TRANSPORTATION: On base shuttle/bus, C-559-998-4196; Off base shuttle/bus, C-559-584-0101; Car Rental: Budget, C-559-583-6123.

DINING OPPORTUNITIES: Bowling Alley; E Club, C-559-998-6850; McDonald's, C-559-998-6850; and Mr. Big's Deli are within walking distance.

In the San Joaquin Valley, near Sequoia and Yosemite National Parks, two hours from the coast or mountains and three hours from Los Angeles and San Francisco. Excellent base facilities.

Los Alamitos Joint Forces Training Base (CA39R4)

California Army National Guard
Western Mobilization and Training Complex
11200 Lexington Drive
HQ Bldg 15
Los Alamitos, CA 90720-5001

MAIN INSTALLATION TELEPHONE NUMBERS: C-562-795-2000, DSN-312-972-2000. Locator 795-2000; Medical 796-1111; Security Police 796-2100.

LOCATION: From I-405 (San Diego Freeway) north or south, take exit to I-605 (San Gabriel River Freeway) north approximately 1.5 miles to exit east onto East Katella Avenue, then east 1.7 miles to right (south) on Lexington Drive and proceed to Main Gate. Clearly marked. *USMRA: Page 117 (E-6,7)*. **NMC:** Los Angeles, 15 miles northwest.

RESERVATION INFORMATION: Bldg 19, 4745 Yorktown Avenue, Los Alamitos, CA 90720-5176. **C-562-795-2124, DSN-312-972-2124,** Fax: C-562-795-2125. WEB: www.calguard.ca.gov/jftb 0800-1630 hours daily. Drill weekends Fri and Sat 0600-2000 hours. Duty can make reservations; Space-A 24 hours in advance. Check in after 1300, after duty hours pick up key at Security, Bldg 57. Check out 1100 hours. Directions: At stop sign a make wide left turn. Turn left on Yorktown. Billeting, Bldg 19, is the last building on the left paralell to flightline.

TLF Shared room, shared bath (Officers) (42); shared room, hall bath (Enlisted) (198); private room, private bath (O6+) (11); Suites: private room, private bath, living room (O6+) (5). Rates: $18-$33 per person, per night, depending on quarters.

AMENITIES: Exercise Room, Meeting/Conference Room, Mini Mart, Snack and Soft Drink Vending Machine.

TML AVAILABILITY: Limited, especially on weekends, call ahead.

CREDIT CARDS ACCEPTED: Visa, MasterCard and American Express.

TRANSPORTATION: Car Rental.

DINING OPPORTUNITIES: On post cafeteria, Katella Deli, Fish Company and Paul's Place are within walking distance. Gilders Inn, Spagettini's and Walts of Seal Beach are within driving distance.

Los Alamitos is used extensively for reserve training, but Anaheim (Disneyland!) and Orange County, including great beach cities are nearby.

March Air Reserve Base (CA08R4)

452 AMW/PA
2145 Graeber Street, Suite 211
March ARB, CA 92518-1671

MAIN INSTALLATION TELEPHONE NUMBERS: C-909-655-1110, DSN-312-947-1110. Locator 655-1110; Medical 7-911; Security Police 7-911.

LOCATION: From north or south on I-215/CA-215 use March AFRB exit east onto Cactus Avenue. Continue east approximately 1.5 miles to traffic light at Main Gate on right (south) side of road. *USMRA: Page 111 (G-14)*. **NMC:** Riverside, 9 miles northwest.

RESERVATION INFORMATION: The March Inn, 655 M Street, Suite 4, March ARB, CA 92518-2113. **C-1-888-AFLODGE (1-888-235-6343), C-909-655-5241,** Fax: C-909-655-4574, DSN-312-947-5241, 24 hours daily. Duty can make reservations any time; Space-A can make reservations 24 hours in advance. Directions from Main Gate: Turn left on Meyer Drive (approximately 0.5 miles), right at 4-way stop onto Q Street, lodging office is on right. Check in at lodging office, check out 1100 hours.

VOQ/VAQ Bldgs 100, 102, 311, 400, 456, 2418-2421. Rooms and suites (450+ beds). Microwave, refrigerator, A/C, housekeeping service, laundry facility, cots. Modern Structure. "McBride Suites" (VOQ). Recent VAQ renovation. Rates: sponsor $14.50; suites $21.

DV/VIP Contact Base Protocol **C-909-655-3060, DSN-312-947-3060.** O6+. DV Suites available at VOQ/VAQ. Rates: $21.

AMENITIES: Meeting/Conference Room. Ice, Snack and Soft Drink Vending Machine.

TML AVAILABILITY: Good year round except for reserve weekends (approximately 1st and 3rd weekends).

CREDIT CARDS ACCEPTED: Visa, MasterCard and American Express.

TRANSPORTATION: Off base shuttle/bus: Airport Shuttle, C-909-626-6599; Super Shuttle, C-909-467-9600 (both go to all airports); Car Rental: Alamo, C-1-800-327-9633; Budget, C-909-682-2610; Enterprise, C-909-486-8686; Hertz, C-909-274-9380; Thrifty, C-909-243-7368; Off base taxi: Yellow Cab, C-909-924-7172.

DINING OPPORTUNITIES: Hap Arnold Combined Club, C-909-653-2121 and Pizzeria, C-909-655-3663 are within walking distance. Don Jose's, C-909-653-2254; Joe's Italian Restaurant, C-909-653-3093; and Sizzler Steak, C-909-653-6011 are within driving distance.

This Inn has more than 450 bed spaces, serving 60,000 visitors a year with a staff of about 65 with lots of recent improvements. A good place to stay. See nearby Riverside, the Mission Inn, Castle Park. Disneyland is less than one hour away. Exceptional location for seeing southern California.

March Air Reserve Base has excellent lodging.

Marines' Memorial Club (CA20R4)

609 Sutter Street
San Francisco, CA 94102-5000

MAIN INSTALLATION TELEPHONE NUMBERS: C-415-673-6672, Fax: C-415-441-3649. Reservations: **C-1-800-5-MARINE (562-7463).** Locator 673-6672; Medical 911; Security Police 553-0123. WEB: www.marineclub.com

LOCATION: From 101 north or 80 west. Take 101 north to 4th Street exit, make left onto 3rd Street. Cross Market Street, make left onto

Sutter. After Bay Bridge on 80 west, take Fremont Street exit. Make left onto Pine, then left onto Mason, continue to 609 Sutter. Club is at corner of Sutter and Mason. *USMRA: Page 119 (C-5).* **NMC:** San Francisco, in city limits. NMI: The Presidio of San Fransisco, five miles west.

Author's Note: This is NOT "military lodging" in the sense that we list other military installations in this book. The Marines' Memorial Club is a club and hotel exclusively for Active Duty and former members of all branches of the U.S. Armed Forces of the United States with an honorable discharge. Memberships are available. Call C-415-673-6672 for information. The club is not a part of the government but is a non-profit 501c19 veterans' organization that is self-supporting through membership dues and donations, which are fully tax-deductible. The Marines' Memorial Club and Hotel is a living memorial to Marines who lost their lives in the Pacific during WWII. It opened on the Marine Corps' Birthday, 10 Nov 1946, and chose as its motto "A tribute to those who have gone before; and a service to those who carry on."

RESERVATION INFORMATION: Check in/out at Registration Desk in lobby. Check out 1200 hours. Occupancy limited to two weeks. Reservations: **C-1-800-5-MARINE (1-800-562-7463).** E-mail: Member@marineclub.com WEB: www.marineclub.com Reservations Dept (Pacific time) 0800-1700 hours Mon-Fri, 0800-1600 hours Sat and Sun. For brochure or more info write to the above Attn: Club Secretary, e-mail or call C-415-673-6672.

(TML) Hotel. Guest rooms (137); deluxe suites (12); family suites (2). Reservations required. Courtesy coffee/tea in room, room service, large closets. Rates: Average room $140-$165, suite range $190 - $390. Lower rates available for all Active Duty personnel (based upon rank) and club members. Retiree membership fee tax deductible. Club facilities include lounge, full service restaurant, performing arts theater, library/museum, health club, coin laundry facility, valet, exchange store, package store, meeting and banquet facilities. Convenience store/newsstand and coffee shop outside hotel adjacent to entrance. Public parking garages are within easy walking distance (list available on website).

AMENITIES: Ice and Soft Drink Vending Machines.

TML AVAILABILITY: Best, winter months. Make reservations well in advance.

CREDIT CARDS ACCEPTED: Visa, MasterCard, American Express and Diners.

TRANSPORTATION: Off base shuttle/bus, C-415-673-6864; Car Rentals: Hertz, C-415-771-2200; Thrifty, C-415-788-6906; Off base taxi, C-415-673-1414.

DINING OPPORTUNITIES: Skyroom restaurant (12th floor); E&O Trading Company, C-415-693-0303; Rumpus, C-415-421-2300; and Scala's Bistro, C-415-395-8555 are within walking distance. Friangle, C-415-543-0573; Lulu, C-415-495-5775; and Rubicon, C-415-434-4100 are within driving distance.

In the heart of Union Square and theatre districts, within walking distance of cable cars, many major attractions.

Miramar Marine Corps Air Station (CA14R4)
Director, CBQ
P.O. Box 452007
San Diego, CA 92145-2007

MAIN INSTALLATION TELEPHONE NUMBERS: C-858-577-1011, DSN-312-267-1011. Locator 577-1011; Medical 577-4655; Security Police 577-1213.

LOCATION: From I-15 north of San Diego, take Miramar Way exit west which leads directly to the Main Gate. *USMRA: Page 118 (C,D-2,3,4; E,F-2,3).* **NMC:** San Diego, 10 miles southwest.

RESERVATION INFORMATION: Bldg 4312, 19920 Schilt Avenue, San Diego, CA 92145-2007. **C-858-577-4233/4235, DSN-312-267-4233/4235,** Fax: C-858-577-4243, DSN-312-267-4243. Check in at facility 1500, check out 1200 hours.

(BEQ/BOQ) Bldg 4312, 4325, 5640. Shared rooms, private bath (24); Shared rooms, shared bath (9); Private rooms, shared bath (100); Suites (50). Housekeeping service, CATV/VCR, laundry facility, microwave, refrigerator, telephones. Continental breakfast. Rates: $11, $14, $16; Suites, $26. Temporary duty on orders can make reservations; all others Space-A.

(Lodge) Miramar Inn. Bldg 2516, Newlin Lane, MCAS Miramar, San Diego, CA 92145. Reservations number **C-1-800-628-9466.** Lodge number is **C-858-271-7111,** Fax: C-858-695-7371, 24 hours daily. Check in 1500-1800 hours, check out 1200 hours. 89 units with two double beds; queen-size bed; king size bed; queen-size bed and queen sofa bed. All rooms have private bath, kitchenette, refrigerator, microwave, stovetop, toaster, complete utensils, coffee/tea, hair dryer, A/C, CATV/VCR, video rental, phone, housekeeping service, coin laundry facility, cribs, rollaways, iron/ironing boards and mini mart. Gazebo, barbecue and hot tub. Modern structure. Handicap and non-smoking rooms available. Rates: $48 per unit. All categories may make reservations.

(DV/VIP) C-858-537-1221. O6+. Retirees Space-A.

TML AVAILABILITY: Good, Nov-Dec. Difficult, summer.

CREDIT CARDS ACCEPTED: Visa, MasterCard and Navy Travel Card. Miramar Lodge accepts Visa, MasterCard, American Express and Discover.

TRANSPORTATION: Car rental; Off base taxi.

DINING OPPORTUNITIES: McDonald's, C-858-271-0481; and Rice King are within walking distance. Bread Basket, C-858-689-7305; and Keith's Family Restaurant, C-858-271-4670 are within driving distance.

San Diego's Old Town, Shelter and Harbor Islands, Sea World, and Balboa Park downtown are all not to be missed. Water sports, golf, tennis, and nearby Mexico will keep visitors from ever being bored in this lovely city.

Moffett Federal Air Field/NASA Ames Research Center (CA15R4)
P.O. Box 0128
Moffett Federal Air Field, CA 94035-0128

MAIN INSTALLATION TELEPHONE NUMBERS: C-650-604-5000, DSN-312-359-5000. Locator 604-5000; Medical 603-8251; Security Police 604-5461.

LOCATION: On north side of US-101 (Bayshore Freeway), 35 miles south of San Francisco. Take Moffett Federal Airfield exit north onto Moffett Federal Field exit which leads directly to Main Gate. *USMRA: Page 119 (F-9).* **NMC:** San Jose, seven miles south; San Francisco, 35 miles north.

RESERVATION INFORMATION: NASA Lodge, P.O. Box 17, Moffet Federal Air Field, CA 94035-5000. **C-650-603-7101,** Fax: 650-603-7110. Duty may make reservations any time; Retirees may make reservations five days prior for a period of four days. Check in at Bldg 19. **Navy Lodge,** Bldg 593, Vernon Avenue, Mountain View, CA 94043-5000. **C-1-800-NAVY-INN.** Lodge number is C-650-962-1542, Fax: C-650-694-7538, 24 hours daily. All categories may make reservations. Check in 1500-1800 hours at facility, check out 1200 hours.

(Lodge) NASA Lodge. Bldgs 19, 583A, 583B. Active Duty and NG on orders only, retired military. Bedroom with one full bed or two twin beds, private bath. A/C, housekeeping (143). Bldg 19 rooms (43) also have TV, phone. Newly renovated. Rates: Bldg 583A-B $40; Bldg 19 $50. No pets.

NAVY LODGE Lodge is located outside Moffett Federal Air Field. Directions: From Moffett Federal Airfield exit, make left on Jones Road, then left onto Vernon Avenue. Bedroom, two double beds, private bath (50). Kitchenette, microwave, CATV/VCR, video rental, housekeeping service, laundry facility, ice machine. Modern structure. Rates: $57 per unit. No pets.

TML AVAILABILITY: Limited.

CREDIT CARDS ACCEPTED: NASA Lodge: Visa, MasterCard, American Express and Discover. Navy Lodge: Visa, MasterCard, American Express, Discover and Diners.

TRANSPORTATION: Car Rental: Enterprise, C-650-967-6800.

DINING OPPORTUNITIES: Exchange Deli, C-650-603-9930; and McDonald's are within walking distance. Downtown Mountain View and Castro Street Restaurants are located within driving distance.

Visit historic Hangar One for a trip into Naval Aviation. Carmel-by-the-Sea and Pebble Beach are nearby.

Monterey Naval Postgraduate School (CA16R4)
Family Service Center, Code N11
1 University Circle
Monterey Bay, CA 93943-5001

MAIN INSTALLATION TELEPHONE NUMBERS: C-831-656-2441, DSN-312-878-2441. Locator 656-2441; Medical 656-5741; Security Police 656-2555.

LOCATION: Take CA-1 south to Monterey/Aquarium exit, right (west) at light onto Camino Aguajito. Then first right (right fork) (east) onto 10th street, turn left (north) at stop sign onto Sloat Avenue, and right at 9th Street gate. Or north on CA-1, use Aguajito Road exit to Mark Thomas Drive north, to left (north) on Sloat Avenue, right (east) at 9th Street gate. *USMRA: Page 111 (B-9).* **NMC:** Monterey, in city limits.

RESERVATION INFORMATION: Bldg 220, Herrmann Hall, 1 University Circle, Room 118A, Monterey Bay, CA 93943-5007. **C-831-656-2060/9, DSN-312-878-2060/9,** Fax: C-831-656-3024, DSN-312-878-3024, 24 hours daily. Duty can make reservations; others Space-A. Directions from Main Gate 1: Take Morse Drive to a left on University Way. Herrmann Hall, Bldg 220 is directly ahead. Check in at billeting 1500 hours with reservation, 1600 hours for Space-A. Check out 1100 hours. Government civilian employee billeting (BOQ). Duty billets available during school vacations.

BOQ Bldgs 220, 221, 222. Official duty. Bedroom, private bath (181). Refrigerator, microwave, TV/VCR, phone, housekeeping service, laundry facility, cribs, cots. Older structure. Rates: $15 per day per person, each additional guest $2.50. No pets.

NAVY LODGE 1100 Farragut Road, Monterey, CA 93940-5000. **C-1-800-NAVY-INN (1-800-628-9455).** Lodge number is C-831-372-6133, Fax: C-831-372-6307, DSN-None. 24 hours daily. Check-in 1500-1800, Check-out 1200. Directions: From the north: Route 1 south to Monterey exit (stay in left lane) to first intersection; left onto Aquajito Road; right on to Farragut Road; right at first stop sign (Lodge is on the corner). From the south: Route 1 north to Aquajito Exit; first right onto Aquajito Road; right onto Farragut Road (La Mesa Village); right at first stop sign (Lodge is on the corner). Accommodations: 72 units with queen-size beds and private bath. Units are QHKN-one queen bed and kitchen (handicap accessible); QQKN-two queen beds and kitchen; QSKN-one queen bed with sleeper sofa (single) and kitchen; entire lodge is smoke free. Amenities include: fully equipped kitchenette (dishes, pots, pans, etc.), microwave, dining table, CATV (HBO), VCR, free daily in-room coffee, free local telephone calls, direct dial AT&T service, free daily newspaper, hair dryer, radio/clock, on-site laundry facilities, playground and picnic grounds. Also available at no charge are cribs, highchairs, rollaways, irons/ironing boards. Rates: $59.00 per night, per unit. All categories may make reservations. No pets. New facility.

DV/VIP Bldg 220, **C-408-656-2511/2/3/4.** O6+, official duty. Two-room suites (4); single room suites (4). Refrigerator, microwave, TV/VCR, phone, housekeeping service, laundry facility, cribs, cots, ice machine. Older structure. Rates: room $28, each additional guest $5; suite $33, each additional guest $6. No pets.

AMENITIES: Meeting Room, Mini Mart. Ice, Snack and Soft Drink Vending Machine.

TML AVAILABILITY: Best, Christmas during school vacation. Extremely limited other times.

CREDIT CARDS ACCEPTED: Visa, MasterCard and American Express.

TRANSPORTATION: Car Rental, C-831-649-6300; Off base taxi, C-831-646-1234.

DINING OPPORTUNITIES: Club Del Monte and Monterey Fish House are within walking distance. Monterey Joe's, Sardine Factory and The Whaling Station are within driving distance.

In the heart of one of the most prestigious areas of California, The BOQ (Herrmann Hall) began life as the Hotel Del Monte. Nearby are Pebble Beach, Seventeen Mile Drive, Steinbeck's Cannery Row, the Monterey Bay Aquarium, Fisherman's Wharf and Carmel Mission.

North Island Naval Air Station (CA43R4)
P.O. Box 357138
San Diego, CA 92135-7138

MAIN INSTALLATION TELEPHONE NUMBERS: C-619-545-1011, DSN-312-735-0444. Locator 545-1011; Medical 545-4287; Security Police 545-6122.

LOCATION: From San Diego, take I-5 north or south to CA-75 across Coronado-San Diego Bay Bridge (toll) to CA-282 northwest directly to Main Gate. Also, take CA-75 north from Imperial Beach to downtown Coronado, then left (northwest) on CA-282 directly to Main Gate. Adjacent to Coronado. *USMRA: Page 118 (B,C-6,7).* **NMC:** San Diego, four miles northeast.

RESERVATION INFORMATION: Bldg I (for Officers), North Island, CA 92135-5220. **C-619-545-7545, DSN-312-735-7545** Fax: C-619-545-7546. Bldg 1500 (for Enlisted), North Island, CA 92135-5220. C-619-545-9551, DSN-312-735-9551. For groups larger than five people for VOQ and VEQ call C-619-545-7548 or Fax: C-619-545-7546 for reservations, 24 hours daily. Check in at facility between 1500-2300 hours for confirmed reservations, check out 1200 hours. Government civilian employee with orders billeting available at BOQ.

NAVY LODGE Navy Lodge. Bldg 1402, Rogers Road, San Diego, CA 92135-5220. **C-1-800-NAVY-INN.** Lodge number is C-619-545-6490, Fax-619-522-7455, 24 hours daily. Directions: From I-5 N or S, exit at Coronado Bridge. Continue past toll plaza to Alameda Blvd, turn left. Right lane directs you to Main Gate (McCain Blvd). From Main Gate go 0.25 miles to Rogers Road, turn left. Follow two miles, lodge is on left. Check in 1500-1800 hours, check out 1200 hours. Bedroom, two queen-size beds, private bath (90), kitchenette. Bedroom, two queen-size beds, private bath (100), refrigerator, microwave, coffee maker. A/C, CATV/VCR, video rental, housekeeping service, coin laundry facility, cribs, soft drink/snack vending, ice machine, picnic grounds, playground, recreational equipment, sunbathing and mini mart. Modern structure on ocean front, all rooms renovated in 1993. Rates: $60. All categories may make reservations. No pets.

DV/VIP PAO, **C-619-545-8167.** O6+. Retirees and lower ranks if approved by commander.

TML AVAILABILITY: Good, except Apr-Sep.

CREDIT CARDS ACCEPTED: Visa, MasterCard, American Express and Discover accepted at Navy Lodge.

TRANSPORTATION: On base shuttle/bus, C-619-545-8425; Car Rental: Admiral, C-619-435-1478, C-619-437-0145; On base taxi, C-619-545-8425; Off base taxi, C-619-437-8885, C-619-474-1544.

DINING OPPORTUNITIES: 19th Hole, C-619-545-9655; Cafe 700, C-619-522-7438; and Island Club, C-619-545-9084 are within walking distance. Bowling Center, C-619-545-7240; Del Taco, C-619-435-6058; and Pizza Parlor, C-619-545-7229 are within driving distance.

North Island is the birthplace of Naval aviation. The San Diego Trolley connects to downtown and bus routes. See Mission Valley, the zoo, Balboa Park.

North Island Naval Air Station has an oceanfront Navy Lodge and a family-friendly atmosphere.

Novato Temporary Quarters (CA89R4)
227 South Oakwood, #7
Novato, CA 94949-5000

MAIN INSTALLATION TELEPHONE NUMBERS: C-415-506-3130. Medical 911; Security Police 911.

LOCATION: Southbound on US-101 take exit onto Bel Marin Keyes Blvd/Hamilton Field. Take a right on Nave Drive, then take a left onto Main Gate Road. Take a right onto Crescent Drive, and another right to stay on Crescent Drive. At the end of Crescent Drive there is a fork in the road; lodging building is in the middle of that fork. Directions if traveling northbound on US-101: Take the Hamilton Field exit and turn left onto Main Gate Road. From there turn right onto Crescent Drive and follow directions as above. *USMRA: Page 110 (B-7).* **NMC:** San Francisco, 25 miles south. NMI: ISC Alameda Tracen Petaluma, ten miles north.

RESERVATION INFORMATION: #7, 227 South Oakwood, Novato, CA 94949-5000. **C-415-506-3130,** 0900-1500 hours Mon-Fri. Fax: C-415-506-3131. E-mail: novatotq@aol.com WEB: www.uscg.mil/mlcpac/iscalameda/comptroller/tempqtrs.htm#novhsgtempqtrs.htm Duty on orders can make reservations up to 90 days in advance; all others can make reservations 30 days in advance.

(TML) Rooms with private bath, shared kitchen (8). Suites with sleeper sofa, private bath, kitchen (2). All units have refrigerator, microwave, CATV/VCR, laundry facility, cribs and cots available. Maximum four per room. Rates vary by rank. Rates: Room $25-$55; Suite $28.75-$63.25. *Plans for Snack Vending Machines and Handicap Accessible Unit.*

AMENITIES: Meeting/Conference Room, Soft Drink Machine, free access to city of Novato Swimming Pool (with Active Duty military ID) and city Tennis Courts coming soon.

TML AVAILABILITY: Busiest May-Sep.

CREDIT CARDS ACCEPTED: Visa, Mastercard and Discover.

TRANSPORTATION: Off base shuttle/bus (to airport): Marin Door to Door, C-415-457-2717; Off base Car Rental: Hertz (will pick up), C-800-704-4473/415-892-1121; Enterprise (will pick up), C-800-736-8222/415-898-3500; Alamo (from San Francisco only), C-800-327-9633; Off base taxi: Radio Cab, C-415-485-1234; Marin Cab Company, C-415-455-4555.

DINING OPPORTUNITIES: McDonald's, Burger King, Chevy's, IHOP and Fresh Choice all within driving distance. Excellent dining in San Francisco.

Located on what used to be Hamilton Air Force Base, this lodging is run by the Coast Guard. Hike the nearby Marin Headlands, which overlook San Francisco and the Pacific Ocean. Beautiful San Francisco offers plenty to see and do.

Petaluma Coast Guard Training Center (CA23R4)
599 Tomales Road
Petaluma, CA 94952-5000

MAIN INSTALLATION TELEPHONE NUMBERS: C-707-765-7215. Locator 765-7215; Medical 765-7200; Security Police 765-7215.

LOCATION: From north or south on US-101 exit at Petaluma onto East Washington Street southwest through city of Petaluma, Washington Street becomes Bodega Avenue. Continue west following signs to Coast Guard Training Center a total of about 11 miles. Turn left (southwest) onto Tomales Road. A flashing amber light marks the Main Gate. *USMRA: Page 110 (B-6,7).* **NMC:** San Francisco, approximately 58 miles south.

RESERVATION INFORMATION: 599 Tomales Road, Petaluma, CA 94952-5000. **C-707-765-7248,** 0800-1600 hours Mon-Fri. Office is located in the Combined Club on Nevada Street. Check in at facility, check out 1100 hours. Government civilian employee billeting.

(BEQ) Bldg 124. Double room, semi-private bath (9). Refrigerator, microwave, TV. Older structure. Rates: E1-E3 $14, E4+ $16. No pets.

(TLQ) Bldg 134. Bedroom, private bath (8). Refrigerator, microwave, TV, ice machine. Older structure. Rates: $25 per room. All categories may make reservations. PCS have priority. No pets.

(DV/VIP) Harrison Hall. O4+. Call Commanding Officer for reservations, **C-707-765-7248.** VIP suite, private bath (1). Refrigerator, TV, phone, housekeeping service. Rates: $35 per night. Retirees Space-A. No pets.

AMENITIES: Exercise Room, Meeting/Conference Room, Mini Mart, Snack and Soft Drink Vending Machine.

TML AVAILABILITY: Generally good. Difficult, summer months.

CREDIT CARDS ACCEPTED: None accepted.

TRANSPORTATION: Car Rental.

DINING OPPORTUNITIES: Base Club (dinner only) and Coast Guard Cooking School are within walking distance.

The Petaluma area is saturated with historical lore and legend. Early California missions, a Russian fort (Fort Ross), Sonoma County wineries and Russian River swimming, fishing and canoeing all draw visitors.

Point Mugu Naval Air Station/Ventura County Naval Base (CA40R4)

Family Service Center, 8F000E
521 9th Street, Bldg 1, Room 117
Point Mugu, CA 93042-5001

MAIN INSTALLATION TELEPHONE NUMBERS: C-805-989-7209, DSN-312-351-7209. Locator 989-7209; Medical 989-8815; Security Police 989-7907.

LOCATION: Eight miles south of Oxnard and 40 miles north of Santa Monica on CA-1 (Pacific Coast Highway). From north or south on CA-1 take Los Posas Road exit south onto Pacific Road directly to Gate 3 (Los Posas Gate). Take Frontage Road parallel to CA-1 northwest to Gate 1 and Main Gate (Gate 2). Or take exit onto Wood Drive southwest to Frontage Road and all three gates which will be on southwest (Right) side of road. *USMRA: Page 111 (E-13).* **NMC:** Oxnard, seven miles north.

RESERVATION INFORMATION: The Missile Inn, Code CBCHG, Bldg 27, D Street, Point Mugu NAS, CA 93042-5001. **C-805-989-8251, DSN-312-351-8251,** Fax: C-805-989-7470, DSN-312-351-7470, 24 hours daily. Check in at facility, check out 1100 hours. Government civilian employee billeting. ***Earned a four-star rating for Excellence in Bachelor Housing.***

BEQ Bedroom, common bath or shared bath. Refrigerator, TV/VCR, housekeeping service, laundry facility. Older structure, renovated. Rates: room $9-$13.50 per person; suite $22. Duty only may make reservations; others Space-A.

BOQ Various buildings, some cottages. Bedroom, double beds, private bath, (46). Refrigerator, TV/VCR, housekeeping service, laundry facility, rollaways. Older structure, renovated. Rates: room $13.50 per person; suite $22. Duty and civilians on orders may make reservations; others Space-A.

TML Recreational Motel: **The Mugu Lagoon Beach Motel,** C-805-989-8407, DSN-312-351-8407. Fax: C-805-989-5413. Check in at facility, 24 hours daily. Check out 1100 hours. Late check out call front desk. Bedroom, two beds, private bath (24); Suite, two beds, private bath (2). Kitchenette, limited utensils, TV, housekeeping service, coin laundry facility, cribs, cots. Handicap accessible. Rates: room $40-45, each additional person $4; suite $57-$65, each additional person $4. All categories may make reservations.

DV/VIP Command Protocol, Bldg 36, **C-805-989-8672.** O6+. Bedroom suites, private bath (8). Kitchenette, refrigerator, TV/VCR, housekeeping service, laundry facility. Older structure, renovated. Rates: room $13.50; suite $22. Duty can make reservations, others Space-A.

AMENITIES: Exercise Room, Meeting/Conference Room, Mini Mart. Ice, Snack and Soft Drink Vending Machine.

TML AVAILABILITY: Fair. Difficult, Mar-Sep. Recreational motel good year round, most difficult in Jun-Aug.

CREDIT CARDS ACCEPTED: Visa, MasterCard, American Express and Discover.

DINING OPPORTUNITIES: Base Galley, C-805-989-7741; Mugu's Pizza, C-805-989-7747; and The Point Restaurant, C-805-989-8570 are within walking distance. The Crazy Bull, C-805-988-4209; Marie Callender's, C-805-487-7437; and Sal's Mexican Inn, C-805-483-5854 are within driving distance.

This facility is on the Pacific Ocean, close to the great shopping in Santa Barbara and within reach of coastal recreation as well as the famous beaches of southern California. Full range of support facilities on base.

Port Hueneme Naval Construction Battalion Center/Ventura County Naval Base (CA32R4)

1000 23rd Avenue
Port Hueneme NCBC, CA 93043-4301

MAIN INSTALLATION TELEPHONE NUMBERS: C-805-982-4711, DSN-312-360-4711. Locator 982-4711; Medical 982-6301; Security Police 982-4494.

LOCATION: From east or west on US-101 (Ventura Freeway) exit onto Wagon Wheel Road which leads into South Bank Drive southwest into Ventura Road for total of approximately 6.25 miles to right on Pleasant Valley Road directly to Main Gate. *USMRA: Page 111 (D,E-13).* **NMC:** Los Angeles, approximately 50 miles southeast.

RESERVATION INFORMATION: Bldg 1435, Pacific Road, Port Hueneme NCBC, CA 93043-4301. **C-805-982-4497/4115, DSN-312-551-4497/4115,** Fax: C-805-982-4948, DSN-312-551-4948, 24 hours daily. Check in at facility. No Government civilian employee billeting. ***Earned a four-star rating for Excellence in Bachelor Housing.***

BEQ Bldg 1435. Active Duty only. Private room, shared or private bath. Microwave, coffee/tea, TV, phone, hair dryer, iron, housekeeping service, coin laundry facility, fitness center, lounge. Non-smoking rooms. Rates: room $13.50; suite $22.

BOQ Bldg 1164. C-805-982-5785, DSN-312-551-5785, Fax: C-805-982-5662. Room, double bed, private bath. Microwave, coffee/tea, TV, phone, hair dryer, iron, housekeeping service, coin laundry facility, soft drink/snack vending, ice machine, fitness center, lounge. Non-smoking rooms. Suite: above plus kitchenettes, living room. Rates: room $13.50; suite $22.

NAVY LODGE Navy Lodge. Bldg 1172, Addor Street, Port Hueneme NCBC, CA 93043-5000. **C-1-800-NAVY-INN.** Lodge number is C-805-985-2624/27, Fax: C-805-984-7364, 24 hours daily. Check in 1500-1800 hours, check out 1200 hours. Two double beds, private bath, kitchenette (21); queen-size bed, sleeper chair, private bath (21); two double beds, private bath (6). Microwave, coffee/tea, CATV/VCR, video rental, phone, housekeeping service, coin laundry facility, cribs, cots, picnic grounds, playground. Modern structure, remodeled. Rates: single $50; double $56. Maximum four per room. Duty and Retirees can make reservations; others Space-A. No pets.

DV/VIP Protocol **C-805-985-4741.** E9, O6+. Check in Bldg 1164. Guesthouse. Doll House, Bldgs 39. Cottage, private bath (1). Kitchen, utensils, TV, housekeeping service, patio. Older structure (1925). Rates: $31. Active Duty can make reservations, others Space-A.

AMENITIES: Fitness Center, Ice, Snack and Soft Drink Vending Machines.

TML AVAILABILITY: Good, winter months. Difficult, summer months.

CREDIT CARDS ACCEPTED: Visa, MasterCard and American Express. The Navy Lodge accepts Visa, MasterCard, American Express, Discover and Diners.

TRANSPORTATION: On base shuttle/bus for students, Off base taxi.

DINING OPPORTUNITIES: Galley House is within walking distance.

In easy access of metropolitan Los Angeles, coastal Ventura County boasts wonderful weather. This is the home of the famous Seabees, a bustling complex of 10,000 military and civilians and more than 1600 acres.

Presidio of Monterey (CA74R4)
ATZP-DCA-AS (Relocation)
Defense Language Institute
Bldg 614, Rasmussen Hall, Room 142
Presidio of Monterey, CA 93944-5006

MAIN INSTALLATION TELEPHONE NUMBERS: C-831-242-5200, DSN-312-878-5200. Locator 242-5000; Medical 242-5234; Security Police 242-5634.

LOCATION: From north or south on CA-1 in Monterey, exit to Del Monte Blvd and go west approximately 1.75 miles onto Lighthouse Avenue. Continue northwest and enter post from Lighthouse Avenue. Watch for signs. *USMRA: Page 111 (B-9)* .**NMC:** Monterey, in city limits.

RESERVATION INFORMATION: Bldg 366, Presidio of Monterey, CA 93944-5006. **C-888-719-8886, C-831-242-5091, DSN-312-878-5091,** Fax: C-831-242-5298, 0700-1900 hours Mon-Fri, 0800-1800 hours Sat-Sun and Holidays. After hours check in at SDO in Bldg 614 for guaranteed reservations only. Official Duty may make reservations at any time; Space-A may make reservations two weeks in advance.

TQ Bedroom, shared bath (38). Rates: $30-$35. Two-bedroom, private bath (7). Rates: $32-$42. Bedroom, private bath (20). Rates: $38-$48. Bedroom, kitchenette, private bath (11). Rates: $40-$50. One bedroon suite (8). Rates: $43-$53. Two bedroom duplexes (6). Rates: $50-$60. Three-bedroom house (1). Rates $53-$63. All units have refrigerator, microwave, coffee, CATV, iron, housekeeping service, laundry facilities, cribs. Rooms with kitchenettes have utensils and cookware. Duplexes and houses have full kitchens, utensils and cookware. No pets; kennel listing provided.

DVQ O6+. Three-bedroom house. Full kitchen, utensils, cookware, refrigerator, microwave, coffee, CATV, iron, housekeeping service, laundry facility. Rates: $70-$80.

TML AVAILABILITY: Good. Limited family units, especially in summer.

CREDIT CARDS ACCEPTED: Visa, MasterCard and American Express.

TRANSPORTATION: Off base shuttle/bus, C-831-656-2689, DSN-312-878-2689; Car Rental, C-831-649-6300; Off base taxi, C-831-646-1234.

DINING OPPORTUNITIES: Monterey Joe's, Sardine Factory and The Whaling Station are within driving distance.

Within minutes of many famous Monterey Peninsula tourist attractions: Monterey Bay Aquarium, Fisherman's Wharf, Cannery Row, Pebble Beach golf courses, Seventeen Mile Drive, Point Lobos, Carmel and Big Sur.

San Clemente Island Naval Auxiliary Landing Field (CA53R4)
P.O. Box 357054
San Diego, CA 92135-7054

MAIN INSTALLATION TELEPHONE NUMBERS: C-619-524-9127. Locator 524-9202; Medical 524-9356; Security Police 524-9214.

LOCATION: This is a closed island accessible by air or boat only. *USMRA: Page 111 (E-15).* **NMC:** Los Angeles, 50 miles east. **Visitors must be sponsored by military stationed on the island.**

RESERVATION INFORMATION: Bldg 60201, P.O. Box 357054, San Diego, CA 92135-7054. **C-619-524-9202,** Fax: C-619-524-9203, 0700-1600 hours Mon-Fri.

BEQ/BOQ Bldgs 60121, 60152, 60196, Cottages 1 & 2. Check in at lodging office, after hours call, C-619-524-9204 or C-619-524-9202. Bedrooms, kitchenette, refrigerator, TV, laundry facility,

soft drink and snack vending, exercise room and mini mart available. Renovated. Rates: $10, $14, $15 per night. Reservations accepted for those eligible.

TML AVAILABILITY: Extremely limited.

CREDIT CARDS ACCEPTED: None.

TRANSPORTATION: On base shuttle/bus, C-619-524-9227.

DINING OPPORTUNITIES: SCI Galley, C-619-524-9197 is within driving distance.

San Diego Fleet Anti-Submarine Warfare Training Center (CA54R4)
53690 Tomahawk Drive, Suite 144
San Diego, CA 92147-5000

MAIN INSTALLATION TELEPHONE NUMBERS: C-619-524-1011, DSN-312-524-0557/5382. Locator 524-1011; Medical 524-0349/911; Security Police 524-2030/911.

LOCATION: From I-8 W or I-5 N take Rosecrans exit to Nimitz Street, left on Nimitz to Harbor Drive, turn left on Harbor Drive (Gate 1). *USMRA: Page 118 (B-6).* **NMC:** San Diego, 4 miles east.

RESERVATION INFORMATION: Admiral Kidd Inn, CBH Bldg 82, 32444 Echo Lane, Suite 100, San Diego, CA 92147-5199. **C-619-226-5382, DSN-312-524-5382,** Fax: C-619-524-0754, DSN-312-524-0754. Front Desk C-619-524-0557, Switchboard C-619-226-0444, 24 hours daily. Directions from Gate 2: Left on Nixie Way to Bldg 82 on the right side. Check in 1600 hours, check out 1100 hours.

CBQ One-bedroom suites, private bath. Kitchenette (some rooms), refrigerator, microwave, utensils, housekeeping service, coffee maker, hair dryer, cribs, cots, CATV/VCR, alarm clock, iron/ironing board, laundry facility. Rates: $22, additional guests $5. Maximum four per unit.

DV/VIP C-619-524-5382. O6/GS15+. Rates: $31, each additional guests $5.

AMENITIES: Exercise Room, Business Center, Meeting/Conference Room and Internet/E-mail access for all customers. Ice, Snack and Soft Drink Vending Machines.

TML AVAILABILITY: Good. Best, Jan-May, Sep-Dec. Difficult, Jun-Aug.

CREDIT CARDS ACCEPTED: Visa, Mastercard and American Express.

TRANSPORTATION: Car Rentals: Hertz, Dollar and Alamo. Off base taxi: Orange Cab, C-619-291-3333, Yellow Cab, C-619-234-6161.

DINING OPPORTUNITIES: Cafe 549, C-619-524-1260; Navy Mess Hall, C-619-524-0031; and Red Hen, C-619-226-0255 are within walking distance. Blue Crab, C-619-224-3000; Humphrey's, C-619-224-3577; and John Tarantinos, C-619-222-0010 are within driving distance.

Mission Bay Park, San Diego Zoo, Sea World and Balboa Park are all nearby and fun to visit!

San Diego Marine Corps Recruit Depot (CA57R4)
Director FSC (RAP)
4025 Tripoli Avenue
San Diego, CA 92140-5023

MAIN INSTALLATION TELEPHONE NUMBERS: C-619-524-1011, DSN-312-524-1720. Locator 524-1719; Medical 524-4079; Security Police 524-4202.

LOCATION: On the west side of I-5. From north or south on I-5 use Old Town Avenue exit south to Hancock Street, then southeast 1 block to Witherby Street, then southwest directly to Main Gate and follow signs. *USMRA: Page 118 (C-6).* **NMC:** San Diego, two miles southeast; adjacent to San Diego International Airport (Lindbergh Field).

RESERVATION INFORMATION: Bldg 625, 3800 Chosin Avenue, San Diego, CA 92140-5196. **C-619-524-4401, DSN-312-524-4401, Fax:** C-619-524-0617, 24 hours daily. Military on orders have priority; others Space-A. Check in at billeting 24 hours daily, check out 1200 hours.

TEQ Bldg 625. Room with two beds, shared bath (212). Enlisted Suites. Microfridge, coffee maker, SATV, housekeeping service, laundry facility, cribs. Modern structure, new carpeting, phone, new furniture in each room. Handicap accessible. Rates: sponsor $8, additional adult $7; SgtMaj Suite $20, each additional person $2. Maximum two per room. No pets.

TOQ Bldg 312. Suites with separate bedroom, private bath (10). Kitchenettes in suites, others common kitchen, microfridge, coffee maker, TV, phone, housekeeping service, laundry facility, cribs. New carpeting, recently remodeled modern structure. Handicap accessible. Rates: sponsor $20, additional adult $2. Maximum $22 per family. Maximum three persons per room. No pets.

DV/VIP Bldg 31, Room 238. Protocol Officer, **C-619-524-8710.** O6+. Active Duty, Retirees, DoD civilians: TOQ and TEQ available. Others Space-A.

TML AVAILABILITY: Good to very good. Best, Jan-May, Sep-Dec. Difficult, Jun-Aug.

CREDIT CARDS ACCEPTED: Visa, MasterCard, American Express and Discover.

TRANSPORTATION: Off base shuttle/bus, C-619-670-3232; On/Off base taxi, C-619-234-6161.

DINING OPPORTUNITIES: Bayview Restaurant, C-619-524-6878; Carrow's, C-619-224-0989; and Volare, C-619-224-0030 are within walking distance. Black Angus, C-619-223-5604; Old Town Mexican Cafe, C-619-297-4330; and Red Lobster, C-619-226-1057 are within driving distance.

This is the Marine Corps' oldest operating installation on the West Coast and is a short distance from downtown San Diego. Check out San Diego Zoo, Sea World, beaches, fishing, and bargain shopping in nearby Tijuana, Mexico.

San Diego Naval Medical Center (CA59R4)
Bldg 26, 41
34425 Farenholt Avenue, Suite 200
San Diego, CA 92134-7200

MAIN INSTALLATION TELEPHONE NUMBERS: C-619-532-6400, DSN-312-522-6400.

LOCATION: From north or south on I-5, exit northeast onto Pershing Drive north for approximately 0.3 miles, then left (west) west on Florida Canyon Drive to entrance on left (west) side of road. *USMRA: Page 118 (D-6).* **NMC:** San Diego, in city limits.

RESERVATION INFORMATION: C-619-532-6282, DSN-312-522-6282, Fax: C-619-532-5195, DSN-312-522-5195, 24 hours.

BEQ Bldg 26. Single room, shared bath, sleeps two (E1-E4). Open bay, central bath, multiple occupancy (E1-E6). Under reconstruction until 2003; spaces are limited to Active Duty staff and students, and medical holding personnel. Bldg 41. Single room, central bath, sleeps two (E1-E4). Rates: no charge.

Fisher House 34800 Bob Wilson Drive, Bldg 46, San Diego, CA 92134-5000. C-619-532-9055, Fax: C-619-

532-5216. Located at San Diego Naval Medical Center. *Note: Appendix B has the definition of this facility. Fisher Houses are only available as lodging for families of patients receiving medical care at military and VA medical centers.*

TML AVAILABILITY: Extremely limited.

In sunny downtown San Diego, near Balboa Park and the San Diego Zoo.

San Diego Naval Station (CA26R4)
3445 Surface Navy Blvd
San Diego, CA 92136-5000

MAIN INSTALLATION TELEPHONE NUMBERS: C-619-556-1011, DSN-312-526-1011. Locator 556-1011; Medical 556-8083; Security Police 524-3620.

LOCATION: From north or south on I-5, seven miles south of San Diego, take 28th Street exit south to Main Street. Station is at 28th & Main Streets. Continue southwest on 28th Street and south to Main Gate at 32nd Street. *USMRA: Page 118 (D-7,8).* **NMC:** San Diego, in city limits.

RESERVATION INFORMATION: 2450 McHugh Street, Suite 1, San Diego, CA 92136-5395. **C-619-556-8672, DSN-312-526-8672** Fax: C-619-556-7263, DSN-312-526-7263, 24 hours daily, Watch Section/Central Assignments, Bldg 3362. E-mail: devincenzo.angela@ns.cnrsw.navy.mil (for group reservation). Check in at facility, check out 1200 hours. Government civilian employees billeting. *Earned a three-star rating for Excellence in Bachelor Housing.*

BEQ Bldg 3362. E1-E6, official duty only. Beds, shared bath (500). Phone, TV lounge, housekeeping service, laundry facility. Rates: $13. DoD civilian VIP rooms available (4). Dependents not authorized. Reservations required.

BEQ Bldg 3203. E7-E9, official duty only. Bedroom, private bath (144). Refrigerator, TV, phone, housekeeping service, laundry facility. Rates: $13 per person. Children not authorized. Duty can make reservations; others Space-A.

BEQ Bldgs 3144, 3150. E7-E9, official duty only. Bedroom, private bath (79). Refrigerator, microwave, coffee, CATV, phone, housekeeping service, laundry facility. Rates: $13 per person. Children not authorized. Duty can make reservations; others Space-A.

BOQ Ford Hall, Bldg 3205. Bedroom, private bath. Refrigerator, microwave, coffee, CATV, phone, housekeeping service, laundry facility. Rates: $13 per person. Children not authorized. Duty can make reservations; others Space-A.

NAVY LODGE Navy Lodge. Bldgs 3526, 28th & Main Street, San Diego, CA 92136-0001. **C-1-800-NAVY-INN.** Lodge number is C-619-234-6142, Fax: C-619-238-0754, 24 hours daily. Check in 1500 hours, check out 1200 hours. Two double beds, private bath (45); One double bed (48). Kitchenette, microwave, utensils, coffee maker, A/C, CATV/VCR, phone, clocks, coin laundry facility, cribs, rollaways, playground, housekeeping service. Handicap accessible (5), non-smoking (86). Rates: $48-$55. Government civilian employees billeting with ID and orders. All categories may make reservations. No pets. *A 104-room addition/replacement is planned for 2001.*

DV/VIP Bldg 3144. VIP Suite (4). Refrigerator, microwave, coffee, CATV, phone, housekeeping service, laundry facility. Rates: $31.

AMENITIES: Meeting/Conference Room, Mini Mart. Ice, Snack and Soft Drink Vending Machine.

TML AVAILABILITY: Good, except PCS rotations, summer months.

CREDIT CARDS ACCEPTED: Visa, MasterCard and American Express. The Navy Lodge accepts Visa, MasterCard, American Express, Discover and Diners.

TRANSPORTATION: Off base shuttle/bus, C-619-222-2744; Car Rental, C-619-544-2184; Off base taxi, C-619-291-3333.

DINING OPPORTUNITIES: Numerous restaurants within driving distance.

America's Finest City welcomes you to vacation paradise! Visit the world famous San Diego Zoo, Wild Animal Park, Sea World, Seaport Village, Old Town, Balboa Park and much more. Enjoy the best year-round climate in the U.S.

San Diego Naval Submarine Base (CA79R4)
Combined Bachelor Houseing
140 Sylvester Road, Bldg 601
San Diego, CA 92106-3521

MAIN INSTALLATION TELEPHONE NUMBERS: C-619-553-1011, DSN-312-933-1011. Locator 553-1011; Security Police 553-7070; Medical 532-6400.

LOCATION: Southwest on Rosecrans Street (CA-209) directly to Main Gate. *USMRA: Page 118 (B-6).* **NMC:** San Diego, five miles southeast.

RESERVATION INFORMATION: Dolphin Lodge and Inn, 140 Sylvester Road, San Diego NB, CA 92106-3521. BOQ: Bldg 601, **C-619-553-9381, DSN-312-553-9381,** Fax: C-619-553-0613. BEQ: Bldg 300, **C-619-553-9381.** Check in at facility 1300 hours, check out 1200 hours. *Earned a five-star rating for Excellence in Bachelor Housing.*

BEQ Bldg 302. E1-E6. Rooms with various bath combinations (72); MCPO suites (2). Refrigerator, CATV, phone, voice-mail, housekeeping service, laundry facility, ice and snack vending machines. Modern structure. Rates: $13 per night; sponsor $7; MCPO suites $31. Duty can make reservations; others Space-A.

BOQ Bldg 501. Officers, O4 and below. Bedroom, private bath (77); separate bedrooms, private bath. Refrigerator, microwave, utensils, CATV, phone, voice-mail, laundry facility, rollaways, ice machine, jacuzzi, two catering facilities. Modern structure. Rates: sponsor $13, each additional person $7; VIP suites $31, each additional person $7.

BOQ Bldg 601. O5+. Bedroom, private bath (58); separate bedrooms, private bath. Kitchenette, refrigerator, microwave, utensils, CATV, phone, voice-mail, rollaways, ice machine, weight room, jacuzzi, two catering facilities. Modern structure. Rates: sponsor $22, each additional person $7; VIP suites $31, each additional person $7.

TML AVAILABILITY: Fairly good. Best, Oct-Dec. Difficult, May-Aug. If eligible, ask for DV/VIP Suites.

CREDIT CARDS ACCEPTED: Visa, MasterCard and American Express.

TRANSPORTATION: Off base taxi.

DINING OPPORTUNITIES: Numerous restaurants within driving distance.

Located on beautiful Point Loma, with a spectacular view of San Diego Harbor and the city, this facility is on the bus line close to beaches, Old Town, Sea World, the San Diego Zoo and many other recreational delights.

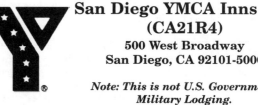

San Diego YMCA Inns (CA21R4)
500 West Broadway
San Diego, CA 92101-5000

Note: This is not U.S. Government/ Military Lodging.

MAIN INSTALLATION TELEPHONE NUMBERS: C-619-234-5252. Locator 234-5252; Medical 911; Security Police 911.

LOCATION: Take CA-5 S to CA-8 E to 163 S. 163 turns into 10th Avenue. Turn right on Broadway, to 500 West Broadway. *USMRA: Page 118 (C-6).* It offers quality accommodations for budget travelers, students and the military. Accessible to the harbor, the Greyhound Bus station, Amtrak, and trolley stations as well as being minutes from the airport. Also, Horton Plaza, the Gaslamp Quarter, Seaport Village, Little Italy, the San Diego Convention Center, Coronado Island, and the Santa Fe Train depot are close by. Services include a full-service restaurant, fitness facilities, indoor pool and hot tub, laundry facilities, a barber shop and 24 hour desk service. It is available to all military personnel, whether on duty or on leave, Retirees and their guests at reduced rates as well as budget travelers and students.

RESERVATION INFORMATION: Address and telephone as above. Fax: C-619-234-5272, 24 hours daily. Write or call for a brochure or more info. Reservations required. Check in/out at lobby desk. Check out 1100 hours.

TML Hotel. Guest rooms (268). TV in room and lounge, housekeeping service, coin laundry facility, snack vending (restaurant on premises). Handicap accessible. Rates (tax not included): single $35, double $45; weekly single $140, weekly double $150 ($55 deposit for weekly/monthly guests). Cash, travelers checks, money orders and government issued checks. No pets.

TML AVAILABILITY: Good. Best, winter months. Make reservations well in advance.

CREDIT CARDS ACCEPTED: Visa and MasterCard.

TRANSPORTATION: Off base shuttle/bus, Car Rental, Off base taxi.

DINING OPPORTUNITIES: Numerous restaurants within driving distance.

In the heart of San Diego and within walking distance of a trolley system that can take you to famous Southern California beaches, a world class zoo and Mexico!

San Pedro Coast Guard Integrated Support Command (CA25R4)
1001 Seaside Avenue
P.O. Box 8
San Pedro, CA 90731-0208

MAIN INSTALLATION TELEPHONE NUMBERS: C-310-732-7400. Locator 732-7400; Medical 911; Security Police 911.

LOCATION: On southwest end of Terminal Island. From San Pedro go east on CA-47 across Vicent Thomas Bridge to south on S. Ferry Street to right (west) on E. Terminal Way which becomes S. Seaside Avenue. Follow Coast Guard and Federal Corrections signs to end of S. Seaside Avenue. Or from Long Beach, go west on Ocean Blvd to south on S. Ferry Street and follow above directions. *USMRA: Page 117 (C-7).* **NMC:** Long Beach, six miles northeast.

RESERVATION INFORMATION: Engineering Office, Integrated Support Command, 1001 S Seaside Avenue, San Pedro, CA 90731-0208. **C-310-732-7444,** Fax-310-732-7449, 0700-1530 hours Mon-Fri. After hours call C-310-732-7400/10 for OOD. Reservations required with application and deposit, may be made up to six months in advance. Check in 1300 hours at ISC San Pedro, check out 1100 hours.

(**Guesthouse**) **Point Fermin Guest Quarters.** Two-bedroom house with two full bathrooms, fully equipped kitchen, dining, living and family room. Sleeps six. Microwave, coffe maker, utensils, CATV/VCR, stereo, alarm clock, pay phone, washer/dryer. Deck with grill. Outstanding view. Rates: vary by rank. No pets.

TML AVAILABILITY: Good year round, but very busy Jun-Sep, holidays and weekends.

CREDIT CARDS ACCEPTED: None.

Close to beach cities, Los Angeles harbor and all that Southern California has to offer. Only one hour from Disneyland.

Sierra Army Depot (CA44R4)
CSRS/AD, Attn: S10S1
74 C Street
Herlong, CA 96113-5166

MAIN INSTALLATION TELEPHONE NUMBERS: C-530-827-2111, DSN-312-855-4910. Locator 827-2111; Security Police 827-4345.

LOCATION: 55 miles northwest of Reno, NV, northeast of US-395. Northbound on US-395 from Reno, turn right (north) on CA-A26 (Garnier Road). When traveling south on US-395, turn left (northeast) on A-25 (Herlong Access Road). Proceed 5 miles to the Main Gate. *USMRA: Page 110 (E-4).* **NMC:** Reno, NV, 55 miles southeast.

RESERVATION INFORMATION: Bldg P144, Herlong, CA 96113-9999. **C-530-827-4544, DSN-312-855-4544,** Fax: C-530-827-5360, DSN-312-855-5360, duty hours. PCS/TDY can make reservations; all others Space-A. Check in 1400, check out 1100 hours. Other hours, Security Bldg P-100, C-530-827-4345.

(**Army Lodging**) **Skedaddle Inn,** Bldg P144. Bedroom, private bath (15). Refrigerator, laundry facility, housekeeping service. New structure. Rates: $44-$48.

(**DV/VIP**) PAO, **C-530-827-4343.**

AMENITIES: Meeting/Conference Room.

TML AVAILABILITY: Very good all year.

CREDIT CARDS ACCEPTED: Visa, MasterCard and American Express.

TRANSPORTATION: On Base Taxi.

DINING OPPORTUNITIES: Limited number of restaurants within driving distance.

Water sports, hiking, skiing and most outdoor activities are popular in this Northern California paradise. Lassen Volcanic National Park, the Eagle Lake Marina and the Reno/Tahoe areas have rich recreational opportunities.

South Lake Tahoe Recreation Housing (CA17R4)
242 Fort Mervine Place, Suite 1
Presidio of Monterey, CA 93944-5000

MAIN INSTALLATION TELEPHONE NUMBERS: C-831-242-5000, DSN-312-878-5000.

LOCATION: Off post. From US-101 100 miles south of San Francisco, take CA-156 W ten miles, follow signs to Presidio of Monterey. Located at

Lake Tahoe; specific directions will be furnished when reservation is made. Obtain keys in Lake Tahoe by making arrangements with Equipment Center, Bldg 228, Presidio of Monterey. USMRA: Page 110 (E-6). **NMC:** Carson City, NV, 30 miles southeast.

RESERVATION INFORMATION: Outdoor Recreation Equipment Center, Bldg 228, 242 Fort Mervine Place, Suite 1, Lewis Hall, Presidio of Monterey, CA 93944-5000. **C-831-242-5506/6133, DSN-312-878-5506/6133,** 1030-1400 hours and 1500-1800 hours Mon-Fri. WEB: www.pom-odr.com Reservations and deposit required, up to six months in advance.

(**TML**) **Motel Lodgings:** Subcontracted units in local motel. Two double beds, CATV, private bath, two blocks from the casinos. Rates: $50-$70 double occupancy.

AMENITIES: Ski Packages available.

TML AVAILABILITY: Year round.

CREDIT CARDS ACCEPTED: MasterCard and Visa.

TRANSPORTATION: Bus and airlines in Reno.

DINING OPPORTUNITIES: Many restaurants and fast food establishments in Reno and Tahoe City.

Heavenly Resort Valley offers a wide range of mountain and water-oriented recreational activities. Close to casinos in downtown Reno.

Travis Air Force Base (CA50R4)
60 MSS/DPF
400 Brennan Circle, Bldg 51
Travis AFB, CA 94535-2045

MAIN INSTALLATION TELEPHONE NUMBERS: C-707-424-1110, DSN-312-837-1110. Locator 424-2026; Medical 423-3462; Security Police 438-2011.

LOCATION: Halfway between San Francisco and Sacramento. From north or south on I-80 take Airbase Parkway exit east at Fairfield directly to Main Gate. Clearly marked. *USMRA: Page 110 (B,C-7).* **NMC:** San Francisco, 45 miles southwest.

RESERVATION INFORMATION: Westwind Inn, Bldg 404, 520 Sevedge Drive, Travis AFB, CA 94535-2216. **C-1-888-AF-LODGE (1-888-235-6343), C-707-437-0700/424-8000, DSN-312-837-2988,** Fax: C-707-424-5489, DSN-312-837-5489, 0730-1630 hours. Duty can make reservations any time; Space-A can make reservations 24 hours in advance. Directions from Main Gate: Travis Blvd approximately 4 blocks and turn left onto Sevedge Drive (Travis Bowling Center is on the right). Check in at facility, check out 1100 hours. Handicap accessible units. Government civilian employee billeting.

(**TLF**) Bldg 440. Studio apartments and two-bedroom apartments, private bath (72). Kitchen, utensils, A/C, TV, phone, housekeeping service. Recreation and dining facilities within walking distance. Modern structure. Rates: $24.50 per unit.

(**VAQ**) Bldgs 403-405. Rooms with various bath combinations (150). Refrigerator, A/C, TV, housekeeping service. Recreation and dining facilities within walking distance. Older structure. Rates: $24.50.

(**VOQ**) Bldgs 406-410. Bedroom, semi-private bath (131). Refrigerator, A/C, TV, housekeeping service. Recreation and dining facilities within walking distance. Older structure. Rates: $32.00.

(**Fisher House**) David Grant USAF Medical Center, 100 Bodin Circle, Travis AFB, CA 94535-5000. C-707-423-7551, Fax: C-707-423-7552. *Note: Appendix B has the definition of this facility. Fisher Houses are only available as lodging for families of patients receiving medical care at military and VA medical centers.*

DV/VIP DV lounge at Air Terminal, Bldg 406, Protocol, **C-707-424-3185, DSN-312-837-3185.** O6+, leave or official duty; E9 Active Duty; Retirees. Suites, private bath (23). A/C, TV, housekeeping service. Recreation and dining facilities within walking distance. Older structure. Rates: $25.

AMENITIES: Exercise Room, Business Center, Meeting/Conference Room, Internet/E-mail access for customers, Laundry Facilities, Soft Drink and Snack Vending.

TML AVAILABILITY: Very limited, Jan-Nov.

CREDIT CARDS ACCEPTED: Visa and MasterCard.

TRANSPORTATION: On base shuttle/bus, C-707-424-3404; Off base shuttle/bus, C-800-258-3826; Car Rental; On base taxi (Official Duty Only), C-707-424-3404; Off base taxi, C-707-422-5555.

DINING OPPORTUNITIES: 24-Hour Food Court, C-707-437-2092; Delta Breeze Club, C-707-437-1977; Bowling Center, C-707-437-4737; and Pizzeria, C-707-424-0976 are within walking distance. Applebee's, C-707-452-1167; Chevy's Fresh Mex, C-707-425-8374; El Tejaban, C-707-437-3514; Ohkura Restaurant, C-707-437-6671; and Chili's, C-707-449-8072 are within driving distance.

San Francisco, almost unlimited cultural and recreational opportunities. California beach towns and wine country, the capital city of Sacramento, and the Sierra Nevada mountains are all within reach of Travis. There is no shortage of entertainment nearby.

Twentynine Palms Marine Corps Air/Ground Combat Center (CA27R4)
Commanding General Manpower Directorate (FSC)
P.O. Box 788102
Twentynine Palms, CA 92277-8102

MAIN INSTALLATION TELEPHONE NUMBERS: C-760-830-6000, DSN-312-230-6000. Locator 830-6853; Medical 830-7254; Security Police 830-6800.

LOCATION: East or west on I-10 to CA-62 (exit to Twentynine Palms/Yucca Valley). Take CA-62 (29 Palms Highway) east approximately 46 miles to town of Twentynine Palms. From town take Adobe Road north (left) to Main Gate of base, approximately 5 miles. *USMRA: Page 111 (H,I-13,14).* **NMC:** Palm Springs, 60 miles northwest.

RESERVATION INFORMATION: P.O. Box X-15, Twentynine Palms, CA 92278-0115. **C-760-830-7375, DSN-312-230-7375,** Fax: C-760-830-5980, DSN-312-230-5980, 24 hours daily. Duty can make reservations; other Space-A. Check in 1400 hours at Bldg 1565, 5th Street near O Club. Check out 1100 hours. Government civilian employee billeting.

BOQ/BEQ Two room suites (O4+) (27); SNCO single rooms, shared bath (48); Single room, private bath (2); Shared room, shared bath (8). Community kitchen, microwave in room and lounge, A/C, TV, housekeeping service, laundry facility. Older structure. Non-smoking rooms available. Rates: Two room suites $20; single rooms $13; shared rooms $6.50. No pets.

TLF Bldg 690, two miles from Main Gate. C-760-830-6573/6583, Fax C-760-830-1647. One-bedroom family units, queen beds, trundle beds, private bath (24). Handicap accessible rooms. Fully equipped kitchen, laundry facility, BBQ, playground. Reception desk 24 hours daily. Walking distance to commissary, seven day store, and Child Development Center. Recreation equipment check-out available. Rates: $40. No pets.

DV/VIP O6/GS15+. VIP Quarters (5); Three bedroom guesthouse (1). Rates: VIP Quarters $25; Guesthouse $36.

AMENITIES: Meeting/Conference Room. Ice, Snack and Soft Drink Vending Machine.

TML AVAILABILITY: Good, winter months. Difficult, summer months.

CREDIT CARDS ACCEPTED: Visa, MasterCard and American Express.

TRANSPORTATION: On/Off base shuttle/bus, C-1-800-794-MBTA (6282); Car Rental, C-760-830-6752; Off base taxi: Alpha Yellow Cab, C-760-367-1976; Top's Taxi, C-760-361-6748.

DINING OPPORTUNITIES: Burger King; Domino's Pizza, C-760-830-1700; Del Taco, Carousel Cafe, C-760-367-3736; Quick Bread Snack Bar, C-760-830-6163 ext 264; and Subway, C-760-830-1782 are within driving distance.

Five miles from Joshua Tree National Monument where the low Colorado and the high Mojave deserts come together. Many come from miles around to see the desert blooming with wild flowers.

Vandenberg Air Force Base (CA29R4)
30th Space Wing
723 Nebraska Avenue, Bldg 105252, Suite 3
Vandenberg AFB, CA 93437-6223

MAIN INSTALLATION TELEPHONE NUMBERS: C-805-606-1110, DSN-312-276-1110. Locator 606-1841; Medical 606-1847; Security Police 606-3911.

LOCATION: From the north on US-101, exit westbound at Santa Maria onto Clark Avenue, then go west approximately 2.3 miles to left (south) on CA-135 which merges into CA-1. Continue southbound on CA-1 directly to Main Gate. Or, from the south, take US-101 north to Buelton. Exit northwest onto CA-246. Just before Lompoc, bear right on Purisima Road which runs into CA-1. Follow CA-1 northwest to the Main Gate on left. *USMRA: Page 111. (C-12).* **NMC:** Santa Barbara, 55 miles southeast.

RESERVATION INFORMATION: Vandenberg Lodge, Bldg 13005, Oregon at L Street, Vandenberg AFB, CA 93437-5079. **C-1-888-AFLODGE (1-888-235-6343), C-805-734-1111 ext 2802, DSN-312-276-1844,** Fax: C-805-606-0720, DSN-312-276-0720, 24 hours daily. E-mail: VAFBBaseLodging@vandenberg.af.mil Duty may make reservations any time; Space-A may make reservations 24 hours in advance. Directions from Main Gate: Continue straight on California Blvd. The road comes to a "Y." Take "Y" to the right on Oregon Street, through stop sign. Vandenberg Lodge is the second building on left. Check in 1500 hours at lodging, check out 1100 hours. Government civilian employee lodging.

TLF One- or four-bedroom, private bath (26). Kitchen, complete utensils, CATV, housekeeping service, laundry facility, cribs, cots. Modern structure. Rates: $25-$38 per room. Maximum five per room.

VAQ Bldg 13800 area. E1-E6. Private bedroom, private bath (96). Rooms arranged in quads, full kitchen, living room, laundry facility. Rates: $18. Maximum one per room. *Note: Renovation project scheduled 01 Mar-02 Oct.*

VQ Bldgs 11041, 11042, 13140A. Private bedroom, private bath (111). Ice machine, snack vending, laundry facility. Modern structure. Rates: $21.50. Maximum two per room.

DV/VIP **Marshallia Ranch,** Bldg 1338, 30 SW/CCP. Protocol C-805-606-3711/2. General Officers Quarters, O7/SES1+. Four-bedroom, private and semi-private bath, suite (4). Kitchen, utensils, SATV, housekeeping service, laundry facility. Historic structure. Rates: $40.50 per room.

DV/VIP For reservations, 30 SW/CCP. Protocol **C-805-606-3711/3712.** E9, GS15/O6+. One bedroom, private bath, kitchenette suite (2). Two bedroom, private bath, full kitchen, suite (7). Rates: One-bedroom $35; Two-bedroom $40.50 per room.

TML AVAILABILITY: Best, Nov-Jan. Difficult, Apr-Oct. Space-A personnel are authorized a maximum of 30 days in a fiscal year in transient quarters. Extensions are not permitted.

CREDIT CARDS ACCEPTED: Visa and MasterCard.

TRANSPORTATION: On base taxi (Official Duty), C-805-606-1843; Off base taxi, C-805-736-3636.

DINING OPPORTUNITIES: Burger King, C-805-734-4263; Pacific Coast Club, C-805-734-4362; and Bowling Center C-805-734-1310 are within walking distance.

Central Coastal California is a treasure trove for visitors. Visitors should see Solvang ("little Denmark"), Pismo Beach, Santa Barbara, Channel Islands National Park and the Hearst Castle (San Simeon), to name only a few attractions within reach of Vandenberg.

COLORADO

Buckley Air Force Base (CO11R3)- New lodging facility scheduled to open in 2003. Call C-303-677-9992/6853/6103 for details.

Farish Recreation Area (CO01R3)
P.O. Box 146
Woodland Park, CO 80866-0146

MAIN INSTALLATION TELEPHONE NUMBERS: C-719-687-9098/9306. Locator 687-9098/9306; Medical 911; Security Police 911.

LOCATION: From north or south on I-25 at Colorado Springs, take exit 141 onto US-24 west for 18 miles to Woodland Park. At second stoplight near McDonald's, turn right (north) onto Baldwin Street. (County Road 22) which changes to Rampart Range Road. Follow road through four stop signs. Road forks at water treatment facility. *USMRA: Page 109 (F-4)*. NMC: Colorado Springs, 30 miles southeast. NMI: U.S. Air Force Academy, 35 miles east; Peterson AFB and Fort Carson, 40 miles southeast.

RESERVATION INFORMATION: C-719-687-9098/9306, Fax: C-719-686-1437, 0800-1700 hours. WEB: www.usafa.af.mil Advance reservations required. Accepted in advance.

TML One Cottage. Two-bedroom, sleeps eight. Fireplace, utensils. Rates: $115 per night.

TML Duplex Units. One- or Two-bedroom with a loft, sleeps five. Utensils. Rates: $70 per night.

Lodge Four-bedroom, each room sleeps four. Utensils. Rates: $46-$60 per night. Campsites, $15 per night.

AMENITIES: Mini Mart.

TML AVAILABILITY: Open year round. Call for conditions during winter months.

CREDIT CARDS ACCEPTED: Visa and MasterCard.

See *Military Living's Military RV, Camping and Outdoor Recreation Around the World* for additional information.

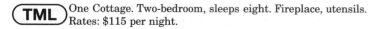

Visit Military Living online at

www.militaryliving.com

Fisher House, Denver (CO16R3)
Denver VA Medical Center
1055 Clermont Street
Denver, CO 80220-3873

Note: Appendix B has the definition of this facility. Fisher Houses are only available as lodging for families of patients receiving medical care at military and VA medical centers.

MAIN INSTALLATION TELEPHONE NUMBERS: C-303-364-4616. Medical 911, Security Police 911.

LOCATION: From I-70, exit south on Colorado Blvd, left on 9th Avenue, left (east) on Clermont Street. From I-25, exit north on Colorado Blvd, right on 9th Avenue, left on Clermont Street. **NMC:** Denver, in city limits. NMI: Buckley ANGB, 18 miles.

Fisher House Denver VA Medical Center, 1055 Clermont Street, Denver, CO 80220-3873. **C-303-393-2817,** Fax: C-303-393-4679, 0800-1600 hours Mon-Fri. After hours contact Medical Center C-303-393-2805. Check in at Medical Center. Rates: $10.

DINING OPPORTUNITIES: Many restaurants within walking and driving distance.

Fort Carson (CO02R3)
AFCZ-PA-B
1217 Weitzel
Fort Carson, CO 80913-5000

MAIN INSTALLATION TELEPHONE NUMBERS: C-719-526-5811, DSN-312-691-3431. Locator 526-0227; Medical 526-7000; Security Police 526-2333.

LOCATION: From north or south on I-25, take exit 135 west onto CO-83 (Academy Blvd) for 2 miles to a left (south) on Co-115 for 2 miles to Main Gate on left (east) side of road. Clearly marked. *USMRA: Page 109 (C,D-6,7)*. **NMC:** Colorado Springs, six miles north.

RESERVATION INFORMATION: Colorado Inn, Bldg 7301, Woodfill Road, Colorado Springs, CO 80913. **C-719-526-4832, DSN-312-691-4832,** Fax: C-719-526-5239. Front desk closed 0130-0630 daily. Reservations 60 days in advance. Check in 1600 hours at facility, check out 1100 hours. Government civilian employee billeting. Smoking and non-smoking rooms available. No pets.

VEQ Bldgs 7301. Bedroom, private bath (19). Shared kitchenette, A/C, CATV, phone, laundry facility. Rates: $33, each additional person 16 and over $5.

VOQ/VEQ Bldg 7302, 7304. Bedroom, private bath (60). Shared kitchenette, A/C, phone, laundry facility. Family rooms: Two-bedroom (50); Three-bedroom. Kitchen, A/C, CATV, phone, laundry facility. Rates: $43, each additional person 16 and over $5.

DV/VIP Bldg 7305. E9, O6+. One- and two-bedroom, private bath (8). A/C, kitchen, housekeeping service, CATV, phone, laundry facility. Older structure, renovated in 1993. Rates: $53, each additional person 16 and over $5. Retirees and lower ranks Space-A.

AMENITIES: Meeting/Conference Room, Mini Mart. Ice, Snack and Soft Drink Vending Machines.

TML AVAILABILITY: Difficult. Best, Nov-Apr.

CREDIT CARDS ACCEPTED: Visa, MasterCard and American Express.

TRANSPORTATION: On base shuttle and local bus services available.

DINING OPPORTUNITIES: Several dining facilities available.

Peterson Air Force Base (CO06R3)
21 MSS/DPF
640 Mitchell Street, Suite 320
Peterson AFB, CO 80914-1130

MAIN INSTALLATION TELEPHONE NUMBERS: C-719-556-7321, DSN-312-834-7321/7011. Locator 556-4020; Medical 556-4333; Security Police 556-4000.

LOCATION: Off US-24 (Platte Avenue) east of Colorado Springs. Eastbound from Colorado Springs on US-24, keep right onto CO-94 for 0.2 miles to right (south) on Peterson Blvd directly to Main Gate. Clearly marked. Or, westbound on US-24, take exit south onto CO-94 then west for 0.2 miles to south (right) on Peterson Blvd directly to Main Gate. *USMRA: Page 109 (G-5); 116 (D,E-5,6).* **NMC:** Colorado Springs, six miles west.

RESERVATION INFORMATION: Bldg 1042, 125 E Stewart Avenue, Peterson AFB, CO 80914-1630. **C-1-888-AFLODGE (1-888-235-6343), C-719-556-7851, DSN-312-834-7851,** Reservations: C-719-597-2010, Fax: C-719-556-7852, 24 hours daily. E-mail: pikes.peak.lodge@peterson.af.mil Duty may make reservations any time; Space-A may make reservations 24 hours in advance for a stay of three days maximum. Unaccompanied dependents may be Space-A with Active Duty or retired sign in. First come, first served. No waitlist. Check in at facility, check out 1100 hours. Government civilian employee lodging.

TLF Bldgs 1091-1094. Bedroom, private bath, sleeps five. Kitchen, refrigerator, complete utensils, TV, A/C, housekeeping service, laundry facility, cribs, ice machine. Older structure, redecorated. Non-smoking facility. Rates: $29 per unit. No pets.

VAQ Bldg 1143. Bedroom, private bath; bedroom, single occupancy, shared bath; SNCO suites, private bath. Refrigerator, A/C, TV in room and lounge, housekeeping service, laundry facility, snack vending, ice machine. Modern structure. Rates: room, sponsor/adult $18; SNCO suites, sponsor/adult $18. All Maximum two per unit, no children, no infants. No pets.

VOQ Bldgs 1026, 1030. Bedroom, private bath. Kitchen, refrigerator, A/C, TV, housekeeping service, laundry facility, ice machine. Modern structures. Non-smoking facility. Rates: sponsor/adult $21.50. Maximum two per unit. No children. No pets.

DV/VIP Protocol, Bldg 1, **C-719-554-3012.** O7+. Kitchen, refrigerator, complete utensils, A/C, TV, housekeeping service, laundry facility, ice machine. Modern structures. Non-smoking facility. Rates: sponsor/adult, $30.50 per person. Maximum two per unit. No Space-A Bldg 999. No children. No pets.

TML AVAILABILITY: Difficult. Best, Dec-Feb.

CREDIT CARDS ACCEPTED: Visa and MasterCard.

TRANSPORTATION: On base shuttle/bus, C-719-556-4307; Off base shuttle/bus, C-709-475-9733; Car Rental, C-719-556-1733; On base taxi, C-719-556-4307; Off base taxi, C-719-634-5000.

DINING OPPORTUNITIES: E Club, C-719-597-7876; McDonald's, C-719-597-4858; and O Club, C-719-547-4100 are within walking distance.

Area skiing and camping are some of the finest in the US; this is the home of NORAD, Space Command HQ. Visit historic Pikes Peak and USAF Academy.

New ski resort, Rocky Mountain Blue, operated by Peterson Air Force Base, opened on 5 November 2001 in Keystone, CO. Call C-719-333-2132 or toll free 1-877-517-3381 for details.

United States Air Force Academy (CO07R3)
2304 Cadet Drive, Suite 316
USAF Academy, CO 80840-4880

MAIN INSTALLATION TELEPHONE NUMBERS: C-719-333-1110, DSN-312-333-1110. Locator 333-4262; Medical 333-5000; Security Police 333-2000.

LOCATION: West of I-25, north of Colorado Springs. From I-25 use exit 150B northwest onto Southgate Blvd which leads to main visitors' entrance. Or take exit 150A west onto Northgate Blvd which leads to Stadium Blvd on the left (south) side of the road. Clearly marked. *USMRA: Page 109 (F-4,5), page 115 (B-2).* **NMC:** Colorado Springs, eight miles south.

RESERVATION INFORMATION: Rampart Lodge, 10 SVS/SVML, Bldg 3130, Academy Drive, Suite 100, Colorado Springs, CO 80840-4880. **C-1-888-AFLODGE (1-888-235-6343), C-719-333-4910, DSN-312-333-4910,** Fax: C-719-333-4936, DSN-312-333-4936, 24 hours daily. E-mail: rampart.lodge@usafa.af.mil Duty can make reservations any time; Space-A can make reservations 24 hours in advance. Check in at facility 1400 hours, check out 1100 hours. Government civilian employee lodging.

TLF Doug Valley and Pine Valley. One-, two- and three-bedroom houses. Kitchen, complete utensils, TV, housekeeping service, washer/dryer, cribs. Modern structures. Rates: $28. Family quarters intended primarily for use by PCS in/out, others Space-A on day-to-day basis. No pets.

VOQ Bldg 3130/3134. Bedroom, private bath. Refrigerator, TV, housekeeping service, laundry facility, ice machine. Modern structures. Handicap accessible. Rates: rooms $25.50 per person.

DV/VIP DVQ. Bldg 3130. O7+. Bedroom, living room, private bath. Kitchen, refrigerator, utensils, TV, housekeeping service, laundry facility, ice machine. Modern structure, renovated. Handicap accessible. Rates: single $30, double $36. Most reservations handled through Protocol Office, Harmon Hall, Bldg 2304, Room 328, **C-719-333-3540,** for O7+ and equivalent.

AMENITIES: Meeting/Conference Room.

TML AVAILABILITY: Best, Jan-Apr. Difficult, other times.

CREDIT CARDS ACCEPTED: Visa and MasterCard.

TRANSPORTATION: On/off base taxi.

DINING OPPORTUNITIES: O Club is within walking distance.

At the foot of the Rocky Mountains, near skiing and mountain resorts. New visitors center, gift shop and exhibits. Guided tours, 18-hole golf courses. Cadet Wing holds 1300 hours formation, visitors may watch from the chapel wall.

CONNECTICUT

Camp Rowland Army National Guard Training Site (CT05R1)
38 Smith Street
Niantic, CT 06357-2597

MAIN INSTALLATION TELEPHONE NUMBERS: C-860-691-4314, DSN-312-636-7314. Locator 691-4314; Medical 691-4357.

LOCATION: From I-95, exit 74, take right onto Rte 161 toward Niantic Center, turn left onto Smith Street. *USMRA: Page 16 (F,G-9).* **NMC:** New London, 11 miles north.

RESERVATION INFORMATION: Bldg 805, 38 Smith Street, Niantic, CT 06357-2597. **C-860-691-4314, DSN-312-636-7314.** Fax: C-860-691-4317, 0800-1600 hours Mon-Fri. E-mail: jenny.collins@ct.ngb.army.mil Duty may make reservations; non-official reservations can be made two business days prior to arrival date. Check in at lodging office.

(BEQ) Bldgs 204, 205 (open bay) & 401 (bedroom). E7-E9. Bedroom, refrigerator, TV in lounge, housekeeping service. Rates: $6-$8. No pets.

(BOQ) Bldgs 61 (open bay) & 201 (bedroom). WOC-O4. Bedroom, refrigerator, TV in lounge, housekeeping service. Rates: $6-$8. No pets.

(Army Lodging) Guesthouse, Bldg 68. Four bedrooms, two baths, full kitchen, living room, housekeeping service. Rates: $14-$27.

(TML) Two person room (45); One person handicap room (8). All have refrigerator, microwave, CATV, housekeeping service, and toiletries. Rates: $14-$27.

AMENITIES: Exercise Room, Meeting/Conference Room, AAFES PX, Beach passes, Snack and Soft Drink Vending Machine.

TML AVAILABILITY: Good. Best, Sept-Apr.

CREDIT CARDS ACCEPTED: None.

TRANSPORTATION: Off base car rentals; Off base taxi.

DINING OPPORTUNITIES: Burke's Tavern, Constantine's Restaurant, Flander's Fish House and Modesto's Bistro are within driving distance.

New London Naval Submarine Base (CT01R1)
Navy Family Service Center, Box 93
Groton, CT 06349-5000

MAIN INSTALLATION TELEPHONE NUMBERS: C-860-694-3777, DSN-312-241-3777. Locator 694-3082; Medical 694-3777; Security Police 694-3333.

LOCATION: From I-95, take exit 86 to CT-12. Turn left on Crystal Lake Road. Main gate on right. Base clearly marked. *USMRA: Page 16 (H-8), page 25 (C,D-1).* **NMC:** Hartford, 50 miles northwest.

RESERVATION INFORMATION: Bldg 379, Groton, CT 06349-5044. **C-860-694-3416, DSN-312-694-3416,** Fax: 860-694-3556. Check in 1500 hours, check out 1100 hours.

(BOQ) Bldg 379. Officers all ranks, E7+. Bedroom, private bath (105); DVQ bedroom, private bath (7). Kitchen, refrigerators, coffee maker, CATV, phone, housekeeping service, laundry facility, ice machine. Newly renovated 1993. Bar/night club in BOQ 1993. Rates: $17 per person; flag officer suite $31.

(TQ) **Susse Chalet International Hotel,** P.O. Box 92, Groton, CT 06349-5000. E1 hotel on New London NSB. C-860-445-6699, Fax: C-860-449-1050. Check in at Bldg 379 after 1500 hours if traveling on orders, check out 1100 hours. Bedroom, private bath (150). Community kitchen, refrigerator, microwave, oven, A/C, CATV, phone, hair dryer, housekeeping service, iron/ironing board, cribs, cots, soft drink and snack vending, ice machine, laundry area. Rates: $64.39, higher rates for personnel on leave. No pets.

(NAVY LODGE) Navy Lodge. Bldg CT-380, 77 Dewey Avenue, Groton, CT 06340-5000. **C-1-800-NAVY-INN.** Lodge number is C-860-446-1160, Fax: C-860-449-9093, 24 hours daily. Located off main base, from CT-12 S, right on Pleasant Valley Road, right on Lestertown Road, right on Dewey Avenue. Check in 1500-1800 hours, check out 1200 hours. Bedroom, two double beds, private bath (49); bedroom, queen-size bed and studio couch, private bath (18). Kitchenette, microwave, coffee/tea, utensils, A/C, CATV/VCR, video rental, clocks, phone, housekeeping service, coin laundry facility, cribs, snack vending, picnic grounds, playgrounds. Modern structure, renovated. Interconnecting (24), handicap accessible (2), non-smoking rooms (34). Rates: $47 per unit. Maximum four per unit. All categories may make reservations. No pets. *Note: A $7.245 million Navy Lodge replacement was approved in the DoD Fiscal Year 2001 NAF Construction Program.*

(DV/VIP) Suites in BOQ Rates: $21. Suites in Susse Chalet, **C-860-445-2105.**

TML AVAILABILITY: Fairly good. Navy Lodge, good all year.

CREDIT CARDS ACCEPTED: Visa, MasterCard and American Express. The Navy Lodge accepts Visa, MasterCard, American Express, Discover and Diners.

TRANSPORTATION: Car rental (limited availability) and off base taxi, bus, train and ferry.

DINING OPPORTUNITIES: Exchange Deli, C-860-694-3811; and McDonald's are within driving distance. Many fine restaurants in the local area.

Visit Mystic seaport for history, USCG Academy, USS Nautilus Memorial/Submarine Force Library and Museum for a view of the modern Navy. Try a game of chance at Foxwood and Mohegan Sun Casinos.

United States Coast Guard Academy (CT02R1)
15 Mohegan Avenue
New London, CT 06320-4195

MAIN INSTALLATION TELEPHONE NUMBERS: C-860-444-8444. Locator 444-8444; Medical 444-8401; Security Police 444-8597.

LOCATION: From southbound I-95 take exit 83 in New London. From northbound I-95 take exit 82-A. Follow signs, CT-32, Mohegan Drive, clearly marked. *USMRA: Page 16 (G,H-8,9), page 25 (C-2).* **NMC:** New Haven, 40 miles west. **NMI:** New London NSB, across the Thames.

RESERVATION INFORMATION: 15 Mohegan Avenue, Munro Hall, New London, CT 06320-4195. **C-860-444-1160,** Fax: C-860-444-8460, 0900-1600, Mon-Fri. E-mail: Bciorciari@cga.uscg.mil WEB: www.cga.edu/mwr/ Directions: From Main Gate take third left onto Harriett Lane. After stop sign go past Cadet Memorial Field and take second right onto Spencer Circle. Munro Hall is immediately to the left. Check in 1400-2200 hours, check out 1100hours. After duty hours, check in Main Gate. DV/VIP C-860-444-8499.

(BOQ) Guest Quarters, Munro Hall. C-860-444-8325. Twin beds, private bath (2). Microwave, refrigerator, TV/VCR, telephone in room and in lounge, housekeeping service, laundry facility. Rates: TAD $24, Leisure $25-$45.

AMENITIES: Mini Mart, Snack and Soft Drink Vending Machine.

TML AVAILABILITY: Good, Jan-Feb and Aug-Dec. Difficult, Mar-Jul.

CREDIT CARDS ACCEPTED: Visa, MasterCard and American Express.

TRANSPORTATION: Off base taxi: Harry's Taxi, C-860-444-2755; Yellow Cab, C-860-443-4371.

DINING OPPORTUNITIES: O Club, C-860-444-8458; and Dry Dock Snack Bar, C-860-444-8473 are on the Academy.

Fifteen miles from Foxwoods and Mohegan Sun Casinos. Other points of interest are Mystic, the CG Museum, USCGC Eagle (WIX-327). There are also a number of public golf courses in the area.

DELAWARE
Bethany Beach Training Site (DE03R1)
Delaware Army National Guard
Route 1
Bethany Beach, DE 19930-9770

MAIN INSTALLATION TELEPHONE NUMBERS: C-302-854-7902, DSN-312-440-7902. Locator 854-7902; Medical 911; Security Police 911.

LOCATION: Located on west side of DE-1, half a mile north of DE-26 and US-1 intersection in Bethany Beach. *USMRA: Page 42 (J-6).* **NMC:** Bethany Beach, in city limits.

RESERVATION INFORMATION: Bldg 114, Bethany Beach, DE 19930-9770. **C-302-854-7902, DSN-312-440-7902,** Fax: C-302-854-7999, DSN-312-440-7999, 0730-1600 hours. Directions: Just inside Main Gate. Check in 1200 hours, check out 1000 hours.

(TML) Hotel. E7+ without children. Two-bedroom suite (3), two full beds with shared bath. Small refrigerator, microwave, A/C, TV/VCR. Rates: $28. No Pets.

(Mobile Home) Three-bedroom mobile home with single bath (22). Kitchen, microwave, coffee maker, toaster, A/C, and CATV/VCR. Rates: $42. No Pets.

(TML) Three-bedroom apartment with single bath. Kitchen, microwave, coffee maker, toaster, A/C, and CATV/VCR. Rates: $42. No Pets.

Note: Bed linens are provided upon request and are exchanged on a weekly basis. The use of personal linens is encouraged. Towels are not available.

AMENITIES: Exercise Room, Meeting/Conference Room and Soft Drink Vending Machine.

CREDIT CARDS ACCEPTED: Visa and MasterCard.

TRANSPORTATION: Car Rental, C-302-855-9300.

DINING OPPORTUNITIES: Boat House, C-302-539-2813; Magnolias, C-302-539-5671; Sedona, C-302-539-1200; Tom & Terry's, C-302-436-4161; and Warren Station, C-302-539-7156 are within driving distance.

The Post is located 3 blocks from the Atlantic Ocean. It is approximately 14 miles from Ocean City, Maryland and 10 miles from Rehoboth Beach, Deleware. Many local activities: jetski/boat rentals, cycling rentals, fishing charter/surf, crabbing/clamming, numerous golf courses miniature/regulation, amusement rides, and boardwalk shops, outlet shopping, swimming/surfing and dining for all tastes and budgets.

Dover Air Force Base (DE01R1)
436 MSS/DPF
447 Tuskegee Blvd, Room 116
Dover AFB, DE 19902-6447

MAIN INSTALLATION TELEPHONE NUMBERS: C-302-677-3000, DSN-312-445-3000. Locator 677-3000; Medical 735-2600; Security Police 677-6664.

LOCATION: From Philadelphia, take I-95 south to Route 13 south. Base is 5 miles south of Dover, on east side of DE-1 toll or US-13. Follow signs to base. Clearly marked. *USMRA: Page 42 (I-3,4).* **NMC:** Dover, five miles northwest.

RESERVATION INFORMATION: Eagles Rest Inn, Bldg 800, 14th Street, Dover AFB, DE 19902-7219. **C-1-888-AFLODGE (1-888-235-6343), C-302-677-5983/2840/2841, DSN-312-445-5983/2840/2841,** Fax: C-302-677-2936, DSN-312-445-2936, 24 hours daily. E-mail: lodging.reservations@dover.af.mil PCS, TDY, DoD civilians (on offical orders) can make reservations any time; Space-A reservations 24 hours prior to arrival for up to three nights stay. Check out 1100 hours.

(TLF) Bldg 803. Family suite, sofabed, private bath (24). Kitchenette, refrigerator, A/C, TV/VCR, housekeeping service. Rates: $24.50.

(TML) Bldg 800. Queen bed, private bath (105). Refrigerator, microwave, coffeemaker, safe, clock radio, TV, A/C, housekeeping service. Rates: $20.

(VAQ) Bldg 481. E1-E4. Bedroom, single bed, common bath (92). Refrigerator, microwave, coffee maker, A/C, TV, clock radio, housekeeping service. Rates: $17.50.

(VAQ) Bldgs 407, 410-412. Bedroom, full size bed, private bath (128). Refrigerator, microwave, coffee maker, A/C, TV, clock radio, housekeeping service. Rates: $17.50.

(TML) Bldg 802. Bedroom suite, queen bed, private bath (27). Rates: $25. Full size bed, private bath (2). Rates: $20. Refrigerator, microwave, coffee maker, A/C, TV/VCR clock radio, housekeeping service.

(DV/VIP) Protocol, **C-302-677-4366, DSN-312-455-4366.** O6+. Suites, private bath (6). Chief suite, private bath (1). Refrigerator, microwave, A/C, TV, housekeeping service. Rates: $25.

AMENITIES: Meeting/Conference Room, Laundry Facilities, Ice Machines, Sundry Items.

TML AVAILABILITY: Good.

CREDIT CARDS ACCEPTED: Visa and MasterCard.

TRANSPORTATION: Off base shuttle/bus, C-1-800-652-3278, C-302-734-1417. Car Rentals: Avis, C-1-800-331-1212; Budget, C-1-800-527-0700; Enterprise, C-1-800-325-8007; Kut Rate, C-302-697-3000; National, C-1-800-227-7368; Seacoast, C-1-800-833-7575. Off base taxi, C-302-734-5968.

DINING OPPORTUNITIES: The Landings Collocated Club C-302-677-6022; Passenger Terminal Cafeteria, C-302-674-3380; Patterson Dining Facility, C-302-677-3925; Kingpin Cafe, C-302-677-5323; The 19th Hole, C-302-677-6039 are within driving distance.

Dover is the jumping off point for many Space-A flights to Europe and beyond. See *Military Space-A Air Opportunities Around the World,* **and** *Military Space-A Air Basic Training* **for information on this money saver for the military.**

DISTRICT OF COLUMBIA

Bolling Air Force Base (DC01R1)
11th Wing
118 Brookley Avenue, Suite 100
Bolling AFB, Washington, D.C. 20332-0503

MAIN INSTALLATION TELEPHONE NUMBERS: C-202-767-6700, C-703-545-6700, DSN-312-297-0101, DSN-312-227-0101. Locator 767-4522; Medical 767-5233; Security Police 767-5000.

LOCATION: Take I-95 (east portion of Capital Beltway, I-495), exit 22 to I-295 south, exit to Portland Street, and main entrance to AFB. Also, I-395 north, exit South Capitol Street, main entrance to AFB on right. Visitors entrance is at south gate, one mile south of Main Gate. Clearly marked. *USMRA: Page 54 (F-6).* **NMC:** Washington, D.C., in southeast section of city.

RESERVATION INFORMATION: Bolling Inn, 11 SPTG/SVML, Bldg 602, 52 Thiesen Street, Bolling AFB, D.C. 20332-5100. **C-1-888-AFLODGE (1-888-235-6343), C-202-767-5316/5771/5741, DSN-312-297-5316/5771/5741,** Fax: C-202-767-5878, DSN-312-297-5878, 24 hours daily. Duty can make reservations any time; Space-A can make reservations 24 hours in advance. Directions: Make a left at the first traffic light onto Duncan Avenue. Make a left onto Theisen Street. The lodging office is the second building on the right, Bldg. 602. Check in at billeting 1400 hours, check out 1200 hours. *Note: A $9.062 million TLF was approved in the DoD Fiscal Year 1998 NAF Construction Program.*

TLF Apartments, private bath (50). Master suite, second bedroom with twin beds. Kitchen, A/C, TV in each bedroom and living room, housekeeping service, washer/dryer in each unit. Rates: $24 per room. Maximum seven per room. Unaccompanied not authorized.

VAQ E1-E6. Bedroom, shared bath (44). Refrigerator, CATV, housekeeping service, laundry facility. Older structure. Rates: $16.

VOQ O1-O4. Suite, private bath (55). Refrigerator, A/C, TV in room and lounge, housekeeping service, laundry facility, ice machine. Rates: $19, DVQ (O5-O6) $21.

DV/VIP Protocol Office, Bldg P-20, **C-202-767-5584.** O7+. VIP Suites, private baths. Virginia House (1); Maryland House (1); Potomac House (10); Columbia House (6); Mathies Manor (6). SNCO Suites, Cheshire Hall (10). Refrigerator, A/C, TV, housekeeping service, laundry facilities. Older structure. Rates: Virginia, Maryland, Potomac and Columbia House $27; Mathies Manor $2. SNCO quarters, $21, reservations via front desk **C-202-767-5316.** Chief Suites (5), reservations should be made via the Command Chief Master Sergeant Office **C-202-767-4398.**

TML AVAILABILITY: Difficult. Better during winter months.

CREDIT CARDS ACCEPTED: Visa and MasterCard.

TRANSPORTATION: Off base shuttle/bus from Bolling AFB to Pentagon 0800-1530. Vehicle Dispatch C-202-433-4116, DSN-312-297-4116.

DINING OPPORTUNITIES: Burger King, C-202-561-4447; and Food Court, C-202-562-4419 are within driving distance.

On the Potomac, across from historic Alexandria, and in sight of the Capitol and famous monuments. Bolling is headquarters for the Air Force District of Washington.

Fort Lesley J. McNair (DC05R1)
103 3rd Avenue
Washington, D.C. 20319-5058

MAIN INSTALLATION TELEPHONE NUMBERS: C-703-545-6700, DSN-312-227-0101. Locator 685-3145; Medical 685-3092; Security Police 911.

LOCATION: At confluence of Anacostia River and Washington Channel, southwest. Enter on P Street SW. Take Maine Avenue SW, to right on 4th Street SW, to dead end at P Street. Left and then immediate right onto the Main Gate. *USMRA: Page 54 (F-5), page 55 (E-4).* **NMC:** Washington, D.C., in southwest section of city.

RESERVATION INFORMATION: Bldg 50, 318 Jackson Avenue, Fort Myer, VA, 22211-5050, **C-703-696-3576/77, DSN-312-426-3576/77,** Fax: C-703-696-3490, 0600-2200 Sun-Thu, 0800-1600 Sat. TDY, PCS can

make reservations, field grade Space-A. Credit card required. Check in 1400 hours, check out 1100 hours. Key pick up is at Fort Myer lodging office. Key drop off, drop box in lounge at Fort McNair.

VOQ/VEQ Bldg 54, Fort McNair (historic building). Suite, two beds, private bath (2); bedroom, private bath (5); bedroom, shared bath (20). Refrigerator, microwave, A/C, CATV in room, housekeeping service, laundry facility, cribs, cots available. Rates: bedroom w/ private bath, sponsor $45, additional person $5; bedroom w/ shared bath, sponsor $41, additional person $5; suites, sponsor $50, additional person $5. Maximum two per unit. No pets.

AMENITIES: ICE, Soft Drink and Snack Vending Machines.

TML AVAILABILITY: Very Good. Difficult, Apr-Nov.

CREDIT CARDS ACCEPTED: Visa, MasterCard and American Express.

TRANSPORTATION: On base shuttle/bus, C-703-475-2004; Off base shuttle/bus, C-703-475-2004; Car Rental, C-703-524-1863; Off base taxi, C-703-522-2222.

DINING OPPORTUNITIES: Golf Course, C-202-685-3138; and O Club, C-202-484-5800 are within walking distance.

Included in the original plans for the District of Columbia, Fort McNair is nearly 200 years old. Site of the trial and execution of President Lincoln's conspirators and where Walter Reed did his research work. Home of the National Defense University, National War College, Industrial College of the Armed Forces and the Inter-American Defense College. See the Washington waterfront, restaurants, seafood markets, monuments and the scenic Potomac River nearby.

United States Soldiers' and Airmen's Home (DC10R1)
3700 N. Capitol Street, NW
Washington, D.C. 20317-5000

MAIN INSTALLATION TELEPHONE NUMBERS: C-202-730-3044. Locator 202-730-3111; Medical 202-782-7761; Security Police 202-730-3111.

LOCATION: Two and one-half miles north of the Capitol. Enter from North Capitol Street. Across the street from VA Hospital and Shrine of the Immaculate Conception. After duty hours, enter through the gate at Upshur Street and Rock Creek Church Road. *USMRA: Page 54 (F-3).* **NMC:** Washington, D.C in city limits. **NMI:** Walter Reed Army Medical Center.

RESERVATION INFORMATION: U.S. Soldiers' and Airmen's Home, Ignatia Guest House, 3700 N. Capitol Street NW, Washington, D.C. 20317-5000. **C-202-730-3044.** Reservations required.

TML There are 37 rooms in this former convent, five of which are available for use by retired and Active Duty Enlisted on leave. Rates: single room $25 per night for up to 5 nights.

TML AVAILABILITY: Difficult.

CREDIT CARDS ACCEPTED: Visa and MasterCard.

TRANSPORTATION: City bus, taxi, Metro.

DINING OPPORTUNITIES: Many excellent restaurants in downtown D.C.

Visit the Smithsonian, the U.S. Capitol, the Washington Monument, the National Zoo and many other D.C. sights.

Walter Reed Army Medical Center (DC03R1)
MCWR-DCA-LD
6900 Georgia Avenue, NW
Washington, D.C. 20307-5001

MAIN INSTALLATION TELEPHONE NUMBERS: C-202-782-3501/02, DSN-312-662-3501/02. Locator 782-1150 (mil); 782-0546 (civ); Medical 782-3501; Security Police-782-3325.

LOCATION: From I-495 (Capital Beltway) take Georgia Avenue/Silver Spring exit south to Medical Center. To reach the Forest Glen support facilities from Georgia Avenue south, right turn onto Linden Lane, cross over B&O Railroad bridge. Support facilities on left (three-quarter miles from Georgia Avenue). *USMRA: Page 54 (F-2)*. **NMC:** Washington, D.C., in city limits.

RESERVATION INFORMATION: Bldg 20, 6900 Georgia Avenue NW, Washington, D.C. 20307-5000. **C-202-726-8700, DSN-312-662-3844,** Fax: C-202-726-8707, 24 hours daily. Check in at facility, check out 1200 hours. No government civilian employee billeting.

TML **Mologne House Hotel,** 1 Main Drive, Washington, D.C. 20307-5000. DoD, Active Duty, retired, reserves. Bedroom, private bath; studio with kitchenette, private bath; suite with kitchenette (200). Refrigerator, microwave, utensils, A/C, CATV, housekeeping service, coin laundry facility, iron/ironing board, coffee maker, cribs, cots, ice machine. Meeting/conference rooms, fitness center, commissary, restaurant and lounge. New modern structure. Handicap accessible (100). Rates: official $59-$76, unofficial $68-$125. This is a commercial hotel with TDY facilities. Reservations required. No pets.

Army Lodging Bldg 17. Bedroom, common bath, semi-private bath or private bath (62). A/C, CATV, housekeeping service, cribs, cots, coin laundry facility, ice machine, includes continental breakfast (Mon-Fri). Facilities for DAVs. Maximum three per unit. Older structure. Rates: official $21-$35, unofficial $28-$43. Priority to PCS, members of immediate family of seriously ill patients and MEDEVAC/AIRVAC personnel. Out-patients may make reservations, others Space-A.

Fisher House 6825 Georgia Avenue NW, Washington, D.C. 20307-5001. Fisher House II on main post WRAMC **C-202-356-7564, DSN-312-295-7374,** Fax: C-301-295-8012 Fisher House I at Forest Glen Annex, **C-301-295-7374.** *Note: Appendix B has the definition of this facility. Fisher Houses are only available as lodging for families of patients receiving medical care at military and VA medical centers. There are two Fisher Houses at WRAMC.*

DV/VIP Mologne House. Two units available. Potomac & Chesapeake Suite. Rates: official $76, unofficial $125.

TML AVAILABILITY: Best, Nov.-Apr. Difficult, other times.

CREDIT CARDS ACCEPTED: Visa, MasterCard and American Express.

TRANSPORTATION: On/off base shuttle/bus.

DINING OPPORTUNITIES: Restaurant located in the Mologne House. Kentucky Fried Chicken, McDonald's and Pizza Hut are within driving distance.

Walter Reed is in D.C. near the National Zoo and National Cathedral, both star attractions for visitors. Other monuments are within 30-minute drive.

Visit Military Living online at
www.militaryliving.com

Washington Naval Support Activity/Anacostia Annex (DC02R1)
2701 S Capitol Street SW
Washington, D.C. 20373-5800

MAIN INSTALLATION TELEPHONE NUMBERS: C-703-545-6700, DSN-312-222-6700. Locator 703-545-6700; Medical 433-3757; Security Police 433-3018.

LOCATION: From I-395, exit South Capitol Street, cross South Capitol Street Bridge, main entrance is on right, before Bolling AFB. *USMRA: Page 54, (F,G-5)*. **NMC:** Washington, D.C., in southeast section.

RESERVATION INFORMATION: BOQ: 2819 Robbins Road SW, Washington, D.C. 20374-5000. **C-202-433-3862, DSN-312-288-3862,** Fax C-202-433-4095. For duty reservations call (SATO)-800-576-93-27. Directions: Exit from I-295 S, take Naval Station Washington exit (3A). Proceed through gate on Defense Blvd, turn right onto Wicks Drive, then left onto Robbins Road. The BOH is Bldg 93 on the right. Check in after 1600 hours, check out 1200 hours. Government civilian employees. WEB: www.ndw.navy.mil Check in 1500-1800 hours, check out 1200 hours.

BOQ Bldg 93. E7-O6 on orders. GS-7+. Bedroom (full size bed), private bath (22). Refrigerator, microwave, coffee maker, A/C, TV, alarm clock, phone with dual jack for PC or laptop Internet connection, housekeeping service, no cost laundry facility, iron/ironing board. Also, kitchen with a microwave, picnic area with grill and gazebo, lounge with a 52-inch screen TV, rec room with ping-pong table, pool table and vending machines. Rates: $15, guest $4. Active Duty on orders and GS7+ may make reservations; Space-A call between 1800-2200 hours on same day only. No Smoking. Renovated January 1998.

DVQ Bldg 2. Reservations: **C-202-433-4052.** O7+. Bedroom suite, private bath (9). Kitchenette (some), microwave, A/C, TV, housekeeping service. Rates: $30, family members $5. Reservations 30 days in advance. PCS, TDY have priority; others Space-A. No pets.

TML AVAILABILITY: Good, Dec-Apr. Difficult, other times.

CREDIT CARDS ACCEPTED: None.

TRANSPORTATION: Off base shuttle/bus; Off base taxi.

DINING OPPORTUNITIES: Cafeteria (Mon-Fri) is within walking distance. Food court and Burger King are within driving distance.

For military history buffs, visit the Navy Memorial Museum, the Navy Yard, the old torpedo factory, the Display Ship Barry (DDSN-933), the Marine Corps Museum (with famous flags raised over Mt. Suribachi and Iwo Jima) and the Combat Art Gallery.

Washington Navy Lodge (DC12R1)
Bldg 4412, 12 Bowline Green SW
Bellevue Housing Community
Washington, D.C. 20032-5000

MAIN INSTALLATION TELEPHONE NUMBERS: C-202-563-6950. Locator 563-6950; Medical 911; Security Police 911.

LOCATION: Take I-95 (east section of Capital Beltway, I-495) north or south, exit to I-295 N, exit 1, onto Overlook Avenue, right at the light. Left at next light into Bellevue Housing Community on Magazine Road. Left on Beyer Road to Navy Lodge. Located within closed based area. All visitors must log in with base police at gate.

NAVY LODGE Navy Lodge. Bldg 4412, 12 Bowline Green SW, Washington, D.C. 20032-5000. **C-1-800-NAVY-INN.** Lodge number is C-202-563-6950, Fax: C-202-563-2970, 24 hours daily. Check in 1500-1800 hours, check out 1200 hours. Bedroom, private bath (50). Kitchen, utensils, A/C, CATV/VCR, video rental, ironing boards, cribs, highchairs, soft drink and snack vending, dining/living room areas, sleep up to four persons (two double beds).

Handicap accessible (2). Modern structure. Rates: $59 per unit. PCS on orders may make reservations any time; Active Duty may make reservations 60 days in advance, others 30 days in advance. No pets.

CREDIT CARDS ACCEPTED: Visa, MasterCard, American Express and Discover.

TRANSPORTATION: Off base shuttle/bus; Off base taxi.

DINING OPPORTUNITIES: Burger King, C-202-561-4447; and Food Court, C-202-562-4419 located on Bolling AFB are within driving distance.

Bolling Air Force Base is one half mile away. Public transportation located outside the entrance gate. All attractions of Washington, D.C., Alexandria, Annapolis and Baltimore are nearby.

FLORIDA

Camp Blanding/National Guard Post (FL42R1)
Route 1, Box 465
Starke, FL 32091-9703

MAIN INSTALLATION TELEPHONE NUMBERS: C-904-682-3430, DSN-312-960-3430. Locator 682-3430; Medical 682-3105; Security Police 682-3462.

LOCATION: From I-95 north or south, exit 95A to FL-16 west for 31 miles. Follow exit signs to support activities. *USMRA: Page 38 (F-3,4).* **NMC:** Jacksonville, 30 miles north.

RESERVATION INFORMATION: Finegan Lodge, Bldg 2392, Route 1, Box 465, Starke, FL 32091-9703. **C-904-682-3381, DSN-312-960-3381,** Fax: C-904-682-3540, DSN-312-960-3540. 0800-1630 hours Mon-Sat. After duty hours report to MP at Main Gate. Check in 1300 hours, check out 1100 hours. Government civilian employee billeting.

(**TLF**) **Finegan Lodge.** Bldg 2392. Bedroom, semi-private bath (98). CATV, housekeeping service, coin laundry facility, ice, soft drink and snack vending. Rates: Active Duty PCS/TDY $12.50, all others $13.85. Reservations can be made by Active Duty, others Space-A.

(**DV/VIP**) Contact Training Site Manager at **C-904-682-3357, DSN-312-960-3357.** O6+. Retirees and lower ranks Space-A.

TML AVAILABILITY: Good, Nov-Feb.

CREDIT CARDS ACCEPTED: Visa, MasterCard and American Express.

TRANSPORTATION: Car Rental, C-904-964-3666.

DINING OPPORTUNITIES: Cedar River Seafood, C-904-964-8282; Sonny's Real Pit BBQ, C-904-964-8840; and Western Steer Steak House, C-904-964-8061 are within driving distance.

Under one hour drive to Gainesville, Jacksonville and St. Augustine. Three hours to Walt Disney World and the Orlando area.

Visit Military Living online at

www.militaryliving.com

Corry Station Naval Technical Training Center (FL19R1)
640 Roberts Avenue, Room 112
Pensacola, FL 32511-5138

MAIN INSTALLATION TELEPHONE NUMBERS: C-850-452-2000, DSN-312-922-2000. Locator 452-6512; Medical 452-6604; Security Police 452-3753.

LOCATION: North of US-98, three miles north of Pensacola NAS at intersection FL-295 and US-98. *USMRA: Page 38 (A,B-13), page 53 (B-4).* **NMC:** Pensacola, five miles northeast.

RESERVATION INFORMATION: Mariner's Roost, 640 Roberts Avenue, Room 112, Pensacola, FL 32511-5138. **C-850-452-6541/6609, DSN-312-922-6541/6609,** Fax: C-850-452-6685, DSN-312-922-6685, 24 hours daily. WEB: www.navy.mil/homepages/nttc/main1.htm Directions: From Main Gate, take first right into parking lot, follow signs to front of building complex. Large sign on right with adjacent parking for housing Bldg 1084.

(**TML**) **Mariner's Roost.** Bldgs 1082, 1084, 1090. Enlisted. Bedroom, private bath. Kitchen, microfridge, microwave, coffee maker, toaster, utensils, TV/VCR, computer hookup, clock radio, hair dryer, iron/ironing board. Rates: single $15; suite $20; additional person 25% of lodging fee. Duty can make reservation, others Space-A.

AMENITIES: Exercise Room, Meeting/Conference Room, Mini Mart, Snack and Soft Drink Vending Machines.

TML AVAILABILITY: Difficult year round.

CREDIT CARDS ACCEPTED: Visa, MasterCard and American Express.

TRANSPORTATION: On base shuttle/bus: People Mover, C-850-452-6609, DSN-312-922-6609; Off base shuttle/bus: E Cat City Bus, C-850-436-9383; Off base taxi: Warrington Taxi, C-850-455-8506.

DINING OPPORTUNITIES: Barnshill's Country Buffet, C-850-456-2760; Crosswinds Casual Dining, C-850-452-6168; and Hong Kong Chinese, C-850-456-3303 are within walking distance. Foster's Barbeque, C-850-456-7758; Oyster Bar, C-850-455-3925; and Quincy's Steak House, C-850-453-5695 are within driving distance.

Destin Army Infantry Center Recreation Area (FL01R1)
557 Calhoun Avenue
Destin, FL 32541-5000

MAIN INSTALLATION TELEPHONE NUMBERS: C-1-800-642-0466, Fort Benning C-706-545-5600. Locator 850-837-6423; Medical 911; Security Police 651-7400.

LOCATION: Located off base on 15-acre site on Choctawhatchee Bay in Destin, FL. US-231 south to I-10, west exit 19 to US-331, south exit 14 to US-98, west to Benning Drive, right to area. Or I-10 to FL-85; south to Fort Walton Beach; US-98 east to Destin, left at Benning Drive to area. *USMRA: Page 39 (C-13).* **NMC:** Pensacola, 45 miles west. **NMI:** Eglin AFB, 17 miles north.

RESERVATION INFORMATION: C-1-800-642-0466, C-706-545-5600; Information only C-850-837-6423. Discounted weekly and off season rates available. Guests are non family members. Check in at facility 1600-2200 hours, check out 1100 hours.

(**TML**) Motel. Bedroom, two double beds, private bath (54); Refrigerator, microwave, coffee maker, CATV, phone (free local calls). Handicap accessible room (5). Rates (subject to change): $41-$57, each additional guest $5. No pets.

Cabins Two-(17) and three-(5) bedroom, furnished, private bath. Kitchen, microwave, pots/pans, CATV, phone (free local calls). Handicap accessible cabins (5). Close to Hurlburt Field support. Rates (subject to change): two-bedroom $47-$66; three-bedroom $53-$73, each additional guest $5. Cabins require four night minumum. No pets.

AMENITIES: Recreation Equipment Rental (Large Fishing and Party Vessels at Cabins). Snack and Soft Drink Vending Machines.

TML AVAILABILITY: Limited.

CREDIT CARDS ACCEPTED: Visa, MasterCard and American Express.

TRANSPORTATION: None available.

DINING OPPORTUNITIES: Capt Dave's on the Gulf, C-706-837-2627; Destin Chops, C-706-654-4944; and Shoney's, C-706-837-9650 are within driving distance.

Fishing, swimming and boat rentals all nearby. Six public golf courses, two greyhound tracks, Destin Fishing Museum, Gulfarium, Zoo and Indian Temple Mound Museum are all within 45 miles. See *Military Living's Military RV, Camping and Outdoor Recreation Around the World* for additional information.

Eglin Air Force Base (FL27R1)
6 MSS/DPF
502 West Van Matre, Suite 1
Eglin AFB, FL 32542-6823

MAIN INSTALLATION TELEPHONE NUMBERS: C-850-882-1110, DSN-312-872-1110. Locator 882-1113; Medical 883-8242 Emergency Medical 883-1113; Security Police 882-2502.

LOCATION: Exit I-10 at Crestview. Follow signs to Niceville and Valparaiso (Eglin AFB). *USMRA: Page 39 (C-13), page 53 (G-2).* **NMC:** Fort Walton Beach, seven miles south.

RESERVATION INFORMATION: Eglin Inn, Bldg 11001, Boatner Road, Eglin AFB, FL 32542-5498. **C-1-888-AFLODGE (1-888-235-6343), C-850-882-8761/4534, DSN-312-872-8761/4534,** Fax: C-850-882-2708, DSN-312-872-2708, 24 hours daily. E-mail: eglininn@eglin.af.mil Duty may make reservations any time; Space-A may make reservations 24 hours in advance. Check in at billeting 1400 hours, check out 1100 hours. *Note: A $2.795 million Recreation Site Lodging was approved in the DoD Fiscal Year 2001 NAF Construction Program.*

TLF Bedroom, private bath (55); two-bedroom, private bath (32); three-bedroom, private bath (1); separate bedroom, private bath (1). Refrigerator, microwave, coffee maker, A/C, TV/VCR, housekeeping service. Rates: $30.

VAQ Suite (SNCO) (18); bedroom, private bath (89); bedroom, shared bath (54). Refrigerator, microwave, coffee maker, A/C, TV/VCR, housekeeping service. Rates: suite $26; room $19. Payment due upon check in.

VOQ Bedroom, private bath (112); suite (several). Refrigerator, microwave, coffee maker, A/C, TV/VCR, housekeeping service. Rates: Bayside Inn (suites) $26; room $19. Payment due upon check in.

TML Duke Field, 919 MSS/MSRH, 506 Drone Street, Suite 6, Eglin AFB, Field 3, FL 32542-5000. C-850-883-6390, 0715-1545 hours Mon-Fri. Bedroom, two twin beds, (175). Refrigerator, housekeeping service. Rates: $16.

DV/VIP HQ AFDTC/CCP, Bldg 1 (Command Section), **C-850-882-3011/3238.**

AMENITIES: Exercise Room, Ice and Snack Vending Machines.

TML AVAILABILITY: Very good, Nov-Jan. Difficult, other times.

CREDIT CARDS ACCEPTED: Visa, MasterCard and American Express.

TRANSPORTATION: On base shuttle/bus, C-850-882-3791; Off base taxi: Airport Taxi Service, C-850-651-0404; Car Rental: Avis, C-850-651-0822; Guardian, C-850-243-5515; Hertz, C-850-651-0612; National, C-850-651-1113.

DINING OPPORTUNITIES: Cafeteria, C-850-651-4821; Dining Hall, C-850-882-5053; Flight Kitchen, C-850-882-5014; NCO/CPO Club, C-850-678-5127; and O Club, C-904-651-1010 are within driving distance.

Call Natural Resources on Eglin for information on the wonderful outdoor activities on Eglin Reserve. Don't miss Fort Walton Beach's Miracle Strip, deep sea fishing off Destin and visit historic Pensacola, 50 miles west.

Fisher House, West Palm Beach (FL55R1)
West Palm Beach VA Medical Center
7305 N. Military Trail
Route 136
West Palm Beach, FL 33410-6400

Note: Appendix B has the definition of this facility. Fisher Houses are only available as lodging for families of patients receiving medical care at military and VA medical centers.

MAIN INSTALLATION TELEPHONE NUMBERS: C-561-882-7180.

LOCATION: From I-95 take exit 55 (west) to Blue Heron Blvd Go right (north) on North Military Trail, medical center is on the left.

Fisher House 7305 N. Military Trail, Route 136, West Palm Beach, FL 33410-6400. **C-561-882-7180.** Fax: C-561-882-6565.

DINING OPPORTUNITIES: VA Medical Center Canteen. Many local fast food establishments and restaurants.

Homestead Air Reserve Base (FL17R1)
360 Coral Sea Blvd
Homestead ARB, FL 33039-1299

MAIN INSTALLATION TELEPHONE NUMBERS: C-305-224-7000, DSN-312-791-7000. Locator 224-7000; Medical 911; Security Police 224-7115.
Ten-digit dialing required for local calls.

LOCATION: Exit 5 (Biscayne Blvd/288th Street) off Florida Turnpike, left at bottom of ramp. Road leads straight to base. Or take exit 6 (Speedway Blvd) off Florida Turnpike, left at bottom of ramp. At first light take a left. Road leads straight to base. *USMRA: Page 39 (I-14), page 51 (A,B-10).* **NMC:** Miami, 40 miles northeast.

RESERVATION INFORMATION: Homestead Inn, 482 SVF/SVML, Bldg 476, 29050 Coral Sea Blvd, Homestead ARB, FL 33039-1299. **C-1-888-AFLODGE (1-888-235-6343), C-1-800-330-8149 ext 7198, C-305-224-7168/2330, DSN-312-791-7168/2330,** Fax: C-305-224-7290, DSN-312-791-7290, 24 hours, 0700-1200 hours on some holidays. Please call to verify. WEB: www.homestead.af.mil/baseFac7.htm Duty may make reservations any time; Space-A can make reservations 24 hours in advance. Check in at front desk. No reservations on the web or via email.

VAQ Bldg 475, 477, 478. Bedroom, private bath. Refrigerator, microwave, TV/VCR, phone, housekeeping service, washer/dryer. Rates: $23.00.

(**VOQ**) Bldg 476. Bedroom, private full bath. Refrigerator, microwave, TV/VCR, phone, housekeeping service, washer/dryer. Rates: $23.00.

(**DV/VIP**) Bldg 476. E9, O6/GM-15+. Bedroom, private bath; Suite, full bath. Refrigerator, microwave, stocked bar, TV/VCR, phone, housekeeping service, washer/dryer. Rates: $31.50 per suite.

AMENITIES: Snack and Soft Drink Vending Machine.

TML AVAILABILITY: Good. Best, May-Aug.

CREDIT CARDS ACCEPTED: Visa, MasterCard, and Services Club Card.

TRANSPORTATION: Off base shuttle/bus, C-305-871-2000; Car Rental: C-305-246-2050; On base taxi, C-305-246-4400; Off base taxi, C-305-256-4444, C-305-378-8888.

DINING OPPORTUNITIES: All Ranks Club, C-305-224-7484; BX Mart, C-305-258-3881; and Dunkin' Donuts, C-305-258-3881 are within walking distance. Capri Restaurant, C-305-247-1542; Denny's, C-305-247-7800; and Golden Corral, C-305-245-0022 are within driving distance.

Hurlburt Field (FL18R1)
16 MSS/DPF
121 Bartley Street, Bldg 90213
Hurlburt Field, FL 32544-5272

MAIN INSTALLATION TELEPHONE NUMBERS: C-850-884-1110, DSN-312-579-1110. Locator 850-884-1110; Medical 850-881-5173; Security Police 884-7114.

LOCATION: Off US-98, five miles west of Fort Walton Beach, north of US-98. Clearly marked. *USMRA: Page 39 (C-13), page 53 (H-4).* **NMC:** Pensacola, 35 miles west.

RESERVATION INFORMATION: Commando Inn, 16 SVS/SVML, Bldg 90509, 301 Tully Street, Hurlburt Field, FL 32544-5844. **C-1-888-AFLODGE (1-888-235-6343), C-850-581-1627, C-850-884-7115/6245, DSN-312-579-7115/6245,** Fax: C-850-884-5043, DSN-312-579-5043, 24 hours daily. E-mail: Commando.Inn@hurlburt.af.mil. Duty, PCS may make reservations any time; Space-A may make reservations 24 hours in advance, space permitting. Directions: Take Cody Avenue north, turn left on Simpson Avenue. Lodging office is at the corner of Simpson and Tully. Check in at lodging after 1400, check out 1200 hours. Government civilian employee lodging available for duty travel and on a Space-A basis.

(**TLF**) Bldgs 90372, 90374, 90375. Bedroom with queen-size bed, sofa sleeper and sleeper chair (24). Kitchen, cribs, rollaways, high chairs. Rates: $25.

(**VAQ**) Bldgs 90345. E1-E6. Bedroom, queen bed, private bath (5), semi private bath (46); Bldg 90346. E9. Suite, queen bed, private bath, living room, kitchenette (2). Limited utensils and dishware, central A/C, TV, housekeeping service, laundry facility, in room beverage and snack sales. Rates: room $12.50; suite $17.50. Maximum two per unit in private bath rooms and suites; one per unit in semi-private bath rooms.

(**VQ**) Bldgs 90346, 90502, 90507, 90508. Bedroom, queen bed, private bath (181); suite with living room (18). Kitchenettes in some units, utensils and dishware, central A/C, TV, housekeeping service, laundry facility, in room beverage and snack sales. Handicap accessible units (8). Rates: room $12.50; suites $17.50. Maximum two per unit.

(**DV/VIP**) AFSOC Protocol Office, Bldg 1, **C-850-884-2308, DSN-312-579-2308.** O7+. Bldgs 90377, 90378, 90507. Suite with living room, private bath. Rates: $17.50 and $25. Maximum two per unit.

AMENITIES: Ice, Snack and Soft Drink Vending Machines.

TML AVAILABILITY: Difficult. Best, Dec-Jan.

CREDIT CARDS ACCEPTED: Visa and MasterCard.

TRANSPORTATION: On base taxi, C-850-884-7223, DSN-312-579-7223.

DINING OPPORTUNITIES: Diner's Reef (Enlisted dining facility); and Jr. Rocker's Sports Pub are within walking distance. Numerous fine restaurants are within driving distance.

The fishing is great here! Destin is known as "The World's Luckiest Fishing Village." Great beaches and numerous fine restaurants. Various facilities under renovation through 2003.

Jacksonville Naval Air Station (FL08R1)
Box 2, PAO
Bldg 850, Room 211
Jacksonville, FL 32214-5000

MAIN INSTALLATION TELEPHONE NUMBERS: C-904-542-2345, DSN-312-942-2345. Locator 542-2340; Emergency Medical 777-7300; Security Police 542-2661/2662.

LOCATION: Access from US-17 south, Roosevelt Blvd. Clearly marked. *USMRA: Page 38 (G-3), page 50 (B,C-6,7).* **NMC:** Jacksonville, nine miles northeast.

RESERVATION INFORMATION: CBQ, Bldg 11, Jacksonville, FL 32212-5000. **C-904-542-3138/3139, DSN-312-942-3138,** Fax C-904-542-5002, DSN-312-942-5002, 24 hours daily. Check in at facility after 1200 hours, check out 1100 hours. Government civilian employee billeting. *Note: A $2.187 million golf course cottage addition was approved in the DoD Fiscal Year 2001 NAF Construction Program.*

(**BEQ**) Bldg 822. E1-E4: double room, shared bath; E5-E6: single or double room, private bath; E7-E9: single room, private bath. Rates: $10-$17 per room. Call billeting for more information.

(**BOQ**) Bldgs 11, 844, 845. Bedroom, private bath (110); bedroom, shared bath (8); separate bedroom, private bath (96). Refrigerator, phone, TV in room and lobby, housekeeping service, laundry facility, snack vending, ice machine, one large and two small conference rooms, sauna, fishing dock. Bldg 11, older structure. Rates: $10-$17 per room. Reservations taken 45 days in advance for official duty; all others Space-A. No pets.

(**NAVY LODGE**) Navy Lodge. Bldg 802, Mustin Road, Jacksonville, FL 32212-5000. **C-1-800-NAVY-INN.** Lodge number is C-904-772-6000, Fax: 904-777-1736, 24 hours daily. Check in 1500-1800 hours, check out 1200 hours. Bedroom, two double beds, private bath (50). Kitchenette, microwave, utensils, coffee/tea, A/C, CATV/VCR, HBO, video rental, clocks, phone, housekeeping service, coin laundry facility, iron/ironing board, cribs, rollaways, snack vending, ice machine, picnic grounds, playground. Modern structure. Interconnecting rooms (12), handicap accessible (2), non-smoking (40). Rates: $48 per unit. Active Duty can make reservations 60 days in advance, Retirees 30 days. No pets. *Note: A $4.788 million Navy Lodge addition of 50-rooms is in progress for the DoD Fiscal Year 2001 NAF Construction Program.*

(**DV/VIP**) PAO, **C-904-542-3147/3138.** O6/GS15+. Retirees and Space-A only after 1800 hours.

TML AVAILABILITY: Fair. Difficult, summer months.

CREDIT CARDS ACCEPTED: Visa and MasterCard. The Navy Lodge accepts Visa, MasterCard and American Express.

TRANSPORTATION: On base taxi, C-904-777-0270.

DINING OPPORTUNITIES: Bambinos and Mulligan's (Golf Course) are within walking distance. McDonald's, O Club and Yesterdays are within driving distance.

Don't miss boating and water sports on over 74 square miles of inland waters, golf courses, wonderful beaches that are among Florida's finest. Also visit museums, symphony, St. Augustine and Cypress Gardens.

Key West Naval Air Station (FL15R1)
P.O. Box 9037
Key West NAS, FL 33040-9037

MAIN INSTALLATION TELEPHONE NUMBERS: C-305-293-2348, DSN-312-483-3700. Locator 292-2256; Medical 293-4500; Security Police-294-2511.
Ten-digit dialing required for local calls.

LOCATION: Take Florida Turnpike, US-1 south to exit signs east for Key West Naval Air Station on Boca Chica Key, 7 miles north of Key West. *USMRA: Page 39 (G-16).* **NMC:** Miami, 150 miles north.

RESERVATION INFORMATION: CBH, Bldg C2076, Trumbo Point Annex, Key West, FL 33040-9001. **C-305-293-4117/8, DSN-312-483-4117/8,** Fax: C-305-293-4430, DSN-312-483-4430, 24 hours daily. Directions: For Trumbo Point Lodging, enter Trumbo Point Annex Gate, building located off to right (six-story cream colored building). For Boca Chica and Truman Annex, enter Boca Chica Gate, take first right, second building on right (three-story building). Check in at facility 1600 hours, check out 1200 hours. Government civilian employee billeting, GS 1+ (on orders only).

TML Reservations required for personnel on orders. Bedroom, private bath (260); Suites, separate bedroom, private bath (18); single suite, private bath (12). Refrigerator, TV in rooms and lounge, housekeeping service, laundry facility. Handicap accessible. Rates: single rooms $18 and $24, each additional person $4 and $6; Suites $30, each additional guest $7; Townhouses $50, each additional guest $9. Maximum three per unit.

TML Truman Annex. Substandard, Bldgs 437-439, 1350, 1351. E1-E6. Bldg 437, bedroom, shared bath (66); Bldg 438, bedroom, shared bath (65); Bldg 439, bedroom, shared bath (57); Bldg 1350, bedroom, double occupancy, shared bath (65); Bldg 1351, bedroom, shared bath (62). Common kitchen, CATV, laundry facility, pool/video room. Rates: Bldgs 438, 439, 1350 $11; Bldg 437, $20; Bldg 1351, $26; each additional guest $6. No Space-A.

TML Boca Chica. Bldgs 638, 639, 648, 649, 727. C-305-293-2085, DSN-312-483-2085. Bldg 638, room, shared bath (44); Bldg 639, room, shared bath (49); Bldg 649, room, two single beds, private bath (49); Bldg 648, single room, private bath (42); VIP suites (2); Bldg 727 room, shared bath (36). Kitchen, microfridge, CATV/VCR, video rental, phone, laundry facility. Bldg 639, substandard rooms. Single, shared bath. CATV, housekeeping service, laundry facility, pool/video room. Rates: room $26, each additional guest $6; VIP suite $50, each additional guest $9.

NAVY LODGE Navy Lodge. Bldg V-4114, Arthur Sawyer Road, P.O. Box 9035, Key West, FL 33040-9001. **C-1-800-NAVY-INN.** Lodge number is C-305-292-7556, Fax: C-305-296-4309, 0700-2000 hours. Directions: Six miles south of NAS Boca Chica, on Sigsbee Park. Check in 1500-1800 hours, check out 1200 hours. Bedroom, two double beds, private bath (26). Kitchenette, microwave, utensils, A/C, CATV/VCR, video rental, phone, hair dryer, coin laundry facility, iron/ironing board, cribs, cots. Handicap accessible (2). Rates: Jan-Apr $70, May-Sep $51. MWR Sunset Lounge, community center with tickets, commissary and exchange across the road. MWR marina boat and snorkel rental gear. Modern structure. All categories may make reservations. No pets.

TML Sigsbee RV Park/White Street Vacation Rentals. MWR Department, Box 9027, Key West NAS, FL 33040-9001. C-305-293-4431, DSN-312-483-3144. Location: At the corner of White & United Street Office closed Sun, Mon and holidays (arrivals for these days will be

arranged). MWR Trailers. Near Old Town Key West. Two-bedroom, double beds, dining room, private bath with tub & shower (12). Kitchen, microwave, complete utensils, limited housekeeping service, within walking distance of Old Key West. Rates: May-Dec $48, Jun-Apr $55. All categories may make reservations three to four months in advance. **See *Military Living's Military RV, Camping and Outdoor Recreation Around the World* for additional information and directions.**

DV/VIP Quarters Guesthouse, Truman Annex. O6+. **C-305-293-5310,** Fax: C-305-293-2084. Open Duty Hours. Bldg 648. Three-bedroom beach house (1). Kitchen, A/C, all amenities. Rates: $36, guests $9. Call CO Secretary, NAS Key West, FL 33040. Reservations required, others Space-A.

AMENITIES: Exercise Room, Meeting/Conference Room, Mini Mart, Snack and Soft Drink Vending Machine.

TML AVAILABILITY: Extremely limited. Best, summer.

CREDIT CARDS ACCEPTED: Visa, MasterCard and American Express.

TRANSPORTATION: Off base shuttle/bus, C-305-293-2268, DSN-312-483-2268; Car Rental: Avis, C-305-296-8744; Enterprise, C-305-293-0220; Hertz, C-305-294-1039; Off base taxi, C-305-296-6666, C-305-292-2000.

DINING OPPORTUNITIES: Harbor Lights Seafood and Raw Bar, C-305-294-2727 and Mini Mart, C-305-292-7226 are within walking distance of Trumbo Point. Cafe Sole, C-305-294-0230; Half Shell Raw Bar, C-305-294-7496; and PT's Late Night, C-305-296-4245 are within driving distance. Commissary, Navy Exchange and Sunset Lodge Marina are within walking distance of Navy Lodge.

This is the place to kick back and relax by the ocean. Visit the Ernest Hemingway House Museum and Harry Truman Little White House.

Key West Navy Lodge is a superb vacation destination.

MacDill Air Force Base (FL02R1)
6 MSS/DPF
2306 Florida Keys Avenue
MacDill AFB, FL 33621-5313

MAIN INSTALLATION TELEPHONE NUMBERS: C-813-828-1110, DSN-312-968-1110. Locator 828-2444; Medical 828-2334; Security Police 828-3322.

LOCATION: From I-75 exit 57 to I-275 south, exit 23 at Dale Mabry Highway (US-92/573), south 5 miles to MacDill AFB Main Gate. *USMRA: Page 38 (E,F-8), page 56 (E,F-3,4).* **NMC:** Tampa, five miles north.

RESERVATION INFORMATION: MacDill Inn, Bldg 411, 8604 Hangar Loop, MacDill AFB, FL 33608-0219. **C-1-888-AFLODGE (1-888-235-6343), C-813-831-4804, 813-828-4259, DSN-312-968-4259/4804,**

Fax: C-813-828-2660/4259, DSN-312-968-2660/4259, 24 hours daily. E-mail: macdill.inn@macdill.af.mil Duty may make reservations any time; Space-A may make reservations 24 hours in advance. Directions: Located at the corner of Hangar Loop Road and Tampa Blvd. Check in at lodging, check out 1100 hours. Government civilian employee billeting.

TLF Bldgs 893, 905, 906. PCS families are Priority 1; all others are Priority 2. Bedroom, private bath (24). Kitchen, refrigerator, utensils, A/C, TV/VCR, housekeeping service, laundry facility, cribs, cots, snacks at front desk, ice machine. Handicap accessible. Rates: $24.50 per family. Maximum five per unit.

VAQ Bldg 372. E1-E6. Bedroom, shared bath (62). Microfridge, A/C, TV, housekeeping service, laundry facility. Older structure. Rates: $17.50.

VOQ Bldgs 312, 366, 390, 411. Bedroom, private bath; suites, private bath. A/C, TV, housekeeping service, laundry facility, ice machine. Modern structure. Rates: rooms $20 per unit; suites $25 per unit. Maximum two per unit. No children.

DV/VIP 6th ARW/CCP, **C-813-828-2056.** E9, O6+.

AMENITIES: Exercise Room, Meeting/Conference Room, Mini Mart.

TML AVAILABILITY: Extremely limited.

CREDIT CARDS ACCEPTED: Visa and MasterCard.

TRANSPORTATION: Off base shuttle/bus; Car Rental, C-813-840-2613; On base taxi, C-813-828-5281, DSN-312-968-5281; Off base taxi, C-813-253-0121.

DINING OPPORTUNITIES: Bowling Center, C-813-840-6907; O Club, C-813-837-1031; and Shoppette/BX Food Court, C-813-840-2143 are within walking distance. Golf Course Clubhouse, Marina Bay Cafe, McDonald's, Burger King, C-813-840-2992; and NCO Club, C-813-840-6900 are within driving distance.

Local attractions include Busch Gardens, Tampa Aquarium, Epcot Center, Disney World, Sea World—this is an area with lots of interesting things to see.

Marathon Recreation Cottages & RV Park(FL28R1)
100 MacArthur Causeway
Miami, FL 33139-5101

MAIN INSTALLATION TELEPHONE NUMBERS: C-305-536-5850. Locator 536-5850; Medical 911; Security Police 911. *Ten-digit dialing required for local calls.*

LOCATION: Situated on Marathon Key in the heart of the Florida Keys on US-1 (Overseas Highway) at mile marker 48 at Marathon. Enter recreation area from US-1. *USMRA: Page 39 (H-15).* **NMC:** Miami, 111 miles northeast. NMI: Key West Naval Air Station on Boca Chica Key, 40 miles south.

RESERVATION INFORMATION: C-305-535-4565, Fax: C-305-535-4566 WEB: www.uscg.mil/mlclant/iscmiami/mwr.htm E-mail: gcoyle@iscmiami.uscg.mil Reservations required, by application only, with payment at least eight weeks in advance of month requesting. Credit cards are not accepted. Check-in 1400-1800 hours at Cottage Caretaker, 1800 Overseas Highway, Marathon, FL 33050. After-hours arrivals check in at Coast Guard Station OOD ($15.00 late arrival fee will be charged on arrivals after 1800 hours.)

TLF One-bedroom cottage, private bath, sleeps five (4). One double bed, two single sofabeds, one rollaway bed, fully furnished. Kitchen, cookware, utensils, A/C, CATV. Screened in patio. Rates: $27-$47 depending on rank. Twelve day limit (including only one weekend). No pets. See *Military Living's Military RV, Camping and Outdoor Recreation Around the World* for additional information.

AMENITIES: Boat and Recreation Equipment Rentals.

TRANSPORTATION: Off base taxi.

DINING OPPORTUNITIES: Pancho's, C-305-289-1629; Porky's Bayside, C-305-289-2065; and 7 Mile Grill, C-305-743-4481 are within walking distance. Herbie's, C-305-743-6373; The Hurricane, C-305-743-2220; and Key Colony Inn, C-305-743-0100 are within driving distance.

Situated on the bay side of Vaca Key in the heart of the Florida Keys. Beaches on Atlantic side only. Activities available at facility include fishing, swimming, snorkeling, scuba diving, boating, kayaking, hiking and bicycling.

Mayport Naval Station (FL13R1)
Bldg 1333, Baltimore Street, Rainey Hall
Mayport, FL 32228-0042

MAIN INSTALLATION TELEPHONE NUMBERS: C-904-270-5011, DSN-312-960-5011. Locator 270-5401; Medical 270-5303; Security Police 270-5583.

LOCATION: From Jacksonville take Atlantic Blvd (FL-10) east to Mayport Road (FL-A1A), left to Naval Station, east of FL-A1A. *USMRA: Page 38 (H-3), page 50 (G-3,4).* **NMC:** Jacksonville, 10 miles west.

RESERVATION INFORMATION: Davis Hall, Bldg 425, Mayport, FL 32228-0098. **C-904-270-5423/5707, SATO (official duty) 1-800-576-9327, DSN-312-960-5423,** Fax: C-904-270-5396. Duty on orders to Mayport can make reservations, others Space-A. Check in at facility at 1400 hours, check out 1200 hours. Government civilian employee billeting. Handicap accessible units.

CBQ Davis Hall Bldg 425, Bldg 1585. Bedroom, shared and private bath. Kitchenette, refrigerator, A/C, CATV, housekeeping service, laundry facility, ice machine. Rates: $8-$20 depending on room and rank.

NAVY LODGE Navy Lodge. Bldg 1980 Baltimore Street, Mayport Naval Station, FL 32228-0077. **C-1-800-NAVY-INN.** Lodge number is C-904-247-3964, Fax: C-904-270-6153, 24 hours daily. Check in 1500-1800 hours, check out 1200 hours. From Main Gate take second right on Massey Avenue, left on Baltimore Avenue. Two-bedroom mobile homes, private bath (19). Kitchen, complete utensils, A/C, CATV/VCR, video rental, housekeeping service, coin laundry facility, hair dryer, cribs. Rates: mobile home $53. Lodge, two queen-size beds, private baths, kitchenette, refrigerator, microwave and coffee maker (32). Rates: $62. One queen-size bed, private bath, refrigerator, microwave, coffee maker, snack and soft drink vending (20). Rates $52. All categories may make reservations. No pets. *Note: The Navy Lodge's 36-room addition opened on 2 April 2002.*

DV/VIP Commander/DO, **C-904-270-4501.** E9, O7+. Bldgs 425, 1585. Bldg 425. Kitchenette, refrigerator, A/C, CATV, housekeeping service, laundry facility, ice machine. Modern structure. Rates: VIP $25, DV $36. Bldg 1585. Separate bedroom, private bath, kitchen (2). Rates: $25.

TML AVAILABILITY: Very good, Nov-Mar. Difficult, other times.

CREDIT CARDS ACCEPTED: Visa, MasterCard and American Express.

TRANSPORTATION: On base shuttle/bus.

DINING OPPORTUNITIES: Bogey's, C-904-270-5143; Mayport Beach Club, C-904-270-7205; and Subway are within walking distance. Arby's; Exchange, C-904-249-3747; and Wendy's, C-904-346-3529 are within driving distance.

Near Jacksonville, historic St. Augustine. Deep sea fishing, and famous Florida beaches-shark's teeth are picked up on local beaches.

The new Navy Lodge is a sight to see at Mayport Naval Station.

Oak Grove Park FAMCAMP (FL09R1)
MWR Department NASP
Pensacola NAS, FL 32508-5000

MAIN INSTALLATION TELEPHONE NUMBERS: C-850-452-0111, DSN-312-922-0111. Locator 452-0111; Medical 452-4138; Security Police 452-2453.

LOCATION: From I-10 E or W, take exit 2 south on FL-297, Pine Forest Road. Turn onto FL-173 (Blue Angel Parkway). Road will lead south approximately 12 miles and enter back entrance to NAS. *USMRA: Page 39 (A,B-13) and Page 53 (A,B-4,5).* **NMC:** Pensacola, 8 miles east.

RESERVATION INFORMATION: C-850-452-2535, DSN-312-922-2535, 0800-1630 hours. Fax C-850-452-4366 DSN-312-922-4366. E-mail: Lance.Don@CNET.Navy.mil WEB: www.mwr-pcola.navy.mil Reservations three months in advance for Active Duty; two months in advance for Retirees with a two night non-refundable deposit. Check in 1300-1630 hours, check out 0730-1000 hours. Space-A taken after 0900 hours.

TML One-bedroom cabins, private bath (12, 1 handicap accessible), two-bedroom cabins (8). Two double beds, one twin bed and one sleeper sofa (queen). Kitchen, refrigerator, complete utensils, A/C, TV, housekeeping service. Modern structures. Handicap accessible. Rates: $50. Two day minimum, two week maximum. Also four new cottages (2-handicap accessible.)

AMENITIES: Ice and Soft Drink Vending Machines.

TML AVAILABILITY: Best, Oct-Apr. Difficult, other times.

CREDIT CARDS ACCEPTED: Visa, MasterCard, American Express and Discover.

TRANSPORTATION: Off base Car Rental: AVIS C-1-800-831-2847; Enterprise C-1-800-736-8222; Thrifty C-850-477-5553. Off base taxi: Gosstown C-850-456-8294; Yellow C-850-433-3333; Blue Angel C-850-456-8294.

DINING OPPORTUNITIES: Cubi Bar Cafe, C-850-452-2643; and Lighthouse Point Restaurant & CPO Club, C-850-452-3251 are within walking distance. Gosalino's Italian Restaurant, C-850-452-8000/1; Mustin Beach O Club, C-850-452-8280; The Oaks Restaurant, C-850-452-3859, and Ducks, C-850-452-2443 are within driving distance.

Coastal Florida, near Pensacola is known for water recreation and fishing.

Panama City Coastal Systems Station
Naval Surface Warfare Center (FL35R1)
Family Transition Office
Bldg 500, 6703 West Highway 98
Panama City, FL 32407-7001

MAIN INSTALLATION TELEPHONE NUMBERS: C-850-234-4011, DSN-312-436-4011. Locator 234-4011; Medical 234-4177; Security Police 234-4332.

LOCATION: Located on US-98 at the west foot of the Hathaway Bridge in Panama City Beach. *USMRA: Page 39 (D,E-14).* **NMC:** Panama City, adjacent.

RESERVATION INFORMATION: BEQ: 484 Vernon Avenue, Bldg 484, Panama City, FL 32407-5000. BOQ: 349 Solomon Drive, Bldg 349, Panama City, FL 32407-5000. **C-850-234-4217, DSN-312-436-4217,** Fax: C-850-234-4991, DSN-312-436-4991, 24 hours daily. Reservations for official duty; all others Space-A. Check in 1600 hours, check out 1100 hours. Handicap accessible units. *Winner of the 1997 and 1999 Admiral Elmo R. Zumwalt Award for Excellence in Bachelor Housing.*

BEQ Bldg 484. Private bedroom, private bath; private bedroom, shared bath; shared bedroom, shared bath (40). Refrigerator, microwave, A/C, CATV/VCR, free movies, laundry facility, housekeeping service, computer room. Modern building with recent remodeling. E7-E9 suite $16; E5-E6 private room $13; E1-E4 shared room $7. No overnight guests, no pets.

BOQ Seashore Inn. Bldg 349. Officers, W1+. Suite, private bath (30); senior suite, private bath (12). Kitchenette, limited utensils, A/C, CATV/VCR, free movies, phone, laundry facility, housekeeping service, jacuzzi. Fully remodeled facility. Some handicap accessible. Rates: suite member $16, guest $3.25; senior suite memeber $20, guest $5. Guests must be ID card holding dependents only. No children under 18. No pets.

CBQ Bldg 304. C-850-236-2920. Bedroom, sofabed, private bath. Community kitchens, refrigerator, microwave, CATV/VCR, free movies, laundry facility, housekeeping service. Recently renovated to accommodate families up to four. Rates: members $16, guest $3.25. No pets.

DV/VIP Seashore Inn, Bldg 349. **C-850-234-4217, DSN-312-436-4217.** 06/GS15+. VIP suites, private bath (5). Kitchenette, limited utensils, A/C, CATV/VCR, free movies, phone, laundry facility, housekeeping service, jacuzzi. Fully remodeled facility. Handicap accessible available. Rates: memeber $20, guest $5. Guests must be ID card holding dependents only. No children under 18. Reservations required for official duty; all others Space-A. No pets.

AMENITIES: Exercise Room, Mini Mart, Meeting/Conference Room, Business Center. Ice, Snack and Soft Drink Vending Machines.

TML AVAILABILITY: Good, Oct-Mar. Difficult, Apr-Sep.

CREDIT CARDS ACCEPTED: Visa, MasterCard, American Express and Discover.

TRANSPORTATION: Off base taxi, C-850-233-8299.

DINING OPPORTUNITIES: Down the Hatch, C-850-235-0961; and Sonic Drive Inn, C-850-235-9786 are within walking distance. Black Angus, C-850-784-1788; and Mikato, C-850-235-1338 are within driving distance.

Visit the Armament Museum, beautiful sandy white beaches and enjoy Florida sport fishing.

Patrick Air Force Base (FL03R1)
45 SVS/SVML
820 Falcon Avenue
Patrick AFB, FL 32925-5000

MAIN INSTALLATION TELEPHONE NUMBERS: C-321-494-1110, DSN-312-854-1110. Locator 494-4542; Medical 494-8229; Security Police 494-2008.
Ten-digit dialing required for local calls.

LOCATION: Take I-95 south to exit 73 east (Wickham Road), 3 miles to FL-404 (Pineda Causeway), left on South Patrick Drive, to Patrick AFB. *USMRA: Page 38 (I-8).* **NMC:** Orlando, 45 miles northwest.

RESERVATION INFORMATION: Space Coast Inn, Bldg 720, 820 Falcon Avenue, Patrick AFB, FL 32925-5000. **C-1-888-AFLODGE (1-888-235-6343), C-321-494-5428/5429/2075/6590, DSN-312-854-5428/5429/2075/6590,** Fax: C-321-494-6093/7597, DSN-312-854-6093/7597, 24 hours daily. WEB: www.patrick.af.mil Directions: After entering Main Gate, go to first stop sign turn left and go one block. Bldg 720 is on right. Check in at lodging 1500 hours, check out 1100 hours. Government/Military civilian employee lodging.

(TLF) Bldgs 306 and 308. One-bedroom, private bath (10); two-bedroom, private bath (10). Kitchen, living room, utensils, A/C, TV, housekeeping service, laundry facility, cribs and high chairs. Newly constructed structures (Sept 2001). Rates: $29. Duty may make reservations any time; Space-A may make reservations 24 hours in advance.

(VAQ) Bldgs 556, 727. E1-E8. Bedroom, living room, private bath (28); bedroom, private bath (8); bedroom, shared bath (66). Refrigerator, microwave, A/C, TV, housekeeping service, laundry facility, ice machine. Older structure, renovated. Rates: $18 and $21.50. Duty may make reservations any time; Space-A may make reservations 24 hours in advance.

(VOQ) Bldgs 264, 265, 404. Two-bedroom, shared bath, living room (94); suite, private bath (10). Refrigerator, microwave, A/C, TV, housekeeping service, laundry facility, ice machine. Renovated. Rates: $21.50-$25.50. Duty may make reservations any time; Space-A may make reservations 24 hours in advance.

(DV/VIP) Protocol **C-321-494-4511.** Bldg 255, E9. Bedroom suite, private bath (3). A/C, TV, kitchen with utensils, laundry facility, housekeeping service. Rates: $35. Bldgs 250, 251, 253. O6+. Bedroom suite, private bath (3); two-bedroom suite, private bath (1); four-bedroom house (1). Full kitchen, refrigerator, utensils, AC, TV, housekeeping service, laundry facility. Older structure, renovated. Rates: $35-$40.50. Duty may make reservations any time; Space-A may make reservations 24 hours in advance.

(TML) **Manatee Cove Recreational Lodging.** C-407-494-4787, DSN-312-854-4787. Three-bedroom beach houses, three full baths (3); sleeps eight, furnished. Kitchen, CATV/VCR, washer/dryer, garage. Rates: $125-$150 per day, $800-$1000 per week. **See *Military Living's Military RV, Camping and Outdoor Recreation Around the World* for additional information and directions.**

TML AVAILABILITY: Good, Nov-Jan. Limited, other times.

CREDIT CARDS ACCEPTED: Visa and MasterCard.

TRANSPORTATION: On base shuttle/bus, C-321-494-7247; Car Rental, C-321-783-2424; Off base taxi, C-321-783-7200.

DINING OPPORTUNITIES: Bowling Center, C-321-494-2958; O Club, C-321-494-4011; and Riverside Dining Facility (For TDYs), C-321-494-4248 are within walking distance. Anthony's Pizza, C-321-494-5620; Golf Course, C-321-494-7856; and NCO Club, C-321-494-7491 are within driving distance.

Florida's "Space Coast" includes US Air Force Space Museum, Kennedy Center, Disney World, Sea World, Epcot Center, Cypress Gardens.

Pensacola Naval Air Station (FL14R1)
190 Radford Blvd, Bldg 191
Pensacola, FL 32508-5217

MAIN INSTALLATION TELEPHONE NUMBERS: C-850-452-0111, DSN-312-922-0111. Locator 452-4693; Medical 452-4138; Security Police 452-3453.

LOCATION: Four miles south of US-98, and 12 miles south of I-10. Take Navy Blvd from US-98 or US-29 directly to NAS. *USMRA: Page 39 (A,B-13,14), page 53 (A,B-4,5).* **NMC:** Pensacola, eight miles north.

RESERVATION INFORMATION: BEQ, Bldg 3910, Pensacola NAS, FL 32508-5000. **C-850-452-7782, DSN-312-922-7782,** Fax: C-850-452-5676, DSN-312-922-7784, 0730-1600 hours Mon-Fri. Front Desk C-850-452-7076/77, DSN-312-922-7076/77, 24 hours daily. Check in at Bldg 3910 after 1200 hours, check out 1100 hours. **BOQ,** Bldg 600. **C-850-452-3625/2755/2756, DSN-312-922-3625/2755/2756,** Fax: C-850-452-3188, DSN-312-922-3188, 24 hours daily. Check in at Bldg 600, check out 1100 hours. Duty, TAD, Reservists (orders) may make reservations; others Space-A.

(BEQ) Bayshores. Bldg 3472. E1-E4. Shared room, shared bath. Refrigerator, microwave, coffee maker, CATV/VCR. Rates: $7.50, no guests. Personnel assigned to NAS. No family.

(BEQ) Bayshores. Bldgs 3470,3471,3473. Single room, private bath. Refrigerator, microwave, coffee maker, CATV/VCR. Rates: $15, guest $3. Personnel assigned to NAS. No family.

(BOQ) Bldg 600. Bedrooms, private bath; flag officer suites, private bath. Microwave, coffee maker, CATV/VCR. Renovated. Rates: rooms $15, suites $29. Personnel assigned to NAS. No family.

(NAVY LODGE) Navy Lodge. Lighthouse Point, Bldgs 3875 and 3945, Pensacola NAS, FL 32508-5217. **C-1-800-NAVY-INN.** Lodge number is C-850-456-8676, Fax: 850-457-7151, 24 hours daily. Check in 1500 hours, check out 1200 hours. Room with two queen beds and kitchenette (42); Business class room with two queen beds, desk and kitchenette (20); Room with one queen bed, microwave and refrigerator (36); Mobile unit (12). Handicap accessible (4). All double queen rooms have kitchen utensils. A/C, CATV/VCR, video rental, phone, housekeeping service, coin laundry facility, snack vending. Cribs, high chairs and rollaways available upon request. Rates: single queen-size bed $48; two queen-size beds and handicap units $60; mobile units $53. All categories may make reservations. No pets. There is a lobby gift shop. *A new 50-room expansion opened Dec 2000.*

(DV/VIP) BEQ. Bayshores, Bldgs 3474, 3475; Barracks E, Bldg 3910. E5-E9. Suite, living room, private bath. Refrigerator, microwave, coffee maker, CATV/VCR, laundry facilities. Bayshores suites have kitchenettes. Rates: Bayshores $20, Barracks E $17; guest $3. Personnel assigned to NAS. No family, check with BEQ on Space-A.

(DV/VIP) BOQ. O6+. Rooms, private bath. Microwave, coffee maker, CATV/VCR. Renovated. Rates: $29. Personnel assigned to NAS. No family.

TML AVAILABILITY: Limited due to ongoing renovations for the next two years.

CREDIT CARDS ACCEPTED: Visa, MasterCard and American Express.

TRANSPORTATION: On/off base shuttle/bus.

DINING OPPORTUNITIES: Lighthouse, C-850-452-2351; and O Club, C-850-455-2276, are within walking distance of Navy Lodge. Barnhill

Buffet, C-850-456-2760; Oyster Bar, C-850-455-3925; and Quincy's, C-850-453-5695 are within driving distance.

See miles of sugar-white sand beaches, fishing, Saenger Theater of performing arts in Pensacola, the Blue Angels, the USS Lexington.

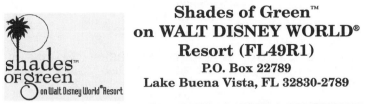

Shades of Green™ on WALT DISNEY WORLD® Resort (FL49R1)

P.O. Box 22789
Lake Buena Vista, FL 32830-2789

MAIN INSTALLATION TELEPHONE NUMBERS: C-407-824-3400, Fax: C-407-824-3460. Medical 911, Security Police 911. Reservations: C-888-593-2242, Fax:C-407-824-3665. WEB: www.shadesofgreen.org
Ten-digit dialing required for local calls.

LOCATION: From Orlando take I-4 west, exit 26-B. Walt Disney World, follow Magic Kingdom Resort signs, go through Magic Kingdom toll booth, stay in far right lane following signs to resort and hotels, at first light turn left, Seven Seas Drive past Polynesian Resort, come to three way stop, turn right on Floridian Way. Driveway is first road to the left, Magnolia Palm Drive. *USMRA: Page 38 (G,H-7), page 53 (A-2).* **NMC:** Orlando, 15 miles northeast.

DESCRIPTION OF AREA: The newest addition to Armed Forces Recreation Centers is Shades of Green on Walt Disney World Resort. The former Disney Inn, Shades of Green is situated almost in the heart of the Magic Kingdom, nestled between two championship golf courses and a nine-hole executive course which are all part of Walt Disney World Resort. There are 287 rooms, two swimming pools, a hot tub, a toddler pool, two tennis courts, a small fitness center and a playground. There are two restaurants with lounges nearby to relax and enjoy great food and the beverage of your choice. The hotel also offers an AAFES gift shop, a video arcade center and laundry facilities. Transportation to all of Walt Disney World Resorts and Attractions is complimentary for all Shades of Green guests. Discount tickets are available for most Orlando area attractions. Shades of Green is a smoke-free resort.

SEASON OF OPERATION: Year round.

RESERVATIONS: Required. Military personnel, Active Duty, retired, Guard and Reserve, family members and DoD employees may make reservations by calling **C-888-593-2242,** Fax: C-407-824-3665. Make reservations up to a year in advance. Write for reservations and information packet: Shades of Green on Walt Disney World Resort, P.O. Box 22789, Lake Buena Vista, FL 32830-2789.

RATES: E1-E5, standard $66, poolside $76; E6-E9, O1-O3, WO1-CW3, GS1-GS10, NF1-NF3, widows(ers), Medal of Honor recipients, 100% disabled veterans, standard $89, poolside $99; O4-O6, CW4-CW5, GS11-GS15, NF4-NF5, standard $95, poolside $105; O7-O10, Active Duty Foreign Military assigned to a U.S. Military Installation, retired DoD civilians, NF6 standard $99, poolside $109. Rates are for double occupancy, add $10 per additional adult 18 years or older. Sponsors are required to provide verification of eligibility and pay grade. Upon check-in, valid military ID or current LES is required.

CREDIT CARDS ACCEPTED: Visa, MasterCard, American Express, Discover and Diners.

TRANSPORTATION: On base shuttle/bus to and from theme parks, C-407-824-3400; Car Rental, C-888-593-2242; Off base taxi, C-407-857-9999.

DINING OPPORTUNITIES: Back Porch Lounge, C-407-824-3400; Evergreens Sports Bar and Grill, C-407-824-3400; and Garden Gallery Restaurant, C-407-824-3400 are available at the resort.

A vacation dream come true, a visit to WALT DISNEY WORLD® Resort, including Magic Kingdom®, Epcot®, Disney-MGM Studios Theme Park and Disney's Animal Kingdom Theme Park®. Other attractions within an hour's drive are Busch Gardens, Cypress Gardens, hot air balloon rides, deep sea fishing, Daytona and Cocoa Beach and Cape Canaveral where you can visit the Space Center and if you're lucky, watch the space shuttle launch. If this is not enough to keep you busy, there is golf, swimming and tennis all without leaving the resort.

The Shades of Green closed 31 March 2002 in order to build an exciting new expanded hotel. The "new" expanded hotel will have 300 new rooms (for a total of 587 rooms). This is, indeed, a real blessing since so many military folks have been unable to get a reservation there because of its popularity. The newly expanded Shades of Green is expected to open 15 December, 2003. Reservation lines are now open for the new and improved facility.

There is good news for those who want to go to Walt Disney World NOW during the time of the closure. Call Shades of Green weekdays at 1-888-593-2242 and learn about their alternate arrangements at Disney's Contemporary Resort, North Garden Wing, adjacent to the Main Tower. You will be able to book at Shades of Green's rates based on two adults occupying a room with $10 added for each additional guest 18 or over *(subject to change).*

Rates at Disney's Contemporary Resort are much higher, between $234 and $370. Shades of Green has negotiated a fabulous deal for military and their families, active, retirees, Guard and Reserve and their family members plus DoD employees. The only additional charge to Shades of Green rates, according to Armed Forces Recreation Center headquarters is the 11 percent state and county tax, which is unavoidable. Call 1-888-593-2242 for any additional information.

Tyndall Air Force Base (FL04R1)

325th FW
721 Suwannee Road
Tyndall AFB, FL 32403-5428

MAIN INSTALLATION TELEPHONE NUMBERS: C-850-283-1110/3, DSN-312-523-1110/3. Locator 283-2138; Medical 283-7523; Security Police 283-4124.

LOCATION: Take I-10, exit to US-231 south to US-98. 13 miles east of Panama City on US Hwy 98. Clearly marked. *USMRA: Page 39 (E-14).* **NMC:** Panama City, 10 miles northwest.

RESERVATION INFORMATION: Sand Dollar Inn, 325 SVS/SVML, Bldg 1332, 204 Oak Drive, Tyndall AFB, FL 32403-5541. **C-1-888-AFLODGE (1-888-235-6343), C-850-283-4211 ext 3346/7/8/9, DSN-312-523-4211 ext 3346/7/8/9,** Fax: C-850-283-4800, DSN-312-523-4800, 24 hours daily. Duty can make reservations any time; Space-A can make reservations 24 hours in advance. Check in 1400 hours, check out 1200 hours Mon-Fri, 1000 hours Sat-Sun and Holidays.

TML VAQ/VOQ/DVQ/TLF. Sand Dollar Inn. All rooms have one queen-size bed in each room. VOQ: Private bedroom, private bath (200); VAQ: Private bedroom, shared bath (376); DV Suites: Private bedroom, private bath, living room (19); SNCO: Private bedroom, private bath, living room (14); TLF: One bedroom efficiency apartments (40), sleeps four. Cribs and rollaways available. A/C, CATV in all rooms, housekeeping service, laundry facility, ice machine. Modern structure. Rates: TLF, $27.50; VOQ, $21.50; VAQ, $18.00; DV Enlisted $23.00, DV Officer $28.50, Large Suites $30.50.

DV/VIP 325th FW, Protocol, **C-850-283-2232.** O6+. Rates: $20.50-$22.50.

TML AVAILABILITY: Very good, 15 Nov-15 Jan. Weekends normally good. Fair, other times.

CREDIT CARDS ACCEPTED: Visa and MasterCard.

TRANSPORTATION: On base taxi, C-850-283-4872; Off base taxi.

DINING OPPORTUNITIES: Burger King, C-850-286-5859; Pizza Pub, C-850-283-2814; E Club, C-850-283-4357; and O Club, C-850-283-4146 are within walking distance.

Beautiful white sand beaches, water sports, fishing and small friendly communities.

Whiting Field Naval Air Station (FL05R1)
FSC, 7511 Enterprise Street
Milton, FL 32570-5000

MAIN INSTALLATION TELEPHONE NUMBERS: C-850-623-7011, DSN-312-868-7011. Locator 623-7011; Medical 623-7333; Security Police 623-7333.

LOCATION: From US-90 east exit, FL-87 north for 8 miles to NAS on east side of FL-87. *USMRA: Page 39 (B-13).* **NMC:** Pensacola, 30 miles southwest

RESERVATION INFORMATION: Wings Inn, Bldg 2942, 7426 USS Lexington Circle, Milton, FL 32570-6015. **C-850-623-7605/6/7, C-877-627-9324, DSN-312-868-7605/6/7,** Fax: C-850-623-7238, DSN-312-868-7238, 24 hours daily. Duty may make reservations; others Space-A. Directions from Main Gate: Go one block, first road on right then 2 blocks on left. Check in 1500 hours, check out 1100 hours. Government civilian employee billeting.

CBH Bldg 2958. Family style two-bedroom suite, private bath (70). Kitchenette, some utensils, A/C, TV/VCR, lounge, sauna, picnic tables, grills, game room, Sega rental. Rentals available for check out at front desk. Some rooms have a twin bed. Rates: $17, each additional person $2.

CBH Bldg 2957. Family style two-bedroom unit (8). Single bedroom units, lounge, private bath (42). Kitchenette, some utensils, A/C, TV/VCR, sauna, picnic tables, grills, game room, sega rental. Rates: two-bedroom unit $17, one-bedroom unit $12; each additional person $2.

DV/VIP Admiral's Office, Bldg 2942, **C-850-623-7201.** BOQ 05+; BEQ E9+. Private bath, kitchenette, utensils, A/C, TV/VCR. No children under 10. Rates: $29. Retirees Space-A.

AMENITIES: Exercise Room, Snack and Soft Drink Vending Machine, Mini Navy Exchange Store (located in bachelor housing), Computer Room with internet access and Theatre with surround sound.

TML AVAILABILITY: Good.

CREDIT CARDS ACCEPTED: Visa, MasterCard and American Express.

TRANSPORTATION: Off base taxi.

DINING OPPORTUNITIES: Bowling Alley, C-850-623-7545, DSN-312-868-7545; Wings club, C-850-623-7311, DSN-312-868-7311 are within walking distance.

Small growing community, 25 miles northeast of Pensacola, 18-hole golf course, swimming pools, bowling alley, clubs, commissary and exchange. Stop in and see the new Whiting Field.

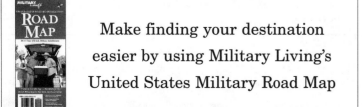

GEORGIA

Albany Marine Corps Logistics Base (GA17R1)
Family Service Center
814 Radford Blvd
Albany, GA 31704-1128

MAIN INSTALLATION TELEPHONE NUMBERS: C-229-639-5000, DSN-312-567-5000. Locator 1-800-352-3877; Medical 439-5911; Security Police 439-5181.

LOCATION: Off US-82 east of Albany, take Mock Road south from 5-Points to Fleming Road. Go east to Main Gate. *USMRA: Page 37 (C-8).* **NMC:** Albany, three miles west.

RESERVATION INFORMATION: Live Oak Lodge, 9201 Williams Blvd, Albany, GA 31705-5000. **C-229-639-5614, DSN-312-567-5614,** Fax: C-229-639-5690, DSN-312-567-5690, 0730-1600 hours Mon-Fri. After hours, contact Duty Office, Bldg 3500. Check out 1130 hours.

TML Bldgs 9251, 9253, 9255. Primarily for PCS. Three-bedroom detached house, two baths (3). Furnished, kitchen, dishes, utensils, TV, housekeeping service, washer/dryer, iron/ironing board. Non-smoking. Rates: $25. Maximum six adults and children per unit. Military on leave, Retirees, Space-A. No pets.

TQ Bldg 7966. E6+, equivalent graded government employees on official orders. One-bedroom, private bath units. Refrigerators, microwaves. Non-smoking. Rates: $12. Maximum two adults per unit. Retired military Space-A. No pets.

TOQ Bldgs 10201, 10202. Officers all ranks, equivalent government employees on official duty. One-, three- and four-bedroom suites with kitchenettes. Renovated. Non-smoking, handicap accessible suite available. Rates: $15-$25 per unit. Retired military Space-A. No pets.

DV/VIP Bldg 10300. O6+. Two-bedroom, two bath, completely furnished detached house (1). All facilities and amenities. Housekeeping service, TV, washer/dryer. Non-smoking. Rates: $30. Official duty may make reservations; leave and retired military, Space-A. No pets.

TML AVAILABILITY: Fairly good. Best Nov-Mar.

CREDIT CARDS ACCEPTED: Visa, MasterCard, American Express and Discover.

TRANSPORTATION: Off base shuttle/bus.

DINING OPPORTUNITIES: Subway C-229-639-5000; The 10th Hole, C-229-639-1576; and Base Restaurant C-229-639-5223 are within walking distance.

Swimming at beautiful Radium Springs, south of Albany, outdoor sports, local Concert Association, Little Theater. Albany is a trade and distribution center for Southwest Georgia.

Athens Navy Supply Corps School (GA12R1)
1425 Prince Avenue
Athens NSCS, GA 30606-2205

MAIN INSTALLATION TELEPHONE NUMBERS: C-706-354-7305, DSN-312-588-7305. Locator 354-1500; Medical 354-7321; Security Police 354-1500.

LOCATION: From Atlanta, take I-85 northeast to GA-316/US-29. Go East to Athens perimeter loop. Follow loop west to Prince Avenue exit.

Turn left (north) onto Prince Avenue. Base is on the right. *USMRA: Page 37 (D-3).* **NMC:** Atlanta, 70 miles west.

RESERVATION INFORMATION: The Oaks, 1425 Prince Avenue, Athens NSCS, GA 30606-2205. **C-706-543-3033, DSN-312-588-7360,** 0800-0100 hours, Fax: C-706-354-7370, DSN-312-588-7370. E-mail: frontdesk@nscs.com Check in at Brown Hall after 1400 hours, check out 1200 hours. Reservations 180 days in advance for those on orders to NSCS; all others Space-A. No pets.

CBQ The Oaks. Brown Hall. Two-room suite, private bath (35); one-room suite, private bath. Microfridge, coffee maker, A/C, CATV/VCR, telephone, hair dryer, iron/ironing board, clock radio, housekeeping service, laundry facilities available. Rates: two-room suite $23.50, each additional person 10 and over $6.00; one-room suite $16.50, each additional person 10 and over $6.00. No pets. No smoking. *Earned a five-star rating for Excellence in Bachelor Housing.*

CBQ Wright Hall. One-room suite, private bath (72). Microfridge (some rooms), coffee maker, A/C, TV/VCR, video rental, housekeeping service, laundry facility, iron/ironing board, ice, soft drink and snack vending machines. Rates: sponsor $16.50 guest $6.00. Maximum two per room. No pets.

TML AVAILABILITY: Dependent on student/class loading.

CREDIT CARDS ACCEPTED: Visa, MasterCard, American Express and Diners.

TRANSPORTATION: Off base shuttle/bus.

DINING OPPORTUNITIES: Various restaurants are within driving distance.

Athens has museums, restaurants, shopping, and the University of Georgia; the state botanical garden, and the Chattahoochee National Forest nearby. Atlanta 70 miles away . . . lots to do and see.

Atlanta Naval Air Station (GA16R1)
1000 Halsey Avenue, Bldg 80
Marietta, GA 30060-5099

MAIN INSTALLATION TELEPHONE NUMBERS: C-770-919-6392, DSN-312-625-6392. Locator 919-5000; Medical 919-5300; Security Police 919-6175.
Ten-digit dialing required for local calls.

LOCATION: From I-75 north or south, take exit on Windy Hill Road. Proceed west on Windy Hill Road to Atlanta Road. Take right onto Atlanta Road, follow approximately 1.5 miles to Richardson Road. Take right onto Richardson Road and follow the fence line to the Main Gate on the left. *USMRA: Page 37 (B-3), page 49 (A-1).*

RESERVATION INFORMATION: Phoenix Inn Reservation Desk, Bldg 54, 1000 Halsey Avenue, Marietta, GA 30060-5099. **C-1-888-436-2246 ext 9-6393 or C-770-919-6393, DSN-312-625-6393,** Fax: C-770-919-6263, 24 hours daily. Duty may make reservations; others Space-A after 1800 hours. Check in at 1800 hours, check out 1200 hours.

BEQ/BOQ Bldgs 53, 54. Bedroom, queen-size bed, private bath (8); Bedroom, two double beds, private bath (8). Refrigerator, microwave, A/C, CATV/VCR, phone, housekeeping service. Modern structure. Rates: $18.70, each additional person $4.25. No smoking, no pets.

DV/VIP Bldg 53, Commander's Office. **1-888-436-2246 ext 9-6413, C-770-919-6413, DSN-312-625-6413.** O5+, Retirees Space-A. Two-room suite, private bath. Bedroom, queen-size bed (5). Refrigerator, microwave, A/C. CATV/VCR, phone, sofabed, housekeeping service. Rates: VIP $30, each additional person $7.50; DVQ $34, each additional person $7.50.

TML AVAILABILITY: Very good during the week, difficult on weekends.

CREDIT CARDS ACCEPTED: Visa, MasterCard, American Express and Discover.

TRANSPORTATION: None.

DINING OPPORTUNITIES: General Mess and Strike Zone Bowling Alley, C-770-919-6493 are within walking distance. Numerous restaurants are located within driving distance in Marietta.

Six Flags over Georgia, Stone Mountain, Kennesaw Mountain National Battlefield Park, Centennial Olympic Park, Turner Field (Atlanta Braves), Georgia Dome (Atlanta Falcons), Phillips Arena (Atlanta Hawks, Atlanta Thrashers), CNN Center and Georgia Tech Campus. Metro Atlanta also has numerous shopping opportunities within a short drive from NAS Atlanta.

Camp Frank D. Merrill (GA23R1)
1 Camp Merrill
Dahlonega, GA 30533-9499

MAIN INSTALLATION TELEPHONE NUMBERS: C-706-864-3327/3367. Locator 864-3327; Medical ext 800; Security Police 100.

LOCATION: From GA-400 north from Atlanta, take Highway 60 north to Dahlonega, turn right at the first light. Follow signs for Camp Frank D. Merrill. Take left onto North Grove (60 and US 19 Bus). Turn right onto Wahsega Road. Camp is approximately 9 miles. *USMRA: Page 37 (C-2).* **NMC:** Gainesville, 25 miles south.

RESERVATION INFORMATION: Bldg 47, 5th Ranger Training Battalion, 1 Camp Merill, Dahlonega, GA 30533-1802. **C-706-867-7748** (direct) 0900-1600 hours or **C-706-864-3327/3367 ext 130** after hours. Fax: C-706-864-3029, 0800-1200 hours and 1300-1700 hours Mon-Fri. Reservations require a two-night minimum stay. Reservations require the following information: Sponsor's Name, Rank, Military Status, Home Address and Phone Number, Number of Dependents, Dates of Reservation and Active Duty Address and Phone Number.

TLQ Bldg 1. Five-room cottage, sleeps six (2). Fully furnished, kitchenette, refrigerator, microwave, stove, utensils, TV, cribs, cots. Completely renovated 1988/1989. Rates: $20 for active duty personnel, $35.00 for all other personnel. All Ranks.

AMENITIES: Exercise Room, Mini Mart and Commissary.

TML AVAILABILITY: Call three months in advance for reservations.

CREDIT CARDS: None.

TRANSPORTATION: None.

DINING OPPORTUNITIES: Camp Merrill Dining Facility, NCO Club and local restaurants are within driving distance.

Camp Merrill and Dahlonega are located in the North Georgia Mountains.

Dobbins Air Reserve Base (GA13R1)
1492 First Street
Dobbins ARB, GA 30069-5010

MAIN INSTALLATION TELEPHONE NUMBERS: C-770-919-5000, DSN-312-925-5000. Locator 919-5000; Medical 919-5305; Security Police 919-4907.
Ten-digit dialing required for local calls.

LOCATION: From Atlanta take I-75 north to Lockheed/Dobbins Exit (110 west). Turn right (north) onto Highway 41. Follow signs to Dobbins Main Gate. *USMRA: Page 37 (B-3), page 49 (A-1).* **NMC:** Atlanta, 16 miles northeast.

RESERVATION INFORMATION: Dobbins Inn, Bldg 800, 1295 Barracks Court, Dobbins ARB, GA 30069-4821. **C-1-888-AFLODGE (1-888-235-6343), C-770-919-1352 (switchboard), C-770-919-4745, DSN-312-625-4745,** Fax: C-770-919-5185, DSN-312-925-5185, 24 hours daily. Duty can make reservations any time; Space-A can make reservations 24 hours in advance of arrival. Check in at facility after 1400 hours, check out 1100 hours. Government civilian employee lodging.

TML Bldg 800. E7-E9. Two-room suite (4). Refrigerator, microwave, honor bar, A/C, TV/VCR, phone, housekeeping service, laundry facility, iron/ironing board, cribs, ice machine. Rates: $21. SNCO rooms (40) single occupancy, share bath, renovated 1992. Rates: $19.50.

VAQ Bldg 801. E1-E6. Bedroom, semi-private bath (75). Refrigerator, microwave, TV/VCR, phone, A/C, laundry facility, irons/ironing board, cribs, ice machine, snacks available at front desk. Older structure, renovated 1990. Rates: $19.50.

VOQ Bldg 401. Bedroom, private bath (12); bedroom, shared bath (32). Refrigerator, microwave, honor bar, A/C, TV/VCR, phone, housekeeping service, laundry facility, iron/ironing board, cribs, ice machine. Renovated 1992. Rates: $19.50

DV/VIP Bldg 401. O6+. **C-770-919-3655.** Bedroom suites, private bath, sitting room (5). Refrigerator, microwave, honor bar, A/C, TV/VCR, phone, housekeeping service, laundry facility, iron/ironing board, cribs, ice machine. Renovated 1992. Rates: $21.

AMENITIES: Exercise Room.

TML AVAILABILITY: Good, Nov-Mar. Difficult, Apr-Oct.

CREDIT CARDS ACCEPTED: Visa and MasterCard.

TRANSPORTATION: Car Rental.

DINING OPPORTUNITIES: Numerous restaurants available within short driving distance in Marietta.

Excellent fishing and boating in the Metro Atlanta area at Lake Alatoona and Lake Lanier. Visit underground Atlanta, the Cyclorama, Stone Mountain Park which has a laser show nightly, Fort Gille, Six Flags and the Jimmy Carter Presidential Library. The Atlanta Zoo now has a new Panda Exhibit.

Fort Benning (GA11R1)
Army Community Service
Attn: ATZB-PAF-A, Bldg 2643
Fort Benning, GA 31905-5000

MAIN INSTALLATION TELEPHONE NUMBERS: C-706-545-2011, DSN-312-835-2011. Locator 545-5217; Medical 544-2041/2; Security Police 545-5222.

LOCATION: Off I-85 or US-27/280. South to Benning Blvd and Main Gate. *USMRA: Page 37 (B-6).* **NMC:** Columbus, five miles northwest.

RESERVATION INFORMATION: Fort Benning Lodging, Bldg 399 (Transient and Guesthouse check in), Gillespie Street, Fort Benning, GA 31905-5122. **C-706-689-0067, DSN-312-835-3146,** Fax: C-706-689-4513, 24 hours daily. WEB: www.benning.army.mil Check in at facility 1400 hours, check out by 1100 hours. Fee charged for late checkouts. Dependents (Space-A), Reservists, and government civilian employees on TDY orders. Pet kennel available.

BEQ/BOQ Bldgs 75, 83, 399. Microfridge, coffee maker, CATV. Rates: $25.

VOQ Bldgs 75, 83, 399. Primarily for TDY students, may have Space-A for transients. Microfridge, coffee maker, CATV. Rates: $25. No children, no pets.

Guesthouse Bldgs 36-38, 96. C-706-689-0067 ext 2501. Priority PCS personnel, others Space-A. Bedrooms, private bath, central kitchen, refrigerator, A/C, TV, housekeeping service (Mon-Fri), living room with sofabed. Older structures, New Structure (Bldg 96), includes kitchenette. Check out 1100 hours. Rates: $30.

TML MWR. **Uchee Creek Army Campground and Marina.** Located south of Columbus, easy access from US-80, I-185, US-280, US-431 and AL165. Bldg 0007. Reservations: C-706-545-4053/7238/5600, DSN-312-835-7238/4053. Write: Community Recreation Division, Attn: ATZB-PAR-U (Uchee Creek Army Campground/Marina), Bldg 241 Baltzell Street, Fort Benning, GA 31905-5226. Visa, MasterCard and American Express. Check in at facility, check out 1100 hours. All ranks, family members, government civilian employees. Secluded cabins, largest sleeps six, private bath (10); medium, sleeps four, private bath (10); small, sleeps four, no bath or kitchen facilities (10) (comfort station on site); small sleeps two (2). Large and medium cabins have refrigerator, stove, microwave, utensils, TV/VCR, A/C, heat. Guests furnish linen and towels, blankets and pillows provided. Recreation and rental equipment, country store, ice, snack and soft drink vending machine, marina, playground, fishing, and pool on campground. Rates: $18-$42. Availability: best on weekdays, worst on weekends, holidays and in summer; Winter, good all season. No pets.

DV/VIP Bldg 83, McIver Apartments, Marshall House, Blg 83 (Towle Suites). O6+. Protocol RSVP **C-706-545-5724, DSN-312-835-5724.** Check out 1100 hours (fee of $15 for late check out) Apartments and Marshall House. Suites available. Kitchen (11), refrigerator, microwave, stocked bar, A/C, TV, housekeeping service (Mon-Fri). Towle Suites (18). Older structure. Rates $23, each additional person $10. Retired and lower ranks Space-A.

AMENITIES: Meeting/Conference Room, Snack and Soft Drink Vending Machines.

TML AVAILABILITY: Best, Dec. Difficult, Jun-Sep.

CREDIT CARDS ACCEPTED: Visa, MasterCard, American Express and Discover.

TRANSPORTATION: On base shuttle/bus; Car Rental, C-706-687-1848; On base taxi, C-706-689-6367; Off base taxi, C-706-689-6367.

DINING OPPORTUNITIES: Burger King, C-706-682-1256; and O Club, C-706-682-1120 are within walking distance. Fast Daves, C-706-545-7278; and Reggies Beverage Company, C-706-687-1232 are within driving distance.

For those interested in military history, visit the Infantry museum, the Infantry Hall of Fame and a number of other Fort Benning points of interest. See more about Camp Uchee in Military Living's *Military RV, Camping and Outdoor Recreation Around the World.*

Fort Gillem (GA21R1)
4705 North Wheeler Drive
Forest Park, GA 30297-5000

MAIN INSTALLATION TELEPHONE NUMBERS: C-404-469-5000, DSN-312-797-1001. Locator 469-5000; Security Police 469-5982; Medical 752-3711.
Ten-digit dialing required for local calls.

LOCATION: From I-75, go east on I-285 to I-675, south to Fort Gillem exit, right to Anvil Block Road, go 1.5 mile to light at Main Gate. Also from I-75 to east on I-285 to GA-54 south, 3 to Main Gate. East gate is located west of US-23, south of I-285. Fort is 5 miles from the William Hartsfield (Atlanta) IAP. *USMRA: Page 37 (C-4), page 49 (C-4).* **NMC:** Atlanta, 10 miles northwest.

RESERVATION INFORMATION: Bldg 816, Hood Avenue, Forest Park, GA 30050-5238. **C-404-464-3833/2253, DSN-312-367-3833,** Fax: C-404-464-

3376, DSN-312-367-3376, 0600-2330 hours. Other hours, SDO, Bldg 65, C-404-464-2980/3602. Check in at MP station. Check out 1000 hours. Government civilian employee billeting. This is a sub-post of Fort McPherson.

VOQ/VEQ Bldgs 131, 134. Apartments, private bath (7). Kitchen, refrigerator, microwave, stove, utensils, A/C, TV, phone, housekeeping service, laundry facilities, ice machine. Older structures, Bldg 134 renovated. Rates: VEQ TDY/PCS $32, VOQ TDY/PCS $38; Space-A $43. Duty may make reservations; others Space-A.

DV/VIP O6/GS15+. Bldg 133. Apartment, two bedrooms, two baths (2). Kitchen, refrigerator, microwave, stove, utensils, A/C, TV, phone, housekeeping service, laundry facility. Rates: TDY/PCS $3;. Space-A $43.

TML AVAILABILITY: Extremely limited.

CREDIT CARDS ACCEPTED: Visa, MasterCard and American Express.

TRANSPORTATION: None available.

DINING OPPORTUNITIES: Burger King and Anothony's Pizza are within walking distance. McDonald's and a variety of other restaurants available within driving distance.

"Gone with the Wind" country, and historic Atlanta attractions, combine with seashore, flatlands and mountains to make this area a joy to visit.

Fort Gordon/United States Army Signal Center (GA09R1)
ATZH-CAF-C
Chamberlain Avenue, Bldg 29808
Fort Gordon, GA 30905-5000

MAIN INSTALLATION TELEPHONE NUMBERS: C-706-791-0110, DSN-312-780-0110. Medical 787-6686; Security Police 791-4537/2681.

LOCATION: From I-20 east or west, exit 194 south, between US-78/278 and US-1. Gates are on both US-78 and US-1. Gate 2 and Gate 1 (McKenna Gate) on US-78 east-west. *USMRA: Page 37 (F-4).* **NMC:** Augusta, 12 miles northeast.

RESERVATION INFORMATION: Fort Gordon Lodging, Griffith Hall, Bldg 250, Chamberlain Avenue, Fort Gordon, GA 30905-5040. **C-706-791-2277/3644, DSN-312-780-2277/3644,** Fax: C-706-796-6595, 24 hours daily. Email: reservations@gordon.army.mil Check in at facility 1400 hours, check out 1100 hours.

TML **Stinson Hall.** Bldgs 37300, 37302. C-706-790-3676, DSN-312-780-3676, 24 hours daily. Check in 1400 hours, check out 1100 hours, one hour additional on request. Bedrooms, private bath (103); handicap accessible rooms, private bath (3); kitchenettes (12). Refrigerator, microwave, A/C, TV, laundromat, cribs, rollaways ($2), playground, BBQ grills, park area, coffee service daily. Modern structure. Rates: $37-$39 per unit. TDY/PCS/hospital visitors can make reservations 30 days in advance. Reservations held until 1800 hours unless prepaid with cash or credit card. Pets must be boarded off post **prior** to check-in. Boarding information available at front desk.

VOQ/VEQ VOQ Bldgs 250 & 36700. Military TDY. Check in at lodging. Bedroom, private bath. Refrigerator, microwave, A/C, TV in room and lounge, housekeeping service, laundry facility, ice, soft drink and snack vending machines. Modern structure. Rates: single $37, additional person $2. Maximum two per room. VEQ Bldgs 24401-24405, same but shared bath and no ice machine (190). Rates: $34.50, Space-A $39.50. Temporary duty can make reservations; others Space-A. Pets must be boarded off post **prior** to check-in.

DVQ Bldg 250, E9, O6. Bldgs 34503/04/06, 34601/05, Quarters 6, O6+. Separate bedrooms, private bath (11). Kitchen, com-

plete utensils, A/C, TV, housekeeping service, cots. Bldg 250 modern structure, others older structures. Rates: $50 single, each additional person $2. Reference Bldg 250, temporary duty can make reservations, others, including lesser ranks, Space-A. Pets must be boarded off post **prior** to check-in. VIP, O6+, make reservations through Protocol Office, 10th floor, Signal Towers, **C-706-791-0022, DSN-312-780-0022;** Retirees and lower ranks (O3+) Space-A.

Fisher House Dwight David Eisenhower Army Medical Center, Fisher House Road, Bldg 280, Fort Gordon, GA 30905-5000. **C-706-787-7100,** Fax: C-706-787-5106. WEB: www.ddeamc.amedd.army.mil/visitor/fisherhouse.htm *Note: Appendix B has the definition of this facility. Fisher Houses are only available as lodging for families of patients receiving medical care at military and VA medical centers.*

TML AVAILABILITY: Good.

CREDIT CARDS ACCEPTED: Visa, MasterCard, American Express and Discover.

TRANSPORTATION: On/Off base bus, C-706-793-0026; Car Rental, C-1-800-325-8005; On/Off base taxi, C-706-722-5588.

DINING OPPORTUNITIES: AAFES Food Court, Gordon Club, Burger King and Commissary Deli.

Fort Gordon Recreation Area (GA04R1)
P.O. Box 67
Appling, GA 30802-5000

MAIN INSTALLATION TELEPHONE NUMBERS: C-706-791-0110. Locator 791-0110; Medical 911; Security Police 541-1057 ext 131.

LOCATION: Off post. From I-20 Augusta, take exit Appling north on US-221 to GA-47 north to end (Washington Road). Left on Washington Road to recreation area. *USMRA: Page 37 (F-4).* **NMC:** Augusta, 25 miles southeast. **NMI:** Fort Gordon, 25 miles south.

RESERVATION INFORMATION: C-706-541-1057, Fax: C-706-541-1963. WEB: www.fortgordon.com/fgra.htm. Hours of operation: Oct through Mar 1000-1800, Apr through Sept 0900-1900. Reservations required for a minimum of two nights. Active Duty may make reservations up to 45 days in advance; others 30 days in advance.

TML Cabins (9) and mobile homes (8), three-bedroom, furnished. Rates: $45-$60. Mini-motel, guest rooms (10). Rates: $30. **See** *Military Living's Military RV, Camping and Outdoor Recreation Around the World* **for additional information.**

TML AVAILABILITY: Limited.

CREDIT CARDS ACCEPTED: Visa, MasterCard and American Express.

TRANSPORTATION: On/Off base taxi, Radio Cab C-706-722-5588.

DINING OPPORTUNITIES: Limited restaurants within driving distance.

Fort McPherson (GA08R1)
Army Community Service
1518 Stovall Lane, SW
Fort McPherson, GA 30330-1049

MAIN INSTALLATION TELEPHONE NUMBERS: C-404-464-3113, DSN-312-367-1110. Locator 464-2743/4174; Medical 464-3711; Security Police 464-2281.
Ten-digit dialing required for local calls.

LOCATION: Off I-75 north or south, take Langford Freeway (GA-154/GA-166), exit 243 west past MARTA Station to north on Lee Street

(US-29) and Main Gate west of Lee Street. *USMRA: Page 49 (B-3)*. **NMC:** Atlanta, in city limits.

RESERVATION INFORMATION: Bldg T-22, 1496 Walker Avenue SW, Fort McPherson, GA 30330-1001. **C-404-464-3833/2253/1050, DSN-312-367-3833,** Fax: C-404-464-3376, DSN-312-367-3376, 0600-2330 hours. Other hours, SDO, Bldg 65, C-404-464-2980/3602. Duty may make reservations; others Space-A. Check in at facility 1400 hours, check out 1000 hours. Government civilian employee billeting. ***Winner of Lodging Operation of the Year Award.***

(VEQ) Chateau, Bldg T-22. One-bedroom, private bath (20). Refrigerator, microwave, A/C, TV, phone, housekeeping service, laundry facility, ice machine, lounge. Older structure. Rates: $30.

(VOQ) Hardee Hall, Bldg 168. Suite, private bath, (8); single room, private bath (9). Community kitchen, refrigerator, microwave, TV, phone. Modern structure. Rates: $30.

(DV/VIP) Lee Hall, Bldg 200. **C-404-464-5388.** O6+. Various size suites, private bath (8). Community kitchen, refrigerator, A/C, TV in room and lounge, housekeeping service, ice machine. Historic structure. Rates: $38. Retirees and lower ranks Space-A.

TML AVAILABILITY: Good. Best, Dec-Feb.

CREDIT CARDS ACCEPTED: Visa, MasterCard and American Express.

TRANSPORTATION: Off base shuttle/bus: MARTA.

DINING OPPORTUNITIES: Anthony's Pizza, C-404-361-4844; Special T's, C-404-363-5610; The Commons C-404-753-4520; Reggie's Beverage Company and Mulligan's are within driving distance.

Fort McPherson is steeped in history, and surrounded by the vibrant city of Atlanta.

Fort Stewart (GA15R1)
DPCA/ACS Relocation
954 William Wilson Avenue, Suite 106
Fort Stewart, GA 31314-5132

MAIN INSTALLATION TELEPHONE NUMBERS: C-912-767-1411, DSN-312-870-1411. Locator 767-2862; Medical 370-6161; Security Police 767-2822.

LOCATION: On US-84. Accessible from US-17 or I-95. Also GA-119 or GA-144 crosses the post but may be closed occasionally. From I-95 exit to GA-144. From I-16 exit 29 to GA-119 south. *USMRA: Page 37 (G-7)*. **NMC:** Savannah, 35 miles northeast.

RESERVATION INFORMATION: Attn: AFZP-DPW-B. Bldg 4951, Coe Avenue, Fort Stewart, GA 31314-5142. **C-912-767-8384/4184, DSN-312-870-8384,** Fax: C-912-876-7469, 0700-2345 hours. E-mail: bellc2@emh5.stewart.army.mil Other hours, SDO, Bldg 01, C-912-767-8666. Duty may make reservations; others Space-A. Directions: From Main Gate, follow Hero Road to second light (will pass commissary on right) at stop sign make a right turn onto Coe Avenue. Guesthouse, Bldg 4951, will be on left across from Club Stewart. Check in at billeting 1400 hours, check out 1100 hours. Government civilian employees billeting TDY, PCS.

(Army Lodging) Bldg 4951. Bedroom, dining room, private bath, sleeps six (70). Kitchen, A/C, CATV, housekeeping service, laundry facility, cribs, ice machine. Modern structure. Handicap accessible. Rates: $35 per room.

(VOQ) Bldg 4950. C-912-368-8384. One bedroom, private bath (45). Kitchen, utensils, A/C, TV, housekeeping service, laundry facility, ice machine. Rates: $33.

(DVQ) Bldg 16, 17. O6+. Cottage, two-bedroom, private bath. Kitchen, A/C, TV, housekeeping service, laundry facility, cribs, ice machine. Modern structure. Rates: $40 per room.

(DV/VIP) Protocol, Bldg 01, **C-912-767-8610.** O6+. O6 Retirees and O5 only Space-A.

AMENITIES: Snack and Soft Drink Vending Machine.

TML AVAILABILITY: Fairly good. Best, Nov-Apr. Difficult, other times.

CREDIT CARDS ACCEPTED: Visa, MasterCard, American Express and Discover.

TRANSPORTATION: Car Rental, C-912-877-4242; Off base taxi, C-912-876-6191.

DINING OPPORTUNITIES: Burger King; Popeye's, C-912-368-0134; and Post Exchange, C-912-876-2782 are within walking distance. Golden Corral, C-912-368-8060; Shoney's, C-912-876-9321; Sonny's BBQ, C-912-877-6000; and Sports USA are within driving distance.

Local recreational activities are hunting, fishing, tennis and golf. Ocean beaches are within driving distance, and historic Savannah is 40 miles northeast with many attractions.

Grassy Pond Recreation Area (GA06R1)
5360 Grassy Pond Road
Lake Park, GA 31636-5000

MAIN INSTALLATION TELEPHONE NUMBERS: C-229-559-5840, DSN-312-460-1110 ext 559-5840. Locator 559-5840; Medical 911; SecurityPolice 911.

LOCATION: Off base. From I-75, take exit 5, go west 3/4 mile in GA 376 (Lakes Blvd), turn South on Loch Laurel Road go 1.5 miles, turn left on Grassy Pond Road. *USMRA: Page 37 (D,E-9)*. **NMC:** Valdosta, 12 miles north. **NMI:** Moody AFB, 25 miles north.

RESERVATION INFORMATION: **C-229-559-5840,** DSN-312-460-1110 ext 559-5840. Reservations required. Check in after 1400 hours, check out 1200 hours.

(TML) Cabins: sleep six (6); sleep nine (7), private bath. Kitchen, dishes, pots/pans. Bring bath and kitchen towels, wash cloths, paper towels, dish detergent. Rates: $25-$35. See *Military Living's Military RV, Camping and Outdoor Recreation Around the World* for additional information.

TML AVAILABILITY: Limited.

CREDIT CARDS ACCEPTED: Visa and MasterCard.

TRANSPORTATION: None available.

DINING OPPORTUNITIES: Limited restaurants within driving distance.

Hunter Army Airfield (GA10R1)
Army Community Service
369 North Middleground Road, Suite 101
Hunter Army Airfield, GA 31409-5014

MAIN INSTALLATION TELEPHONE NUMBERS: C-912-352-6521, DSN-312-971-1110. Locator 767-2863; Medical 352-5551; Security Police 352-6133.

LOCATION: From I-95 exit I-16 east, exit I-16 at exit 164A to I-516. Go approximately 4 miles to the end of I-516. Before 2100 hours exit right onto Montgomery Street. ID, safety belt and proof of insurance are required at the gate. Enter Post on Duncan Drive. Landmark Inn is on left first block; Hunter Suites is on left across from gas station. After

2100 hours at end of I-516, go to second traffic light, right on White Bluff Road, go to second traffic light, right onto base on Wilson Blvd, right on N Lightning Road (short block), right on Leonard Neal Street. Hunter Lodging on second block across from PX gas station, for Landmark Inn, right at (gas station) Duncan Drive, right frist driveway. *USMRA: Page 37 (H-7)*. **NMC:** Savannah, in southwest part of city.

RESERVATION INFORMATION: Hunter Suites, Bldg 6010, 525 Leonard Neal Street, Hunter AAF, GA 31409-5109. **C-912-355-1060 or C-912-352-5910/5834, DSN-312-971-5910/5834,** Fax: C-912-352-6920, DSN-312-971-6864, 0600-2100 hours daily. After 2100 hours stop at SDO, Garrison Headquarters, Bldg 1201 to pick up keys. Check in 1400 hours, check out 1100 hours. Lodging Cancellation Policy: All lodging reservation cancellations must be made by the traveler by calling Hunter Suites, C-912-353-4121 or Landmark Inn, C-912-692-0139 by 1400 hours on the day of arrival or be charged for one night lodging. Traveler must receive a cancellation number when callling to cancel a reservation. Non-guaranteed reservations will be cancelled at 1400 hours on the day of arrival.

(TML) Bldgs 6005, 6010. Two-bedroom suites, private bath (32); bedroom, semi-private bath (10). Kitchen, microwave, complete utensils, A/C, TV in room and lounge, phone, hairdryer, housekeeping service, laundry facility, cribs, cots. Older structures, renovated and remodeled. Handicap accessible. Rates: $31-$52. TDY can make reservations up to one year in advance; all others up to 60 days in advance. No pets.

(TML) **Landmark Inn.** Bldg 6007, 165 Duncan Drive, Hunter AAF, GA 31409-5101. **C-912-692-0139,** Fax: 912-692-8077, 24 hours daily. New 75 room facility opened Jan 2001. All government civilian and military employees and all Retirees; also non-military uniformed peronnel of the U.S. Public Health Service and the National Oceanic and Atmospheric Administration, foreign military personnel and U.S. Coast Guard and their Retirees. All suites have two queen beds, private bath, microwave, and refrigerator. All others, queen beds, private bath. A/C, TV in room and lounge, iron/iron board, coffee, phone, hairdryer, housekeeping service, laundry facility, cribs, lounge. 17 adjoining rooms, four adjoining handicap rooms. Rates: $53-$79. All categories may make reservations up to one year in advance (see cancellation policy above).

(DV/VIP) Protocol Office, Fort Stewart, **C-912-767-7742, DSN-312-870-7742.** O5+. Retirees Space-A.

AMENITIES: Mini Mart, Pool, Ice and Snack Vending Machines.

TML AVAILABILITY: Difficult during summer, very good other times for Hunter Suites. Very good at all times for Landmark Inn.

CREDIT CARDS ACCEPTED: Visa, MasterCard, American Express and Discover.

TRANSPORTATION: Off base taxi available.

DINING OPPORTUNITIES: Bowling Alley, C-912-352-5205 and Burger King are within walking distance. Savannah is renown for variety and quality of restaurants.

Near historic Savannah. Near malls, hunting, fishing and Georgian coastal beaches.

Kings Bay Naval Submarine Base (GA03R1)
1063 USS Tennessee Avenue
Kings Bay, GA 31547-2606

MAIN INSTALLATION TELEPHONE NUMBERS: C-912-673-2000 ext. 2000, DSN-312-573-2001 ext. 2000. Locator 673-2001 ext 6970; Medical 673-2928; Security Police 673-2147.

LOCATION: Off I-95 north of GA/FL border. Take exit 1 east, which leads right into base. Off I-95 south, take exit 6, east to Kings Bay Road and follow the road north to base. *USMRA: Page 37 (G-9)*. **NMC:** Jacksonville, Fl, 40 miles south.

RESERVATION INFORMATION: Attn: Housing Office QL31, Bldg 1051, 952 James Madison Road, Kings Bay, GA 31547-5015. **C-912-673-2001 ext 9282,** Fax: C-912-882-6800, DSN-312-573-2752, 24 hours daily. Call SATO first if on orders. Duty may make reservations anytime; others Space-A. Directions: Stimson Gate: Follow until second traffic light (USS James Madison Road). Follow signs to BOQ Bldg 1056 (about two blocks) on right. Check in at billeting, check out 1100 hours.

(TVQ) Bldg 1056. Bedroom, private bath (120); seperate bedroom, private bath (92); multiple occupancy rooms (36). Refrigerator, microwave, coffee maker, A/C, CATV/VCR, phone, housekeeping service, iron/ironing board, rollaways, utensils, ice machine. Modern structure. Rates: double occupancy $10; three or more $13, mulitple occupancy rooms $5 per person.

(NAVY LODGE) Navy Lodge. Bldg 0158, 1290 Andrew Jackson Road, Kings Bay, GA 31547-5000. **C-1-800-NAVY-INN.** Lodge number is C-912-882-6868, Fax: C-912-882-6800, 0700-2000 hours. Directions: At second traffic light turn left onto USS James Madison Road. Go 1 mile and turn left onto USS Andrew Jackson Road, second building on the left. Check in 1500-1800 hours, check out 1200 hours. Bedroom, two double beds, private bath (26). Kitchenette, microwave, utensils, A/C, CATV/VCR, video rental, housekeeping service, coin laundry facility, hair dryer, cribs, ice machine, new playground. Modern structure, all rooms renovated 1997. Four sets interconnecting, handicap accessible (2), non-smoking. Rates: $40 per night. Maximum four per room. VCRs, tape rental at desk. Duty and Retirees can make reservations. No pets. *Winner of the 1998 Carlson Award, 1999 American Hotel & Motel Association Educational Institute's Performance Plus Gold Pineapple Award and the 1999 Hospitality Award.*

(DV/VIP) E9, 06/GS15+. Bldg 1056. **C-912-673-4871**, Fax: C-912-882-6800. Rates: mini VIP suite: double occupancy $14, triple occupancy $18; DV suites: double occupancy $23, triple occupancy $30; VIP suite: double occupancy $16, triple occupancy $21.

AMENITIES: Exercise Room, Meeting/Conference Room, Snack and Soft Drink Vending Machines.

TML AVAILABILITY: Good. Best, Oct-Dec. Difficult, Jun-Sep.

CREDIT CARDS ACCEPTED: Visa, MasterCard, American Express and Discover.

TRANSPORTATION: Car Rental: Enterprise, C-912-729-1883; On base taxi, C-912-673-2001 ext 8294; Off base taxi, C-912-673-6900.

DINING OPPORTUNITIES: McDonald's C-882-275; Subway C-673-9500; Taco Bell C-673-1975; and Clippers Cafe C-673-2001 ext 4548 are within walking distance. Angelo's Pizza; Pasta & Subs, C-912-673-7007; Applebee's, C-729-9515; St. Mary's Seafood and Shoney's are within driving distance.

From the beauty and history of old Savannah to the beaches of the Golden Isles near Brunswick and the Cumberland Island National Seashore, coastal Georgia offers everything from sightseeing to fishing and hunting.

Lake Allatoona Army Recreation Area (GA05R1)
40 Old Sandtown Road, SE
Cartersville, GA 30121-5000

MAIN INSTALLATION TELEPHONE NUMBERS: C-770-974-3413. Security Police at Fort McPherson 404-464-2282. Locator at Fort McPherson 404-464-2282; Medical 911; Police 911. *Ten-digit dialing required for local calls.*

LOCATION: Located on 85-acre site at Lake Allatoona reservoir. Heading north on I-75 from Atlanta, take exit 283 (Emerson exit). Turn right (east) off exit, travel 2.7 miles, turn left on Old Sandtown Road.

Travel 1 block and bear left into park; follow signs to office. *USMRA: Page 37 (B-3).* **NMC:** Atlanta. NMI: Dobbins ARB, 28 miles southeast.

RESERVATION INFORMATION: C-770-974-3413, Fax: C-770-974-1278. Reservations required and accepted up to four months in advance. Check in after 1500 hours.

(TML) Apartment, furnished, three-bedroom (3); two-bedroom deluxe cabin, furnished (5); two-bedroom cabin, furnished (12); one-bedroom cabin, furnished (8). Microwave, dishes, pots/pans, utensils, A/C, CATV. Bring towels, extra blankets, can opener, soap, detergent, sharpened knives. Several two-bedroom cabins and three-bedroom apartments are handicap accessible. Active Duty, retired, reserve, NG, DoD civilians at Fort McPherson and Fort Gillem. Rates: cabin $52-$72; apartment $52-$80. No pets. See *Military Living's Military RV, Camping and Outdoor Recreation Around the World* for additional information.

AMENITIES: Marina with covered rental slips, summer boat rentals, dry storage, covered pavillon rentals (2), bath houses (2), coin laundry, mini golf, volleyball and multi-purpose courts, picnic areas, playgrounds.

TML AVAILABILITY: Limited.

CREDIT CARDS ACCEPTED: Visa, MasterCard and American Express.

TRANSPORTATION: None.

DINING OPPORTUNITIES: Restaurants within driving distance.

Moody Air Force Base (GA02R1)
347 MSS/DPF
5124 Austin Ellipse
Moody AFB, GA 31699-1507

MAIN INSTALLATION TELEPHONE NUMBERS: C-229-257-4211, DSN-312-460-4211/1110. Locator 257-3585; Medical 257-3232; Security Police 257-3108.

LOCATION: On GA-125, 10 miles north of Valdosta, east of GA-125. Also, can be reached from I-75 north or south via GA-122 east to GA-125 south. *USMRA: Page 37 (D,E-9).* **NMC:** Valdosta, 10 miles south.

RESERVATION INFORMATION: 347 SVS/SVML, Bldg 3131, Cooney Street, Moody AFB, GA 31699-1511. **C-1-888-AFLODGE (1-888-235-6343), C-229-257-3893, DSN-312-460-3893,** Fax: C-229-257-4971, DSN-312-460-4971, 24 hours daily. Duty may make reservations any time; Space-A can make reservations 24 hours in advance. Check in at lodging at 1400 hours, check out 1200 hours. *Note: A $2.348 million TLF was approved in the DoD Fiscal Year 1998 NAF Construction Program.*

(TLF) Bldgs 3080, 5000, 5001. Community motel design. Two-bedroom, private bath (10). One bedroom, private bath (22). Kitchen, A/C, TV, housekeeping service, laundry facility, cribs. Rates: $28.00 per night. All Ranks..

(VAQ) Bldg 3080. Community motel design. Units, private bath (17). Refrigerator, microwave, A/C, TV/VCR, housekeeping service, laundry facility. Rates: $21.50 per night.

(VOQ) Bldg 3132. Community motel design. Bedroom, private bath (32). Refrigerator, microwave, wet bar, A/C, TV/VCR, housekeeping service, laundry facility. Rates: $24.00 per night.

(DV/VIP) Protocol Office, 347 WG/CCP, Bldg 5113, **C-229-257-4144.** Bldgs 3132/3080. E9, O6+. Community motel design. DV bedroom suites, private bath (Officer) (7); bedroom suites, private bath (E9). Kitchenette, microwave, A/C, TV/VCR, housekeeping service, laundry facility. Rates: $28.00 per night. PCS in/out, TDY can make reservations anytime, Space-A may make reservations 24 hours in advance of their arrival date.

AMENITIES: Snack and Soft Drink Vending Machine.

TML AVAILABILITY: Good, May, Sep, Dec. Difficult, Jun-Aug.

CREDIT CARDS ACCEPTED: Visa and MasterCard.

TRANSPORTATION: Car Rental: Enterprise, C-229-257-2989, DSN-312-460-2989; On base taxi (TDY only), C-229-257-3461, DSN-312-460-3461.

DINING OPPORTUNITIES: Bowling Center Snack Bar, C-229-257-3872; Moody Field Club, C-229-257-3794; Quiet Pines Snack Bar, C-229-257-3856; and Wright Bros Cafe, C-229-257-4530 are within walking distance. Family Pizza House, C-229-244-1845 is within driving distance.

Visit the mansion Crescent, in Valdosta, for tours, particularly during Azalea season. There are many freshwater lakes for fishing and water sports. Dove, quail, turkey and other wild game hunting in season is also popular.

Robins Air Force Base (GA14R1)
725 9th Street, Suite 100
Robins AFB, GA 31098-2235

MAIN INSTALLATION TELEPHONE NUMBERS: C-478-926-1113/1110, DSN-312-468-1001/1110. Locator 926-6027; Medical 926-3845; Security Police 926-2187.

LOCATION: Off US-129 on GA-247 at Warner Robins. Go south on I-75. Get off exit 46. Go east on Hwy 247 (Watson Blvd) until dead-end at Robins AFB, east of US-129. *USMRA: Page 37 (D-6).* **NMC:** Macon, 15 miles northwest.

RESERVATION INFORMATION: Pine Oaks Lodge, 78 SPTG/SVML, Bldg 557, Club Drive, Robins AFB, GA 31098-1469. **C-1-888-AFLODGE (1-888-235-6343), C-478-926-2100, DSN-312-468-2100,** Fax: C-478-926-0977, 24 hours daily. Duty may make reservations any time; Space-A may make reservations 24 hours in advance. Check in at facility, check out 1100 hours.

(TLF) Bldgs 1000, 1002, 1003, 1008. One- and two-bedroom, private bath. Kitchen, complete utensils, A/C, TV, housekeeping service, laundry facility, cribs, cots, ice machine. New structure. One bedroom maximum five per unit. Two bedroom maximum seven per unit. Rates: $30.

(VAQ) Bldg 755. Bedroom, private bath (18); Bedroom, shared bath (54). Refrigerator, A/C, TV, housekeeping service, laundry facility, ice machine. Older structure. Rates: $19 per person.

(VOQ) Bldgs 551-553, 557. Bedroom, private bath (40); Bedroom, shared bath, shared living room (82). Refrigerator, A/C, TV, housekeeping service, laundry facility. Older structure. Handicap accessible. Rates: $19.

(DV/VIP) Bldgs 551, 552, 557, **C-478-926-2761,** Mon-Fri. VOQ. O6+. Chief suites, Bldg 551 (2); VIP suites, Bldg 552 (4); VIP suites, Bldg 557 (6). Refrigerator, A/C, TV, housekeeping service, laundry facility. Older structure. Handicap accessible. Rates: $26.

TML AVAILABILITY: Good, Nov-Feb. Difficult, other times.

CREDIT CARDS ACCEPTED: Visa and MasterCard.

TRANSPORTATION: On base taxi.

DINING OPPORTUNITIES: Golf Course Snack Bar and O Club are within walking distance. Burger King, E Club and Pizza Depot are within driving distance.

Macon, 18 miles northwest, is the geographic center of Georgia, where shopping, parks (this is the Cherry Blossom Capital of the World) welcome visitors with true Southern hospitality. Also visit the Museum of Aviation, home of the Georgia Aviation Hall of Fame.

World Famous Navy Lake Site (GA01R1)

166 Sandtown Road
Cartersville, GA 30121-5000

MAIN INSTALLATION TELEPHONE NUMBERS: C-770-974-6309. Locator 974-6309; Medical 911; Security Police 911. *Ten-digit dialing required for local calls.*

LOCATION: Off base. From I-75 north or south of Atlanta, take exit 283 east. Turn right on Sandtown Road going east for approximately three miles to marked entrance on the left. *USMRA: Page 37 (B-3)*. **NMC:** Atlanta, 40 miles southeast. NMI: Atlanta NAS, Marietta, 20 miles east.

RESERVATION INFORMATION: C-770-974-6309, Fax: C-770-974-1927. WEB: www.nasatlanta.navy.mil/lakesite.html E-mail: wfnls@aol.com Reservations required. Accepted beginning the first day of the month four months in advance for Active Duty; three months in advance for other categories. Check in 1400-1700 hours.

(TML) Cabins: one- to four-bedroom, furnished (9). Refrigerator, microwave, stove, dishes, pots/pans, A/C, TV. Summer rates: One-bedroom $52, two-bedroom $61, three-bedroom $69, four-bedroom $78. Winter rates: subtract $4.00. No pets. See *Military Living's Military RV. Camping and Outdoor Recreation Around the World* for additional information.

AMENITIES: Boat Rental, Exercise Room, Game Room, Small Store, Soft Drink Vending Machine.

TML AVAILABILITY: Extremely difficult, summer and weekends year-round.

CREDIT CARDS ACCEPTED: Visa, MasterCard, American Express and Discover.

TRANSPORTATION: None available.

DINING OPPORTUNITIES: Numerous restaurants within driving distance.

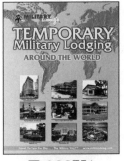

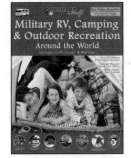

HAWAII

Barbers Point Recreation Area (HI01R6)
Morale Welfare Recreation Department
850 Ticonderoga Street, Suite 300
Pearl Harbor, HI 96860-5100

MAIN INSTALLATION TELEPHONE NUMBERS: C-808-449-7110. Locator 682-2019; Medical 684-4300; Security Police 471-5141.

LOCATION: Take HI-1 W to Kalaeloa/Makakilo City exit. Left at sign for 2.5 miles on HI-901 then go through Main Gate. Turn right on Roosevelt, left on Lexington, right on Yorktown. Then take second left, Power Point Fitness Center, Bldg 1762. *USMRA: Page 129 (C-7).* **NMC:** Pearl Harbor, 10 miles northeast.

RESERVATION INFORMATION: C-808-682-2019. Fax: C-808-682-4235, 0900-1700 hours Mon, Wed, Fri 0900-1600 hours Tue, Thu. Inquiries on beach cottage reservations may be taken 180 days in advance via written request. Priority system in effect. Confirmation 90 days in advance. Mail applications to MWR Cottage Reservations, 850 Ticonderoga Street, Suite 300, Pearl Harbor, HI 96860-5100. Check in at facility 1400 hours, check out 1000 hours. Cottages cannot be used as party facility.

Cottages Two-bedroom Enlisted cottage (12); two-bedroom Officer cottage (6); one-bedroom handicap accessible cottage (2). Kitchen, complete utensils, BBQ grills. Rates: Enlisted $40-$45 per unit; Officer $60-$70 per unit. Maximum six persons, handicap accessible cottages maximum four persons.

DV/VIP O7/GS16+. Reservations: **C-808-473-2206 or C-808-473-1940, DSN-315-473-2206.** VIP Cottage 1943. Space-A to O6+ (2). Kitchen, complete utensils, TV, cribs, cots, BBQ grills. Rates: $70 per unit. Maximum six persons. Retirees and lower ranks Space-A.

AMENITIES: Exercise Room, Meeting/Conference Room and Mini Mart.

TML AVAILABILITY: Good, Jan-Apr and Oct-Nov. Difficult, other times.

CREDIT CARDS ACCEPTED: Visa, MasterCard, American Express and Discover.

TRANSPORTATION: Car Rental, C-808-671-5399; Off base taxi, C-808-422-2222, Off base Shuttle/Bus C-808-848-5555.

DINING OPPORTUNITIES: Bowling Alley Food Frame, 19th Puka Snack Bars. Kapolei Shopping Center, Kentucky Fried Chicken and Taco Bell are within driving distance.

Complete beach recreation area. Check with Special Services, Ticket Office for tourist/island activities. For full details see *Military Living's Military RV, Camping and Outdoor Recreation Around The World.*

Barking Sands Pacific Missile Range Facility (HI22R6)
P.O. Box 128
Kekaha, Kauai, HI 96752-0128

MAIN INSTALLATION TELEPHONE NUMBERS: C-808-335-4111, DSN-315-471-6111. Locator 335-4111; Medical 335-4203; Security Police 335-4523.

LOCATION: Six miles west of Kekaha on Kaumualii Highway (HI-50 west). *USMRA: Page 129 (B-2).* **NMC:** Lihue, 30 miles east.

RESERVATION INFORMATION: BEQ Bldg 1261, Kekaha, Kauai, HI 96752-0128. **C-808-335-4383, DSN-315-471-6383,** Fax: C-808-335-4194, DSN-315-471-6194, 0700-1600 hours, Mon-Fri. For reservations, after hours leave message. E-mail: glocke@pmrf.navy.mil WEB: www.pmrf.navy.mil For information on MWR Beach Cottages call C-808-335-4752, DSN-315-471-6769 or go to our web site. Reservations are made by application only, either in writing or by internet. Submit application 90 days in advance, processed 60 days in advance, notification by mail if dates can be accommodated. You may call or write to: MWR Department, Beach Cottage Reservations PMRF, Barking Sands, P.O. Box 128, Kekaha, HI 96752-0128. *Earned a five-star rating for Excellence in Bachelor Housing. Note: A $1.467 million Beach Cottage addition was approved in the DoD Fiscal Year 2001 NAF Construction Program.*

TQ One-bedroom (15). Duty must make reservations 30 days in advance; others Space-A. Rates: no charge.

Cottages MWR Beach Cottages. C-808-335-4752, Fax: 808-335-4769. Twelve cottages. Two-bedroom, private bath, sofabed, sleeps six (6). Kitchen, refrigerator, microwave, utensils, TV, washer/dryer, iron/ironing board, outdoor BBQ, balcony, lanai, indoor/outdoor gear rentals, gym, craft center, pool, theater. No daily maid service. Dish/laundry/bath soap, shampoo and paper towels not provided. Limited Handicap Accessibility. Rates: single/double occupancy $55, each additional person age 3 and above $5. Check in at MWR Admin Bldg 1267, 1400-1600 hours, for after hours arrivals: Mon-Fri 1600-2000 hours and Sat/Sun/Holiday 1400-1700 hours check in at Rec Center, Bldg 1264. Check out 1000 hours. A late check out will be charged one day's rental fee, unless prior notice is made to reservationist. No pets.

DV/VIP Two cottages set aside for O6+. Reservations made by phone with "gentleman's agreement," **C-808-335-4752, DSN-315-471-6752,** Fax: C-808-335-4769, DSN-315-471-6769, or write to: MWR Department Beach Cottages Reservations, PMRF Barking Sands, P.O. Box 128, Kekaha, HI 96752-0128.

TML AVAILABILITY: Very good, Sep-Feb. Difficult, Mar-Aug.

CREDIT CARDS ACCEPTED: Visa, MasterCard, American Express and Discover.

TRANSPORTATION: Off base Bus, Car Rental, Off base taxi.

DINING OPPORTUNITIES: All Hands Club; Fatty's Galley/mess hall, C-808-335-4163; Menehune Inn, C-808-335-4249; and Shenanigans, C-808-335-4707, are within driving distance.

This is truly the Navy's "Best Kept Secret In Paradise!" Captain Cook's historic landing place and Waimea Canyon, "the Grand Canyon of Hawaii" and a seven mile strip of white sandy beach are nearby.

Bellows Air Force Station (HI18R6)
220 Tinker Road
Waimanalo, HI 96795-5000

MAIN INSTALLATION TELEPHONE NUMBERS: C-1-800-437-2607, C-808-259-8080. Security Police 259-4200.

LOCATION: On the Eastern shore of Oahu. From Honolulu, take H-1 east to exit 21-A Pali Highway (HI-61), go north. Take a right onto Kalanianaole (HI-72), south to AFS on east at beach. Off HI-72 to Main Gate, then left on Hughes Road to registration on right. Clearly marked. *USMRA: Page 129 (E-7).* **NMC:** Kaneohe, nine miles northwest.

RESERVATION INFORMATION: C-1-800-437-2607 from U.S. Mainland, **All Others, C-808-259-8080,** Fax: C-808-259-4119, 0800-2100 hours. WEB: www.bellowsafs.com Priorities: Active Duty Air Force has priority during summer season (Memorial Day weekend-Labor Day weekend); Active Duty 90 days in advance in summer; others 75 days in advance. Other times reservations taken up to one year in advance. A sponsor may reserve only one cabin at a time and may not stay more than 21 days in a 30-day period. A sponsor must be on station with their guests during quiet hours (2200-0800). Deposit (one night's rent) required at the time reservations are made (MasterCard and Visa accepted), cancellations 14 days prior to occupancy. Also, effective 1 Oct 2001, no walk-in reservations will be accepted, unless time of arrival is one week or less. *Note: When reservation period includes a Friday, Saturday or Federal Holiday—the beginning date of a reservation may not be cancelled without cancelling the entire reservation.* Check in 1500 hours, check out 1100 hours. *Earned the medium-sized Army Lodging of the Year Award 2001.*

TML Leave only- all ranks. Cottage, furnished, single and duplex units, private bath, one-bedroom (4) or two-bedroom (103) configuration. Also four cabins are fully wheelchair accessible. Kitchen, complete utensils, dishes, CATV, VCR. Rates: back row $49; ocean view $54.

TML AVAILABILITY: Difficult year round.

CREDIT CARDS ACCEPTED: Visa and MasterCard.

TRANSPORTATION: No local transportation. Rental cars available at airport.

DINING OPPORTUNITIES: Bellows Beach Club, C-808-259-4110 is within walking distance.

On Oahu's northwest coast, about 16 miles from downtown Waikiki, turquoise waters and gorgeous beaches await your arrival! Beach front recreation center.

Fort Shafter (HI09R6)
Bldg 5-380
Attn: APVG-GF
Fort Shafter, HI 96858-5100

MAIN INSTALLATION TELEPHONE NUMBERS: C-808-449-7110, DSN-315-430-0111. Locator 438-1904; Medical 433-6620; Security Police 438-2885.

LOCATION: Take H-1 east or west, exit at Fort Shafter on middle street to Main Gate. Clearly marked. *USMRA: Page 129 (D-7), page 131 (D,E-1,2).* NMC: Honolulu, seven miles east.

RESERVATION INFORMATION: Billeting, Bldg 719, Morton Drive, Fort Shafter, HI 96858-5000. **C-808-438-1685** or **C-808-893-2336, DSN 315-839-2336.** Fax: C-808-438-0492. Check in at facility, check out 1100 hours.

DV/VIP 06/GS13+. Three-bedroom suite (1); Two-bedroom suite (1); One-bedroom suite (3); single room (2). Rates: $35-$55, each additional person $5.

TML AVAILABILITY: Fair, most of the year.

CREDIT CARDS ACCEPTED: Visa, MasterCard and American Express.

TRANSPORTATION: On/Off base shuttle/bus.

DINING OPPORTUNITIES: Combined Club, Bowling Alley, Strike Zone and Mulligan's are located on base. Numerous restaurants are within driving distance in Honolulu.

The oldest Army post in Hawaii, part of the post is a National Historic Place. Visit the Bishop Museum in Honolulu, the Honolulu Academy of Arts, Mission Houses Museum and don't miss the beach!

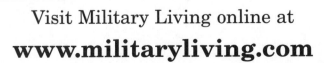

Visit Military Living online at
www.militaryliving.com

Hale Koa Hotel AFRC
(HI08R6)
2055 Kalia Road
Honolulu, HI 96815-1998

MAIN INSTALLATION TELEPHONE NUMBERS: C-808-955-0555. Reservations: 0800-1600 hours daily except Sun and federal holidays, **1-800-367-6027, DSN-315-438-6739** (official travel), Fax: C-1-808-HALE-FAX(425-3329), 24 hours daily, except holidays. E-mail: information@halekoa.com WEB: www.halekoa.com Medical 911 or Hotel Operator; Security Police 911 or Hotel Operator.

LOCATION: On Fort DeRussy at 2055 Kalia Road, on the beach at Waikiki, Oahu. Fort DeRussy is between Ala Moana Blvd, Kalakaua Avenue, and Saratoga Road, nine miles east of Honolulu IAP. *USMRA: Page 129 (D,E-7,8), page 131 (F-4).* NMC: Honolulu, in city limits.

DESCRIPTION OF AREA: This morale-boosting hotel was opened in October 1975. Fourteen stories with 817 guest rooms with views of the Pacific Ocean and Koolau Mountains. All rooms identical in size, with private bath, lanai (veranda), A/C, TV, coin laundry facility. Some rooms handicap accessible. Beautifully landscaped gardens, famous Waikiki Beach, swimming pool, and recreational activities: tennis, snorkeling, swimming, volleyball and racquet ball. Casual or fine dining: Poolside Snack Bar, Happy's Self-Service Snack Bar, Snack Shack, Koko Cafe, Bibas Restaurant, or the Hale Koa Room, the hotel's signature restaurant. Private banquets, meetings, and conferences arranged through the hotel's catering services. Live entertainment and dancing in the Warriors Lounge, poolside drinks at the Barefoot Bar. Fitness center with sauna and locker rooms, Post Exchange, jewelry store, barber and beauty shops, car rental desk and tour and travel desk. Three dinner shows each week: Hale Koa Luau, Tama's Polynesian Revue, and Magic in Paradise. The Hale Koa is a complete resort. Dress: aloha-wear at all times.

RATES: The rates below are for double occupancy. For single occupancy, deduct $2 from double rate. For more than two occupants, add $10 per person to double rate (maximum of four persons permitted). Children under 12 are free in parents' room if no additional beds are required. Cribs available at $4 a night. Most rooms have two double beds. Ocean front rooms have king size beds only. Daily rates based on room location (generally the higher floors reflect increased rates).

Rates are subject to change on or before Oct. 1, 2001
*Rooms for sponsored guests of E1-E5 will be charged at Category II rates.
**Current Leave and Earnings Statement or employee ID card required for check-in.
***100% DAVs with DD-1173, DD-2765 or DD-2 with VA letter.
****Foreign military with U.S. travel orders or assigned to U.S. military installation (with unlimited DD-1173).

2000-2001 Double Occupancy Rates/Night Effective 1 October 2000				
CATEGORIES	I	II	III	IV
	Leave/Pass	Leave/Pass	Leave/Pass	Official Travel
Active, Retired, Reserve & NG (select your rank/grade-your rate is below)				All Grades TDY/PCS/TLA
Enlisted Grades	E1-E5*	E6-E9		
Officer Grades		W01-WO3 O1-O3	CW4-CW5 O4-O10	
DoD** Civilians		Up to GS10/NF3**	GS11-SES** NF4-NF5	
Others		Widows/DAV***	Retired DoD Civilians	Foreign Svcs****
Standard	$66	$77	$83	$93
Moderate	$71	$83	$90	$101
Garden View	$75	$88	$95	$107
Partial Ocean View	$79	$94	$102	$114
Ocean View	$88	$105	$115	$130
Oceanfront	$108	$129	$141	$158
Deluxe Oceanfront	$118	$140	$153	$169

SEASON OF OPERATION: Year round

RESERVATIONS: Required. Reservations will not be accepted more than 365 days in advance of arrival date of requested stay. Reservations may be made for a maximum of 30 days. Extensions permitted on Space-A basis. Write for reservation and information packet: 2055 Kalia Road, Honolulu, HI 96815-1998. **C-1-800-367-6027, DSN-315-438-6739** (official travel) or Fax: C-808-HALE-FAX(425-3329), 0800-1600 hours.

ELIGIBILITY: Active Duty, retired military (DD form 2 Ret-gray or blue), reserve and NG (DD form 2 reserve-pink/red), dependents (DD-1173 or authorized dependent card for reserve & NG), DoD civilians (current employee ID card) and all foreign military with orders to U.S.

Hale Koa Luau on Mon and Thu, $31.50 adults, $19.95 children under 12. Tama's Polynesian Revue Dinner Show on Wed night in the Banyan Tree Showroom, $19.95 adults and $11.50 children under 12. The Tuesday Night Magic Show with dinner buffet, $20.95 adults and $11.50 children under 12. ID cardholders may sponsor guests.

CREDIT CARDS ACCEPTED: Visa, MasterCard and American Express.

TRANSPORTATION: Off base shuttle/bus, C-808-848-5555; Car Rental, C-808-955-9419; On/Off base taxi, C-808-946-8282.

DINING OPPORTUNITIES: Bibas (casual dining); Hale Koa Room (fine dining); and Koke Cafe (family dining); all C-808-955-0555 ext 546 are within walking distance.

Check out the Army Museum, Diamond Head, Honolulu Zoo, Waikiki Aquarium, and Ala Moana Center, not to mention Downtown Honolulu.

Hickam Air Force Base (HI11R6)
15th ABW/PAC
Family Support Center
655 Vickers Avenue, Bldg 1105
Hickam AFB, HI 96853-5385

MAIN INSTALLATION TELEPHONE NUMBERS: C-808-449-7110, DSN-315-449-7110. Locator 449-0165; Medical 448-6000; Security Police 449-7114.

LOCATION: Adjacent to the Honolulu International Airport. Accessible from H1 exit 5 or Nimitz Highway south. Main Gate on Vandenberg Blvd. Clearly marked. *USMRA: Page 129 (D-7), page 131 (B,C-2,3,4).*

RESERVATION INFORMATION: Royal Alakai, Attn: 15 SVS/SVML, 15 G Street, Bldg 1153, Hickam AFB, 96853-5328. **C-1-888-AFLODGE (1-888-235-6343), C-808-448-5400, DSN-315-448-5400,** Fax: C-808-448-5999, 24 hours daily. WEB: www.hickamservices.com/lodging/ Duty may make reservations any time; Space-A may make reservations 24 hours in advance. Check in at facility 1400 hours, check out 1000 hours. Government civilian employee billeting.

(VAQ) Bldgs 1153, 1168. Fully equipped room, central bath, housekeeping service. Rates: $17. Bldgs 1166, 1172. Suite, private bath. Rates: $21.00.

(VQ) Bldgs 470, 471. Two bedroom apartment, private bath (18). Kitchen, microwave, TV. Single room, shared bath (24). Housekeeping service. Rates: $22.50.

(VQ) Bldgs 814, 815, 925, 926. Two-bedroom apartment, shared bath. Living room, microwave, TV, housekeeping service. Rates: half apartment $22.50, whole apartment $37.

(TLF) Bldgs 1156, 1158. One- and two-bedroom apartment, shared bath. Living room, kitchen, microwave, TV, housekeeping service. Rates: $35.

(DV/VIP) HQ PACAF Protocol Office, **C-808-449-4526.** Bldg 922, C-808-449-4531. Bldgs 725, 728, 922, 934. One- and two-bedroom apartment, private bath. Living room, kitchen, microwave, private laundry facilities, TV, housekeeping service. Rates: $29.00 per person; Large DV: $34.00.

TML AVAILABILITY: Difficult, most of the year.

CREDIT CARDS ACCEPTED: Visa and MasterCard.

TRANSPORTATION: On base shuttle/bus; Off base shuttle/bus; Car Rental.

DINING OPPORTUNITIES: Cafe Express, C-808-449-1145; E Club, C-808-449-1292; O Club, C-808-449-1998/1592; and Sea Breeze Restaurant, C-808-449-9900 are within driving distance.

Waikiki, Pearl Harbor's historic war memorial, shopping and sightseeing in Honolulu, hikes in local parks that put you in touch with Oahu's natural wonders. Whether you want relaxation or excitement, it's all here.

Kaneohe Bay Beach Cottages (HI12R6)
Marine Corps Community Services
TLF Bldg 3038, P.O. Box 63073
Kaneohe Bay MCB, HI 96863-3037

MAIN INSTALLATION TELEPHONE NUMBERS: C-808-449-7110, DSN-315-430-0110. Locator 257-1294; Medical 257-3133; Security Police 257-2123.

LOCATION: At the end of H-3 on the Windward (east) side of Oahu. From Honolulu IAP: Take H-1 west to H-3 interchange. Take H-3 east to Kaneohe, continue to Main Gate. Off Mokapu Blvd and Kaneohe Bay Drive. Clearly marked. *USMRA: Page 129 (E-6).* NMC: Honolulu, 14 miles southwest

RESERVATION INFORMATION: Beach Cottages. **C-808-254-2806/2716, DSN-315-457-2409,** Fax: C-808-254-2716. E-mail: mia.ng@usmc-mccs.org Check in after 1400 hours, before 1800 hours, check out no later than 1000 hours. After hours check in call Duty Officer, C-808-257-1824. Closed on all federal holidays. Reservations required. Active Duty stationed at Kaneohe Bay MCBH can make reservations up to 60 days in advance; Active Duty stationed elsewhere can make reservations up to 45 days in advance; all others can make reservations up to 30 days in advance.

(Cottages) Two-bedroom, living room, dining areas, private bath, CATV, housekeeping service (11). Rates: $65 per day

AMENITIES: Soft Drink Vending, Laundromat.

TML AVAILABILITY: Fairly good.

CREDIT CARDS ACCEPTED: Visa, MasterCard, American Express and Discover.

TRANSPORTATION: On/off base bus: The Bus (public).

DINING OPPORTUNITIES: E Club, C-808-254-7660; and Subway are within walking distance. Officers' and Staff Clubs, C-808-254-7649; McDonald's; and K-Bay Chinese Garden are within a short driving distance.

MCB full support facilities. (For details see *Military Living's Military RV, Camping and Outdoor Recreation Around The World*.) Beaches, boating, or just plain relaxing. You won't regret your stay at Kaneohe.

Kaneohe Bay Marine Corps Base (HI12R6)
Commanding General, Attn: FSC
4th Street, Bldg 216, Box 63002
Kaneohe Bay, HI 96863-3002

MAIN INSTALLATION TELEPHONE NUMBERS: C-808-449-7110, DSN-315-430-0110. Locator 257-2008; Medical 257-2505; Security Police 257-2123.

LOCATION: At the end of H-3 on the Windward (east) side of Oahu. From Honolulu IAP: Take H-1 west to H-3 interchange. Take H-3 east to Kaneohe, continue to Main Gate. Off Mokapu Blvd and Kaneohe Bay Drive. Clearly marked. *USMRA: Page 129 (E-6)*. **NMC:** Honolulu, 14 miles southwest.

RESERVATION INFORMATION: Transient UPH Division, Facilities Department, P.O. Box 63062, Kaneohe MCB, HI 96863-3062. **C-808-257-2409, DSN-315-457-2409,** 0700-2300 hours Mon-Sun, 0800-2300 hours holidays. All categories may make reservations. Check in at facility 1400 hours, check out 1000 hours. Closed Christmas and Thanksgiving. Beach Cottages: C-808-254-2806/2716

BOQ Bldg 503. C-808-257-2409, 0700-2300 hours Sun-Mon, 0800-2300 hours holidays. Bedroom, shared bath (36). Refrigerator, community kitchen, TV in room and lounge, housekeeping service, laundry facility, ice machine, spa/jacuzzi and meeting/conference room available. Older structure, newly refurbished. Rates: sponsor $25, each dependent $6. Maximum four per unit.

TML Bldg 386. SNCO bedroom, shared bath (6); VIP suite (1).

TML The Lodge. Bldg 3038, 0.25 miles from Main Gate. Mailing address: The Lodge, Marine Corps Community Services, Bldg 3038, Kaneohe Bay MCB, HI 96863-5000. **C-808-254-2806/2716, DSN-315-457-2409,** 24 hours daily. Fax: C-808-254-2716. After hours check in call Duty Officer, C-808-257-1824. Closed on all federal holidays. Studio unit (24), private bath, fully equipped kitchen, CATV, housekeeping service. Soft drink vending, laudromat. One mile from commissary, exchange and seven day store. Rates: $55. Reservations are required. No pets. *Note: Renovation of 24 units will be completed spring of 2001. Groundbreaking for 50 additional units is scheduled mid-2001.*

DV/VIP FMF PAC Protocol, Kaneohe MCB, HI 96863-5001. **C-808-257-1827.** O6+. Retirees Space-A.

TML AVAILABILITY: Varies.

CREDIT CARDS ACCEPTED: Visa, MasterCard and American Express.

TRANSPORTATION: On base shuttle/bus and local taxis available. Car Rental: Enterprise C-808-254-0808.

DINING OPPORTUNITIES: E Club, C-808-254-7660/7661; K-Bay Chinese Garden Restaurant, C-808-254-7657; McDonald's, C-808-254-4053; O Club, C-808-254-7649/7650 and Subway, C-808-254-2468 are within driving distance.

See Kaneohe Bay Beach Cottages listing on previous page.

Kilauea Military Camp
Joint Services Recreation Center (HI17R6)
Attn: Reservations Office, Bldg 40
Hawaii Volcanoes National Park, HI 96718-5000

MAIN INSTALLATION TELEPHONE NUMBERS: C-808-967-8333/34/35, direct dial from Oahu C-438-6707. Medical 967-8368; Security Police 967-7315.

LOCATION: On island of Hawaii, 216 air miles southeast of Honolulu, 32 miles southwest off HI-11 from Hilo International Airport. Scheduled bus transportation to camp: reservations required 48 hours prior. Hilo to Kilauea Military Camp (KMC). *USMRA: Page 129 (I,J-6,7)*. **NMC:** Hilo, 32 miles northeast.

RESERVATION INFORMATION: KMC Lodging, Hawaii Volcanoes National Park, HI 96718-5000. **C-808-967-8333,** Direct Dial from Oahu C-438-6707, Fax: C-808-967-8343 E-mail: reservations@kmc-volcano.com WEB: www.kmc-volcano.com Reservations required. Reservations are accepted on first come, first serve basis, reguardless of rank, up to one year prior to the requested arrival date during non-peak periods. During peak periods, reservations are accepted in the following priorities: Active Duty Military, Reservists, Guardsmen one year in advance; Retired Military, DoD Civilians 60 days in advance. Reservations Office, 0800-1600 hours daily. Check in 1500 hours, check out 1100 hours. From Oahu, call toll free above number 0800-1600 hours. Others call direct.

TML Apartments and Cottages (78) all with private bath. One-bedroom with or without jacuzzi; two-bedroom with or without kitchen; two-bedroom or three-bedroom, with kitchen and jacuzzi; three bedroom apartment units; One dormitory with common baths and showers for large groups. Handicap accessible units available. Refrigerator, coffee maker, CATV, housekeeping service, coin laundry facility, cribs and rollaways for $1.25 (per night). Fireplaces, playground, basketball, tennis, bowling alley, country store, snack shop, recreation lodge, 18-hole golf course, deep sea fishing and helicopter tours, bus tours Mon-Fri, mainland and inter-island airline packages. Rates: E1-E5 $43-$81; E6-E9, W1-W3, O1-O3, NF1-3, GS1-10, DAV, WIDOWS $55-$93; W4, O4-O6, NF4-6, GS11-15, TLA/PCS $68-$106; O7-O10, Foreign Services, DOD Ret, CIV, TDY, Guest, Other $74-$112. Rates are based on double occupancy, each additional person $8/$9/$10/$11. No charge for children under 12 years of age with parents. Dormitory $10-$12.75 overnight, per person and $7.50-$10 nightly, per person.

AMENITIES: Weight Room and Meeting/Conference Room.

TML AVAILABILITY: Good all year.

CREDIT CARDS ACCEPTED: Visa, MasterCard and American Express.

TRANSPORTATION: Shuttle service is available to and from Hilo airport for authorized patrons at $5 per person, one way. No charge for E1-E6 Active Duty and immediate family members. It will be dispatched only with an advance request of at least 48 hours. Allow 50 minutes travel time each way. Car Rental: Avis, C-1-800-321-3712, Budget, C-800-827-0700, Harper Car and Truck Rental, C-800-852-9993, National, C-800-227-7368. Taxis are available at airport ($50-$60 fare one way).

DINING OPPORTUNITIES: Volcano Golf Course Restaurant, C-808-967-8228 and Volcano House, C-808-967-7321 are within walking distance. Kilauea Lodge, C-808-967-7366; Surfs C-808-967-8511; Thai Thai, C-808-967-7969; and Lava Rock Cafe, C-808-967-8526 are within driving distance. Cafeteria and snack bar are also available.

On the rim of Kilauea Crater at 4,000 feet, temperature 50-75 degrees, quiet guest cottages, hiking, support facilities, this is the place to get away from it all. For more details see *Military Living's Military RV, Camping and Outdoor Recreation Around the World*.

Pearl Harbor Naval Station (HI20R6)
Family Service Center
820 Willamette Street
Pearl Harbor, HI 96860-5108

MAIN INSTALLATION TELEPHONE NUMBERS: C-808-449-7110, DSN-315-430-0111. Locator 471-7110; Medical 471-9541; Security Police 471-7114.

LOCATION: Off H-1, adjacent to Honolulu International Airport. Take Pearl Harbor exit, enter Nimitz Gate. Clearly marked. *USMRA: Page 129 (C-7) and Page 131 (A-1,2,3; B-2,3; C-2)*. **NMC:** Honolulu, 5 miles east.

RESERVATION INFORMATION: Code 40/43, Bldg 1623, Barracks Road, Pearl Harbor NS, HI 96860-6000. **C-808-473-5210, DSN-315-473-5210,** Fax C-808-423-1704, 24 hours daily. E-mail: yamilavv@pearlharbor.navy.mil WEB: www.pearlharbor.navy.mil/BQ/ Check in after 1500 hours, check out 1300 hours. *Note: Construction of a 150-room Navy Lodge, to be located on Ford Island, commenced on 2 Nov 2001.*

BEQ Arizona Hall, Bldg 1623. Front desk C-808-473-5983. Singles only. Refrigerator, TV, housekeeping service, laundry facility. Modern structure. Rates: E1-E4 $10; E5-E9 $20. Duty may make reservations; others Space-A.

CBOQ Lockwood Hall, Bldg 662. Front desk C-808-791-8300 ext 1000. Bedroom, private bath. Refrigerator, A/C, TV, phone, housekeeping service, laundry facility. Modern structure. Rates: sponsor $25, adult $10. Maximum two persons. Duty may make reservations; others Space-A.

BOQ Makalapa Complex, Bldg 372. Front desk C-808-471-3041. Bedroom, private bath. Refrigerator, A/C, TV, phone, housekeeping service, laundry facility. Modern structure. Rates: $25; DV suite $50.

BOQ Hale Alii, Bldg 1315. Front desk C-808-473-5342. Bedroom, private bath. Refrigerator, A/C, TV, phone, housekeeping service, laundry facility. Modern structure. Rates: $25.

DV/VIP CINCPACFLT Protocol, **C-808-473-2207.** O7+. Rates: $50.

AMENITIES: Exercise Room, Meeting/Conference Room, Mini Mart. Ice, Snack and Soft Drink Vending Machine.

TML AVAILABILITY: Difficult. Best, Nov-Feb.

CREDIT CARDS ACCEPTED: Visa.

TRANSPORTATION: Off base bus, Car Rental, Off base taxi.

DINING OPPORTUNITIES: The Banyans; Beeman Center; Club Pearl, C-808-471-1742; and Marina Restaurant, C-808-471-0593 are within driving distance.

Visit the Bishop Museum and Planetarium to see what old Hawaii was like, Pier 9 at the foot of Fort Street Mall has spectacular views of Honolulu and the harbor from the Aloha Tower. Don't forget the Arizona Memorial and USS Bowfin.

Schofield Barracks (HI13R6)
25th Infantry Division (Light) & U.S. Army Hawaii
APVG-GAF-FA
Bldg 824
Schofield Barracks, HI 96857-5000

MAIN INSTALLATION TELEPHONE NUMBERS: C-808-449-7110, DSN-315-471-7110. Locator 655-2299; Medical 433-8883; Security Police 655-0911.

LOCATION: Exit airport on H-1 west bound. Proceed to H-2 going north to Wahiawa, H-2 ends. Turn left on Kunia Road, turn right onto Foote Avenue at Foote Gate. *USMRA: Page 129 (C-6).* **NMC:** Honolulu, 20 miles southeast.

RESERVATION INFORMATION: Inn at Schofield Barracks, 563 Kolekole Avenue, Wahiawa, HI 96786-6000. **C-1-800-490-9638, C-808-624-9650/9640, DSN-315-655-5036,** Fax: C-808-624-5606, 24 hours daily. E-mail: theinn@aloha.com WEB: www.innatschofield.com Directions: At Foote Gate follow Foote Avenue. Foote Avenue changes to Kolekole Avenue. The Inn is on the right. The main lobby is on your left as you enter the parking lot. Check in 1500 hours, check out 1200 hours.

TML Inn at Schofield Barracks. The Inn has 192 rooms with private bath. Refrigerator, microwave, A/C, CATV/VCR, coin laundry facility, ice machine, video rental. Interconnecting units available. Rates: Single occupancy, queen-size bed $68.50; double occupancy, one or two queen-size beds unofficial $68.50, official $95; Single or double occupancy, one queen-size bed, sofabed $105. Reservations, PCS and TDY one year prior; all others six months in advance. No pets.

DV/VIP Bldg 719, Fort Shafter. Reservations **C-808-438-1685** or **C-808-839-2336, DSN 315-839-2336,** Fax: C-808-438-0492. 06/GS13+. Three-bedroom suite (1); Two-bedroom suite (1); One-bedroom suite (3); single room (2). Rates: $35-$55, each additional person $5. Primarily for TDY personnel.

TML AVAILABILITY: Good. Most difficult, summer.

CREDIT CARDS ACCEPTED: Visa, MasterCard, American Express, Discover and Diners.

TRANSPORTATION: On base shuttle/bus, C-808-655-2248; Off base shuttle/bus, C-808-848-4400; Car Rental, C-808-624-2324; Enterprise, C-808-622-0024; On base taxi, C-808-655-4944; Off base taxi, C-808-422-2222.

DINING OPPORTUNITIES: On-site Deli/Mini Mart within walking distance. Burger King and Food Court are within driving distance.

In winter don't miss major surfing meets held in Haleiwa on the north shore, just nine miles away, golf at Kalakaua, the post museum and recreation equipment rental.

The Inn at Schofield Barracks is located in the heart of WWII history.

Tripler Medical Center (HI03R6)
1 Jarrett White Road
Tripler Medical Center, HI 96859-5000

MAIN INSTALLATION TELEPHONE NUMBERS: C-808-839-1110, DSN-315-433-0111. Locator 433-6661; Medical 433-6620; Security Police 438-7116.

LOCATION: Take H-1 west to Tripler exit. Turn right on Jarret White Road to Tripler Medical Center. *USMRA: Page 129 (D-7), page 131 (D-1,2).* **NMC:** Honolulu, three miles southeast.

RESERVATION INFORMATION: Billeting, Bldg 228B, Jarrett White Road, Tripler AMC, HI 96859-5000. **C-808-839-2336,** Fax: C-808-433-6905, 24 hours daily. E-mail: tamcbillet@shafter.army.mil Directions: Turn right on Jarret White Road. Second building on the left, Bldg. 228-

B. Check in at billeting 1500 hours, check out 1100 hours. Government civilian employee billeting **NMC:** Honolulu, three miles south. NMI: Fort Shafter, 2 miles.

Army Lodging Bldg 228B. One-bedroom suite, private bath (90). Refrigerator, microwave, TV, housekeeping service, laundry facility, cribs, cots, ice machine. Handicap accessible units. Older structure, recently renovated. Rates: $41, each additional person $5. Reservations accepted anytime for offical travel; all others 30 days with deposit or cerdit card.

Fisher House Tripler Medical Center, 315 Krukowski Road, Honolulu, HI 96819-5000. **C-808-433-1291,** Fax: C-808-433-3619. *Note: Appendix B has the definition of this facility. Fisher Houses are only available as lodging for families of patients receiving medical care at military and VA medical centers.*

DV/VIP Bldg 719, Fort Shafter. Reservations **C-808-438-1685** or **C-808-839-2336, DSN 315-839-2336,** Fax: C-808-438-0492. 06/GS13+. Three-bedroom suite (1); Two-bedroom suite (1); One-bedroom suite (3); single room (2). Rates: $35-$55, each additional person $5.

AMENITIES: Meeting/Conference Room, Snack and Soft Drink Vending Machines, Continental Breakfast.

TML AVAILABILITY: Varies.

CREDIT CARDS ACCEPTED: Visa, MasterCard, American Express and Discover.

TRANSPORTATION: On base shuttle/bus; Off base shuttle/bus, C-808-848-5555; Car Rentals, C-808-422-6915, C-808-946-2777, C-808-537-3600; Off base taxi, C-808-847-3566, C-808-593-9727.

DINING OPPORTUNITIES: Tripler Dining & Mess and Tripler Food Court are within walking distance. City of Honolulu offers numerous restaurants within driving distance. Fort Shafter has a new combined club, bowling alley and snack bar, two miles.

Hawaii's rare and endangered plant life may be better appreciated at Haiku Gardens, Kaneohe, Foster Garden botanical park and Paradise Park in Manoa Valley. Don't forget the Honolulu Zoo, in Kapiolani Park.

Waianae Army Recreation Center (HI05R6)

85-010 Army Street
Waianae, HI 96792-5000

MAIN INSTALLATION TELEPHONE NUMBERS: C-808-696-4158; Medical 911; Security Police 696-2811.

LOCATION: On the west coast of Oahu. Take H-1 west to HI-93 west (Farrington Highway) to Waianae. Look for the Aloha gas station on your left (west); turn left at Army Street. *USMRA: Page 129 (B-6).* **NMC:** Honolulu, 35 miles southeast. NMI: Schofield Barracks, 20 miles northeast.

RESERVATION INFORMATION: Rec Center, Bldg 4070, 85-010 Army Street, Waianae, HI 96858-5000. **C-1-800-333-4158 (mainland), 1-800-847-6771 (outer island), C-808-696-4158 (Oahu),** 0900-1600 hours Mon-Fri. Reservations may be made up to one year in advance during off-peak season; 90 days in advance during peak season. Deposit required 14 days from booking date. Twenty-one night occupancy limit in a 60 day period. Year round operation. Check in 1630-1930 hours, check out 1200 hours.

Cabins Two-bedroom cabin (25); studio cabin (5); deluxe cabin, two-bedroom (6); deluxe cabin, three-bedroom (3). Full kitchen with dishes, utensils, A/C, TV, (TV/VCR-deluxe rooms), phone, housekeeping service, cribs ($5), rollaways ($10 per night), BBQ, picnic

facilities, deck and parking. Handicap accessible units (3). Rates: standard two-bedroom $55-$75; studio $45-$55; deluxe two-bedroom $70-$90; deluxe three-bedroom $85-$95. Bring personal items and beach towels. No pets.

TML AVAILABILITY: Good all year.

CREDIT CARDS ACCEPTED: Visa, MasterCard, American Express and Discover.

TRANSPORTATION: None available.

DINING OPPORTUNITIES: Waianae Beach Club, C-808-696-4778 is within walking distance.

On the "Leeward" western side of Oahu, with the look of old Hawaii, and Waianae Mountain Range at 4,000 feet. The heart of "Pokai Bay" has one of the best beaches, snorkeling, surfing, swimming. Rentals, catering and meeting facilities. See *Military Living's Military RV, Camping and Outdoor Recreation Around the World* for more information.

An oceanfront cabin at the Waianae Army Recreation Center, HI

IDAHO

Boise Air Terminal/Gowen Field Airport/Air National Guard (ID04R4)

4040 Guard Street
Boise, ID 83705-5004

MAIN INSTALLATION TELEPHONE NUMBERS: C-208-422-5011/5366, DSN-312-422-5011/5366. Locator 422-5011; Medical 911; Security Police 422-5366.

LOCATION: From I-84 east or west, take Orchard Street exit (exit 52) south. Turn left and remain on Gowen Road as it goes behind the airport. Watch for "Gowen Field" sign near tanks. Turn left into Main Gate. *USMRA: Page 98 (B-8).* **NMC:** Boise, five miles north.

RESERVATION INFORMATION: 4200 West Ellsworth, Boise, ID 83705-8033. **C-208-422-4451, DSN-312-422-4451,** Fax: C-208-422-4452, DSN-312-422-4452, 0800-1630 hours Mon-Fri. Reservations accepted.

Army Lodge Mostly single rooms, CATV, housekeeping service. Rates: $8-$24.

DV/VIP Office of the Adjutant General, Command Group Protocol, 4040 Guard Street, C-208-422-6364, Fax C-208-422-6179.

DV rooms available with kitchenette. Rates: $24. All ranks Space-A, lower ranks may be bumped.

AMENITIES: Exercise Room and Mini Mart.

TML AVAILABILITY: Good, Nov-Mar. Difficult, May-Jul.

CREDIT CARDS ACCEPTED: Visa, MasterCard and American Express.

TRANSPORTATION: Off base taxi.

DINING OPPORTUNITIES: Denny's, McDonald's and Outback Steakhouse within driving distance.

Mountain Home Air Force Base (ID01R4)
366th MSS/DPF
575 Gunfighter Avenue
Mountain Home AFB, ID 83648-5237

MAIN INSTALLATION TELEPHONE NUMBERS: C-208-828-2111, DSN-312-728-1110. Locator 828-6647; Medical 911; Security Police 828-2256.

LOCATION: From Boise, take I-84 southeast, 39 miles to Mountain Home, exit 95 west, follow road through town to Airbase Road, (ID-67 west), 10 miles to Main Gate on left. *USMRA: Page 98 (C-9).* **NMC:** Boise, 51 miles northwest.

RESERVATION INFORMATION: Sagebrush Hotel, 445 Falcon Street, Mountain Home AFB, ID 83648-5000. **C-1-888-AFLODGE (1-888-235-6343), C-208-828-5200, DSN-312-728-5200,** Fax: C-208-828-4797, DSN-312-728-4797, 24 hours daily. Check in at facility, check out 1200 hours. DoD civilian billeting. Duty can make reservations any time; Space-A can make reservations 24 hours in advance.

TLF Two-, three- or four-bedroom houses (16). PCS in/out, some Space-A. Private units with fully equipped kitchen, housekeeping service. Rates: $21. No pets.

VOQ/VAQ Hotel. Bedroom, semi-private bath (90). Community kitchen, refrigerator, microwave, A/C, CATV, HBO, housekeeping service, laundry facilities, cribs, cots, ice machine. Rates (expected to change): VOQ $13.50. VAQ $13. Older structure. No pets.

DV/VIP Protocol, **C-208-828-4536.** 06+. Units designated. Rates: $24.50 per room. Active Duty can make reservations, Space-A can reserve non-confirmed 24 hours prior to arrival. Retirees Space-A.

TML AVAILABILITY: Very good, winter. Difficult, Jun-Aug.

CREDIT CARDS ACCEPTED: Visa and MasterCard.

TRANSPORTATION: On base shuttle/bus, C-208-828-2339. On base taxi, C-208-343-2215/2239.

DINING OPPORTUNITIES: Bowling Center, C-208-828-2567; Pizza Etc., C-208-828-6546; and Base Exchange Food Court are within walking distance. Burger King, C-208-832-7572; Gunfighters Club, C-208-828-2105; and Wagon Wheel Dining Hall, C-208-828-2313 are within driving distance.

Yellowstone Country Trailers (ID05R4)
c/o US Air Force Outdoor Recreation
366 SVS/SVRO
655 Pine Street, Bldg 2800
Mountain Home AFB, ID 83648-5125

MAIN INSTALLATION TELEPHONE NUMBERS: C-208-828-2111, DSN-312-728-1110. Locator 828-2111; Medical 911; Security Police 911.

LOCATION: Off base. Trailers are placed at commercial RV parks around Yellowstone National Park Idaho, Montana and Wyoming. *USMRA: Page 98 (C-9).* **NMC:** Idaho Falls, 80 miles south. NMI: Malmstrom AFB, 254 miles north.

RESERVATION INFORMATION: c/o US Air Force Outdoor Recreation, 366 SVS/SVRO, 655 Pine Street, Bldg 2800, Mountain Home AFB, ID 83648-5125. Reservations may also be made in person at Outdoor Recreation, 655 Pine Street, Mountain Home AFB, ID. **C-208-828-6333, DSN-312-728-6333.** Reservations required, made up to sixty days in advance in person or by phone. Accommodations must be paid in full at time of reservation with cash, check or credit card and cannot be made by mail.

Trailers Flagg Ranch (8), Henry's Lake (1), Lionshead Resort (4). Twenty-six foot travel trailers fully self-contained, sleep six, equipped with cooking and eating utensils. Non-smoking. Rates: $55. No pets.

TML AVAILABILITY: Memorial Day to 15 Sept (depending on occupancy and weather).

CREDIT CARDS ACCEPTED: Visa and MasterCard.

TRANSPORTATION: None available.

DINING OPPORTUNITIES: Numerous restaurants and snack bars at Henry's Lake, Flagg Ranch and Lionshead.

Each location contains beautiful scenery plus rivers and lakes that are perfect for fishing.

ILLINOIS

Great Lakes Naval Training Center (IL07R2)
2701 Sheridan Road, Bldg 42
Great Lakes, IL 60088-5001

MAIN INSTALLATION TELEPHONE NUMBERS: C-847-688-3500, DSN-312-792-3500. Locator 688-3500; Medical 688-4560/6855; Security Police 688-3333.
Ten-digit dialing required for local calls.

LOCATION: From I-94 north or US-41 north of Chicago, exit to IL-137 east to Sheridan Road north, turn right into the gate. Clearly marked. *USMRA: Page 64 (G-1).* **NMC:** Chicago, 30 miles south.

RESERVATION INFORMATION: Central Billeting, Bldg 30 Admiral Boorda Hall, 2601A Paul Jones Street, NTC, Great Lakes, IL 60088-5000. **C-847-688-3777/2170/2241, DSN-312-792-3777/2170/2241,** Fax: C-847-688-5815, DSN-312-792-5815, 24 hours daily. Directions: Main Gate located on Farragut Avenue. Turn left at end of bridge onto Rodgers Street; go 1 1/2 blocks to Bronson Avenue and turn right; go 1 1/2 blocks to Bldg 30 "ADM. Mike Boorda Hall" (Intersection of Bronson Avenue. and Sampson Street. to your left.) Check in at facility, check out 1200 hours. Government civilian employee billeting (if on official duty).

BEQ Bldgs 833, 834, 430, 431, 433-435. Bldg 833, E5-E9, bedroom, private bath (108); DVEQ units (2). Bldg 834, E5-E9, bedroom, private bath (57). E1-E4 shared bedroom, private bath (53). Bldg 430, E5-E9, private bedroom, and bath (54). E1-E4 shared bedroom, private bath (12). Bldg 431, E5-E9, private bedroom and bath (56). Refrigerator, microwave, coffee/tea, A/C, CATV/VCR in room and lounge, housekeeping service, laundry facilities. Brick barracks structure, renovated. Rates: E1-E6 $8; E7-E9 $13; VIP $29. Active Duty, Reservists and NG on orders may make reservations; others Space-A. No pets.

BOQ All ranks, Government civilians, all grades, official duty. Suites: separate bedroom, sitting room, private bath (140). Refrigerator, microwave, A/C, CATV/VCR in room and lounge, housekeeping service, laundry facilities, iron/ironing board, cribs, cots, game room. Brick barracks structure. Rates: sponsor $23, each additional over age five $5.75; VIP $29, each additional $7.25. Maximum five per unit. Active Duty, Reservists and NG on orders can make reservations; others Space-A. No pets.

NAVY LODGE Navy Lodge. Bldg 2500, Meridian Drive, Great Lakes NTC, IL, 60088-5000. **C-1-800-NAVY-INN.** Lodge number is C-847-689-1485, Fax: C-847-689-1489, 24 hours daily. Check in 1500-1800 hours, check out 1200 hours. Bedroom, two double beds, private bath (50). Kitchenette, utensils, A/C, TV, phone, housekeeping service, coin laundry facility. Renovated July 1996. New building, bedroom, two queen-size beds, private bath (100). Microwave, coffee, A/C, CATV/VCR, video rental, phone, housekeeping service, coin laundry facility. Four sets interconnecting units, handicap accessible. Rates: $54 per room (50 rooms for long-term guests, 100 rooms for short-term guests). Maximum five per room. All categories may make reservations. No smoking. No pets.

AMENITIES: Exercise Room (BOH), Meeting/Conference Room, Mini Mart. Ice, Snack and Soft Drink Vending Machines.

TML AVAILABILITY: Good, Sept-Feb. Difficult, Jun-Aug.

CREDIT CARDS ACCEPTED: Visa, MasterCard and American Express. The Navy Lodge accepts Visa, MasterCard, American Express and Discover.

TRANSPORTATION: Car Rentals: Enterprise, C-847-360-8008; Hertz, C-1-800-654-3131; Avis, C-1-800-831-2847; Off base taxi, Checker C-847-689-1050; GL Yellow Cab, C-847-623-2000; Airport Express, C-1-800-654-7871.

DINING OPPORTUNITIES: McDonald's and Base Clubs are within walking distance. List of local restaurants available at front desk.

Boating, swimming and all water sports are available through the marina Beach House. An 18-hole golf course, bowling center, and extensive other support facilities are available on base.

Rock Island U.S. Army Armament & Chemical Acquisition & Logistics Activity (IL08R2)
Community and Family Activities
SMARI-CF
Rock Island, IL 61299-5000

MAIN INSTALLATION TELEPHONE NUMBERS: C-309-782-6002, DSN-312-793-6002. Locator 782-6002; Medical 782-0801; Security Police 782-5507.

LOCATION: From I-74 north in Moline, exit 1 to 4th Avenue west and follow signs to Arsenal Island, located in middle of Mississippi River. *USMRA: Page 64 (C-2).* NMC: Quad Cities of Rock Island, Moline, Davenport and Bettendorf.

RESERVATION INFORMATION: SMARI-CF, Bldg 110, Rock Island, IL 61299-6000. **C-309-782-0833, DSN-312-793-0833,** Fax: C-309-782-

1706, DSN-312-793-1706. 0800-1600 hours, after hours report to Police (Bldg 225). E-mail: rollinsj2@ria.army.mil Directions: Follow Rodman Avenue to Bldg 110 located at intersection of Rodman and East. Check in Transient Quarters Office, Bldg. 110, 1400 hours. Check out at 0900 hours.

VOQ Bldg 60. Fully equipped apartment (1), sleeps six; bedroom, two beds, full-size crib, bath. Kitchen, refrigerator, utensils, microwave, dining area, CATV/VCR, A/C, laundry facility. Handicap accessible entrance. Rate: $35.

AMENITIES: Exercise Room, Snack and Soft Drink Vending Machines.

TML AVAILABILITY: Fairly Good, Nov-Jan. Difficult, other times.

CREDIT CARDS ACCEPTED: Visa and Master Card.

DINING OPPORTUNITIES: Post restaurant for breakfast and lunch (Mon-Fri) and Arsenal Club for lunch (Tue-Fri) are located next door. Evening meals not available within walking distance. Many restaurants including fast food within one mile of installation.

While here visit the Rock Island Arsenal Museum, National Cemetery, Confederate Cemetery and the Colonel Davenport House.

Scott Air Force Base (IL02R2)
1510 Beech Street
Scott AFB, IL 62225-5359

MAIN INSTALLATION TELEPHONE NUMBERS: C-618-256-1110, DSN-312-576-1110. Locator 256-4108; Medical 256-7595; Security Police 256-2223.

LOCATION: From I-64 east or west, take exit 19 east or 19-A west to IL-158 south, two miles and watch for signs to AFB entry. *USMRA: Page 64 (D-8).* NMC: St. Louis, 25 miles west.

RESERVATION INFORMATION: The Scott Inn, Bldg 1510 Beech Street, Scott AFB, IL 62225-5000. **C-1-888-AFLODGE (1-888-235-6343), C-618-256-1844, DSN-312-576-1844,** Fax: C-618-256-6638, DSN-312-576-6638 (for duty reservations only), 24 hours daily. E-mail: reservations@wing.scott.af.mil TDY/PCS may make reservations any time; Space-A may make reservations 24 hours in advance only. Directions from Main Gate: Go straight on Scott Drive, turn right at first light. Lodging front desk is third building on right. Check in 1430 hours daily, check out 1200 hours. NO PETS. ALL UNITS NON-SMOKING.

TLF Located at Scott Lake. Front desk will supply directions. Three- and Four-bedroom townhouses. All units have washer/dryer. Four bedroom unit has extra bathroom in master bedroom. Rates: $24.50. Used mainly for PCS In/Out.

VAQ Bedroom, private bath. Refrigerator, microwave, coffee maker, housekeeping service, laundry facilities. Rates: $17.50.

DVAQ Senior NCO quarters. Suite with bedroom, living room, private bath. Housekeeping service, laundry facilities. Rates: $21.50.

VOQ Bedroom, private and shared bath. Housekeeping service, laundry facilities. Rates: $20.

DVOQ **Essex House** AMC/Protocol **C-618-229-2555, DSN-312-576-2555.** O6+ and civilian equivalents. Suite with bedroom, living room, private bath. Housekeeping service, laundry facilities. Rates: $25.

AMENITIES: Exercise Room, Snack and Soft Drink Vending Machines.

TML AVAILABILITY: Fairly Good, Nov-Jan. Difficult, other times.

CREDIT CARDS ACCEPTED: Visa and MasterCard.

TRANSPORTATION: Off base shuttle/bus, C-1-800-852-6810; Car Rental, C-618-624-8960; Off base taxi, C-1-800-991-8660.

DINING OPPORTUNITIES: Scott Club (near main gate), C-618-256-5501, DSN-312-576-5501 is within walking distance. Restaurant guide supplied in each room.

Near the "Gateway to the West," visitors enjoy the cultural, sporting, and outdoor activities St. Louis affords. Nearby small communities reflect the stability and warmth of middle America.

INDIANA

Camp Atterbury (IN05R2)
Army National Guard
Bldg 708
Edinburgh, IN 46124-1096

MAIN INSTALLATION TELEPHONE NUMBERS: C-812-526-1499, DSN-312-569-2499. Locator 526-1117; Medical 526-1117; Security Police 526-1117.

LOCATION: From I-65, take exit 76 (31 north), left at Hospital Road. Enter post on Eggleston Street at Main Gate. *USMRA: Page 65 (E-6,7).* **NMC:** Indianapolis, 45 miles south.

RESERVATION INFORMATION: Camp Atterbury Contract Quarters, Attn: CA-DOL, Building 230, Edinburgh, IN 46124-4096. **C-812-526-1128, DSN-312-569-2128,** Fax: C-812-526-1764, DSN-312-569-2765, 0730-1600 hours Sat-Thu, 0730-1900 hours Fri. Reservations required. Directions from Main Gate: Go south on Eggleston Street to 3rd Street, west on 3rd Street to Fairbanks Street and Building 230. Check in at lodging office.

BOQ/BEQ Bldgs 220-222, 228-230, 514, 515. Suites (4); bedroom (170). Refrigerator, TV (in some rooms), housekeeping service, laundry facility. Handicap accessible. Rates: $10-$12.

DV/VIP Bldgs 6, 326, 331, 4082. SNCO/O4+. Kitchenette, refrigerator, TV, housekeeping service, laundry facility. Rates: $12-$16. Retirees and lower ranks Space-A.

AMENITIES: Exercise Room, Meeting/Conference Room, Mini Mart, Swimming Pool. Ice, Snack and Soft Drink Vending Machines.

TML AVAILABILITY: Good, Sep-May. Poor, Jun-Aug.

CREDIT CARDS ACCEPTED: Visa and MasterCard.

TRANSPORTATION: Car Rental: C-812-375-1200; Off Base Taxi, C-812-526-3800.

DINING OPPORTUNITIES: Two snack bars are within walking distance. Cracker Barrel Old Country Store, C-812-526-7968; and Schaffer's Old Towne Inn & Museum, C-812-526-0275 are within driving distance.

Over 70 Antique malls, a car museum and a prime outlet mall with twenty stores are all within five miles of camp.

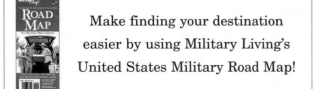
Make finding your destination easier by using Military Living's United States Military Road Map!

Crane Division Naval Surface Warfare Center (IN03R2)
Attn: N00164
300 Highway 361
Crane, IN 47522-5001

MAIN INSTALLATION TELEPHONE NUMBERS: C-812-854-1225, DSN-312-482-1225. Locator 854-2511; Medical 854-1220; Security Police 854-3301.

LOCATION: From Indianapolis, take Highway 465 south to 37 south to Bloomington, exit right on 45 southwest. Follow to Crane. Or from US-231 east, IN-645 to gate. *USMRA: Page 65 (D-8).* **NMC:** Bloomington, 30 miles northeast.

RESERVATION INFORMATION: CBQ, Code 01QL4, Bldg 3319, 300 Highway 361, Crane NSWC, IN 47522-5001. **C-812-854-1176, DSN-312-482-1176,** Fax: C-812-854-4416, DSN-312-482-4416, 24 hours daily. Directions: From Bloomington Gate, about five to seven miles on Main Road. At the second stop light, make a right and proceed to a 4-way stop. Turn left. The Combined Bachelor Quarters (Bldg 3319) is on the right side of the road.

TML Bldg 3319. Bedroom, double bed, private bath, kitchenette (includes microfridge, utensils, etc), living room, CATV/VCR, housekeeping service. New structure. Rates: $19.

DV/VIP CBQ. Bldg 3319: Rooms 201, 202. O6+. Bedroom suite, private bath, central kitchen, living room. Rates: $26. Retirees Space-A same day reservation, for one night only on weekends.

DV/VIP Bldg ZZ. Captains' Cottage. O6+. One-bedroom cottage, kitchen, living room, CATV, phone. Rates: $26.

AMENITIES: Snack and Soft Drink Vending Machines. Laundry room in facility, Kitchen in facility, Gas Grill. Gym, Swimming Pool and Marina are within driving distance.

TML AVAILABILITY: Very good, all year.

CREDIT CARDS ACCEPTED: Visa, MasterCard, American Express and Discover.

TRANSPORTATION: On base taxi.

DINING OPPORTUNITIES: Club Lakeview, Mess Hall, C-812-854-3435 or C-812-854-1501; Crane Cafe and Cafeteria, C-812-854-1519 are within walking distance. Other restaurants are within driving distance off base in local communities.

Sportsman's paradise, 22,500 acres for hunting, fishing, boating. Camping available through the Marina. Nine-hole golf course. Approximately one mile of nature trails.

Grissom Air Reserve Base (IN01R2)
434th ARW/PA
Grissom ARB, IN 46971-5000

MAIN INSTALLATION TELEPHONE NUMBERS: C-765-688-5211, DSN-312-928-5211. Locator 688-2992; Medical 688-3334; Security Police 688-3385.

LOCATION: On US-31, 15 miles north of Kokomo and 7 miles south of Peru. Turn at Grissom Aeroplex, proceed on Hoosier Blvd, turn right on Matador Street, take half left turn to continue on Matador Street, proceed past the intersection of Matador and Lightning Streets and turn left into the parking lot and proceed across the street to Bldg 333. *USMRA: Page 65 (E-3).* **NMC:** Indianapolis, 64 miles south.

RESERVATION INFORMATION: Grissom Inn, Bldg 333, Matador Street, Grissom ARB, IN 46971-5000. **C-765-689-8865/2884, DSN-312-928-8865/2844,** Fax: C-765-689-8751, 0600-2000 Mon-Sun; 24 hours daily on training weekends; closed holidays. Duty may make reservations any time; Space-A may make reservations 24 hours in advance. Directions: Turn right on Matador Street and follow to Lightning Avenue. Registration is in the first building on the right, Bldg 333. Check in at facility, check out 1200 hours.

VAQ Bldgs 328, 329, 331, 332. Bed spaces (300). Refrigerator, A/C, TV, alarm clock, coffee maker, hair dryer, housekeeping service, laundry facility. Modern structure. Rates: $14.50. No pets.

VOQ Bldgs 327-333. E7-O10. Rooms (76). Refrigerator, A/C, TV, alarm clock, coffee maker, hair dryer, housekeeping service, laundry facility. Rates: $14.50. No pets.

DV/VIP Bldg. 333. E9, O6+. Reservations same as central. All regular amenities plus premium cable channel, free toiletries, dishes. Rates: $21.

AMENITIES: Ice, Snack and Soft Drink Vending Machines.

TML AVAILABILITY: Good, Aug-April. Difficult, May-July.

CREDIT CARDS ACCEPTED: Visa and MasterCard.

TRANSPORTATION: Car Rental: Ace, Enterprise, and National Car Rental Companies in Kokomo; Off base taxi: B&E Cab Co. and City Cab Co. in Kokomo.

DINING OPPORTUNITIES: Combined Club, Noble Roman's Express and Chester's Chicken are within walking distance. Grissom Pizza, Fast Stop and Barb's Corner Kitchen are within driving distance.

If the Indianapolis 500 isn't excitement enough, try the new Circle Center Shopping Center, the Indiana Repertory Theater, the Bluegrass Music Festival, walking tours of Victorian Mansions and Independence Day in Evansville.

IOWA

Camp Dodge/Army National Guard Base (IA02R2)

7700 Northwest Beaver Drive
Johnston, IA 50131-1902

MAIN INSTALLATION TELEPHONE NUMBERS: C-515-252-4000 or C-1-800-294-6607, DSN-312-946-2000. Locator 252-4000; Medical 252-4235; Security Police 911.

LOCATION: From I-35/I-80 east or west, take Merle Hay Road/Camp Dodge exit 131 north on Iowa 401 (Merle Hay Road) to northwest Beaver Drive, left to Camp Dodge. Clearly marked. *USMRA: Page 77 (E-5).* **NMC:** Des Moines, eight miles southeast.

RESERVATION INFORMATION: CBQ, Bldg A-8, 7700 Northwest Beaver Drive, Johnston, IA 50131-1902. **C-515-252-4238 or C-1-800-294-6607 ext 4010, DSN-312-946-2238,** Fax: C-515-252-4092, DSN-312-946-2092, 0730-1700 hours. Active Duty, Reservists on orders can make reservations, others Space-A. Check in at Billeting Office, after hours security check in. Check out 0800 hours (late checkout call C-515-252-4238).

BEQ Bldg B-30. E7-E9. Bedroom, hallway bath (6). Refrigerator, A/C, TV, housekeeping service. Renovated structure. Rates: Active Duty $8, others $15. No pets.

BOQ Bldg M-1. O1-O3 (male only). Bedroom, hallway bath (13). Refrigerator, TV, housekeeping service. Rates: Active Duty $8, others $15. No pets.

BOQ Bldg M-3. O4-O5. Bedroom, hallway bath (13), bedrooms, semi-private bath (4). Refrigerator, TV, housekeeping service. Rates: Active Duty $8, others $15. No pets.

BOQ Bldg A-5. Bedroom, private bath (6), bedroom, semi-private bath (4). Refrigerator, TV, housekeeping service, laundry facility. Rates: Active Duty $8, others $15. No pets.

BOQ Bldg S-51. Bedroom, shared bath (56); Bedroom, private bath (4). Refrigerator, TV, housekeeping service, laundry facility. Rates: Active Duty $8, others $15. No pets.

DV/VIP Bldgs SOQ A-2, A-4, A-7, A-18, A-62, B-70; SEQ Bldg. B33. O6+. Bedroom, private bath (5). Refrigerator, microwave, TV, housekeeping service. Rates: Active Duty $16, others $30. No pets.

TML AVAILABILITY: Good.

CREDIT CARDS ACCEPTED: Visa and MasterCard, Government Travel Guard.

TRANSPORTATION: Off base taxi, C-515-282-8111, C-515-243-1111.

DINING OPPORTUNITIES: Greenbriar Restaurant C-515-253-0124; Okobeji Bar and Grill C-515-276-5255; and North End Diner, C-515-276-5151 are within driving distance.

While here visit Adventureland Theme Park, White Water University Park, aquarium, zoo and State Fairgrounds.

KANSAS

Fort Leavenworth (KS04R3)

615 McClellan Avenue
Fort Leavenworth, KS 66027-2303

MAIN INSTALLATION TELEPHONE NUMBERS: C-913-684-4021, DSN-312-552-4021. Locator 684-3651/4021; Medical 684-6000; Military Police 684-2111.

LOCATION: From I-70, exit 223 to US-73 north to Leavenworth. From I-29, exit 19, KS-92 west to Leavenworth. Fort is adjacent to city of Leavenworth. Main Gate on US-73 (Metropolitan Avenue). *USMRA: Page 78 (J-3).* **NMC:** Kansas City, 30 miles southeast.

RESERVATION INFORMATION: Lodging Operations, Bldg 695, Hoge Barracks, 210 Grant Avenue, Fort Leavenworth, KS 66027-1231. **C-913-684-4091 or 1-800-854-8627, DSN-312-552-4091,** Fax: C-913-684-4097, DSN-312-552-4097, 24 hours daily. E-mail: leavresv@leavenworth.army.mil WEB: www.leav.army.mil/housing/ Travelers on orders can make reservations; others Space-A. Check in at lodging after 1400 hours, check out 1000 hours.

Army Lodging Hoge Barracks, Truesdell Hall, Riverside Apartments, Root, Schofield, and Blochberger Hall. Units have private and semi-private baths. Kitchen (some), A/C, TV, housekeeping service, phone, laundry facility. Rates (subject to change): Duty $33 (semi-private bath), $37 (private bath); unofficial $49-$52. Additional occupant charge is $6.00 per person. No pets.

DV/VIP Executive Services, **C-913-684-4063/4.** O6+. Cooke Hall Bldg 22; Thomas Custer House Bldg 3; Otis Hall Bldg 213. Bedroom, private bath. Kitchen (some), refrigerator, utensils, A/C, TV, housekeeping service, phone, laundry facility. Historic structure. Rates (subject to change): Duty $42, unofficial $57; more than one person $63 per room. No pets.

AMENITIES: Continental Breakfast, Exercise Room, Meeting/Conference Room. Ice, Snack and Soft Drink Vending Machines.

TML AVAILABILITY: Difficult. Best, Dec. Limited, other times.

CREDIT CARDS ACCEPTED: Visa, MasterCard and Discover.

TRANSPORTATION: Off base shuttle/bus, C-913-682-1229; Car Rental, C-913-727-2222.

DINING OPPORTUNITIES: Burger King, C-913-651-9511; Robin Hood Deli/Anthony's Pizza, Taco Bell Express C-913-682-3278; and Trails West Golf Course, C-913-651-7176 are within walking distance. High Noon, C-913-682-4876; Mamie's Italian, C-913-682-2131; and Pullmans, C-913-682-8658 are within driving distance.

Fort Riley (KS02R3)
Commander
Attn: AFZN-CAH (ACS), Bldg 405
Fort Riley, KS 66442-6421

MAIN INSTALLATION TELEPHONE NUMBERS: C-785-239-1110, DSN-312-856-1110. Locator 239-9867; Medical 239-7777; Security Police 239-6767.

LOCATION: Near Junction City. From I-70, take exit 301 (Fort Riley/Marshall Army Air Field) northwest onto Henry Drive directly to Main Post. Follow signs. *USMRA: Page 78 (G,H-3,4)*. **NMC:** Topeka, 50 miles east.

RESERVATION INFORMATION: Billeting Office, Bldg 45, Barry Avenue, Fort Riley, KS 66442-5921. **C-785-239-2830, DSN-312-856-2830**Fax: C-785-239-8882, 24 hours daily. E-mail: lodging@riley-emh1army.mil Check in at billeting office 1500 hours, check out 1100 hours.

(VOQ) Bldgs 45, 470, 471, 541, 542, 620, 621. Two-room suite, private bath, kitchenette (24); two-bedroom, private bath, living room, kitchen (24); one-bedroom, private bath, living room, kitchen (2); single rooms, kitchenette (61). TV, laundry facility. Older structures. Rates: $26-$36 per unit. **Pets allowed in Bldg 620 only,** fee $10 per night. Duty on PCS/TDY may make reservations; others Space-A.

(Army Lodging) Bldg 170. Bedroom, living room, kitchen, private bath (6); two-bedroom, living room, kitchen, private bath (2). Older structure. Rates: $30-$35 per unit. Duty on PCS orders may make reservations; others Space-A.

(Army Lodging) Bldg 5309. Two-room suite, private bath (27); single room, private bath (3). Community kitchen, laundry facility, cribs. Older structure. Rates: suite $35, room $26. PCS may make reservations; others Space-A.

(DV/VIP) Grimes Hall, Bldg 510; Bacon Hall, Bldg 28. O4+. Bacon Hall is a three-bedroom house for $46 per night; Grimes Hall offers Custer Suite for $36 per night; Stuart Suite for $31 per night; one-bedroom suite for $26 per night (5). Kitchen, laundry facilities. Older structure. 05+ may make reservations by calling Protocol, **C-785-239-8843.**

AMENITIES: Snack and Soft Drink Vending Machines.

TML AVAILABILITY: Limited.

CREDIT CARDS ACCEPTED: Visa, MasterCard, American Express and Discover.

TRANSPORTATION: On base shuttle/bus, C-785-239-2636, DSN-312-856-2636; Car Rental: National, C-785-539-8814; On base taxi, C-785-239-2636, DSN-312-856-2636; Off base taxi, C-785-238-6122.

DINING OPPORTUNITIES: Country Kitchen, C-785-762-4477; Riley's, C-785-784-5999; and Sirloin Stockade, C-785-238-1817 are within driving distance.

Don't miss the US Cavalry Museum, in Bldg 205, which traces the history of this illustrious post, the battle of the Little Big Horn, Wounded Knee and then tour the Custer House.

McConnell Air Force Base (KS03R3)
22nd Air Refueling Wing
51347 Kansas Street, Suite 105
McConnell AFB, KS 67221-3600

MAIN INSTALLATION TELEPHONE NUMBERS: C-316-759-3840/6100, DSN-312-743-3840/6100. Locator 759-3555; Medical 759-5421 or 691-6300; Security Police 759-3978.

LOCATION: From north, on I-135, take KS-96 east to Rock Road. Go south to the base. From north or south on I-35, take the East Wichita exit. Go west on US-54 to Rock Road and south to the base. *USMRA: Page 78 (G-6)*. **NMC:** Wichita, six miles northwest.

RESERVATION INFORMATION: 22 SVS/SVML, Bldg 196, Suite 1, 53050 Glen Elder, McConnell AFB, KS 67221-3504. **C-1-888-AFLODGE (1-888-235-6343), C-316-759-6999, DSN-312-743-6999,** Fax: C-316-759-4190, DSN-312-743-4190, 24 hours daily. Check in 1400 hours, check out 1100 hours. Active Duty may make reservations any time; Space-A may make reservations 24 hours in advance.

(VOQ) Bldg 196. Active Duty personnel and retired; civilians on official duty. Single room, private bath (19); suite, private bath (8). Kitchenette, refrigerator, microwave, A/C, CATV, phone, housekeeping service, laundry facility, ice machine, in-room sundry sales. Rates: room $26.50; suite $32.00.

(VOQ) Bldg 202. Active Duty personnel and retired; civilians on official duty. Suite, two-bedroom (10). Kitchenette, refrigerator, microwave, A/C, CATV, phone, housekeeping service, laundry facility, ice machine, sundries for sale in room. Rates: $26.50.

(VQ) Bldg 202. SNCOs. Suite (4). Refrigerator, microwave, A/C, CATV, phone, housekeeping service, laundry facility, ice machine, sundries for sale in room. Rates: $26.50.

(VQ) Bldg 319. Active Duty personnel on leave or official duty; civilians on official duty. Suite (38). Refrigerator, microwave, A/C, CATV, phone, housekeeping service, laundry facility, ice machine, sundries for sale in room, entertainment room with pool tables, fitness center, meeting room. Rates: $26.50.

(TLF) Bldg 190. Suite, one-bedroom, furnished (45). Kitchen, A/C CATV, phone, housekeeping service, laundry facility, snack vending. Rates: $32.00.

(DV/VIP) Protocol **C-316-759-3110, DSN-312-743-3110.** Bldg 202. O6+. One-bedroom suite (4); two-bedroom suite, private bath (2). Refrigerator, microwave, A/C, CATV, phone, housekeeping service, laundry facility, ice machine, sundry sales. Rates: $32.00.

(DV/VIP) Bldg 185. O7+. Two-bedroom house, fully furnished, two private baths, kitchen with utensils, refrigerator, microwave, washer/dryer, garage, CATV, A/C, housekeeping service, phone, sundry sales. Rates $38.00.

TML AVAILABILITY: Great, Nov-Feb. Good, other times.

CREDIT CARDS ACCEPTED: Visa and MasterCard.

TRANSPORTATION: On base taxi, C-316-759-4051; Best Cabs Inc, C-316-838-2233. Off base taxi: American Cab Inc., C-316-262-7511.

DINING OPPORTUNITIES: Emerald City, C-316-759-6007; Burger King, C-316-683-7750; and Base Exchange, C-316-685-0231 are within walking distance.

Visit Charles Russell and others in the Wichita Art Museum, Wyatt Earp in the Old Cowtown Museum or stroll through one of the 100 municipal parks available to you. Still restless? There are more than 99 nightclubs in Wichita.

KENTUCKY

Fort Campbell (KY02R2)
101st Airborne Division & Fort Campbell
Bldg 5661, 25th Street and Wickham
Fort Campbell, KY 42223-5470

MAIN INSTALLATION TELEPHONE NUMBERS: C-270-798-2151, DSN-312-635-2151. Locator 798-2151; Medical 270-798-6111; Security Police 798-2677.

LOCATION: In the southwest part of Kentucky, four miles south of intersection of US-41A and I-24, exit 86 on I-24, 10 miles northwest of Clarksville, TN. *USMRA:* Page 40 (E,F-7). **NMC:** Hopkinsville, 15 miles north.

RESERVATION INFORMATION: Richardson Army Lodging. Bldg 1581, William C. Lee Road, Fort Campbell, KY 42223. **C-270-798-5618, DSN-312-635-5618,** Fax: C-270-798-0602, DSN-312-635-0602, 0800-1600 hours. TDY/PCS/Retirees. Does not accommodate families. Directions: Enter at main Gate 4 to obtain visitor pass, then proceed on Screaming Eagle Blvd to first light, turn left onto Bastogn, go to end, turn left on William C. Lee Road. First street turn right immediately after parking lot. The street has no name. **Turner Army Lodging,** Bldg 82, Texas Avenue, Fort Campbell, KY 42223. **C-270-439-2229,** Fax: C-270-439-7758, 0800-1600. PCS/Retirees/TDY. Accomodates families. E-mail: howesm@emh2.Campbell.army.mil WEB: www.campbell.army.mil Check in 1400, check out 1000.

VOQ Richardson Army Lodging. Bldgs 1582-1585. Room with one double bed, private bath. Refrigerator, microwave, stove, coffee maker, toaster, utensils, TV/VCR, iron/ironing board. Rates: $34. Laundry room available. TDY can make reservations 60 days in advance.

Army Lodging Turner Army Lodging. Bldgs 83, 90. Bedroom, two double beds, private bath, kitchenette (90); Bedroom, one double bed, private bath (45). All rooms have A/C, TV/VCR, iron/ironing board, ice machine. Rollaways and cribs available upon request. Laundry room available. Rates: double occupancy $35. PCS can make reservations 30 days in advance; all other 14 days in advance. No pets.

DV/VIP Protocol Office, Bldg T-39, **C-270-798-9913, DSN-312-635-9913.** O6+. Suites. Refrigerator, microwave, stove, coffee maker, toaster, utensils, TV/VCR, alarm clock, iron/ironing board. Rates: $40.

AMENITIES: Snack and Soft Drink Vending Machines.

TML AVAILABILITY: Difficult.

CREDIT CARDS ACCEPTED: Visa, MasterCard and American Express.

TRANSPORTATION: Car Rental, C-270-439-9988; On base taxi, C-270-798-6101, DSN-312-635-6101.

DINING OPPORTUNITIES: Cole Park Grill, C-931-431-6239; Campbell Club, C-931-431-5603 are within walking distance. 101 Pub, C-270-439-1772; and Sportsman's Lodge, C-931-431-4140 are within driving distance.

Stroll Clarksville's Public Square and architectural district for turn-of-the-century buildings. Visit local watershed lakes for fishing and picnicking.

Please see the order coupon at the end of this book for a list of all of Military Living's helpful military travel publications

Fort Knox (KY01R2)
Headquarters US Army Armor Center
1384 Vine Grove Road
Fort Knox, KY 40121-5000

MAIN INSTALLATION TELEPHONE NUMBERS: C-502-624-1181/1000, DSN-312-464-0111. Locator 624-1141; Security Police 624-2111.

LOCATION: From I-65, in Louisville, exit Gene Snyder Expressway west to US-31 west, go south to Fort Knox. From I-64, exit I-264 (Waterson Expressway west) to US-31 west, south to Fort Knox. Or from I-71, exit I-65 south to Gene Snyder Expressway to US-31 west then south to Fort Knox. *USMRA:* Page 40, 41 (H,I-3,4). **NMC:** Louisville, 25 miles north.

RESERVATION INFORMATION: Attn: ATZK-BOH-U, Bldg 4770 **Newgarden Tower,** Dixie Highway 31 W, Fort Knox, KY 40121-5000. **C-502-943-1000, DSN-312-464-3491,** Fax: C-502-942-8752, 24 hours daily. WEB: knox-www.army.mil/mwr Check in/out as indicated. Reservations taken 24 hours daily for Transient Lodging and Wickam Guest House. Cribs and rollaways are on a first come, first served basis. No pets. DV/VIP: Protocol Office: C-502-624-6951. *Awarded the 2001 Army Lodging of the Year Award in the super-sized category.*

Army Lodging Wickam Guesthouse, 7961 Wilson Road, P.O. Box 939, Fort Knox, KY 40121. C-502-942-0490, Fax: C-502-943-7475, 24 hours daily. From Chaffee Gate entrance go left at light onto Eisenhower, turn right at third light onto Wilson, follow sign into Anderson Family Complex. Guesthouse is at the complex, which includes an 18-hole professional PGA golf course, a restaurant, an indoor Olympic-sized pool and a cardiovascular fitness center. Check out 1200 hours. New 105 room guesthouse has 55 standard rooms and 50 suites. All units equipped with A/C, private bath, microwave, refrigerator, coffee maker, phone and computer/fax jack. Some rooms have queen or king size beds. Two-room suites have two double beds, dining area and stove. On site laundry facility, cribs, ice machine, game room, continental breakfast. Modern structure. Rates: official $37-$47; unofficial $39-$74.

VOQ Standard rooms or apartments, building 4770, 855-857, 2602-2607, 2441-2448. Check out at 1200 hours daily. Kitchen with refrigerator, stove, microwave, and coffee maker. Color TV, Cable, VCR, housekeeping service, laundry facility, ice machine. Modern structures. Rates: sponsor $29-$37, each additional person $6. Duty can make reservations, others Space-A.

DVQ Yeomans Hall. Bldg 1117. **C-502-624-6951, DSN-312-464-6951.** O6+. Check out 1200 hours. Bedroom suites, private bath (10). A/C, TV, housekeeping service. Older structure. Rates: official travel $41-60, each additional person $6. Duty can make reservations, others Space-A.

DVQ Henry House. Bldg 1120. **C-502-624-6951, DSN-312-464-6951.** O7+. Check out 1200 hours. Four-bedroom house (1). Kitchen, TV, housekeeping service, laundry facility. Older structure. Rates: official travel $41-60, each additional person $6. Duty can make reservations, others Space-A.

AMENITIES: Continental Breakfast, Exercise Room, Meeting/Conference Room, Mini Mart, Snack Vending Machine and Soft Drink Machine.

TML AVAILABILITY: Good. Best, Nov-Mar. Difficult, other times.

CREDIT CARDS ACCEPTED: Visa, MasterCard and American Express.

TRANSPORTATION: Van service available for guests, C-502-943-1000, DSN-312-464-3491; Car Rentals: Budget, C-502-351-4777; Enterprise C-502-352-4088; Off base shuttle/bus, C-502-351-7373; Off base taxi, C-502-351-7373.

DINING OPPORTUNITIES: Gallotta's Italian Restaurant, C-502-942-7417 is within walking distance from Guesthouse. Leader's Club, C-502-

942-0959 is within walking distance from Yeomans Hall; Anthony's Pizza, C-502-942-7484; Burger King, C-502-942-4281; and Kentucky Fried Chicken, C-943-9079 are within driving distance. There are various restaurants within a 10-20 minute drive.

Visit the Patton Museum of Cavalry and Armor, the US Bullion Depository and Louisville, home of the Kentucky Derby and historic points of interest.

LOUISIANA

Barksdale Air Force Base (LA01R2)
2nd MSS/DPF
413 Curtiss Road
Barksdale AFB, LA 71110-2426

MAIN INSTALLATION TELEPHONE NUMBERS: C-318-456-2252, DSN-312-781-1000. Locator 456-2252; Medical 456-4051; Security Police 456-2551.

LOCATION: Exit I-20, at Airline Drive exit 22, go south to Old Minden Road (one quarter mile), left on Old Minden Road (one block), then right on North Gate Drive (one mile) to North Gate of AFB. Co-located with Bossier City and Shreveport. *USMRA: Page 79 (B-2).* **NMC:** Shreveport, one mile west.

RESERVATION INFORMATION: Bldg 5155, 555 Davis Avenue, Barksdale AFB, LA 71110-2164. **C-1-888-AFLODGE (1-888-235-6343), C-318-456-3091, DSN-312-781-3091,** Fax: C-318-456-1263/2267, DSN-312-781-1263, 24 hours daily. E-mail: coriesselman@barksdale.af.mil Duty may make reservations any time; Space-A may make reservations 24 hours in advance. Directions: From North Gate on Davis Avenue, second building on the left. Check in at facility, check out 1200 hours.

VAQ Barksdale Inn. Bldgs 5155, 4359. Separate bedroom, private bath (SNCO) (26); separate bedroom, shared bath (E1-E6) (74). Refrigerator, A/C, TV, housekeeping service, laundry facility, cribs, ice machine. Older structure, renovated. Rates: $13.

VOQ Bldgs 5123, 5224, 4167. Separate bedroom, private bath (114); Bldg 5224, separate bedroom, private bath (O4+) (8); Refrigerator, A/C, TV, housekeeping service, laundry facility, ice machine. Older structure, renovated. Rates: Bldg 5123, $13.50, chief suite $23; Bldg 5224, $13.50; Bldg 4167, $13.50 per person.

TLF Bldg 5243. Large family unit, sleeps five (16); small unit, sleeps four (8). Kitchen, refrigerator, complete utensils, A/C, TV, housekeeping service, laundry facility, cribs, ice machine. Older structure, renovated. Rates: E1-E9 $21.50; Space-A $21.50.

DV/VIP PAO, 2nd Wing, **C-318-456-4228/5335/5077, DSN-312-781-4228.** O6+. Three-bedroom house, fully furnished, O7+ official duty only, no Retirees; one-bedroom suite, private bath (12); two-bedroom, private bath (4). Kitchen, refrigerator, complete utensils, A/C, TV, housekeeping service, laundry facility, ice machine. Older structure, renovated. Rates: suite, $23; house $25.50.

AMENITIES: Internet/E-mail access for customers.

TML AVAILABILITY: Good, all year.

CREDITS CARDS ACCEPTED: Visa and MasterCard.

TRANSPORTATION: Off base shuttle/bus, C-318-221-7433; Car Rentals: C-318-746-5100, C-318-631-1839, C-318-636-2846; On base taxi, C-318-456-4084, DSN-312-781-4084; Off base taxi, C-318-425-3325, C-318-425-7000.

DINING OPPORTUNITIES: O Club, C-318-746-2203 is within walking distance. Dragon House, C-318-752-9001; El Chico, C-318-742-4685; Griff's Hamburgers, C-318-747-5990; Ralph & Kacoos Seafood Restaurant, C-318-747-6660 and many other restaurants are within driving distance.

Visit Barnwell Garden and Art Center and the Shreveport-Bossier City American Rose Center, located in a 118-acre wooded park. Hunting and fishing in season on Barksdale, call Base Forestry C-318-456-2231/3353.

Camp Beauregard (LA12R2)
409 F Street
Pineville, LA 71360-3737

MAIN INSTALLATION TELEPHONE NUMBERS: C-318-640-2080, DSN-312-485-8222/8223. Locator 640-2080; Medical 911; Security Police 442-6603.

LOCATION: West off US-165, seven miles south of Pollock. *USMRA: Page 79 (D-4).* **NMC:** Alexandria, five miles southwest.

RESERVATION INFORMATION: Bldg 1111 F Street, Pineville, LA 71360-3737. **C-318-641-5669, DSN-312-435-5669,** Fax: C-318-641-3422, DSN-312-485-8222/3 ext 302, 0730-1600 Mon-Fri. WEB: cbbilleting.com Duty may make reservations. Directions: Enter Main Gate, proceed down F Street; office at corner of F Street and 15th Street. Check in at billeting, after hours Bldg 409.

BEQ Bldg 1250. E6-E9. Bedroom, shared bath (11). Rates: $6 ($7.36 surcharge for unofficial use). No pets.

BOQ Bldg 1101-1103. Bedroom, shared bath (15); semi-private bedroom, shared bath (20). Refrigerator, TV in lounge. Rates: $6 ($7.36 surcharge for unofficial use). No pets.

DV/VIP Bldg 201, cottage. Bldg 1124, private room, suite bath. Refrigerator, CATV. Rates: $10.

AMENITIES: Exercise Room, Meeting/Conference Room, Snack and Soft Drink Vending Machines.

TML AVAILABILITY: Best, Sept-Apr. More difficult, May-Aug.

CREDIT CARDS ACCEPTED: None.

TRANSPORTATION: Car Rental: C-318-641-1463; Off base taxi, C-318-445-1000.

DINING OPPORTUNITIES: McDonald's, Pizza Hut and Popeye's Chicken are within walking distance. Lee J's of the Levee, C-318-487-4628; Paradise Catfish House, C-318-640-5032; and Tunk's Cypress Inn, C-318-487-4014 are within driving distance.

Fort Polk/Joint Readiness Training Center (LA07R2)
AFZX-PA-FSS
6939 Mississippi Avenue
Fort Polk, LA 71459-5227

MAIN INSTALLATION TELEPHONE NUMBERS: C-337-531-2911, DSN-312-863-1110. Locator 531-1272/3; Medical 537-3143; Security Police 531-2677.

LOCATION: Off US-171, nine miles south of Leesville. East of US-171 south. *USMRA: Page 79 (C-4).* **NMC:** Alexandria, 60 miles southwest.

RESERVATION INFORMATION: Welch Guest House, Bldg 522, Utah Avenue, Fort Polk, LA 71459-7100. **C-337-531-2941, DSN-312-863-2941,** Fax: C-337-535-0968, 24 hours daily. Check in at Welch Guest House, check out 1100 hours. Government civilian employee billeting.

Army Lodging Welch Guest House. Bldg 522. Bedroom, sofabed, private bath (70). Kitchen, microwave, TV, housekeeping service, laundry facility, snack vending. Rates: $33, each additional person $3. Active Duty on PCS, visiting relatives and guests of patients in the hospital and Active and retired military recieving outpatient care can make reservations; others Space-A. No pets in rooms, pet kennels available.

(TML) Bradshaw Court Area. Two bedroom house available for transient PCS In/Out lodging. Shared bath. Rates: $33, each additional person $5. Bldgs 331, 33, Cypress Inn Complex, Duty only (two conference rooms with fax and computer ($10). Room (58). Rates: $33. Inquire about reservations. No pets.

(DV/VIP) Protocol, **C-337-531-1720/21, DSN-312-863-1720.** Bldgs 8-12, 15, 17, 18, 426, 567. O6/GS15+, DoD civilian and Sergeant Major of the Army, official duty only. One-, two-, three- and four-bedrooms, private bath. Kitchen, complete utensils, A/C, TV, housekeeping service. Older structure, renovated. Rates: first person $41, each additional person $5. Bldgs 11, 12 and 426 are $41 per bedroom and $5 each additional person. Upon request, personnel in grades O5+, on PCS in/out, may be given tentative, unconfirmed reservations. No pets.

TML AVAILABILITY: Good, Oct-Mar. Difficult, other times.

CREDIT CARDS ACCEPTED: Visa, MasterCard and American Express.

TRANSPORTATION: Car Rental, C-318-537-8694; On/off base taxi, C-337-239-6006.

DINING OPPORTUNITIES: AAFES Food Court, C-337-537-1001; Sports USA, Primo's Express, and Burger King, C-337-537-7948 are within walking distance. Catfish Junction, C-337-239-0985; Szechuan Chinese Restaurant, C-337-238-2568; and Wagon Master Steak House are within driving distance.

Best known for its outdoor recreation, the area is a paradise for hunters, and fishermen. Early Indian sites, a history that reads like a who's who of American legendary characters and Lake Charles festivals are all of interest.

Jackson Barracks/Army National Guard Base (LA13R2)
Military Department, State of Louisiana
Bldg 57, Jackson Barracks
New Orleans, LA 70146-0330

MAIN INSTALLATION TELEPHONE NUMBERS: C-504-278-1110, DSN-312-485-1110. Locator 278-8364; Medical 911; Security Police 278-8460/911.

LOCATION: From Baton Rouge, take I-10 east to I-10/I-610 east to exit 2. Go straight over an overpass, then cross a drawbridge. Entrance to Jackson Barracks is about 2 miles past drawbridge. Claiborne Avenue will go through Jackson Barracks. *USMRA: Page 90 (F-3,4).* **NMC:** New Orleans, in city limits.

RESERVATION INFORMATION: Bldg 57. **C-504-278-8364, DSN-312-485-8364,** Fax: C-504-278-8715, DSN-312-485-8715, 0730-1630 hours Mon-Fri, 0730-1530 Sat-Sun, after hours report to Security (Bldg 57). Reservations required; can be made two weeks in advance. Directions: Enter Area A towards the river. Second building, Bldg 57, on left. Check in 1500 hours at Billeting Office, check out 0900 hours.

(BEQ) Bldg 214. E1-E5 leave or official duty. Bedroom (11), hall bath, hall telephone, TV and vending machine in lounge. Bldgs 301, E1-E4, open bay barracks, male and female separate sides; 70 beds (35 male and 35 female). Refrigerator, microwave, billard table, TV, pay phone and vending machine in lounge. Rates: Bldg 214 $12 per person; Bldg 301, $8 per person. No smoking. No pets.

(BOQ) SNCOQ, Bldg 27. E6-O4 leave or official duty. Bedrooms, private bath (4); bedrooms, shared bath (16). Rates: $15-$20 per person, maximum $30. Reservations required. No smoking. No pets.

(TVQ) Bldg 209. E6+, leave or official duty. Apartments. One bedroom with one bed, sleeper sofa, private bath; Two bedroom with three beds, sleeper sofa, private bath. Handicap accessible. Kitchenette, utensils, TV. Rates: $35 per night. No smoking. No Pets

(DV/VIP) Bldgs 24, 30, 34, 50. O5+, leave or official duty. Bedroom with private bath (7). Kitchenette, utensils, TV. Rates: $30 per person, maximum $40. No smoking. No pets.

Note: Laundry Facilities for all lodging available in Bldg 212.

TML AVAILABILITY: Fairly good Jan-May and Sept-Dec. Most difficult Jun-Aug. No availability first weekend of every month.

CREDIT CARDS ACCEPTED: Visa, MasterCard, and American Express.

TRANSPORTATION: Off base bus, RTA C-504-248-3900; Off base car rental, Thrifty Car Rental C-504-463-0800; Off base taxi, Arabi Cab C-504-279-7225; United Cab C-504-522-9771.

DINING OPPORTUNITIES: Bubba John's, Docker's and Mutt's are within driving distance.

New Orleans Naval Air Station/Joint Reserve Base (LA11R2)
400 Russell Avenue
New Orleans, LA 70143-5012

MAIN INSTALLATION TELEPHONE NUMBERS: C-504-678-1110, DSN-312-678-1110. Locator 678-3011; Medical 911; Security Police-678-3827.

LOCATION: Take I-10 to US-90 Business West, cross the Crescent City Connection Bridge to the Westbank Expressway. Exit at Lafayette Street. Make a left turn at the traffic light after the tunnel, make a right turn to go to the back gate or stay on Highway 23 (Belle Chasse Highway) about 5-6 miles to go into the Main Gate. Clearly marked. *USMRA: Page 79 (H-7), page 90 (F-6).* **NMC:** New Orleans, 10 miles north.

RESERVATION INFORMATION: CBH, Bldg 40, 400 Russell Avenue, Belle Chasse, LA 70143-1001. **C-504-678-3419, DSN-312-678-3419,** Fax: C-504-678-9745, DSN-312-678-9745, 24 hours daily. Check in at facility 1400 hours, check out 1200 hours. Reservations 45 days in advance on official orders; Space-A available 24 hours in advance. Government civilian employee billeting.

(CBH) Bldgs 21, 22, 40, 45. Bedrooms, shared or private bath (BOQ). Double room, shared bath (BEQ). Refrigerator, A/C, housekeeping service, laundry facility, gym, mini mart, exchange. Barracks structure, renovated. Rates: BOQ: room $15, suite $31; BEQ: shared room $6, private room $12. No smoking. No pets.

(Mobile Home) MWR Campground. **C-504-678-3448/3142, DSN-312-678-3448/3142, Fax: C-504-678-3552, DSN-312-363-3552.** Check in at Auto Hobby Shop, Bldg 143. Directions (to campground): From Main Gate, stay in right lane and bear right at fork in road. MWR pool and parking lot will be on the right, make next right. Road dead ends to camp. Mobile home, two-bedroom, kitchen (1). Rates: $30 daily. **See *Military Living's Military RV, Camping and Outdoor Recreation Around the World* for additional information and directions.**

AMENITIES: Meeting/Conference Room. Ice, Soft Drink and Snack Vending Machines.

TML AVAILABILITY: Good, except on drill weekends.

CREDIT CARDS ACCEPTED: Visa, MasterCard, American Express and Discover.

TRANSPORTATION: Off base taxi, C-504-368-3300.

DINING OPPORTUNITIES: Bowling Center, C-504-678-3514; Galley, C-504-678-3421; and Navy Exchange, C-504-678-3580 are within walking distance. Burger King, C-504-393-1009; McDonald's, C-504-394-7951; and Subway, C-504-391-2090 are within driving distance.

Should you be unable to get lodging here, don't forget there is a Navy Lodge at the Naval Support Activity nearby, call 1-800-NAVY-INN.

New Orleans Naval Support Activity (LA06R2)
Family Service Center, Bldg 732
2300 General Meyer Avenue
New Orleans, LA 70142-5007

MAIN INSTALLATION TELEPHONE NUMBERS: C-504-678-1110, DSN-312-678-1110. Locator 678-3011; Medical 911; Security Police 678-2570.

LOCATION: On the west bank of the Mississippi River. From I-10 east, take Mississippi River Bridge to the west bank. Take Gen. DeGaulle east exit after passing over bridge and turn left at Shirley Drive, which leads to NSA. *USMRA: Page 90 (E,F-3,4).* **NMC:** New Orleans, in city

RESERVATION INFORMATION: CBQ. 89 Constitution Avenue, Bldg 700, New Orleans, LA 70142-5007. **C-504-678-2220/2252, DSN-312-678-2220/2252,** Fax: C-504-678-2781, DSN-312-678-2781, 24 hours daily. Check in at facility, check out 1400 hours, check out 1200 hours. Reservations 45 days in advance on official orders; Space-A 24 hours in advance. Government civilian employee lodging.

(BOQ/BEQ) Bldgs 700, 703, 705, 712. E7+ Bedroom, private bath (255); suite, private bath (12). A/C, TV, housekeeping service, laundry facility, exercise room, mini mart, exchange. Barracks structure, renovated. Rates: BOQ: suite $31, room $15; BEQ: shared room $6, private room $10. No pets.

(NAVY LODGE) Navy Lodge. Bldg 771, Hebert Drive, New Orleans, LA. 70142-5060. **C-1-800-NAVY-INN.** Lodge number is C-504-366-3266, Fax: C-504-362-3752, 0600-2300 hours. WEB: www.navy-nex.com/lodge/united_states/index.html Directions: Through Main Gate, left on Hebert Drive, lodge is 1.5 blocks on right. Check in 1500-1800 hours, check out 1200 hours. Bedroom, two queen beds, private bath or bedroom one queen bed and one queen-size sleeper sofa (26). Kitchen, refrigerator, microwave, coffee/tea in room, USA Today in lobby (Mon-Fri) utensils, A/C, CATV/VCR, video rental, clock, housekeeping service, coin laundry facility, iron/ironing board, cribs, highchairs, rollaways, safety deposit box, playground, ramps for DAVs. Business Class rooms feature couch and sitting area and desk with computer access. Modern structure, remodeled; expansion opened December 2000. Rates: $56 per unit. Maximum four per unit. All categories may make reservations, availability difficult. No pets. *Note: A $2.235 million Navy Lodge addition was approved in the DoD Fiscal Year 2001 NAF Construction Program. Completion of the 24-room addition is expected to be by Jan 2002.*

(DV/VIP) BOQ VIP, C-504-678-2104; BEQ VIP, C-504-678-2208. E7/O6+. BOQ VIP suites (2). A/C, TV, housekeeping service, laundry facility, ice machine, exercise room, meeting/conference room, mini mart. Rates per room: BOQ VIP $31, BEQ VIP $10. Lower ranks Space-A. No Retirees.

AMENITIES: Ice, Snack and Soft Drink Vending Machines.

TML AVAILABILITY: Good, Nov-Jan. Difficult, Apr-Sep.

CREDIT CARDS ACCEPTED: The BOQ accepts Visa and MasterCard. The BEQ accepts American Express. The Navy Lodge accepts Visa, MasterCard, American Express, Discover and Diners.

TRANSPORTATION: Off base taxi.

DINING OPPORTUNITIES: Fairwinds Club (All hands), C-504-678-2218; McDonald's, C-504-368-6237; and Subway are within walking distance. Applebee's, C-504-361-9700; and Shoney's, C-504-362-5830 are within driving distance.

Visit stately old homes, take a paddle-wheel boat dinner cruise, visit the zoo, and the Aquarium of the Americas. Take in the Garden District and Bourbon Street. The French Quarter is made for strolling. One-half block to Special Services and tickets!

MAINE

Bangor International Airport/Air National Guard (ME10R1)
101st ARW
103 Maineiac Avenue, Suite 505
Bangor, ME 04401-3099

MAIN INSTALLATION TELEPHONE NUMBERS: C-207-942-1110, DSN-312-698-7700. Locator 990-7700; Medical 911; Security Police 990-7212.

LOCATION: Northbound from I-95 take exit 47, Ohio Street, drive west two blocks and turn left, one block to right turn on Union Street (ME-222), past Bangor IAP, turn left on Griffin Road; entrance is 300 yards on right. *USMRA: Page 18 (E-6,7).* **NMC:** Bangor, in city limits

RESERVATION INFORMATION: Pine Tree Inn, Bldg 346, 22 Cleveland Avenue, Bangor ANGB, ME 04401-3099. **C-207-942-2081.** Duty can make reservations; others Space-A. Check out 1200 hours.

(TML) Pine Tree Inn. Bedroom, semi-private bath (46). Community kitchen, refrigerator, housekeeping service, TV lounge, laundry facility, soft drink vending machine. Rates: official $8, unofficial $13.

TML AVAILABILITY: Fairly good any time, except drill weekends, which are poor.

CREDIT CARDS ACCEPTED: Visa and Mastercard.

TRANSPORTATION: Off base shuttle/bus; Car rental; Taxi.

DINING OPPORTUNITIES: Captain Nick's, 207-942-6444; Ground Round, C-207-942-5621; and Nickie's Diner, C-207-942-3430 are within walking distance. Governor's Restaurant, 207-947-3113; Miller's Restaurant, C-207-942-6361; Olive Garden, C-207-942-6209; Red Lobster, 207-942-6511; and Paul's Restaurant, C-207-942-6726 are within driving distance.

Freeport Maine, home of millions of outlet shops, is an easy drive from Bangor ANGB. Acadia National Park and Baxter State Park are approximately 1.5 hours away. New Brunswick is within an easy drive.

Brunswick Naval Air Station (ME07R1)
FSC, 400 Foxtrot
Brunswick NAS, ME 04011-5000

MAIN INSTALLATION TELEPHONE NUMBERS: C-207-921-1110, DSN-312-476-1110. Locator 921-2214; Medical 921-2865; Security Police 921-2587.

LOCATION: From I-95 N, exit Coastal Route 1 north. Take Route 1 four miles to Cooks Corner. Turn right to Main Gate of Brunswick NAS. *USMRA: Page 18 (C-9).* **NMC:** Portland, 30 miles southwest.

RESERVATION INFORMATION: Family Housing Office, Bldg 512, 351 Sewall Street, Brunswick, ME, 04011-5000. **C-207-921-2245, DSN-312-476-2245,** Fax: 207-921-2942, 24 hours daily. Duty may make reservations; families authorized as Space-A only. Check in at facility (Space-A check in 1800 hours), check out 1100 hours. No government civilian employee billeting.

BEQ Single or double bedroom, living area, private bath. Refrigerator, microwave, coffee maker, TV, housekeeping service, laundry facility, cots, picnic tables, tennis courts. Older structure. Rates: single $12; double $7; suite $17.

BOQ Bedroom, living area, private bath. Community kitchen, refrigerator, limited utensils, TV/VCR, video rental, housekeeping service, laundry facility, cots, picnic tables, tennis, sauna. Older structure. Rates: transient and PCS $12; suite $24.

NAVY LODGE Navy Lodge. 1400 Burbank Avenue. Bldg. 31, Brunswick, ME 04011. **1-800-NAVY-INN.** Lodge C-207-921-2206, Fax: 207-721-9028, 0800-2000 hours. Other hours OD, C-207-921-2206. Fax: C-207-721-9028. On base across from NEX. Check in 1500-1800 hours, check out 1200 hours. All rooms have 2 queen-size beds with private bath. Kitchenette, microwave, utensils, dining area, A/C, CATV/VCR, telephone, clock/radio, housekeeping service, coin laundry facility, iron/ironing board, cribs, rollaways. Brand new facility. Rates: $49; summer season (Jun-Oct) $55. All categories may make reservations. Handicap accessible unit (1). No pets.

DV/VIP O6+. Refrigerator, TV/VCR, video rental, housekeeping service, laundry facility. Retirees Space-A.

AMENITIES: Exercise Room, Meeting/Conference Room. Ice, Snack and Soft Drink Vending Machines.

TML AVAILABILITY: Good, Sep-Jan. Difficult, Apr-Aug.

CREDIT CARDS ACCEPTED: Visa, MasterCard, American Express and Discover.

TRANSPORTATION: Car Rental, C-207-725-1344; Off base taxi, C-207-729-3688.

DINING OPPORTUNITIES: McDonald's, C-207-729-8746; Subway; and Neptune Hall Galley, C-207-921-2293 are within walking distance. Cook's Lobster House, C-207-833-2818; J. R. Maxwell's, C-207-443-2014; and Richard's, C-207-729-9673 are within driving distance.

Fishing and hunting are considered "tops" here. Sixty ski areas, including Sugarloaf (it has a 9,000 foot gondola line) make winter skiing here a favorite. If you've never tasted shrimp or lobster, do it here! Freeport (home of L.L. Bean) is just 15 minutes south.

Prospect Harbor Naval Satellite Operations Center (ME16R1)
Detachment Alfa (NAVSOC)
P. O. Box 229
Prospect Harbor, ME 04669-0229

MAIN INSTALLATION TELEPHONE NUMBERS: C-207-963-7700, Fire C-963-7788.

LOCATION: From I-95 at Bangor, exit 45A to I-395, exit 6A to US-A1 southeast through Ellsworth to ME-195 southeast to Prospect Harbor and NAVSOC, Detachment Alfa. *USMRA: Page 18 (F-8).* **NMC:** Bangor, 50 miles northwest. NMI: Winter Harbor Naval Security Group Activity, 5 miles south.

RESERVATION INFORMATION: Gull Cottage. Reservations are accepted 0800-1100 hours on the first working day of the month preceding the month in which reservations are desired. **C-207-963-7700.** 06+ reservations with NAVSOC HQ Senior Enlisted Advisor, **C-805-989-4212/4211, DSN 312-351-4212/4211.** Check in after 1300 hours, check

out no later than 1000 hours to avoid extra charges. Period of scheduled occupancy is from two to five nights.

Cottage **Gull Cottage.** The cottage and associated lighthouse are landmarks of unparalleled quality. Renovated in 1969, the cottage is a two-story building with two bedrooms, a living room, study, kitchen, and bath. Fully furnished, it includes complete kitchen facilities with microwave oven, range, refrigerator, cooking utensils and dinner service. Designed for six occupants. Larger groups require CO's approval. Rates: $20-$60 depending on rank.

AMENITIES: Laundry facilities in the basement of cottage.

TML AVAILABILITY: Extremely limited and difficult, year round.

CREDIT CARDS ACCEPTED: Only exact cash or checks accepted.

TRANSPORTATION: None

DINING OPPORTUNITIES: Food and beverages available at Winter Harbor Naval Security Group Activity, 5 miles south. Local restaurants.

Near Acadia National Park, favorite location for hunters, fishermen, snow and water skiers.

Winter Harbor Naval Security Group Activity (ME09R1)
10 Fabbri Green, Suite 10
Winter Harbor, ME 04693-0900
This facility closed June 2002.

MAIN INSTALLATION TELEPHONE NUMBERS: C-207-963-1110, DSN-312-476-1110. Locator 963-5534/5535; Medical ext 297/298; Security Police ext 425/294.

LOCATION: From Ellsworth, take US-1 north to ME-186 east to Acadia National Park. Naval Security Station on Schoodic Point in the park. *USMRA: Page 18 (F-8).* **NMC:** Bangor, 45 miles northwest.

RESERVATION INFORMATION: 10 Fabbri Green, Suite 84, Winter Harbor, ME 04693-7020. **C-207-963-5534 ext 223/203, DSN-312-476-9223/9203,** Fax: C-207-963-3039, DSN-312-476-9281, 0730-2330 hours. E-mail: jsutton@nsgawh.navy.mil Duty may make reservations; others Space-A. Directions: From Main Gate, take first left; drive through parking lot past the stop sign. lodging office (Fabbri Hall, Bldg 84) is last brick building on the right. Check in at billeting, check out 1300 hours. Government civilian employee billeting. *Note: This facility is downsizing until the final closure in June 2002. Be sure to call ahead for most recent information. The recreation area is scheduled to remain open.*

BEQ Fabbri Hall. Bldg 84. Bedroom, shared bath (E1-E6) (12). Community kitchen, refrigerator, microwave, coffee maker, CATV/VCR, HBO, movie rentals, housekeeping service, laundry facility, iron/ironing board. Modern structure. Rates: $9, each additional adult $2.25, each child $1.00.

CBQ Bldg 192. E7-E9. Suite, private bath (12). Kitchen, refrigerator, microwave, coffee maker, limited utensils, CATV/VCR, HBO, movie rentals, housekeeping service, laundry facility, iron/ironing board, garage. Modern structure. Rates: $12, each additional adult $4.25, each child $1.00. Maximum two per room.

Cabins & Trailers MWR cabins and trailers. **Winter Harbor Recreation Area. C-207-963-5534 ext 287/282.** Cabin, three-bedroom, private bath (6), fully furnished, sleep six. Kitchen, microwave, dishes, utensils, TV/VCR, crib/playpen, gas fireplace. Trailers, 14 by 70 feet, three-bedroom, 1.5 baths (5), sleep six. (Built in 1997.) Full kitchen, washer/dryer, living room. Full range of recreational opportunities, both summer and winter. Close to base support activities. Knox cabin is handicap accessible. Rates: May-Oct $65, Nov-Apr $50. All categories may make reservations (90 days in advance during peak season). ***Pets allowed in trailers*** for additional $10 fee.

AMENITIES: Exercise Room, Meeting/Conference Room, Mini Mart, Snack and Soft Drink Vending Machines.

TML AVAILABILITY: Good, Nov-Mar. Difficult, May-Sep.

CREDIT CARDS ACCEPTED: Visa, MasterCard, American Express and Discover.

TRANSPORTATION: Off base shuttle/bus: Down East Transportation, C-207-667-5796; Car Rental: Enterprise, C-207-667-1217; Off base taxi: Towne Taxi, C-207-667-1000.

DINING OPPORTUNITIES: Galley Restaurant, C-207-963-5534 ext 244, DSN-312-476-9253; Schooner Club, C-207-963-5534 ext 283; and Chases Restaurant C-207-963-7171 are within walking distance. Fisherman's Inn Restaurant, C-207-963-5585; and Ocean Wood Gallery Restaurant, C-207-963-2653 are within driving distance.

Located in Schoodic Point section of Acadia National Park, this is a favorite with hunters, fishermen, snow and water skiers. For additional information on the rec area, read *Military Living's Military RV, Camping and Outdoor Recreation Around the World.*

MARYLAND

Aberdeen Proving Ground (MD11R1)
Commander, U.S. Army Test & Evaluation Command
Army Community Service
Bldg 2754 Rodman Road
Aberdeen PG, MD 21005-2001

MAIN INSTALLATION TELEPHONE NUMBERS: (Aberdeen/Edgewood Area) C-410-278-1110, DSN-312-298-1110. Medical 410-278-1725; Security Police 410-306-0564.
Ten-digit dialing required for local calls.

LOCATION: Aberdeen Area: From I-95, take exit 85 to MD-22 east for two miles to Main Gate. From Main Gate at third light turn right, at next light turn left. Then at third light turn left, the building is behind the Post Office (Bldg 2207). Edgewood Area: From I-95 take exit 77 to MD-24 east then turn left onto MD-755 to the Main Gate. From the Main Gate make a right onto Austin Road, then a left onto Parrish Road. Office will be on your left. (Bldg E-4650 the office is in the back of the building in room 9). *USMRA: Page 42 (G-2,3).* **NMC:** Baltimore, 23 miles southwest.

RESERVATION INFORMATION: Aberdeen Area: Bldg 2207, Bel Air Street, Aberdeen PG, MD 21005-5001. **C-410-278-5148/5149, DSN-312-298-4373/5148,** Fax: C-410-278-5515, 24 hours daily. Edgewood Area: Bldg E 4650, Parrish Road, EA-Aberdeen PG, MD 21010. **C-410-436-3848, DSN-312-584-3848,** Fax: C-410-612-0979, 0630-2245 daily. E-mail: angela.ferrell@usag.apg.army.mil Check in 1300 hours, check out 1100 hours.

(TLQ) **Swan Creek Inn** Bldg 2207 (Aberdeen Area) and **River Lodge** Bldg E4650 (Edgewood Area). Several buildings; official duty. Bedroom, private bath (212); bedroom, shared bath (83). Kitchenette, A/C, TV in room, housekeeping service, laundry facility. Older structure, recently remodeled. Rates: $44-$48. Active Duty, Reservists, NG and TDY civilians may make reservations. No pets.

(PCS) Bldg 2505 (Aberdeen Area). Check in at Bldg 2207. Room with one double bed, private bath, living room, and shared kitchen (3); Two bedroom each with double bed, private bath, living room, kitchen (16). A/C, TV, housekeeping service, cribs, cots, highchairs, laundry facility. PCS in/out reservations can be made up to 30 days in advance. Rate: $44. No Pets.

(DV/VIP) Bldg 30 (Aberdeen Area), Bldg E4650 (Edgewood Area). Reservations **C-410-278-5148.** E9, O6/GS15/CW4+. Bldg 30: private suite (6). Bldg E4650: private suite (2). Kitchen, complete utensils, A/C, TV, housekeeping service, cribs, cots. Rates: $62. Duty, leave and Retirees may make reservations. No pets.

AMENITIES: Exercise Room, Meeting/Conference Room, Snack and Soft Drink Machines.

TML AVAILABILITY: Good, Nov-Jan. Difficult, other times.

CREDIT CARDS ACCEPTED: Visa, MasterCard and American Express.

TRANSPORTATION: Off base taxi, Victory Cab C-410-272-0880.

DINING OPPORTUNITIES: Burger King, C-410-273-7464; and The Patio, C-410-273-7050 are within walking distance. Bob Evans, C-410-569-7008; Japan House Restaurant, C-410-575-7878; Colonel's Choice, C-410-272-6500; McDonald's, C-410-272-7668 and Olive Tree Restaurant, C-410-272-6217 are within driving distance.

On the Chesapeake Bay. Hunting, fishing, boating, three golf courses, two swimming pools, theater, bowling alley, fitness center. Baltimore is 30 miles south, D.C. 75 miles south, and Philadelphia 92 miles north. Lots to do here.

Andrews Air Force Base (MD02R1)
89 MSS/DPF
Attn: RAP Manager
1610 California Avenue, Suite 100
Andrews AFB, MD 20762-6421

MAIN INSTALLATION TELEPHONE NUMBERS: C-301-981-1110, DSN-312-858-1110. Locator 301-981-1110; Medical 911; Security Police 911.
Ten-digit dialing required for local calls.

LOCATION: From I-95 N (east portion of Capital Beltway, I-495) take exit 9; first traffic light after leaving exit ramp turn left. At next traffic light turn right into Main Gate of AFB. Also, from I-395 N, exit South Capitol Street, cross Anacostia River bear left to Suitland Parkway E, exit at Morningside on Suitland Road east to Main Gate of AFB. From I-495 S, take exit 9; turn right at stop sign, turn right at next light onto Allentown Road; turn left into Main Gate on Suitland Road. *USMRA: Page 42 (E-5), Page 55 (I,J-6,7).* **NMC:** Washington, D.C., 10 miles northwest.

RESERVATION INFORMATION: Gateway Inn, 89th SVS/SVML, 1375 Arkansas Road, Andrews AFB, MD 20762-7002. **C-1-888-AFLODGE (1-888-235-6343), C-301-981-0785, DSN-312-858-0785,** Fax: C-301-981-9277, DSN-312-858-9277, 24 hours daily. Reservations: Fax: C-301-981-9277. E-mail: JosieForcle@andrews.af.mil WEB: www.andrews.af.mil Duty may make reservations any time; Space-A may make reservations 24 hours in advance. Directions: Immediate left on Brookley Avenue, follow to Arkansas Road and take a left. The Gateway Inn is located on the left hand side. Check in 1500 hours, check out 1100 hours. All guests are required to pay in advance. Handicap accessible units available. Government civilian employee billeting.

(TLF) Bldgs 1801-1804, 1328, 1330. Check out 1000 hours. Separate bedrooms, private bath (68). Kitchen, utensils, A/C, TV, housekeeping service, laundry facility, cribs, ice machine, iron/ironing board. Modern structure. Rates: $24.50. Maximum five per room. ***Recent improvements to rooms: new carpet, wallpaper and walls painted.***

(VAQ) Bldgs 1373, 1376, 158, 1629. E1-E6. Suite, private bath (7); Chief suite (1); room, shared bath (65). Refrigerator, microwave, A/C, TV/VCR, soft drink and snack vending, iron/ironing board. Rates: singles $17.50. Reservations required.

VQ Bldgs 1349, 1360-1371. E1-O6. Bedroom, private bath (30); suites, private bath (60). Refrigerator, microwave, A/C, TV/VCR, iron/ironing board. Rates: single $20.

Fisher House Malcolm Grow Medical Center, 1076 West Perimeter Road, Andrews AFB, MD 20762-5000. **C-301-981-1243**, Fax: C-301-981-7629. *Note: Appendix B has the definition of this facility. Fisher Houses are only available as lodging for families of patients receiving medical care at military and VA medical centers.*

DV/VIP Protocol, 89 AW/CCP, **C-301-981-4525**. Bldg 1349. O7+. Bedroom, private bath (31), DV suite, private bath (8). Kitchen, A/C, TV, housekeeping service, laundry facility, iron/ironing board. Rates: single $25.

TML AVAILABILITY: Best, Dec-Feb. Difficult, Mar-Nov.

CREDIT CARDS ACCEPTED: Visa and MasterCard.

TRANSPORTATION: On base shuttle/bus C-301-981-4661, DSN-312-858-4661; On/Off base Car Rental. Off base taxi.

DINING OPPORTUNITIES: O Club, C-301-420-4744; and Sports Page, C-301-981-4638 are within walking distance. BX Food Court; Burger King; and E Club, C-301-568-3100 are within driving distance.

Andrews is the military aerial gateway to Washington, D.C. for most overseas VIPs, and the home of "Air Force One," the President's aircraft. If you're lucky you can witness "important people" coming and going here.

Bethesda National Naval Medical Center (MD06R1)

8901 Wisconsin Avenue, Bldg 1
Bethesda, MD 20889-5600

MAIN INSTALLATION TELEPHONE NUMBERS: C-301-295-1110, DSN-312-295-1110 (Hospital Information). Locator 301-295-4611; Medical 301-295-2156; Security Police 301-295-1246.
Ten-digit dialing required for local calls.

LOCATION: From VA: Take I-495 N to Wisconsin Avenue exit. Stay in left lane through two lights to NNMC entrance on left. From MD: Take I-95 S to I-495 W to Connecticut Avenue exit. Stay in center lane to light, turn left onto Connecticut Avenue. At next light turn right onto Jones Bridge Road, right on Wisconsin Avenue, right at next light into NNMC. *USMRA: Page 55 (D,E-1).* **NMC:** Washington, D.C., one mile southeast.

RESERVATION INFORMATION: Lodging Office, 8901 Wisconsin Avenue, Bldg 60, Bethesda, MD 20889-5600. **C-301-295-5855/1111, DSN-312-295-0321/0307**, Fax: C-301-295-6316, DSN-312-295-6316. Check in at facility, check out 1200 hours. Government civilian employee lodging. No government employee billeting.

CBQ Bldg 11, 60. Official duty. Reservations required. Bedroom, private bath (81); bedroom, private bath (5). Community kitchen, refrigerator, microwave, coffee maker, utensils, A/C, CATV/VCR in lounge, video rental, alarm clock, hair dryer, housekeeping service, laundry facility, cribs, rollaways (upon request). Rates: transient single $18, double $20; Enlisted (E4 and below) transient single $12, double $20.

NAVY LODGE Navy Lodge. Bldg 52, 8901 Wisconsin Avenue, Bethesda, MD 20889-5600. **C-1-800-NAVY-INN.** Lodge number is C-301-654-1795, 24 hours daily, Fax: C-301-295-5955. Medical and PCS have priority. Check in 1500 hours, check out 1200 hours. There are 72 units: Bedroom, two double beds, private bath, kitchenette; single room, queen-size bed. Microwave, A/C, CATV/VCR, video rental, phone/fax service, housekeeping service, coin laundry facility, cribs, highchairs, rollaways, iron/ironing board, lounge. All units non-smoking. Modern structure. Four sets interconnecting units. Rates: $64. PCS/patients may make reservations any time; Active Duty 60 days in advance; Retirees/Reservists 30 days in advance. No pets. *The Navy Lodge is currently undergoing a 57-room expansion, due to be completed in 2001.*

Fisher House National Naval Medical Center, 24 Stokes Road, Bethesda, MD 20814-5002. C-301-295-5334, Fax: C-301-295-5632. *Note: Appendix B has the definition of this facility. There are two Fisher Houses at NNMC. Fisher Houses are only available as lodging for families of patients receiving medical care at military and VA medical centers.*

AMENITIES: Exercise Room, Meeting/Conference Room, Mini Mart. Ice, Snack and Soft Drink Vending Machines.

TML AVAILABILITY: Very limited.

CREDIT CARDS ACCEPTED: Visa, MasterCard, American Express, Diners. The Navy Lodge accepts Visa, MasterCard, American Express and Discover.

TRANSPORTATION: On/Off base shuttle/bus, C-301-295-4611; Car Rental, 301-907-7780; Off base taxi, C-301-984-1900.

DINING OPPORTUNITIES: Base Galley, Chinese Express, Crab House and McDonald's are within walking distance. Kokopellis Pizza, TGI Friday's and Subway are within driving distance.

Bethesda is located just north of Washington D.C., shopping and the Metro are close by.

Curtis Bay Coast Guard Yard (MD01R1)

2401 Hawkins Point Road
Baltimore, MD 21226-5000

MAIN INSTALLATION TELEPHONE NUMBERS: C-410-636-4194. Locator 410-636-7494; Medical 410-636-3144; Security Police 410-636-3993.
Ten-digit dialing required for local calls.

LOCATION: Take I-695, exit 1, bear to your right, first right on Hawkins Point Road, 0.25 mile to left into Coast Guard Yard. *USMRA: Page 42 (F-3), page 49 (C-4).* **NMC:** Baltimore, two miles north.

RESERVATION INFORMATION: Family Transient Lodging, 2401 Hawkins Point Road, Bldg 143/Mail Stop 3, Baltimore, MD 21226-1797. **C-410-636-7373**, Fax: 410-636-7496, 0900-1500 hours, Mon-Fri. E-mail: Jcurrie@cgyard.uscg.mil Check in at 1400 hours at Columbus Recreation Center, check out 1000 hours. Reservations required.

CBQ Berry Hall. Bldg 28A. Active Duty or Retirees. One Bedroom, two single beds, private bath (5). Refrigerator, microwave, A/C, TV/VCR, laundry facility, SATV, pool table in lounge. Modern structure. Rates: E1-E4, $13; E5-E7, $16; E8-O3, $18; all others $21.

TLF Steibyck Grove. Bldg 84. Three-bedroom suite (1); two-bedroom suite (4). Master bedroom, queen-size bed, all other rooms, twin beds. Living room, dining area, sofabed, private bath. Fully equipped kitchen, complete utensils, A/C, TV, pay phone, housekeeping service, laundry facility. Rates based on rank: three-bedroom suite $33-$48; two-bedroom suite $28-$43.

AMENITIES: Base Exchange, Recreation Center, Small children's playground and Soft Drink Vending Machines.

TML AVAILABILITY: Good, Oct-Apr. More difficult, other times.

CREDIT CARDS ACCEPTED: Visa and MasterCard. Payment for Family Transient Lodging due upon check in.

TRANSPORTATION: Car Rental; Off base taxi.

DINING INFORMATION: Dry Dock All Hands Club is within walking distance, hours: Lunch-11:30-12:30 (daily specials); Bar 1600-2400 (limited menu).

Southeast of Baltimore, a city rich in history and entertainment, where the Inner Harbor buzzes with shopping, dining and recreational opportunities.

Fort Detrick Army Garrison (MD07R1)
Commander, USAG
Attn: MCHD-PCS (ACS)
810 Schreider Street
Fort Detrick, MD 21702-5016

MAIN INSTALLATION TELEPHONE NUMBERS: C-301-619-8000, DSN-312-343-1110. Locator 301-619-2233; Medical 301-619-7175; Security Police 301-619-7114.
Ten-digit dialing required for local calls.

LOCATION: From Washington, D.C., take I-270 N to US-15 N. From Baltimore take I-70 W to US-15 N. From US-15 N, in Frederick, exit Seventh Street to post. Clearly marked. *USMRA: Page 42 (D-2).* **NMC:** Baltimore, 50 miles east; Washington, D.C., 50 miles southeast.

RESERVATION INFORMATION: MCHD-PCH, 810 Schreider Street, Suite 400, Frederick, MD 21702-5033. **C-301-619-2154, DSN-312-343-2154,** Fax: C-301-619-2010, 0800-1600 hours Mon-Fri. Check out 1000 hours. Government civilian employee billeting.

(Army Lodging) Bldgs 800, 801. Two-bedroom, private bath (1); three-bedroom, private bath (3). Kitchen, microwave, dishwasher, utensils, A/C, CATV, phone, housekeeping service, iron/ironing board, laundry facility, sofabed. Completely modernized. Rates: $36 per unit. PCS can make reservations; others Space-A. No pets.

(VOQ) Bldg 660. Bedroom suite, double beds, private bath (16). Kitchen, microwave, limited utensils, A/C, CATV, phone, housekeeper service, laundry facility, iron/ironing board, sofabed. Older structure, remodeled. Rates: $24.50 per room. TDY may make reservations; others Space-A. No pets.

(DVQ) Bldg 715. Officers. Suite, queen-size bed, private bath (1). Kitchen, microwave, limited utensils, A/C, CATV, phone, housekeeping service, iron/ironing board. Older structure, remodeled. Rates: $32. TDY may make reservations; others Space-A. No pets.

(DV/VIP) HQ Fort Detrick. **C-301-619-2154.** O6+. Retirees and lower ranks Space-A.

AMENITIES: Snack and Soft Drink Vending Machines.

TML AVAILABILITY: Good, Oct-Mar. Difficult, Jun-Aug.

CREDIT CARDS ACCEPTED: Visa, MasterCard, American Express and MOST (debit).

TRANSPORTATION: Off base shuttle/bus, C-301-694-2065; Off base taxi, C-301-662-2250.

DINING OPPORTUNITIES: Fast food and other restaurants are within driving distance.

Historic Frederick County offers visitors a variety of cultural, sports and recreational options. Both Baltimore and Washington, D.C. are nearby.

Fort George G. Meade (MD08R1)
Attn: ANME-PEC-A-(RAP)
3179 MacArthur Road
Fort Meade, MD 20755-5078

MAIN INSTALLATION TELEPHONE NUMBERS: C-301-677-1110, DSN-312-923-1110. Locator 301-677-6261; Medical 301-677-2570; Security Police 301-677-6622.
Ten-digit dialing required for local calls.

LOCATION: From north: I-95 S to Baltimore. Take I-695 W (Baltimore-Washington Pkwy) around Baltimore. Take Fort Meade exit (Route 175 east).Two miles, turn right at Mapes Road. From south: I-295 Baltimore-Washington Pkwy N. Exit at Route 198 (Fort Meade). Turn right on 32 E. Exit onto Route 175 (Odenton). Turn left. At third traffic light, turn left onto Mapes Road. From east: (Annapolis) Route 50 W, take I-97 N to Route 32 W. Follow Route 32 to Route 175. Follow sign to Fort Meade (bear right). At second traffic light, turn left onto Mapes Road. From west: (Howard County and I-95) Follow Route 32 S, exit Route 175 (Fort Meade/Odenton). Turn left. Left onto Mapes Road. *USMRA: Page 42 (E, F-4).* **NMC:** Baltimore, 15 miles north; Washington, D.C., 25 miles south.

RESERVATION INFORMATION: Army Lodging, Brett Hall, 4707 Ruffner Road, P.O. Box 1069, Fort George G. Meade, MD 20755-5502. **C-301-677-6529/5884, DSN-312-923-5884,** Fax: C-301-677-4704, 24 hours daily. E-mail: bearde@emh1.ftmeade.army.mil Check in at billeting, check out 1200 hours. Government civilian employee billeting.

(BOQ) Bldgs 4717, 4720. C-301-677-9395, DSN-312-923-9395. Official duty. Separate bedroom, private bath (62). Rates: No charge. PCS to Fort Meade.

(SEBQ) Bldg 4721. C-301-677-9395, DSN-312-923-9395. E7-E9, official duty. Separate bedroom, private bath (30). Older structure. Rates: No charge. For SNCO on PCS to Fort Meade.

(VOQ) Bldgs 4703-4705, 4707, 4709. Bedroom, semi-private bath (142); one bedroom, private bath (4); separate bedroom suite, private bath (46). Kitchen (44), refrigerator, A/C, CATV, housekeeping service, laundry facility, ice machine. Older structures, bathrooms renovated. Rates: shared bath $32.50, private bath $40 on orders; all others $42.50; suite $44 on orders; all others $52 . TDY room confirmation duration of stay, confirmed 60 days in advance.

(Army Lodging) Abrams Hall, Family Quarters. Bldg 2793 Hawkins Drive. C-410-672-1929/1975, DSN-312-923-5660/2045. Check in 1400 hours. Bedroom with two beds, private bath (54). Community kitchen, refrigerator, microwave, A/C, CATV, phone, housekeeping service, laundry facility, cribs, snack vending, ice machine. Has a fenced playground. Older structure, completely renovated 1993-1994. Handicap accessible. Rates: PCS/TDY, single $35, double $39; Visitors, single $39, double $43, each additional person $5. Priorities: PCS, hospital visitors, visitors of Active Duty assigned, TDY may stay 30 days. Reservations 30 days in advance, one night confirmed stay. (This does not pertain to personnel who are PCS, hospital visitors, Active Duty assigned, TDY, etc.)

(DVQ) Kuhn Hall, Bldg 4415, Llewellyn Avenue. O5+. Separate bedrooms, private bath (5); two-bedroom, private bath (2). Kitchen, limited utensils, A/C, TV, housekeeping service, laundry facility. Older structure, renovated. Rates: TDY/PCS $44; all others $52. Reservations 60 days in advance.

TML AVAILABILITY: Good. Best months, Oct-Mar.

CREDIT CARDS ACCEPTED: Visa, MasterCard and American Express.

TRANSPORTATION: On base shuttle/bus; Car Rental: Enterprise (in nearby Crofton, free delivery and pickup), C-301-721-3628; On base taxi, C-1-800-818-5255, C-301-850-5255.

DINING OPPORTUNITIES: AAFES/Concessions Mart and Shoppette, C-301-674-7170 are within walking distance. AAFES Main Exchange, C-301-674-7170; Burger King/Fort Meade, C-301-677-6261; and McDonald's (in Odenton), C-301-677-6261 are within driving distance.

Visit Baltimore's Fort McHenry National Monument and new Inner Harbor or see Annapolis' quaint shopping areas. Washington, D.C. is also a short drive from Fort Meade.

Indian Head Division Naval Surface Warfare Center (MD04R1)
101 Strauss Avenue
Indian Head, MD 20640-5000

MAIN INSTALLATION TELEPHONE NUMBERS: C-301-744-4000, DSN-312-354-4000. Locator 301-744-4303; Medical 301-744-4601; Security Police 301-744-4381.
Ten-digit dialing required for local calls.

LOCATION: Take I-495 (Capital Beltway) east, exit to MD-210 S for 25 miles to station. *USMRA: Page 42 (D-5,6).* **NMC:** Washington, D.C., 25 miles north.

RESERVATION INFORMATION: Housing Welcome Center, CBQ (Code 115) Indian Head Division, Bldg 902, Indian Head, MD 20640-5035. **C-301-744-4845, DSN-312-354-4845,** Fax: C-301-744-4486, DSN-312-354-4486, 24 hours daily. Duty may make reservations; others Space-A. Directions: Go straight on Strauss Avenue past golf course to Bldg 902. *Note: As of 2001, the BEQ/BOQ facilities have become permanent party only, though this may change.*

BEQ Bldgs 902, 1752. Bedroom, one bed, semi-private bath (108). A/C, TV, housekeeping service, laundry facility. Rates: $4.50. No Space-A for families or dependents.

CBQ Bldg 1542. Rooms, private bath. A/C, TV/VCR, housekeeping service, laundry facility. Rates: transient $8.75. Duty can make reservations, others Space-A. No Space-A for families or dependents.

DV/VIP PAO. Bldg 20. **C-301-744-4627.** Inquire about qualifying rank. Lodging considered substandard by Navy standards. Retirees Space-A.

AMENITIES: Exercise Room, Snack and Soft Drink Vending Machine.

TML AVAILABILITY: Fair, Jan-May, Sept-Dec. Difficult, other times.

CREDIT CARDS ACCEPTED: Visa, MasterCard and American Express.

TRANSPORTATION: None available.

DINING OPPORTUNITIES: All Hands Dining Facility (Bldg 902); Jerry's Subs & Pizza, C-301-744-6290; Long Horn Inn, C-301-744-5341; and Powder Keg, C-301-744-4648 are within walking distance. Burger King, C-301-375-9066; Golden Star Chinese Restaurant, C-301-283-3327; and Subway, C-301-375-9001 are within driving distance.

Only 25 miles from Washington, D.C. makes this place within "shouting distance" of the many cultural and sporting events available to the area. The nearby Potomac River also provides recreational opportunities.

Patuxent River Naval Air Station (MD09R1)
Family Service Center
21993 Bundy Road
Patuxent River, MD 20670-1132

MAIN INSTALLATION TELEPHONE NUMBERS: C-301-342-3000, DSN-312-342-3000. Locator 301-342-3000; Medical 301-342-1422; Security Police 301-342-3911.
Ten-digit dialing required for local calls.

LOCATION: From I-95 (east portion of Capital Beltway, I-495) take exit 7-A to Branch Avenue (MD-5) south. Follow MD-5 until it becomes MD-235 near Oraville, on to Lexington Park, and the NAS. Main gate is on MD-235 and MD-246 (Cedar Point Road). *USMRA: Page 42 (F-6,7).* **NMC:** Washington, D.C., 65 miles northwest.

RESERVATION INFORMATION: Central Reservations, BOQ Office, Bldg 406, Patuxent River NAWC, MD 20670-5199. **C-301-863-9343, DSN-312-342-3601,** Fax: C-301-342-1015. Check in at facility, check out 1200 hours.

BEQ Bldg 464. Bedroom, double bed, private bath (14). Refrigerator, microwave, A/C, TV/VCR, phone, housekeeping service, cots, laundry facility, ice machine. Rates: $10 per person, each additional person $4. No children.

BOQ Bldg 406. Suite, bedroom double bed, living room area, private bath (60). Kitchen, refrigerator, microwave, A/C, TV/VCR, phone, housekeeping service, cots, laundry facility, ice machine. Handicap accessible (2). Rates: $15 per person, each additional person $8. No children. Reservations only from persons on TAD orders; Retirees Space-A.

NAVY LODGE Navy Lodge. Bldg 2119, 22148 Cuddihy Road, Patuxent River NAS, MD 20670-5000. **C-1-800-NAVY-INN.** Lodge number is C-301-737-2400, Fax: C-301-862-7866, 24 hours daily. From Main Gate turn left on Cuddihy Road, lodge is 0.5 miles on right, across from commissary. Bedroom, two double beds, private bath (50). Kitchenette, microwave, utensils, A/C, CATV/VCR, video rental, HBO, phone, clock radio, hair dryer, laundry facility, iron/ironing board, cribs, highchairs, rollaways, snack vending, ice machine, playground, complimentary coffee and copy of USA Today newspaper. Free local phone calls. Handicap accessible, interconnecting units and non-smoking rooms available. Rates: $48 per room. No pets.

DV/VIP C-301-342-1108. O7+. Suite, king size bed, private bath (4 on site, 2 off site). Living/dining area, kitchen. Rates: $25. Retirees Space-A.

TML AVAILABILITY: Weekends fairly good, very difficult during week.

CREDIT CARDS ACCEPTED: Visa, MasterCard, American Express and Discover. The Navy Lodge also accepts Diners.

TRANSPORTATION: Taxi, C-301-342-5008.

DINING OPPORTUNITIES: Eddy's Three (lunch, Mon-Fri), C-301-342-3200 is within walking distance of BEQ/BOQ. O Club; C-301-342-3656; PAX Landing Restaurant, C-301-342-3293; McDonald's; and Subway are within driving distance.

The Special Interest Coordinator's Office in Bldg 423 (C-301-863-3510) has discount tickets to Kings Dominion, Wild World, Busch Gardens, Hershey Park, local ski resorts, Colonial Williamsburg, sporting events.

Have **YOU** seen this dog? If not, visit **www.militaryliving.com** and read all about Tootie, a military dependent dog. There are letters from other military pets, as well as lots of helpful pet-related travel information!

Solomons Navy Recreation Center (MD05R1)
P.O. Box 147
Solomons, MD 20688-0147

MAIN INSTALLATION TELEPHONE NUMBERS: C-410-326-5000. Locator 410-326-1260; Medical 911; Security Police 410-326-5410. *Ten-digit dialing required for local calls.*

LOCATION: In southern Maryland where the Patuxent River meets the Chesapeake Bay. From US-301 take MD-4 southeast to Solomons; or take MD-5 southeast to MD-235, then MD-4 northeast to Solomons. *USMRA: Page 42 (F-6).* **NMC:** Washington, D.C., 65 miles northwest. NMI: Patuxent River NAS, 10 miles south.

RESERVATION INFORMATION: Lodging Office, Bldg 411, Solomons, MD 20688-0147. **C-410-326-5203/5204, D.C. Area 1-800-NAVY(6289)-230,** Fax: C-410-326-4280, 0700-2200 hours (summer), 0900-1800 hours (off season). Check in at billeting, check out 1100 hours. WEB: www.ndw.navy.mil/MWR/nrcsolomons.html Minimum two nights stay year round and maximum ten night stay from 27 May-4 Sep. All categories except unaccompanied dependents can make reservations. No pets.

Cottages **Classic Cottages.** One to five bedroom cottages with kitchen, refrigerator, microwave. The five bedroom cottage is heated. The other cottages are not heated and they are not available for winter occupancy. Not all units have showers, some have tubs only. Not all bedrooms are private. Rates: In season, E1-E5 $47-$91; E6-E9 $53-$97; Officer $63-$107; DoD $79-$131; Off season, E1-E5 $40-$56; E6-E9 $46-$62; Officer $56-$72; DoD $70-$86. **Remodeled Classic Cottage #2.** Five bedroom cottage remodeled to include gas fireplace, new furnishings and fixtures. Central heat and A/C make it available for year round use. Rates: In season, E1-E5 $93; E6-E9 $99; Officers $109; DoD $133; Off season, E1-E5 $58; E6-E9 $64; Officers $74; DoD $88. **Contemporary Cottages.** Two to five bedroom cottages with kitchen, living room, dining room. Modern style, comfortably furnished. Handicap accessible unit (1). Rates: In season, E1-E5 $58-$91; E6-E9 $64-$97; Officer $74-$107; DoD $92-$131; Off season, E1-E5 $44-$56; E6-E9 $50-$62; Officers $60-$72; DoD $74-$86.

Cabins **Cozy Cabins.** New cedar cabins with master bedroom and loft, kitchen, stove, refrigerator, central heat, A/C, screened in porch. Sleeps six. Rates: In season, E1-E5 $64-$97; E6-E9 $70-$106; Officer $80-$121; DoD $100-151; Off season E1-E5 $43-$65; E6-E9 $49-$74; Officer $59-$89; DoD $73-$110.

TML Apartments. One- to four-bedroom units with fully equipped kitchen, living room, dining room. Playground. Handicap accessible unit (1). Rates: In season, E1-E5 $45-$78; E6-E9 $51-$84; Officer $61-$94; DoD $77-$116; Off season, E1-E5 $38-$50; E6-E9 $44-$56; Officer $54-$66; DoD $68-$80.

TML Bungalows. Three- and four- bedroom units with fully equipped kitchen, heat, A/C. Rates: In season, E1-E5 $55-$66; E6-E9 $61-$72; Officer $71-$82; DoD $91-$104; Off season E1-E5 $34-$38; E6-E9 $40-$44; Officer $50-$54; DoD $64-$68.

Note: All lodging facilities are furnished and equipped with a full kitchen, picnic table and outdoor grill. Soap, TV, small appliances and telephones are not provided. Linens are not provided except for pillows and bed spreads.

AMENITIES: Meeting/Conference Room, Soft Drink Vending Machine.

TML AVAILABILITY: Good, Oct-Apr. Difficult, other times.

CREDIT CARDS ACCEPTED: Visa, MasterCard, American Express and Discover.

TRANSPORTATION: None available.

DINING OPPORTUNITIES: Numerous restaurants are within driving distance.

Complete river recreational/camping area. Full support facility available at nearby Patuxent River NAWC. St. Maries City, Calvert Cliffs, Calvert Marine Museum, Farmers' Market, charter fishing, Point Lookout State Park. For complete details see *Military Living's Military RV, Camping and Outdoor Recreation Around The World.*

United States Naval Academy/ Annapolis Naval Station (MD10R1)
Navy Family Service Center
348 Kinkaid Road
Annapolis, MD 21402-5073

MAIN INSTALLATION TELEPHONE NUMBERS: C-410-293-1000, DSN-312-281-0111. Locator 410-293-1000; Medical 410-293-3333; Security Police 410-293-4444. *Ten-digit dialing required for local calls.*

LOCATION: The USNA and Annapolis NS are separated by the Severn River. From Washington, D.C.: Take US-50 E, exit 27 to Route 450 to Annapolis. Go 1.5 miles to traffic light. Proceed straight over Naval Academy Bridge to reach USNA or turn left at the light (Route 648) to go to Naval Station. From BWI Airport: Take 170 east to Annapolis. Turn right on Hammonds Ferry Road. Turn left on Dorsey Road, go into right lane. Take entrance ramp onto I-97 S to US-50 E. On US-50 take exit 27 to Route 450. Go 1.5 miles to first light. Cros over the Naval Academy Bridge to reach academy or go left for station. *USMRA: Page 42 (F-4), Page 48 (D,E,F.G-1,2,3).* **NMC:** Annapolis, in city limits.

RESERVATION INFORMATION: 2nd floor, **Officers' and Faculty Club,** 2 Truxton Road, Annapolis, MD 21402-5071. **C-410-293-3906, DSN-312-281-3906,** Fax: 410-293-2444, 0800-1600 hours. Check in 1300 hours at billeting, check out 1100 hours at billeting. Billeting for Officers, equivalent civilian employees on orders and Space-A.

NAVY LODGE Navy Lodge. 347 Kinkaid Road, U.S. Naval Station, MD 21402-5000. **C-1-800-NAVY-INN.** Lodge number is C-410-757-7900, Fax: C-410-757-9394, 24 hours daily. From Main Gate turn right on Kincaid Road, lodge is on left. Bedroom, two double beds, private bath (50). Kitchenette, microwave, utensils, A/C, CATV/VCR, video rental, HBO, phone, clock radio, hair dryer, laundry facility, iron/ironing board, cribs, highchairs, rollaways, snack vending, ice machine, playground, complimentary coffee in lobby. Two handicap accessible rooms, ten business class rooms, interconnecting units and non-smoking rooms available. Rates: $61 per room. No pets.

BOQ Leave or official duty, equivalent government employees on orders. Suite, queen-size bed, sofabed, private bath, sleep up to four. Shared kitchen, microwave, A/C, TV, phone, laundry facility, housekeeping service. Older historic structure, remodeled. Rates: $30.50, each additional person $8. PCS, TAD/TDY have priority; others Space-A.

BOQ Reservations through Superintendent's Protocol Office, **C-410-293-1510.** O6+. VIP suite, private bath (2). Kitchenette, coffee bar. VIP guest suite, private bath (1), coffee bar. Rates: $45, each additional person $11. Retirees Space-A.

TML AVAILABILITY: Best, Oct-Apr. Extremely difficult during summer months.

CREDIT CARDS ACCEPTED: Visa, MasterCard and American Express.

TRANSPORTATION: None available.

DINING OPPORTUNITIES: Restaurant on site serves lunch and dinner Mon-Fri, Sunday brunch. Numerous restaurants are located within walking distance in Annapolis.

Don't miss a visit to the waterfront shopping and restaurant area, where dreaming over yachts is "SOP." Visit the Naval Academy Chapel and historic buildings, and walk around historic Maryland's capital.

Washington Naval Air Facility (MD22R1)
Supply Officer, Naval Air Facility, Attn: Code 76
Bldg 1384, 1 San Diego Loop
Andrews AFB, MD 20762-5518

MAIN INSTALLATION TELEPHONE NUMBERS: C-301-981-1110, DSN-312-858-1110, Fax: C-301-981-3588, DSN-312-858-3588. Locator 981-2750; Medical 981-2850; Security Police 981-2001. *Ten-digit dialing required for local calls.*

LOCATION: From I-95 (east part of Capital Beltway, I-495), exit 9. At first traffic light after leaving exit ramp, turn right into Main Gate of Andrews AFB. Also, from I-395 N, exit South Capitol Street, cross Anacostia River on South Capitol Street, bear left to Suitland Parkway E, exit Parkway at Morningside on Suitland Road east to Main Gate of Andrews AFB. Follow signs to east side of Andrews AFB. Clearly marked. *USMRA: Page 42 (E-5); Page 55 (I,J-6,7).* **NMC:** Washington D.C., 6 miles northwest.

RESERVATION INFORMATION: Bldg 1384, 1 San Diego Loop, Andrews AFB, MD 20762-5518. **C-240-857-2750, DSN-312-857-2750,** Fax: C-240-857-3588, 24 hours daily. Personnel on official orders may make reservations; others Space-A. Check in 1600 hours, check out 1100 hours.

CBQ Bldgs 1675, 1687. BOQ. Bldgs 1384, 1385. No family quarters available. Coffee maker, CATV, housekeeping service, soft drink and snack vending. Rates: Enlisted $5; Officer $10.

DV/VIP Controlled by NAF Washington, D.C. Commanding Officer. Rates: $20. Reservations must be made through the CO for VIP suites.

TML AVAILABILITY: Limited, weekdays and Reservist drill weekends.

CREDIT CARDS ACCEPTED: Visa, MasterCard and American Express.

TRANSPORTATION: On base shuttle/bus, C-301-981-4661; Car Rental: Thrifty, C-301-568-7900; Off base taxi: Bluebird, C-301-864-7700; NAF Duty Driver, C-301-981-2744.

DINING OPPORTUNITIES: Freedom Hall, C-301-981-6516; O Club, C-301-420-4744; and Sports Page, C-301-981-4638 are within walking distance. Burger King, C-301-736-4864; Checkers, C-301-736-4179; and Roy Rogers, C-301-899-7698 are within driving distance.

MASSACHUSETTS

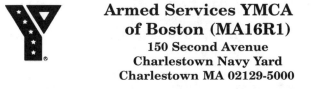

Armed Services YMCA of Boston (MA16R1)
150 Second Avenue
Charlestown Navy Yard
Charlestown MA 02129-5000

(This is not U.S. Government/Military Lodging.)

MAIN INSTALLATION TELEPHONE NUMBERS: C-617-241-8400, Fax: C-617-241-2856. Locator 241-8400; Medical 911; Security Police 911.

LOCATION: From the Massachusetts Turnpike to Boston; I-93 exit 25 and follow signs to USS Constitution; from South I-93 to exit 28 Sullivan Square, follow signs to USS Constitution. *USMRA: Page 24 (E-5).* **NMC:** Boston, in the city.

RESERVATION INFORMATION: 150 Second Avenue, Charlestown Navy Yard, Charlestown, MA 02129-5000. **C-1-800-495-9622, C-617-241-8400,** Fax: C-617-241-2856, 24 hours daily. E-mail: military@asymcaboston.org All categories may make reservations. Check in 1500 hours at facility, check out 1100 hours. Government civilian employee billeting.

TML Single and family accommodations. Bedroom, two beds or one queen bed, private bath; adjoining rooms. A/C, kitchenette (must provide own cooking and eating utensils). Rates (subject to change): military $40 and up; civilian $100 and up; each additional person $15 per night.

DV/VIP Suites, private bath. CATV, housekeeping service, coin laundry facility, YMCA space rentals, meeting/conference rooms, gym, pool, function room. Rates (subject to change): military $40 and up; civilian $100 and up.

TML AVAILABILITY: Very good.

CREDIT CARDS ACCEPTED: Visa, MasterCard and American Express.

TRANSPORTATION: Car Rental; taxi.

DINING OPPORTUNITIES: Numerous restaurants are within driving distance.

Boston is one of America's most "walkable" cities—see bustling Faneuil Hall Marketplace and waterfront areas, the shops of Back Bay and picturesque squares of Beacon Hill. The Hub's many athletic and cultural events are only a few minutes away by car or Boston's rapid transit system, the "T."

Camp Edwards (MA14R1)
Bldg 5218
Camp Edwards, MA 02542-5003

MAIN INSTALLATION TELEPHONE NUMBERS: C-508-968-4000, DSN-312-557-4000. Medical 911; Security Police 911.

LOCATION: Off MA-28 (MacArthur Blvd) at the base of Cape Cod. From I-495 E, exit 3 to MA-28 S to camp, east of MA-28. *USMRA: Page 17 (M-6,7).* **NMC:** Boston, 70 miles northwest.

RESERVATION INFORMATION: Bldg 5218, Turpentine Road, Camp Edwards, MA 02542-5003. **C-508-968-5915/16, DSN-312-557-5916/15,** Fax: 508-968-5666, DSN-312-557-5666, M-Th 0700-1700, Fri 0700-2200, Sat 0730-2000, Sun 0730-1600. Personnel on official duty can make reservations; others Space-A. Check in at billeting office during operation hours. **No dependents.**

BEQ/BOQ DV/VIP E7/O6+. Apartment (108). Kitchenette, refrigerator, utensils, CATV in lounge, housekeeping service, soap. Wood frame barracks structure. Rates: official $10, unofficial $13. Maximum four to five per unit.

AMENITIES: Mini Mart.

TML AVAILABILITY: Limited.

CREDIT CARDS ACCEPTED: Visa and MasterCard.

TRANSPORTATION: Off base taxi.

DINING OPPORTUNITIES: Honeydew Donuts is on post. Fast food and fine dining establishments are within driving distance.

On base there is a gas station, PX, commissary, pizza/snack bar, gym, bowling, movie theater, barber shop and ATM machine.

Cuttyhunk Island Recreational Facility (MA04R1)

USCG Integrated Support Command
Attn: Morale Officer
427 Commercial Street
Boston, MA 02109-5000

MAIN INSTALLATION TELEPHONE NUMBERS: C-617-223-1110.

LOCATION: Off base. On Cuttyhunk Island. From I-195 or MA-6 at New Bedford, south to State Pier (near Elm Street). Transportation to the island is via Cuttyhunk Boat Lines M/V ALERT (508-992-1432). *USMRA: Page 17 (L-8).* **NMC:** New Bedford. NMI: Newport Naval Station, RI, 35 miles southwest of New Bedford.

RESERVATION INFORMATION: Commanding Officer, FM USCG Integrated Support Command, Attn: Morale Officer, 427 Commercial Street, Boston, MA 02109. **C-617-223-3181,** Fax: C-617-223-3182. Facility is open Memorial Day-Labor Day. Reservations required, by application only (fax accepted), with advance payment. Active Duty Coast Guard may make reservations 90 days in advance; all other Active Duty may make reservations 80 days in advance; Reservists, Retirees, Coast Guard civilian employees and 100% DAVs 75 days in advance.

TML Four-bedroom apartment, private bath, furnished, kitchen (1). Two-bedroom apartment, private bath, furnished, kitchen (1). Laundry facility, cribs, cots. Rates: $300-$500 weekly. No pets.

AMENITIES: Game room. Telephone located on dock.

TML AVAILABILITY: Very difficult during summer.

CREDIT CARDS ACCEPTED: None.

TRANSPORTATION: Transportation is via Cuttyhunk Boat Lines M/V ALERT. M/V ALERT does not transport vehicles. Prepaid reservations three weeks to a month ahead of time are required. Contact boat line at 508-992-1432 or www.cuttyhunk.com for information.

DINING OPPORTUNITIES: There are two small restaurants and a small convenience store on the island.

Devens Reserve Forces Training Area (MA09R1)

Army Community Service
Box 11, 30 Quebec Street
Devens, MA 01432-4429

MAIN INSTALLATION TELEPHONE NUMBERS: C-978-772-1110. Locator 772-4300/0188; Medical 777-8870; Security Police 772-6600.

LOCATION: Take Route 2 (west from Route 495, or east from Leominster) to Devens/Jackson Road exit, to end of Jackson Road, at first stop sign make right onto Givry, left onto MacArthur, take MacArthur to a right turn onto 10th Mountain Division Road. *USMRA: Page 17 (I-2,3).* NMC: Boston, 35 miles northwest.

RESERVATION INFORMATION: Devens Inn, (Formerly the McGrath Guesthouse) 22 10th Mountain Division Road, Bldg 2002, Devens, MA 01432-5010. **C-978-772-4300,** Fax: C-978-772-4749, 24 hours daily. Check in 1500, check out 1100 hours. Government civilian employee billeting.

TML Devens Inn. Bldg 2002. Official duty. Suites, private bath (60). Kitchenette, refrigerator, CATV, housekeeping service, cribs. Rates: $59.

AMENITIES: Meeting/Conference Room, Snack Vending Machine.

TML AVAILABILITY: Good, Dec-Mar. Very difficult, summer.

CREDIT CARDS ACCEPTED: Visa, MasterCard, American Express and Diners.

TRANSPORTATION: Car Rental: Gervais Ford, C-978-772-6600; Off base taxi, C-978-772-3801, C-978-772-0873.

DINING OPPORTUNITIES: Devens Conference Center (lunch, lounge/pub), C-978-772-0188 is within walking distance. Atlantic Sea Grill C-978-263-3162; Bull Run Restaurant, C-978-425-4311; and Piccolino's Restaurant, C-978-425-9000 are within driving distance.

Fourth Cliff Recreation Area (MA02R1)

P.O. Box 479
Humarock, MA 02047-0479

MAIN INSTALLATION TELEPHONE NUMBERS: C-781-377-4441, DSN-312-478-4441. Locator 377-4441; Medical 911; Security Police 911.

LOCATION: Off base. I-95 S or I-93 N to MA-Route 3 S. Take exit 12, MA-139 east to Marshfield. Go straight, through the traffic lights, for 1.5 miles to Furnace Street, turn left. Continue to "T" intersection, left on Ferry Street. From Ferry Street to Sea Street, right over South River Bridge, left on Central Avenue, bear left at fork. (Do not go straight up hill on Cliff Road.) Proceed to gate. *USMRA: Page 17 (M-4).* **NMC:** Boston, 30 miles north. NMI: Hanscom AFB, 55 miles northwest.

RESERVATION INFORMATION: Bldg 107. Reservations required. Confirmation with credit card, cash, or check within five days. Ask for brochure. **C-1-800-468-9547, C-781-837-9269,** Fax: C-781-837-4921, 0800-1630 hours Mon-Fri. WEB: www.hanscom.af.mil/orgs/66abw/sv/fourth.htm RV sites, rec hall, and cabins are open year round. Tenting is seasonal, open Memorial Day through Columbus Day. Closed on Christmas Day.

TML Efficiency apartment (4), one is handicap accessible; three bedroom cottage (4), two are handicap accessible; townhouse (2); chalet (11). CATV, laundry facilities, hair dryer, microwave, ice machine, snack bar, cribs/cots. Rates: $50-$105. All categories can make reservations. *Pets not allowed in cabins but may be leashed in other areas. (Check out Military Living's RV Camping and Outdoor Recreation Around the World for more info).*

TML AVAILABILITY: Limited. Book early.

CREDIT CARDS ACCEPTED: Visa and MasterCard.

TRANSPORTATION: None available.

DINING OPPORTUNITIES: Bridgewaye Inn, Lou's and Nautical Mile are within driving distance.

Easy access to Boston, Cape Cod, Martha's Vineyard and Nantucket Islands, and located on a cliff overlooking the Atlantic and scenic North River, this is a super location for a summer or winter vacation.

Hanscom Air Force Base (MA06R1)

66 MSS/DPF
20 Kirtland Street, Bldg 1218
Hanscom AFB, MA 01731-2012

MAIN INSTALLATION TELEPHONE NUMBERS: C-781-377-4441, DSN-312-478-4441. Locator 377-5111; Medical 377-2333; Security Police 377-2315.

LOCATION: From I-95 S, exit 30 B (MA-2A) west for 2 miles then turn right at the Hanscom Field Sign. From I-95 N take exit 31B, keep to right, follow signs to base, 2 miles. *USMRA: Page 17 (J-3), page 24 (A-2).* NMC: Boston, 20 miles southeast.

RESERVATION INFORMATION: Hanscom Inn, 66 SVS/SVML, Bldg 1427, Kirtland Street, Hanscom AFB, MA 01731-5000. **C-1-888-AFLODGE (1-888-235-6343), C-781-377-2112, DSN-312-478-2112,**

Fax: C-781-377-4961, DSN-312-478-4961, 24 hours daily. E-mail: hanscominn@hanscom.af.mil Duty may make reservations any time; Space-A may make reservations 24 hours in advance, for up to a three day stay. Check in 1400 hours, check out 1100 hours.

TLF Bldgs 1412, 1423. **C-781-377-2044, DSN-312-478-2044.** Official duty. Bldg 1423, single bedroom, sofabed, private bath. Full kitchen, A/C, housekeeping service, laundry facility, cribs. Handicap accessible. Rates: $30. PCS in/out: 30 days in, seven days out.

VQ Bldgs 1412, 1426. Official duty. Bldg 1426, bedroom, semi-private bath. A/C, housekeeping service, laundry facility. Rates: $19 per person. TDY personnel have priority. Bldg 1412, single bedroom, private bath, laundry facility in building. Rates: $19 per person.

DV/VIP Bldgs 1420, 1427. **C-781-377-5151.** O6+, SES equivalent. Rates: $26.

AMENITIES: Exercise Room, Snack and Soft Drink Vending Machines.

TML AVAILABILITY: Fair. Best in Nov-Mar.

CREDIT CARDS ACCEPTED: Visa and MasterCard.

TRANSPORTATION: On base shuttle/bus, C-781-377-2588, DSN-312-478-2588; Car Rental: Avis, C-781-274-0010; Off base taxi, C-781-272-0700.

DINING OPPORTUNITIES: E Club, C-781-377-2123; Hanscom Bowling Center, C-781-377-2237; and Pizza Sub Shop, C-781-274-0133 are within walking distance. Cafe Luigi, C-781-271-0666; Chili's, C-781-273-9309; and Great Wall, C-781-275-7007 are within driving distance.

Delve into U.S. history by visiting Minute Man National Historical Park, Battle Road near Fiske Hill in Lexington, the Wayside Unit, home of the Alcotts, Nathaniel Hawthorne and others and Lexington Green.

Martha's Vineyard/Nantucket Vacation Houses (MA17R1)
USCG Air Station Cape Cod
Air Station Cape Cod, MA 02542-5024

MAIN INSTALLATION TELEPHONE NUMBERS: C-508-968-6447.

LOCATION: Off base. One house on Nantucket, three houses on Martha's Vineyard. Island accessible via ferry from West Yarmouth, Cape Cod. USMRA (edition year 2000): Page 17 (M-8, O-9). NMI: Otis ANG/Cape Cod CGAS. **NMC:** Boston, 80 miles northwest.

RESERVATION INFORMATION: Reservations: Commanding Officer, Attn: MWR-Morale House Reservations, USCG Air Station Cape Cod, Air Station Cape Cod, MA 02542-5024. Call **C-508-968-6447/8** for information only, Fax: C-508-968-6443. WEB: www.uscg.mil/d1/units/ascapecod/mwr.htm#Vineyard Registration info and application forms are also obtainable from web site. Reservations may be made for a minimum of one night and a maximum of 13 nights. Reservations will be confirmed 90 days prior to check in. Check in 1500-1800, check out 1100 hours. Eligible military personnel: Active Duty, Reservists, retired, auxiliary personnel of Armed Forces, DoT civilian employees of CG, uniformed personnel of PHS and NOAA when assigned to CG.

Guesthouse Martha's Vineyard House (2). The four-bedroom, two bath house located on Pontiac Street is available for ranks E1-E6. The four-bedroom, two bath house located on

Pennsylvania Street is available to ranks O1-O4, E7-E9. All houses have TV/VCR, fully equipped kitchens (all major appliances including microwave, coffeemaker, toaster), washer/dryer, two adult and two child bicycles, porta crib. Maximum occupancy is 12. No pets, no smoking.

Guesthouse Nantucket House. Four-bedroom, two bath house, sleeper sofa. Within walking distance to beach. Maximum occupancy is 12. No pets, no smoking.

Lighthouse West Chop Lighthouse. This three-bedroom, one bath cottage is available to VIP senior officers (O5+). Maximum occupancy is eight. No pets. No smoking. Reservations on first come first served basis.

RATES: E1-E6: $45/$50 per day; E7-E9, O1, O2, W1, W2, GS1 to GS7: $50/$60 per day; O3, O4, W3 to W5, GS8-GS12, NAF/Wage Grade, Auxiliary: $60/$70 per day; O5-O10, GS13+: $80/$100 per day. Winter rates (11/1-4/30)/Season rates (5/1-10/30).

TML AVAILABILITY: Difficult year round.

CREDIT CARDS ACCEPTED: Visa, MasterCard, American Express and Discover.

TRANSPORTATION: In order to take your vehicle to the islands, you must make reservations with the island ferry. These reservations are very difficult to get, so call the ferry at C-508-477-8600 as soon as possible once your lodging reservations are confirmed. Nantucket shuttle bus-C-508-228-7025, Martha's Vineyard bus service-C-508-627-7448. Car rental, taxi service, bicycle rental available on both islands.

DINING OPPORTUNITIES: Numerous restaurants.

Martha's Vineyard and Nantucket offer wonderful island communities with great beaches, nature preserves, historical sights and museums, fishing and boating.

Otis Air National Guard Base/
Cape Cod Coast Guard Air Station (MA07R1)
Temporary Quarters
ENT Street, Bldg 5204
U.S.C.G Station Cape Cod, MA 02542-5024.

MAIN INSTALLATION TELEPHONE NUMBERS: C-508-968-1000, DSN-312-557-4401, National Guard Base. Coast Guard Air Station, C-508-968-6300, DSN-312-557-6300. Locator 968-1000; Medical 968-6570; Security Police 968-4010.

LOCATION: South of Plymouth, from Bourne Bridge MA-28 take MA Military Reservation exit, south on Connley Avenue approximately 2 miles to Bourne Gate. From Sagamore Bridge Route 6, exit 2 (Route 130), make a right on to 130 S. Follow for approximately 4 miles to Snake Pond Road (MA Military Reservation). Take right on to Snake Pond Road and follow to gate. *USMRA: Page 17 (M-7).* NMC: Boston, 60 miles northwest. *Note: Otis Air National Gaurd Base and Cape Cod Coast Guard Air Station share several support facilities.*

RESERVATION INFORMATION: Commanding Officer, Temporary Quarters, Bldg 5204, ENT Street, U.S. Coast Guard Air Station Cape Cod, MA 02542-5024. **C-508-968-6461,** Fax: C-508-968-6337, 0800-1600 hours Mon-Fri, 0900-1400 hours Sat-Sun. Credit card number or advance payment required. Check in at billeting at 1300 hours, check out 1000 hours. Reservations: Jun-Sep PCS 90 days in advance, TDY 30 days in advance, all others 14 days in advance. Oct-May PCS 90 days in advance, all others 30 days in advance. Directions: From Bourne Gate, take first right (Hospital Road), at split, bear left. At stop sign go straight to first right onto ENT Street. Temporary Quarters, Bldg 5204, is the second building on the left. From Sagamore Bridge: At gate, make a left. At stop sign, make a right (Herbert Road), take the first left. At rotary take first exit off to Connery Road. Make a left at first stop sign (Turpentine Road) follow to stop sign and make a right (Lee Road). Make

first left (Hospital Road) then take first right onto ENT Street. Temporary Quarters, Bldg 5204, is the second building on the left. After hours check in at CG Air Station, directions: from Main Gate continue to rotary, take third exit (CG Air Operations). At stop sign make a right on to Herbert Road. Continue through the gate, JOOD (Bldg 3159) is the first building on the left, C-508-968-6331.

TML Leave or official duty. Standard room with queen-size bed, private bath (3); suite, private bath (17). Suite: one bedroom, two double beds, living area with sofa bed, dinette. Sleeps six. All units have refrigerator, microwave, TV, housekeeping service, cots, cribs, playroom, coin laundry facility, soft drink vending. Complimentary morning coffee in lobby. Older structure remodeled. No A/C. Suite rates: summer $50, winter $40. Room rates summer $40, winter $35. Smoking and non smoking units available. No pets.

TML Leave or official duty. Two-bedroom townhouse (12). Full bed, two twin beds, sofa sleeper, fully equipped kitchen, dining area. TV, no housekeeping. Rates: summer $65, winter $55. Cleaning deposit required. **See *Military Living's Military RV, Camping and Outdoor Recreation Around the World* for additional information and directions.**

TML AVAILABILITY: Best Oct-Apr, very difficult in summer.

CREDIT CARDS ACCEPTED: Visa, MasterCard, American Express and Discover.

TRANSPORTATION: None available.

DINING OPPORTUNITIES: Activity Center Snack Bar, C-508-968-6478 and Pizza Hut, C-508-563-3373 are within walking distance. Golf Course Snack Bar, C-508-968-6454 and Galley at CGAS, C-508-968-6426 are on base.

Otis has nine-hole golf course and driving range. Newport mansions, beaches, Martha's Vineyard, and Nantucket Islands nearby make this a special place to visit.

Westover Air Reserve Base (MA03R1)
439th Airlift Wing (AFRC)
100 Lloyd Street
Chicopee, MA 01022-1825

MAIN INSTALLATION TELEPHONE NUMBERS: C-413-557-1110, DSN-312-589-1110, C-1-800-367-1110 ask for ext 2700 (base lodging). Locator 557-3874; Medical 557-3565; Security Police 557-3557.

LOCATION: From Boston take I-90 W (Massachusetts Turnpike) to exit 5 in Chicopee; bear right after toll booth to traffic light; take a left onto Memorial Drive (Route 33) and follow signs to Westover ARB. *USMRA: Page 16 (F-4).* NMC: Springfield, eight miles south.

RESERVATION INFORMATION: Flyers Inn, Bldg 2201, 650 Airlift Drive, Chicopee, MA 01022-1309. **C-1-888-AFLODGE (1-888-235-6343), C-413-557-2700, DSN-312-589-2700,** Fax: C-413-557-2835, DSN-312-589-2835, weekends only. Duty may make reservations any time; Space-A may make reservations 24 hours in advance. Space-A check in 1700 hours, check out 1100 hours. Check in at security desk after 2300 hours. Government civilian employee lodging.

VAQ Bldgs 5101-5105. E1-E8. Room, shared bath (250); SNCO suite, private bath (32). Refrigerator, TV, housekeeping service, laundry facility, snack vending, ice machine. Older structures, Bldg 5101, renovated. Rates: $14.50. Maximum two per unit.

VOQ Bldgs 2200, 2201. Bedroom, semi-private bath (10); two-bedroom suite, semi-private bath (29). A/C, TV/VCR rental, housekeeping service, ice machine. Older structure, remodeled. Rates: $14.50 per person; DV Suite $21 per person. Maximum depends on number per family.

DV/VIP Bldg 2200. **C-413-557-5421.** O6+ or unit commander. Rates: $21 per person. Maximum two per unit.

AMENITIES: Meeting/Conference Room.

TML AVAILABILITY: Good, except Jun-Sep. Due to renovation of the Officers' complex call in advance to determine availability of rooms.

CREDIT CARDS ACCEPTED: Visa and MasterCard.

TRANSPORTATION: None available on base. Taxi service, bus station and train station nearby in Springfield.

DINING OPPORTUNITIES: Bowling Center, C-413-557-2039; and Combined Club, C-413-557-3010 are within walking distance.

Museums, parks, ski areas, Basketball Hall of Fame, professional stage and Symphony Hall in Springfield, are of interest to visitors. Several golf courses. Visit Forest Park Zoo, and the Naismith Memorial Hall of Fame (basketball).

MICHIGAN

Camp Grayling/Army National Guard (MI10R2)
Headquarters, Bldg 117
Camp Grayling, MI 49739-0001

MAIN INSTALLATION TELEPHONE NUMBERS: C-517-344-6100, DSN-312-623-6100. Locator 344-6100; Medical 911; Security Police 911.

LOCATION: Located three miles west of city of Grayling, just off of I-75. From gate at the end of Michigan highway M-93. *USMRA: Page 66 (D-5).* NMC: Grayling, three miles east.

RESERVATION INFORMATION: Housing Management Office, Bldg 560, Camp Grayling, MI 49739-0001. **C-517-344-6202.** Check in by 1600 hours on duty days, check out 1000 hours. O Club, Bldg 311, **C-517-348-9033.** Check out 1000 hours. *Note: Camp Grayling is not a federal military installation, it is a state facility. Open during duty hours only–0745-1130; 1230-1600 Mon-Fri.*

TML Operated and maintained by Housing: Billeting for those on official duty. Individual rooms, shared bath. Most buildings are unheated and consequently closed during colder months.

TML Operated and maintained by Housing: CTQ, unaccompanied housing. Official duty and Retirees. Reservations are a first come basis. Single bed. Kitchenette, microwave, TV/VCR, clock radio. Rates: official $13; unofficial $33; each additional person $23.

TML Operated and maintained by O Club, Officers during summer months only. Lake front cottage, sleep six, fully furnished and equipped (4); lakefront mobile home, sleep six, fully furnished and equipped (2). Rates: $35 (minimum two night stay), $200 weekly. Open mid-Apr-mid-Oct. Unaccompanied users need to see O Club manager.

TML Operated and maintained by O Club, Officers during summer months only. Rooms (unheated) (10) available with two to four beds in each. Rates: $7. Open May-Sept.

TML AVAILABILITY: Limited, especially during colder months.

CREDIT CARDS ACCEPTED: The Housing/Lodging Office does not accept credit cards. The O Club accepts Visa, MasterCard and Discover

TRANSPORTATION: Off base taxi.

DINING OPPORTUNITIES: Snack Bar and Clubs are within driving distance.

Hunting, camping, fishing and winter sports are available in this area. Limited on post support facilities. Commercial airlines available in Traverse City. Excellent local community canoeing. Live on-stage entertainment with a wide variety of popular music at the Speak Easy Saloon Lounge, Holiday Inn Lounge.

Point Betsie Recreation Cottage (MI04R2)
Grand Haven Coast Guard Group
650 Harbor Drive
Grand Haven, MI 49417-1762

MAIN INSTALLATION TELEPHONE NUMBERS: C-616-850-2500.

LOCATION: Off base. One hundred fifty miles north of Grand Rapids. Take US-131 N to highway 115 W into Frankfort, go north on MI-22 for 4 miles to Point Betsie Road; cottage is at the end of Point Betsie Road. *USMRA: Page 66 (C-5).* NMC: Traverse City, 45 miles east. NMI: Traverse City Coast Guard Air Station, 45 miles east.

RESERVATION INFORMATION: Reservations required by telephone up to 90 days in advance for Coast Guard; 60 days for all others. Address for information and advance payment: Make checks payable to Point Betsie Morale. Mail to: USCG Group Grand Haven, 650 S Harbor Drive, Grand Haven, MI 49417-1752. **C-616-850-2510,** Fax: 616-850-2528. Check in after 1400 hours and get cottage key at CG Station in Frankfort. Check out 1000 hours.

Cottage Furnished two-bedroom (1), sleeps six. Refrigerator, microwave, utensils, gas grill. Rates: $20-30 daily. Five-day limit in summer, seven-day limit in winter. No telephone at cottage. No smoking in cottage. No pets.

AMENITIES: None available at CG Station.

TML AVAILABILITY: Book early.

CREDIT CARDS ACCEPTED: None.

TRANSPORTATION: None available.

DINING OPPORTUNITIES: In town of Frankfort, five miles south.

Located in northwest Michigan on eastern shores of Lake Michigan south of Sleeping Bear Dunes National Lakeshore. Plenty of outdoor recreation such as water sports, hunting, fishing, hiking and skiing. Crystal Lake and Betsie Bay resorts nearby. Full range of support facilities available at Traverse City Coast Guard Air Station.

Selfridge Air National Guard Base (MI01R2)
CDR, Attn: AMSTA-CY-AF
Bldg 780, Room 12
Selfridge ANGB, MI 48045-5000

MAIN INSTALLATION TELEPHONE NUMBERS: C-586-307-5110, DSN-312-273-5110. Locator 307-4021; Medical 307-4650; ANG Security Police 307-4673; DoD Police 307-2621.

LOCATION: Take I-94 N from Detroit to Selfridge ANG at exit 240, then east on Hall Road extension MI-59 to Main Gate of base. *USMRA: Page 66 (G-9), page 70 (G-1).* NMC: Detroit, 25 miles southwest.

RESERVATION INFORMATION: Attn: AMSTA-CY-ATLF, Bldg 410, 410 George Avenue, Selfridge ANG Base, MI 48045-5016. **C-586-307-4062 DSN-312-273-4062,** Fax: C-586-307-6102, DSN-312-273-6102, 24 hours daily. WEB: www.selfridge. army.mil PCS may make reservations 90 days out; official travel (TDY/TAD) 30 days; Space-A 7 days. Credit card required for reservations guarantee. Directions: Enter Selfridge ANGB through the Main Gate on Jefferson Avenue. Stay straight on Jefferson until George Avenue. Turn left onto George Avenue. Hotel and check-in desk is at Lufberry Hall (Bldg 410), just past the stop sign on the left.

VOQ/VEQ Bldg 410. Lufberry Hall. Separate parlor and bedroom, private bath (23). Microfridge, TV/VCR, daily housekeeping service, A/C, sofa sleeper, crib, limited fitness room, laundry facility. Older structure, renovated. Ongoing revitalization projects. Rates: $40.

BEQ/BOQ Bldgs 1060, 942. Limited amenities. Some share a room with another bed, shared bath, CATV, telephones. Ongoing revitalization projects. Rates: $15 per bed.

Guesthouse Bldgs 916, 936. One-, two-, three- and four-bedroom units, formerly family housing units, now fully furnished apartments for temporary lodging. Pet limitation. Kennels available. Housekeeping services provided every 72 hours. Rates: One-and two-bedroom units $25-$35. Three- and four-bedroom units $45-$55. Majority of units have A/C. Ongoing revitalization projects.

DV/VIP Bldg 410. Lufberry Hall. VIP suite (4). Master bedroom, oversize parlor, microfridge, separate bedroom with two twin beds, one bath. Daily housekeeping services provided. Older structure renovated. Ongoing revitalization projects. Rates: $50.

AMENITIES: Exercise Room, Meeting/Conference Room. Ice, Snack and Soft Drink Vending Machines.

TML AVAILABILITY: Fairly good. Reduced during peak of PCS season, May-Nov.

CREDIT CARDS ACCEPTED: Visa, MasterCard and American Express.

TRANSPORTATION: Local bus service, off base car rental, off base taxi and off base handicap transportation available.

DINING OPPORTUNITIES: Mulligans Sports Bar/Restaurant, Burger King, Bowling Alley Bar and AAFES Snack Bar are within walking distance. Many local restaurants and fast food restaurants within driving distance.

Located on the beautiful shores of Lake Saint Claire. On base recreation facilities offer boat, ski and snow gear rental, camping and fishing. Newly renovated 18-hole PGA golf course. Many parks and recreation facilities located not far from the base. Visit museums, the Detroit Zoo and don't forget Canada across Lake St. Clair or cross the border at Port Huron.

MINNESOTA

Camp Ripley (MN02R2)
Attn: Billeting
15000 Hwy 115
Little Falls, MN 56345-0150

MAIN INSTALLATION TELEPHONE NUMBERS: C-320-632-7000, DSN-312-871-7000. Locator 632-7000; Medical 632-7337; Security Police 632-7375.

LOCATION: West of Hwy 371, 25 miles south of Brainerd, seven miles north of Little Falls, in central Minnesota. *USMRA: Page 80 (C,D-6)*. **NMC:** Little Falls, seven miles south.

RESERVATION INFORMATION: Camp Ripley Billet Office-Bldg 6-76, 15000 Hwy 115, Little Falls, MN 56345. **C-320-632-7378, DSN-312-871-7378,** Fax C-320-632-7787, DSN-312-871-7787, Mon-Fri 0600-2300 hours, Sat 0700-2300 hours, Sun 0600-2200 hours. E-mail: Jessica.Serie@mn.ngb.army.mil Directions: From Main Gate, go straight to four way stop. Proceed straight approximately 3/4 mile. Education Center (Bldg 6-76) on right. Check in at billeting, after hours report to Education Center, use phone in front lobby to call Security. They will come to Education Center to issue room and key.

BEQ Bldgs 10-72, 15-71, 15-72. Bedroom, community bath (50). Refrigerator, TV, laundry facility, day room, housekeeping service. Maximum one per unit. Rates: Duty $15, all others $23.

BOQ Bldgs 7-171, 7-71, 10-73, 10-173. Bedroom, shared bath (155). Refrigerator, microwave, TV, laundry facility, housekeeping service. Rates: Duty $15, all others $23. Maximum one per unit.

DV/VIP Personnel & Community Activities,15000 Hwy 115, Little Falls, MN 56345. **C-320-632-7296.** Bldgs 8-71, 8-72, 19-71, 19-72, 19-73. Two or four-bedrooms. Area 19 has kitchenette, refrigerator, microwave, TV, phone, housekeeping services daily, laundry facility. Rates: Duty $20 per person; all others $28. VIP rooms are located in BOQ buildings. Small refrigerator, microwave, coffeepot, wall locker, reading lamp, TV, laundry facility, daily housekeeping service. Rates: Duty $17; all others $25.

AMENITIES: Exercise Room, Meeting/Conference Room, Alternative Center, Combined Club, Snack and Soft Drink Vending Machines.

TML AVAILABILITY: Good, Oct-May. Difficult, Jun-Sept.

CREDIT CARDS ACCEPTED: Visa, MasterCard and American Express.

TRANSPORTATION: None available.

DINING OPPORTUNITIES: On post: AAFES Snack Bar. South of Camp Ripley: Canteen Bar and Grill, Krazy Rabbit Bar and Grill, Cabin Fever Supper Club, Jason's Supper Club, Perkins, Pizza Hut, Kentucky Fried Chicken, Taco Johns, McDonalds, Burger King, Subway. North of Camp Ripley: The Fort Steakhouse, Poncho's and Lefty's, Black Bear, The Green Mill.

The Mississippi River runs through Camp Ripley. Easy access to fishing and water recreations. Miles of wooded area perfect for camping, hiking, or just getting away to relax. Seven miles from one of Minnesota's most beautiful and friendly towns complete with all the small town hospitalities.

Minneapolis-St. Paul International Airport/Air Reserve Station (MN01R2)
934th Airlift Wing AFRC
760 Military Highway
Minneapolis, MN 55450-2000

MAIN INSTALLATION TELEPHONE NUMBERS: C-651-713-1000, DSN-312-783-1000. Locator 713-1000; Security Police 713-1-911/1102.

LOCATION: From I-35 W or MN-55 S to crosstown MN-62, exit at 34th Avenue and entrance. Or I-494 east to exit 1A on MN-5 and entrance west to airport. *USMRA: Page 89 (C-3,4)*. **NMC:** Minneapolis-St Paul, in city limits.

RESERVATION INFORMATION: North Country Lodge, 934 SVS/SVML, Bldg 707, 760 Military Highway, Minneapolis, MN 55450-2100. **C-1-888-AFLODGE (1-888-235-6343), C-612-713-1978, DSN-312-783-1978,** Fax: C-612-713-1966, DSN-312-783-1966, Open 7 days a week, 0700-2200 hours. Closed on Federal Holidays. Duty may make reservations any time; Space-A may make reservations 24 hours in advance. Check in at billeting 1430, check out 1000 hours. Active Duty, Reservist, retired military, authorized dependents and duty government civilian employee billeting. *Note: Construction of two new wings with 127 guest rooms completed.*

VQ Bldg 707, AFRC's newest lodging facility. 139 private guest rooms including 5 DV suites. 169 additional rooms to follow when construction is complete. All units have refrigerator, A/C, TV, housekeeping service, laundry facility, ice machine. All Ranks.

VOQ Bldg 711. Officers, civilians, females (all ranks), SNCO E7+. Private room, private and semi-private baths; Officers, private bath (96); SNCO suite, private bath (3). All units have refrigerator, A/C, TV, housekeeping service, laundry facility, ice machine. Rates: room $23.00, suite $31.50. Maximum two per room.

Fisher House Minneapolis VA Medical Center, One Veterans Drive, Minneapolis, MN 55417-2300. **C-612-725-2106,** Fax: C-612-725-2016. *Note: Appendix B has the definition of this facility. Fisher Houses are only available as lodging for families of patients receiving medical care at VA medical centers.*

DV/VIP VOQ. Bldg 711. DV suite, private bath (7). Refrigerator, A/C, TV, housekeeping service, laundry facility, ice machine. Older structure. Rates: first person $22.00, couple $31.50. Maximum two per room.

TML AVAILABILITY: Good, except Fri and Sat during Air Force (934th and 133AW) UTA drill weekends. Very limited in summer.

CREDIT CARDS ACCEPTED: Visa, MasterCard and American Express.

TRANSPORTATION: Car Rental, C-651-830-2345, C-651-727-2000, C-800-331-1212; Off base taxi, C-651-721-6566.

DINING OPPORTUNITIES: E Club, C-651-713-1655 is within walking distance. Fort Snelling O Club, C-651-713-3678 is within driving distance.

While you're here check out the Mall of America, the Minnesota Zoo, various art museums and theaters. Also stop by the Metrodome to see either the Twins or Vikings play.

MISSISSIPPI

Camp Shelby Training Site (MS07R2)
Bldg 1001, Lee Avenue
Camp Shelby, MS 39407-5500

MAIN INSTALLATION TELEPHONE NUMBERS: C-601-558-1110, DSN-312-921-1110. Locator 558-2000; Medical 288-7000; Security Police 558-2232.

LOCATION: From Hattiesburg take US-49 S, or take US-98 east from Hattiesburg to MS-29 S, which bisects the training site. Follow signs. *USMRA: Page 43 (F-8).* **NMC:** Hattiesburg, 10 miles north.

RESERVATION INFORMATION: Building 6606, Camp Shelby, MS 39407-5500. **C-601-558-2540, DSN-312-921-2540,** Fax: C-601-558-2339, DSN-312-921-2339, 0730-1600 hours Sat-Wed, 0730-2100 hours Thu-Fri. Billeting Office is the building to left front after crossing the railroad tracks.

TML Camp Shelby is a weekend and annual training base.

CREDIT CARDS ACCEPTED: Visa, MasterCard and American Express.

DINING OPPORTUNITIES: Combined Club is within walking distance. Corner, Subway and Three Little Pigs are within driving distance.

Columbus Air Force Base (MS01R2)
14 MSS/DPF
166 C Circle, Suite 204
Columbus AFB, MS 39701-7901

MAIN INSTALLATION TELEPHONE NUMBERS: C-662-434-1110, DSN-312-742-1110. Locator 434-7322; Medical 911; Security Police 434-7129.

LOCATION: From Columbus north on US-45, five miles north and west of US-45. *USMRA: Page 43 (G-3).* **NMC:** Columbus, 10 miles south.

RESERVATION INFORMATION: Magnolia Inn, Attn: 14th SPTG/SVML, 179 F Street, Suite 1607, Columbus AFB, MS, 39710-5000. **C-1-888-AFLODGE (1-888-235-6343), C-662-434-2548/2372, DSN-312-742-2548/2372,** Fax: C-662-434-2777, DSN-312-742-2777, 24 hours daily. Duty may make reservations any time; Space-A may make reservations 24 hours in advance. Check in at lodging 1400 hours, check out 1100 hours. Government civilian employee lodging.

TLF Bldg 955. Bedrooms, private bath (20). Kitchen, utensils, A/C, TV, housekeeping service, cribs, rollaways, laundry facility, snack vending, ice machine, facilities for DAVs. Older structure. Rates: $23.50 per unit.

VAQ Bldg 956. Space, semi-private bath (27); SNCO suite, private bath (3). TV, housekeeping service, laundry facility, snack vending, ice machine. Older structure. Rates: $10; SNCO suite $15-$20.50.

VOQ Bldgs 954, 966. Bedroom private bath (17); bedroom, private bath, kitchenette (44). TV, housekeeping service, laundry facility, snack vending, ice machine. Older structure. Rates: first person $15.50, two people $21.75.

DV/VIP WG Executive, Bldg 724, **C-662-434-7024.** O6+ Active Duty only. SNCO contact WG SEA at **C-662-434-7005.**

TML AVAILABILITY: Good, Nov-Feb. Difficult, other times.

CREDIT CARDS ACCEPTED: Visa and MasterCard.

TRANSPORTATION: On base taxi (official duty only), C-662-434-7432.

DINING OPPORTUNITIES: Bowling Center, C-662-434-2426; and Columbus Club, C-662-434-2489 are within walking distance. Applebee's, C-662-327-3348; and Little Kitchen, C-662-434-9954 are within driving distance.

Columbus, with many antebellum structures not destroyed during the Civil War, is of interest to visitors. The area also hosts excellent fishing, boating and hunting along the Tennessee Tombigbee Waterway.

Gulfport Naval Construction Battalion Center (MS03R2)
5200 CBC 2nd Street
Gulfport, MS 39501-5001

MAIN INSTALLATION TELEPHONE NUMBERS: C-228-871-2555, DSN-312-868-2555. Locator 871-2286; Medical 871-2809; Security Police 871-2361.

LOCATION: Take US-49 south to Gulfport and west to Center off 28th Street West. From US-90 exit to Broad Avenue. From I-10 exit to US-49 south. *USMRA: Page 43 (F-10).* **NMC:** New Orleans, 70 miles west.

RESERVATION INFORMATION: Bachelor Housing, Code 20.2, 5401 Sixth Street, Gulfport, MS 39501-5001. **C-228-871-2505, DSN-312-868-2505,** Fax: C-228-871-2130, DSN-312-868-2130, 24 hours daily. Duty can make reservations, others Space-A. Check in at Bldg 313, check out 1100 hours. Government civilian employee billeting.

CBH Bldg 313, located on Marvin Sheilds and Calaghan Streets. Private room with bath. Coffee maker, hair dryer, A/C, TV/VCR, phone, microwave, refrigerator, housekeeping service, laundry facility, travel kit. Ice and vending machines. Modern structure. Rates: $8-$12 per person.

 NAVY LODGE Navy Lodge. Bldg 328, Gulfport, MS 39501-5001. **C-1-800-NAVY-INN.** Lodge number is C-228-864-3101, DSN-312-868-3101, Fax: C-228-868-7392, 0700-1900 hours. Check in 1500-1900 hours, check out 1200 hours. Bedroom, private bath (30). Kitchenette, microwave, coffee/tea (in lobby), coffee maker in room, utensils, A/C, CATV/VCR, video rental, phone, clock, hair dryer, housekeeping service, coin laundry facility, iron/ironing board, cribs, rollaways, highchairs, soft drink/snack vending, ice machine, playground. Modern structure. Two interconnecting units, handicap accessible, accessible kitchen, roll-in shower, and one bed sleeper sofa, non-smoking (8). Rates: $44 (Oct-Apr); $52 (May-Sept) per unit. Maximum five per room. All categories can make reservations. No pets. Remodeled and expanded early 1999.

(DV/VIP) Commanding Officer's Guesthouse. Bldg 301, Pass Road Gate. **C-228-871-2202.** O6+. Room, private bath, kitchenette (2). Coffee, housekeeping service, TV/VCR, phone, travel kit. Rates: $22. Retirees and lower ranks Space-A.

AMENITIES: Exercise Room, Snack and Soft Drink Vending Machines, picnic grounds, playground, barbeque grill with tools.

TML AVAILABILITY: Good, Nov-Dec. Difficult, other times.

CREDIT CARDS ACCEPTED: Visa, MasterCard, American Express, Discover and Diners. The Navy Lodge accepts Visa, MasterCard and American Express.

TRANSPORTATION: Off base shuttle/bus, C-228-432-2649; Car Rentals: Budget, C-1-800-527-0700; Dollar, C-1-800-800-4000; Enterprise, C-228-868-6001; Hertz, C-228-863-2761; Off base taxi: Sun Cab, C-228-863-8002; Yellow Cab, C-228-863-1511.

DINING OPPORTUNITIES: McDonald's, C-228-864-7355; and Stingers Dugout, C-228-871-2396 are within walking distance. Chappy's, C-228-865-9755; Grand Casino, C-1-800-946-2946; and Vrazels, C-228-863-2229 are within driving distance.

Swimming, fishing, sailing, windsurfing, sunning and beach combing in summer are popular. There are also casinos in the area. Visit Beauvoir (Confederate President Jefferson Davis' home), Gulf Islands National Seashore, Shearwater Pottery showroom.

Keesler Air Force Base (MS02R2)
81 MSS/DPF
500 Fisher Street, Room 111
Keesler AFB, MS 39534-2554

MAIN INSTALLATION TELEPHONE NUMBERS: C-228-377-1110, DSN-312-597-1110. Locator 377-2798; Medical 377-6555; Security Police 377-3720.

LOCATION: From I-10 exit 46 south on I-110 to base, west of I-110. From US-90, north on White Avenue to Main Gate. *USMRA: Page 43 (F-10).* NMC: Biloxi, in city limits.

RESERVATION INFORMATION: Inns of Keesler, 81 SPTG/SVML, Bldg 2101, 509 Larcher Blvd, Muse Manor, Keesler AFB, MS 39534-2346. **Muse Manor, C-1-888-AFLODGE (1-888-235-6343), Reservations (Mon-Sat) C-228-377-9986, DSN-312-597-9986 or Front Desk (Sat-Sun) C-228-377-2420, DSN-312-597-2420,** Fax: C-228-377-0084/3588, DSN-312-597-0084/3588, Mon-Fri. WEB: www.kee.aetc.af.mil Allow 72 hours for reply of electronic reservations. Check in 1600 hours at facility, check out 1100 hours. Government civilian employee billeting. No pets and no smoking. *Note: A $6.192 million TLF was approved in the DoD Fiscal Year 1998 NAF Construction Program.*

(VAQ) Bldgs 2101, 2002, 2003, 5024, 5025. Bedroom, one bed, semi-private bath (638); separate bedrooms, DVAQ private bath for E7+ (8). Refrigerator, A/C, TV, housekeeping service, laundry facility, snack vending, ice machine. Rates: enlisted $10, DVAQ $15. Maximum two per room. Duty can make reservations any time, Space-A can make reservations 24 hours in advance.

(VOQ) Bldgs 3821, 3823, 0470, 2004. Bedroom, private bath (224); bedroom, semi-private bath (328); DVOQ private bath for O6+ (12). A/C, TV, housekeeping service, laundry facility, ice machine. Modern structure. Rates: officers $13.50 each; DVOQ $20.50. Duty can make reservations any time, Space-A can make reservations 24 hours in advance.

(TLF) Bldgs 0305, 0306, 5725, 5730, 5735, 5740, 5745. Two bedroom units (25) and one bedroom units (45). Kitchen, utensils, A/C, TV in room and lounge, housekeeping service, laundry facility, snack vending, ice machine, playground. Rates: $23.50. Duty can make reservations any time, Space-A can make reservations 24 hours in advance. Primary use for PCS members and medical appointments, Space-A extrememly limited April-Sept.

(TML) Guesthouse. Bldg 0470. Two-bedroom, living room, dining room, semi-private bath (21). Refrigerator, housekeeping service, washer/dryer, cribs, ice machine. Rates: E7+ $22 single; E6 and below $18. Primarily for hospital patients and families of patients.

(Fisher House) Keesler Medical Center, 509 Fisher Street, Keesler AFB, MS 39534-2599. **C-228-377-8264, DSN-312-597-8264,** Fax: C-228-377-7691, DSN-228-597-7691. E-mail kelley.frank@keesler.af.mil Guestrooms (9). Kitchen and laundry room. Rate: $10 per room, per night. *Note: Appendix B has the definition of this facility. Fisher Houses are only available as lodging for families of patients receiving medical care at military and VA medical centers.*

TML AVAILABILITY: Fairly good, all year. Best, Dec-Jan.

CREDIT CARDS ACCEPTED: Visa and MasterCard.

TRANSPORTATION: Car Rental, C-228-864-5181; On base taxi, C-228-377-2430 (Active Duty on PCS/TDY only); Off base taxi: Coastliners, C-228-432-2649/1-800-647-3958; Commercial Taxi, C-228-436-3788; Limo service, C-228-432-2649.

DINING OPPORTUNITIES: Cafeteria, C-228-377-3854; E Club, C-228-377-2424; NCO/CPO Club, C-228-377-3439; and O Club, C-228-377-2219 are within driving distance.

Biloxi is rich in history: eight flags have flown over the city. Visit the Old French House off Highway 90, Ship Island, 12 miles offshore, the Jefferson Davis Shrine. White sand beaches, golf, fishing, boating and sailing are available.

Meridian Naval Air Station (MS04R2)
Combined Bachelor Quarters
218 Fuller Road
NAS Meridian, MS 39309-5000

MAIN INSTALLATION TELEPHONE NUMBERS: C-601-679-2211, DSN-312-637-2211. Locator 679-2528; Medical 679-2633; Security Police 679-2958.

LOCATION: Take MS-39 north from Meridian, for 12 miles to four-lane access road. Clearly marked. Right for three miles to NAS Main Gate. *USMRA: Page 43 (G-6).* NMC: Meridian, 15 miles southwest.

RESERVATION INFORMATION: Bldg 218 (CBQ), Fuller Road, NAS Meridian, MS 39309-5000. **C-601-679-2186, DSN-312-637-2186,** Fax: C-601-679-2745, 24 hours daily. Directions: Enter at Main Gate, go straight to flashing red light, turn left and proceed approximately .5 miles. Turn left at large complex (first building past Lake Helen), enter First Deck Central Complex. Check in at facility, check out 1300 hours, Space-A at 1400, check out 1000 hours. Government civilian employee billeting.

(BEQ) Bldgs 218. Bedroom, semi-private bath (2); bedroom, private bath (129). Community kitchen, refrigerator, microwave, coffee maker, A/C, TV, clock radio, housekeeping service, laundry facility, iron, ice machine. Remodeled. Handicap accessible. Rates: E1-E9 $6.30 double occupancy; $10.30 single room. Maximum two per room. Duty can make reservations, others Space-A.

(BOQ) Bldg 218. Separate bedrooms, private bath (40). Community kitchen, microwave, coffee maker, A/C, TV, clock radio, housekeeping service, laundry facility, iron, cribs $1, rollaways $1, ice machine. Remodeled. Handicap accessible. Rates: single $10.30 per night, suite $14.30 per night, each additional person $4. Maximum five per room.

(TML) Family Quarters. Bldg 208. Enlisted all ranks. Separate bedrooms, private bath (25). Community kitchen, refrigerator, microwave, coffee maker, A/C, TV, clock radio, housekeeping service, laundry facility, iron, cribs $1, rollaways $1. Older structure, renovated in 1988. Rates: $14.30 per room per night first three persons, each additional person $4. Maximum five per room. Duty can make reservations, others Space-A.

(DV/VIP) BOQ. Bldg 218. O6+. Bedroom, private bath, kitchen (2). Community kitchen, refrigerator, utensils, A/C, TV/VCR, housekeeping service, laundry facility, cribs $1, rollaways $1, ice machine. Remodeled. Handicap accessible. Rates: $20.30 per room, maximum two per room. Duty can make reservations, others Space-A.

(TML) Family Housing. Separate bedrooms, private bath (10), kitchen, microwave, coffee maker, A/C, TV, clock radio, housekeeping service, laundry facility, iron. Rates: $30.00 per unit per night. Maximum five per unit. Duty can make reservations, others Space-A.

AMENITIES: Dynatouch Information Center, Exercise Room, Meeting/Conference Room, Snack Vending Machine and Soft Drink Machine.

TML AVAILABILITY: Excellent year round.

CREDIT CARDS ACCEPTED: Visa, MasterCard, American Express and Discover.

TRANSPORTATION: On/Off base city bus, C-602-693-6904; Off base taxi, C-601-679-2645.

DINING OPPORTUNITIES: Numerous restaurants within driving distance.

Take a driving tour of the historic Natchez Trace, a local flea market, nearby Flora's Petrified Forest, and the Choctaw Fair for American Indian life and lore. ITT (in MWR) has information on theatrical, sports, special events tickets. Horseback riding, fishing, rollerblading, jogging trails, and bowling alley are all on base.

Pascagoula Naval Station (MS06R2)
Navy Family Service Center
Singing River Mall, Suite 1466
Pascagoula, MS 39595-5000

MAIN INSTALLATION TELEPHONE NUMBERS: C-228-761-1110, DSN-312-358-1110. Medical 761-2222; Security Police 761-3333.

LOCATION: From north on Hwy 63, take Hwy 90 west. Proceed to Chicot Road (second light) and make a left. Approximately .75 mile, the facitlity will be on the left. Look for the twelve acre lake and the two three story buildings. *USMRA: Page 43 (G-10).* **NMC:** Mobile, Alabama, 30 miles east. NMI: Kesler, 30 miles west.

RESERVATION INFORMATION: Bldg 63, 100 Singing River Island, Pascagoula, MS 39545-5000. **C-228-761-2444, DSN-312-358-2444,** Fax: C-228-761-2582, DSN-312-457-4627, 0700-2300 hours daily. Check in 1400 hours, check out 1100. Government civilian employee billeting.

(TLF) There are only four suites available at the Naval Station, and 96 permanent party rooms for Naval Station staff. At the Lakeside facility there are DV/Family suites (16) and regular suites (2). All other rooms are for Precommissioning permanent party and transient personnel. Active Duty, retired military and civilians are welcome. Families on house hunting orders are welcome. Make reservations no more than 45 days in advance. Rates: single $12 per; multiple $6; suites $26; DV/Family Suites $30 per night.

CREDIT CARDS ACCEPTED: Visa, MasterCard, Discover and American Express.

TRANSPORTATION: No on base transportation. Local taxis available.

DINING OPPORTUNITIES: McDonald's and NEX are located on base. Other fast food chains and local restaurants located within driving distance.

Casinos, Sea World of Biloxi, Jefferson Davis Museum, Salt and Freshwater Fishing, Boating and Sailing. All MWR facilites are on the Naval Station. There is a picnic area, softball field, and lake at the Lakeside Support Facility. All you need to fish in the lake is a government I.D. card.

MISSOURI

Fort Leonard Wood (MO03R2)
Community Service Center
Bldg 470, Room 1201
Fort Leonard Wood, MO 65473-8935

MAIN INSTALLATION TELEPHONE NUMBERS: C-573-596-0131, DSN-312-581-0110. Medical 596-2157; Security Police 596-6141; Emergency 911.

LOCATION: Two miles south of I-44, adjacent to St. Robert and Waynesville, at Fort Leonard Wood exit. *USMRA: Page 81 (E-6).* **NMC:** Springfield, 85 miles southwest.

RESERVATION INFORMATION: Bldg 470, Room 1201, Replacement Avenue, Lodging Division, PO Box 221, Fort Leonard Wood, MO 65473-8935. **C-1-800-677-8356, DSN-312-581-8356,** Fax: C-573-596-0943, 24 hours daily. Directions from Main Gate: Go 1.5 miles south to Building 470. Duty can make reservations; others Space-A. Check in at lodging, check out 1200 hours. Government civilian employee lodging for TDY. Handicap accessible units available. *Pets allowed in some facilities.*

(TDY) Thirteen buildings. Official duty only. Bedroom, private bath (678). Kitchen, refrigerator, limited utensils, A/C, TV, housekeeping service, laundry facility. Modern structure. Rates: $22-$32.50, additional person $3.50. Maximum two persons.

(TDY) Twelve Buildings, NCO Academy. Official duty only. Separate bedroom, shared bath (888), community kitchen . Rates: $25, with housekeeping service; DSS/PLDC $16 with supplies only.

(VOQ) Bldgs 4102, 4104. TDY only. Bedroom, private bath (74); separate bedroom suite, private bath (8). Kitchen (82), refrigerator, microwave, utensils, coffee maker, A/C, TV, housekeeping service, laundry facility, iron/ironing board, ice machine. Modern structure, remodeled. Rates: official $22, additional person $3.50. Maximum two per room.

(Army Lodging) Guesthouse. Several buildings. Separate bedroom, private bath (79). Refrigerator, stove, microwave, utensils, coffee maker, A/C, TV, housekeeping service, laundry facility, iron/ironing board, cribs, cots, rollaways, playroom, continental breakfast. Handicap accessible (4). Rates: official $22, each additional person $3.50; unofficial $36, each additional person $3.50.

(DV/VIP) Protocol Office, **C-573-596-8070/8071.** O6/GS15+, official duty. Bldg 4104 and 2051. Separate bedroom suite, private bath (8); three-bedroom suite, private bath (1). Kitchen, utensils, A/C, TV, housekeeping service. Modern structure. Rates: official $40, additional person $3.50; unofficial $47.50, additional person $3.50. Maximum two per room. Ike Skelton House—two bedroom suite, private bath, dining room (2). Media room, conference/board room.

AMENITIES: Meeting/Conference Room, Internet/E-mail access for guests. Detergent, Ice, Snack and Soft Drink Vending Machines.

TML AVAILABILITY: Fair. Best Dec. Difficult May-Oct.

CREDIT CARDS ACCEPTED: Visa, MasterCard, American Express and MWR.

TRANSPORTATION: On base shuttle, C-573-596-1927; Car Rental: Hertz, C-573-329-6688; On/Off base taxi, C-573-336-3229.

DINING OPPORTUNITIES: Pershing Club, C-573-329-6500; and Tri-Corp Lounge, C-573-329-6005 are within walking distance. Burger King, C-573-329-5677; Davis Club, C-573-329-6080; Audie Murphy Club, C-573-329-2455; Warriors' Lounge, C-573-329-3100; and Post Exchange Food Court, C-573-329-6663 are within driving distance.

Crystal clear rivers and streams provide fishing, float trips, canoeing. Campers, hikers, hunters and horseback riders find the Ozarks a paradise. Guided tours through caves, and all levels of spelunking are available.

Lake of the Ozarks Recreation Area (MO01R2)
Route 1, Box 380
Linn Creek, MO 65052-5000

MAIN INSTALLATION TELEPHONE NUMBERS: C-573-596-0131, DSN-312-581-0110. Locator 596-0131; Medical 596-9331; Security Police 346-3693.

LOCATION: From I-70 at Columbia, take US-63 S to Jefferson City, then take US-54 SW to Linn Creek area, left at County Road A for 6 miles. Left on McCubbins Drive for 4.7 miles to travel camp. From I-44 northeast of Springfield, exit 150, MO-7 northwest to Richland, right on State Road A and travel 19.8 miles to Freedom, right on McCubbins Drive, approximately 5 miles to travel camp. *USMRA: Page 81 (D-6)*. **NMC:** Jefferson City, 40 miles northeast.

RESERVATION INFORMATION: Route 1, Box 380, Linn Creek, MO 65052-5000. **C-573-346-5640, DSN-312-581-5640** WEB: www.wood.army.mil/mwr (First Mon in March to Memorial Day weekend 0900-1700 hours Mon-Wed; Memorial Day weekend to Labor Day weekend 0900-1700 hours Mon-Fri.) No mail reservations. Reservations may be made as far in advance as desired, full payment is required within two weeks after reservation is made. Full service Memorial Day weekend-Labor Day weekend. Fri-Sun operations, Apr-May and Sep-Oct. Check in at facility 1500 hours, check out 1100 hours.

TML Mobile home, sofabed, private bath (16); cabin, sofabed, private bath (3); duplex, sofabed, private bath (2); Kitchen, microwave, A/C, TV/VCR. Furnished except cleaning supplies. One bedroom waterfront motel like units, no kitchen (3). Rates: two-bedroom duplex $49-$79; cabin $47-$76; three-bedroom deluxe mobile home $43-$71, waterfront unit $25-$39. Rates applicable for active and retired personnel. *Some pet facilities;* no pets in duplexes, cabins or waterfronts.

TML AVAILABILITY: Fairly good, in season. Very good, off season.

CREDIT CARDS ACCEPTED: Visa and MasterCard.

TRANSPORTATION: None available.

DINING OPPORTUNITIES: None within short driving distance; numerous within 25-minute drive.

New lakefront trailers, cabins, duplexes, rustic and hookup campsites, rental office, and a 20-bay berthing dock for private boat storage. Jet Skis are available. This is a large and fully equipped recreational area, see *Military Living's Military RV, Camping and Outdoor Recreation Around the World.*

Visit Military Living online at
www.militaryliving.com

Marine Corps Activities at Richards-Gebaur Airport (MO02R2)
15431 Andrews Road, Bldg 601
Kansas City, MO 64147-5000

MAIN INSTALLATION TELEPHONE NUMBERS: C-816-843-3800, DSN-312-894-3800. Locator 843-3800; Medical 348-1200; Security Police 234-5550.

LOCATION: From Kansas City take US-71 S to 155th Street exit for Richards-Gebaur Memorial Airport. Between Grandview and Belton. *USMRA: Page 81 (B-5), Page 89 (B-5)*. **NMC:** Kansas City, 17 miles north.

RESERVATION INFORMATION: Lodging Facility, 15820 Elmwood Avenue, Bldg 250, Kansas City, MO 64147-1400. **C-816-843-3850/1/2, DSN-312-894-3850/1/2,** Fax C-816-843-3857, 0630-2345 Mon-Fri, 0730-2345 Sat-Sun, 0730-1600 hours holidays. Duty may make reservations; all others Space-A. Check in at lodging office 1400 hours, check out 1200 hours.

TML Bldgs 250, 252. Bedroom, shared bath and private bath (102); family suite, private bath (4). Refrigerator, microwave, alarm clock radio, A/C, CATV/VCR, phone, housekeeping service, laundry facility, ice machine, free coffee. Bldg 250 modern structure, renovated. Bldg 252 modern structure, renovation planned. Rates: single shared bath $15, double $20; single private bath $20, double $25; family suite $22.

DV/VIP DV suite (4). Refrigerator, microwave, phone, housekeeping service, laundry facility, ice machine. Rates: single $30, double $40.

AMENITIES: Exercise Room, Mini Mart, Snack and Soft Drink Vending Machine.

TML AVAILABILITY: Good.

CREDIT CARDS ACCEPTED: Visa, MasterCard and American Express.

TRANSPORTATION: Car Rental: Enterprise, C-816-765-4404; Off base taxi/limousine service.

DINING OPPORTUNITIES: Country Kitchen, C-816-322-3369; Jess & Jim's Steak House, C-816-941-9499; Oden's BBQ, C-816-322-3072; Ryan's Steak House, C-816-322-7543; and Smoke-Stack, C-816-942-9141 are within driving distance.

Note: Many people do not know that this lodging still exists because the old Richards-Gebaur AFB is closed.

Whiteman Air Force Base (MO04R2)
509th MSS/DPF
750 Arnold Avenue
Whiteman AFB, MO 65305-5000

MAIN INSTALLATION TELEPHONE NUMBERS: C-660-687-1110, DSN-312-975-1110. Locator C-687-1841, DSN-312-975-1841; Medical 687-3733; Security Police 687-3700.

LOCATION: From I-70, exit to 58 S on MO-23, cross US-50 and continue to AFB on east side of MO-23. *USMRA: Page 81 (C-5)*. **NMC:** Kansas City, 60 miles west.

RESERVATION INFORMATION: The Whiteman Inn, Bldg 325, Spirit Blvd, P.O. Box 5032, Whiteman AFB, MO 65305-5097. **C-1-888-AFLODGE (1-888-235-6343), C-660-687-1844, DSN-312-660-975-1844,** Fax: C-660-687-3052, DSN-312-660-975-3052, 24 hours daily. Duty may make reservations any time; Space-A 24 hours in advance. Directions from Main Gate: follow Spirit Blvd approximately 0.33 mile to Whiteman Inn on right side. Check in at lodging 1500-2330 hours, check out 1100 hours.

VAQ The Enterprise Hall, Bldg 1551. E1-E6. Private bedroom, semi-private bath (56); E7-E8 suite, private bath (6). Refrigerator, A/C, CATV, housekeeping service, laundry facility, cribs, rollaways, ice machine. Rates (subject to change): $13.

TLF Bldgs 3003, 3004, 3201/3/5/6. Three-bedroom, two private bath (2); bedroom, private bath, pull out couch (29). Handicap accessible, bedroom, private bath, pull out couch (1). All have refrigerator, A/C, CATV, housekeeping service, laundry facility, cribs, rollaways, ice machine. New and older structures, renovated. Rates (subject to change): $21.50.

VOQ Whiteman Inn, Bldg 325. Suite, private bath (50). Refrigerator, A/C, CATV, housekeeping service, laundry facility, cribs, rollaways, ice machine. Rates(subject to change): $13.50.

CPOQ Chief Suites at Whiteman Inn, Bldg 325. E9 suite, private bath (4). Refrigerator, A/C, CATV, housekeeping service, laundry facility, ice machine, cribs, rollaways. Rates(subject to change): $23.

DV/VIP Whiteman Inn, Bldg 325. O6+. DV Suite, private bath (7). Refrigerator, A/C, CATV, housekeeping service, laundry facility, cribs, rollaways, ice machine. Rates(subject to change): $23.

DV/VIP Protocol: 509 BW/CCP, **C-660-687-7144, DSN-312-975-7144.** Spirit House on Grey Lane, Travis House and Truman House on Travis Lane. O6+. Three-bedroom house, two bath. Refrigerator, A/C, CATV, housekeeping service, laundry facility, ice machine, rollaways and cribs. Rates(subject to change): $25.50.

AMENITIES: Meeting/Conference Room.

TML AVAILABILITY: Good all year except late Jul because of State Fair. Best, winter.

CREDIT CARDS ACCEPTED: Visa, MasterCard and Club Card.

TRANSPORTATION: On base shuttle supplied by 509 Transportation Squadron; Off base taxi: Central Taxi Cab C-660-429-5523; Yellow Cab, C-816-471-5000.

DINING OPPORTUNITIES: The Missions End (on base), BX food court and Stars and Strikes (bowling center).

MONTANA

Malmstrom Air Force Base (MT03R3)
341st MSS/DPF
Family Support Center
312 73rd Street, N
Malmstrom AFB, MT 59402-7511

MAIN INSTALLATION TELEPHONE NUMBERS: C-406-731-1110, DSN-312-632-1110. Clinic Appointments 454-8240; Security Police 731-3827.

LOCATION: From I-15 take 10th Avenue South, exit 278 to Malmstrom AFB. From the east take Malmstrom exit off US-87/89. Clearly marked. *USMRA: Page 99 (D,E-4).* **NMC:** Great Falls, one mile west.

RESERVATION INFORMATION: Malmstrom Inns, Bldg 1680, 7028 4th Avenue N, Malmstrom, AFB, MT 59402-7528. **C-1-888-AFLODGE (1-888-235-6343), C-406-727-8600/731-3394, DSN-312-632-3394,** Fax: C-406-731-3848, DSN-312-632-3848, 24 hours daily. Duty may make reservations any time; Space-A may make reservations 72 hours in advance for up to three nights, space permitting (certain facilities more liberal during off season). Directions: Follow Goddard Drive to the stoplight, turn left on 70th Street at the light, left on 4th Avenue. The main office is the second building on the left. Check in 1400 hours, check

out 1100 hours. *Winner of nine Air Force Major Command Awards and two Air Force Innkeeper Awards in the last nine years.*

VQ Bldg 1680. Check in facility for entire property. All suites, private bath, living room area, refrigerator, microwave, CATV, HBO, laundry facility, housekeeping service, A/C and in-room sundry sales. Lobby features fireplace, coffee bar and three tier deck leading to beer garden. Prairie mission atmosphere. Maximum two persons. No children. *Open June 2001.*

VQ Bldg 1620, next to main lodging office. Suite (8); single room (22). Private bath, refrigerator, wet bar, microwave, CATV/VCR, Sony Playstation, laundry facility, housekeeping service, A/C and in-room sundry sales. Stained glass lobby. Renovated 1994. Rates: room $21.50; suite $35. No children.

TLF Bldgs 1681-1683. Extended stay suites. Seperate bedroom, private bath, kitchen, utensils, A/C, CATV, HBO, housekeeping service, washer dryer in room, cribs, dishwasher and Sony Playstation. Rates: Two bedroom, maximum eight people $29; one bedroom maximun five people $25.

DV/VIP Bldg 1620, next to main lodging office. Officers all ranks. Separate bedroom suite, private bath (4). Refrigerator, microwave, wet bar, TV/VCR, housekeeping service, laundry facility, ice machine, sundry sales. Older structure, renovated 1994. Rates: single $16; double $23. Children not authorized. Duty can make reservations any time; Space-A can make reservations 24 hours in advance.

AMENITIES: Meeting/Conference Room, beer garden (summer), kitchen, exercise room, business center, snacks and travel items available for sale at front desk. During season Custom Suite Stay Packages can be arranged for special occasions.

TML AVAILABILITY: Good, winter. Difficult, May-Sep. Space-A reservations more lenient during winter call for information.

CREDIT CARDS ACCEPTED: Visa, MasterCard and priority Club Card.

TRANSPORTATION: Off base shuttle/bus, C-406-727-7480; Car Rental (Airport); On base taxi, C-406-731-2843; Off base taxi: Diamond Cab, C-406-632-2843.

DINING OPPORTUNITIES: Burger King, C-406-727-7480; Club Malmstrom, C-406-761-6430; and Aces High Bowling Center, C-406-731-2494; are within walking distance. Eddie's Supper Club, C-406-453-1616; Jaker's, C-406-727-1033; and Perkins Restaurant, C-406-453-2411 are within driving distance. A variety of dinning is available in the Great Falls and surrounding area.

Centrally located between Glacier and Yellowstone National Parks. Close to Lewis and Clark's Trail sites and interpretive center. Outdoor Recreation provides trips rafting, skiing, fishing and snowmobiling. They also offer classes many classes in outdoor activities. The Inn is one of Space Command's certified (four star) facilities in the command. Visit the Malmstrom Museum on base.

Timber Wolf Resort (MT09R3)
341st SVS/SVRO, Outdoor Recreation
Malmstrom AFB, MT 59402-6863

MAIN INSTALLATION TELEPHONE NUMBERS: Malmstrom AFB C-406-387-9633 or toll free C-877-846-9653.

LOCATION: Off base near Glacier National Park. From I-15 north of Great Falls and Conrad, take Route 44 west past Valier to Hwy 89 north to Browning. From Browning, take Hwy 2 to Hungry Horse. Resort is on left. *USMRA: Page 99 (D-3).* **NMC:** Great Falls, one mile west.

RESERVATION INFORMATION: 341 SVS/SVRO, Outdoor Recreation, Malmstrom AFB, MT 59402-6863, **C-406-387-9653** or toll free **C-877-846-9653,** Fax: 406-453-6684, 0800-1900. Check in 1500 hours, check out 1000 hours.

(**Trailers**) Four trailers are reserved for military use, operated by Malmstrom AFB, May-Oct. All trailers have bathroom, kitchenette, refrigerator, heat, electric, water and sewage hookups. Rates: $35-$60 per trailer.

AMENITIES: Mini Mart, Gift Shop, Gazebos and BBQ Grills.

TML AVAILABILITY: Trailers May-Oct. Other facilities year round.

CREDIT CARDS ACCEPTED: Visa, MasterCard, American Express and Discover.

TRANSPORTATION: Shuttles between resort and airport; off base taxi service.

DINING OPPORTUNITIES: Local restaurants within five miles.

Editor's Note: Timber Wolf Resort is a commercial resort. Malmstrom AFB reserves four trailers for use by Military. Contact Malmstrom MWR at the above telephone numbers for reservations regarding the trailers. Timber Wolf Resort also has cabins and Bed and Breakfast rooms in the Main Lodge, however, for rental information on these facilities, comtact Timber Wolf Resort directly by e-mail: elek@timberwolfresort.com or visit their website at www.timberwolfresort.com.

This is big sky country with snow skiing, wildlife, rafting, hunting and Canadian fishing trips.

NEBRASKA

Camp Ashland (NE03R3)
220 County Road "A," Bldg 508
Ashland, NE 68003-6000

MAIN INSTALLATION TELEPHONE NUMBERS: C-402-944-2110. Medical/Security Police 911.

LOCATION: From I-80, exit 432. Highway 31, north 0.25 mile to Highway 6. Go west 4 miles to road signs indicating Nebraska National Guard Camp. *USMRA: Page 82 (I-5).* **NMC:** Lincoln, 26 miles southwest. NMI: Offutt Air Force Base, Omaha, 35 miles northeast.

RESERVATION INFORMATION: Lodging Office, Bldg 508, Room 110, Ashland, NE 68003-6000. **C-402-944-2479 ext 200,** Fax: 402-944-2835. E-mail: detne@mail.state.ne.us Reservations can be made at any time; duty has priority. Directions from Main Gate: Left at the battle tank, right at the flag pole. Check in/out room 110, 0730-1630 hours Mon-Fri.

(**BEQ/BOQ**) BEQ Bldgs 505, 506. BOQ Bldg 507. Single bed, shared bath. Refrigerator, TV, clock radio, A/C, iron/ironing board, telephone, housekeeping service. Rates: official $11.55, unofficial $13.65.

(**DV/VIP**) Bldg 507. General Officers' Quarters. E9, O5+. Bedroom, living area, private bath. Refrigerator, microwave, coffee maker, TV, clock radio, A/C, iron/ironing board, telephone, cribs and cots available, housekeeping service. Rates: official $15.75, unofficial $17.85; each additional adult $7.

(**Cabin**) Cabin 450. Located away from other billets near river. Two bedrooms, family area, fully equipped kitchen (utensils and cookware). Coffee maker, microwave, large screen TV, A/C, cribs and cots available, housekeeping service, fireplace, porch with charcoal grill. Rates: official $22.05, unofficial $26.20; each additional adult $7.

(**Army Lodging**) Bldg 13. Three bedrooms, living room, formal dining room, fully equiped kitchen (utensils and cookware). Coffee maker, microwave, TV/VCR, A/C, cribs and cots

available, housekeeping service, porch with charcoal grill. Located near camp entrance, Turner Lake and picnic area. Rates: official $22.05, unofficial $26.20; each additional adult $7.

AMENITIES: Exercise Room, Laundry Facilities, Ice, Snack and Soft Drink Vending Machines.

TML AVAILABILITY: Good.

CREDIT CARDS ACCEPTED: Visa, Mastercard and American Express.

TRANSPORTATION: None available.

DINING OPPORTUNITIES: Ashland Keno Kove, C-402-944-2838; Gateway Inn, C-402-944-9950; Granny's Cafe, C-402-944-3523; and Linoma Beach, C-402-332-4500 are all within driving distance.

SAC Museum, Mahoney State Park, Wildlife Safari Park, Ashland Country Club, Henry Doorly Zoo, State Capital, as well as fishing, swimming and boating in nearby Platte River.

Offutt Air Force Base (NE02R3)
55th MSS/DPF
109 Washington Square, Suite 111
Offutt AFB, NE 68113-2124

MAIN INSTALLATION TELEPHONE NUMBERS: C-402-294-1110, DSN-312-271-1110. Locator 294-5125; Medical 294-7332; Security Police 294-5677.

LOCATION: From I-80, exit to US-75 south to AFB exit, 6.5 miles south of I-80/US-75 interchange, on east side of US-75. *USMRA: Page 82 (I,J-5).* **NMC:** Omaha, eight miles north.

RESERVATION INFORMATION: Offutt Inns, 105 Grants Pass Street, Offutt AFB, NE 68113-2084. **C-1-888-AFLODGE (1-888-235-6343), C-402-291-9000 or 294-3671, DSN-312-271-3671,** Fax: C-402-294-3199, DSN-312-271-3199, 24 hours daily. Duty may make reservations any time and are encouraged to re-confirm three days prior to arrival; Space-A confirmed/non-confirmed 24 hours prior to arrival. Check in 1500 hours, check out 1100 hours. Government civilian employee lodging. Reservations accepted on first-call, first-served basis.

(**TLF**) **Platte River Lodge.** Bldgs 5089-5093. Cottage, two-room, private bath (60). Complete kitchen, microwave, A/C, TV/VCR, housekeeping service, laundry facility, cribs, highchairs, ice machine. Older structure, renovated. Rates (subject to change): $21.50. Maximum five per unit. No smoking. No pets.

(**VQ**) **Offutt Inn.** Bldg 479. Bedroom, private bath (39). Refrigerator, microwave, A/C, TV, laundry facility, ice machine, housekeeping service. Renovated structure. Handicap accessible (2). Rates (subject to change): $13. Maximum two per room. No smoking. No pets.

(**VQ**) **O'Malley Inn.** Bldg 436. Bedroom, private bath (79). Refrigerator, microwave, A/C, TV, housekeeping service, laundry facility, ice machine. Modern structure. Handicap accessible (1), non-smoking. Rates (subject to change): $13.50. Maximum two per unit. No smoking. No pets.

(**DVQ**) **Fort Crook House,** Quarters 13. O6+. Separate bedroom suite, private bath (6); separate bedroom suite, shared bath (2). Refrigerator, microwave, utensils, A/C, TV, laundry facility, housekeeping service. Historic Building (1900's), renovated. Rates (subject to change): $23. Maximum two per unit. No smoking. No pets.

(**VQ**) **Malmstrom Inn.** Bldg 432. Officers all ranks, SNCO E7+. Separate bedroom suite, private bath, Officers (28), SNCOQ (18). Refrigerator, microwave, A/C, TV, housekeeping service, laundry facility, ice machine. Older structure, renovated. Rates (subject to change): $23. Maximum two per unit. No smoking. No pets.

DVQ **Fort Crook House,** Quarters 13. O7+. Two-bedroom, private bath (2). Full kitchen, microwave, A/C, TV, housekeeping service. Historic Building (1900's), renovated. Rates: $23-$25.50 (subject to change). Maximum two per unit. No smoking. No Pets.

DVQ **Offutt Inn.** Bldg 479. O7+. Separate bedroom suite, private bath (5). Refrigerator, microwave, A/C, TV, housekeeping service, laundry facility, ice machine. Older structure, renovated. Rates (subject to change): $23. Maximum two per suite.

DV/VIP USSTRATCOM Protocol, Bldg 500, **C-402-294-4212.** O7+. 55 Wing Protocol **C-402-294-5797.** O6+.

TML AVAILABILITY: Good. Best, Nov-Jan. More difficult, other times.

CREDIT CARDS ACCEPTED: Visa and MasterCard.

TRANSPORTATION: On base shuttle/bus; Car Rental.

DINING OPPORTUNITIES: Exchange Snack Bar (open Mon-Fri) is located within walking distance. Godfather Pizza, C-402-292-5850; O Club, C-402-294-2268; E Club, C-402-294-3766; and Golf Course, C-402-294-3362.

Try nearby Omaha's Old Town for shopping and dining, Fontenelle Park for hiking and the historic Southern Railroad Depot for getting in touch with this interesting area. Don't miss the Joslyn Art Museum. The Henry Dooly Zoo is located next to Rosenblatt Stadium, which hosts the College World Series in June.

NEVADA

Fallon Naval Air Station (NV02R4)
4755 Pasture Road, Bldg 309
Fallon NAS, NV 89496-5000

MAIN INSTALLATION TELEPHONE NUMBERS: C-775-426-5161; DSN-312-890-5161; Medical 775-426-3100 & 775-428-0100; Security Police 775-426-2803, Quarterdeck 775-426-2715.

LOCATION: From Reno/Tahoe Airport take I-80 east through Reno/Sparks. Approximately 30 miles, take exit 48 to Fernley. Turn left on the first light onto US Highway alternate 50 and continue for 30 miles to Fallon. Continue through the town of Fallon (four stop lights). Go past the Churchhill Community Hospital (on the left) until you come to Crook Road (1.5 miles past hospital). Follow Crook Road to dead end and make a left at the stop sign. Take the first right on to Pasture Road (1 mile) to the Main Gate (located on left) at Cottonwood Drive. *USMRA: Page 113 (C-4).* **NMC:** Reno, 72 miles west.

RESERVATION INFORMATION: Combined Bachelor Housing, Bldg 354, 4755 Pasture Road, Fallon NAS, NV 89496-5000. **C-775-428-3003/3004, C-775-426-3199, DSN-312-890-3003/3004,** 0600-1800 daily. Fax: C-775-426-2378, DSN-312-890-2378; Combined Bachelor Housing Officer, C-775-426-2966, Mon-Fri 0730-1600; Reservations: C-775-426-3199, Fax: C-775-426-2378, 24 hours daily. E-mail: cbhinns@ fallon.navy.mil Duty may make reservations; retired and leave Space-A. Directions: From Main Gate, straight on Churchill turn left at Credit Union on Lahontan; Stillwater Inns on right. Check out 1000 hours. Government civilian employee billeting.

BEQ Bldgs 306, 310, 357-359, 474-477, 490. Leave or official duty. Bedroom, two beds, shared bath. Refrigerator, A/C, TV/VCR, housekeeping service, laundry facility. Modern structure. Rates: $6.

BOQ Bldgs 69, 72-75, 78-80, 356, 468, 469, 471, 472. Leave or official duty. Bedroom, semi-private bath; separate bedroom, private bath. Kitchen, refrigerator, A/C, TV/VCR, housekeeping service, laundry facility. Modern structure. Rates: sponsor $15, each additional person $3.

NAVY LODGE Navy Lodge. Pasture Road, Fallon NAS, NV 89496-5000. **C-1-800-NAVY-INN.** Lodge number is C-775-428-2704, Fax: 775-423-3720. Located outside Main Gate near Exchange Mall. Check in 1700 hours, check out at main exchange. Large double room, private bath (6). Kitchen, microwave, A/C, CATV/VCR, HBO, phone, clock radio, coffee maker. Rates: $40 per unit. All categories may make reservations. No pets.

DV/VIP BEQ: **C-775-428-2859**. VIP rooms. Refrigerator, A/C, TV/VCR, housekeeping service, laundry facility, ice machines, vending. BOQ: DV/VIP suites, private bath; DVQ suites with full-size kitchen. Refrigerator, A/C, TV, housekeeping service, laundry facility. Rates: BEQ room $15; BOQ suite $20.

AMENITIES: Exercise Room, Meeting/Conference Room, Mini Mart, free USA Today newspaper. Ice, Snack and Soft Drink Vending Machines.

TML AVAILABILITY: Impossible during CVW deployments; excellent rest of the time.

CREDIT CARDS ACCEPTED: Visa, MasterCard and American Express.

TRANSPORTATION: On base shuttle, C-775-426-2792; Off base taxi, C-775-423-9333; Car Rental C-775-867-3245.

DINING OPPORTUNITIES: Parcheezi Pizza, C-775-426-2454; Subway, C-775-423-9600; Galley; and Sportline Bar & Grill are within walking distance.

At the Carson River and Lake Lahontan, fishing, boating, swimming, water skiing and local rock collecting are of interest. Call MWR for special rates to Reno, Tahoe, Carson City, Virginia City, and other points of interest.

Indian Springs Air Force Auxiliary Field
(NV03R4) Det 1, 99 RANS
P.O. Box 569
Indian Springs, NV 89018-7001

MAIN INSTALLATION TELEPHONE NUMBERS: C-702-652-1110, DSN-312-682-1110. Locator 652-0401; Medical 118; Security Police 116.

LOCATION: Off US-95, 47 miles northwest of Nellis Air Force Base. On the north side of US-95, take Indian Springs exit north. *USMRA: Page 113 (F-8).* **NMC:** Las Vegas, 45 miles southeast.

RESERVATION INFORMATION: Lodging Office, Bldg 65, Indian Springs, NV 89018-7001. **C-1-888-AFLODGE (1-888-235-6343), C-702-652-0401, DSN-312-682-0401,** Fax: C-702-652-0456, DSN-312-682-0456, 0730-1630 hours. Write to: P.O. Box 569, Indian Springs, NV, 89018. Duty may make reservations any time; Space-A may make reservations 24 hours in advance. Check in at billeting, check out 1100 hours.

VAQ/VOQ Bldgs 4-8, 24, 127. Bedroom, two beds, private and shared bath (107). Kitchenette (Bldg 127), refrigerator, utensils on request, TV in room and lounge, housekeeping service, laundry facility, toiletries, ice machine (Bldg 24). Rates: $8-$10. No pets.

VOQ House. Bldg 37. O5+. Three-bedroom, two bath, living room, kitchen. Utensils and cookware, TV/VCR, housekeeping service, laundry facility. Rates: $10 per person.

AMENITIES: Exercise Room, Meeting/Conference Room, Mini Mart, Snack and Soft Drink Vending Machines.

TML AVAILABILITY: Fairly good. Best winter months, more difficult, summer.

CREDIT CARDS ACCEPTED: Visa and MasterCard.

TRANSPORTATION: None available.

DINING OPPORTUNITIES: Brusso Hall, C-702-652-0237; Indian Springs Casino, C-702-879-3456; and Oasis Bar & Restaurant, C-702-879-3711 are within walking distance.

There is a casino off base with gaming available here, and the Las Vegas area offers many other activities. But the desert also attracts rock hounds, and would-be archeologists who look at Indian drawings among the red rock formations. Mt. Charleston/Lee Canyon Ski Resort approximately 45 minutes from base.

Nellis Air Force Base (NV01R4)
99 MSS/DPF
4311 N Washington Blvd, Suite 102
Nellis AFB, NV 89191-7073

MAIN INSTALLATION TELEPHONE NUMBERS: C-702-652-1110, DSN-312-682-1110. Locator 652-1841; Medical 653-2343; Security Police 652-2311.

LOCATION: Off I-15. Also accessible from US-93/95. Exit 48 east on Craig Road to north on Las Vegas Blvd to Main Gate on right. Clearly marked. *USMRA: Page 113 (G-9).* **NMC:** Las Vegas, eight miles southwest.

RESERVATION INFORMATION: 99 SVS/SVML, 5990 Fitzgerald Blvd, Bldg 780, Nellis AFB, NV 89191-6514. **C-1-888-AFLODGE (1-888-235-6343), C-702-652-2711, DSN-312-682-2711,** Fax *(for those on official orders only)*: C-702-652-9172, DSN-312-682-9172, 24 hours daily. E-mail: svml@svs99.nellis.af.mil Duty may make reservations any time; Space-A may make reservations 24 hours in advance. Check in at billeting, check out 1200 hours. Government civilian employee billeting. Handicap accessible units.

TLF 2900s (9 buildings). Bedroom, private bath (60). Wall beds in all living rooms. Kitchen, refrigerator, complete utensils, A/C, TV/VCR, housekeeping service, laundry facility, cribs, cots, ice machine, playground. Modern structure, remodeled. Handicap accessible. Rates: $21.50. Rates are subject to change. Maximum five per unit.

VAQ Bldgs 536, 552, 465. Bedroom, semi-private bath (258); SNCO room, private bath (64); Chief's suite, private bath (1); single room, double bed, shared bath (8). Refrigerator, microwave, phone, clock radio, A/C, TV (with VCR, Bldg 552), housekeeping service, laundry facility, ice machine. Modern structure, remodeled. Rates (subject to change): $13 per person; Chief's suite $23. Maximum two per unit. Children not allowed during deployments. *Note: The number of rooms available is subject to change due to renovation projects.*

VOQ Bldgs 465, 523, 538, 540, 545. Bedroom, private bath (261). Kitchen, refrigerator, microwave, utensils only in suites, A/C, TV/VCR, phone, clock radio, housekeeping service, laundry facility, iron/ironing board. Modern structures. Rates (subject to change): $13.50. Maximum two per unit. No children.

DV/VIP Protocol Office, Bldg 620, Room 112, **C-702-652-2525/702-643-2987.** Suite, private bath (5). Kitchen, refrigerator, microwave, utensils, A/C, TV/VCR, phone, clock radio, housekeeping service, laundry facility, iron/ironing board. Modern structures. Rates (subject to change): $23-$25.50. Maximum two per unit. No children.

AMENITIES: Mini Mart, Snack and Soft Drink Vending Machines.

TML AVAILABILITY: Extremely limited. Best, spring and Nov-Dec. Difficult, other times.

CREDIT CARDS ACCEPTED: Visa and MasterCard.

TRANSPORTATION: Car Rental: AAFES, C-702-644-5567.

DINING OPPORTUNITIES: E Club, C-702-652-9733; O Club, C-702-652-9188; and Time Out Sports Lounge, C-702-652-2880 are within walking distance.

The Las Vegas area offers Lake Mead for boating and swimming, Mt. Charleston for snow skiing, Red Rock Canyon for scenic hiking and Hoover Dam for sheer wonderment. Of course, Las Vegas is noted for night life and gambling!

Stead Training Center/Army National Guard Base (NV08R4)
4600 Alpha Avenue
Reno, NV 89506-1276

MAIN INSTALLATION TELEPHONE NUMBERS: C-775-677-5213, DSN-312-830-5413, Toll Free-800-797-8323. Medical 911, Security Police 911.

LOCATION: From I-80, exit to NV-395 to Stead exit to Alpha Avenue to Main Gate. *USMRA: Page 113 (B-4).* **NMC:** Reno, 10 miles south. NMI: Fallon NAS, 60 miles east.

RESERVATION INFORMATION: Bldg 8205, 4600 Alpha Avenue, Reno, NV 89506-5000. **C-775-677-5213 or 1-800-797-8323, DSN-312-830-5213** Fax: C-775-677-5203, 0600-1630 hours Mon-Fri. E-mail: steadreservations@nv.ngb.army.mil Duty must make reservations; others Space-A. Check in at billeting during operation hours.

BEQ/BOQ Bldg 8203, 8204, 8206, 8207. Bedroom (43). Refrigerator, A/C, coffee pot, phones, TV/VCR in room and lounge, housekeeping, towels, laundry facility. Rooms recently renovated. Rates: BEQ $15 per night; BOQ $20 per night; additional occupant $5. Maximum two persons.

AMENITIES: All buildings are equipped with washer and dryer. Snack, soda and ice machines are located in the billeting office hallway which is open 24 hours a day.

TML AVAILABILITY: Good, except drill weekends (first full weekend of each month).

CREDIT CARDS ACCEPTED: None.

TRANSPORTATION: Off base bus, Car Rental (in Reno at airport), Off base taxi.

DINING OPPORTUNITIES: Numerous restaurants within driving distance in Reno.

NEW HAMPSHIRE

Portsmouth Naval Shipyard (NH02R1)
Portsmouth Naval Shipyard, NH 03804-5000

MAIN INSTALLATION TELEPHONE NUMBERS: C-207-438-1000, DSN-312-684-1110. Medical 438-2555; Security Police 438-2351.

LOCATION: From I-95 north, cross Piscataqua River Bridge into Maine. Take exit 2 to US-236 to US-1 south to US-103, left onto Walker Street to Gate 1. Or, from I-95 south, take exit 2, follow above directions. Located on an island on Piscataqua River between Portsmouth and Kittery, ME. *USMRA: Page 23 (H-9).* **NMC:** Portsmouth, in city limits.

RESERVATION INFORMATION: Helmsman Inn, CBH, Bldg H-23, Portsmouth, NH 03804-5000. **C-207-438-1513/2015, DSN-312-684-1513/2015,** Fax: C-207-438-3580. Check in after 1400 hours, check out 1200 hours. *Earned a five-star rating for Excellence in Bachelor Housing in 1998 and 2000.*

DVQ Official duty only. Refrigerator, microwave, TV/VCR, movie rental, phone, hair dryer, housekeeping service, laundry facility, toiletries, fitness center, sundry sales available at Central Registration, Bldg H-23. Rates: suite $21, each additional person $4; single room $14, each additional person $4. Duty may make reservations up to 60 days in advance. No pets.

TML Family quarters. Two-room suite with kitchen and the above amenities (8). Rates: $21 per room, per additional guest $4. Children under five free. Due to room size, families with more than five persons must rent two rooms. No pets. Mainly for use by PCS; others Space-A.

TML AVAILABILITY: Fairly good, depending on number of ships in overhaul.

CREDIT CARDS ACCEPTED: Visa, MasterCard and American Express.

TRANSPORTATION: Off base taxi, C-603-431-2345.

DINING OPPORTUNITIES: Asia House, C-603-436-3343; Captain Simeon's Seafood, C-207-439-3655; and Weathervane, C-207-439-0330 are within driving distance.

Local skiing at White Mountain, outlet shopping in nearby Kittery, and trips to Boston are some of the favorite pursuits in this area.

NEW JERSEY

Cape May Coast Guard Training Center (NJ13R1)
1 Munro Avenue
Cape May, NJ 08204-5002

MAIN INSTALLATION TELEPHONE NUMBERS: C-609-898-6900, DSN-312-898-6900. Locator 898-6900; Medical 898-6959; Security Police 911.

LOCATION: Take Garden State Parkway or US-9 to Cape May. In Cape May, take Pittsburgh Avenue to Pennsylvania Avenue to Main Gate of Center. *USMRA: Page 19 (D-10).* **NMC:** Atlantic City, 45 miles northeast.

RESERVATION INFORMATION: MWR Office, Bldg 269, 1 Munro Avenue, Cape May, NJ 08204-5002. **C-609-898-6922, DSN-312-898-6922** 0800-1630 hours Mon-Fri. No after hours, Sat, Sun or holiday. PCS and TDY have priority; others Space-A. Check in/out at MWR Office. Government civilian employee billeting.

TLQ Two-bedroom cottage, private bath (6). Kitchenette, refrigerator, utensils, CATV, cribs, cots. Wood frame buildings. Rates $17-$44, depending on rank and status. No pets

TML AVAILABILITY: Difficult year round.

CREDIT CARDS ACCEPTED: None.

TRANSPORTATION: Car Rental: Gentilini, C-1-800-648-0242, C-609-861-2185; Off base taxi.

DINING OPPORTUNITIES: Mad Batter Restaurant, C-609-884-5970; Spiaggi, C-609-884-3504; and Waters Edge, C-609-884-1717 are within driving distance.

Resort Area. Fishing, boating, beaches. Museums and parks abound.

Earle Naval Weapons Station (NJ11R1)
201 State Highway 34 South
Colts Neck, NJ 07722-5020

MAIN INSTALLATION TELEPHONE NUMBERS: C-732-866-2000, DSN-312-449-2000. Medical 866-2911; Security Police 866-2911.

LOCATION: From New Jersey Turnpike (I-95), exit 8 to NJ-33, east through Freehold to NJ-34, north to Main Gate. Or exit Garden State Parkway to NJ-33, west to NJ-34, north to Station. *USMRA: Page 19 (F,G-5).* **NMC:** Newark, 50 miles north.

RESERVATION INFORMATION: NWS Earle, 201 Highway 34 S, Colts Neck, NJ 07722-5020, Attn: I.T.T. **C-732-866-2103, DSN-312-449-2167,** Fax: C-732-866-1259, DSN-312-449-1259, 0900-1600 hours Mon-Fri. PCS and TDY have priority; others Space-A. Directions: Bldg. C-62 Youth Center. From Main Gate drive straight ahead, pass large electronic sign on right. Turn left onto Macassar Road continue on Macassar across railroad track to first building on left, use far end door. Check in at facility. No civilian employee billeting.

BQ BQ desk C-732-866-2121. Active Duty, PCS or Active assigned to Earle receive priority. Mobile home, private bath (4). Kitchen, refrigerator, microwave, utensils, A/C, CATV/VCR. Rates $22-$35, depending on rank. Maximum six per unit. No pets.

AMENITIES: Fittness Center, small NEX and Club nearby.

TML AVAILABILITY: Difficult. Best winter.

CREDIT CARDS ACCEPTED: Visa and MasterCard.

TRANSPORTATION: Off base taxi.

DINING OPPORTUNITIES: Huddy's, C-732-431-0194; Christophus, C-732-308-3668; Colts Neck Inn, C-732-462-0383; Perkins, C-732-577-1011; Tutta Italia, C-732-780-8877; and Buon Appetito, C-732-303-0533 are within walking distance.

Seven miles from the New Jersey shore, where sport fishing, swimming and boating are available. One hour from New York City.

Fort Dix Army Garrison (NJ03R1)
Attn: AFZT-CFA (ACS)
5407 Pennsylvania Avenue
Fort Dix, NJ 08640-5130

MAIN INSTALLATION TELEPHONE NUMBERS: C-609-562-1011, DSN-312-944-1110. Locator 562-1011; Medical 562-2695; Security Police 562-6001.

LOCATION: From NJ Turnpike (I-95), exit 7, right onto NJ-206, short distance left on NJ-68, continue to General Circle and Main Gate. *USMRA: Page 19 (E,F-6).* **NMC:** Trenton, 17 miles northwest.

RESERVATION INFORMATION: Attn: AFRC-FA-CF-LD, Lodging Division, Bldg 5255, P.O. Box 419, Maryland Avenue and 1st, Fort Dix, NJ 08640-0419. **C-609-562-3188/723-2026, DSN-312-944-3188,** Fax: C-609-562-3752, DSN-312-944-3752, 24 hours daily. All categories may make reservations. Check in at facility, check out 1100 hours.

VEQ Bldg 5255. Bedroom, semi-private bath (80). Refrigerator, A/C, TV in room and lounge, housekeeping service, laundry facility, cribs, cots, ice machine. Older structure, renovated. Rates: TDY $34, each additional person $5.

VOQ Bldg 5255. Separate bedrooms, private bath (13). Refrigerator, A/C, TV in room and lounge, housekeeping service, laundry facility, cribs, cots, ice machine. Older structure, renovated. Rates: TDY $34, each additional person $5.

Army Lodging Doughboy Inn. Bldg 5997. C-609-723-5579, Fax: C-609-562-3367. Bedroom, two double beds, private bath (76). Community kitchen, A/C, TV, phone, housekeeping service, coin laundry facility, cribs ($2.50), cots ($2.50), ice machine. Modern structure. Rates: TDY double $41; three persons $46; four or more $51. All categories may make reservations.

DVQ Bldg 5256. O6+. Bedroom suite, private bath (4); two-bedroom apartments, private bath (4). Kitchen (apartments), refrigerator (suites), utensils, A/C, TV in room and lounge, housekeeping service, laundry facility, cribs, cots, ice machine. Modern structure. Rates: $37, each additional person $5.

DV/VIP HQ USATC and Fort Dix, Attn: Office of The Secretary General Staff, **C-609-562-5059/6293.** O6+/civilian equivalent. Retirees Space-A.

AMENITIES: Snack and Soft Drink Vending Machines.

TML AVAILABILITY: Good, Oct-Mar. Difficult, other times.

CREDIT CARDS ACCEPTED: Visa, MasterCard and American Express.

TRANSPORTATION: Car Rental; On/Off base taxi.

DINING OPPORTUNITIES: Mulligan's on Post. Various within driving distance.

Nearby Brindle Lake, a 30-acre lake surrounded by about 2,000 acres of pine forest provides rental boats (no power boats), camping, picnic and barbecue facilities. Six Flags Great Adventure Amusement Park is located in Jackson, NJ, approximately 15 miles away. Visit Trenton and its historic sites 17 miles northwest.

Fort Monmouth (NJ05R1)
Bldg 812, Murphy Drive
Fort Monmouth, NJ 07703-5113

MAIN INSTALLATION TELEPHONE NUMBERS: C-732-532-9000, DSN-312-992-9000, Locator 532-1492; Medical 532-2789; Security Police 532-1112.

LOCATION: From Newark Airport: take New Jersey Turnpike south to exit 11, to Garden State Parkway south, exit 105 for Eatontown. Take Route 36 E to intersection of Route 35 N to Main Gate. From North: Take New Jersey Turnpike north to exit 7A, at exit take Route 195 E to Shore Points. Take Garden State Parkway N to exit 105, Eatontown. Take Route 36 E to intersection of Route 35, take Route 35 N to Main Gate. 105*USMRA: Page 19 (G-5).* **NMC:** New Brunswick, 23 miles northwest.

RESERVATION INFORMATION: Lodging Office, Bldg 270, Allen Avenue, Fort Monmouth, NJ 07703-5108. **C-732-532-1092/5501/1635, DSN-312-992-1092/5501/1635,** Fax: C-732-532-0012, 0730-2345 hours. Other hours, Work Center Office, Bldg 166, C-732-532-1122. Check in 1500 hours at lodging office, check out 1100 hours. Government civilian employee billeting on official business.

VQ Bldgs 360, 363, 364. Officers, TDY civilians, Enlisted, SNCOs on official duty. Inquire about rooms and services. Rates: single occupancy $44, double occupancy $54. All military and goverment civilians leisure travel with families. Rates: single occupancy $40, double occupancy $50. No children. Duty may make reservations; others Space-A. No pets.

Army Lodging Bldg 365. Suite bedroom, sofabed, private bath, sitting room (60). Kitchen, microwave, TV, housekeeping service, cots, ice machine. Handicap accessible (5). Rates: PCS single occupancy $40, double occupancy $50; Unofficial single occupancy $45, double occupancy $55. All categories may make reservations Space-A. No pets.

DVQ Blair Hall, Bldg 259. O6/GS15+. Inquire about rooms and services available. Modern structure, renovated. Rates: single occupancy $50, double occupancy $60; super suite: single occupancy $75, double occupancy $85. Duty may make reservations; others Space-A. No pets.

AMENITIES: Meeting/Conference Rooms. Snack and Soft Drink Vending Machines and Laundry Facilities in every building.

TML AVAILABILITY: Good.

CREDIT CARDS ACCEPTED: Visa and MasterCard

TRANSPORTATION: On base shuttle/bus, Off base taxi.

DINING OPPORTUNITIES: Lane Hall Combined Club, C-732-532-3892; and Olde Wharf Inne Oceanport, C-732-542-1661 are within walking distance. Gibbs Hall O Club, C-732-532-4520; The Olde Union House, C-732-747-3444; and Zachary's, C-732-229-0286 are within driving distance.

Within three miles of the ocean, the area also has two race tracks for thoroughbreds and trotters. Atlantic City 1.5 hours south, New York City, one hour north. Nearby Garden State Art Center and Count Basie Theatre for concerts year round.

Lakehurst Naval Air Engineering Station (NJ08R1)
FSC, Code 8.0D.3, B488/2
Attn: RAP
Lakehurst, NJ 08733-5076

MAIN INSTALLATION TELEPHONE NUMBERS: C-732-323-2011, DSN-312-624-2011; Medical 323-4000; Security Police 323-4000, DSN-312-624-4000.

LOCATION: Take the Garden State Parkway S to NJ Route 70, west to city of Lakehurst, right on NJ-547 and proceed 1 to base. *USMRA: Page 19 (F-6).* **NMC:** Trenton, 30 miles northwest.

RESERVATION INFORMATION: Combined Bachelors' Housing, NAES Bldg 481, Lakehurst, NJ, 08733-5041. **C-732-323-2266, DSN-312-624-2266,** Fax: C-732-323-4371/1402/5067, DSN-312-624-4371/1402/5067, 24 hours daily. Located 0.5 miles inside Main Gate on right. Check in 1600 at facility, check out 1100 hours. Government civilian employee billeting on official business.

CBH Maloney Inn, Bldg 481. All military, permanent party, transient. Dual occupancy rooms, shared private bath (15); private rooms, private bath (26). TV/VCR, microwave, refrigerator, housekeeping service, laundry facility, ice machine. Rates: call for current information. Active Duty, all others on official business may make reservations; Space-A, daily only, after 1600 hours. No children. No pets.

BOQ Bldg 33. O1-7, official duty. Private suite, private bath (11); Commanding Officers' Guest Suite (1); Handicap accessible (1). TV/VCR, microwave, refrigerator, housekeeping service, laundry facility,. Rates: call for current information. Active Duty, all others on official business may make reservations; Space-A, daily only, after 1600 hours. No children. No pets.

TFQ Transient Family Accomadations Units, two bedroom (4). Kitchenette, complete utensils, TV/VCR, microwave, refrigerator, housekeeping service, laundry facility. Rates: call for current information. Active Duty only, make reservations with their families. No pets.

AMENITIES: Snack and Soft Drink Vending Machines.

TML AVAILABILITY: Very good, all year.

CREDIT CARDS ACCEPTED: Visa, MasterCard and American Express.

TRANSPORTATION: Car Rental: Enterprise, C-732-408-0464; Off base taxi: Ace Taxi, C-732-657-2626; Roadrunner Taxi, C-732-657-1616

DINING OPPORTUNITIES: Galley and Subway are within walking distance of Bldgs 481/33. Angelo's Pizza of Manchester, C-732-657-6060; Circle Landmark, C-732-657-8377; Great Wok, C-732-657-1616; Plaza Diner, C-732-657-7771; and other restaurants are within fifteen mile drive.

This is the site of the crash of the Airship Hindenburg, memorial on base. One of the last Airship "Blimp" hangers, Hanger One. On base golf course, biking, boating, fishing and hunting in season. There is nearby Lakehurst conservation area.

McGuire Air Force Base (NJ09R1)
305th AMW/PA
2901 Falcon Lane
PSC Box 3000
McGuire AFB, NJ 08641-5000

MAIN INSTALLATION TELEPHONE NUMBERS: C-609-754-1100, DSN-312-650-1100. Locator 754-1110; Medical 562-4061; Security Police 911.

LOCATION: From New Jersey Turnpike (I-95), exit 7 to NJ-206 south to Route 68 south, then to Route 537, turn left. Take Route 537 northeast to intersection (traffic light) of Routes 545 and 680, turn right. Take Route 680 to base's Main Gate, about 2 miles. Clearly marked. *USMRA: Page 19 (E-6)*. NMC: Trenton, 18 miles northwest. NMI: Fort Dix, adjacent.

RESERVATION INFORMATION: All-American Inn, SVS/SVML, Bldg 2717, McGuire AFB, NM 08641-5012. C-1-888-AFLODGE (1-888-235-6343), C-609-754-3336/7, DSN-312-650-3336/7, Fax: C-609-754-2035, DSN-312-650-2035. E-mail: reservations@mcguire.af.mil. 24 hours daily. Check in at facility by 1800 hours, check out 1100 hours. Government civilian employee billeting. *Note: All rooms are smoke and tobacco free.*

(TLQ) One bedroom, sofabed, private bath (30). Kitchen, A/C, TV, housekeeping service, laundry facility. Older structure. Rates: $24.50 per unit. Duty may make reservations any time; Space-A on walk in basis only.

(VAQ) Bedroom, semi-private bath (359). A/C, TV, housekeeping service. Older structure. Rates: $17.50 per person. Duty may make reservations any time; Space-A 24 hours in advance.

(VOQ) Bedroom, semi-private bath (100). A/C, TV, housekeeping service. Older structure. Rates: $20 per person. Duty may make reservations any time; Space-A 24 hours in advance.

(DV/VIP) Protocol Office, C-609-754-2405. E9, O6+. Bedroom suite, private bath (17). A/C, TV, housekeeping service. Rates: Chief Suite $21.50; DV Suite $25 per unit. Duty may make reservations any time; Space-A on walk in basis only.

AMENITIES: Meeting/Conference Room.

TML AVAILABILITY: Good, Oct-Apr. Difficult, other times.

CREDIT CARDS ACCEPTED: Visa and MasterCard.

TRANSPORTATION: Car Rental: B&J Rental, C-609-723-1313, Enterprise, C-609-291-1112, Hertz, C-609-298-8585; Off base taxi, C-609-723-2001, C-609-723-3000.

DINING OPPORTUNITIES: Dining Hall, C-609-754-3784; NCO Club, C-609-754-2396; Wright Brothers Cafe, C-609-754-4278; and O Club, C-609-754-3297 are within walking distance.

New Jersey coastal fishing is popular here. Trenton, the state capital, has many historic sites and an excellent Cultural Center.

Miles of roads and trails show off a number of well kept state forests. Atlantic City, New York and Philadelphia are nearby.

Picatinny Arsenal (NJ01R1)
US Army TACOM/ARDEC
Attn: AMSTA-AR-MWR-R, Bldg 34N
Picatinny Arsenal, NJ 07806-5000

MAIN INSTALLATION TELEPHONE NUMBERS: C-973-724-4021, DSN-312-880-4012. Medical 724-2113; Security Police 724-6666.

LOCATION: From I-80 west, exit 34-B to Route 15 N, follow signs to Center, 1 mile north. From I-80 east, exit 34 to Route 15 N, follow signs to Center. *USMRA: Page 19 (E-2)*. NMC: Newark, 30 miles east.

RESERVATION INFORMATION: US Army TACOM/ARDEC, Attn: AMSTA-AR-MWR-R, Bldg 3359, Picatinny Arsenal, NJ 07806-5000. C-973-724-8855/4186, DSN-312-880-8855/4186, Fax: C-973-724-3263, DSN-312-880-8855, 0800-1530 hours Mon-Fri. Check in 1500 hours, check out 1100 hours. After hours, persons with reservations may check in with Desk Sgt for key, Bldg 173, C-973-724-6666. DV/VIP: C-ext 7026.

(Army Lodging) Guesthouse. Bldg 110. Four-room suite, three beds, private bath (1). Kitchen, living room, dining area. Room 2: One-room, three beds, private bath (1). Room 3: One-room, four beds, private bath (1). Room 4: One-room, two beds (1). Community kitchen, refrigerator, A/C, TV in room and lounge, housekeeping service, laundry facility, cribs, cots. Older structure, renovated. Rates: room $36; suite $52. Reservations open the first working day of the month for the following month

(Mobile Home) MWR Campground. Attn: Trailer Park Office, Bldg 34N, Picatinny Arsenal, NJ 07806-5000. C-973-724-4014, DSN-312-880-4014. Directions: From Main Gate, follow Parker Road to Cannon Gate. Go left on 1st Street, take first right on Ramsey Avenue, follow around sharp corner to Bldg 34N on right. Mobile homes, two-bedroom (6); three-bedroom (9). Kitchen. Rates: $33-$40.

TML AVAILABILITY: Fairly good, mobile homes difficut May-Sep.

CREDIT CARDS ACCEPTED: Visa and MasterCard.

TRANSPORTATION: On base taxi, C-973-724-2049, DSN-312-880-2049; Car Rental: C-1-800-361-6264; Avis, C-973-361-0250; Off base taxi, C-973-366-0800.

DINING OPPORTUNITIES: Cafeteria within walking distance of guesthouse.

Townsends Inlet
Recreation Facility (NJ20R1)
8101 Landis Avenue
Sea Isle City, NJ 08243-5000

MAIN INSTALLATION TELEPHONE NUMBER: C-609-263-3722.

LOCATION: From North Garden State Parkway, exit 17 then east to Sea Isle City. South (right) on Landis Avenue. On the corner of 82nd and Landis. NMI: USCG Air Station Atlantic City, 25 miles north. NMC: Atlantic City, 25 miles north; Cape May, 25 miles south.

RESERVATION INFORMATION: USCG Townsends Inlet Recreation Facility, 8101 Landis Avenue, Sea Isle City, NJ 08243-5000. C-(Nov-Feb) 609-677-2028, (Mar-Oct) 609-263-3722, 0800-1600 Mon-Fri. Web: www.uscg.mil.d5/group/atlanticcity/htmls/rr_inst.html Check in on premises 1400-1600 hours, check out 1000 hours. Prepayment required. Reservations: Active Duty USCG 90 days in advance, all other Active Duty 75 days in advance, retired CG 60 days in advance, all other retired 50 days in advance, dependents 45 days in advance, all others 30 days in advance.

(**Beach House**) Apartment, shared bath (2), private bath (2). Community kitchen and dining room. Refrigerator, cookware/utensils, microwave, CATV/VCR, telephone, washer/dryer, toiletries, cribs, high chairs, cots, lounge, picnic area with grill, bikes available. All facilities non smoking. Rates per day: Winter (Sep-May): E1-E3, $36; E4-E6, $38; E7-O2, $40; O3-O4 and W3-W5, $42; O5-O10, $46. Summer (Jun-Aug): E1-E3, $38; E4-E6, $40; E7-O2, $42; O3-O4 and W3-W5, $45; O5-O10, $48. No Pets.

TML AVAILABILITY: Year Round, most difficult in summer.

CREDIT CARDS ACCEPTED: None

TRANSPORTATION: None

DINING OPPORTUNITIES: Resort area with many restaurants nearby.

Peaceful location, short walk from the beach, space for outdoor games, fishing, ocean kayaking, sailing and wind surfing.

NEW MEXICO

Cannon Air Force Base (NM02R3)
27 MSS/DPF
200 W Terminal Avenue
Cannon AFB, NM 88103-5000

MAIN INSTALLATION TELEPHONE NUMBERS: C-505-784-1110, DSN-312-681-1110. Locator 784-1110; Medical 784-4033; Security Police 784-4111.

LOCATION: From Clovis, near the Texas border, west on US-60/84 for 7 miles to AFB south of US-60/84. From NM-467 enter the Portales gate. *USMRA: Page 114 (H-5)*. **NMC:** Clovis, seven miles east.

RESERVATION INFORMATION: Caprock Inn, 401 S Olympic Blvd, Cannon AFB, NM 88103-5328. **C-1-888-AFLODGE (1-888-235-6343), C-505-784-2918/2919, DSN-312-681-2918/2919,** Fax: C-505-784-4833, DSN-312-681-4833, 24 hours daily. Duty may make reservations any time; Space-A may make reservations 24 hours in advance. Directions from Main Gate: Right on Ingram Blvd, right on Casablanca Avenue, left on Olympic Blvd. Check in at billeting, check out 1200 hours. Government civilian employee billeting.

(**TLQ**) Bldgs 1812, 1818, 1819. Family unit (44). Kitchen, utensils, A/C, TV, housekeeping service, laundry facility. Older structure. Rates: $21.50 per room. List of kennels available.

(**VQ**) Bldg 1816. All ranks, DoD civilians. Suite (8), standard room (31). Refrigerator, A/C, CATV/VCR, coffeemaker, microwave, housekeeping service, laundry facility. Rates: $13.50.

(**DV/VIP**) Protocol Office, **C-505-784-2727.** CMSGT; COL+. Bldg 1812, 1800. Separate bedroom suite, private bath (6). Kitchen, utensils, TV, housekeeping service, laundry facility. Older structure. Rates: smaller room $20.50, larger room $24.50.

AMENITIES: Ice, Snack and Soft Drink Vending Machines.

TML AVAILABILITY: Good, Nov-Feb. Difficult, other times.

CREDIT CARDS ACCEPTED: Visa and MasterCard.

TRANSPORTATION: On base taxi, C-505-784-2775, DSN-312-681-2775.

DINING OPPORTUNITIES: Anthony's Pizza, C-505-784-5777; Bowling Center, C-505-784-2280; and The Landing, C-505-784-2853 are within walking distance. Amici's Pizza, C-505-784-2448; Burger King, C-505-784-3878; and Golf Snack Bar, C-505-784-2800 are within driving distance.

Visit the Blackwater Draw Museum, Roosevelt County Museum, or the Oasis State Park outside Portales for fishing, hiking, picnics and camping. Local lakes offer good fishing.

Holloman Air Force Base (NM05R3)
49th MSS/DPF
850 First Street
Holloman AFB, NM 88330-8035

MAIN INSTALLATION TELEPHONE NUMBERS: C-505-572-1110, DSN-312-572-1110. Locator 572-7510; Medical 572-7768; Security Police 572-7171.

LOCATION: Exit US-70, eight miles southwest of Alamogordo. Route to AFB north of US-70 is clearly marked. *USMRA: Page 114 (D,E-7)*. **NMC:** Las Cruces, 50 miles southwest.

RESERVATION INFORMATION: Holloman Inn, Bldg 583, 1040 New Mexico Avenue, Holloman AFB, NM 88330-8159. **C-1-888-AFLODGE (1-888-235-6343), C-505-572-7160/3311/3468/3880, DSN-312-572-7160/3311/3468/3880,** Fax: DSN-312-572-7753, 24 hours daily. Active Duty may make reservations any time; Space-A may make reservations 24 hours in advance. Check in at facility 1400, check out 1100 hours. Government civilian employee billeting.

(**TLF**) Bldgs 590-594. Bedroom, private bath, sofa and chair sleepers (50). Kitchen, complete utensils, A/C, TV, housekeeping service, laundry facility, cribs, cots, highchairs, ice machine. Rates: Priority 1 $17.50 (E1, E2 and O1); all others $21.50. No smoking. No pets.

(**VAQ**) Bldgs 583, 584. Enlisted all ranks (Bldg 584); SNCO (Bldg 583). Rates: $13.50. No smoking. No pets.

(**VOQ**) Bldgs 582, 585-587. Bedroom, private bath (133). Kitchen, microwave, coffee maker, A/C, TV, housekeeping service, cots. Modern structure. Rates: DVOQ $23-$25.50. No smoking. No pets.

(**DV/VIP**) 49 FW/CC, Bldg 29. E9, O6/GS15+. **C-505-572-5573/74, DSN-312-572-5573/74.** No smoking. No pets.

TML AVAILABILITY: Good, Nov-Jan. Difficult, other times.

CREDIT CARDS ACCEPTED: Visa and MasterCard.

TRANSPORTATION: Car Rental (check with front desk).

DINING OPPORTUNITIES: Bowling Center, Shifting Sands Dining Facility and NCO Club are within walking distance. Westerner Dining Facility is within driving distance.

Kirtland Air Force Base (NM03R3)
377th SVS/SVML
1951 2nd Street, SE
Kirtland AFB, NM 87117-5521

MAIN INSTALLATION TELEPHONE NUMBERS: C-505-846-0011, DSN-312-246-0011. Locator 846-0011; Medical 846-3730; Security Police 846-7913.

LOCATION: From I-40, exit on Wyoming Blvd, south for 2 miles to Wyoming gate to AFB. *USMRA: Page 114, (D-4)*. **NMC:** Albuquerque, one mile northwest.

RESERVATION INFORMATION: Kirtland Inn, Box 5418, Bldg 22016, Club Drive, Kirtland AFB, NM 87185-5000. **C-1-888-AFLODGE (1-888-235-6343), C-505-846-9652/9653, DSN-312-246-9652/9653,** Fax 505-846-4142, DSN-312-246-4142, 24 hours daily. Duty may make reservations any time; Space-A may make reservations 24 hours in advance. Check in at billeting, check out 1100 hours. Active Duty, Retirees, Reservists, NG, government civilian employee billeting. Handicap accessible units available.

TLF Houses. Three- and four-bedroom houses, private bath (39). Kitchen, A/C, TV, housekeeping service, washer/dryer. Rates: $30 per unit. No pets.

VAQ Bldgs 918, 924. A/C, TV, housekeeping service, laundry facility, ice machine. Rates: $19 per person. No pets.

VOQ Bldgs 1911, 22001-22003, 22010-22012. Suite, living room, bedroom, private bath (216). Refrigerator, A/C, TV, housekeeping service, laundry facility, ice machine. Older structure. Rates: $19 per person. No pets.

DV/VIP 377 ABW/Protocol Office, reservations **C-505-846-4119, DSN-312-246-4119.** O6+/civilian equivalents. Bldgs 22000, 22011. Suite (25). Rates: $26 per person. No pets.

AMENITIES: Exercise Room

TML AVAILABILITY: Best, late fall and winter. Fri and Sat nights always better than during the week. Worst, June-Oct.

CREDIT CARDS ACCEPTED: Visa and MasterCard.

TRANSPORTATION: On base taxi, C-505-846-TAXI (8294). Off base taxi available.

DINING OPPORTUNITIES: E Club, C-505-846-5165; and O Club, C-505-846-1467 are within walking distance.

Take the tram to the Sandia Mountains, investigate the National Atomic Museum and Old Town Albuquerque, founded in 1706. Enjoy local skiing, the State Fair in September, the International Hot Air Balloon Fiesta each October.

White Sands Missile Range (NM04R3)
White Sands Missile Range, NM 88002-5000

MAIN INSTALLATION TELEPHONE NUMBERS: C-505-678-2121, DSN-312-258-2121. Locator 678-1630; Medical 678-2882; Security Police 678-1234.

LOCATION: From US-70, 18 miles south of Alamogordo, follow signs to Visitors Center and White Sands Missile Range, north of US-70. Clearly marked. *USMRA: Page 114 (D-7).* **NMC:** El Paso, TX, 45 miles south.

RESERVATION INFORMATION: Attn: White Sands Lodging Office, Bldg 501, 1st Floor, P.O. Box 37, White Sands Missile Range, NM 88002-5000. **C-505-678-4559, DSN-312-258-4559,** Fax: C-505-678-2367, DSN-312-258-4559, 0700-1630 Mon-Thurs, 0700-1530 every other Fri. Closed weekends and holidays—check in at Law Enforcement & Security Directorate, Bldg 384 Picatinny Avenue. E-mail: parrelltl@wsmr.army.mil Directions: From El Paso Gate, 4-Mile access road to main post, left on Aberdeen Avenue, five blocks down on right; from Las Cruces Gate: proceed down to Aberdeen Avenue (about four blocks), right on Aberdeen Avenue and five blocks down on right. Check out 1200 hours. Charge for late checkouts. Handicap accessible units available.

VOQ/DVQ Bldgs 501, 502, 504. Military and DoD civilians on official duty; also Space-A. Bedroom, private bath (2); suite, private bath (41). Refrigerator, microwave, CATV, coffee maker, iron/ironing board, DATA hookup. Two-bedroom apartment, private bath (3). Kitchen, refrigerator, microwave, complete utensils, A/C, CATV, housekeeping service, iron/ironing board. Rates: TDY $41, spouse $5 additional. Reservations confirmed only for TDY or PCS military families in/out. Three-bedroom houses (11) at $41 and up, depending upon number of beds used. Strict no pet policy.

Army Lodging Bldg 506. Reservations confirmed only for military in PCS/TDY status. Two double beds, private bath, (15). Kitchenette, stove, complete utensils, microwave, A/C, CATV, laundry facility, iron/ironing board. Modern structure. Rates: $41, each additional person/bed $5.

DV/VIP Protocol, **C-505-678-1028, DSN-312-258-1028.** O6/GS15+. Three houses. Full kitchen, refrigerator, microwave, complete utensils, A/C, TV, housekeeping service, washer/dryer, iron/ironing board. Rates: $51, each additional person $10, each additional bed $20, per night.

AMENITIES: Community Kitchen in each building. Laundry facilities, Snack and Soft Drink Vending Machines.

TML AVAILABILITY: Fall and winter months, very good. Spring and summer months, good.

CREDIT CARDS ACCEPTED: Visa, MasterCard, American Express and Discover.

TRANSPORTATION: None available. Must have own transportation.

DINING OPPORTUNITIES: Mountain View Cafeteria, C-505-678-2081; Italian Cafe, C-505-678-0544; Frontier Club, C-505-678-2055; and Bowling Alley are within walking distance.

Las Cruces' blending of three cultures, and New Mexico State University supply much entertainment locally. Visit the International Space Hall of Fame in Alamogordo, White Sands National Monument and El Paso, gateway to the Southwest and Mexico.

NEW YORK

Fisher House, Albany (NY34R1)
Stratton VA Medical Center
113 Holland Avenue
Albany, NY 12208-5000

Note: Appendix B has the definition of this facility. Fisher Houses are only available as lodging for families of patients receiving medical care at military and VA medical centers.

MAIN INSTALLATION TELEPHONE NUMBERS: C-518-462-3311 ext 2800. Security Police 462-3311 ext 2377.

LOCATION: From north and airport take I-87 approaching exit 1 then left onto Western Avenue (Route 20). Stay to the right and merge onto Madison. Then right on New Scotland Avenue, entrance to medical center on left, parking on right. From south take I-87 exit 23. Go left onto 9W and follow blue "H" signs to medical center. **NMC:** Albany, in city limits.

Fisher House Stratton VA Medical Center, 113 Holland Avenue, Albany, NY 12208-5000. **C-518-462-3311 ext 2800,** Fax: C-518-462-3596, 0800-1600 hours Mon-Fri. Rates: $8 per night per person.

DINING OPPORTUNITIES: VA Medical Center Canteen C-518-462-3311 ext 2430. Numerous fast food restuarants also nearby.

Fort Drum (NY06R1)
Bldg P-4205 Povalley Road
Fort Drum, NY 13602-5286

MAIN INSTALLATION TELEPHONE NUMBERS: C-315-772-6011, DSN-312-772-6011/774-6011. Locator 772-5869; Medical 772-5236; Security Police 772-5156.

LOCATION: From I-81 take exit 48 (north of Watertown) east, and follow signs to Fort Drum. *USMRA: Page 21 (J-3).* **NMC:** Watertown, eight miles southwest.

RESERVATION INFORMATION: Lodging Office, Bldg T-227, Officers' Loop, Fort Drum, NY 13602-5097. **C-315-772-5435, DSN-312-772-5435/774-3435,** 24 hours daily. E-mail: lodging@drum.army.mil Check in at billeting, check out 1100 hours. Government civilian employee billeting.

TLF **The Inn.** C-315-773-7777. Room, queen-size bed (111). Kitchenette (64), microwave (111). A/C, CATV, phone. Civilian funded motel operated by the Army. Rates: $30, each additional person $5.

VOQ Fax C-315-772-9647. Cottage (9), one- and two-bedroom, private bath (2). Kitchen, complete utensils, TV, housekeeping service, laundry facility, cribs, cots. Rates $31, each additional person $5.

DV/VIP Protocol Office, Bldg P-10000, **C-315-772-5010,** Fax 315-772-9647. O6+. Retirees and lower ranks Space-A.

AMENITIES: Business Center with two computers with Internet/E-mail access, Mini Mart, Play Room, Snack and Soft Drink Vending Machines.

TML AVAILABILITY: Good, Oct-Apr. Difficult, other times.

CREDIT CARDS ACCEPTED: Visa, MasterCard, American Express, Discover and Diners.

TRANSPORTATION: On/Off base taxi, C-315-786-3362, C-315-785-9710.

DINING OPPORTUNITIES: Primo's Express, C-315-772-0405; and The Commons, C-315-772-6222 are within walking distance.

Sackets Harbor Battleground, site of War of 1812 battle. Nearby is the fascinating area called 1,000 Islands, rich in water recreation. Canada is 45 minutes away.

Fort Hamilton (NY02R1)
HQ New York Area Command
Public Affairs
Bldg 302, Room 8
Brooklyn, NY 11252-5700

MAIN INSTALLATION TELEPHONE NUMBERS: C-718-630-4101, DSN-312-232-1110. Locator 630-4958; Medical 630-4615; Security Police 630-4456.

LOCATION: From Belt Parkway exit 2 (Fort Hamilton Parkway) to 100th Street, right to Fort Hamilton Parkway, right to Main Gate. *USMRA: Page 26 (D-7).* **NMC:** New York, in city limits.

RESERVATION INFORMATION: Adams Guesthouse, Bldg 109, Schum Avenue, Brooklyn, NY 11252-5330. **C-718-630-4564/4052/4892, DSN-312-232-4564/4052/4892,** 24 hours daily; C-718-630-4564 (recording). Check in at facility after 1400 hours, check out 1000 hours. Government civilian employee billeting (on orders).

Army Lodging Adams Guesthouse. Bldg 109, Bldg 110. Bedroom, private bath (39), shared bath (48). Kitchen, microwave, A/C, CATV in room and lounge, coin laundry facility, ice machine. Rates: official $45, unofficial $50. Maximum four per room. All can make reservations. TDY has priority; others Space-A. No pets.

DV/VIP Liaison and Protocol Office, Bldg 302, Room 13, **C-718-630-4436.** Adams Guesthouse. Bldg 109. O6+. Separate bedroom, private bath (2). Refrigerator, coffee, CATV, A/C, housekeeping service. Rates: official $50, unofficial $60. Duty and Retirees may make reservations. No pets.

TML AVAILABILITY: Good, winter months. Difficult, summer months.

CREDIT CARDS ACCEPTED: Visa, MasterCard and American Express.

TRANSPORTATION: On/off base shuttle/bus; the subway.

DINING OPPORTUNITIES: Burger King, Combined Club and Tiffany's are within walking distance.

New York Coast Guard Activities (NY01R1)
Commander
212 Coast Guard Drive
Fort Wadsworth
Staten Island, NY 10305-5000

MAIN INSTALLATION TELEPHONE NUMBERS: C-718-354-4037. *Ten digit dialing required for local calls.*

LOCATION: Take I-95, exit 13 east to Goethals Bridge (I-278 east) to Staten Island. Last exit before Verrazano Bridge, (Lily Pond Avenue). At light go left onto School Road, follow School Road to next light, go right onto Bay Street to Main Gate. *USMRA: Page 26 (D-5).* **NMC:** New York City.

RESERVATION INFORMATION: Reservations required. MWR CG Activities NY, 204 Molony Drive, Fort Wadsworth, Staten Island, NY 10305-5000. Call MWR **C-718-354-4407** Mon-Fri, 0900-1500 for more information. Fax: C-718-354-4406. E-mail: mwrres@actny.uscg.mil WEB: www.uscg.mil/d1/units/actny

Guesthouse Guest House is a former family housing unit, comprised of a two- and a three-bedroom apartments. Each unit is fully furnished with CATV, private bath, fully equipped kitchen, A/C, telephone, and backyard deck with grill. Parking is shared with the Navy Lodge. No smoking. No pets.

AMENITIES: Nearby CG Exchange, MWR Fitness Center and Gym.

TML AVAILABILITY: Fair.

CREDIT CARDS ACCEPTED: Visa, MasterCard, American Express, and Discover.

TRANSPORTATION: Local taxis available.

DINING OPPORTUNITIES: Galley, 718-354-4360; and numerous restaurants within driving distance.

Take the Staten Island Ferry, a ten minute drive with parking available, to get to downtown Manhattan.

Niagara Falls International Airport/Air Reserve Station (NY12R1)
2720 Kirkbridge Drive
Niagara Falls ARS, NY 14304-5001

MAIN INSTALLATION TELEPHONE NUMBERS: C-716-236-2000, DSN-312-238-2000. Locator 236-2002; Medical 236-2086/7; Security Police 236-2278.

LOCATION: Take I-190, exit 23. Travel east on Porter-Packard Road. After approximately 1.5 miles, the name of the road will change to Lockport Road. Another 1.5 miles, the installation Main Gate will be on the right. *USMRA: Page 20 (D-6).* **NMC:** Niagara Falls, six miles west.

RESERVATION INFORMATION: Niagara Falls Lodge, 914th AW/SVML, 10780 Kinross Street, Bldg 312, Niagara Falls ARS, NY 14304-5058. **C-1-888-AFLODGE (1-888-235-6343), C-716-236-2014, DSN-312-238-2014,** Fax: C-716-236-6348, DSN-312-238-6348, 0700-2300 hours. Duty may make reservations any time; Space-A may make reservations 24 hours in advance. Check out 1000 hours. Government civilian employee lodging.

VAQ Bldgs 502, 504. Bedroom, two beds, common bath (34). Refrigerator, A/C, TV, housekeeping service, laundry facility, ice machine. Rate: $14.50.

VAQ Bldg 508. Bedroom, semi-private bath (36). Housekeeping service, laundry facility, ice machine. Rates: single $15.50, double $21.50. SNCO: bedroom suite, living room, private bath (2). Refrigerator, A/C, TV, phone. Rate: $23.00.

VOQ Bldgs 300 (new) and 312. Bedroom, private bath (103). Refrigerator, A/C, TV, phone, housekeeping service, laundry facility, cribs, cots, ice machine, lounge with microwave. Rate: $23.00.

VOQ/VIP Bldg 312. O5/GS13+. Suites, bedroom, living area, private bath (6). Refrigerator, microwave, A/C, TV, phone, housekeeping service. Rate: $31.50.

VOQ/VIP Bldgs 304E, 304W, 306E, 306W. DV Suites. Three-bedroom, queen-size bed, shared living room, private bath (4). Refrigerator, microwave, A/C, TV, phone, housekeeping service, laundry facility.

VOQ/VIP Bldg 308. Bedrooms, king-size bed, shared living room and dining area, private bath (2). Refrigerator, A/C, TV, phone, housekeeping service, laundry facility. Rate: $31.50.

AMENITIES: Meeting/Conference Room, Snack and Soft Drink Vending Machines.

TML AVAILABILITY: Good, Oct-Mar. Difficult, Apr-Sep. Avoid weekends.

CREDIT CARDS ACCEPTED: Visa, MasterCard and Air Force Club Cards (Credit or Proprietary).

TRANSPORTATION: Car Rental, Off base taxi available.

DINING OPPORTUNITIES: Most major chains and numerous local establishments within ten miles.

Niagara Falls, Winter Gardens, Niagara Power Vista, Old Fort Niagara, Our Lady of Fatima Shrine, Art Park, Casino Niagara and the Aquarium are all attractions in this area. Also visit the amusement parks and scenic area surrounding the Niagara frontier.

Soldiers', Sailors', Marines' and Airmen's Club (NY17R1)
283 Lexington Avenue
New York, NY 10016-3540

(This is not U.S. Government/Military Lodging.)

MAIN INSTALLATION TELEPHONE NUMBERS: C-212-683-4353, Fax: C-212-683-4374. In US toll free **1-800-678-8443**. Locator 683-4353; medical 911; Security Police 911.

LOCATION: Midtown Manhattan, on Lexington Avenue between 36th (one way eastbound) and 37th Streets (one way westbound); 5 blocks from Grand Central Terminal at 42nd Street and Lexington Avenue. *USMRA: Page 26 (E-4).* **NMC:** New York, in city limits. NMI: Fort Hamilton, seven miles south.

RESERVATION INFORMATION: 283 Lexington Avenue, New York, NY 10016-34540. E-mail: ssmaclub@ix.netcom.com WEB: www.ssmaclub.org Lobby desk open 24 hours daily. Call above numbers for reservations and information on lodging and related club activities, or visit the website. Check in 1430 hours at lobby desk, check out 1030 hours.

AUTHOR'S NOTE: The **Soldiers', Sailors', Marines' and Airmen's Club** is a tax exempt, not-for-profit organization founded in 1919 to serve the needs of service personnel while visiting New York City.

TML Rooms contain different numbers of beds and if checking in alone, you may be placed in a room with guests of the same gender. Room, two beds (21); room, three beds (6); room, four beds (1); room, six beds (1). **Facilities are spartan and baths *must* be shared.** *Note for the mobility impaired: There is no elevator at this location and all rooms are on the second, third and fourth floors.*

RATES: Eligibility	Rate
(Proof required)	(daily)
Enlisted E1-E4 (Active Duty, Reservist, NG)	$25
Service Academy and ROTC Cadets	$25
Enlisted E5 and above	$30
Merchant Seamen	$30
Officers (Active Duty, Reservist, NG)	$40
Retired Military (all ranks)	$40
Widows/Widowers (of eligible personnel)	$40
Veterans-honorably discharged,	$45
Visitors of eligibles	$45
Children: Under 3 (occupying bed with parent)	FREE
Ages 3-13	$10
Ages 14+	same as sponsor

AMENITIES: Meeting/Conference Rooms (25-150 people).

CREDIT CARDS ACCEPTED: Visa, MasterCard and Discover.

Located in the Murray Hill section of New York, SSMAC is close to the Empire State Building, Radio City Music Hall, Fifth Avenue and Madison Avenue shops, Grand Central Station and Penn Station. See NYC without spending a bundle on hotels.

Staten Island Navy Lodge (NY07R1)
Bldg 408, North Path Road
Staten Island, NY 10305-5000

MAIN INSTALLATION TELEPHONE NUMBERS: C-718-442-0413. Locator 614-5815; Medical 226-9200; Security Police 390-1762 (Coast Guard Police), 338-3988 (National Park Police).

LOCATION: Take I-95, exit 13 east to Goethals Bridge (I-278 east) to Staten Island. Last exit before Verrazano Bridge, (Lily Pond Avenue). At light go left onto School Road, follow School Road to next light, go right onto Bay Street to Main Gate. *USMRA: Page 26 (C-7).* **NMC:** New York City.

RESERVATION INFORMATION: Navy Lodge, Bldg 408, North Path Road, Staten Island, NY 10305-5000. **C-1-800-NAVY-INN.** Lodge number is C-718-442-0413, Fax: C-718-816-0830, 24 hours daily. All categories may make reservations. Check in 1500-1800 hours, check out 1200 hours.

NAVY LODGE Navy Lodge. Bedroom, two queen-size beds, private bath, dining area (40); handicap accessible bedroom, queen-size bed, sofabed (2); bedroom, queen-size bed (8). Kitchenette, microwave, utensils, A/C, CATV/VCR, video rental, phone, housekeeping service, laundry facility, iron/ironing board, cribs, parking, playground. Interconnecting and smoking or non-smoking rooms available. All rooms renovated 1997. Rates: $67. No pets; kennel available in area.

AMENITIES: Meeting/Conference Room, Mini Mart, Ice, Snack and Soft Drink Vending Machines.

TML AVAILABILITY: Good all year, weekends difficult.

CREDIT CARDS ACCEPTED: Visa, MasterCard and American Express.

TRANSPORTATION: City bus to ferry picks up on base between 0600-0900 hours. After 0900, bus stop is one block from back gate. Car Rental: Enterprise, C-1-800-736-1217; Off base taxi C-718-442-4242.

DINING OPPORTUNITIES: Carriage House, C-718-876-6489; Coast Guard Exchange, C-718-815-6519; Galley, C-718-354-4360; and Gym-MWR C-718-354-4407 are within walking distance. Basilo Restaurant,

C-718-447-9292; Country Club Diner, C-718-442-3212; and Evergreen, C-718-720-6242 are within driving distance.

National Park Service has opened Fort Wadsworth. For information call 718-354-4500. While visiting, take a 30-minute ferry ride to Manhattan, or see sites such as the Statue of Liberty, the Empire State Building, Times Square or Rockefeller Center

Staten Island Navy Lodge is just a ferry ride away from New York City.

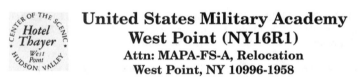

United States Military Academy West Point (NY16R1)
Attn: MAPA-FS-A, Relocation
West Point, NY 10996-1958

MAIN INSTALLATION TELEPHONE NUMBERS: C-845-938-4011, DSN-312-688-1110, Fax: C-845-564-6328. Locator 938-4011; Medical 938-4004; Security Police 938-3333.

LOCATION: Off I-87 or US-9 west. From I-81 take exit 16 west on Route 6 E to 9 W north to Main Gate. Clearly marked. *USMRA: Page 28 (C,D-3,4).* **NMC:** New York City, 50 miles south.

RESERVATION INFORMATION: Five Star Inn, Bldg 2113, Pershing Center, West Point, NY 10996-2002. **C-845-938-6816/446-5943 or C-1-800-247-5047,** 24 hours daily. WEB: www.usma.army.mil/dcfa/activity/5star/5star.htm Check in at facility after 1300 hours, check out 1000 hours. No government civilian employee billeting.

Army Lodging Five Star Inn, Bldg 2113 & 785. Bldg 785 has 20 efficiency apartments and 10 family rooms. Bldg 2113 has 14 suites and 19 family rooms. Each room has queen, double or twin beds, CATV/VCR, iron, A/C, coffeepot, microwave, toaster, refrigerator. Laundromat, cribs, rollaways, fax machine available. Official rates: Efficiency apt $51 single, $56 double (Bldg 785); Family rooms $56 single, $61 double (Bldg 785 & 2113); Suites $61 single, $66 double (Bldg 2113); Executive suites $66 single, $71 double (Bldg 2113). Unofficial rates: Add one dollar to above prices. Each additional person $5. No pets.

TML Hotel Thayer, 674 Thayer Road, West Point, NY 10996. C-845-446-4731, or toll free 1-800-247-5047. Fax C-845-446-0338. E-mail: info@hotelthayer.com WEB: www.hotelthayer.com Newly refurbished, 128 rooms, 9 suites. Amenities include CATV, hairdryer, coffeemaker, iron, voice mail, refrigerator, room service, in-room movies, office area with internet access and data ports, gift shop. Reservations accepted one year in advance. Open to the public. Government rates: 10% discount off rack rates with ID card. TDY rates available upon request/orders. Rates: Room $99-$225 per night; long term stay available

at $85 per night (min 14 nights). No Pets. *Note: Hotel Thayer was privatized in March 1998 and has undergone major renovation. More construction is planned to add 132 rooms, conference facilities, restaurant, pool, ballroom and other amenities.*

DV/VIP Protocol Office, Bldg 600, **C-845-938-4315/4316.** O7/GS16+. Retirees Space-A.

AMENITIES: Snack and Soft Drink Vending Machines.

TML AVAILABILITY: Difficult, May-Sept and during sporting events.

CREDIT CARDS ACCEPTED: Visa and MasterCard.

TRANSPORTATION: On base shuttle/bus, C-845-938-2018/2047, DSN-312-688-2018/2047; On base car rental, C-845-938-3601; Off base taxi, Bosch's Taxi, C-845-446-4588; Metro North Train Station, C-1-800-638-7646.

DINING OPPORTUNITIES: West Point Club on post C-446-5504, Dining at Hospital (on orders), Grant Hall.

Part of the U.S. Armed Forces Recreation System, the history of the Military Academy, sporting events and special vacation packages are available at this castle-like hotel rising above the Hudson River.

NORTH CAROLINA

Camp Lejeune Marine Corps Base (NC10R1)
Attn: FSC
PSC Box 20004
Camp Lejeune MCB, NC 28542-0004

MAIN INSTALLATION TELEPHONE NUMBERS: C-910-451-1113, DSN-312-451-1113. Locator 451-3074; Medical 451-4372; Security Police 451-2555.

LOCATION: Main Gate is 6 miles east of junction of US-17 and NC-24, off NC-24. *USMRA: Page 45 (L,M-5).* **NMC:** Jacksonville, six miles northwest.

RESERVATION INFORMATION: Attn: AC/S Facilities, Bachelor Housing, PSC Box 20004, Bldg 2617, Seth-Williams, Camp Lejeune, NC 28542-0004. **C-910-456-1070 ext 0, DSN-312-751-2368.** Fax: C-910-451-1755, 24 hours daily. Check in 1400 hours, check out 1100 hours. Government civilian employee billeting.

BEQ Bldg HP-51. C-910-456-1080 ext 0. E6-E9. Efficiency, private bath, kitchenette (18); Suite, living room, bedroom, private bath, kitchenette, refrigerator (52); bedroom SNCO transient billeting (21). Coffee maker, utensils, AC, TV in room and lounge, housekeeping service, laundry facility, cribs, cots, facilities for DAVs. Older structure, renovated. Rates: $16-$21. Duty may make reservations; others Space-A.

BOQ Bldg 2617. C-910-456-1070 ext 0. Efficiency, private bath, kitchenette (18); suite, bedroom, living room, private bath, kitchenette, refrigerator (53); bedroom SNCO transient billeting (21). Coffee maker, utensils, AC, TV in room and lounge, housekeeping service, cribs, cots, laundry facility, facilities for DAVs. Older structure, renovated. Rates: $25-$35. Duty may make reservations; others Space-A.

Guesthouse Hospitality Inn. Bldg 896, on Holcomb Blvd near Marine Corps Exchange, 4 miles from Main Gate. **C-910-451-3041, Fax: C-910-451-0360.** Check in after 1500 hours, 24 hour desk. Bedroom, two double beds, private bath (90). Kitchenette, utensils, refrigerator, microwave, A/C, TV/VCR, housekeeping service, cribs ($1), cots ($1), coin laundry facility, video rentals. Non-smoking facility. In walking distance of Exchange Food Court with commissary,

Burger King and Dominos Pizza. Rates: $44.95 per unit. Reservations highly resommended. Duty has priority; others Space-A. No pets.

(**DV/VIP**) Protocol Office, **C-910-451-2523**. O6+. Bldg 2601: Suite, two-bedroom, kitchen, private bath (1); bedroom suite, kitchen, private bath (2). A/C, housekeeping service, laundry facility, cribs. Bldg 2607: Separate bedroom suite, kitchenette, private bath (6). A/C, housekeeping service, laundry facility, cribs. Rates: DV $20-$40 per unit. Bldg HP-51. C-910-456-1070 ext 0. SNCO bedroom, private bath (2). All categories can make reservations; Retirees Space-A.

AMENITIES: Exercise Room, Meeting/Conference Room, Snack and Soft Drink Vending Machines.

TML AVAILABILITY: Limited, year round.

CREDIT CARDS ACCEPTED: Visa, MasterCard and American Express.

TRANSPORTATION: On base taxi, C-910-451-3674.

DINING OPPORTUNITIES: Paradise Point O Club (guest of BOQ), C-910-451-2465 is within walking distance. Applebee's, C-910-347-6011; Captain Charlie's, C-910-326-4303; and Ragazzi's, C-910-577-2782 are within driving distance.

Nearby Onslow Beach offers swimming, surfing and picnicking, and local marinas offer boat rentals. Two 18-hole golf courses are also nearby.

Cape Hatteras Coast Guard Group (NC09R1)

P.O. Box 604, Old Lighthouse Road
Buxton, NC 27920-0604

MAIN INSTALLATION TELEPHONE NUMBERS: C-252-995-1110. Locator 995-6408; Medical 995-6425; Security Police 911

LOCATION: From US-158 south or US-64 east, take NC-12 south to Buxton (approximately 50 miles south of Nags Head). East on Old Lighthouse Road, 0.5 mile to base. *USMRA: Page 45 (P-3)*. **NMC:** Elizabeth City, 110 miles northwest.

RESERVATION INFORMATION: Cape Hatteras Recreational Quarters, USCG Group Cape Hatteras, P.O. Box 604, Buxton, NC 27920-0604. **C-252-995-3676**, 0830-1630 hours Mon-Fri (peak season), 0830-1230 hours (off season). Fax: C-252-995-3748. Reservations required with advance payment 30-90 days by mail. Credit card required. Summer months reservations only taken by phone.

(**TML**) Room, sleep five, private bath (6). Portable refrigerator, TV, rollaways. Rates: $30-$37. Suite, sleep seven, private bath (1). Kitchen, TV. Rates: $42-$57. Winter rates available. Active Duty, Retirees, reserve, non-commissioned and Coast Guard civilians only. All categories can make reservations. No pets.

(**DV/VIP**) O4+. VIP suite, sleeps five, private bath, kitchen area, TV. Non-smoking. Rates: $55. Winter rates available. No pets.

TML AVAILABILITY: Limited. Book early.

CREDIT CARDS ACCEPTED: Yes.

TRANSPORTATION: None available.

DINING OPPORTUNITIES: Diamond Shoals, C-252-995-5217; Cape Sandwich Co., C-252-995-6140; Angelo's Pizza, C-252-6364; Billy's Fish House, C-252-995-5151; Pilot House, C-252-995-5664; and Soundside, C-252-995-6778 are within driving distance.

Within walking distance of historic Cape Hatteras Lighthouse. Famous for fishing, a mecca for wind surfers- "the best surfing on the east coast." For the sedentary, you will find peaceful, clean beaches and solitude (off season).

Cherry Point Marine Corps Air Station (NC02R1)

Family Service Center
PSC, Box 8022
Cherry Point, NC 28533-0022

MAIN INSTALLATION TELEPHONE NUMBERS: C-252-466-2811, DSN-312-582-1110. Locator 466-2109; Medical 466-0266; Security Police 466-3615.

LOCATION: On NC-101 between New Bern and Morehead City. US-70 connects with NC-101 at Havelock. *USMRA: Page 45 (N-4)*. **NMC:** New Bern, 17 miles northwest.

RESERVATION INFORMATION: Billeting Fund, Bldg 487, BOQ 1 Madison Drive, Havelock, NC 28533-5079. **BEQ C-252-463-3061/252-466-3060, DSN-312-582-3060,** Fax: C-252-466-3060. **BOQ C-252-466-3359, DSN-312-582-5169,** Fax: C-252-466-5221, DSN-312-582-5221, 24 hours daily. Check in 1400 hours at facility, check out 1200 hours. Government civilian employee billeting.

(**BEQ/TEQ**) Bldg 3673. 104 total spaces. Room, private bath; SNCO bedroom, private bath (40). Microwave, coffee maker, A/C, TV (not PCS), phone, housekeeping service, laundry facility, ice machine. Older structure, renovated. Rates: single $12-$14, double $9 per person, family rooms $14; each additional dependent $2 (except family rooms). TAD/PCS have priority; others Space-A. PCS rooms, three to a room, shared bath. No amenities. Rates: $3 per night.

(**BOQ/TOQ**) Bldgs 487, 496. Bedroom, private bath (53); separate bedroom suite, private bath (22). Refrigerator, microwave, coffee maker, A/C, TV, phone, housekeeping service, laundry facility, ice machine, meeting/conference room. Older structure, renovated. Rates: single $16; suite $19; each additional dependent $2. Duty may make reservations; others Space-A.

(**Guesthouse**) DGQ. Bldg 313. O6+. Commander, **C-252-466-2848, DSN-312-582-2848.** Four-bedroom house, private bath (1). Kitchenette, microwave, complete utensils, A/C, TV/VCR, phone, housekeeping service, washer/dryer. Rates: $30. O6+ may make reservations; others Space-A.

(**DV/VIP**) Commander's Office, **C-252-466-2848, DSN-312-582-2848.** BOQ VIP Suits (4), alternate VIP suite (4). Microwave, coffee maker, honor bar, A/C, TV, phone, housekeeping service, laundry facility, ice machine. Rates: $21, each additional dependent $2. BEQ VIP rooms. Rates: $16, each additional dependent $2.

TML AVAILABILITY: Limited, book early.

CREDIT CARDS ACCEPTED: Visa, MasterCard and American Express.

TRANSPORTATION: Off base taxi: Carolina Cab, C-252-447-7744; Cherry Cab, C-252-447-3101; Union Cab, C-252-447-0444.

DINING OPPORTUNITIES: Burger King; Dairy Queen, C-252-446-9122; Domino's, C-252-466-9000; McDonald's, C-252-447-0214; and O Club, C-252-466-2395 are within driving distance.

New Bern museums, shopping and dining, area historical attractions, the sailing center at Oriental, where you can catch Neuse River blue crabs, fishing, boating, the nearby Outer Banks and Cape Lookout National Seashore and Morehead City—don't miss them!

Elizabeth City Coast Guard Support Center (NC03R1)

Commanding Officer, Admin Office, Bldg 35
Elizabeth City, NC 27909-5000

MAIN INSTALLATION TELEPHONE NUMBERS: C-252-335-6886, Fax: C-252-335-6296. Locator 335-6397; Medical 335-6460; Security Police 335-6398.

LOCATION: Take I-64 east to US-17 south to Elizabeth City, left on Halstead Blvd, 3 miles to Main Gate of Center. Or, from I-95, exit 176 east on US-158 to Elizabeth City. *USMRA: Page 45 (O-1).* **NMC:** Elizabeth City, in city limits.

RESERVATION INFORMATION: Lodging Office, Bldg 5, Elizabeth City CGSC, NC 27909-5006. **C-252-335-6397,** 0800-1600 hours. PCS may make reservations up to 90 days in advance; all others 60 days. Check in at facility, check out 0800-1000 hours. No government civilian employee billeting.

Mobile Homes 16A-F. Two-bedroom, private bath, sleeps six (6). Kitchen, limited utensils, A/C, TV, coin washer/dryer. Modern structure. Rates: $23-$55 depending on pay grade.

TML AVAILABILITY: Good, Oct-Apr. Difficult, other times.

CREDIT CARDS ACCEPTED: Yes.

TRANSPORTATION: None available.

DINING OPPORTUNITIES: Hangar 7 Snack Bar, C-252-335-6301 is within walking distance. Golden Corral, C-252-338-6651; and Mulligan's, C-252-331-2431 are within driving distance.

Visit Kitty Hawk and the Outer Banks. Read *Military Living's Military RV, Camping and Outdoor Recreation Around the World* for more information on this area.

Fort Bragg (NC05R1)

XVIII Airborne Corps HQ
Bldg 1-1326 Macomb Street
Fort Bragg, NC 28307-5000

MAIN INSTALLATION TELEPHONE NUMBERS: C-910-396-0011, DSN-312-236-0011. Locator 396-1461; Medical 432-0301; Security Police 396-0391.

LOCATION: From I-95, exit 52 to NC-24 west for 15 miles. NC-24 runs through Post as Bragg Blvd. From US-401 (Fayetteville Bypass) exit to All American Expressway, west five miles to Fort. *USMRA: Page 45 (I,J-4).* **NMC:** Fayetteville, 10 miles southeast.

RESERVATION INFORMATION: Airborne Inn, Lodging Office, Moon Hall, Bldg D-3601, Room 101, Fort Bragg, NC 28310. **C-910-396-7700, DSN-312-236-7700,** Fax: C-910-396-3033, DSN-312-236-3033. Front desk facility 24 hours daily, C-910-396-7700. E-mail: airborninn@bragg.army.mil WEB: www.bragg.army.mil/mwr/HOSPITALITY/LODGE_guest.htm Check in after 1300 hours, check out 1100 hours. Government civilian employee billeting.

Army Lodging Airborne Inn. **Delmont House,** Bastogne Drive, Bldg D-4215. **Normandy House,** Totten and Armistead Street, Bldg 1-4428. **Leal House,** Reilly Road, behind NCO Club, check in at Moon Hall. Bedroom, private bath (111); separate bedroom suite, private bath (8). Kitchen (some), microfridge or refrigerator, A/C, TV in room and lounge, housekeeping service, laundry facility, cribs, cots, ice machine, facilities for DAVs (Delmont House). Modern structures. Rates: $32-$43. Reservations for PCS 30 days in advance; UVs and all others Space-A. **Bldgs D-3601, D-3705, 1-1939.** C-910-396-7700/9574. Bedroom, private bath (520); separate bedroom suite; private bath (27). Kitchen (suites), refrigerator, A/C, TV,

housekeeping service, laundry facility, ice machine, facilities for DAVs. Modern structures. Rates: standard room $20.50-$35, suite $36-$45; dependent charge $5. Reservations for TDY 60 days in advance; all others Space-A. No pets in facilities, kennels available in area.

Army Lodging **Landmark Inn.** 1208 Glider Street, Fort Bragg, NC 28307-5000. **C-910-495-1215,** Fax: C-910-495-1216, 24 hours daily. Directions from NC-24 N: Left on Randolph Street, right on Saunders Lane, left on Glider Street. Inn is on the right. Hotel type facility. Kitchenette, refrigerator, microwave, utensils, hair dryer, A/C, SATV, housekeeping service, laundry facilities. Cribs and cots available. Handicap accessible units. Rates (not including tax): official standard rooms $54, unofficial standard rooms $64, suites $79. Group rates available.

Fisher House Womack Army Medical Center, 12 Bassett Street, Fort Bragg, NC 28307-5000. **C-910-432-1486,** Fax: C-910-432-3825. *Note: Appendix B has the definition of this facility. Fisher Houses are only available as lodging for families of patients receiving medical care at military and VA medical centers.*

DV/VIP Protocol Office. **C-910-396-2804.** O7+. Bldg 1-4425. Two-bed suite, private bath (1). Kitchen, complete utensils, A/C, TV, housekeeping service, laundry facility, cribs, cots. Modern structure. Rates: $40-$43, dependent charge $15. All categories may make reservations; Retirees Space-A. No pets, kennels available in area.

AMENITIES: Meeting/Conference Room, Snack and Soft Drink Vending Machine.

TML AVAILABILITY: Good, Sep-Apr. Difficult, other times.

CREDIT CARDS ACCEPTED: Visa, MasterCard and American Express. Landmark Inn accepts all major credit cards.

TRANSPORTATION: Car Rental, C-910-864-4144; Off base taxi, C-910-850-1313, C-910-488-5555.

DINING OPPORTUNITIES: Mini Mall, McGregor's and NCO Club, C-910-436-3300 are within walking distance. Bragg Main Exchange, C-910-436-4888; O Club, C-910-436-1700; Yntema Club, C-910-436-3200; Sports USA/Primo's Express, C-910-907-0739; and Mulligan's are within driving distance.

The 82nd Airborne Division War Memorial Museum has over 3,000 objects on view. The Historic Fayetteville Foundation gives walking tours of historical sites and Sandhills area golf resorts are world famous.

Fort Fisher Air Force Recreation Area (NC13R1)

118 Riverfront Road
Kure Beach, NC 28449-5000

MAIN INSTALLATION TELEPHONE NUMBERS: C-910-458-6549/6546. Emergency Medical 911; Security Police 911.

LOCATION: Fort Fisher is located on Pleasure Island between Cape Fear River and Atlantic Ocean. On US-421 south of Wilmington, NC, go through Carolina and Kure Beaches to Fort Fisher AF Rec Area, on the east side of US-421. *USMRA: Page 45 (L-6).* **NMC:** Wilmington, NC, 20 miles north. NMI: Camp Lejeune, 65 miles northeast.

RESERVATION INFORMATION: 118 Riverfront Road, Kure Beach, NC 28449-3321. **C-910-458-6549/6546,** Fax: C-910-458-6298, 0800-1900 hours. E-mail: ffafra@wilmington.net WEB: www.ftfishermilrec.com Check in 1600-1900 hours at reception center, check out 1100 hours. Late check in call reservations. Rooms may not be ready before 1600 hours, but use of resort facilities allowed until check in. Operated by Seymour Johnson Air Force Base, year round. Rates: call for current rate schedule.

Cottages) Beach cottage, sleep six-twelve (26); mobile home, sleep eight (12). Full kitchen with utensils, two baths, CATV, housekeeping service. No pets, kennel available $5 per night.

TML) River Marsh Landing: Suite, sleep four (2); room, sleep two (6). Private bathroom, CATV, housekeeping service, shared kitchen and living area.

Lodge) Room, sleep two (27); room, sleep four (6), room, sleep six (7). Shared bathroom, CATV. Additional persons in all units charged extra. Weekdays are Sun through Thurs, weekends are Fri, Sat, and nights prior to a holiday. (extra linens and towels available, $5 per person).

ELIGIBILITY: All categories. Active Duty Air Force 90 days ahead. All other Active Duty 85 days ahead. Retirees 75 days ahead. All others, 60 days ahead. Confirmed with Visa, MasterCard, Seymour Johnson AFB Club Card, or advance payment. Limits to number of rooms reserved during Memorial Day to Labor Day. Cancellations 15 days prior, or one night fee.

AMENITIES: Convenience store, gift and beach shop, restaurant, basketball and tennis courts, dock, boat ramp. Access to beach, boating, fishing, swimming. Bicycle rentals. ***Pets permitted on leash in designated areas, owners must clean up after pet.***

TML AVAILABILITY: Very good. Best, 1 November-31 March.

CREDIT CARDS ACCEPTED: Visa and MasterCard.

TRANSPORTATION: Ferry, C-910-458-3329.

DINING OPPORTUNITIES: Beach House Bar and Grill on base. Kure and Carolina Beaches local restaurants.

Aside from all the recreational activities at this resort, the North Carolina Aquarium at Fort Fisher, the Fort Fisher State Historic Site Civil War Museum and USS NC Battleship Memorial, Orton and Poplar Grove Plantations are worth visiting.

New River Marine Corps Air Station (NC06R1)
Family Service Center, Attn: RAP
PSC Box 21001
Jacksonville, NC 28545-1001

MAIN INSTALLATION TELEPHONE NUMBERS: C-910-451-1113, DSN-312-751-1113. Locator 451-3074; Medical 451-6511; Security Police 450-6111.

LOCATION: Off US-17, two miles south of Jacksonville, on east side of US-17. Clearly marked. *USMRA: Page 45 (L,M-5).* **NMC:** Jacksonville, two miles northeast.

RESERVATION INFORMATION: Lodging Office, Bldg 705, Flounder Road, Jacksonville, NC 28545-5079. **C-910-937-5024, DSN-312-752-6405,** Fax: C-910-449-6969, DSN-312-750-6969, 24 hours daily. Duty may make reservations; others Space-A. Check in at facility, check out 1200 hours. Government civilian employee billeting.

BOQ) Bldg 705. E6+, Officers all ranks. Bedroom, private bath (50). Refrigerator, microwave, coffee maker, A/C, TV/VCR in room and lounge, housekeeping service, laundry facility, cribs, cots. Modern structure, remodeled. Rates: (leave status) single room $20, two-room suite $25; each additional person $5. Maximum four per unit.

AMENITIES: Exercise Room. Ice, Snack and Soft Drink Vending Machine.

TML AVAILABILITY: Difficult. Best, Sep-Mar.

CREDIT CARDS ACCEPTED: Visa, MasterCard and American Express, Discover Card.

TRANSPORTATION: Off base taxi, C-910-455-3333.

DINING OPPORTUNITIES: New River O Club, C-910-450-6409 is within walking distance. Wendy's, C-910-450-0405; Applebee's, C-910-347-6011; Maitai, C-910-346-6675; and Red Lobster, C-910-353-9454 are within driving distance.

Some area interests include Fort Macon, Hammocks Beach, Hanging Rock, Jones Lake and Cape Hatteras National Seashore. North Carolina National forests and local festivals are all drawing cards for visitors.

Pope Air Force Base (NC01R1)
43rd MSS/DPF
374 Maynard Street, Suite G
Pope AFB, NC 28308-2375

MAIN INSTALLATION TELEPHONE NUMBERS: C-910-394-1110, DSN-312-424-1110. Locator 910-394-4131; Medical 910-394-2778; Security Police 394-2800.

LOCATION: Take I-95, exit to NC-87/24 west. Follow signs northwest for 15 miles to Pope AFB and Fort Bragg. *USMRA: Page 45 (J-4).* **NMC:** Fayetteville, 12 miles southeast.

RESERVATION INFORMATION: Carolina Inn, 43 SVS/SVML, 302 Ethridge Street, Bldg.235, Pope AFB, NC 28308-2310. **C-1-888-AFLODGE (1-888-235-6343), C-910-394-4131, DSN-312-424-4131,** Fax: C-910-394-4912, DSN-312-424-4912, 24 hours daily. Duty may make reservations any time; Space-A may make reservations 24 hours in advance. Check in at lodging 1400, check out 1100 hours. Directions: From Main Gate take Reilly Road to Ethridge Street, turn right on Ethridge. Take first right. Government civilian employee lodging with reservations. ***All units non-smoking and no pets.***

TLF) Bldg 243-247. PCS in/out. Recently renovated. Four bedroom, private bath (10). Two bedroom, private bath (12). Kitchenette, utensils, A/C, TV, housekeeping service, laundry facility. Rates: $24.50 per room.

VAQ) Bldg 287. Bedroom, shared bath (68); separate bedroom, private bath (4). Refrigerator, A/C, TV, housekeeping service, laundry facility, ice machine. Older structure, renovated 1991. Rates: $17.50 per room.

VOQ) Bldgs 229-233. Bedroom, private bath (96); separate bedroom, private bath (12); eight-bedroom units (8). Refrigerator, A/C, TV, housekeeping service, laundry facility, cribs, ice machine. Rates: standard room $20, suite $21.50.

DV/VIP) Protocol Office. 259 Maynard Street, Suite C. **C-910-394-4739, DSN-312-424-4737.** Bldgs 219,221. O6+. Recently renovated. Bedroom, private bath (8). Kitchen, utensils, A/C, TV, housekeeping service, laundry facility, ice machine. Rates: $25, $36 double per person.

TML AVAILABILITY: Good, winter. Difficult, other times.

CREDIT CARDS ACCEPTED: Visa and MasterCard.

TRANSPORTATION: On base shuttle/bus. C-910-394-6906. Taxi, C-910-497-6565, C-910-488-5555, C-910-482-0444. Car rental available at Fort Bragg.

DINING OPPORTUNITIES: Cafeteria, C-910-394-4377; Pope Club, C-910-394-2154 and numerous fast food establishments are within driving distance.

Nearby Asheville is good for rafting, hiking and skiing, while Carowinds, in Charlotte, is a large family entertainment center.

Ashboro's zoological park, and Raleigh, the state capital, are well worth visits.

Seymour Johnson Air Force Base (NC11R1)
4th MSS/DPF
1200 Wright Brothers Avenue, Suite 100
Seymour Johnson AFB, NC 27531-2442

MAIN INSTALLATION TELEPHONE NUMBERS: C-919-722-5400, DSN-312-722-1110. Locator 722-1175; Medical 722-1802; Security Police 722-1211.

LOCATION: From US-70 Bypass, take Seymour Johnson AFB exit east onto Berkeley Blvd to Main Gate. Clearly marked. *USMRA: Page 45 (L-3).* **NMC:** Raleigh, 50 miles west.

RESERVATION INFORMATION: Southern Pines Inn, 4 SVS/SVML, 1535 Wright Brothers Avenue, Seymour Johnson AFB, NC 27531-2325. **C-1-888-AFLODGE (1-888-235-6343), C-919-722-0385, DSN-312-722-0385,** Fax: C-919-722-0375, DSN-312-722-0375, 24 hours daily. E-mail: joyce.medeiros@seymourjohnson.af.mil WEB: www.seymourjohnson.af.mil Duty may make reservations any time; Space-A may make reservations 24 hours in advance. Directions from Main Gate: go left on Wright Brothers Avenue, located on left past the O Club. Check in 1500 hours, check out 1200 hours. Government civilian employee billeting VOQ. Handicap accessible units available.

TML Bldg 3815. Student Officers. Apartment style suite (20). Rates: $13.50 per room.

TLF Bldg 3802. PCS families Priority 1; all others Space-A basis. Bedroom, private bath (3); separate bedroom, private bath (25); two-bedroom, private bath (11). Kitchen, limited utensils, A/C, TV/VCR, housekeeping service, laundry facility, ice machine. Newly renovated structure. Rates: $21.50 per unit. No pets.

VAQ Bldg 3803. Official duty Priority 1; Retirees and leave Space-A. Bedroom, private bath (6); bedroom, semi-private bath (28); SNCO suite, separate bedroom, private bath (6); Chief suite, separate bedroom, private bath (1). A/C, TV/VCR, housekeeping service, laundry facility, ice, soft drink and snack vending machines. Exercise room available. Older structure. Rates: room $13; suite $23. No pets.

VOQ Bldg 3804. Official duty Priority 1. Suite, kitchen, separate bedroom, private bath (5); bedroom, private bath (38). A/C, TV/VCR, conference room, housekeeping service, laundry facility, ice machine, sundry items sold at front desk, meeting/conference room. Modern structure. Rates: room $13.50; suite $23. No pets.

DV/VIP Protocol **C-919-722-0003, DSN-312-722-0003.** Bldg 2820. O6+. Separate bedroom suite, private bath (10). Kitchen, TV/VCR, housekeeping service, laundry facility. Modern structure. Rates: suite $23.

TML AVAILABILITY: Good, Nov-Apr. Difficult, other times.

CREDIT CARDS ACCEPTED: Visa and MasterCard.

TRANSPORTATION: Base Taxi (military appointments) DSN-312-722-1303; Car Rentals: American Auto, C-919-736-8077; Enterprise, C-919-778-4828; Off base taxi: City Cab Company, C-919-735-2202; Webb Town Taxi, C-919-734-8444.

DINING OPPORTUNITIES: Anthony's Pizza, C-919-735-8511; Burger King, C-919-735-8511; and SJAFB Bowling Center are within walking distance. Captain Bob's Seafood, C-919-778-8332; and Texas Steak House, C-919-778-7998 are within driving distance.

Near Goldsboro, Cliffs of the Neuse River, picnicking, refreshments, fishing swimming and rental rowboats, museum. Also visit historic Fort Macon, the Cape Hatteras National Seashore, and Fayetteville.

NORTH DAKOTA

Camp Gilbert C. Grafton National Guard Training Site (ND03R3)
4417 Highway 20
Devils Lake, ND 58301-9235

MAIN INSTALLATION TELEPHONE NUMBERS: C-701-662-0200. Locator 662-0200; Security Police 911.

LOCATION: From the intersection of US Hwy 2 east or west and ND Hwy 20 in Devils Lake, turn south. Drive approximately 5 miles south. Main Gate will be on the west (right hand) side of the highway. *USMRA: Page 83 (G-3)*. **NMC:** Devils Lake, five miles north.

RESERVATION INFORMATION: 4417 Highway 20, Devils Lake, ND 58301-9235. **C-701-662-0239,** Fax: C-701-662-0597, 0700-1700 hours Mon-Thu, 0700-2100 hours Fri-Sun. Reservations required for duty; others Space-A. Directions: Follow signs from the front gate to the information center. After hours use phone in information center, Bldg 6010. Check in at billeting office after 1430 hours, check out 1000 hours. Late check out pays extra day.

BOQ/BEQ Bldgs 3600, 3800. C-701-662-0239. Bedroom, two beds, shared bath (80). Refrigerator (40), kitchenette (2), TV, A/C, housekeeping service, laundry facility in separate building. Modern structure. Rates: official duty $8, unofficial duty and dependents $9 per person, maximum $20. Maximum six per unit. No pets.

Army Lodging Double-wide trailers (19), three-bedroom, two baths. Kitchen, refrigerator, stove, A/C, TV, daily housekeeping service, washer/dryer (10), living/dining room. Rates: Same as above. No pets.

DV/VIP Two-bedroom house, private bath (1). Fully equipped kitchen, A/C, TV, daily housekeeping service, living/dining room. Rates: Same as above. No pets.

AMENITIES: Mini Mart, Snack and Soft Drink Vending Machines.

TML AVAILABILITY: Good. Best, Sep-May. Difficult, May-Sep.

CREDIT CARDS ACCEPTED: Visa, MasterCard and American Express.

TRANSPORTATION: Off base taxi C-701-662-7812/1192; Car Rental C-701-662-1144/5346/2124.

DINING OPPORTUNITIES: On base dining facilities and numerous restaurants are within driving distance.

This area is known for its summer and winter fishing and seasonal waterfowl hunting (must have ND license). At certain times of the year the skies are black with migrating ducks and geese. Enjoy boating, snowmobiling, historical sites and casinos. Only 90 miles from the Canadian border, an outdoor paradise.

Grand Forks Air Force Base (ND04R3)
319 MSS/DPFR
575 Holzapple Street, Suite 3
Grand Forks AFB, ND 58205-6319

MAIN INSTALLATION TELEPHONE NUMBERS: C-701-747-3000, DSN-312-362-3000. Locator 747-3344; Medical 747-5600; Security Police 747-5351.

LOCATION: From I-29, take US-2 west exit for 14 miles to Grand Forks, County Road B-3 (Emeraldo/Air Base) north 1 mile to AFB on east (right) side of road. *USMRA: Page 83 (I-3)*. **NMC:** Grand Forks, 15 miles east.

RESERVATION INFORMATION: Warrior Inn, Attn: 319 SVS/SVML, Bldg 117, Holzapple & 6th Avenue, Grand Forks AFB, ND 58205-0001. **C-1-888-AFLODGE (1-888-235-6343), C-701-747-7200, DSN-312-362-7200,** Fax: C-701-747-3069, DSN-312-362-3069, 24 hours daily. Duty may make reservations any time; Space-A may make reservations 24 hours in advance. Check out 1200 hours. Government civilian employee lodging. *Note: A $1.8 million TLF conversion was approved in the DoD Fiscal Year 2001 NAF Construction Program.*

TLF Across street from billeting. Efficiency apartments, private bath (24). Kitchen, limited utensils, A/C, TV, housekeeping service, laundry facility, ice machine. Modern structure. Rates: $24.50 per unit. PCS in/out reservations required.

VQ Bldg 117. Two-bedroom suite, private bath (24). Refrigerator, TV, housekeeping service, laundry facility, ice machine. Rates: $20. PCS in/out reservations required.

DV/VIP VAQ/VOQ. Bldg 117. E9. Two-bedroom suite, living room, private bath (2). Refrigerator, TV, A/C, housekeeping service, laundry facility, ice machine. Rates: $25. For reservations contact Protocol.

DV/VIP VAQ/VOQ. Bldg 117. 06+. One-bedroom suite, living room, private bath. Refrigerator, TV, A/C, housekeeping service, washer dryer, ice machine. Rates: $25. For reservations contact Protocol.

DV/VIP 319 Active Duty Protocol Office, Bldg 307, **C-701-747-5055, DSN-312-362-5055.** Bldg 132. O7+. Four-bedroom house, private bath (1). Kitchen, living room, dining room, laundry facility. Rates: $29.50 per person. For reservations contact Protocol.

TML AVAILABILITY: Good, winter. Difficult, spring and summer.

CREDIT CARDS ACCEPTED: Visa and MasterCard.

TRANSPORTATION: Car Rental: Enterprise, C-701-775-3977; On base taxi, C-701-747-3976; Off base taxi, C-701-772-3456.

DINING OPPORTUNITIES: Dakota Lanes, C-701-747-3050; and E Club, C-701-747-3392 are within walking distance. Dairy Queen, C-701-594-4021; Paladinos Pizza, C-701-594-5854; and Subway, C-701-594-5952 are within driving distance.

Minot Air Force Base (ND02R3)
5th MSS/DPF
22 Peacekeeper Place, Unit 1
Minot AFB, ND 58705-5003

MAIN INSTALLATION TELEPHONE NUMBERS: C-701-723-1110, DSN-312-453-1110. Locator 723-1841; Medical 723-5633; Security Police 723-3096.

LOCATION: On US-83, 13 miles north of Minot. *USMRA: Page 83 (D-2)*. **NMC:** Minot, 13 miles south.

RESERVATION INFORMATION: Sakakawea Inn, 5 SVS/SVML, 201 Summit Drive, Suite 203, Minot AFB, ND 58705-5037. **C-1-888-AFLODGE (1-888-235-6343), C-701-723-6161/2184, DSN-312-453-6161/2184,** Fax: C-701-723-1844, DSN-312-453-1844, 24 hours daily. Duty may make reservations any time; Space-A may make reservations 24 hours in advance. Directions from Main Gate: Go to first stoplight and take a right. Lodging is immediately on the right. Check out 1200 hours.

TLF Bldgs 158-163, Missile Avenue. Separate bedroom apartment, private bath (38). Kitchen, microwave, complete utensils, A/C, TV/VCR, housekeeping service, laundry facility, ice machine. Modern structure. One unit meets all ADA (Americans with Disabilities Act) requirements. No smoking. Rates: $12-$21.50 per unit.

VAQ Bldg 173, Summit Drive. Bedroom, private and semi-private bath (32). Refrigerator and/or complete kitchen, microwave, A/C, TV, housekeeping service, laundry facility. Chief suites. Modern structure. No smoking. Rates: $10-$13 per person.

VOQ Bldg 175, Summit Drive. Bedrooms, private and semi-private bath (40). Refrigerator and/or complete kitchen, microwave, A/C, TV/VCR, housekeeping service, laundry facility, ice machine. Modern structure. No smoking. Rates: $10-$13.50 per person.

DVQ Bldg 171, Summit Drive (Rough Rider Suite and Magic City Suite). O6+. Suite, private bath (4); bedroom suite with office (2). Kitchen, microwave, A/C, TV/VCR, housekeeping service, laundry facility. Rates: $25.50 per person.

DV/VIP Protocol Office, 201 Summit Drive, **C-701-723-3474, DSN-312-453-3474.** Rates: $10-$25.50.

AMENITIES: Exercise Room.

TML AVAILABILITY: Generally good. Difficult, Jul and Oct.

CREDIT CARDS ACCEPTED: Visa and MasterCard.

TRANSPORTATION: On base taxi, C-701-723-3121, DSN-312-453-3121; off base taxi: Ace Checker Cab, C-701-852-9000.

DINING OPPORTUNITIES: Dakota Inn, C-701-723-2359 (TDY authorized to subsist for breakfast only); In-Flight Kitchen, C-701-723-3079 (Hot meals not available on weekends and holidays; except during exercises); Jimmy Doolittle Center, C-701-723-3731; J.R. Rocker's Sports Cafe, C-701-727-6158; Rough Rider Pizza, C-701-727-4377/8; and Sub Shop, C-701-723-6707/18 are within driving distance.

Swimming pools, tennis courts, city zoo are in Roosevelt Park. Visit General Custer's command post at Fort Lincoln State Park and the International Peace Garden on the Manitoba/North Dakota border. Lake fishing, abundant hunting for deer and fowl.

OHIO

Camp Perry Training Site (OH06R2)
1000 Lawrence Road
Port Clinton, OH 43452-9578

MAIN INSTALLATION TELEPHONE NUMBERS: C-614-336-6280, Medical 911; Security Police 911.

LOCATION: On Lake Erie, just north of State Route 2; 6 miles west of Port Clinton. *USMRA: Page 67 (D-3).* **NMC:** Toledo, 25 miles northwest. NMI: Mansfield Lahm, Airport/ANG, 70 miles southeast.

RESERVATION INFORMATION: Preferred, up to one year in advance. Write to: Clubhouse Manager, Bldg 600, 1000 Lawrence Road, Camp Perry Military Training Site, Port Clinton, OH 43452-9578. **C-614-336-6214.** Fax: C-614-336-6238. Check in 1400-2200 hours. Open to the public. Military discount. Directions: North on Niagara Road to the flagpole. Turn right on Lawrence, proceed to Bldg 600.

Army Lodging 1000 Lawrence Road, Bldg 600. Rates: $20-$100 daily. Phones in rooms.

Cottages Bldgs 501-527. One- and two-bedroom, private bath (27). Toaster, dishes, utensils, A/C, phone, sofabed.

TML Motel. Bldgs 120, 150, 160, 170. Double bed, private bath (20). Some kitchens, toaster, dishes, utensils, sofabed. Rates: $50 daily. Motel units without kitchen, private bath (207); A/C. *Note: Daily housekeeping service is not provided. Cleaning and trash removal is a personal responsibility. Cleaning materials*

provided upon request. Linen exchange: towels exchange daily, bed linens exchange bi-weekly. No pets allowed.

TML AVAILABILITY: Good, Jan-Mar. Difficult, other times.

CREDIT CARDS ACCEPTED: Visa, MasterCard and American Express.

TRANSPORTATION: None available.

DINING OPPORTUNITIES: Snack Bar is within walking distance.

Situated along Lake Erie approximately 30 miles from the Canadian border. Limited support facilities available on post. Fishing/license, swimming, fishing pier, grills, picnic area.

Columbus Defense Supply Center (OH05R2)
3990 East Broad Street
Columbus, OH 43216-5000

MAIN INSTALLATION TELEPHONE NUMBERS: C-614-692-3131, DSN-312-850-3131. Locator 692-3131; Medical 692-2227; Security Police 692-2111.

LOCATION: From I-270 (Beltway) take exit 39 to Broad Street west, Main Gate on north side of street. *USMRA: Page 67 (D-6).* **NMC:** Columbus, in city limits.

RESERVATION INFORMATION: DSCC-WLQ/Lodging, Bldg 20, 1st floor, B134 North, 3990 East Broad Street, Columbus, OH 43216-5000. **C-614-692-4758, DSN-312-850-4758,** Fax: C-614-692-6945, DSN-312-850-6945, 0630-1400 hours Mon-Fri. After hours, weekends and holidays, check security at Broad Street Gate for vacancy list, after 1430 hours C-614-692-3608. Reservations required. Directions: Go to Bldg 20, 1st floor area B134 North. Check in at DSCC Lodging 1400 hours, check out 1200 hours.

Army Lodging Bldg 201. Single room, shared bath (6). Refrigerator, microwave, TV. Rates: PCS/DY with orders $25, all others $30. Suite, private bath (2). Refrigerator, microwave, TV, telephone. Rates: PCS/TDY with orders $30, all others $35. Apartment, one- and two-bedrooms, private bath (2). Kitchen with utensils, TV/VCR, telephone. Rates: PCS/TDY with orders $35, all others $40. Additional $5 patron fee. Housekeeping service and laundry facilities.

DV/VIP DSCC-WLQ/Lodging, **C-614-692-4758, DSN-312-850-4758.** Qtrs 108. Three-bedroom, kitchen, living room, private bath(2),dining room, utility room with washer/dryer and basement. Rates: PCS/TDY with orders $35, all others $40. Retirees and lower ranks Space-A.

AMENITIES: Exercise Room, Meeting/Conference Room, Mini Mart, Snack and Soft Drink Vending Machines.

CREDIT CARDS ACCEPTED: Visa and MasterCard.

TRANSPORTATION: On/Off base shuttle bus, C-614-692-2350, DSN-312-850-2350; On base taxi, C-614-692-2350, DSN-312-850-2350; Off base taxi: Yellow Cab, C-614-444-4444, C-1-800-551-4222.

DINING OPPORTUNITIES: O Club is within walking distance. House of Yan, Applebee's, Paul's and various fast food establishments are within driving distance.

Rickenbacker International Airport/ Air National Guard Base (OH02R2)
121 OSS/OM
7556 South Perimeter Road
Rickenbacker ANGB, OH 43217-5875

MAIN INSTALLATION TELEPHONE NUMBERS: C-614-492-4468, DSN-312-950-4595. Security Police C-614-492-4321.

LOCATION: From I-270 (Columbus Beltway) south take Alum Creek Road exit 49 then south to Rickenbacker ANGB. Also accessible from I-270 to US-22 south to OH-317 east to Alum Creek. *USMRA: Page 67 (D-7).* **NMC:** Columbus, 13 miles northwest. NMI: Wright-Patterson AFB, 73 miles west.

RESERVATION INFORMATION: The Buckeye Inn, 7370 Minuteman Way, Rickenbacker ANGB, OH 43217-5875. **C-614-409-2660, DSN-312-850-4451.** Fax: C-614-409-2657, 0700-1800 hours Mon-Thu, 0700-2400 hours Fri, 1000-1800 hours Sat, 0800-1630 Sun. E-mail: buckeye.inn@tagoh.org Reservations may be made at any time. Directions: From Alum Creek Road entrance, turn right on Port Road, then left on Tank Truck Road, Buckeye Inn across from BX.

(TML) The Buckeye Inn. Bedroom, private bath; suite, private bath. Refrigerator, microwave, housekeeping, laundry facilities. Rates: room $16, second person $11; suite $21. Children 12 and under are free.

AMENITIES: Snack and Drink Vending Machines.

TML AVAILABILITY: Best during week.

CREDIT CARDS ACCEPTED: Visa and Mastercard.

TRANSPORTATION: Off base taxi.

DINING OPPORTUNITIES: Fast food within walking distance. Restaurants within driving distance.

In nearby Columbus, State Fairgrounds, Ohio Historical Center, Franklin Park Conservatory, Ohio State University, Center of Science and Industry, Palace Theater, German Village, Brewery district and Columbus Museum of Art.

Wright-Patterson Air Force Base (OH01R2)
2000 Allbrook Drive, Suite 3
Bldg 2, Area C
Wright-Patterson AFB, OH 45433-5315

MAIN INSTALLATION TELEPHONE NUMBERS: C-937-257-1110, DSN-312-787-1110. Locator 257-3231; Medical 257-0839; Security Police 257-6516.

LOCATION: South of I-70, off I-675 at Fairborn. Also access from OH-4 north or south. AFB clearly marked. *USMRA: Page 67 (B-7).* **NMC:** Dayton, 10 miles southwest.

RESERVATION INFORMATION: 88 SPTG/SVML, Bldg 825, 2439 Schlatter Drive, Wright-Patterson AFB, OH 45433-5519. **C-1-888-AFLODGE (1-888-235-6343), C-937-879-5921** or **C-937-257-3810/3451, DSN-312-787-3451,** Fax: C-937-257-2488, DSN-312-787-2488, 24 hours daily. Directions: From Gate 12A, follow Chidlaw Road to a right onto Schlatter Drive. Lodging is at the corner of the two streets. Check in at billeting, check out 1200 hours. Government civilian employee billeting.

(TLF) Bldg 825. C-937-257-3810. Bedroom, bath, sleeps four (40). Kitchen, microwave, complete utensils, A/C, TV, housekeeping service, laundry facility, cribs, ice machine. Rates: $34 per unit. Duty can make reservations any time; Space-A can make reservations 24 hours in advance.

(VOQ) Bldg 825. Refrigerator, microwave, coffee maker, A/C, TV, housekeeping service, laundry facility, ice, soft drink and snack vending machines. Fax service available at no charge for VOQ/VAQ guests. Rates: $27 per room. Maximum three per room. Duty can make reservations any time; Space-A can make reservations 24 hours in advance.

(TML) **Hope Hotel and Conference Center.** The Air Force's first private sector financed hotel. Bldg 823. All ranks. DoD civilian lodging. Official duty reservations call billeting at C-937-257-3810, DSN-312-787-3810. Others, C-937-257-1285, DSN-312-787-1285. One- and two-bedroom, double bed, private bath (260). A/C, CATV, iron/ironing board, ice machine. Seven full service conference rooms available, catering available from on-site restaurant. Handicap accessible. Official Duty Rates: single $38 + tax, double $46.10 + tax. Unofficial Rates: single $45 + tax, double $50 + tax.

(Fisher House) USAF Medical Center, 415 Schlatter Drive, WPAFB, OH 45433-5000. **C-937-257-0855,** Fax: C-937-656-2150. Rates: $3 per night. Credit cards not accepted. *Note: Appendix B has the definition of this facility. Fisher Houses are only available as lodging for families of patients receiving medical care at the Wright-Patterson Air Force Base Medical Center and Veteran's Administration Hospital in Dayton, OH.*

TML AVAILABILITY: Poor during summer due to official travel.

CREDIT CARDS ACCEPTED: Visa and MasterCard.

TRANSPORTATION: On base shuttle/taxi (0600-2300 hours Mon-Fri), C-937-257-3755, DSN-312-787-3755; Off base shuttle/bus (Airport to base only), C-937-898-4043; Car Rental, C-937-879-0023.

DINING OPPORTUNITIES: O Club, C-937-257-9762; and Packy's (at Hope Hotel & Conference Center), C-937-257-1285.

The Air Force Museum on base, and the city of Dayton with its art and natural history museums, local arts and the Nutter Sports Center all make this area an interesting place to visit.

Youngstown-Warren Regional Airport/Air Reserve Station (OH11R2)
910th Airlift Wing
3976 King Graves Road
Vienna, OH 44473-0910

MAIN INSTALLATION TELEPHONE NUMBERS: C-330-609-1000, DSN-312-346-1000. Medical 911; Security Police 609-1299. *Ten-digit dialing required for local calls.*

LOCATION: From OH-11, exit to King Graves Road Hwy 82 east to Hwy 193 north at signs pointing to base, Main Gate left (west) one mile. Base is clearly marked. *USMRA: Page 67 (H-3).* **NMC:** Youngstown, three miles south.

RESERVATION INFORMATION: Eagles Nest Inn, 3976 King Graves Road, Vienna, OH 44473-0910. **C-1-888-AFLODGE (1-888-235-6343), C-330-609-1268, DSN-312-346-1268,** Fax: C-330-609-1120, DSN-312-346-1120. Duty may make reservations any time; others Space-A.

(BEQ/BOQ) Bedroom, two twin beds, private bath. (68). Rates: $23.00.

(DV/VIP) E9, O6+. Bedroom, queen-size bed, private bath (6). Rates: $31.50.

TML AVAILABILITY: Very difficult in summer, fair other times.

CREDIT CARDS ACCEPTED: Visa and MasterCard.

TRANSPORTATION: Car Rental and off base taxi available.

DINING OPPORTUNITIES: Airport Inn, C-330-394-2099; Brothers

Pizza, C-330-394-2733; and Yankee Kitchen, C-330-726-1300 are within driving distance.

Be sure to visit Six Flags Amusement Park.

OKLAHOMA

Altus Air Force Base (OK02R3)
97th MSS/DPF
308 North First Street
Altus AFB, OK 73523-5001

MAIN INSTALLATION TELEPHONE NUMBERS: C-580-481/482-8100, DSN-312-866-1110. Locator 481-7250; Medical 911; Security Police 911.

LOCATION: From US-62 traveling west from Lawton, turn right (north) at first traffic light in Altus and follow the road to the Main Gate on Falcon Road. *USMRA: Page 84 (E-5).* **NMC:** Lawton, 56 miles east.

RESERVATION INFORMATION: Red River Inn, 97 SVS/SVML, 308 North First Street, Altus AFB, OK 73523-5146. **C-1-888-AFLODGE (1-888-235-6343), C-580-481-7356, DSN-312-866-7356,** Fax: C-580-481-5704, DSN-312-866-5704, 24 hours daily. Duty may make reservations any time; Space-A may make reservations 24 hours in advance. Check in at lodging, check out 1200 hours. Government civilian employee billeting.

(TLF) One-bedroom unit (28); three-bedroom duplex (2). Rates: $23.50 per unit.

(VAQ) Bldg 82. Bedroom, common bath (49). A/C, TV in room and lounge, housekeeping service. Modern structure. Rates: $10 per unit.

(VAQ) Bldg 314. Bedroom, central latrine (144). Bldg 327, bedroom, common bath (76). Rates: $10 per unit.

(VOQ) Bldgs 81-85. Bedroom, private bath (128); separate bedrooms, private bath (24). Kitchen, A/C, TV, housekeeping service, laundry facility. Modern structure, hotel type lodging. Rates: $13.50 per unit.

(VOQ) Bldgs 76, 79. Suite, private bath. Kitchen, A/C, TV, housekeeping service, laundry facility. Rates: $13.50 per unit.

(DV/VIP) Wing EXO, Bldg 1, **C-580-481-7044.** O6+. Bldg 81, 84, 85. O4+. Separate bedrooms, private bath (8). Kitchen, A/C, TV, housekeeping service, laundry facility. Modern structure, hotel type lodging. Rates: $20.50 per unit.

(DV/VIP) Bldgs 20, 21. **C-580-481-7044.** O6+. House style with three bedrooms, private bath, kitchen, housekeeping service (2). Rates: $23.50.

AMENITIES: ICE, Soft Drink and Snack Vending Machines. Internet/E-mail access for customers.

TML AVAILABILITY: Good, Dec. Difficult, other times.

CREDIT CARDS ACCEPTED: Visa, MasterCard and American Express.

TRANSPORTATION: Off base shuttle/bus C-405-482-5043, C-405-482-5503; On base taxi C-405-481-6272; Off base taxi C-405-0383/3300.

DINING OPPORTUNITIES: Bowling Alley, C-405-481-6420; E Club, C-405-481-6295; Golf Course, C-405-481-6411; O Club, C-405-481-6224; and Solar Inn Dining Hall, C-405-481-6169 are within driving distance.

Visit the Museum of the Western Prairie for the saga of the area's wild west roots. Quartz Mountain State Park hosts the county fairs, rodeos and roundups that are part of life here.

Fort Sill (OK01R3)
Attn: ATZR-PNC-A, Bldg 455
Fort Sill, OK 73503-5100

MAIN INSTALLATION TELEPHONE NUMBERS: C-580-442-8111, DSN-312-639-7090. Locator 442-3924; Medical 458-2500; Security Police 442-2101.

LOCATION: From Lawton, take I-44 north to exit 41, then west on Sheridan Road to Key Gate. Clearly marked. Free shuttle to and from Fort Sill/Lawton Municipal Airport. *USMRA: Page 84 (E,F-5.)* **NMC:** Lawton, on the south boundary of Fort Sill.

RESERVATION INFORMATION: Aultman Hall, Attn: AT2R-PL, Bldg 5676, Fergusson Road, P.O. Box 33334, Fort Sill, OK 73503-5100. **C-580-442-5000, C-1-877-902-3607, DSN-312-639-5000,** Fax: C-580-442-7033, DSN-312-639-7033, 24 hours daily. E-mail: atzrpl@sill.army.mil Directions: Take Sheridan Road to left on Geronimo Road to a right on Fergusson Road. Check in at building, check out 1100 hours. *Note: A $1.459 million Gunner's Inn renovation was approved in the DoD Fiscal Year 2001 NAF Construction Program.*

(Army Lodging) 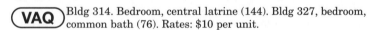 Standard rooms, apartments, suites and houses (750). TV/VCR, telephone with data ports, coffee maker, A/C, hair dryer, iron/ironing board, daily housekeeping service. Some with kitchen/kitchenette. *Rooms for families with pets available at additional charge.* Rates (higher for unofficial stays): room $27; apartment $30-$34; suite, house $45. Each additional person over 13 $7 per night.

(DVQ) Suites and houses. TV/VCR, telephone with data ports, coffee maker, A/C, hair dryer, iron/ironing board, daily housekeeping service. Kitchen or kitchenette. *Pets at additional charge.* Rates (higher for unofficial stays): $45. Each additional person over 13 $7 per night.

AMENITIES: Room Service, Cleaner/Tailor Service, Barber Shop, Exercise Room, Game Room, Laundry Room, Meeting/Conference Room, Walking/Jogging Track, Tennis Courts, Basketball Courts, Storm Shelter, Covered Picnic Area, Swimming Pools and Video Checkout.

TML AVAILABILITY: Difficult, summer. Fairly good, other times.

CREDIT CARDS ACCEPTED: Visa, MasterCard, American Express and Discover.

TRANSPORTATION: On base shuttle/bus; Off base shuttle bus; On base taxi, C-580-355-5555; Off base taxi, C-580-357-7777.

DINING OPPORTUNITIES: Observation Post, C-580-355-3493 is within walking distance. China Garden, C-580-248-0931; Crockett's Smokehouse, C-580-357-7427; Golden Corral Steakhouse, C-580-357-5113 are within driving distance.

Don't miss the original stone buildings constructed by the "Buffalo Soldiers" of the 10th Calvary, the Guardhouse where Geronimo was confined, the large museum on post and the Museum of the Great Plains in Lawton.

Tinker Air Force Base (OK04R3)
72nd MSS/DPF
3359 N Avenue, Suite 1
Tinker AFB, OK 73145-3001

MAIN INSTALLATION TELEPHONE NUMBERS: C-405-732-7321, DSN-312-884-1110. Locator 734-2456; Medical 734-8370; Security Police 734-3737.

LOCATION: Southeast of Oklahoma City, off I-40. Use Tinker gate exit 157A off South Air Depot Blvd. Clearly marked. *USMRA: Page 84 (G-4).* **NMC:** Oklahoma City, 12 miles northwest.

RESERVATION INFORMATION: Indian Hills Inn, 72nd SPTG/SVML, 4002 Mitchell Avenue, Tinker AFB, OK 73145-3001. **C-1-888-AFLODGE (1-888-235-6343), C-405-734-2822, DSN-312-882-2822,** Fax: C-405-734-7426, DSN-312-884-7426, 24 hours daily. Duty may make reservations any time; Space-A may make reservations 24 hours in advance. Check in at lodging 1500 hours, check out 1100 hours. Government civilian employee lodging.

(TLF) Bldgs 5824, 5826, 5828, 5830, 5832. Room (39). Kitchen, A/C, TV, housekeeping service, laundry facility, playground. Rates: $30 per unit.

(VAQ) Bldg 5915. Bedroom, private and semi-private bath (48); chief suites (2). Refrigerator, A/C, CATV/VCR, housekeeping service, laundry facility. Rates: $19 per person.

(VOQ) Bldgs 5604-5606. Bedroom, private and semi-private bath (104). Refrigerator, A/C, CATV/VCR, housekeeping service, laundry facility. Rates: $19 per person.

(DV/VIP) OC-ALC/CCP, Bldg 3001, **C-405-739-5511.** O6/GS15+. Business Suites. Rates $26-$29 per person.

TML AVAILABILITY: Limited in summer.

CREDIT CARDS ACCEPTED: Visa and MasterCard.

TRANSPORTATION: On base shuttle/bus, C-405-734-2803; Car Rental: Hertz, C-405-732-0366; On base taxi, C-405-734-2803; Off base taxi, C-405-235-1431.

DINING OPPORTUNITIES: Dining Hall, C-405-734-MENU(6368); and NCO/CPO Club, C-405-734-3418 are within driving distance.

Note: All lodging rates subject to change without notice.

In Oklahoma City visit Remington Park, the National Cowboy Hall of Fame and Western Heritage Center, the city Zoo, tour the mansions of Heritage Hills. Five municipal golf courses, four lakes, and many sports events are available.

Vance Air Force Base (OK05R3)
71st MSS/DPF
446 McAffrey Avenue, Suite 15
Vance AFB, OK 73705-5712

MAIN INSTALLATION TELEPHONE NUMBERS: C-580-213-5000, DSN-312-448-7110/2121. Locator 213-7791; Medical 213-7416; Security Police 213-7415.

LOCATION: Off of US-81 south of Enid (on west side of US-81). Clearly marked. *USMRA: Page 84 (F-3).* **NMC:** Oklahoma City, 90 miles Southeast.

RESERVATION INFORMATION: 71 FTW/NW-SL, 426 Goad Street, Suite 131, Vance AFB, OK 73705-5028. **C-1-888-AFLODGE (1-888-235-6343), C-580-213-7358, DSN-312-448-7358,** Fax: C-580-213-6278, DSN-312-448-6278, 24 hours daily. Duty may make reservations any time; Space-A may make reservations 24 hours in advance. Check in at lodging 1400, check out 1100 hours. Government civilian employee lodging.

(TLF) Bldg 790. Separate bedrooms, private bath (10). Kitchen, utensils, A/C, TV, housekeeping service, laundry facility, cribs, ice machine. Rates: $27.50 per unit.

(VOQ/VAQ) Bldgs 713, 714. Bedroom, private bath (48). Microwave, stove (28), wet bar, A/C, TV/VCR, housekeeping service, ice machine, facilities for DAVs. Modern structure. Rates: $21.50 per room.

(DV/VIP) Two-bedroom, two bath (2); bedroom suite, private bath (4); handicap accessible (1). Rates: $30.50 per room.

TML AVAILABILITY: Difficult.

CREDIT CARDS ACCEPTED: Visa and MasterCard.

TRANSPORTATION: On base shuttle/bus, C-580-213-7472; Off base shuttle/bus, C-580-233-7433; Car Rental: Avis, C-1-800-831-2847; Enterprise, C-1-800-325-8007; Johnsons, C-1-800-375-5718; On base taxi, C-580-213-7472; Off base taxi, C-580-233-1795.

DINING OPPORTUNITIES: Combined Club, C-580-213-7595; and Bowling Alley, C-580-213-7331 are within walking distance. Applebee's Grill and Bar, C-580-233-1525; Golden Corral, C-580-234-1803; and Richill's Cafeteria, C-580-237-4005 are within driving distance.

In Enid visit Government Springs Park where cowboys watered cattle 75 years ago, Leonardo's Discovery Warehouse, Gaslight Theatre, Midgly Museum, Railroad Museum of Oklahoma, the Museum of the Cherokee Strip and Meadowlake Park with its 18-hole golf course, amusement park and 14-acre lake.

OREGON

Camp Rilea Armed Forces Training Center (OR07R4)
Route 2, Box 497-E
Warrenton, OR 97146-9711

MAIN INSTALLATION TELEPHONE NUMBERS: C-503-861-4018, DSN-312-355-3972. Locator 861-4018; Medical 911; Security Police 911. *Ten-digit dialing required for local calls.*

LOCATION: From Portland, take US-26 northwest to Oregon Coast, approximately 65 miles. When you reach US-101, proceed north 12 miles. Located between Seaside and Astoria. *USMRA: Page 100 (B-1).* **NMC:** Astoria, five miles north.

RESERVATION INFORMATION: 91372 Rilea Pacific Road, Warrenton, OR 97146-9711. **C-503-861-4048/4052, DSN-314-355-4048/4052,** Fax: C-503-861-4049, 0830-1630 hours. E-mail: nikkilas@or-arng.ngb.army.mil All reservations may be made 90 days in advance. Check in at billeting.

(BEQ) Bedroom (53). Refrigerator, CATV in lounge, housekeeping service. Rates: $15-$20.

(BOQ) E7+. Room (18). Refrigerator, CATV, housekeeping service. Rates: $20-$30.

(DV/VIP) VOQ/DVQ. State homes. O6+ Chateau; E8+ Cottage; O4/CW4+ Hilltop. Separate bedroom, private bath, refrigerator, microwave, TV. Rates: Chateau, $100-$115; Cottage, $60-$69; Hilltop, $50-$57.

AMENITIES: Exercise Room, Meeting/Conference Room, Mini Mart, Snack and Soft Drink Vending Machines.

TML AVAILABILITY: Good.

CREDIT CARDS ACCEPTED: Visa and MasterCard.

TRANSPORTATION: Off base taxi.

DINING OPPORTUNITIES: Kilroy's Pub, C-503-361-4040 is within walking distance. Blue Water Grill, C-503-717-1635; Captain Morgan's, C-503-736-0206; Gregorio's Pizza, C-503-738-5217; McDonald's, C-503-738-9496; and Taco Time, C-503-738-8833 are within driving distance.

Visit the many National Forests and State Parks that dot the coastline and state.

Note: **North Bend Coast Guard Group and Portland Coast Guard Marine Safety Office have lodging facilities. Call C-541-756-9201(North Bend), C-541-756-9282 (Portland)for details.**

Klamath Falls International Airport/ Kingsley Field/Air National Guard (OR03R4)

302 Vandenburg Drive, Suite 38
Klamath Falls, OR 97603-0400

MAIN INSTALLATION TELEPHONE NUMBERS: C-541-885-6350, DSN-312-830-6350. Locator 885-6350; Medical 885-6312; Security Police 885-6663.

LOCATION: Take I-5 through Medford to Hwy 140 E, 75 miles to southside bypass. Go east approximately 4.5 miles to the airport. West of Highway 39 and east of US-97, adjacent to Klamath Falls IAP. *USMRA: Page 100 (D-8).* **NMC:** Medford, 80 miles west.

RESERVATION INFORMATION: Kingsley Dormitory, Bldg 208, McConnell Circle, Klamath Falls, OR 97603-0400. **C-541-885-6365, D-312-830-6365** 0700-1600 hours Mon-Fri. All categories may make reservations; no Space-A. After hours check in at Security Gate.

TML Kingsley Dormitory. Newly renovated. Official duty only. Suite, private bath (4); bedroom, two beds, semi-private bath (16); bedroom, one bed, semi-private bath (12). Refrigerator, A/C, iron/ironing board, housekeeping service, TV, coffee maker. Wood frame structure. Rates: no charge.

AMENITIES: Laundry Room. Ice, Snack and Soft Drink Vending Machines.

TML AVAILABILITY: Very good. *Note: Lodging available to personnel on official business only.*

CREDIT CARDS ACCEPTED: No charge for billeting.

TRANSPORTATION: Off base shuttle/bus, C-541-883-2877; Car Rentals: Avis, C-1-800-831-2847; Budget, C-1-800-527-0770; Enterprise, C-1-800-736-8222; Hertz, C-1-800-654-3131; off base taxi, C-541-885-5607.

DINING OPPORTUNITIES: Satellite, C-541-882-5509 is within walking distance. Sizzler, C-541-884-1848; Sam's Place, C-541-884-3276; and Denny's, C-541-882-3537 are within driving distance.

There is a clinic and small BX on base. Experience topnotch fishing, bald eagles that winter nearby, world class skiing, golf, horseback riding, camping, hunting. Then there's Crater Lake and Mt. Shasta within an hour's drive.

PENNSYLVANIA

Carlisle Barracks (PA08R1)

632 Wright Avenue
Carlisle, PA 17013-5046

MAIN INSTALLATION TELEPHONE NUMBERS: C-717-245-3131, DSN-312-242-3131. Locator 245-3131; Medical 245-3915/3400; Security Police 245-4115.

LOCATION: From I-81 exit 52B to US-11, 2 miles southwest to Carlisle. Signs clearly marked to Carlisle Barracks and Army War College. *USMRA: Page 22 (F-6).* **NMC:** Harrisburg, 18 miles northeast.

RESERVATION INFORMATION: ATZE-DCA-AL, Ashburn Hall, 36 Flower Road, Carlisle, PA 17013-5081. **C-717-245-4245, DSN-312-242-4245,** Fax: C-717-245-3757/4770, DSN-312-242-3757/4770, 0700-1800 hours weekdays, 0800-1600 hours weekends and holidays. Other hours Bldg 400, pick up key at MP desk. E-mail: lodgingoffice@carlisle.army.mil Directions: Through Main Gate to stop sign. Turn right onto Lovell Avenue, at stop sign, turn left on Flower Road. 1/2 block down the road on the left. Check in 1400 hours, check out 1100 hours. Government civilian employee billeting.

Note: Only family members with valid ID card can stay at this facility.

VAQ Bldg 7, Washington Hall (14 units); Bldg 36, Ashburn Hall (19 units); Building 37, Pratt Hall (12 units). Bedroom, private bath; suite, private bath. Community kitchen, refrigerator, coffee maker, A/C, TV/VCR in room and lounge, hair dryer, housekeeping service, iron/ironing board, toiletries, cribs, cots, ice machine. Rates: $50-$60, each additional person $5. Rates vary according to type of room. TDY, PCS and guests of USAWC have priority. All categories can make reservations.

DV/VIP Bldg 7. Bedroom, private bath; suite, private bath. Community kitchen, refrigerator, coffee maker, A/C, color TV/VCR in room and lounge, hair dryer, housekeeping service, iron/ironing board, toiletries, cribs, cots, ice machine. Rates: $51, each additonal person $5.

AMENITIES: Meeting/Conference Room, Snack Vending Machine.

TML AVAILABILITY: Good, Jan-Mar. Difficult, other times.

CREDIT CARDS ACCEPTED: Visa, MasterCard and American Express.

TRANSPORTATION: Off base shuttle/bus; Off base car rental; Off base taxi: West Shore Taxi, C-717-795-8294 or 717-249-4474.

DINING OPPORTUNITIES: Sunnyside, C-717-243-5712; Sandwich Man, C-717-245-2472; and Hoss's Steak & Seafood House, C-717-258-4468 are within walking distance. Rillo's, C-717-243-6141; Little John's, C-717-249-4575; and California Cafe, C-717-249-2028 are within driving distance.

An arsenal during the Revolutionary War, near the Gettysburg Battlefields, site of the Military History Institute, home of the Army War College, Carlisle Barracks has an illustrious history worth tracing.

Defense Distribution Center, Susquehanna (PA06R1)

Bldg 268, G Avenue
New Cumberland, PA 17070-5000

MAIN INSTALLATION TELEPHONE NUMBERS: C-717-770-6011, DSN-312-977-6011. Locator 770-6011; Medical 770-7281; Security Police 770-6222.

LOCATION: From I-83, exit 39 Ato PA-114 east for one mile to Old York Road, left 3/4 of a mile to Ross Avenue, right for 1 mile to Main Gate of Center. *USMRA: Page 22 (G-6).* **NMC:** Harrisburg, seven miles northeast.

RESERVATION INFORMATION: Attn: HF, Bldg 268, J Avenue, New Cumberland, PA 17070-5002. **C-717-770-7035, DSN-312-977-7035,** Fax: C-717-770-4579, 0800-1630 hours. Duty with TDY, PCS orders can make reservations; others Space-A. Government civilian employee billeting in VOQ.

VOQ Bldg 268. Bedroom, private bath (15). Refrigerator, microwave, coffee maker, A/C, TV, housekeeping service, cribs, cots, laundry facility, living area. Older structure, renovated. Rates: $30, each additional adult $5.Maximum two adults and one child per unit.

DV/VIP Protocol Office, Bldg 268, **C-717-770-7192.** O6/GS15+. Bedroom, living area (4); bedroom suite (2); bedroom, living area, kitchen (1). Refrigerator, A/C, TV, housekeeping service, cribs, cots, laundry facility. Older structure, renovated. Rates: regular room $40.00, suite $52.00. Retirees and lower ranks Space-A.

AMENITIES: Snack and Soft Drink Vending Machines.

TML AVAILABILITY: Good, Nov-Feb. Difficult, other times.

CREDIT CARDS ACCEPTED: Visa, MasterCard, American Express and MAC debit card.

TRANSPORTATION: Off base bus, C-717-238-8304; off base taxi, C-717-737-3699.

DINING OPPORTUNITIES: Bob Evan's, C-717-774-0593; Coakley's, C-717-774-5556 and Pierre's Cafe, C-717-774-0132 are withing driving distance.

Visit Hershey Park, famous Pennsylvania Dutch Country, Gettysburg National Military Park and General Lee's Headquarters and Museum.

Fort Indiantown Gap (PA04R1)
1 Service Road, Bldg 11-7
Annville, PA 17003-5002

MAIN INSTALLATION TELEPHONE NUMBERS: C-717-861-2000, DSN-312-491-2000. Locator 861-2000; Medical 861-2091; Security Police 861-2727.

LOCATION: From I-81, take exit 29 B north on PA-934 to post. *USMRA: Page 22 (G-6).* **NMC:** Harrisonburg, 18 miles southwest.

RESERVATION INFORMATION: 1 Service Road, Bldg 11-7, Annville, PA 17003-5000. **C-717-861-2512/2540/8158, DSN-312-491-2512/2540/8158,** Fax: C-717-861-2821, DSN-312-491-2821, 0800-1630 hours, Mon-Sun; 0800-2000 hours Fri. E-mail: house@nbn.net Space-A walk in only; unable to take reservations. Directions: At light make a left onto service road; approx. 3/4 mile from the light. Check in at billeting 1500 hours, check out 1100 hours.

TML Reserve/NG post. VOQ/BEQ. Official duty. Bedroom, common bath (500); suite, shared bath (24); Cottages (12). A/C, CATV, housekeeping service, laundry facility, facilities for DAVs. Older structure, renovated. Rates: rooms $7; suites $15; cottages $25, each additional person in suites/cottages over age eight $4. Dependents allowed.

DV/VIP C-717-861-2512/2540. O6+. Cottages, half kitchen, AC, TV/VCR, full maid service, sleeps two to four. Rates: $25.

TML AVAILABILITY: Difficult, most of the time. Best, Nov-Mar.

CREDIT CARDS ACCEPTED: Visa, MasterCard and American Express.

TRANSPORTATION: None available.

DINING OPPORTUNITIES: Funck's, C-715-865-2764 is within driving distance.

Hershey Park, Museum and Chocolate World, Indian Echo Caverns with a spectacular underground display and local Pennsylvania German farm and village festivals and crafts demonstrations are "must sees."

Pittsburgh International Airport/ Air Reserve Station (PA15R1)
911th Airlift Wing
2275 Defense Avenue, Suite 218
Coraopolis, PA 15108-4463

MAIN INSTALLATION TELEPHONE NUMBERS: C-412-474-8000, DSN-312-277-8000. Locator 472-0170; Medical 474-8117; Security Police 474-8250.

LOCATION: Take I-279 west, which merges into PA-60 (Airport Parkway), then take exit 3 (Business Route 60) to Thorn Run Interchange, follow signs to Air Reserve Station. *USMRA: Page 22 (A-5,6).* **NMC:** Pittsburgh, 15 miles southeast.

RESERVATION INFORMATION: Bldg 206, 2275 Defense Avenue, Corapolis, PA 15108-4463. **C-1-888-AFLODGE (1-888-235-6343), C-412-474-8229/8230, DSN-312-277-8230,** Fax: C-412-474-8752, DSN-312-277-8752, 0700-2300 hours. Duty may make reservations any time; Space-A may make reservations 24 hours in advance. Directions: 100 yards past the Main Gate on the left. Check out 1200 hours.

TML VAQ/SNCO. Bldgs 209, 216-219. Bedroom, two beds, common bath (72); bedroom, private bath (44); two-room SNCO suite, private bath (10). Refrigerator, microwave in lounge, A/C, TV/VCR, phone, housekeeping service. Rates: VAQ $14.50; SNCO $21.

VOQ Bldg 206. Bedroom, semi-private bath (20); bedroom, private bath (2). Refrigerator, microwave in lounge, A/C, TV/VCR, phone, housekeeping service. Rates: $14.50.

DV/VIP VOQ. Bldg 206. Two-room DV suite, private bath (2). Refrigerator, microwave in lounge, A/C, TV/VCR, phone, housekeeping service. Rates: $21.

AMENITIES: Ice, Snack and Soft Drink Vending Machines.

TML AVAILABILITY: Very limited on training weekends.

CREDIT CARDS ACCEPTED: Visa, MasterCard and American Express.

TRANSPORTATION: Car Rental, C-412-269-9200; Off base taxi, C-412-665-8100.

DINING OPPORTUNITIES: Hoss's; Eat N Park, C-412-262-3270; and King's, C-412-269-9523 are within driving distance.

Tobyhanna Army Depot (PA05R1)
Attn: AMSEL-TY-CS-R
11 Hap Arnold Blvd
Tobyhanna, PA 18466-5044

MAIN INSTALLATION TELEPHONE NUMBERS: C-570-895-7000, DSN-312-795-7110. Locator 895-7000; Medical 895-7121; Ambulance/Fire Station 895-7300; Security Police 895-7550.

LOCATION: Take I-80 to I-380 north, exit 7 to PA 507 and 1 mile to depot. *USMRA: Page 22 (I-4).* **NMC:** Scranton, 24 miles northwest.

RESERVATION INFORMATION: 11 Hap Arnold Blvd, Tobyhanna, PA 18466-5044. **C-570-895-8529, DSN-312-795-8529,** Fax: C-570-895-7419, DSN-312-795-7419, 0730-1630 hours Mon-Fri. Other hours Security, Bldg 20, C-570-895-7550. Reservations may be made 30 days in advance. Check in at billeting 1500 hours, check out 1000 hours.

TML Guesthouse. Bldgs 1013, 1014, 2020. Two-bedroom (5); three-bedroom (1). Private bath, kitchen, utensils, microwave, TV, housekeeping service. Two units have washer/dryer, one unit has jacuzzi tub. One new structure, four newly renovated structures. Rates: $40 per day, each additional person over two years old $5. Housekeeping service must be requested 24 hours in advance or automatically every third day at an additional charge of $15 each time.

TML AVAILABILITY: Good, Mar-May. Difficult, other times.

TRANSPORTATION: Off base taxi.

DINING OPPORTUNITIES: Cafeteria, C-570-895-7998; and Combined Club, C-570-895-7045 are within walking distance. Nearby restuarants are within ten minutes of depot.

In the Pocono Mountains resort area. Nearby lakes and streams provide fishing and water sports. Skiing and winter sports January to March. State parks and forest picnic areas in the immediate area will lure visitors.

Willow Grove Naval Air Station/ Joint Reserve Base (PA01R1)
Willow Grove, PA 19090-5000

MAIN INSTALLATION TELEPHONE NUMBERS: C-215-443-1000, DSN-312-991-1000. Locator 443-6000; Medical 443-6360/1600; Security Police 443-1911.
Ten-digit dialing required for local calls.

LOCATION: Take PA Turnpike (I-76) to Willow Grove exit 27 north approximately 3.5 miles on PA-611 to NAS. *USMRA: Page 22 (I,J-6)*. **NMC:** Philadelphia, eight miles south.

RESERVATION INFORMATION: CBQ Bldg 609, Willow Grove, PA 19090-5000. **C-215-442-5800/5801, DSN-312-991-5800, Toll-Free C-1-800-227-9472,** Fax: C-215-442-5817, 24 hours daily. Check in at facility 1500 hours, check out 1100 hours. PCS, TDY Active Duty and Reservists can make reservations; Retirees and others Space-A. Active Duty, retired, reserve, NROTC, NG, DoD civilian billeting.

(BEQ) Bldg 172. E7 and below. E5-E7: Bedroom, private bath (14); E4 and below: double room, private bath (20). Refrigerator, microwave, coffee maker, A/C, CATV, alarm clock, telephone, housekeeping service, laundry facility, iron/ironing board. Rates: single $13, double $7; each additional person $6.

(BEQ) Bldg 609. E9 and below. Bedroom/living room suites, queen-size bed, private bath (3); two-bedroom (one queen-size bed, two singles), private bath (7). Refrigerator, microwave, coffee maker, A/C, CATV, alarm clock, telephone, housekeeping service, laundry facility, iron/ironing board. Rates: family suite $19, each additional person $6.

(BOQ) Bldg 5. Single bedroom, common bath (36); suites, private bath, window A/C (10). Refrigerator, microwave, CATV, telephone, housekeeping service, laundry facility. Older structure, renovated. Rates: single $10, suite $22; each additional person $6.

(DV/VIP) Contact the CBQ directly. VIP suites (2). Rates: $28, each additional person $6.

AMENITIES: Snack and Soft Drink Vending Machines, Mini Mart, Internet/E-mail access for customers.

TML AVAILABILITY: Fair. Except weekends when extremely limited due to ASW Training School and Reserve Unit training.

CREDIT CARDS ACCEPTED: Visa, MasterCard and American Express.

TRANSPORTATION: Off base Shuttle/Bus: Septa Train from Hatboro; Septa Bus runs from Doyles Town to Philly. Septa Info C-215-580-7800, 0600-2000 hours; Car Rental: Enterprise, C-215-674-8400 (Warminster); Off base taxi, C-215-659-0245.

DINING OPPORTUNITIES: Liberty Hall Galley, C-215-443-6282; Pitcarin Club, C-215-443-6081; and Subway, C-215-328-0544; and Orion Club, C-215-443-6089 are on base. Off base dining:Ruby Tuesday, IHOP, TGI Fridays and McDonalds.

See Philadelphia's Liberty Bell, Art Museum and Zoo. Visit the 9th Street Market in Little Italy (Rocky Balboa made his famous run here), Independence Hall and Penns Landing. A short drive to Washington's crossing, Valley Forge, Sesame Place, Six Flags, Dorney Park, Poconos, Crystal Cave and the Amish Country. Society Hill, New Market, summer open air concerts along the Parkway and at Robin Hood Dell. For sports events some tickets for the Flyers, Eagles, Phillies and 76ers are available through ITT Office ext 6082.

Visit Military Living online at
www.militaryliving.com

RHODE ISLAND

Newport Naval Station (RI01R1)
690 Peary Street
Newport, RI 02841-5000

MAIN INSTALLATION TELEPHONE NUMBERS: C-401-841-2311, DSN-312-948-2311. Medical 841-3771; Security Police 841-4035.

LOCATION: From US-1 exit to RI-138 east over Jamestown/Newport bridge (toll) to Newport. Follow signs north to Navy Base, Gate 1. *USMRA: Page 17 (J-8), page 25 (B,C-1,2,3)*. **NMC:** Newport, adjacent.

RESERVATION INFORMATION: 1312 Meyerkord Avenue, Newport, RI 02841-1513. Bldg 1312, **C-401-841-7900, DSN-312-948-7900,** Fax: C-401-841-7577, DSN-312-948-7577, 24 hours daily. E-mail cbqreservations@nsnpt.navy.mil Directions: From Gate 1, Training Station Road take the first right, follow Peary Road to the small bridge (just past the Susse Chalet). Proceed across the bridge and turn left onto Elliot Street. Take third right onto Perry Street, Bldg 1312 is 200 feet up on the left. Check in at facility 1500 hours, check out 1100 hours. Government civilian employee billeting in CBQ.

(TML) Private Rooms, private bath. Refrigerator, CATV, telephone. Rates: winter: $10, each additional guest $2.50. Summer: $15, each additional guest $3.75. E7-E9 (VIP 3). Rates: winter: $25, each additional guest $6.25. Summer: $35, each additional guest $8.75. VIP amenities: everything E1-E9 room has plus kitchenette with all utensils, honor bar, hair dryer, VCR. Duty can make reservations, others Space-A.

(CBQ) Bldg 1312. Single (412); suite (92). Refrigerator, microwave, coffee maker, CATV/VCR, hair dryer, housekeeping service, iron/ironing board. Winter Rates: single $10, additional guest $2.50; suite $20, additional guest $5. Summer Rates: single $15; additional guest $3.75; suite $24, additional guest $6.

(NAVY LODGE) Navy Lodge. Bldg 685, Coddington Highway, Middletown, RI 02842. **C-1-800-NAVY-INN.** Lodge number is C-401-849-4500, Fax: C-401-841-1807, 24 hours daily. Directions: In southern Middle-Town, I-95 , exit to I-138 E to Jamestown/Newport Bridge (toll) to Newport. Exit west onto Admiral Kalbfus Road to circle, then left on Lake Erie street to Navy Lodge Bldg 685 on right. Check in 1500-1800 hours, check out 1200 hours. Apartment: bedroom, two double beds, private bath, no A/C (16); bedroom, two double beds, studio couch (28). Kitchenette, microwave, coffee/tea, utensils, A/C, CATV/VCR, video rental, HBO, phones, clock radio, hair dryer, housekeeping service, coin laundry facility, iron/ironing board, cribs, highchairs, ice machine. Rates: Apr-Nov, apartments $70; efficiencies $56. Dec-Mar, apartments $54; efficiencies $42. All categories can make reservations. No pets. *Replacement 50 room Navy Lodge scheduled to open in Fall 2001.*

(DV/VIP) Contact CO, **C-401-841-3715** or **C-401-841-6464,** Naval War College, President's Office. Suite (6), flag cabin, apartment (2). Refrigerator, microwave, honor bar, coffee maker, CATV/VCR, hair dryer, housekeeping service, iron/ironing board. Rates: winter: suite $25, additional guest $6.25; cabin $50. Summer: suite $35, additional guest $8.75; cabin $50. Susse Chalet available $58.42 year-round on orders.

AMENITIES: Meeting/Conference Room, Snack and Soft Drink Vending Machine.

TML AVAILABILITY: Good, winter 15 Oct-30 Apr. Difficult, summer 1 May-14 Oct.

CREDIT CARDS ACCEPTED: Visa, MasterCard and American Express.

TRANSPORTATION: Off base shuttle/bus, C-401-846-2500; on base taxi, C-401-841-3913, DSN-312-948-3913; off base taxi, C-401-849-1333, C-401-846-1500.

DINING OPPORTUNITIES: Blimpie's; McDonald's, C-401-846-4460; and O Club, C-401-846-7987 are within walking distance. Chili's; Coddington Brew Pub & Restaurant, C-401-847-6690; and East Side Mario's, C-401-841-0700 are within driving distance.

Stroll along cobblestone streets, or oceanfront walks; admire turn-of-the-century mansions; visit many national historic landmarks, and the Naval War College Museum. Admire the wonderful sailing vessels—this is Newport!

SOUTH CAROLINA

Beaufort Marine Corps Air Station (SC01R1)
P.O. Box 55018
Beaufort MCAS, SC 29904-5023

MAIN INSTALLATION TELEPHONE NUMBERS: C-843-228-7100, DSN-312-335-7100. Locator 228-7188; Medical 228-7311; Security Police 228-7373.

LOCATION: From I-95 take Beaufort exit 33 to SC-21 southeast and follow signs. Sixteen miles to MCAS east of SC-21. Clearly marked. *USMRA: Page 44 (G-9).* **NMC:** Savannah, GA, 40 miles south.

RESERVATION INFORMATION: 1108 Delalio, Beaufort MCAS, SC 29904-5000. **C-843-522-1663, DSN-312-335-7676,** Fax: C-843-522-1663, 24 hours daily. Check in at facility, check out 1200 hours. Government civilian employee billeting.

TML de Treville House. Bldg 1108. Bedroom, private bath (21); seperate bedroom, private bath, kitchen with refrigerator, microwave, complete utensils (21). All rooms include A/C, TV/VCR, housekeeping service, laundry facility, cots ($5), cribs, ice machine, playground, picnic area with grills. Hard Corp Cafe adjacent. Modern structure. Handicap accessible, special facilities for DAVs. Rates: single $35; double $40; kitchen room $45. Maximun five adults per unit. Make reservations. Non-military personnel visiting relatives stationed at Beaufort may stay on a Space-A basis. *Note: New carpet is being installed. Construction for 21 new units is planned for 2001.*

BOQ Bldg 431. Bedroom (39); suite, private bath (5); bedroom, private/shared bath (SR/SNCO) (17). Community kitchen, refrigerator, microwave, limited utensils, A/C, TV lounge, housekeeping service, laundry facility, iron/ironing board, ice machine. Modern structure, renovated. Rates: Duty room $15; suite $20; each additional family member $3. No children. Duty may make reservations; others Space-A. No pets.

DV/VIP Contact CO, Bldg 601, **C-843-228-7158.** Retirees and lower ranks Space-A.

AMENITIES: Snack and Soft Drink Vending Machines, Video Rental.

TML AVAILABILITY: Very good, most of the year. Best, Sep-Apr.

CREDIT CARDS ACCEPTED: Visa, MasterCard and American Express.

TRANSPORTATION: Car Rental: Enterprise, C-843-524-0494; Thrifty, C-843-522-9996; On base Taxi, C-843-522-7550; Off base taxi, C-843-522-1121.

DINING OPPORTUNITIES: Cafeteria, C-843-228-7895; O Club, C-843-228-7541; and Snack Bar, C-843-228-7895 are within driving distance.

Visit Military Living online at
www.militaryliving.com

Charleston Air Force Base (SC06R1)
437th MSS/DPF
104 E Simpson Street, Bldg 500
Charleston AFB, SC 29404-4924

MAIN INSTALLATION TELEPHONE NUMBERS: C-843-963-6000, DSN-312-673-2100/1110. Locator 963-6000; Medical 963-6747; Security Police 963-3600.

LOCATION: From I-26, exit 211 to West Aviation Avenue to traffic light, continue through light to second light right, follow perimeter road around end of runway to gate 2 (Rivers Gate). *USMRA: Page 44 (H-8,9).* **NMC:** Charleston, 10 miles southeast.

RESERVATION INFORMATION: The Inns of Charleston, Hill Blvd, Bldg 362, Charleston AFB, SC 29404-4825. **C-1-888-AFLODGE (1-888-235-6343), C-843-963-3806, C-843-552-9900, DSN-312-673-3806/8000,** Fax: C-843-963-3394, 24 hours daily. Duty may make reservations any time; Space-A may make reservations 24 hours in advance. E-mail: joe.abell@charleston.af.mil Check in 1600 hours at Bldg 362, check out 1200 hours. Government civilian employee billeting in contract quarters.

TLF Bldg 330. Bedroom suite, private bath, kitchen, sleeps five (18). A/C, TV, housekeeping service, laundry facility, ice machine. Rates: $24.50 per family. No pets.

VAQ Bldg 344. Bedroom, private bath (4); bedroom, shared bath (40). A/C, TV, housekeeping service, laundry facility, ice machine. Rates: $17.50. No pets.

VQ Bldgs 362, 343. Bedroom, private bath (68). Microfridge, A/C, housekeeping service, laundry facility, cribs, cots, ice machine. Modern structure. Rates: $20. Maximum two per room. No pets.

DV/VIP Bldgs 343, 344, 362. O6+. Bedroom suite, private bath (4). Kitchen, microfridge, A/C, housekeeping service, laundry facility, cribs, cots, ice machine. Modern structure. Rates: $25. Maximum five per room. No pets.

AMENITIES: Meeting/Conference Room, Soft Drink Vending Machine.

CREDIT CARDS ACCEPTED: Visa and MasterCard. Credit Card required to make reservation.

TRANSPORTATION: On base shuttle/bus: Agency, C-843-571-7243; Off base shuttle bus: Enterprise, C-843-767-5460; Car Rentals: Alamo, C-843-767-4417; Charleston Transportation, C-843-767-6111; On base taxi: North Area Taxi, C-843-554-7575; Off base taxi: Yellow Cab, C-843-577-6565.

DINING OPPORTUNITIES: Burger King; Charleston Club, C-843-963-3920; and Wrenwoods Golf Course Snack Bar, C-843-760-4174 are within walking distance. Applebee's, C-843-207-0990; Youngblood's American Grill and Bar, C-843-767-1713; and Yum Yum Express Chinese Restaurant, C-843-767-1828 are within driving distance.

Visit stately mansions along the Battery and Boone Hall, where scenes from "Gone With the Wind" and "North and South" were filmed. Take a water tour and visit historic Fort Sumter in Charleston Harbor.

Charleston Naval Weapons Station (SC11R1)
Naval Weapons Station Charleston
2316 Redbank Road, Suite 100
Goose Creek, SC 29445-8601

MAIN INSTALLATION TELEPHONE NUMBERS: C-843-764-7901, DSN-312-794-7901. Locator 764-7218; Medical 743-7000; Security Police 764-7521.

LOCATION: From I-26, exit 205 south, east on US-78, to US-52 north, to SC-37 southeast (Red Bank Road) to Main Gate. *USMRA: Page 44 (H-8,9).* **NMC:** Charleston, 25 miles south.

RESERVATION INFORMATION: Commanding Officer, Housing Department (Code 55), 2316 Red Bank Road, Suite 100, Goose Creek, SC 29445-8601. **C-843-556-7646, DSN-312-794-7218.** Fax: C-843-764-7285, DSN-312-794-7285, 0730-1600 hours. MWR on the web: www.nwschs.navy.mil/mwr/index.html. Directions: Located in Housing Welcome Center on Fletcher Street. Turn left off Redbank Road into Fletcher Street. Active Duty, Retirees (Space-A), DoD civilians.

DV/VIP O5-O10 and Command Master Chiefs on official travel. Kitchen, refrigerator, microwave, utensils, A/C, CATV/VCR in lounge and room, housekeeping service, laundry facility. Rates: $26, each additional person over 18 years of age $6.50. No pets.

AMENITIES: Exercise Room, Mini Mart, Internet/E-mail access for customers. Ice, Snack and Soft Drink Vending Machines.

TML AVAILABILITY: Limited.

CREDIT CARDS ACCEPTED: None.

TRANSPORTATION: Car Rental: Thrifty, C-843-552-7531; Off base taxi, C-843-577-6565.

DINING OPPORTUNITIES: Redbank Club, C-843-764-7797; and Redbank Plantation Golf Club Snack Bar, C-843-764-7802 are within walking distance. McDonald's, C-843-572-9671 is within driving distance.

Visit Charleston for excellent historical and shopping experiences.

Fort Jackson (SC09R1)
United States Army Training Center
Bldg 3499 Green Avenue
Fort Jackson, SC 29207-5000

MAIN INSTALLATION TELEPHONE NUMBERS: C-803-751-7511, DSN-312-734-1110. Locator 751-7511; Medical 751-2168/911; Security Police 751-3113/911.

LOCATION: Exit from I-20 north of fort, or from US-76/378 at the Main Gate. From I-20 and I-77 interchange exit 16 take newly constructed Beltway south to Percival Road, right onto Percival Road to Gate 2. *USMRA: Page 44 (G-6).* **NMC:** Columbia, 12 miles southwest.

RESERVATION INFORMATION: Kennedy Hall, Bldg 2785, Semmes Road and Lee Road, Fort Jackson, SC 29207-5000. **C-803-751-6223, DSN-312-734-6223,** Fax: C-803-751-6797, DSN-312-734-6797. Toll free reservations for government official duty personnel (on post) and local hotels **1-800-276-6984 (subject to change),** 24 hours daily. Duty may make reservations; others Space-A. Check in at billeting, check out 1000 hours. Active Duty, retired, reserve, NG and DoD civilian on TDY billeting.

TML Kennedy Hall. Bldg 2785. Bedroom, one bed, private bath (transient units) (142). Refrigerator, microwave, A/C, TV, housekeeping service, laundry facility. Modern structure, remodeled. Rates per room: official $26, unofficial $36. Maximum two per unit. No pets.

VEQ Dozier Hall, Bldg 2464. **C-803-782-7326,** Fax: C-803-751-8476. Official duty. Bedroom, one bed, private bath (76). Refrigerator, microwave, TV, housekeeping service. Rates per room: official $38, unofficial $48. No pets.

Army Lodging Palmetto Lodge. Bldg 6000. **C-803-751-5205/4429,** Fax: C-803-751-5500. Bedroom, private bath, sleeps six (70). Kitchen, limited utensils, A/C, TV in room and lounge, phone, housekeeping service, laundry facility, ice machine. Rates: Duty/PCS $30, unofficial $40; $5 each additional person. No pets.

Cabins Weston Lake Recreation Area and Travel Camp. C-803-751-LAKE(5253), DSN-312-734-LAKE (5253). Directions: On base. From I-20 north of Fort take exit 80 onto Clemson Road; left on Percival Road (SC-12), then right onto Wildcat Road; drive 7 miles across Fort Jackson, then left on Leesburg Road (SC-262) 2.5 miles to Weston Lake Recreation Area on the left. Leesburg Road (SC-262) is also accessible from US-76/378 south of post AND from US-601 east of post. Cabins: Four-bedroom (1), three-bedroom, furnished (2), two-bedroom, furnished (2), two-bedroom log, furnished (1), one-bedroom duplex, furnished, private bath. Kitchen, microwave, dishes, pots and pans, linens available for fee, TV. Lakefront cabins come with use of a rowboat. Rates: $30-$50 daily. Reservations suggested. See *Military Living's Military RV, Camping and Outdoor Recreation Around the World* for additional information and directions.

DV/VIP Executive Service Office, HQ Bldg, **C-803-751-6618, DSN-312-734-5218.** Bldgs 3640-3645, 4416, Legion Landing and Dozier House. O6+, official duty. Check out 1100 hours. Cottages: Bedroom, private bath (2), two-bedroom, private bath (4), three-bedroom suite, private bath (1). Kitchen, utensils, A/C, TV, phone, housekeeping service. Remodeled. Rates: $30-$50. No smoking. No pets.

TML AVAILABILITY: Very good, Oct-May.

CREDIT CARDS ACCEPTED: Visa, MasterCard and American Express.

TRANSPORTATION: On base shuttle/bus, C-803-751-3191; Car Rental, C-803-782-4178; On base taxi, C-803-799-3311 or C-803-754-8163.

DINING OPPORTUNITIES: Burger King, C-803-782-5396; NCO Club, C-803-782-1932/2218; and O Club, C-803-751-4906/782-8761 are within walking distance. Golden Corral Restaurant, C-803-787-4446; Olive Garden Italian Restaurant, C-803-736-9440; and Red Lobster Restaurant, C-803-736-1343 are within driving distance.

Riverbanks Zoological Park, Town Theater amateur productions and a carriage ride along historic Broad Street compete with local golf courses, Lake Murray and numerous public recreation areas as local popular pastimes.

Parris Island Marine Corps Recruit Depot (SC08R1)
P.O. Box 19001
Parris Island MCRD, SC 29905-9001

MAIN INSTALLATION TELEPHONE NUMBERS: C-843-525-2744, DSN-312-832-2744. Locator 525-3358; Medical 525-3315; Security Police 525-3444.

LOCATION: From I-95, exit 33 to US-17 east to US-21 south to SC-280 to SC 802 south, which leads to the Main Gate of the depot. *USMRA: Page 44 (G-10).* **NMC:** Savannah, GA 43 miles southwest.

RESERVATION INFORMATION: MWR, Bldg 330, P.O. Box 1500, Parris Island MCRD, SC 29905-0059. **C-843-228-2744, DSN-312-335-2744,** Fax: C-843-525-3815, DSN-312-832-3815. Duty may make reservations any time; others 14 days in advance. **All Space-A required to confirm 72 hours in advance.** Directions from Main Gate: Take Blvd de France to intersection with four stop signs. Turn left on Mexico Street, Bldg 330 is on left. Check in at facility after 1400 hours, check out no later than 1100 hours.

BEQ Osprey Inn II. Bldg 330. Leave or official duty, civilian government employees, retired, DAVs, military widows. Bedroom, hotel style with all amenities (1); bedroom, hotel style, private bath (5); bedroom, college style, shared bath (64). Refrigerator, microwave, coffeemaker, A/C, CATV, phone, clock radio, ironing board, housekeeping service, laundry facility, ice machine. Modern structure. Rates: without kitchen $14, with kitchen $19; each additional person $5.

BOQ **Osprey Inn I.** Bldg 289. Leave or official duty, civilian government employees, retired, DAVs, military widows. Bedroom, private bath (19); bedroom, common bath (4). Refrigerator, coffee maker, A/C, TV, phone, clock radio, laundry facility, ironing board, ice machine, meeting/conference room. Older structure. Rates: without kitchen $17, with kitchen $22, civilian $27; each additional person $5. Children 12 & under are free. Maximum four per room.

VOQ **Beaufort River Inn.** Bldg 254. Leave or official duty, retired, DAVs, military widows, accompanied dependents, government civilians GS12+ on official duty. Bedroom, private bath, kitchen, complete utensils (4). Bedroom, private bath (2). Refrigerator, A/C, TV in room and lounge, housekeeping service, laundry facility, cots, ice machine. Older structure, renovated. Rates: without kitchen $17, with kitchen $22, civilian $27; each additional person $5. Children 12 & under are free. Maximum four per unit. All categories can make reservations.

TML **Hostess House.** Bldg 200, two miles from Main Gate. **C-843-228-2976, Fax: C-843-228-2872.** All categories. Bedroom, two beds, sofabed, private bath (30). Kitchenette, A/C, TV/VCR in room, housekeeping service, laundry facility, cribs, ice machine, facilities for DAVs. Video rental and snacks in lobby. Rates: $50 per room; with kitchen $55, each additional person $5. Duty may make reservations anytime; others may make reservations 30 days in advance.

AMENITIES: Exercise Room, Meeting/Conference Room, Snack and Soft Drink Vending Machines.

TML AVAILABILITY: Good except graduation days.

CREDIT CARDS ACCEPTED: Visa, MasterCard and American Express.

TRANSPORTATION: Car Rental; Off base taxi.

DINING OPPORTUNITIES: On base dining facilities and numerous restaurants in Beaufort are within driving distance.

Weekly recruit graduations at 0915 most Fridays. Museum on base. Visitors Center Bldg 283.

Shaw Air Force Base (SC10R1)
20th MSS/DPF
524 Stuart Avenue
Shaw AFB, SC 29152-5023

MAIN INSTALLATION TELEPHONE NUMBERS: C-803-895-1110, DSN-312-965-1110. Locator 895-4844; Medical 895-6675; Security Police 895-9893.

LOCATION: Off US-76/378, eight miles west of Sumter, north side of US-76/378. Clearly marked. *USMRA: Page 44 (H-6)*. **NMC:** Columbia, 35 miles west.

RESERVATION INFORMATION: Carolina Pines Inn, Bldg 930, 471 Myers Street, Shaw AFB, SC 29152-5000. **C-1-888-AFLODGE (1-888-235-6343), C-803-895-3803, DSN-312-965-3803** Fax: C-803-895-3805, DSN-312-965-3805, 24 hours daily. Check in at facility, check out 1200 hours. Duty may make reservations any time; Space-A can request availability 24 hours in advance for up to three days. Directions from Main Gate: Take left on Polifka, right on Myers, the reception office is fourth building on right.

TLF Bldgs 931-934. Separate bedrooms, sofabed, private bath (39). Kitchenette, honor bar, A/C, TV, laundry facility, housekeeping service, cribs, cots. Modern structure. Handicap accessible. Rates: $28 per unit. Maximum five per apartment.

VAQ Bldg 911 and 927. Bedroom, one bed, private bath (24). Honor bar, A/C, TV, housekeeping service, laundry facility, ice machine. Modern structure. Rates: $24 per unit.

VOQ Bldgs 924, 927. Bedroom, private bath. Kitchen, honor bar, limited utensils, A/C, TV, housekeeping service, laundry facility, ice machine. Modern structure. Rates: $24 per unit. Maximum two per room.

DV/VIP Protocol Office, **C-803-895-2007/8, DSN-312-965-2007/8.** O6+. Bldg 924. Bedroom, private bath (6). Kitchen, honor bar, utensils, A/C, TV, housekeeping service, laundry facility, ice machine. Older structure, remodeled. Rates: $28 per unit. Maximum two per unit.

AMENITIES: Exercise Room.

TML AVAILABILITY: Good. Best, Dec-Mar.

CREDIT CARDS ACCEPTED: Visa and MasterCard.

TRANSPORTATION: On base taxi (official use only); off base taxi, C-803-783-3333.

DINING OPPORTUNITIES: Shaw Annex (all ranks dining) C-803-666-3661; E Club C-803-666-3651 and Bowling Center C-803-895-2732 are all within walking distance. Demara's Italian Restaurant C-803-499-4741, Subway C-803-494-2204; and Twin Dragon Chinese Restaurant, C-803-494-8484 are within driving distance.

An 18-hole golf course, three swimming pools, tennis courts and fitness center on base. Columbia, the state capital, and Charleston, not to mention Myrtle Beach, the Blue Ridge and Smokey Mountains.

Short Stay Navy Outdoor Recreation Area (SC02R1)
211 Short Stay Road
Moncks Corner, SC 29461-5000

MAIN INSTALLATION TELEPHONE NUMBERS: C-843-764-7601. Locator 764-7601; Medical 911; Security Police 911.

LOCATION: Off Base. On Lake Moultrie five miles north of Moncks Corner. Take US-52 north from Charleston. Follow the signs. *USMRA: Page 44 (H-8)*. **NMC:** Charleston, 30 miles south. NMI: Charleston Naval Station, 35 miles south.

RESERVATION INFORMATION: 211 Short Stay Road, Moncks Corner, SC 29461-5000. **C-1-800-447-2178** or **C-843-761-8353,** Fax: C-843-761-4792, 0730-1700 hours daily. WEB: www.shortstay.com Write for brochure. A non-refundable reservation fee equal to the first night's lodging is required. Check in at facility 1500 hours, check out 1100 hours. After hours Security is located near office. Active Duty, retired, reserve, DoD civilian billeting.

Short Stay Recreation Area has a lot to offer!

Cabins Cabins and villas. Cabin, private bath, sleep four (6); log cabins, sleep four to six (2); two-bedroom villa, private bath, sleeps four (24); three-bedroom villa, private bath, sleeps six (12); handicap accessible (3). Kitchenette, CATV, picnic tables, deck, grills. Amenities include swimming beach, convenience store, laundry room, game room, party pavilions, boat and equipment rentals. Rates Military/DoD. Summer Rates (Mar-Oct): two-bedroom villa $47/$53; three-bedroom villa $58/$65; cabin $62/$68; log cabin $20/$22; two-bedroom cabin $30/$32. Winter Rates (Nov-Feb): two-bedroom villa $36; three-bedroom villa $44; cabin $62/$68. Discounted prices for week long stays. Pets are not allowed in the cabins or villas.

TML AVAILABILITY: Good. Best, Sep-May. Difficult, Jun-Aug.

CREDIT CARDS ACCEPTED: Major credit cards.

TRANSPORTATION: None available.

Located on Lake Moultrie (60,000 acres), fishing, watersports, Charleston offers beaches, golf, historic sites. Read Military Living's *Military RV, Camping and Outdoor Recreation Around the World* for more information.

Wateree Recreation Area (SC05R1)
Outdoor Recreation
P.O. Box 52696
Shaw AFB, SC 29152-5000

MAIN INSTALLATION TELEPHONE NUMBERS: C-803-895-0449, DSN-312-965-0449. Medical 911; Security Police 911.

LOCATION: Off I-20, exit 98, take US-521 north through Camden to intersect SC Hwy 97 northwest for 9 miles, then turn left for Lake Wateree access. *USMRA: Page 44 (G-5,6)*. **NMC:** Columbia, 35 miles south west. NMI: Shaw AFB, 37 miles southeast.

RESERVATION INFORMATION: **C-803-895-0449, DSN-312-965-0449.** (Wateree Rec Area phone number is C-803-432-7976.) Reservations taken up to 60 days in advance for Active Duty stationed at Shaw AFB; others up to 45 days in advance. Reservations can be made at Shaw AFB Outdoor Recreation 0800-1800 hours Mon-Fri, 0700-1100 hours Sat. Active Duty, retired, ANG, reserves, DoD civilians.

Cabins Three-bedroom cabin, private bath (2); two-bedroom cabin, private bath (11). Microwave, dishes, pots and pans, TV/VCR, fully equipped. Handicap accessible. Rates: $60-$85 daily. See *Military Living's Military RV, Camping and Outdoor Recreation Around the World* for additional information.

TML AVAILABILITY: Good, winter months. Difficult, summer months.

CREDIT CARDS ACCEPTED: Visa and MasterCard.

TRANSPORTATION: None available.

DINING OPPORTUNITIES: Several restaurants are within ten miles driving distance in Camden.

SOUTH DAKOTA

Ellsworth Air Force Base (SD01R3)
28th Bomb Wing
1561 Ellsworth Drive, Suite 1
Ellsworth AFB, SD 57706-4808

MAIN INSTALLATION TELEPHONE NUMBERS: C-605-385-1000, DSN-312-675-1110. Locator 385-1379; Medical 385-3430; Security Police 385-4001.

LOCATION: Two miles north of I-90. Seven miles east of Rapid City. From I-90 take exit 66 north approximately 2 miles to gate. Clearly

marked. *USMRA: Page 85. (B-5)*. **NMC:** Rapid City, seven miles west.

RESERVATION INFORMATION: Pine Tree Inn, 2349 Risner Drive, Ellsworth AFB, SD 57706-4708. **C-1-888-AFLODGE (1-888-235-6343), C-605-385-2844, DSN-312-675-2844,** Fax: C-605-385-2718, 24 hours daily. Duty may make reservations any time; Space-A may make reservations 24 hours in advance. Check in at facility 1400 hours, check out 1100 hours.

TLF **Aspen Inn.** Bldg 8008. One-bedroom, two hide-a-beds. Full kitchen, A/C, CATV, housekeeping service, laundry facility, ice machine. Rates: $21.50. No Smoking. No pets.

VOQ **Pine Tree Inn.** Bldg 1103. One-bedroom, private bath (34); **Cedar Inn,** Bldg 5907, bedroom, private bath (48). Refrigerator, A/C, CATV, housekeeping service, laundry facility, ice machine. Rates: $13.50 per room. No Smoking. No pets.

DV/VIP Protocol, **C-605-385-1205, DSN-312-675-1205.** O6+. Retirees and Active Duty. Rates: $23 per room. No Smoking. No pets.

TML AVAILABILITY: Good, Oct-Apr. Difficult, other times.

CREDIT CARDS ACCEPTED: Visa and MasterCard.

TRANSPORTATION: On base taxi (duty only), C-605-385-2907; Car rental and off base taxi available in Rapid City.

DINING OPPORTUNITIES: Bowling Center, C-605-385-1031; Burger King, C-605-923-3724; and Dakota's Club, C-605-385-1764 are within walking distance. Pauley's Sub Shop, C-605-923-5853; and Pizza Hut, C-605-923-5832 are within driving distance.

While you're here visit the Air and Space Museum, Mount Rushmore, the Badlands, Crazy Horse Monument, Deadwood and the Black Hills.

TENNESSEE

Arnold Air Force Base (TN02R2)
Arnold Engineering Development Center
100 Kindel Drive, Room B-213
Arnold AFB, TN 37389-5000

MAIN INSTALLATION TELEPHONE NUMBERS: C-931-454-3000, DSN-312-340-3000. Locator 454-3000; Medical 454-5351; Security Police 454-5662.

LOCATION: From US-231 north of Huntsville, take TN-50/55 east to AEDC access highway in Tullahoma. From I-24 take AEDC exit 117, four miles south of Manchester. Clearly marked. *USMRA: Page 41 (I-9)*. **NMC:** Chattanooga, 65 miles southeast;Nashville, 65 miles northwest.

RESERVATION INFORMATION: Wingo Inn, 4176 Westover Road, Tullahoma, TN 37389-2213. **C-1-888-AFLODGE (1-888-235-6343), C-931-454-3099, DSN-312-340-3094,** Fax: C-931-454-4004, DSN-312-340-4004, 0600-2200 hours Mon-Fri, 1000-2000 hours Sat-Sun, 1000-1800 hours holidays. WEB: www.arnold.af.mil/aedc/lodging.htm Directions: From Main Gate, head west on AEDC highway for 2 miles. Turn left after passing Gate 2 and follow signs to lodging. After hours, Security C-931-454-5662. Check in at billeting 1400 hours, check out 1100 hours.

VAQ/VOQ Bldg 3027. Bedroom, shared bath (36); bedroom, private bath (4); business suites. Rooms have community kitchen, refrigerator, microwave, coffee maker, limited utensils, A/C, TV/VCR, housekeeping service, laundry facility, cribs, ice machine. Rates: room $19, business suite $26. Duty may make reservations any time; Space-A may make reservations 24 hours in advance.

(DV/VIP) Billeting Office. O6+. Bedroom, private bath (5). Community kitchen, refrigerator, microwave, coffee maker, limited utensils, A/C, TV/VCR, housekeeping service, laundry facility, cribs, ice machine. Duty may make reservations any time with approval from Protocol; Space-A may stay on one night basis after 1600 hours.

AMENITIES: Meeting/Conference Room, Snack and Soft Drink Vending Machines.

TML AVAILABILITY: Good, all year.

CREDIT CARDS ACCEPTED: Visa and MasterCard.

TRANSPORTATION: On/Off base taxi, C-931-454-5579, DSN-312-340-5579.

DINING OPPORTUNITIES: Arnold Lakeside Club, C-931-454-3090, DSN-312-340-3090 is within walking distance. Mulligan's Grill, C-931-455-5870; and Tucker's, C-931-967-4045 are within driving distance.

On this 44,000-acre installation, Woods Reservoir has a 75-mile shoreline for fishing and all water sports. Visit the Grand Ole Opry, Music Row, the Parthenon, the Hermitage in Nashville, Jack Daniels Distillery, Rock City, Look-out Mountain and NASA Space Center in Huntsville, AL. Civil War buffs–there's lots to see!

Mid-South Naval Support Activity (TN01R2)
Family Service Center (TAC)
5720 Integrity Drive
Millington, TN 38054-5045

MAIN INSTALLATION TELEPHONE NUMBERS: C-901-874-5111, DSN-312-882-5111. Locator 874-5111; Medical 911; Security Police 911.

LOCATION: From Memphis International Airport, take Airways Blvd north to I-240 (exit 23). Turn right onto I-240 E. Take I-40 (exit 12B) west tp SR 14 N (exit 8). Turn left on Singleton Parkway and go straight to South Gate of NSA Mid-South. *USMRA: Page 40 (B-9,10).* **NMC:** Memphis, 20 miles southwest.

RESERVATION INFORMATION: Navy Lodge. Bldgs N-762, N-931, Attu Street, Millington, TN 38054-6024. **C-1-800-NAVY-INN.** Lodge number is C-901-872-0121, Fax: C-901-874-5346, 0600-2400 hours daily. All categories may make reservations. Check in 1500-1800 hours, check out 1200 hours. After hours get key at Bldg 452 (Navy Inns) at the corner of Wasp and Intrepid. *Note: All transient quarters are being managed and operated by the NEXCOM (Navy Inn Program). Twelve suites and 246 regular rooms are available at the rate of $48 and $35 per day respectively.*

(NAVY LODGE) Navy Lodge. Bldgs N-762, N-931. All ranks and NEX associates. Bedroom, one queen-size bed and a sofabed, private bath (22); bedroom, two extra-long double beds, private bath (25), Handicap accessible rooms, double bed with sofa bed (2). Kitchenette, microwave, microfridge, dining table, utensils, coffee, A/C, SATV/VCR, video rental, phone, clock radio, hair dryer, Internet access, housekeeping service, coin laundry facility, iron/ironing board, cribs, highchairs, rollaways, playgrounds, picnic area, BBQ. Four interconnecting units, non-smoking (23). Tennis, golf, Navy Lake, stables nearby. No pets, kennel nearby. Rates: $42.

AMENITIES: Ice, Snack and Soft Drink Vending Machines.

TML AVAILABILITY: Good, Dec. Difficult, other times.

CREDIT CARDS ACCEPTED: Visa, MasterCard, American Express. The Navy Lodge accepts Visa, MasterCard, American Express and Discover.

TRANSPORTATION: Airport and Base Shuttle C-901-874-5752; Car Rental; on base taxi, C-901-874-5752; off base taxi, Millington Taxi.

DINING OPPORTUNITIES: MWR Food Court, The Nineteenth Hole, Subway and McDonald's are within walking distance. Burger King, Old Timer's and Taco Bell are within driving distance.

Check out the nearby attractions of Graceland, Beale Street (Home of the Blues), Shelby Forest State Park provides thousands of acres of native woodlands for walking, riding, picnicking and boating. The Memphis area is famous for bird and duck hunting.

TEXAS

Armed Services YMCA of El Paso (TX50R3)
7060 Comington Street
El Paso, TX 79930-4239

(This is not U.S. Government/Military Lodging.)

MAIN INSTALLATION TELEPHONE NUMBERS: C-915-562-8461. Locator 568-2121; Medical 569-2331; Security Police 568-2115.

LOCATION: Five miles from downtown or El Paso International Airport. From I-10 exit onto Patriot Freeway. Head north on the Freeway to Fred Wilson exit.Turn right on Hayes Avenue, to William Beaumont Army Medical Center gate. YMCA Residence Center straight ahead. *USMRA: Page 86 (B-6).* NMI: Fort Bliss 1.5 miles. **NMC:** El Paso, in city limits.

RESERVATION INFORMATION: Bldg 7060, Comington Street, El Paso, TX 79930-4239. **C-915-562-8461,** Fax: C-915-565-0306, 24 hours daily. E-mail: aymca3@elp.rr.com All categories may make reservations. Check in at front desk, check out 1100 hours. *Note: This facility is on Fort Bliss (Beaumont Army Medical Center). For additional TML see Fort Bliss listing.*

(TML) Motel-style ASYMCA residence. King size room, private bath (16); double bed, private bath (36). A/C, CATV, refrigerator (all), kitchenette (30 units). Housekeeping service, coin laundry facility, cots. Handicap accessible. Rates: Active Duty $30.50; retired $31.50; civilian personnel $33.50, additional person $5.50. Children 12 & under are free. Maximum four per room, arrangements can be made to adjust. *Pets allowed.*

AMENITIES: Exercise Room, Meeting/Conference Room. Ice, Soft Drink and Snack Vending Machines.

TML AVAILABILITY: Excellent year round.

CREDIT CARDS ACCEPTED: Visa, MasterCard, American Express, Discover.

TRANSPORTATION: Car Rental; Off base taxi.

DINING OPPORTUNITIES: Restaurant serving all meals opened January 1998. Numerous restaurants are within driving distance in El Paso,

Visit old Juarez and the Tiqua Indian Reservation. There are numerous military museums on post. The William Beaumont Army Medical Center is close by.

Belton Lake Recreation Area (TX07R3)
Reservations Office
Attn: AFZF-CA-BOD-OR-BLORA
Fort Hood, TX 76544-5056

MAIN INSTALLATION TELEPHONE NUMBERS: C-254-287-1110 or 287-288-1110, DSN-312-737-1110 or 312-738-1110. Locator 287-2137; Medical 288-8000; Security Police 287-2176.

LOCATION: From I-35 take Loop 121 N to Sparta Road. Stay on Sparta, turn right on Cottage Road, area marked. *USMRA: Page 87 (K-4,5).* **NMC:** Austin, 60 miles south.

RESERVATION INFORMATION: Community Fitness and Recreation Division, AFZF-CA-CFRD-OR-BLORA, III Corp & Fort Hood, Fort Hood, TX 76544-5056. **C-254-287-2523, DSN-312-737-2523,** Fax: C-254-288-1955. WEB: www.hoodmwr.com All categories may make reservations. 50% of total deposit required within 72 hours of reservation. Check in at cottages after 1500 hours, check out 0730-1200 hours.

(**Cottages**) Bedroom, private bath, sleeps four (10). Kitchen, dishwasher, appliances, A/C, TV, fully equipped. Rates: E1-E4 $30; all other authorized users $35. No Pets.

AMENITIES: Meeting/Conference Room, Mini Mart, Snack and Soft Drink Vending Machines.

TML AVAILABILITY: Good, winter. Difficult, May-Sep.

CREDIT CARDS ACCEPTED: Visa, MasterCard, American Express, Esprit and MWR card.

TRANSPORTATION: Off base taxi, C-254-690-5717, C-254-699-2227.

DINING OPPORTUNITIES: Fort Hood on base dining facilities are within driving distance.

A full round of recreational opportunities is offered here: jet skiing, deck boats, fishing, paddle and ski boats can be rented; the picnic areas, RV camp sites, tent camping sites and party pavilions are fun, fun, fun.

Brooks Air Force Base (TX26R3)
311th AGB/SVML
2804 5th Street, Bldg 214
Brooks AFB, TX 78235-5120

MAIN INSTALLATION TELEPHONE NUMBERS: C-210-536-1110, DSN-312-240-1110. Locator 536-1841; Medical 536-3278; Security Police 536-2851.

LOCATION: At the intersection of I-37 north or south and Military Drive (Loop 13) exit 135. *USMRA: Page 91 (C-4).* **NMC:** San Antonio, five miles northwest.

RESERVATION INFORMATION: Brooks Inn, Bldg 214, 2804 5th Street, Brooks AFB, TX 78235-5000. **C-1-888-AFLODGE (1-888-235-6343), C-210-536-1844, DSN-312-240-1844,** Fax: C-210-536-2327, DSN-312-240-2327, 24 hours daily. E-mail: lodging.reservations@brooks.af.mil WEB: www.brooks.af.mil/ABG/SV/lodging.htm Duty may make reservations any time; Space-A may make reservations 5 days in advance for weekends and 24 hours in advance for weekdays. Check in at facility, check out 1100 hours. Government civilian employee billeting.

(**TLF**) Bldg 211. Bedroom, living room, private bath (8). Kitchen, utensils, A/C, housekeeping service, laundry facility, cribs. Handicap accessible. Rates: $30. PCS in 30-day limit. PCS out seven day limit. PCS have priority; others Space-A.

(**VAQ**) Bldg 718. Separate bedrooms, private bath (2); one-bedroom, shared bath. Refrigerator, A/C, TV, housekeeping service, laundry facility, ice machine. Modern structure. Rates: $19 per person.

(**VOQ**) Bldgs 212, 214, 218, 220. Separate bedrooms, private bath (109); two-bedroom, shared bath (50). Refrigerator, A/C, TV, housekeeping service, laundry facility, cribs, cots, ice machine. Modern structure. Rates: sponsor $19.

(**DV/VIP**) PAO Office, **C-210-536-3238.** O6+. Separate bedrooms, living room, private bath (6). Housekeeping service, laundry facility. Rates: $26 per person.

AMENITIES: Exercise Room, Internet/E-mail access for customers.

TML AVAILABILITY: Limited. Base has contract hotel/motel lodging. Contact Lodging Office.

CREDIT CARDS ACCEPTED: Visa and MasterCard.

TRANSPORTATION: None available.

DINING OPPORTUNITIES: Brooks Club and Sidney's (Bldg 714) are within walking distance. Capparelli's, C-210-648-7630; Lotus, C-210-337-7168; and Pesos Cafe, C-210-333-6481 are within driving distance.

Popular with Brooks' people are the recreation areas at Canyon Lake, on the Guadalupe River northwest of New Braunfels, San Antonio Riverwalk and the Alamo. Also, Six Flags Fiesta and Sea World.

Canyon Lake Recreation Area (TX29R3)
ITR, Bldg 124, Stanley Road
Fort Sam Houston, TX 78234-5000

MAIN INSTALLATION TELEPHONE NUMBERS: C-1-888-882-9878 or C-1-830-964-3318, DSN-312-471-3318. Locator 964-3318; Medical 911; Security Police 911.

LOCATION: Take I-35 to Canyon Lake exit 191 west. Turn west onto FM 306, and drive approximately 16 miles to Canyon City. Continue another 1.5 miles past the blinking light in Canyon City to Jacob Creek Park Road. Turn left, and the recreation area will be on the right. *USMRA: Page 87 (J-6).* **NMC:** San Antonio, 48 miles south. **NMI:** Randolph AFB, 35 miles south.

RESERVATION INFORMATION: Fort Sam Houston Recreation Area at Canyon Lake, 698 Jacobs Creek Park Road, Bldg 300, Canyon Lake, TX 78133-3535. **C-1-888-882-9878** or **C-830-964-3318, DSN-312-471-3318,** Fax: 1-830-964-4405, peak season (1 Mar-30 Sept) Sun-Thurs 0800-1630, Fri 0800-2000, Sat 0800-1800; off season (1 Oct-28 Feb) 0800-1630. WEB www.ftsamcanyonlake.com Reservations are required and may be made up to one year in advance. Check in at facility 1600-2000 hours, check out 1200 hours. Active Duty, retired, reserve, NG, DoD civilians, Foreign Military lodging.

(**Mobile Homes**) Three-bedroom mobile home, private bath (32). Furnished except for towels and soap. Kitchenette, refrigerator, microwave, utensils, A/C, TV/VCR, washer/dryer, ice machine, cribs, cots. One handicap accessible unit. Rates: Active Duty peak $35-$40, off season $20-$25; All others peak $45-$50, off season $30-$35. See *Military Living's Military RV, Camping and Outdoor Recreation Around the World* for additional information.

AMENITIES: Mini Mart.

TML AVAILABILITY: Good, winter. Difficult, May-Sep.

CREDIT CARDS ACCEPTED: Visa, MasterCard, American Express, and MWR Credit Card.

TRANSPORTATION: None available.

DINING OPPORTUNITIES: Several restaurants within driving distance from Canyon Lake.

Corpus Christi Naval Air Station (TX10R3)
Family Service Center
11001 D Street, Suite 143
Corpus Christi, TX 78419-5021

MAIN INSTALLATION TELEPHONE NUMBERS: C-361-961-2811, DSN-312-861-2811. Locator 939-2383; Medical 939-3735/3839; Security Police 939-3460.

LOCATION: From San Antonio, take Interstate 37 southeast to exit 4 A, Highway 358 southeast. Exit northwest for NAS after 12 miles. *USMRA: Page 87 (K-8)*. **NMC:** Corpus Christi, 10 miles west.

RESERVATION INFORMATION: CBQ, 11801 Ocean Drive, Corpus Christi, TX 78419-9999. **C-361-961-2388/89, DSN-312-861-2388/89,** Fax: C-361-961-3275, DSN-312-861-3275, 24 hours daily.

(**VQ**) Bldg 1281. Bedroom, private bath (205). Refrigerator, microwave, coffee maker, A/C, TV/VCR in room and lounge, housekeeping service, laundry facility. Modern structure, renovated. Rates: E1-E9 $11.00, each additional person $2.75; W1-O5 suite $16, each additional person $4; O6/GS15+ DV Suite $24, each additional person $6. Maximum three per unit. Duty may make reservations; others Space-A.

(**NAVY LODGE**) Navy Lodge. Bldg 1281, Corpus Christi, TX 78419-9999. **C-1-800-NAVY-INN.** Lodge number is C-361-937-6361, Fax: C-361-961-3275/937-7854, 24 hours daily. Suites, one queen-size bed, sofabed, private bath (10); bedroom, queen-size bed, private bath (11). Kitchenette, microwave, utensils, coffee/tea, A/C, CATV/VCR, video rental, clock, hair dryer, housekeeping service, coin laundry facility, iron/ironing board, cribs, highchairs, rollaways, ice machine. Modern structure. Handicap accessible, one suite and one room (2); non-smoking (4). Rates: rooms, $33; suites, $41. All categories may make reservations. PCS on orders may make reservations any time. No pets.

(**DV/VIP**) Protocol Office. Bldg 1281, Admin Office, **C-361-961-2388/89, DSN-312-861-2388/89.** Commander's discretion. Retirees, E9, O6+ may make reservations up to 24 hours in advance; Active Duty on orders 60 days in advance; others Space-A.

AMENITIES: Exercise Room, Meeting/Conference Room, Snack and Soft Drink Vending Machines.

TML AVAILABILITY: Very Good, Jan-Mar and Jun-Dec. Difficult, Apr-May.

CREDIT CARDS ACCEPTED: The Navy Lodge accepts Visa, MasterCard, American Express, Discover and Diners.

TRANSPORTATION: Off base bus: RTA, C-361-289-2600; Car Rentals: Dollar Rent A Car, C-361-289-2886; Hertz, C-361-289-0777; Rent-A-Wreck, C-361-855-7368; Super Star Rent-A-Car, C-361-853-5300; Off base taxi: City Cab, C-361-881-8294; Liberty Taxi Service, C-361-882-7654; Pinkie's Taxi, C-361-881-5250.

DINING OPPORTUNITIES: The Corpus Christi Bay Club and McDonald's are within walking distance.

The Padre Island National Seashore, the famous King Ranch, the Confederate Air Force Flying Museum, and the Texas State Aquarium are all local sights worth seeing.

Dyess Air Force Base (TX14R3)
7th SVS/SVML/DPF
441 5th Street
Dyess AFB, TX 79607-1244

MAIN INSTALLATION TELEPHONE NUMBERS: C-915-696-3113, DSN-312-461-3113. Locator 696-3098; Medical 696-4677; Security Police 696-2131.

LOCATION: Turn left off of I-20/US-277 west onto Arnold Blvd. Main Gate will be up 3 miles on the right. *USMRA: Page 87 (I-3)*. **NMC:** Abilene, six miles northeast.

RESERVATION INFORMATION: Dyess Inn, Bldg 441, 5th Street, Dyess AFB, TX 79607-1244. **C-1-888-AFLODGE (1-888-235-6343), C-915-696-1874, DSN-312-461-1874/2681,** Fax: DSN-312-461-2836, 24 hours daily. Duty may make reservations any time; Space-A may make reservations 24 hours in advance. Check in at facility, check out 1100 hours. Government employee lodging.

(**TLF**) Bldg 6240. Separate bedroom, private bath, sleeps five (39). Kitchen, utensils, A/C, TV/VCR, laundry facility, cribs, sleeper sofa/chair, ice machine. Modern structure. Handicap accessible. Rates: $18-$21.50.

(**VAQ**) Bldg 7407. Junior Enlisted ranks. Single room, shared bath (52); Bldg 7218, suite (40). Refrigerator, A/C, TV/VCR, housekeeping service, laundry facility, sundries. Rates: $13-$23. Senior enlisted suites also available through protocol.

(**VOQ**) Bldgs 7420-7422, 6135, 7409. Officers all ranks, senior Enlisted only. One-bedroom, private bath (79). Kitchen, refrigerator, A/C, TV/VCR, housekeeping service, laundry facility, in room sundries. Older structure, remodeled. Handicap accessible. Rates: $13.50-$25.50. Maximum two per room.

(**DV/VIP**) 7th WG. Protocol Office, **C-915-696-5610.** O6+. Separate bedroom suite, private bath (8). Kitchen, refrigerator, A/C, TV/VCR, housekeeping service, laundry facility. Rates: $23-$25.50. Maximum two per room.

AMENITIES: In Room Sundry Bar, Internet/E-mail access for customers.

TML AVAILABILITY: Very good all year.

CREDIT CARDS ACCEPTED: Visa and MasterCard.

TRANSPORTATION: On base Car Rental; Off base taxi.

DINING OPPORTUNITIES: Bowling Center, Burger King, NCO Club and O Club are within walking distance.

Abilene has an award-winning Zoo, a collection of vintage aircraft on display at the base Air Park, boating, fishing and sailing at Lake Fort Phantom Hill and a visit to Buffalo Gap Historic Village a "must."

Fort Bliss (TX06R3)
ACS
Bldg 2494, Ricker Road
Fort Bliss, TX 79916-6816

MAIN INSTALLATION TELEPHONE NUMBERS: C-915-568-2121, DSN-312-978-2121. Locator 568-1113; Medical 569-2331; Security Police 568-2115.

LOCATION: Take I-10 to US-54 north, exit Fort Bliss/Forrest Road. *USMRA: Page 86 (B,C-5,6)*. **NMC:** El Paso, within city limits.

RESERVATION INFORMATION: The Inn at Fort Bliss, P.O. Box 6034, 1744 Victory Avenue, Fort Bliss, TX 79906-1150. **C-915-565-7777, DSN-312-978-7777.** Reservations C-1-800-723-8130, Fax: C-915-565-7778, 24 hours daily. E-mail: innatbliss@bliss.army.mil WEB: www.blissmwr.com Directions: After entering Robert E. Lee Gate follow directional signs to front desk. Located next to commissary and PX complex. Check in at billeting after 1500 hours, check out 1100 hours. Handicap accessible. *Note: See Armed Services YMCA for additional TML on Fort Bliss.*

(**TML**) Fort Bliss Lodging. Kitchenette, microwave, coffee maker, TV, A/C, cribs, rollaways, housekeeping service, laundry facility, iron/ironing board, ice machine and pool. Rates: single $26-$51, double $31-$56.

(**Fisher House**) Located at William Beaumont Army Medical Center, Bldg. 7360 Rodriguez Street, El Paso, TX 79930. **C-915-569-1860,** Fax: **C-915-569-1862.** *Note: Appendix B has the definition of this facility. Fisher Houses are only available as lodging for families of patients receiving medical care at military and VA medical centers.*

(**DV/VIP**) Protocol Office, **C-915-568-5319/5330, DSN-312-978-5319/5330.** O6+ Active Duty or retired, equivalent civilian grade, leave or official duty. Four houses, 12 suites. Completely furnished DV/VIP facility. Rates: $41-$51 per day, each additional person $5. Retirees and lower ranks Space-A.

AMENITIES: Exercise Room, Business Center, Internet/E-mail access for customers. Snack and Soft Drink Vending Machines.

TML AVAILABILITY: Good.

CREDIT CARDS ACCEPTED: Visa, MasterCard, American Express.

TRANSPORTATION: Billeting and The Inn courtesy van, C-915-565-7777; On base Car Rental, C-915-562-5400. *Note: Free transportation to and from El Paso Airport and Biggs Army Airfield Flight operations for anyone staying in Fort Bliss Billeting TDY Quarters. Hours are limited.*

DINING OPPORTUNITIES: The Desert Rose Cafe, located at the Inn at Fort Bliss, C-915-565-7777 is within walking distance. Burger King, C-915-562-2311; Food Court (Post Exchange), C-915-568-3005; Domino's Pizza, C-915-562-0171; and Popeye's Chicken, C-915-566-1829 are within driving distance.

Visit old Juarez and the Tiqua Indian Reservation, check out the Scenic Drive that gives you a view of all of El Paso and old Mexico. There are numerous military museums on post.

Fort Hood (TX02R3)
Relocation Assistance Program
Bldg 36006
Fort Hood, TX 76544-5005

MAIN INSTALLATION TELEPHONE NUMBERS: C-254-287-1110, DSN-312-737-1110. Locator 287-2137; Medical 288-8000; Security Police 287-2176.

LOCATION: From I-35, exit to US-190 west, go 12 miles through Killeen. Main Gate is clearly marked. *USMRA: Page 87 (K-4,5).* **NMC:** Killeen, at main entrance.

RESERVATION INFORMATION: Directorate of Community Activities, Bldg 194, Fort Hood, TX 76544. Office C-254-532-8233, Reservations **C-254-532-3067, DSN-312-737-3067;** Fax: C-254-288-7604 or C-254-287-6566, DSN-312-738-7604 or 312-737-6566; 24 hours daily. Duty may make reservations; others Space-A. Check in at facility, check out 1100 hours. Government civilian employee lodging. Directions from Main Gate: Take Santa Fe Loop. At the light take a right on Wratten Drive. Building is on right. *Winner of Lodging Operation of the Year Award.*

VQ Bldg 36006. Bedroom, private bath (208). Refrigerator, A/C, TV, housekeeping service, laundry facility, ice machine. Older structure renovated. Rates: TDY $36; PCS $36, each additional person $5.

VQ Bldgs 5790, 5792. Suite (60). Community kitchen, refrigerator, A/C, TV, housekeeping service, laundry facility, ice machine. Older structure, renovated. Rates: TDY $36, PCS $35, each additional person $5.

Cottages One-bedroom (10). Kitchen, refrigerator, A/C, TV, VCR. Patrtons must provide toileteries. Rates: $35 per day Mon-Thu, $40 per day, Fri-Sun and holidays. Maximum four persons per cottage.

TML Poxon Guesthouse. Bldg 111. **C-254-287-3067.** Bedroom, private bath (75). Community kitchen, refrigerator, A/C, TV in room and lounge, housekeeping service, laundry facility, cribs, cots, ice machine. Older structure, renovated. Handicap accessible. Rates: $35.

Fisher House Darnall Army Community Hospital, 36000 Darnall Loop, Fort Hood, TX 76544-4752. **C-254-286-7927,** Fax: C-254-286-7929, DSN-566-7927. E-mail fhhood@aol.com Rates: $10 per night. *Note: Appendix B has the definition of this facility. Fisher Houses are only available as lodging for families of patients receiving medical care at military and VA medical centers.*

DV/VIP Bldg 36006. Protocol, **C-254-287-5001.** O6+. Two-bedroom, private bath (10). A/C, TV, housekeeping service, laundry facility, ice machine. Older structure, remodeled. Rates: TDY/PCS $45, each additional person $5.

AMENITIES: Exercise Room, Snack and Soft Drink Vending Machines.

TML AVAILABILITY: Good, winter. Difficult, May-Sep.

CREDIT CARDS ACCEPTED: Visa, MasterCard and American Express.

TRANSPORTATION: Car Rental: C-254-532-3615; On base taxi, C-254-287-2154; Off base taxi, C-254-699-8294.

DINING OPPORTUNITIES: Applebee's, China Star, El Chico, Outback, Roadhouse, TGI Fridays and Black-eyed Pea are within driving distance.

Visitors should tour Lake Belton and other lakes in the regions where boating, fishing, swimming and camping are main pursuits for residents.

Fort Sam Houston (TX18R3)
ACS
Bldg 2797 Stanley Road
Fort Sam Houston, TX 78234-5020

MAIN INSTALLATION TELEPHONE NUMBERS: C-210-221-1211, DSN-312-471-1110. Locator 221-2302; Medical 916-4141; Security Police 221-2222.

LOCATION: Accessible from I-410 or I-35. From I-35 exit 159 A north to gate or New Braunfels Avenue. *USMRA: Page 91 (C,D-2,3).* **NMC:** San Antonio, in city limits.

RESERVATION INFORMATION: Bldg 592, Dickman Road, Fort Sam Houston, TX 78234-5000. **C-210-357-2705, C-1-800-462-7691, DSN-312-471-2705,** Fax: C-210-221-8578, 24 hours daily. Check in at facility 1300 hours, check out 1100 hours. Government civilian employee billeting.

Army Lodging Guesthouse. Bldg 3625, 3050 George C. Beach Avenue. Room, private bath (150); two-bedroom suites. Refrigerator, microwave, A/C, TV, housekeeping service, coin laundry facility, cribs, rollaways, game room. Rates: $30-$35. All categories may make reservations.

VOQ Bldgs 592, 617, 688, 1384. TDY Officer students and Officers all ranks. Bedroom, private bath (513). Kitchenette, microfridge, CATV, housekeeping service, laundry facility. Rates: $32. Duty can make reservations; others Space-A.

TML Officers' Club Bed and Breakfast Suites. **C-210-224-3295.** Active Duty or non-official. Suite (7). Refrigerator, microwave, CATV, HBO. Continental breakfast seven days a week. Reservations up to 90 days in advance. No bumping.

Fisher House Brooke Army Medical Center, 3623 George C. Beach Road, Fort Sam Houston, TX 78234-5000. **C-210-225-4855 ext 101,** Fax: C-210-270-2560. *Note: Appendix B has the definition of this facility. There are two Fisher Houses at BAMC. Fisher Houses are only available as lodging for families of patients receiving medical care at military and VA medical centers.*

DV/VIP Protocol, **C-210-357-2705 ext 5003.** Bldgs 48 (Sam Houston House), 107 (Foulois House). O6+ and comparable grade DoD civilians, leave or official duty. Two-bedroom suite, private bath (2); One-bedroom suite, private bath (22). Microfridge, honor bar, CATV, housekeeping service. Continental breakfast served (Mon-Fri). Recently renovated. Rates: $55. All categories may make reservations; Retirees and lower ranks Space-A. All except TDY subject to bumping.

AMENITIES: Meeting/Conference Room (at Guesthouse), Snack and Soft Drink Vending Machines.

TML AVAILABILITY: Good. Best, Oct-Mar.

CREDIT CARDS ACCEPTED: Visa, MasterCard, and American Express.

TRANSPORTATION: On base shuttle/bus (to hospital only).

DINING OPPORTUNITIES: Golf Course Snack Bar; and O Club C-210-224-4211 are within walking distance. AAFES Main PX Food Court, Burger King and Mulligan's are within driving distance.

Surrounded by San Antonio, this historic post has seen much colorful military history, from its namesake to the "Rough Riders" and Teddy Roosevelt and key roles in WWI and WWII, to today's role as a medical training center. While you're here why not visit the Alamo, Retama Horse Racing Park, Sea World and Six Flags Fiesta Texas. Also visit the Quadrangle Military Museum.

Fort Worth Naval Air Station/Joint Reserve Base (TX21R3)
3175 Vandenberg Avenue
Fort Worth NAS/JRB, TX 76127-6200

MAIN INSTALLATION TELEPHONE NUMBERS: C-817-782-5000, DSN-312-739-1110. Locator 782-5000; Medical 782-5923; Security Police 782-5200.

LOCATION: On TX-183. From Fort Worth, west on I-30, exit at 78 north on TX 183, 1.5 miles to gate on left (north) of TX-183. *USMRA: Page 88 (A-3).* **NMC:** Fort Worth, seven miles east.

RESERVATION INFORMATION: Family Housing, 1324 Military Parkway, Fort Worth NAS/JRB, TX 76127-5000. **C-817-782-5392/3, DSN-312-739-5392/3,** Fax: C-817-782-5391, DSN-312-739-5391, 24 hours daily. Duty may make reservations; others Space-A. Directions: First building on right after Main Gate. Check in at facility 1400 hours, check out 1100 hours. Government civilian employee billeting.

CBQ Bldgs 1520, 1521, 1565, 1566. Bedroom, shared bath. Refrigerator, microwave, coffee maker, A/C, CATV, phone, clock radio, housekeeping service, laundry facility in building, ice machine. Modern structure. Rates: Two person room $8 per bed, single room $12 per night.

CBQ 1324, 1326. Bedroom, private bath. Refrigerator, microwave, coffee maker, A/C, CATV, phone, clock radio, housekeeping service, laundry facility in building, ice machine. Modern structure. Rates: CWO1-CWO5, O1-O5 $24.

Guesthouse Bldg 1326. Queen bed suite (1), two twin beds suite (2), queen-size bed suite, sofabed (3). Refrigerator, microwave, A/C, TV, phone, clock radio, housekeeping service, laundry facility in building, ice machine. Modern structure. Rates: $29.

DV/VIP Protocol, **C-817-782-7614.** Bldg 1324. O6+. One-bedroom suite, private bath (5). Refrigerator, microwave, coffee maker, limited utensils, A/C, TV, phone, clock radio, housekeeping service, laundry facility, ice machine, sitting room. Modern structure. Rates: $30.

AMENITIES: Exercise Room, Meeting/Conference Room, Snack and Soft Drink Vending Machines.

TML AVAILABILITY: Limited space due to rehabilitation of many buildings. It's best to make reservations 30-45 days in advance.

CREDIT CARDS ACCEPTED: Visa, MasterCard and American Express.

TRANSPORTATION: Car Rental.

DINING OPPORTUNITIES: AAFES Exchange, C-817-738-1943; Bowling Center, C-817-782-5505; and Desert Storm Club, C-817-732-7781 are within walking distance. Don Pablo's; C-817-731-0497; Olive Garden, C-817-732-0618; and Ryan's Steakhouse, C-817-246-5080 are within driving distance.

Visit the historic Stockyard District and then world-renowned art museums. How about Southfork? Or the Water Gardens? Or Six Flags Over Texas and the Opera? Fort Worth has come a long way since 1841!

Goodfellow Air Force Base (TX24R3)
17th MSS/DPF
255 Fort Lancaster Avenue
Goodfellow AFB, TX 76908-4304

MAIN INSTALLATION TELEPHONE NUMBERS: C-915-654-3231, DSN-312-477-4000. Locator 654-3410; Medical 654-3135; Security Police 654-3504 or 911.

LOCATION: Off US-87 or US-277. Clearly marked. *USMRA: Page 86 (H-6,7).* **NMC:** San Angelo, two miles southeast.

RESERVATION INFORMATION: Angelo Inn, Bldg 3305, 313 E Kearney Blvd, Goodfellow AFB, TX 76903-4410. **C-1-888-AFLODGE (1-888-235-6343), C-915-654-3686/3332, DSN-312-477-3686/5870,** Fax: C-915-654-5177, DSN-312-477-5177, Information: C-915-654-3332, 24 hours daily. Duty may make reservations any time; Space-A may make reservations 24 hours in advance. Check in at facility, check out 1100 hours. Government civilian employee billeting.

TLF Bldgs 910, 920, 922, 924. Separate bedrooms, private bath (29). Kitchen or kitchenette, complete utensils, microwave, TV, housekeeping service, laundry facility, cribs, ice machine. Modern structure. Handicap accessible. Rates (subject to change): $27.50.

VAQ Bldgs 3307, 3311. Enlisted all ranks, NCO Academy. Bedroom, shared bath (105); room with two beds, shared bath (250). Bldg 239, bedroom, shared bath (58). Refrigerator, microwave, A/C, TV, housekeeping service, laundry facility. Rates: $18.00 per person.

VOQ Bldgs 702, 711. Separate bedrooms, private bath (116). Kitchenette, microwave, A/C, TV, housekeeping service, laundry facility. Modern structure. Rates: $21.50 per person.

DV/VIP Bldg 702, 910 (DVQ Officers), Bldg 3307 (DVQ Enlisted). Separate bedrooms, private bath (18). Kitchen, complete utensils, A/C, TV, housekeeping service, laundry facility, ice machine. Modern structure. DVQ Officers' Rates: $28.50 per room, DVQ Enlisted Rates: $15 per room.

TML AVAILABILITY: Fairly good all year.

CREDIT CARDS ACCEPTED: Visa and MasterCard.

TRANSPORTATION: Off base bus; Car Rental, C-915-655-6663; On base taxi, C-915-654-5744; Off base taxi.

DINING OPPORTUNITIES: Burger King, C-915-659-6613; Bowling Alley; and Military Dining Facilities are within walking distance. Golden Corral, C-915-658-7654; Cheddars' C-915-655-6200; Catfish Corner C-915-651-4817; and Mejor Que Nada, C-915-655-3553 are within driving distance.

Visit historic Fort Concho, a preserved Indian fort and home of the "Buffalo Soldiers," the Concho River Walk and Plaza, and three lakes within 20 minutes of downtown feature camping, boating and fishing.

Ingleside Naval Station (TX30R3)
Family Service Center
2370 Highway 361
Ingleside, TX 78362-5000

MAIN INSTALLATION TELEPHONE NUMBERS: C-361-776-4200, DSN-312-776-4201. Locator 776-4200; Medical 776-4575; Security Police 776-4454.

LOCATION: I-37 south to exit 1 A to US-181 northeast to Route 1069 east and Naval Station. *USMRA: Page 87 (K,L-8).* **NMC:** Corpus Christi, 37 miles south.

RESERVATION INFORMATION: 1455 Ticonderoga, Suite W123, Ingleside, TX 78362-5001. **C-361-776-4420, DSN-312-776-4420,** Fax: C-361-776-4519, DSN-312-776-4519, 24 hours daily. Duty can make reservations; others Space-A. Check in at billeting office.

BEQ Bldgs 134, 138. Bedroom (20); CPO suites (6), VIP suites (2). Refrigerator, microwave, TV/VCR in room and lounge, stereo, phone, housekeeping service, laundry facility, ice machine. Modern structure. Rates: $12 per person. Each additional person in CPO suites $2.75 per night; VIP suites $15 per night. No pets.

AMENITIES: Exercise Room, Meeting/Conference Room. Ice, snack and soft drink vending machines.

TML AVAILABILITY: Fair. All months limited due to facility size.

CREDIT CARDS ACCEPTED: Visa, MasterCard and American Express.

TRANSPORTATION: On/Off base shuttle/bus, C-361-776-4299; Car Rental (USO), C-361-776-4777; Off base taxi, C-361-758-5858.

DINING OPPORTUNITIES: Master Miner Inn (Galley), C-361-776-4425 and USO, C-361-776-4777 are within walking distance. Floyd's Ranch House, C-361-776-3511; Ted's BBQ, C-361-776-5333; and Twin Pizza, C-361-776-3487 are within driving distance.

Visit the USS Lexington, Texas State Aquarium, Mustang Island Beach, Corpus Christi Beach, Greyhound Race Track, King Ranch, Harbor Playhouse or the Corpus Christi Botanical Gardens during your stay!

Kelly Air Force Base (TX03R3)
250th Goodrich Drive
PSC 1, Box 4100
Kelly AFB, TX 78241-5828
Closed July 2001. Now annex to Lackland AFB

MAIN INSTALLATION TELEPHONE NUMBERS: C-210-925-1110, DSN-312-945-1110. Locator 925-1841; Medical 925-4544; Security Police 925-6811.

LOCATION: All of the following, I-10, I-35, I-37, I-410 intersect with US-90 in southwest San Antonio. From US-90 take either the Gen. Hudnell or Gen. McMullen exit and go south to AFB. *USMRA: Page 91 (B-3,4).* **NMC:** San Antonio, seven miles northeast.

RESERVATION INFORMATION: Kelly Inns, Bldg 1650, Goodrich Road, Kelly AFB, TX 78241-5000. **C-1-888-AFLODGE (1-888-235-6343), C-210-925-1844/8279, DSN-312-945-1844,** Fax: C-210-925-9556 or 924-7201, DSN-312-945-9556, 24 hours daily. Duty may make reservations any time; Space-A may make reservations 24 hours in advance. Check in 1400 hours, check out 1100 hours. Active Duty, Retirees, Reservists, NG, DoD civilian billeting.

VAQ Bldg 1650. Refrigerator, microwave, A/C, CATV, housekeeping service, laundry facility, ice machine. Older structure. Rates $19.

VOQ Bldg 1676. Bedroom, private bath. Kitchen, microwave, A/C, CATV, housekeeping service, laundry facility, ice machine. Older structure. Rates: $19.

DV/VIP VOQ. Bldg 1676. Rates: $26.

AMENITIES: Exercise Room, Laundry Room and Meeting/Conference Room.

TML AVAILABILITY: Limited all year.

CREDIT CARDS ACCEPTED: Visa and MasterCard.

TRANSPORTATION: On base shuttle/bus, C-210-925-6372; Off base shuttle/bus, C-210-227-2020; On base taxi, C-210-925-6372; Off base taxi, C-210-222-2151 or C-210-226-4242; On base limo, C-210-671-3555.

DINING OPPORTUNITIES: NCO Club, C-210-925-8354; and O Club, C-210-925-8254 are within walking distance. Bldg 171, C-210-925-6218; Pizza Hut, C-210-433-3371; and V&A Restaurant, C-210-432-9815 are within driving distance.

Your trip to San Antonio will be well remembered if you visit Sea World, Fiesta Texas, the Alamo and the historic mission sites.

Kingsville Naval Air Station (TX22R3)
Bldg 4724, 746 Rosendahl Street
Kingsville NAS, TX 78363-5110

MAIN INSTALLATION TELEPHONE NUMBERS: C-361-516-6136, DSN-312-876-6136. Locator 516-6136; Medical 911; Security Police 911.

LOCATION: Off US-77, exit to TX-141 southeast to Main Gate. *USMRA: Page 87 (K-9).* **NMC:** Corpus Christi, 50 miles northeast.

RESERVATION INFORMATION: Bldg 2700, 1140 Moffett Avenue, Kingsville NAS, TX 78363-5021. **C-361-516-6321/6581, DSN-312-876-6581/6321,** Fax: C-361-516-6428, 24 hours daily. Directions: Make right at first intersection. Follow signs. Check in at facility after 1200 hours, check out by 1200 hours. Government civilian employee billeting. Handicap accessible units.

BOQ/BEQ Bldgs 2700, 3730, 3730A, 3730W. Active Duty, PCS on orders. Bedroom, private bath, living area (49); bedroom, private bath, shared lounge (33). Refrigerator, microwave, A/C, CATV, housekeeping service, cribs, cots, laundry facility, ice, snack and soft drink vending machines. Thirty-five upgraded rooms with new carpet, furniture. Rates: single $14, each additional person $3; DoD civilian $22, each additional person $5. PCS in/out personnel should make reservations; others Space-A. *Note: Bldg 2700 is planned to re-open April 2001.*

TML Escondido Ranch. Off base. Located 90 miles NW of Kingsville NAS C-830-373-4419. Seventeen-room lodge with an adjacent cook house containing four BBQ pits, electric stove, electric grill. The lodge also has a huge lounge with tables, TV/VCR, sofas, pool table, electronic darts, microwave. Rooms are furnished, but limited water prevents linen service. Rates: $10-$50.

DV/VIP Protocol Office, Bldg 3730W, **C-361-516-6321.** O6+ Two bedroom suite (5); E9 Two-bedroom suite (1). Rates: $20-$25. Retirees Space-A.

TML AVAILABILITY: Difficult, Oct-Dec. Good, other months.

CREDIT CARDS ACCEPTED: Visa, MasterCard, American Express, Discover and Government Credit Card.

TRANSPORTATION: Off base car rental.

DINING OPPORTUNITIES: El Jardin Mexican Restaurant, C-572-595-5955; Sirloin Stockade, C-572-595-1182; and Yen Chinh Chinese Restaurant, C-572-595-1541 are within driving distance.

Home of the King Ranch, for Santa Gertrudis cattle, beautiful thoroughbred and quarter horses, the historic ranch house and other interesting sites. Texas A&M University is located here.

Lackland Air Force Base (TX25R3)
37th MSS/DPF
2160 Bong Avenue
Lackland AFB, TX 78236-5113

MAIN INSTALLATION TELEPHONE NUMBERS: C-210-671-2523/2296, DSN-312-473-2523/2296. Locator 671-1110; Medical 292-7100; Security Police 671-2018.

LOCATION: Lackland is located in the southwestern quadrant of the city. Take either IH-10 or I-35 to US-90 south. Loop 13 (Military Drive) bisects Lackland AFB. *USMRA: Page 87 (J-6,7), page 91 (A,B-3).* **NMC:** San Antonio, six miles northeast.

RESERVATION INFORMATION: Bldg 10203, 1750 Femoyer Street, Lackland AFB, TX 78236-5431. **C-1-888-AFLODGE (1-888-235-6343), C-210-671-3622/4277/2556, DSN-312-473-3622/4277/2556,** Fax: C-210-671-1447, DSN-312-473-1447, 24 hours daily. Duty may make reservations any time; Space-A may make reservations 24 hours in advance. Check in at facility, check out 1100 hours.

VAQ Bldg 10203, west side of base. Two-person room, semi-private bath (770); one-person room, semi-private bath; SNCO room, semi-private bath (78); suite with bedroom, private bath. A/C, TV, housekeeping service, laundry facility, snack vending, ice machine. Modern structure. Rates: $10-$15 per unit.

VOQ/TLQ Bldg 2435. Separate bedroom, shared bath; separate bedroom, private bath (157). Refrigerator, microwave, A/C, TV, housekeeping service, laundry facility, snack vending, ice machine. Older structure, remodeled. Rates: VOQ $13.50-$20.50; TLQ $23.50 per person. Air Force policy requires advance payment.

Fisher House Wilford Hall Medical Center (WHMC), 2580 Luke Blvd, Bldg 3810, Lackland AFB, TX 78236-5000. **C-210-292-3000,** Fax: C-210-292-3031. *Note: Appendix B has the definition of this facility. There are three Fisher Houses at WHMC. Fisher Houses are only available as lodging for families of patients receiving medical care at military and VA medical centers.*

DV/VIP Protocol Office, **C-210-671-5397/3622.** O6+. Bedroom suite, private bath (13). Two-bedroom suite, private bath (4). Refrigerator, A/C, TV, housekeeping service, laundry facility, ice machine. Older structure, remodeled. Rates: $20.50. Air Force policy requires advance payment.

TML AVAILABILITY: Difficult, Jan-Nov.

CREDIT CARDS ACCEPTED: Visa and MasterCard.

TRANSPORTATION: On base shuttle/bus; Car Rental: Enterprise, C-210-670-4232; On base taxi, C-210-670-8855.

DINING OPPORTUNITIES: Bowling Center, C-210-671-2271; and Dining Hall, Bldg 6474, C-210-671-4939 are within walking distance. Dining Hall, Bldg 10810, C-210-671-4720, and Bldg 1465, C-210-671-2686 are within driving distance.

San Antonio takes its name from Mission San Antonio de Valero or, the Alamo. Visiting the local Missions and brushing up on the long history of this gracious city, is only one of a number of activities for visitors.

Laughlin Air Force Base (TX05R3)
47th SPTG/DPF
427 Liberty Drive, Bldg 246, Room 301
Laughlin AFB, TX 78843-5135

MAIN INSTALLATION TELEPHONE NUMBERS: C-830-298-3511, DSN-312-732-1110. Locator 298-3511; Medical 298-6362; Security Police 298-3511.

LOCATION: Take US-90 west from San Antonio, 150 miles or US-277 south from San Angelo, 150 miles to Del Rio area, or exit I-10 east or west to US-277 south. The AFB is clearly marked off US-90. *USMRA: Page 86 (H-9).* **NMC:** Del Rio, six miles northwest.

RESERVATION INFORMATION: Laughlin Manor, 47th SVS/SVHM, 416 Liberty Drive, Laughlin, TX 78843-5227. **C-1-888-AFLODGE (1-888-235-6343), C-830-298-5731, DSN-312-732-5731,** Fax: C-830-298-5272, DSN-312-732-5272, 24 hours daily. Lodging Registration C-830-732-5781; Lodging Switch Board C-830-732-5781. Duty may make reservations any time; Space-A may make reservations 24 hours in advance. Directions: Go straight on Liberty Drive to a right on Laughlin Drive and go straight to Seventh Street and make right. Lodging office is on left. Check in at lodging, check out 1100 hours. Government civilian employees lodged in TDY status.

TLF Bldgs 460-463. Separate bedroom, private bath (20). Kitchen, utensils, A/C, TV, limited housekeeping service, microwave, cribs, ice machine. Modern structure. Rates: $25.50 per unit.

VOQ Bldg 470. Bedroom, shared bath (32). Refrigerator, A/C, TV in room and lounge, housekeeping service, laundry facility, cribs, cots, ice machine. Older structure, renovated. Rates: VOQ $13.50 per person.

DV/VIP 47 FTW/CCP, Bldg 338, Room 1, **C-830-298-5041.** Bldg 470. O6+. Separate bedroom, private bath (2); three-bedroom, private bath (4). Kitchen, utensils, TV, housekeeping service, laundry facility, ice machine. Older structure, renovated. Rates: $22.50 per person.

AMENITIES: Snack and Soft Drink Vending Machines.

TML AVAILABILITY: Good, Nov-Jan. Difficult, other times.

CREDIT CARDS ACCEPTED: Visa, MasterCard and Government Travel Card.

TRANSPORTATION: On base taxi, C-830-298-5763, DSN-312-732-5763.

DINING OPPORTUNITIES: Cactus Bowling Lanes, C-830-732-5526; and Club XL, C-830-732-5134 are within walking distance. Burger King Express, C-830-732-3627; Chaparral Dining Facility, C-830-732-5295; and Silver Wings Snack Bar, C-830-732-5661 are within driving distance.

Visit the historical district in Brown Plaza, particularly for Cinco de Mayo and Diez Y Seis de Septiembre celebrations. The Brinkley Mansion, Valverde Winery and the visitors center at Lake Amistad, are all worthwhile to visit.

Randolph Air Force Base (TX19R3)
12th MSS/DPF
555 F Street, Suite 1
Randolph AFB, TX 78150-4537

MAIN INSTALLATION TELEPHONE NUMBERS: C-210-652-1110, DSN-312-487-1110. Locator 652-1110; Medical 652-2734; Security Police 652-5700.

LOCATION: From I-35 take exit 172 south on TX-1604 to AFB or I-10 exit 587 north on TX-1604 to AFB. *USMRA: Page 91 (E-2).* **NMC:** San Antonio, five miles southwest.

RESERVATION INFORMATION: **Randolph Inn,** 12 SPTG/SVML, 415 B Street E, Bldg 112, Randolph AFB, TX 78150-4424. **C-1-888-AFLODGE (1-888-235-6343), C-210-652-1844, DSN-312-487-1844,** Fax: C-210-652-2616, DSN-312-487-2616, 24 hours daily. Duty may make reservations any time; Space-A may make reservations 24 hours in advance. Check in at lodging, check out 1200 hours Mon-Fri, weekends 1100 hours. Government civilian employee lodging in TDY status.

(**TLF**) Bldgs 152-155. Bedroom with queen bed, living room, private bath (30). Full kitchen, utensils, A/C, TV, housekeeping service, iron/ironing board, hair dryer, cribs, limited rollaways, laundry facility, ice machine. Older structure, renovated. Handicap accessible (1). Call for current rates.

(**VAQ**) Bldgs 861, 862. Bedroom with queen bed, living room, kitchen, private bath (5); bedroom, queen-size bed, private bath, stocked bar and snacks (57); bedroom, queen-size bed, shared bath (98). Refrigerator, microwave, utensils for two, A/C, TV, housekeeping service, hair dryer, laundry facility, iron/ironing board, cribs, limited rollaways, ice machine. Modern structure. Call for current rates.

(**VOQ**) Bldgs 110, 111, 120, 121, 161, 162, 381. Bedroom with queen bed, living room, private bath (357); bedroom with queen bed, private bath (256), Refrigerator, microwave, utensils for two, A/C, TV, hair dryer, iron/ironing board, housekeeping service, laundry facility, cribs, limited rollaways, ice machine. Some modern, some older structures. Call for current rates.

(**DV/VIP**) Protocol. Bldg 900, Room 306, **C-210-652-4126.** O7+, SES.

TML AVAILABILITY: Good, Nov-Feb. Fair, other times.

CREDIT CARDS ACCEPTED: Visa and MasterCard.

TRANSPORTATION: On base shuttle/bus/taxi, C-210-652-8294, DSN-312-487-8294; Car Rental: Enterprise.

DINING OPPORTUNITIES: Enlisted Dining Hall, C-210-652-5533 and Robin Hood Deli, C-210-658-7509 are within walking distance.

San Antonio is nestled between the Texas Hill Country and the coast and there is a wealth of local things to do. Visit New Braunfels to the north, for a fascinating look at Texas' German past, and Sequin to the east.

Red River Army Depot (TX15R3)
Building 15, 100 Main Street
Texarkana, TX 75507-5000

MAIN INSTALLATION TELEPHONE NUMBERS: C-903-334-2141, DSN-312-829-2141, Security Police (for recreation area) C-903-334-2911.

LOCATION: Eighteen miles west of Texarkana, TX. From east or west on I-30 take Red River Army Depot exit 206 off of Interstate 30 and turn left at the red light on Highway 82. At East Gate, take a right. *USMRA: Page 86 (N-2).* NMC: Dallas, 170 miles southwest.

RESERVATION INFORMATION: Required for cabins. Address: Camping Reservations Office, Bldg 1433 Elliott Lake, Red River Army Depot (RRAD), Texarkana, TX 75507-5000. **C-903-334-2688/2254, DSN-312-829-2688/2254,** Fax: C-903-334-3290. E-mail: amstarru@redriver-ex.army.mil or Customer Service Representative: E-mail: mcclaranr@redriver-ex.army.mil. Check in 1300 hours at Elliott Lake (southeast corner of RRAD) Country Store, check out 1200 hours.

(**Cottages**) Theme Cottages (16). Log Cabins all with 2 bedrooms, full kitchen, bath, deck and 125-channel SATV. Cabins $75 per night ($35 if you bring your own linens). ***No pets in cottages, allowed outside on leash.*** No firearms.

AMENITIES: Conference Center rental with full audio/visual support, rentals for motor boats, party barge, canoe, aqua cycle, country store, picnic area and weight lifting room.

TML AVAILABILITY: Heavy bookings in summer months.

CREDIT CARDS ACCEPTED: American Express, MasterCard and Visa.

TRANSPORTATION: None available.

DINING OPPORTUNITIES: Post restaurants: Bldg 499, C-334-3472; and Bldg 345, C-334-3371 are open for Breakfast/Lunch Service.

Country Store has tickets and trip information for Six Flags and other attractions.

Sheppard Air Force Base (TX37R3)
82nd MSS/DPF
718 I Avenue
Sheppard AFB, TX 76311-2540

MAIN INSTALLATION TELEPHONE NUMBERS: C-940-676-2511, DSN-312-736-1001. Locator 676-1841; Medical 676-1847; Security Police 676-4522.

LOCATION: Take US 281 or US 287 north of Witchita Falls, exit Spur 325, leads to Main Gate. Clearly marked. *USMRA: Page 87 (J-1).* NMC: Wichita Falls, five miles southwest.

RESERVATION INFORMATION: **Sheppard Inn,** 82 SPTG/SVML, 400 J Avenue, Sheppard AFB, TX 76311-2624. **C-1-888-AF-LODGE (1-888-235-6343), C-940-855-7370, DSN-312-736-1844,** Fax: C-940-676-7434, DSN-312-736-7434, 24 hours daily. E-mail: lori.parker@ sheppard.af.mil or olga.wood@sheppard.af.mil WEB: www.sheppard.af.mil/82svs/lodging.htm Directions from Main Gate: Take a right at stoplight and a left on J Avenue. Sheppard Inn, Bldg 1600, is on right at corner of 4th and J. Check in at lodging, check out 1200 hours. Government civilian employee lodging.

(**TLF**) Bldgs 127-134, 160-165, 1511. C-940-676-2707, DSN-312-736-1844. Separate bedrooms, private bath (73). Four-bedroom, two bath (8). Kitchen, microwave (23), utensils, A/C, TV, housekeeping service, laundry facility, cribs, cots, ice machine. Modern structure. Call for current rates.

(**VAQ**) Bldgs 1601-1604. C-940-676-2707, DSN-312-736-1844. E4 and below. Bedroom, two beds, shared bath (1022). Bldg 1603. E5+. Separate bedrooms, private bath (37); bedroom, one bed, shared bath (580). Refrigerator, microwave, coffee maker, A/C, TV, housekeeping service, ice machine. Modern structure. Call for current rates.

(**VOQ**) Bldgs 240, 260, 370. C-940-676-2707, DSN-312-736-1844. Bedroom, kitchenette, private bath (407); separate bedrooms, kitchenette, private bath (12). Refrigerator, microwave, coffee maker, A/C, TV, laundry facility. Call for current rates.

(**DV/VIP**) Bldg 331, 332, 1603. **C-940-676-2707/2970.** Protocol **C-940-676-2123.** Fax: C-940-676-1814. O6+. Separate bedroom suite, private bath (8). Kitchenette, housekeeping service, A/C, TV, utensils, laundry facility, some with amenities. Modern structure. Call for current rates.

AMENITIES: Exercise Room, Meeting/Conference Room, Mini Mart, Snack and Soft Drink Vending Machines.

TML AVAILABILITY: Good, winter. Difficult, Apr-Sep.

CREDIT CARDS ACCEPTED: Visa and MasterCard. Official business requires government credit card.

TRANSPORTATION: On base shuttle/bus, C-940-676-2701, DSN-312-736-2701; Off base shuttle bus, C-940-761-7921; Car Rental: Budget C-1-800-527-0770, Enterprise C-1-800-rent-a- car; On base taxi, C-940-676-1843, DSN-312-736-1843; Off base taxi, Presidential C-940-322-taxi, All American C-940-723-2678.

DINING OPPORTUNITIES: On base: Burger King, Taco Bell, Robin Hood. Off base: China Star, IHop, McDonald's, Denny's, Long John Silver's and El Chico.

Visit the Wichita Falls Museum and Art Center, Lucy Park, and the 3.5 miles drive to Wichita Falls' waterfall. The original washed away 100 years ago and this one is manmade.

Sheppard Air Force Base Recreation Annex (TX16R3)
1030 SAFB Road
Whitesboro, TX 76273-5000

MAIN INSTALLATION TELEPHONE NUMBERS: C-903-523-4613. Locator 523-4613; Medical 911; Security Police 911.

LOCATION: Located approximately 120 miles east of base at Wichita Falls, near the Texas/Oklahoma line. From US-82 east of Gainesville, take US-377 north approximately 11 miles (past Gordonville exit) to TX FM-901 and turn left. (Just prior to this exit is a green SAFB Annex sign.) Go two miles; turn right at SAFB Annex sign. Follow signs approximately five miles to recreation annex. Rec area is located on Texas side of Lake Texoma. *USMRA: Page 87 (K-1,2)*. **NMC:** Dallas, 95 miles south.

RESERVATION INFORMATION: 1030 SAFB Road, Whitesboro, TX 76273. **C-903-523-4613,** Fax: C-903-523-5200. 0800-1700 hours. Check in at facility 1500 hours, check out 1200 hours. Handicap accessible.

(Cabins) One-bedroom cabin, private bath (42); two-bedroom cabin, private bath (3). AC, TV, refrigerator, utensils, laundry facility, cribs, cots, ice machine, housekeeping service. Rates: $36-$55 daily. ***Pets allowed. See Military Living's Military RV, Camping and Outdoor Recreation Around the World for additional information.***

AMENITIES: Exercise Room, Meeting/Conference Room, Mini Mart, Soft Drink and Snack Vending Machines. Driving Range, Tennis and basketball courts and Playgrounds for the kids.

TML AVAILABILITY: Good, winter. Difficult, Apr-Sep.

CREDIT CARDS ACCEPTED: Visa and MasterCard.

TRANSPORTATION: Off base taxi: Sherman Taxi, C-903-892-1544.

DINING OPPORTUNITIES: Steakhouse and lounge located inside of the annex. Off base: Catfish Haven, C-903-564-3107; Don's BBQ, C-903-564-5813; and Pelicans Landing C-903-523-4500 are within driving distance.

UTAH

Camp W.G. Williams (UT11R4)
17800 S. Camp Williams Road
Bldg 601
Riverton, UT 84065-4999

MAIN INSTALLATION TELEPHONE NUMBERS: C-801-253-5455, DSN-312-766-5455. Locator 253-5455; Medical 911; Security Police 253-5455.

LOCATION: From I-15 take exit 294 (Draper/Riverton UT-71). Turn left at UT-68, drive approximately 7 miles, Camp Williams is on the right. *USMRA: Page 112 (D-4)*. **NMC:** Salt Lake City, 25 miles north.

RESERVATION INFORMATION: Bldg 802, 17800 S Camp Williams Road, Riverton, UT 84065-4999. **C-801-253-5410, DSN-312-766-5410,** Fax: C-801-253-9543, 1000-1600 hours. Check in at billeting office, check out 1200 hours.

(TLF) Bldg 820. E7-E9, Officers all ranks. Bedrooms, semi-private bath (60); bedroom, private bath (5). Refrigerator, TV, housekeeping service, laundry facility, soft drink/snack vending. Rates: $6-$12. Active Duty/reserve may make reservations, others Space-A.

AMENITIES: Snack Vending Machine and Soft Drink Machine.

TML AVAILABILITY: Difficult. Best, fall and winter. *NOTE: No lodging available during Olympics—February and March 2002.*

CREDIT CARDS ACCEPTED: Visa, MasterCard and American Express.

TRANSPORTATION: None available.

DINING OPPORTUNITIES: None available within walking distance. Eriks, C-801-572-6123; Heides Deli, C-801-572-6927; Mullboons, C-801-562-5147; Porters Place, C-801-768-8348; and Shoney's, C-801-572-3844 are within driving distance.

While you're here visit Salt Lake City's Temple Square, planetarium, Hogle Zoo, Trolley Square for shopping, Salt Palace for pro sports. Close to skiing and hiking.

Dugway Proving Ground (UT04R4)
Attn: STEDP-DBO-PCA-FS
Bldg 5124, Room 220
Dugway, UT 84022-5000

MAIN INSTALLATION TELEPHONE NUMBERS: C-435-831-2151, DSN-312-789-2151. Locator 831-2901; Medical 831-2222; Security Police 831-2933.

LOCATION: Isolated, but can be reached from I-80. Take exit 77 south, UT-196, Skull Valley Road for 40 miles south to Dugway and entrance to Proving Ground. *USMRA: Page 112 (B,C-4,5)*. **NMC:** Salt Lake City, 80 miles northeast.

RESERVATION INFORMATION: Antelope Inn, Bldg 5228, Valdez Circle, P.O. Box 128, Dugway, UT 84022-5000. **C-435-831-2333, DSN-312-789-2333,** Fax: C-435-831-2669, DSN-312-789-2669, 0630-1730 hours Mon-Thu, 0730-1130 hours Fri, closed weekends and holidays. E-mail: billeting@dugway-emh3.army.mil After hours, Main Gate, C-431-831-2718. Duty may make reservations; others including contractors and social guests Space-A. Directions from Main Gate: Turn left on Valdez Circle until you see Visitor's Quarters sign on left. Check in at billeting 1500 hours, check out 1300 hours. Government civilian employee billeting.

(TML) DVQ/VOQ/Houses. Bldgs 5226, 5228. Bedroom, private bath (5); separate bedroom suite (30); house with two- to three-bedrooms (8). Refrigerator, A/C, CATV/VCR in room and lounge, hair dryer available upon request, housekeeping service (weekdays only), laundry facility, iron/ironing board, cribs, cots, ice machine, microwave in lobby. Older structures, remodeled. Handicap accessible. Rates do vary and may be obtained by calling.

(DV/VIP) House 1. **C-435-831-2141, DSN-312-789-2141.** O6+. Kitchen, microwave, bar, coffee/tea, TV/VCR, hair dryer available upon request, iron/ironing board. Rates do vary and may be obtained by calling.

AMENITIES: Snack and Soft Drink Vending Machines.

TML AVAILABILITY: Good. Best, fall and winter.

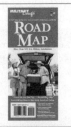

Make finding your destination easier by using Military Living's United States Military Road Map!

CREDIT CARDS ACCEPTED: Visa, MasterCard and American Express.

TRANSPORTATION: None available.

DINING OPPORTUNITIES: Bowling Alley Snack Bar, C-431-831-2687; and Combined Club, C-431-831-2901 are within walking distance. Ditto Diner, C-431-831-5391 is within driving distance.

Pristine alpine mountains, vast deserts, the mysterious Great Salt Lake—this area offers many outdoor activities without entry fees or hype and is only minutes away from metropolitan Salt Lake City!

Hill Air Force Base (UT02R4)
7336 Sixth Street, Bldg 308 N
Hill AFB, UT 84056-5720

MAIN INSTALLATION TELEPHONE NUMBERS: C-801-777-7221, DSN-312-777-1100. Locator 777-1411; Medical 777-5285; Security Police 777-3056.

LOCATION: Adjacent to I-15 between Ogden and Salt Lake City. From I-15, take exit 334, go north to UT-232 to South Gate Drive; or exit 338 to West Gate. *USMRA: Page 112 (D-3)*. **NMC:** Ogden, eight miles north. NMI: Tooele Army Depot, 60 miles southwest.

RESERVATION INFORMATION: Mountain View Inn, 5847 D Avenue, Bldg 146, Hill AFB, UT 84056-5206. **C-1-888-AFLODGE (1-888-235-6343), C-801-777-1844; DSN-312-777-0801,** Fax: C-801-942-2014, DSN-312-775-2015, 24 hours daily. WEB: www.hill.af.mil/services/index.htm Check in 1400 hours at lodging office, check out 1100 hours. Call for rate information. Lodging is available for both official military and civilian duty. Space-A reservations for Active Duty Retired and DOD civilians are accepted 24 hours in advance for up to three consecutive nights' stay based on availability. Exception: Space-A reservations may be made up to two weeks in advance for up to two consecutive weeks stay based on availability during Nov-Feb. Government civilian employee billeting.

VQ Private single room, private bath, microwave, refrigerator. Private two-room, private bath, living room, microwave, refrigerator.

TLF Private bedroom, private bath, living room, kitchenette. Private two-bedroom, (one queen, two twin), private bath, living room, kitchenette.

DVQ/VIP Chief Suite reservations (E9) Command Chief Master Sergeant **C-801-777-5567.** Private room, private bath, living room, microwave, refrigerator, wet bar.

DVQ/VIP Hobson House Suite reservations (O6+) Protocol **C-801-777-5565.** Private room, private bar, living room, microwave, refrigerator, wet bar.

TML AVAILABILITY: Good, summer months. Excellent, winter months. *NOTE: No lodging available during Olympics—February 2002.* (PCS families will have only consideration.)

CREDIT CARDS ACCEPTED: Visa and MasterCard.

TRANSPORTATION: On base shuttle/bus, C-801-777-1843; Car Rental C-801-773-8999; On base taxi, C-801-777-1843; Off base taxi, C-801-394-9411; Limo service, C-1-800-678-2360, C-801-364-6520.

DINING OPPORTUNITIES: Crosswinds Restaurant, C-801-777-2043; O Club, C-801-777-2809; and Wasatch Beach Club, C-801-777-3840 are within walking distance. Hometown Buffet, C-801-547-9976; Olive Garden, C-801-546-1447; and Outback Steakhouse, C-801-779-9394 are within driving distance.

Tooele Army Depot (UT05R4)
Bldg 1012
Tooele, UT 84074-5000

MAIN INSTALLATION TELEPHONE NUMBERS: C-435-833-3211, DSN-312-790-3211. Locator 833-2094; Medical 833-2572; Security Police 833-2314.

LOCATION: From west I-80, exit 99 south, to UT-36 south for about 15 miles to main entrance on right (west) side of UT-36. *USMRA: Page 112 (C-4)*. **NMC:** Salt Lake City, 40 miles northeast.

RESERVATION INFORMATION: Bldg 35, Tooele, UT 81074-5008. **C-435-833-2056, DSN-312-790-2056,** Fax: C-435-833-2251, DSN-312-790-2251, 0630-1700 hours Mon-Thu, closed Fri. Other hours, SDO, Bldg 1000, C-435-833-2304. E-mail: hugelend@emh3.tooele.army.mil Make reservations during regular duty hours or through E-mail. All categories must make reservations, no walk in business. Credit card required to guarantee reservation. Limits on length of stay to be determined at time of call. Directions: First street on the left, Bldg 1000 is first on the left. Check in at billeting 1300 hours, check out 1100 hours. Government civilian employee billeting Handicap accessible.

VOQ/DVQ Bldg S-35. Two-bedroom apartment, private bath (9). One-bedroom apartment, private bath (2). Kitchen, utensils, A/C, CATV, housekeeping service, soft drink and snack vending. Rates: $38.00 for primary occupant, $5.00 for each additional occupant. No charge for children. *Pets accepted on a limited basis.*

TML AVAILABILITY: Good, Nov-Mar; Fair, Apr-Oct.

CREDIT CARDS ACCEPTED: Visa, Mastercard and American Express.

TRANSPORTATION: Off base taxi: Tooele Taxi, C-435-882-8294; Green Top Cab, C-435-882-3100.

DINING OPPORTUNITIES: Eagle's Nest Combined Club is within walking distance. Numerous restaurants are within driving distance in Tooele.

Some special sights in Salt Lake City: the Mormon Temple and Temple Square, the Pioneer Memorial Museum. There are several local ski resorts within reach of Tooele.

VIRGINIA

Camp Pendleton Army National Guard (VA50R1)
PO Box 9
Virginia Beach, VA 23458-5000

MAIN INSTALLATION TELEPHONE NUMBERS: C-757-491-5140. Locator 491-5140; Medical 911; Security Police 491-5144.

LOCATION: SMR is north of Dam Neck Fleet Combat Training Center and south of Virginia Beach resort strip. Take exit 22 off I-264 E onto Birdneck Road, proceed approximately 5 miles until you cross General Booth Blvd, go to next left turn lane and enter Main Gate. *USMRA: Page 52 (J-7)*. **NMC:** Virginia Beach, in city limits.

RESERVATION INFORMATION: State Military Reservation Billeting, ATTN: Mrs. Jane Page, P.O. Box 9, Virginia Beach, VA 23458-0009. **C-757-491-5140 ext 20.** Fax: C-757-491-5958.

TML Rooms, Apartments and House. Single room with community bathroom, A/C, SATV (192). Rates: $10-$15. One-bedroom apartment (3); four-bedroom house (1). Units have private bath, full kitchen, A/C, SATV. Rates: Apartment $25-$35, House $65-$70. Official use has priority. All forms of payment accepted with the exception of Discover Card. All available all-year round.

TML Cottages and Trailers. **State Military Reservation Cottage and Trailer Program,** ATTN: Ms. Rina Cason, P.O. Box 9, Virginia Beach, VA 23458-0009. **C-757-491-5140 ext 14.** Fax: C-757-491-5152. WEB: smrvabeach.homestead.com Cottages (6), Trailers (7). Two or three bedrooms with private baths, sleep four to six persons (most newly remodeled). All have A/C, TV, full kitchen, some with screened porches and one on the lake with a dock. NO HOUSEKEEPING SERVICE (renters leave units clean); towels (bath and kitchen) not provided. Rates: Cottage $55-$70; Trailer $45. Completed application and $100 deposit required. Only checks and money orders are accepted for payment. Reservations for peak season not taken until 15 March with V/ANG members having priority on that day ONLY. Peak season is for weekly rentals ONLY. Season runs 1 May-30 Sept. Two week written notice for cancellations. Year-round rentals (5), off season rates are reduced.

TML AVAILABILITY: Best, Sep-Mar. Difficult, summer.

TRANSPORTATION: Off base taxi: Beach Taxi, C-757-486-4304; James Taxi, C-757-340-4929; and Yellow Cab, C-757-460-4929.

DINING OPPORTUNITIES: Numerous restaurants are within driving distance in Virginia Beach.

Its closeness to historic Williamsburg, Jamestown, the resort area and the Eastern Shore makes this place a find for visitors lucky enough to be able to rent one of the cottages or trailers.

Cheatham Annex/Yorktown Naval Weapons Station (VA02R1)

NWSY Cheatham Annex MWR Department
108 Sanda Avenue
Williamsburg, VA 23185-5830

MAIN INSTALLATION TELEPHONE NUMBERS: C-757-887-4000, DSN-312-953-4000. Locator 887-4000; Medical 887-7222; Security Police 887-7222.

LOCATION: From I-64 east or west take exit 242B northeast to US-199 east to Main Gate. *USMRA: Page 47 (N-8)*. **NMC:** Williamsburg, six miles west.

RESERVATION INFORMATION: MWR, Bldg 284, 108 Sanda Avenue, Williamsburg VA 23185. **C-757-887-7224, DSN-312-953-7224,** 0800-1530 hours mon-fri. After duty hours, Bldg 130, C-757-887-7418 or 757-887-7222. Reservations taken four weeks in advance for Active Duty Militar; three weeks for Retirees and Reserves; two weeks for DoD civilians. Summer seven day rentals only, Mon-Mon, winter two day minimum, seven day maximum. Directions: From main road (Sanda Avenue) go left on D Street, follow D Street to cabins. Check in 1600 hours, check out 1100 hours.

Cabins Recreation Cabins. One to three bedroom cabins, furnished, private bath, each sleeps four to ten (12). Kitchen, refrigerator, dishes, utensils, CATV, phone, boat (with motor, battery charger, paddles and cushions). A/C, central heat, eleven have woodburning stove or fireplace (wood furnished in winter). Handicap accessible cabin (1). Rates: winter, 1 Nov-31 Mar, $35-$75 daily, $210-$450 weekly; summer, 1 Apr-31 Oct $40-$80 daily, $240-$480 weekly. **Nineteen new fully furnished cabins are available for occupancy. No pets allowed. See *Military Living's Military RV, Camping and Outdoor Recreation Around the World* for additional information and directions.**

AMENITIES: Exercise Room, Mini Mart and Soft Drink Machine. Golf Course, Swimming Pool (summer only), fishing, boating and bicycles.

TML AVAILABILITY: Good, Nov-Mar, Mon-Fri. Difficult, other months, Fri-Sun.

CREDIT CARDS ACCEPTED: Visa, MasterCard, American Express and Discover.

TRANSPORTATION: Off base taxi and car rental.

DINING OPPORTUNITIES: The Cascades, Williamsburg Lodge Bay Room, The Taverns of Colonial Williamsburg (King's Arms Tavern, Shield's Tavern, Chowning's Tavern, Christina Campbell's Tavern), C-757-229-2141 (telephone number applicable to all taverns, reservations recommended) are within driving distance.

Near Colonial Williamsburg/Jamestown/Yorktown, Busch Gardens/Water Country, many museums. Great deer hunting. Fitness Center, pool, golf course, racquetball and tennis courts, bowling alley, snack bar.

Chesapeake Naval Security Group Activity Northwest (VA42R1)

1300 Northwest Blvd, Suite 100
Chesapeake, VA 23322-5000

MAIN INSTALLATION TELEPHONE NUMBERS: C-757-421-8000, DSN-312-564-1110. Medical 421-8220, Security Police 421-8333.

LOCATION: From I-64, take exit 291-B to Hwy 168. Proceed through the toll and make a right at the second light to Ballahack Road and follow to base gate (a left on Relay Road). *USMRA: Page 47 (N,O-10)*. **NMC:** Norfolk, 35 miles north.

RESERVATION INFORMATION: Bldg 207, Billeting Office, Chesapeake, VA 23322-5000. **C-757-421-8282, DSN-312-564-0111,** Fax: C-757-421-8792, 0600-2130 hours daily. **Duty required to make reservations through (SATO)-800-576-9327.** Check in at billeting office during duty hours. After duty hours check in at quarterdeck, Bldg 145.

BEQ Bldg 144. Refrigerator, A/C, microwave, TV, housekeeping service, laundry facilities. Rates: $17.

BOQ Bldgs 207, 208, 342. Kitchenette, refrigerator, utensils, TV, housekeeping service, laundry facility, handicap accessible units. Rates: $25, each additional person $6.

TML Bldg 66. Kitchen, refrigerator, TV, housekeeping service, laundry facility. Rates $38, each additional person $9.

AMENITIES: Ice, Snack and Soft Drink Vending Machines.

TML AVAILABILITY: Good, year round

CREDIT CARDS ACCEPTED: Visa, MasterCard, Discover and American Express.

TRANSPORTATION: None available.

DINING OPPORTUNITIES: Base Club, Bowling Alley and McDonald's are within distance.

Dahlgren Naval Surface Warfare Center (VA06R1)

17320 Dahlgren Road/C25
Dahlgren, VA 22448-5100

MAIN INSTALLATION TELEPHONE NUMBERS: C-540-653-8291, DSN-312-249-1110. Locator 653-8216/8701; Medical 911; Security Police 653-8500.

LOCATION: From I-95 in Fredericksburg, east on VA-3 to VA-206 (17 miles), left at Arnold's Corner, east to Dahlgren (11 miles). Also US-301 south to VA-206, east to Main Gate of Center. *USMRA: Page 47 (M-6)*. **NMC:** Washington, D.C., 38 miles north.

RESERVATION INFORMATION: Bldg 960, Dahlgren, VA 22448-5100. **C-540-653-7671/72, DSN-312-249-7671/72,** Fax: C-540-653-4274, DSN-312-249-4274, 24 hours daily. Check in at billeting 1600 hours, check out 1100 hours. Reservations accepted 45 days in advance. Duty may make reservations; others Space-A. Billeting for government civilian employees on orders. ***Earned a five-star rating for***

Excellence in Bachelor Housing.

BQ Bldgs 215, 217. Bedroom, double bed, private bath (32). Bldg 215 rooms have kitchens, Bldg 217 ten rooms have kitchens. Refrigerator, microwave, limited utensils, A/C, TV/VCR in room and lounge, housekeeping service, laundry facility, ice machine. Older structures, renovated. Rates: $16 for Officer transients, each additional adult $8.

TLQ Bldg 909. Leave or official duty, PCS in/out have priority. Two-bedroom, private bath (4). Kitchen, microwave, no utensils, housekeeping service, TV. Older structure, renovated. Rates: E1-E4 $15; E5-E6 $18; E7+ $20; children $2; adult $8.

DV/VIP Public Affairs Office, Bldg 217. O6+/SES equivalent. Retirees Space-A. Two-bedroom, private bath suite (1). Community kitchen, refrigerator, limited utensils, A/C, TV/VCR in room and lounge, housekeeping service, laundry facility, ice machine. Older structure, renovated. Rates: $25 for Officer transients, slightly higher for DV/VIP. Each additional adult $8, children $2.

AMENITIES: Exercise Room, Meeting/Conference Room, Snack and Soft Drink Vending Machines.

TML AVAILABILITY: Fairly good. Best, Nov-Feb.

CREDIT CARDS ACCEPTED: Visa, MasterCard and American Express.

TRANSPORTATION: None available.

DINING OPPORTUNITIES: McDonald's and Subway are within walking distance.

Take a walk through Dahlgren's Beaver Pond Nature Trail and then savor the history of Washington's and Lee's birthplace in historic Fredericksburg. The area is full of interesting historic sites.

Dam Neck Annex, Oceana Naval Air Station (VA25R1)
Navy Family Service Center, Code N15
1912 Regulus Avenue, Bldg 522, Room 126
Virginia Beach, VA 23461-5000

MAIN INSTALLATION TELEPHONE NUMBERS: C-757-444-0000, DSN-312-492-6234. Locator 492-6000; Medical 314-7204; Security Police 492-6302.

LOCATION: Route 44 East to exit 8 (Birdneck Road), turn right and follow to General Booth Blvd. Turn right and follow to Dam Neck Road. Turn left and follow to Main Gate. *USMRA: Page 47 (O-9,10), page 52 (J-7,8).* **NMC:** Virginia Beach, four miles north northwest.

RESERVATION INFORMATION: Dam Neck at the Dunes, Bldg 566C, 1912 Regulus Avenue, Code N2, Virginia Beach, VA 23461-2098. **C-1-877-986-9258 (toll free),** Fax: C-757-492-6746, DSN-312-492-6746. Duty on orders can make reservations; others Space-A. Check in at facility 1400 hours, check out 1100 hours. Advance reservations are recommended aith a copy of orders faxed or emailed. Email: AvendanoA@cbhdn.nasoceana.navy.mil

VQ Bldgs 566, 508. Shared room, shared bath (E1-E4) (30). Privat room, private bath (E1+) (304). Refrigerator, A/C, CATV/VCR, phone, housekeeping service, laundry facility, lounges, sun deck, BBQ. Modern structures. Rates: $17.50-$35.

VQ Bldgs 225. E5+. Bedroom, private bath (96); bedroom, living room, private bath (53). Refrigerator, coffee maker, A/C, CATV/VCR, housekeeping service, laundry facility, cots, ice machine, sun deck. Modern structures. Rates: standard room, $17.50 per person, suites $25.50. Children under five no charge. **Bldg 241 (99 rooms, including 4 DV suites) is undergoing renovation.**

NAVY LODGE Navy Lodge. Bldg 226, 1697 Regulus Avenue, Virginia Beach, VA 23461, **C-1-800-NAVY-INN.** Lodge number is C-757-437-8100, Fax: C-757-437-1072, 24 hours daily. Email: navy_lodge-dam neck@nexnet.navy.mil Directions: From Norfolk Airport, take I 64 E to 44 E to Birdneck Road exit. Right onto Birdneck to right on General Booth. Get in left lane and go left on Dam Neck Road to front gate. Take first left to lodge. Check in at facility. Bedroom, two double or queen-size beds, private bath (43); bedroom, one queen-size bed and sofabed (5); handicap accessible (2). Interconnecting and non-smoking rooms available. Kitchenette, microwave, coffee maker, toaster, utensils, dining table, A/C, CATV/VCR, video rental, phone, clock radio, hair dryer, housekeeping service, coin laundry facility, iron/ironing board, cribs, highchairs, rollaways, snack vending, ice machine, FAX/copy service, playground, complimentary coffee (in lobby), deck overlooking Red Wing Lake. Modern structure, opened May 1998. Rates: Call for current rates. Special rate for personnel under PCS orders into or out of the Tidewater area of $46.00 per night. Maximum four per unit. All categories can make reservations. No pets.

DV/VIP VQ/BEQ. Bldgs 508. VP suite, private bath (E7-E9) (8). Kitchenette, refrigerator, coffee maker, A/C, CATV,/VCR, housekeeping service. Rates: $25.50. Children under five no charge.

TML AVAILABILITY: Because this is a training command, availability is usually poor and only fair at best.

CREDIT CARDS ACCEPTED: Visa, MasterCard and American Express.

TRANSPORTATION: Off base shuttle/bus: TRT Bus; Car Rental: Enterprise, C-757-455-4572; Off base taxi: Yellow Cab, C-757-460-0605/0911; Beach Taxi, C-757-486-4304/6585.

DINING OPPORTUNITIES: Bowling Alley, C-757-492-6341; Mess Hall, C-757-492-6388/6748; McDonald's, C-757-491-0359; O Club, C-757-492-6913; and Shifting Sands, C-757-492-7434 are within walking distance of Navy Lodge. Applebee's, C-757-721-6469; Captain George's, C-757-428-3494; and Golden Corral, C-757-428-7608; Pizza Hut, C-757-427-1111 are within driving distance.

Dam Neck is two miles from Ocean Breeze Water Park and the Marine Science Museum.

Fort A.P. Hill (VA17R1)
Attn: ANAP-PEL
Fort A.P. Hill, VA 22427-3110

MAIN INSTALLATION TELEPHONE NUMBERS: C-804-633-8710, DSN-312-578-8710. Locator 633-8797; Medical 633-8339; Security Police 633-8239.

LOCATION: From I-95 south, take Carmel Church/Bowling Green exit 104 to 207 east to 301 north to Main Gate on left. From I-95 north take exit 126, right on Route 1 to Highway 17. Six miles to Route 2 (right). Fifteen miles to 207 (left) to 301 north to installation (left). *USMRA: Page 47 (L,M-6,7).* **NMC:** Fredericksburg, 14 miles northwest.

RESERVATION INFORMATION: Bldg P00179, 18350 First Street, Fort A.P. Hill, VA 22427-3110. **C-804-633-8335, DSN-312-578-8335,** Fax: C-804-633-8418, DSN-312-578-8418, 0800-1630 hours, M-F. WEB: www.aphill.army.mil Check in 1400 hours, after hours check in thru Provost Marshal's Office, Bldg P00156 at 4th and Montague Streets. Check out 1100 hours. Government civilian employee billeting. DV/VIP: Protocol Office: C-804-633-8205.

TML Bldg P00179. Single bedroom, private bath (16). Refrigerator, microwave, A/C, TV/VCR, telephone, housekeeping service, ice machine. Rates: $40, charge for additional occupants.

TML Bldgs P00174. Single bedroom (6), private bath (two connecting rooms make a suite). Kitchenette, complete utensils, refrigerator, microwave, telephone, A/C, TV/VCR, housekeeping service. Rates: $40, charge for additional occupants.

TML Cottages/Farmhouses. Farmhouse (2), five-bedroom, multiple beds per room, A/C, TV/VCR, telephone, full kitchen, living and dining areas. Cottage, one-bedroom (3), A/C, TV/VCR, full kitchen, living area, telephone; Cottage, two-bedroom (2), A/C, TV/VCR, two beds in each room, full kitchen, living and dining area, telephone; Cottage, three-bedroom (1), A/C, TV/VCR, full kitchen, living and dining area, telephone. All cottages have complete kitchen utensils and daily housekeeping services. Rates: vary.

Lodge Recreation Lodge. Bldg SS-0251. C-804-633-8219. Nine-bedrooms, semi-private baths, sleeps 18 (1). Kitchen, freezer, complete utensils, TV, ice machine, two woodburning fireplaces, lounge chairs. Rates: $180 per day for groups of six (minimum) or $30 per person. All categories may make reservations.

Cabins Recreation Cabins. Report to Bldg TT-106, C-804-633-8219. Check out 1100 hours. Three-bedroom, private bath (3). Kitchen, complete utensils, A/C, TV, laundry facility. Modern structures. Rates: $30 per person, family rates available. Maximum six per family. Minimum two nights stay, minimum two people. All categories can make reservations.

TML AVAILABILITY: Good, Oct-Mar. Difficult, other times.

CREDIT CARDS ACCEPTED: Visa, MasterCard and American Express.

TRANSPORTATION: Car Rental.

DINING OPPORTUNITIES: Gerber New Yorker Restaurant, C-804-633-5549; Pizza Hut, C-804-633-6110 and McDonald's are within driving distance.

This is a very rustic area with good hunting and fishing in season. Dolly's House is named for Kitty "Dolly" Hill, wife of General A.P. Hill, for whom the Fort is named. Support facilities: snack bar and post exchange.

Fort Belvoir (VA12R1)
9725 Harris Road, Suite 101
Fort Belvoir, VA 22060-5908

MAIN INSTALLATION TELEPHONE NUMBERS: C-703-545-6700, DSN-312-227-0101. Locator 805-2043; Medical 805-1106; Security Police 805-1104.
Ten-digit dialing required for local calls.

LOCATION: From Washington, D.C., take I-95 South to Fort Belvoir/Newington exit 166. Turn right, connect with the southern leg of Fairfax County Parkway. Take Parkway to the end at Richmond Highway. Turn left. At the first light, Tulley Gate is on right. At second light, Pence Gate (main entrance) is to the right. Visitor Center is just inside Pence Gate. *USMRA: Page 47 (L,M-5), page 54 (B-8).* **NMC:** Washington, D.C., 10 miles northeast.

RESERVATION INFORMATION: Fort Belvoir Lodging, Bldg 470, 9775 Gaillard Road, Fort Belvoir, VA 22060-5905. **C-1-800-295-9750 or 703-805-2333/2307, DSN-312-655-2333,** Fax: C-703-805-3566, DSN-312-655-3566, 24 hours daily. Lodging Manager, C-703-805-2640. Email: fb-dpca-lodging@belvoir.army.mil WEB: www.belvoir.army.mil TDY and PCS may make reservations. Directions: Enter Main Gate (Pence Gate). Follow Belvoir Road through two stoplights. Make a left onto 18th Street. Follow signs to Lodging Office (Bldg 470). Check in 1700 hours, check out 1200 hours. Government civilian employee billeting VOQ. *Note: Renovations planned for Fiscal Years 2001-2004.*

VOQ Various buildings. Bedroom, private bath (332). Bedroom, semi-private bath (121). Two room suite, private bath (49). Two-bedroom apartments (13). One-bedroom apartments (16). All rooms have refrigerator, microwave, (some available with full kitchenettes), utensils, A/C, TV/VCR, telephones, daily housekeeping service, laundry facility, cribs, rollaways, ice machine. Modern structure, continual renovations. Rates: bedroom/private bath, sponsor $48, spouse $5, child $3; bedroom, semi private bath, sponsor $44, spouse $5, child $3; Two-bedroom suite and one-bedroom apartment, sponsor $53, spouse $5, child $3; Two-bedroom apartment, sponsor $60, spouse $5, child $3. No pets.

DV/VIP Bldgs 20B (O Club), 470, 807. **C-703-805-2333.** E9, O6+. Bldg 20: Two-room suite, king size bed, private bath (4), two-room suite, queen-size bed, private bath (8); Bldg 470: bedroom, double bed, private bath (6); Bldg 807: One-bedroom apartment, private bath (2). Kitchen, refrigerator, microwave, complete utensils, A/C, TV/VCR (with HBO), phone, housekeeping service, cribs, rollaways, ice machine. Modern structure, renovated 1997. Rates: two-room, sponsor $64, spouse $5, child $3; one-room, sponsor $48, spouse $5. No pets.

AMENITIES: Exercise Room, Meeting/Conference, Snack and Soft Drink Vending Machines.

TML AVAILABILITY: Good, Dec. Difficult, May-Sep.

CREDIT CARDS ACCEPTED: Visa, MasterCard and American Express.

TRANSPORTATION: On base Lodging Shuttle, Mon-Fri 1600-2000, Sat/Sun 1000-1800; Off base Super Shuttle C-1-800-blue-van(2583-826); On base car rental, Enterprise C-703-781-0480; Off base car rental, Budget C-1-800-527-0700; On base taxi, Belvoir Cab C-703-781-7040; Off base taxi, Springfield Cab C-703-451-2255.

DINING OPPORTUNITIES: PX Food Court 703-806-5800; NCO Club, C-703-780-0962; and O Club, C-703-780-0930 are within driving distance.

Exit Walker Gate to see George Washington's Mill and visit nearby Mount Vernon, Woodlawn Plantation and Gunston Hall. See the Smithsonian Museums and Capitol Hill in downtown Washington, D.C.; northern Virginia is rich in colonial and Civil War history.

Fort Eustis (VA10R1)
ATZF-PCF-A, Bldg 601

Knadle Hall at Fort Belvoir, VA

Fort Eustis, VA 23604-5114

MAIN INSTALLATION TELEPHONE NUMBERS: C-757-878-1212, 312-927-1212. Locator 878-5215; Medical 757-878-4555; Security Police 757-878-4555.

LOCATION: From I-64, exit 250A to VA-105, west to Fort Eustis. *USMRA: Page 47 (N-9), page 52 (B,C-2,3).* **NMC:** Newport News, 13 miles southwest.

RESERVATION INFORMATION: 2110 Pershing Avenue, P.O. Box 4278, Fort Eustis, VA 23604-5200. **C-757-878-5807, DSN-312-927-5807,** Fax: C-757-878-3251, DSN-312-927-3251, 24 hours daily. Directions: Left on Madison Street. Left onto Pershing Avenue, office is located at the end of Pershing Avenue. Check in 1600 hours, check out 1100 hours.

Government civilian employee billeting. Handicap accessible. ***Note: A $22.763 million TLF was approved in the DoD Fiscal Year 2001 NAF Construction Program.***

(VOQ/VEQ) Bldg 2110. Suite (20) and cottage (4) for transient persons; VOQ: bedroom (236); VEQ: bedroom (302). Kitchen (cottages and DVQ only), community kitchen, refrigerator, microwave, A/C, CATV in room and lounge, housekeeping service, laundry facilities, cribs, cots, ice machine. Handicap accessible. Rates: VOQ suite single occupancy $40; double occupancy $47; VEQ $31.50 single. Priority for VOQ: Officers attending Transportation Office Basic Course. Priority for VEQ: Enlisted personnel attending Advanced Non-commissioned Officer Course. Duty can make reservations; others Space-A. Space-A check in 1800 hours. ***Pets allowed in cottages, $5 per day.***

(DV/VIP) Protocol Office. Bldg 210, Room 207, **C-757-878-6030, DSN-312-927-6030.** O6+. Rates: single occupancy $44; double occupancy $51. Retirees and lower ranks Space-A.

AMENITIES: Soft Drink and Snack Vending Machine. ***Free Internet and E-mail access for customers.***

CREDIT CARDS ACCEPTED: Visa, MasterCard and American Express.

TRANSPORTATION: On/Off base taxi, C-757-887-1111.

DINING OPPORTUNITIES: Restaurants of Busch Gardens, Williamsburg and Water Country are within driving distance.

Visit Busch Gardens, the Army Transportation Museum, tour historic Yorktown Battlefield and Colonial Williamsburg for a crash course in early history of the United States.

Fort Lee (VA15R1)
ACS, 2021 A Avenue
Fort Lee, VA 23801-1709

MAIN INSTALLATION TELEPHONE NUMBERS: C-804-765-3000, DSN-312-539-3000. Locator 804-734-6855; Medical 734-9000; Security Police 804-765-6869.

LOCATION: From I-95 take Fort Lee/Hopewell exit 52 east, follow VA-36 to Main Gate on right (south). *USMRA: Page 47 (L-8).* **NMC:** Petersburg, three miles west.

RESERVATION INFORMATION: Bldg P-8025, Mahone Avenue, P.O. Box 5019, Fort Lee, VA 23801-1515. **C-804-734-6694, DSN-312-687-6700,** Fax: C-804-734-6676, DSN-312-687-6676, 24 hours daily. E-mail: lodging@lee.army.mil Directions: Take Lee Avenue to Mahone Avenue, turn right onto Mahone Avenue. The lodging desk is located in second building on the right. Check in at lodging 1530-2300 hours, check out 1200 hours Mon-Sat, 1000 hours Sun and holidays. No pets.

(BEQ) Bldgs P-3004, P-3005. NCOA Students, TDY personnel only. Single room and shared rooms. Refrigerator, coffee pot, CATV/VCR, telephone, housekeeping service, laundry facility, iron/ironing board, ice machine, fax/photocopy service available. Rates: $28.

(VOQ/VEQ) Bldgs P-8026, P-9001, P-9002, P-9051, P-9053-P-9055, P-4229. Leave or official duty, but primarily for TDY personnel. Bedroom, private bath (482). Kitchenette, coffee pot, A/C, CATV/VCR, phone, fax/photocopy service, housekeeping service, laundry facility, iron/ironing board, ice machine. Modern structures. Handicap accessible (2). Rates: official visitors $32, unofficial visitors $37; second person $5. Maximum two per room. Duty may make reservations; others Space-A. No pets.

(Army Lodging) Extended Stay Quarters. Bldgs 9056, P-8134. Leave or official duty, but primarily for PCS personnel. Bedroom, two beds, sofabed, living room, private bath (46). Kitchen, refrigerator, coffee pot, A/C, CATV/VCR, telephone, housekeeping service, laundry facility, iron/ironing board, cribs, cots, ice machine, fax/photocopy service available. Modern structure. Rates: official visitors $45, unofficial visitors $50. Duty may make reservations; others Space-A. No pets.

(DVQ) Bldgs P-9052. E8/O6+, official duty only, but primarily for TDY personnel. Bedroom, private bath (16). Kitchen, coffee pot, A/C, CATV/VCR, mini bar, housekeeping service, laundry facility, iron/ironing board, ice machine, fax/photocopy service available, living room. Modern structure. Rates: official visitors $37, unofficial visitors $42; second person $5. Maximum two per room. Conference room rental $35 (4 hours or less), $50 (more than 4 hours) Duty may make reservations; others Space-A. No pets.

(DV/VIP) Protocol Office, Bldg P-105000, Room 221, **C-804-734-1765, DSN-312-687-1765.** DVQ 1. E9, O6+, official duty only, but primarily for TDY personnel. One-story, three-bedroom house, living room, dining room, two private bathrooms diverted AFH (1). Kitchen, microwave, complete utensils, A/C, CATV/VCR, fax/photocopy service, housekeeping service. Modern structure. Handicap accessible. Rates: sponsor and each TDY person $55; second person $5 (Non TDY). Maximum two per room. Duty may make reservations; others Space-A. No pets.

AMENITIES: Meeting/Conference Room, Snack and Soft Drink Vending Machines.

TML AVAILABILITY: Best, Dec and weekends, holidays. Difficult, Jan-Nov.

CREDIT CARDS ACCEPTED: Visa, MasterCard and American Express.

TRANSPORTATION: Off base taxi, C-804-458-2535/748-0779/862-1108.

DINING OPPORTUNITIES: Fort Lee Officers'/Civilian Club, C-804-734-7545; Leisure Club (NCO), C-804-765-1539 and Burger King, C-804-733-3839 are within walking distance.

Visit the Quartermaster Museum and Battlefield Park, which is rich in Civil War history. Wonderful bass and crappie fishing is on the Chickahominy River. Virginia Beach swimming, fishing and boating is 85 miles east.

Fort Monroe (VA13R1)
Post Headquarters
3 Ruckman Road
Fort Monroe, VA 23651-1039

MAIN INSTALLATION TELEPHONE NUMBERS: C-757-788-2111, DSN-312-680-2111. Locator 788-3175; Medical 788-2840; Security Police 788-2238.

LOCATION: From I-64, exit at 268 east and follow VA-143 to tour signs through Phoebus to fort. *USMRA: Page 47 (N-9), page 52 (F-4).* **NMC:** Hampton, one mile north.

RESERVATION INFORMATION: Armistead Hall, Bldg 80, Fort Monroe, VA 23651. **C-757-788-2128, DSN-312-680-2128,** Fax: C-757-788-4089, DSN-312-680-4089, 0800-1630 hours Mon-Fri. All categories may make reservations. Priority to TDY and PCS. Directions: Go left at guardhouse on Ingalls Road. Registration is in Bldg 80; Ingalls Road 3rd block from the guardhouse. Check in at lodging 1400 hours, check out 1000 hours.

(VQ) All units (17) are suites or duplex houses. All recently redecorated. Refrigerator, utensils, A/C, CATV/VCR, housekeeping service, laundry facility, toiletries, hair dryer, cribs, ice machines. Handicap accessible units. Rates: $47-$66.

TML AVAILABILITY: Fairly good, Oct-Apr. Difficult, May-Sep.

CREDIT CARDS ACCEPTED: Visa and MasterCard.

TRANSPORTATION: Car Rental, off base taxi.

DINING OPPORTUNITIES: Casemate Museum and Giftshop C-757-788-3391. Numerous fine restaurants are within driving distance in the Hampton Roads area.

A National Historic Landmark, touring Fort Monroe is a U.S. history lesson. The historic areas of Hampton and Williamsburg are also nearby. This area is a treasure trove for history buffs.

Fort Myer (VA24R1)
201 Custer Road
Fort Myer, VA 22211-1199

MAIN INSTALLATION TELEPHONE NUMBERS: C-703-545-6700, DSN-312-227-0101. Locator 545-6700; Medical 696-3628; Security Police 696-3525.
Ten-digit dialing required for local calls.

LOCATION: Adjacent to Arlington National Cemetery. Take Fort Myer exit US-258 south from Washington Blvd at 2nd Street, or enter from US-50 (Arlington Blvd) first gate. Also exit from Boundary Drive to 12th Street North entrance near the Iwo Jima Memorial. *USMRA: Page 54 (E-5).* NMC: Washington, D.C., one mile northeast.

RESERVATION INFORMATION: Bldg 50, 318 Jackson Avenue, Fort Myer, VA 22211-1199. C-703-696-3576/77, DSN-312-426-3576/77, Fax: C-703-696-3490,0600-2200 Sun-Fri, 0800-1600 Sat, credit card required. Check in 1400 hours, check out 1100 hours. No pets. This facility is in charge of Fort Lesley J. McNair lodging in Washington, D.C.

(VOQ) Myer VOQ. Bldg 48. Apartment style, living room, private bath (12). Kitchenette, refrigerator, utensils, microwave, CATV/VCR, A/C, cribs, rollaway, housekeeping service. Rates: sponsor $50, each additional person over age 10 $5.

(VOQ) McNair VOQ. Bldg 54. Rooms, shared bath (20); rooms, private bath (5); bedroom suites, private bath (2). All units have refrigerator, microwave, coffee maker, A/C, CATV, phone, crib, rollaway, housekeeping service. Older structure, remodeled, new furniture. Rates: sponsor $41-$50, each additional person over the age of 10 $5.

(DV/VIP) Write to: DA Protocol, Pentagon, Washington, D.C. 20310-5000. C-703-697-7051, DSN-312-227-7051. O7+. Wainwright Hall. Bedroom suites, living room, private bath (18). Refrigerator, bar, A/C, CATV/VCR in room and lounge, housekeeping service. Breakfast service is included Mon-Fri. Older structure, remodeled. Rates: sponsor $62-$70, each additional person $5-$8, child/infant up to ten years of age free. Active Duty, reserve and NG can make reservations, Space-A after 1400 hours.

AMENITIES: Meeting/Conference Room, Laundry Facilities, Ice Machine, Snack Vending Machine and Soft Drink Machine.

TML AVAILABILITY: Very Good. Difficult Apr-Nov.

CREDIT CARDS ACCEPTED: Visa, MasterCard and American Express.

TRANSPORTATION: On base shuttle/bus, C-703-696-8848; Car Rental, C-703-524-1863; Off base taxi, C-703-522-3333.

DINING OPPORTUNITIES: At Fort Myer: Strike Zone, O Club and Community Club are within walking distance. At Fort Lesley J. McNair: Golf Course and O Club. A variety of restaurants are within driving distance of both.

Tour Arlington National Cemetery for a fascinating look at military history and traditions. Don't miss the stables of ceremonial horses used in military funerals, the Old Guard Museum. Fort Myer is home to the U.S. Army Band.

Fort Pickett (VA16R1)
Bldg 469, Military Road
Blackstone, VA 23824-5000

MAIN INSTALLATION TELEPHONE NUMBERS: C-804-292-8621, DSN-312-438-8621. Locator 292-8621; Security Police 292-8444.

LOCATION: On US-460, one mile from Blackstone. From I-95, exit 27 north on VA-46 to Blackstone and gate. Clearly marked. *USMRA: Page 47 (K-9).* NMI: Fort Lee, 45 miles northeast. NMC: Petersburg, 40 miles northeast.

RESERVATION INFORMATION: Attn: VAFP-LH PRN:10C, Fort Pickett, Blackstone, VA 23824-9000. C-804-292-2443, DSN-312-438-2443, 0730-1600 hours duty days. Other hours, PMO, Bldg T-471. C-804-292-8444, DSN-312-438-8444, Fax: C-804-292-8617, DSN-312-438-8617. Check in at billeting, check out 1000 hours. Duty may make reservations; others Space-A. *Note: Confirm all reservations by phone at least 24 hours in advance.* Government civilian employee billeting.

(VOQ/VEQ) Cottage, bedroom, two beds, private bath (7). Kitchen, complete utensils, A/C, TV, housekeeping service, cots $5 per extra person. Older structure. Rates: $20 per unit, additional $4 for unofficial users. *Pets allowed outside.*

(VOQ/VEQ) Bedroom, double bed, sitting area, private bath (16). Microwave, A/C, TV, housekeeping service, laundry facility, cots $5 per extra person. Older structures. Rates: $20 per unit, additional $4 for unofficial users. *Pets allowed outside.*

(VOQ/VEQ) Bedroom, common bath (26); Bedroom suite, double bed, private bath (5). Community kitchen, complete utensils, A/C, TV in lounge, housekeeping service, laundry facility, cots $5 per extra person. Older structure. Rates: $8-$13 per room, additional $2 for unofficial users. *Pets allowed outside.*

TML AVAILABILITY: Good, Sep-Mar. Difficult, other times.

CREDIT CARDS ACCEPTED: Visa, MasterCard, American Express, Discover and Diners.

TRANSPORTATION: Car Rental: C-804-292-7603; Off base taxi, C-804-292-1835.

DINING OPPORTUNITIES: Bradshaw Too, C-804-292-3236; Brother's Pizza and Italian Restaurant, C-804-292-7240/9; Country Inn, C-804-292-7601; Hardee's, C-804-292-4958; McDonald's, C-804-292-4977 and various other eating establishments available within driving distance.

Some of the best hunting and fishing in the state of Virginia. Charlottesville, Richmond, Williamsburg, the James River Plantations and Washington, D.C. are within easy reach of this facility.

Fort Story (VA08R1)
ACS, Bldg 522
Fort Story, VA 23459-5042

MAIN INSTALLATION TELEPHONE NUMBERS: C-757-422-7305, DSN-312-438-7305. Locator 422-7682; Medical 422-7802; Security Police 422-7141.

LOCATION: From the south exit of Chesapeake Bay Bridge Tunnel (US-13), east on US-60 (Atlantic Avenue) to Fort Story. Clearly marked. From I-64 take US-60 east. From VA-44 (Norfolk-VA Beach Expressway) exit US-58, turn left, North Atlantic Avenue (US-60) to 89th Street to Fort Story. *USMRA: Page 47 (O-9), page 52 (I,J-5,6).* NMC: Virginia Beach, three miles south.

RESERVATION INFORMATION: Bldg 1116, Fort Story, VA 23549-5010. **C-757-422-8818,** Fax: C-757-422-6397, 0700-2300 hours. WEB: www.capehenryinn.com Reservations: First come, first served basis up to one year in advance. One night's stay deposit required upon making reservation, 14 day cancellation policy. Check in after 1600 hours, check out 1100 hours.

Cape Henry Inn. DoD, Active Duty, retired, reserve. All units provide housekeeping services, iron/ironing board, A/C, heat, complimentary coffee, CATV, HBO, telephones with data ports and voicemail. Rooms have dune or bay view; cottages have bay view; bungalows and log cabins have no water view. **Sandpiper:** Bedroom, sleeps four (10), two full beds, refrigerator. Rates: $29-$65. **Dunes:** Bedroom, sleeps six (30), two full beds, separate sitting area with pull-out couch, kitchenette, refrigerator, microwave, dishes, utensils. Rates: $39-$78. **Pelican:** Bedroom, queen-size bed, sofa bed (10), kitchenette, refrigerator, microwave, dishes, utensils, handicap accessible. Rates: $35-$73. **Chesapeake:** Cottage: Two-bedroom, sleeps six (12), living room with pull-out couch, kitchen, microwave, dishwasher, dishes, utensils. Rates: $75-$85. **Tidewater:** Cottage: Three-bedroom, sleeps eight (6), living room with pull-out couch, kitchen, microwave, dishwasher, dishes, utensils. Handicap accessible (1). Rates: $80-$90. **Bungalow**: Two-bedroom (8), living room with pull-out couch, kitchen, microwave, dishwasher, dishes, utensils. Rates: $64-$84. **Log cabins** are located in travel camp east of lighthouses. Log cabins have large decks with picnic table, swing, outdoor shower and view of both lighthouses. Cabins have great room/kitchen with sleeper couch, upstairs loft with two single beds, bath has shower only. Bedroom has one full bed. One bedroom cabins (4), sleep six. Rates: $50-$71. Two bedroom cabins (13), sleep eight. Rates: $55-76. Smoking and *pets allowed in Bungalows and cabins.* Limited cribs, highchairs available $5 per night. Limited rollaways available $10 per night for Pelican and Sandpiper. New 20'x40' foot pool located within walking distance from hotel and cottages. *Note: 27 new cottage units opened on 30 Oct, 2002, marking the completion of the $4.9 million NAF construction project.*

Cape Henry Travel Camp. C-757-422-7601. Kamping Kabins (3), one 12x12 room, sleeps four. Rates: $30-$55 daily.

AMENITIES: Outdoor Pool, Poolside Cabana, grill items, bar, soft drinks and free laundromat.

TML AVAILABILITY: Good, Oct-Mar. Difficult, summer months and holidays.

CREDIT CARDS ACCEPTED: Visa and MasterCard.

TRANSPORTATION: None available.

The Cape Henry Inn waterfront lodging at Fort Story, VA

Besides a beautiful waterside hotel, Fort Story, VA also has recreational lodging near the lighthouse.

DINING OPPORTUNITIES: Bowling Alley, Tiki Bar & Grill (seasonal). Many fine restaurants are within driving distance.

See the Old Cape Henry Lighthouse, Douglas MacArthur Memorial, Virginia Beach Marine Science Museum, Williamsburg Pottery Factory. Busch Gardens, Ocean Breeze Park and Norfolk Naval Base nearby. See *Military Living's Military RV, Camping and Outdoor Recreation Around the World* for additional information and directions.

Judge Advocate General's School (VA01R1)
Attn: SSL-H, 600 Massie Road
Charlottesville, VA 22903-1781

MAIN INSTALLATION TELEPHONE NUMBERS: C-804-972-6300, DSN-312-934-7115 ext 450. Locator 972-6400; Medical 924-2231; Security Police 911.

LOCATION: On the grounds of the University of Virginia in Charlottesville. Take the 250 bypass off I-64 to the Baracks Road exit southeast. Take right at first light onto Milmont Street, first right onto Arlington Blvd, at the three-way stop sign turn right into the parking lot. *USMRA: Page 47 (J-7).* **NMC:** Charlottesville, in city limits.

RESERVATION INFORMATION: Attn: SSL-H, 600 Massie Road, Charlottesville, VA 22903-1781. **C-804-972-6450, DSN-312-934-6450,** Fax: C-804-972-6328, 0750-1650 hours Mon-Fri, Room 156 in TJAGSA, adjacent to Hall of Flags. Other hours, SDO front desk. E-mail: goddind@hqda.army.mil Check in 1500 hours, check out 1200 hours. Government civilian employee billeting only on orders to JAGS.

BOQ/BEQ Bedroom, one bed, private bath (72). Community kitchen, refrigerator, A/C, CATV, housekeeping service, laundry facility, cots ($2), ice machine. Modern structure. Handicap accessible. Rates: TDY, sponsor $20, Active Duty on leave and Retirees $25; family members $5. Most space reserved for JAGS students.

DV/VIP Attn: JAGS-ZA, **C-804-972-6301.** O6+. Rates: TDY, sponsor $25-$30, Retirees $30-$35; family members $5. Retirees and leave Space-A.

AMENITIES: Exercise Room, Meeting/Conference Room, Mini Mart and Soft Drink Machine

TML AVAILABILITY: Very limited, last two weeks in Dec. Difficult, other times.

CREDIT CARDS ACCEPTED: Visa and MasterCard.

TRANSPORTATION: Off base bus: City Transit, C-804-296-RIDE(7433); Car Rentals: Avis, C-804-973-3336; Hertz, C-804-973-6040; Off base taxi: Yellow/Airport Taxi, C-804-295-4131.

DINING OPPORTUNITIES: Domino's Pizza, C-804-971-8353; Cafe North and North Grounds are within walking distance. Oregano Joe's, C-804-971-9308; Ruby Tuesday, C-804-295-9118 and Boston Market, C-804-296-2464 are within driving distance.

Visit historic Monticello, Ash Lawn and the Michie Tavern. For outdoor activities, try Wintergreen, Shenandoah National Park, Barboursville Vineyard, Montfair Camp Grounds, Lake Albemarle.

Langley Air Force Base (VA07R1)
1st SVS/SVML
52 Willow Street, Suite 101
Langley AFB, VA 23665-5528

MAIN INSTALLATION TELEPHONE NUMBERS: C-757-764-9990, DSN-312-574-1110. Locator 764-5615; Medical 764-6833; Security Police 764-5092.

LOCATION: From I-64 in Hampton take Armistead Avenue exit 205B northeast, keep right to stop light; right into LaSalle Avenue and enter AFB. *USMRA: Page a47 (N-9).* **NMC:** Hampton, one mile west.

RESERVATION INFORMATION: Langley Inns, 1 SVS/SVML, 44 Taylor Road, Langley AFB, VA 23665-5528. **C-1-888-AFLODGE (1-888-235-6343), C-757-764-4667, DSN-312-574-4667,** Fax: C-757-764-3038, DSN-312-574-3038, 0800-1600 hours Mon-Fri. WEB: www.langley.af.mil/services/lodging.html Duty may make reservations any time; Space-A may make reservations 24 hours in advance. Directions: Nealy Avenue, approximately 1 mile on right hand side. Check in 1500 hours, check out 1200 hours. Government civilian employee lodging.

(TLF) North and South. Separate bedrooms, private bath, sleeps five (100). Kitchen, utensils, A/C, TV, housekeeping service, laundry facility, playpen, cots, ice machine. Modern structures, renovated. Rates: PCS $21.50 per unit.

(VAQ) Bedroom, one- and two-bed units, common bath (47); separate bedrooms, private bath (SNCO)(5). Refrigerator, A/C, TV, housekeeping service, laundry facility, ice machine. Modern structure, renovated. Rates: VAQ $13; SNCO suite $23.

(VAQ) Boots Hall. E4+. Bedroom, shared bath (123). Refrigerator, A/C, TV, housekeeping service, laundry facility, ice machine. Modern structure, renovated. Rates: $13, maximum one per room.

(VOQ) Bedroom, private bath (78). Kitchen, A/C, TV, housekeeping service, laundry facility, cots, ice machine. Modern structures. Rates: $13.50.

(DV/VIP) Protocol Office, **C-757-764-5044.** O6+. Retirees and lower ranks Space-A. Lawson Hall, Dodd Hall. O6/GS15+. Lawson Hall: separate bedroom suite, private bath (11). Dodd Hall: separate bedroom suite, private bath (10). Kitchen, limited utensils, A/C, TV, housekeeping service, laundry facility, cribs, cots, ice machine. Older structures, renovated. Rates: one person $23; Super Suites, one person $25.50.

AMENITIES: Exercise Room.

TML AVAILABILITY: Good, winter. Difficult, summer.

CREDIT CARDS ACCEPTED: Visa, MasterCard and American Express.

TRANSPORTATION: Car Rental: Avis, C-757-877-0291; Hertz, C-757-877-9229; On base taxi, C-757-764-8394; Off base taxi, C-757-723-3377; Limo Service, C-757-877-9477.

DINING OPPORTUNITIES: Bowling Center, C-757-764-2392; and Exchange Concessions are within walking distance. E Club, C-757-764-

1220; Golf Course, C-757-764-4547; and O Club, C-757-766-1361 are within driving distance.

Historic Colonial Williamsburg, Busch Gardens, beautiful Virginia Beach and the Mariner's Museum are all close by and worth a visit.

Little Creek Naval Amphibious Base (VA19R1)
Navy Family Service Center
1450 D Street, Bldg 3129
Norfolk, VA 23521-2231

MAIN INSTALLATION TELEPHONE NUMBERS: C-757-444-0000, DSN-312-564-0111. Locator 444-0000; Medical 462-4444; Security Police 363-4444.

LOCATION: From I-64 to exit US-60 to base. From Chesapeake Bay Bridge/Tunnel US-60 west to base. *USMRA: Page 47 (N,O-9), page 52 (G,H-5,6).* **NMC:** Norfolk, 11 miles southwest.

RESERVATION INFORMATION: Drexler Manor, CBQ, Bldg 3408, 1120 A Street, Norfolk, VA 23521-2698. **C-757-462-7522, DSN-312-253-7522,** Fax: C-757-462-8635. Check in at facility, check out 1330. All categories may make reservations. Billeting for government civilian employees on orders.

(BEQ) Shields Hall. Bldg 3601, 1350 Gator Blvd, NAB, Little Creek, Norfolk, VA 23521-2698. C-757-318-7589 ext 5100. Official duty. Check out 1330 hours. Bedroom, two beds, private bath (140); single rooms, private bath (E5-E9) (195). Microfridge, A/C, CATV, housekeeping service, laundry facility, ice machine. Modern structure, renovated. Rates: $8 per person; dependents not authorized. Duty may make reservations 90 days advance; others Space-A.

(BOQ) Drexler Manor. Bldg 3408. Check out 1330 hours. Bedroom, private bath (230); Microwave, A/C, CATV, housekeeping service, laundry facility, ice machine. Modern structure, renovated. Rates: $18 per person, each additional guest 12 years or older $4.50. Duty on orders can make reservations; others Space-A on one day basis. O6+ can make Space-A reservations.

(NAVY LODGE) Navy Lodge. 1125 Gator Blvd, Norfolk, VA 23521-5000. **C-1-800-NAVY-INN.** Lodge number is C-757-464-6215, Fax: C-757-464-1194, 24 hours daily. Check in prior to 1800 hours to avoid cancellation. Check out 1200 hours. Standard room with two queen beds, private bath (80); Business Class room with one queen bed and living room area with desk, private bath (16). Handicap accessible room (4). Kitchenette, complete utensils, refrigerator, microwave, stove, coffee maker, A/C, CATV/VCR, housekeeping service, iron/ironing board, hair dryer, guest laundry facility, ice machine. Computer hook-up in each room, playground, video rental, vending machines, complimentary coffee and USA Today in lobby. All local calls are free. Modern structure. Rates: $54-$63. All categories can make reservations. *No pets except birds in cages, fish in tanks. A new replacement lodge with 100-rooms opened Dec 2000.*

(DV/VIP) BEQ. Shields Hall. Bldg 3601. **C-757-462-7522, DSN-312-253-7522.** Master Chief suites, private bath (2). Rates: $25, each additional person $6.25.

(DV/VIP) BOQ. Drexler Manor. Bldg 3408. Separate bedroom suites, private bath (14). Microwave, A/C, CATV, housekeeping service, laundry facility, ice machine. Modern structure, renovated. Rates: $28, each additional guest 12 years or older $7.

(DV/VIP) **C-757-462-7522, DSN-312-253-7522.** Bldg 3186. O6+. Check out 1200 hours. Separate bedroom suites, queen-size beds, private bath (4). Community kitchen, refrigerator, limited utensils, A/C, CATV, housekeeping service, cots, ice machine. Older structure, remodeled. Rates: Active Duty $35 per person, each additional person $8.75. Retirees Space-A.

TML AVAILABILITY: Good, Oct-May. Difficult, Jun-Aug.

CREDIT CARDS ACCEPTED: Visa, MasterCard and American Express. The Navy Lodge accepts Visa, MasterCard, American Express and Discover.

TRANSPORTATION: On base shuttle/bus.

DINING OPPORTUNITIES: Galley in Shields Hall and McDonald's are within walking distance. Arby's and Taco Bell are within driving distance.

History is all around Little Creek, with Jamestown and Williamsburg one hour north. Nearby beautiful Virginia beaches beckon, but don't forget to check out Norfolk.

Norfolk Naval Station (VA18R1)
7918 Blandy Road, Suite 100
Norfolk, VA 23551-2419

MAIN INSTALLATION TELEPHONE NUMBERS: C-757-444-0000, DSN-312-564-0111. Locator 444-0000 ext 1; Medical 444-0000 ext 2; Security Police 444-3333.

LOCATION: From north take I-64 east, Naval Base exit 276 for I-564 northwest, follow signs. From south take I-64 exit I-564 northwest to Gate 3A. *USMRA: Page 52 (F-5,6).* **NMC:** Norfolk, in city limits.

RESERVATION INFORMATION: BOH: Spruance Hall, Bldg A128, 1756 Powhattan Street, Norfolk, VA 23511-2995. **C-757-402-7005 or 1-877-ZUMWALT(986-9258), DSN-312-564-7005,** Fax: C-757-445-9888, 24 hours daily. E-mail: norvares@series2000.com BEH: Wall Manor, Franklin Avenue, Norfolk, VA 23511. **C-757-402-4553,** Fax: C-757-444-0797. Check in 24 hours daily, check out 1200 hours. Government civilian employee billeting. ***Winner of the 1997 Admiral Elmo R. Zumwalt Award for Excellence in Bachelor Housing.***

(BEH) Penn Hall. Bldg R63. E4 and below, shared room, two single beds; E5/6, private room, full beds, shared bath, hair dryer. Refrigerator, microwave, A/C, clock radio, TV/VCR, housekeeping service, laundry facility, ice machine, daily newspaper. Modern structures. Rates: E4: $8 per person; E5/6: $9 per person. Duty on orders can make reservations, others Space-A.

(BOH) Bldg A128. Bedroom, private bath (290) with double bed, sofabed; kitchen suites (62). Refrigerator, microwave, A/C, clock radio, CATV/VCR in room and lounge, hair dryer, housekeeping service, laundry facility, iron/ironing board, ice machine, sauna, jacuzzi, sun deck, daily newspaper. Modern structures. Rates: $15 per unit; kitchen suites $30, each additional person $3.50. Duty on orders can make reservations, others Space-A.

(NAVY LODGE) Navy Lodge. 7811 Hampton Blvd, Norfolk, VA 23505-5000. **C-1-800-NAVY-INN.** Lodge number is C-757-489-2656, Fax: C-757-489-9621 (for large groups only!), 24 hours daily. Directions: Take I-64 to 564 exit to Terminal Blvd, right on Hampton Blvd. Lodge on left. Check in 1500-1800 hours, check out 1200 hours. Bedroom, two double beds, private bath (156, 4 handicap accessible); bedroom, two queen-size beds, private bath (60); bedroom, queen-size bed and sofa bed (34); bedroom, two double beds (158); bedroom double bed (42). Kitchenette, microwave, utensils, A/C, CATV/VCR, video rental, clock, coffee maker, housekeeping service, cribs, phones, fax service, hair dryer, coin laundry facility, iron/ironing board, ice machine, picnic area, playground, mini mart. Modern structure. Smoking or non-smoking rooms available. Rates: $48 per unit; mini apartment $54. All categories can make reservations. No pets. **This is the largest Navy Lodge in the world with 294 rooms!**

(DV/VIP) Maury Hall, Bldg A54. **C-757-402-7004,** 24 hours daily. Check in at BOQ, Bldg A128. E7-E9. One-room (19), two-room (E9) (6). Refrigerator, freezer, microwave, coffee maker, CATV/VCR, HBO, clock radio, housekeeping service, iron/ironing board. Rates: one-room $15, two-room $27; each additional person $5.50-$6.50.

(DV/VIP) O6-010. Suite, king size bed, private bath; suite, king size bed, private bath. Three Flag Officer Houses (2). Refrigerator, freezer, microwave, stocked bar, sundry cabinet, A/C, CATV, HBO, stereo system, safe, clock radio, hair dryer, housekeeping service, iron/ironing board, toiletries, hot tub, sauna, roof-top sun deck, playground, daily newspaper. Rates: VIP suites $27; single $22; each additional person over 13 $5.50; Flag Officer $40, each additional person $6.50.

AMENITIES: Fitness center, Meeting/Conference Room, Snack and Soft Drink Vending Machines.

TML AVAILABILITY: Good, fall and winter. Difficult, other times.

CREDIT CARDS ACCEPTED: Visa, MasterCard and American Express. The Navy Lodge accepts Visa, MasterCard, American Express and Discover.

TRANSPORTATION: On base shuttle/bus, C-757-441-4118; Car Rental, C-1-800-736-8222; Off base taxi, C-757-622-3232, C-757-489-7777.

DINING OPPORTUNITIES: Thimble Shoals, C-757-445-1302; Norfolk Live, C-757-444-2125; Food Court with Pizza Hut, Taco Bell, KFC, and Subway are within walking distance. Applebee's, C-757-489-0422; and Pizza Hut, C-757-489-8941 are within driving distance.

This is the largest naval base in the world. There is an interesting tour given daily. If you can see a ship launching, do so! Also, visit Hampton Roads Naval Museum and the MacArthur Memorial. Nearby are Williamsburg, Yorktown and Jamestown.

Norfolk Naval Shipyard (VA26R1)
Code 1160, Bldg 1500
Portsmouth, VA 23709-5000

MAIN INSTALLATION TELEPHONE NUMBERS: C-757-396-3000, DSN-312-961-3000. Locator 396-3221; Medical 396-3268; Security Police 396-5111.

LOCATION: From I-264 in Portsmouth exit on 5 south on US-17 or on Effingham Street south to enter the Shipyard. *USMRA: Page 52 (F-7).* **NMC:** Portsmouth, in city limits.

RESERVATION INFORMATION: CBQ, Bldg 1504A, Code 834, Norfolk Naval Shipyard, Portsmouth, VA 23709-5000. **C-1-877-986-9258 (toll free) or C-757-396-4449, DSN-312-961-4449,** Fax: C-757-396-4968, DSN-312-961-4968. TAD personnel must make reservations through local SATO. Check in at facility 24 hours daily, check out 1200 hours. Directions from Main Gate: Turn right on Lee Street, follow to dead end and make a left. Registration Bldg 1504A is located directly behind the front parking lot. Late checkout C-757-396-4562. Government civilian employee billeting.

(VQ) Seamarks Inn. Bldgs 1531, 1579, 1503 (E1-E9), 1439 (ships in overhaul, official duty only). Reservations accepted. Check out 1200 hours. Rooms, semi-private bath (200); rooms, private bath (158); rooms for official ship overhaul duty only (Bldg 1439) (242). Refrigerator, microwave, housekeeping service, TV in room and lounge, laundry facility, snack vending. Modern structure, remodeled 1994. Rates: transient $8.50; suite $12.75; guest $4. Family members not allowed to stay in facility. Active Duty can make reservations; others Space-A. No pets.

(VQ) The Landing. Bldgs 1579. Rooms, private bath (100). Refrigerator, microwave, housekeeping service, TV in room and lounge, laundry facility, snack vending. Newly built, 1996. Rates: $8.50 per bed; suite $12.75; guest $4. Active Duty can make reservations; others Space-A. No pets.

(Fisher House) Located at Portsmouth Naval Medical Center, 313 Green Street, Portsmouth, VA 23704-5000. **C-757-399-5461.** *Note: Appendix B has the definition of this facility. Fisher Houses are only available as lodging for families of patients receiving medical care at military and VA medical centers.*

Fisher House Located at Portsmouth Naval Medical Center, 853 Williamson Drive, Bldg. 287, Portsmouth, VA 23708-5000. **C-757-953-6889,** Fax: C-757-953-7174. *Note: Appendix B has the definition of this facility. Fisher Houses are only available as lodging for families of patients receiving medical care at military and VA medical centers.*

DV/VIP Code 800, Bldg 1500, Portsmouth Naval Shipyard, Portsmouth, VA 23709, **C-757-396-8605, DSN-312-961-8605.** O7+, Retirees are eligible for suites. VIP suites. Kitchenette, no stove, utensils, TV/VCR in room and lounge, housekeeping service, laundry facility, cots. Rates: $29, guest $7.25. Maximum three per unit. All categories can make reservations; Active Duty, reserve and NG on orders have priority; others Space-A. TAD personnel must make reservations through local SATO. No pets.

AMENITIES: Exercise Room, Meeting/Conference Room, Snack and Soft Drink Vending Machines.

TML AVAILABILITY: Good. Best, Dec. Difficult, Sep.

CREDIT CARDS ACCEPTED: Visa, MasterCard and American Express.

TRANSPORTATION: On base shuttle bus.

DINING OPPORTUNITIES: Mariner's Reef (NNSY Galley), C-757-396-7343; McDonald's, C-757-396-4842; and Ten Pin Grill, C-757-396-5396 are within walking distance. The Olive Garden, C-757-465-2139; Red Lobster, C-757-465-0627; and Shoney's Restaurant, C-757-488-1060 are within driving distance.

Virginia Beach's famed boardwalk and beaches will tempt summer visitors. See the Portsmouth Naval Shipyard museum, attend a play, dine on excellent seafood, or take in a ballgame at Harbor Park.

Oceana Naval Air Station (VA09R1)
Bldg 133
Virginia Beach, VA 23460-5000

MAIN INSTALLATION TELEPHONE NUMBERS: Quarterdeck C-757-433-2366, DSN-312-433-2366. Base OPS, C-757-433-2196, DSN-312-433-2196. Locator 433-2366; Medical 433-2221; Security Police 433-9111.

LOCATION: From I-64 exit to I-264 to Virginia Beach Blvd. (exit 58A) E to Oceana Blvd. Turn right (south) to Oceana NAS. *USMRA: Page 47 (O-9), page 52 (I,J-7).* **NMC:** Virginia Beach, in city limits.

RESERVATION INFORMATION: Bldg 460, E Avenue, Virginia Beach, VA 23460-5120. **C-1-877-986-9258 (toll free) or C-757-433-2574, DSN-312-433-2574,** Fax: C-757-433-3351, DSN-312-433-3351, 24 hours daily. Check in at billeting 1500, check out 1100 hours.

CBQ Bldgs 460, 536. Official orders. Space-A is on a first come, first serve basis. Single room (210); Handicap accessible single unit (8); Suite (65). All units have private bath and/or shower, refrigerator, coffee maker, telephone, TV/VCR, hair dryer, iron/ironing board, housekeeping service, laundry facility. Rates: single $15, each additional person $3; suite $18, each additional person $5. No pets.

DV/VIP Bldgs 460, 536. VIP suites with kitchenette (11); VIP suites without kitchenette (25). Refrigerator, coffee maker, telephone, TV/VCR, hair dryer, iron/ironing board, housekeeping service, laundry facility. Rates: $25, each additional person $5.

AMENITIES: Exercise Rooms, Meeting/Conference Rooms, Lounge Areas, Community Kitchen (Bldg 460). Ice, Snack and Soft Drink Vending Machines.

TML AVAILABILITY: Good, Nov-Apr. Difficult, May-Oct.

CREDIT CARDS ACCEPTED: Visa, MasterCard, American Express and Discover.

TRANSPORTATION: Off base (airport) shuttle/bus, C-757-857-1231; On base car rental: Enterprise Rental, C-757-437-0051.

DINING OPPORTUNITIES: Bowling Alley, C-757-433-2167; Golf Clubhouse C-757-433-2588; and McDonald's, C-757-428-6389 are within walking distance. There are numerous restaurants and fast food chains to choose from that are within a few miles from base.

There are great beaches at Virginia Beach.

Quantico Marine Corps Base (VA11R1)
Family Service Center
Bldg 2034
Quantico, VA 22134-5012

MAIN INSTALLATION TELEPHONE NUMBERS: C-703-784-2121, DSN-312-278-2121. Locator 748-2506; Medical 911; Security Police 911. *Ten-digit dialing required for local calls.*

LOCATION: From I-95, take exit 150-A (Quantico/Triangle) east. US-1 runs parallel to I-95 and is adjacent to the base. Directions to the base from I-95 and US-1 are clearly marked. *USMRA: Page 47 (L-5,6).* **NMC:** Washington, D.C., 30 miles north.

RESERVATION INFORMATION: Liversedge Hall, 15 Liversedge Drive, Quantico, VA 22134-5103. **C-703-784-3148/9 ext 221, DSN-312-278-3148/9 ext 221,** Fax: C-703-784-1347, DSN-312-278-1347, 24 hours daily. Housing Office, 0800-1630 hours Mon-Fri, C-703-784-2711. WEB: www.quantico.usmc.mil/g5/bachelor/right.html Directions from Main Gate: Go 1.5 miles, make a right onto Liversedge Drive. Check in at 1400 hours, check out 1200 hours. Military and Government civilian employee billeting. *Note: A $4.3 million TLF addition is in progress for the DoD Fiscal Year 2001 NAF Construction Program.*

CBQ Liversedge Hall. Bldg 15. E6-O1, official or unofficial duty. Bedroom, semi-private bath (transient duty) (72); guest suites, private bath (TAD/TDY) (39). Microfridge, microwave, heat, A/C, CATV, phones, data port connectivity, voice mail and DSN lines in all rooms. VCR and video rental available, complimentary fax/copier service, continental breakfast and computer work stations. 52" screen TVs in conveniently located lobbies. Housekeeping service provided. Laundry rooms, rollaways and cribs available as needed. Older structure. Rates: TAD/TDY, $18-$22; guest suite $26-$33. TAD/TDY Group reservations 90 days in advance. Names submitted 35 days prior to arrival. Duty on orders may make reservations 30 days in advance; others Space-A.

Guesthouse Neville Road. C-703-784-6093/4477, DSN-312-278-6093/4477. Two bedroom, two bath, living room with gas fireplace, dinning room, den, full family size kitchen with stovetop, full size refrigerator, microwave, queen-size beds, 50" screen CATV/VCR, stereo and mini-bar, heater, A/C, phone, data port connectivity and STU phone. Video rentals available. Housekeeping services provided, laundry facilities and rollways. Two patios, one with gas grill and electric awning. Six-foot privacy fence surrounds units. Rates: $30-$35.

TML Crossroads Inn. Bldg 3018, **C-1-800-965-9511, C-703-630-4444,** Fax: 703-630-4499. All categories. Bedroom, private bath (78), two double beds, TV/VCR, refrigerator, microwave, coffee maker and phone. Suite, private bath (18), two double beds, sofabed, table with four chairs, TV/VCR (2), refrigerator, microwave, dishwasher, coffee maker, toaster, stove, wet bar. All units have access to laundry facility, cribs, rollaways, soft drink and snack vending, meeting/conference rooms. Handicap accessible. Rates: room $47; suite $64. Reservations: policy varies with purpose of stay.

(DV/VIP) DGQ. Bldg 17 Harry Lee Hall, Lejeunne Road. **C-703-784-6096/4477, DSN-312-278-6093/4477.** One- and two-bedroom suites available. Living room, kitchen unit, microwave, mini-bar. Computer workstations, phones, data port connectivity, voice mail, DSN lines in all suites. Heater, A/C, CATV/VCR in all rooms. Small excercise room for guest use. Laundry room and housekeeping services provided. Rates: $30-$35. Duty on orders, military on leave, Retirees and dependents Space-A

AMENITIES: Ice machines, complimentary 26" bicycles with safety equipment available for trail or street riding. Large excercise room with sauna, snack vending machines and detergent vending machines in laundry room. Conference Center with one large room which seats eighty and one small room which seats forty; audio visual equipment on site.

TML AVAILABILITY: Good, Oct-Apr. Difficult, summer.

CREDIT CARDS ACCEPTED: Visa, MasterCard, American Express, and Discover.

TRANSPORTATION: Car Rental: Enterprise, C-703-441-1782; On/Off base taxi, C-703-640-6464.

DINING OPPORTUNITIES: Gallery Cafe (at Medal of Honor Golf Course), C-703-784-2426 is within walking distance. The Clubs of Quantico, C-703-784-2676 are adjacent to Crossroads Inn. Quantico Town and Triangle/Dumfries are located within driving distance.

Located on the Potomac River, near Washington, D.C. Woodbridge is the major shopping and recreation district close by. The battlefield of Manassas, Occoquan (craft shops and marinas) are also near.

Richmond Defense Supply Center (VA30R1)
Attn: DSCR-DB
8000 Jefferson Davis Highway, Bldg 118
Richmond, VA 23297-5000

MAIN INSTALLATION TELEPHONE NUMBERS: C-804-279-3861, DSN-312-695-3861. Locator 279-3861; Medical 279-3821; Security Police 279-4888.

LOCATION: From I-95 (Richmond-Petersburg Turnpike) exit 64 or 67 to US-1/301. Clearly marked. *USMRA: Page 47 (L-8).* **NMC:** Richmond, 8 miles north.

RESERVATION INFORMATION: 8000 Jefferson Davis Highway, Richmond, VA 23297-5000. **C-804-279-3371 or 804-279-4198; DSN-312-695-4198,** Fax: C-804-279-3944, DSN-312-695-3944.

(Army Lodging) Rooms available 1-4; sleep four. Suites: Gregory, sleeps five; Sheffield, Colonels and above, sleep two. Rates: $25 single; suite $35 single; each additional person over 18 $5.

TML AVAILABILITY: Limited.

CREDIT CARDS ACCEPTED: Visa, MasterCard, American Express and Discover.

TRANSPORTATION: None available.

DINING OPPORTUNITIES: Arby's is within walking distance. Halfway House Restaurant, Applebee's, Pelding Restaurant, Shoney's, McDonald's, Hardee's and many others are within driving distance.

The community Rec Office (located in the Fitness Center, Bldg 33D) has discounted tickets to: Busch Gardens, Water Country, Kings Dominion. Tickets are sold from 0800-1600 hours Mon-Fri; ID required.

Wallops Island Surface Combat System Center (VA46R1)
Bldg R-20
Wallops Island, VA 23337-5000

MAIN INSTALLATION TELEPHONE NUMBERS: C-757-824-2058. Locator 824-2079; Medical 824-2130; Security Police 824-2074/58, (at site 824-7028).

LOCATION: From the south: Take Chesapeake Bay Bridge/Tunnel north, stay on US Route 13 to Route 175 (a right at T's Corner) for five miles, a left at Route 798 (Ocean Deli). BQ facilities will be on right. From the north: Take Route 13 south, five miles over MD/VA line to Route 175, same directions as above. *USMRA: Page 47 (P-7).* **NMC:** Norfolk, VA, 100 miles south.

RESERVATION INFORMATION: Combined Bachelor Housing Surface Combat System Center, Bldg R-20, Wallops Island, VA 23337-5000. **C-757-824-2064,** Fax: C-757-824-1764, 24 hours daily. WEB: www.scsc.navy.mil/FHI.htm Write to: CBQ, ACSC Wallops Island, VA 23337-5000 Personnel on official travel orders must call (SATO)-1-800-576-9327. Personell calling for space availability must call the CBH front desk by 1600 on the day of arrival. Space-A will not be accepted over the telephone. The CBH front desk is available 24 hours daily. Check out is at 1100 hours. Government civilian employee billeting. *Note: All guests must be registered at check-in.*

(CBQ) Eagles Nest Bldg R-20. Bedroom, private bath (13); bedroom, shared bath (26). All suites have kitchenette, refrigerator, microwave, limited utensils, CATV/VCR in room and lounge, housekeeping service, cribs, rollaways, snack vending, free laundry facilities. Training trailer (weights, treadmill, stairstepper, and bicycles). Recreation room, pool table, ping pong and large screen TV. Screened in deck. Modern structure. Handicap accessible. No smoking. Galley next door. Bicycles available for residents. Rates E1-E6 $15, E7+ $18; each additional person $3. Active Duty, reserves and NG on orders, military widows can make reservations; others Space-A. No pets.

(CBQ) Osprey Manor. Bedroom, private bath (16). Kitchenette, limited utensils, A/C, CATV in room and lounge, housekeeping service, laundry facility, cribs, rollaways, snack vending, ice machine, outdoor screened gazebo. Award winning modern stick-built structure. Handicap accessible, non-smoking. Rates: $18, each additional person $3. Active Duty, reserves and NG on orders, military widows can make reservations, others Space-A. No pets.

(DV/VIP) Eagles Nest Bldg R-20. Suites. Kitchenette, refrigerator, microwave, limited utensils, CATV/VCR, housekeeping service, cribs, rollaways, snack vending, free laundry facility. Rates $24. Duty can make reservations; others Space-A. No pets.

TML AVAILABILITY: Good. Best, Sep-Dec. Difficult, Jan-Sep.

CREDIT CARDS ACCEPTED: Visa, MasterCard, American Express and Discover.

TRANSPORTATION: Car Rentals.

DINING OPPORTUNITIES: Base Galley, Ray Chanty (Seafood), Don's Seafood, Ocean Deli and Pizza Hut are all within driving distance.

Close to Chincoteague National Wildlife Refuge and Assateague National Seashore Park, where wild ponies are auctioned each May. A variety of outdoor activities abound-boating, crabbing. This is the Eastern Shore!

Yorktown Coast Guard Reserve Training Center (VA28R1)
Loyd Lamont Design
LaFayette Hall, Room 152
Yorktown, VA 23602-5000

MAIN INSTALLATION TELEPHONE NUMBERS: C-757-898-3500, DSN-312-827-3500.

LOCATION: From I-64, exit 25-D east on VA-105, follow signs to Highway 17. Left on Highway 17, then right at second light onto Cook Road. Follow this until road ends, then take a right. This will lead to the base. *USMRA: Page 47 (N-8,9), page 52 (D-1).* **NMC:** Newport News, 15 miles southeast.

RESERVATION INFORMATION: Loyd Lamont Design, LaFayette Hall, Room 152, Yorktown, VA 23602-5000. **C-757-856-2378, DSN-312-827-2378,** Fax C-757-856-2299, 0700-1700 Mon-Fri. Reservations for PCS-TDY; others Space-A. Check in at Cain Hall, Bldg 235.

(BOQ) Private bedroom, private bath (8), refrigerator, microwave, TV, phone. Rates: $13. No pets. No smoking.

(DV/VIP) Captain's Office, **C-757-856-2212, DSN-312-827-2212.** No smoking. No pets.

AMENITIES: Exercise Room, Mini Mart.

TML AVAILABILITY: Better Mon-Thu than weekends.

CREDIT CARDS ACCEPTED: None.

TRANSPORTATION: On base shuttle/bus: Liberty Van, makes periodic runs to town and nearby installations.

DINING OPPORTUNITIES: Base Galley, C-757-898-2321; O Club, C-757-898-2106; and Subway are within walking distance.

Yorktown Naval Weapons Station (VA14R1)
P.O. Drawer 160
Yorktown, VA 23691-0160

MAIN INSTALLATION TELEPHONE NUMBERS: C-757-887-4545, DSN-312-953-4545. Locator 887-4000; Medical 887-7404; Security Police 887-4676.

LOCATION: From I-64 east, take exit 247 east, turn left. One half mile to Gate 3 and pass office. For Station HQ: Go past Gate 3, 0.8 mile to stoplight. Turn left on Route 238 (Yorktown Road) 2.3 miles to Gate 1 on left. Or from I-64 west: Take exit 247, turn right to stoplight. For pass office, turn left, 0.8 mile to Gate 3. For Station HQ: Go straight through stoplight on Route 238 (Yorktown Road), 2.3 miles to Gate 1 on left. *USMRA: Page 47 (N-8), page 52 (B,C-1).* **NMC:** Newport News, two miles southeast.

RESERVATION INFORMATION: Family Housing Office, Nelson House, Bldg 704, P.O. Drawer 160, Yorktown, VA 23694-0032. **C-757-887-7621, DSN-312-952-7621,** Fax: C-757-887-4340, 24 hours daily. Duty may make reservations; others Space-A. Check in at facility, check out 1100 hours. Government civilian employee billeting if GS7+ with advance reservations.

(CBQ) Bldg 704. E7+, Officers all ranks. Separate bedroom suites, private bath (10). Community kitchen, microfridge, A/C, CATV in room and lounge, housekeeping service, cots, laundry facility, ice machine. Modern structure. Rates: $30 maximum per family.

(DV/VIP) CBQ. Bldg 704. O6/GS13+. Bedroom suite, private bath (2). Community kitchen, microfridge, A/C, CATV in room and lounge, housekeeping service, laundry facility, cots, ice machine. Modern structure. Rates: $34 maximum per family.

AMENITIES: Exercise Room.

TML AVAILABILITY: Good, winter. Limited, summer.

CREDIT CARDS ACCEPTED: Visa, MasterCard and American Express.

TRANSPORTATION: Car Rental: Avis, C-757-877-0291; Enterprise, C-757-873-3003; Hertz, C-757-877-9229; Thrifty, C-757-877-5700. Off base taxi, C-767-245-7777.

DINING OPPORTUNITIES: City Limits, C-757-887-4555 is within walking distance. Das Waldcafe, C-757-930-1781; Le Yaca, C-757-220-3616; and White Hall Restaurant, C-757-229-4677 are within driving distance.

The Battlefield at Yorktown, restored Colonial Williamsburg and the first permanent English settlement in America, are all within a 20-mile radius of the station. Also check out Busch Gardens and WIlliamsburg Pottery. Stop by the MWR Department for special tickets to events and parks.

WASHINGTON

Bangor Naval Submarine Base (WA08R4)
2901 Barbel Street
Silverdale, WA 98315-2901

MAIN INSTALLATION TELEPHONE NUMBERS: C-360-396-6111, DSN-312-744-6111. Locator 396-6111; Medical 396-4444; Security Police 396-4444.
Ten-digit dialing required for local calls.

LOCATION: From Sea-Tac Airport, take I-5 south to Tacoma. take exit 132 for Bremerton and WA-16 north and go approximately 30 miles. After passing through small town of Gorst, go approximately five miles. Turn left at stoplight on WA-3 N. Go approximately 7 miles, make a right at the exit for Keyport and Bangor, follow left over freeway to Main Gate. *USMRA: Page 103 (A-1,2).* **NMC:** Bremerton, 12 miles south.

RESERVATION INFORMATION: Evergreen Lodge, Bldg 2750, Bangor Naval Submarine Base, Bldg 2750, Silverdale, WA 98315-5000. **C-360-396-6581/4035, DSN-312-744-6581/4035,** Fax: C-360-396-6629, DSN-312-744-6629, 24 hours daily. Directions from Main Gate: Take Luoto Road then, for BEQ, turn left on Scorpion Avenue, or (for BOQ and Navy Lodge) turn left on Trigger Avenue, then left on Ohio Street. Check in at facility, check out 1200 hours. Government civilian employee billeting.

(NAVY LODGE) Navy Lodge. Bldg 2906, Trigger Avenue, Silverdale, WA 98315-5000. **C-1-800-NAVY-INN.** Lodge number is C-360-779-9100, Fax: 360-779-9117, 24 hours daily. Check in 1500-1800 hours, check out 1200 hours. Bedroom, two queen-size beds, private bath (45); bedroom, one queen-size bed, sofabed, private bath (5). Kitchenette, microwave, coffee, utensils, A/C, CATV/VCR, video rental, phones, hair dryer, housekeeping service, coin laundry facility, iron/ironing board, cribs, highchairs, rollaways, ice machine, playground. Six sets interconnecting, handicap accessible (2). Rates: $50. Maximum five per room. *No pets, but seeing eye dogs are allowed.* No smoking.

(BEQ) Bldg 2200, Scorpion Avenue. Rooms undergoing renovation. When completed, all rooms will have one or two beds (depending on rank), private bath, refrigerator, microwave and TV (60). Housekeeping service, laundry facility, cribs, ice machine. Modern structure. Rates: E1-E4 $5; E5-E9 $10. Duty can make reservations; others Space-A.

(BOQ) Evergreen Lodge. Bldg 2750, Sargo Circle. Bedroom, private bath, (64). Microfridge, TV in room and lounge, housekeeping service, laundry facility, cribs, ice machine, jacuzzi. Modern structure. Rates: sponsor $10-$16, each additional person $2. PCS are confirmed if available; duty, Reservists can make reservations; others Space-A.

(DV/VIP) PAO, Bldg 2750, Room 208. **C-360-396-6581.** O7+, Civilians determined by commander. Bldg 2750: Evergreen Lodge, Suite (4). Kitchen (2), microwave, refrigerator, TV in room and lounge, computer, housekeeping service, laundry facility, ice machine, jacuzzi. Rates: $12. Bldg 4189: VIP Cottage, private bath (1). Kitchen, complete utensils, housekeeping service, TV. Renovated and remodeled. Rates: sponsor $28 adult, each additional person $7. Maximum four persons.

AMENITIES: Mini Mart, Snack and Soft Drink Vending Machines.

TML AVAILABILITY: Fairly good. Best. Oct-Apr, Difficult, May-Sep.

CREDIT CARDS ACCEPTED: Visa, MasterCard, American Express and Discover. The Navy Lodge accepts Visa, MasterCard, American Express, Discover and Diners.

TRANSPORTATION: On base shuttle/bus, C-360-396-0186; Off base shuttle/bus, C-360-479-4348; Car Rental, C-1-800-rent-a-car, C-360-692-7790; Off base taxi, C-360-692-1075, C-360-478-8600.

DINING OPPORTUNITIES: 48 Degrees North, C-360-697-8025; McDonald's, C-360-697-4012; and Olympic Lanes Snack Bar, C-360-779-2838 are within walking distance. Red Lobster, C-360-613-0105; Silver City Brew, C-360-692-1182; and Tony Roma, C-360-698-3033 are within driving distance.

Visit Poulsbo, known as "Little Norway," and stroll the boardwalk along Liberty Bay. Try Bremerton's Naval Shipyard Museum (Ferry Terminal on First Street). For picnicking and boating visit Silverdale Waterfront Park.

Bremerton Naval Station (WA11R4)
120 South Dewey Street
Bremerton, WA 98314-5020

MAIN INSTALLATION TELEPHONE NUMBERS: C-360-476-3711, DSN-312-439-3711. Locator 476-0126; Medical 911; Security Police 911. *Ten-digit dialing required for local calls.*

LOCATION: From Sea-Tac Airport follow signs for I-5 S; after taking I-5 south exit, go approximately 30 miles to exit 132, Highway 16, Bremerton and Gig Harbor. Follow Highway 16 approximately 34 miles to Highway 3 N, take Highway 3 N to Kitsap Way exit. Go right at stop sign, right onto Naval Avenue to 24-hour gate. One hour ferry ride from Seattle. *USMRA: Page 101 (C-4), page 103 (A-3).* **NMC:** Bremerton, in city limits.

RESERVATION INFORMATION: Code N47311, 120 South Dewey Street, Bremerton, WA 98314-5001. For reservations call: **C-360-476-9527, C-360-476-7660 ext 5000, DSN-312-439-7660,** Fax: C-360-476-6895. Check in at Shield's Hall, Bldg 1000, 24 hours daily, check out 1200 hours. Government civilian employee billeting. From Naval Avenue Gate turn right on Green Street to lodging office. *Earned a five-star rating for Excellence in Bachelor Housing.*

(BEQ) Shield's Hall, Bldg 1000. Bldgs 865, 885, 942, 1001. Bedroom, shared bath (447); family room (6). Community kitchen 1st floor, refrigerator, microwave (per floor), coffee maker, TV/VCR in room and lounge, housekeeping service, laundry facility (per floor), ice machine, hot tub, picnic facilities. Modern structure. Rates: E1-E5 $5; E6-E9 $10; single room $10, multi room $5, family room $10; each additional person $2. Active Duty can make reservations; others Space-A.

(BOQ) Bldg 847. Officers all ranks, GS7+. Bedroom, private bath (70); family suite, private bath (5). Community kitchen 1st floor, refrigerator, TV/VCR in room and lounge, phones, housekeeping service, laundry facility, ice machine, complimentary coffee/doughnuts weekdays, sauna/spa, library and reading room, playground. Rates: $16 per person.

(DV/VIP) BOQ. Bldg 847. **DSN-312-439-3251.** O6+. Rates: $18. Retirees Space-A.

AMENITIES: Exercise Room, Meeting/Conference Room, Snack Vending, Hot Tub.

TML AVAILABILITY: Fairly good, Nov-Mar. Difficult, Jun-Sep.

CREDIT CARDS ACCEPTED: Visa and American Express.

TRANSPORTATION: On base shuttle/bus, C-360-476-4078; Off base shuttle/bus, C-360-476-4078; Car Rental, C-360-377-1900; On base taxi, C-360-476-0126; Off base taxi, C-360-479-5676.

DINING OPPORTUNITIES: Subway, McDonald's and TCBY Frozen Yogurt are within walking distance. Coffee Oasis, Cloverleaf and Perry Mall Pub are within driving distance.

A beautiful Northwest location is supplemented by these lodging facilities.

Clear Lake Recreation Area (WA01R4)
Reservation Office
92 SVS/SVROE
121 N Doolittle Avenue
Cheney, WA 99004-5000

MAIN INSTALLATION TELEPHONE NUMBERS: C-509-247-1212, DSN-312-657-1110. Locator 247-1212; Medical 911; Security Police 911.

LOCATION: Off base. From I-90, take exit 264 north on Salnave Road (WA-902), right on Clear Lake Road, 0.5 miles to recreation area. *USMRA: Page 101 (I-4).* **NMC:** Spokane, 12 miles northeast. NMI: Fairchild AFB, 7.5 miles north.

RESERVATION INFORMATION: 14824 S Clear Lake Road, Cheney, WA 99004. **C-509-299-5129,** Fax: C-509-247-5759, 28 April-Labor Day. Reservations accepted 1 April-27 April at C-509-247-2511, DSN-312-657-2511. Area is open from late April thru Memorial Day, Th-Mon 0700-1800 (opening day is base on the state fishing opener). Memorial Day thru Labor Day open every day 0700-1900. Subject to change after Labor Day.

(Cabins) Active Duty, retired, reserve, NG on orders. Two-bedroom cabin (1). Kitchen, picnic area, playground, beach. Rates: $30 daily, $130 weekly. Call to check availability.

AMENITIES: Snack Bar, Vending Machines, Restrooms, Showers, Laundry Facilities.

TML AVAILABILITY: Summer months. Call early for holiday weekend reservations.

CREDIT CARDS ACCEPTED: Visa, MasterCard and AF Club Card.

TRANSPORTATION: Car Rental (Spokane).

DINING OPPORTUNITIES: Snack bar within walking distance.

Beautiful scenic area with beach offering a variety of water sports, boating, sailing and fishing.

Everett Naval Station (WA10R4)
FSC, Code 01F
2000 West Marine View Drive
Everett, WA 98207-5001

MAIN INSTALLATION TELEPHONE NUMBERS: C-425-304-3000, DSN-312-727-3000. Locator 304-3000; Medical 304-4045; Security Police 304-3260/3211. *Ten-digit dialing for local calls with 360 area code.*

LOCATION: Take I-5 north, exit 193 to Pacific Avenue. Turn right onto

West Marine View Drive, base is on the left. To Smokey Point Family Support Complex (13910 45th Avenue NE, Marysville, WA 98271-5000), which is located about 11 miles north of the main base:From main base, take I-5 north, take exit 202, turn right. Turn left on State Street/Smokey Point Blvd. Turn right onto 136th Street. Turn left on 45th to Family Support Complex. *USMRA: Page 101 (D-3), page 103 (C-2).* **NMC:** Seattle, 25 miles south.

RESERVATION INFORMATION: BEH, 2000 West Marine View Drive, Everett, WA 98207-5001. **C-425-304-3111, DSN-312-727-3111,** Fax: C-425-304-3119, 24 hours daily. Directions: Through Main Gate, turn right on Fletcher Way, check in parking approximately 100 yards on right. **BOH,** 13918 45th Avenue NE, Marysville, WA 98271-5000. **C-425-304-4860, DSN-312-727-4860,** Fax: C-425-304-4869, 24 hours daily. Directions: From I-5 take exit 202. Turn right on 116th NE, turn left on 136th Street, then left on 45th Avenue NE. Follow signs to BOH.

(BEH) Bldg 2026. Private bath, toiletries, TV/VCR, phone, free laundry room. Rates: E4 and below $5; E5+ $10.

(BOH) Bldg 13918. Private bath, hot tub, toiletries, kitchen, TV/VCR, phone, computer, free laundry facilities. Rates: single $10, each additional person $2; suite $16, each additional person $3. All authorized guests must be registered at the front desk. *Note: BOH is located at the Naval support facility, in Marysville, 12 miles north of Everett Naval Station.*

(NAVY LODGE) Navy Lodge. 14320 45th Avenue NE, Marysville, WA 98271-5000. **C-1-800-NAVY-INN.** Lodge number is C-360-653-6390, Fax C-360-659-2062, 24 hours daily. Directions: From I-5, take exit 202; turn right off exit onto 116th Street, then left at the first light onto State Avenue. At next light make a right onto 136th Street. Then turn left on 45th Avenue at Navy Support Complex. Navy Lodge is last building on left. Two queen-size beds, private bath (48); one double bed, sofabed, private bath, handicap accessible (2). Kitchenette, refrigerator, microwave, utensils, A/C, CATV/VCR, video rental, phone, hair dryer, laundry facility available, iron/ironing board, housekeeping service, cribs, rollaways, ice machine, playground. Interconnecting smoking and non-smoking rooms available. Rates: $53. No pets. *Note: The Navy Lodge is located at the Naval support facility, in Marysville, 12 miles north of Everett Naval Station.*

AMENITIES: Exercise Room, Mini Mart, Snack and Soft Drink Vending Machines.

TML AVAILABILITY: Fair.

CREDIT CARDS ACCEPTED: Visa, MasterCard and American Express. Navy Lodge accepts Visa, MasterCard, American Express, Discover and Diners.

TRANSPORTATION: On/Off base shuttle: Shuttle Express, C-1-800-487-7433; Airporter Shuttle, C-425-335-4070.

DINING OPPORTUNITIES: McDonald's, C-425-304-4918; Subway Sandwich Shop, C-425-304-4950; and Baskin Robbins, C-425-304-4919 are within walking distance. Naval Station Galley, C-425-304-3168; Olympia (Italian), C-360-659-8800; Paraiso (Mexican), C-360-653-6133; Outback Steakhouse, C-425-513-2181; and Red Robin, C-425-335-7730 are within driving distance.

Fairchild Air Force Base (WA02R4)
92nd MSS/DPF
400 W Castle Street, Suite 101
Fairchild AFB, WA 99011-8536

MAIN INSTALLATION TELEPHONE NUMBERS: C-509-247-1212, DSN-312-657-1110. Locator 247-5875; Medical 247-5661; Security Police 247-5493.

LOCATION: Take US-2 exit from I-90 west of Spokane. Follow US-2 through Airway Heights, after 2 miles turn left to base Main Gate and visitors control center. *USMRA: Page 101 (I-4).* **NMC:** Spokane, 18 miles east.

RESERVATION INFORMATION: 92 SVS/SVML, Bldg 2392, 300 N. Short Street, Fairchild AFB, WA 99011-5000. **C-1-888-AFLODGE (1-888-235-6343), C-509-247-5519, DSN-312-657-5519,** Fax-509-247-2307, 24 hours daily. Reservations: C-509-244-2290 ext 2120. Duty may make reservations any time; Space-A may make reservations 24 hours in advance. Directions: From Main Gate, stay to the right for 0.25 miles and turn on Short Street. Registration, Bldg 2392, is on the left. Check in at lodging, check out 1200 hours. Government civilian employee lodging official duty only. *Winner of the 1997 Air Force Innkeeper Award (large operation).*

(TLF) Bldg 2399. One-bedroom suite, private bath (18). Kitchen, complete utensils, TV, housekeeping service, laundry facility, cribs, cots, ice machine. New structure. Rates: $24.50.

(VAQ) Bldg 2272. Bedroom, semi-private bath (42). Refrigerator, A/C, TV, housekeeping service, laundry facility. Modern structure. Rates: $17.50. Maximum two per room.

(VOQ) Bldgs 2392, 2393. Bedroom, shared bath (42). Laundry facility, iron/ironing board, cots, ice machine. Renovated structures. Rates: O5 and below, SNCO $20 per person, $29 couple.

(DV/VIP) Bldg 2393. **C-509-247-2127.** Only O6+. **Call 509-247-2127.**

AMENITIES: Exercise Room, Meeting/Conference Room, Mini Mart, Snack and Soft Drink Vending Machines.

TML AVAILABILITY: Good, Sep-Mar. Difficult, other times.

CREDIT CARDS ACCEPTED: Visa and MasterCard.

TRANSPORTATION: Off base shuttle/bus, C-509-328-7433, Car Rental, C-509-838-8223; Off base taxi, C-509-535-2535.

DINING OPPORTUNITIES: Burger King, NCO Club and Warrior Dining Hall are within walking distance. Lai Lai Garden, Little Joe's and Longhorn BBQ are within driving distance.

Visit Manito Park and Botanical Gardens, while there look at the local pottery, the Cheney Cowles Museum and historic Campbell House. Try Factory Outlet shopping in Post Falls, Greyhound racing in Coeur D'Alene.

Fort Lewis (WA09R4)
Attn: AFZH-PAW-C
Box 339500
Fort Lewis, WA 98433-9500

MAIN INSTALLATION TELEPHONE NUMBERS: C-253-967-1110, DSN-312-357-1110. Locator 967-6221; Medical 968-1390; Security Police 967-3107.

LOCATION: On I-5, exit 120 in Puget Sound area, 14 miles northeast of Olympia, 12 miles southwest of Tacoma. Clearly marked. *USMRA: Page 101 (C-5), page 103 (A,B-7).* **NMC:** Tacoma, 12 miles north.

RESERVATION INFORMATION: Bldg 2111, P.O. Box 33085, Utah & Pendleton Avenues, Fort Lewis, WA 98433-0085. **C-253-967-2815/6754/5051,** Fax: C-253-967-2253, DSN-312-357-2253, 24 hours daily. Check in at facility, check out 1000 hours. Government civilian employee billeting.

(Army Lodging) Fort Lewis Lodge. C-253-964-0211. Bedroom, private bath (149). Community kitchen on each floor (some units have kitchenettes), CATV, housekeeping service, coin laundry facility, cribs, cots, and ice machine. Modern structure. Handicap accessible (5). Rates: based on rank $35-$45. Maximum five per room. TDY can make reservations; others Space-A.

(VOQ/VEQ) Main Post, two buildings. Bedroom, private bath suite (43); single rooms (3). Community kitchen in each building, limited utensils, CATV, housekeeping service, laundry facility, cribs, cots. Older structures. Rates: $41, each additional person $5. TDY can make reservations; others Space-A.

DVQ Bronson Hall. Bldg 1020. O4+. VIP suite, private bath (3); main post cabin (2). Cabins have kitchen. Refrigerator, wet bar, CATV, housekeeping service. Older structure. Rates: sponsor $46, each additional person $5. Duty can make reservations; others Space-A.

Cabins Klatawa Village. Officer cabins. Main Post, family units (6). Small kitchen, limited utensils, TV, housekeeping service. Family units (10). Rates: call. PCS in/out families may make reservations; others Space-A.

Cabins Log Cabins. C-253-967-7744/5415. Studio, sleep 2 (4); one-bedroom, sleep 4 (6). Handicap accessible (2). Fully furnished, fully equipped kitchen, shower, bathroom. Bedding and fresh towels provided daily, along with daily garbage service. Rates: 1 Oct-30 April, 1 BR-$50 per day $340 per week, Studio-$40 per day, $270 per week. 1 May-30 September 1 BR-$55 per day $375 per week, Studio-$45 per day $305 per week. No smoking. No pets. Check in 1400, check out 1000.

DV/VIP Protocol Office, Bldg 2025, **C-253-967-5834, DSN-312-357-5834.** O7+.

AMENITIES: Off base shuttle/bus, C-253-581-8100; Car Rental, C-1-253-964-1331; On base taxi, C-253-967-8294; Off base taxi, C-253-582-3000, C-253-472-3303.

TML AVAILABILITY: Fair, Oct-Apr. Difficult, other times.

CREDIT CARDS ACCEPTED: Visa, MasterCard and American Express.

TRANSPORTATION: Car Rental, C-253-964-1331.

DINING OPPORTUNITIES: Burger King, C-253-964-8998; Post Exchange, C-253-964-0740; and Sparetime Cafe, C-253-964-3253 are within walking distance. American Lake (NCO Club), C-253-964-2555; Champs, C-253-964-0473; and O Club, C-253-964-0331 are within driving distance.

From majestic Mount Rainier, to the inland sea waters of Puget Sound, perfection for the outdoorsman. Tacoma, Olympia and Seattle are nearby.

Madigan Army Medical Center (WA15R4)
Lodging Office, Bldg 2110
Tacoma, WA 98431-0001
This is part of Fort Lewis Lodging Services.

MAIN INSTALLATION TELEPHONE NUMBERS: C-253-967-5051/2815, DSN-312-357-5051. Locator 967-6221; Medical 968-1110; Security Police 967-3107.

LOCATION: From I-5 N or S take the Madigan exit (124). Clearly marked. *USMRA: Page 103 (A-7).* **NMC:** Tacoma, 12 miles north.

RESERVATION INFORMATION: Bldg 2111, Tacoma, WA 98431-0001. **C-253-964-0211, DSN-312-357-5051.** Fax: 253-967-2253, 24 hours daily. Check in at Bldg 2111, check out 1000 hours. Government civilian employee billeting.

VOQ/VEQ Bldg 9901, 9906. Bedroom, shared bath; separate bedrooms, private bath. Community kitchen, refrigerator, limited utensils, housekeeping service, laundry facility, cribs, cots. Older structure. Rates: sponsor $26-$41, each additional person $5. Duty may make reservations 30 in advance; others Space-A.

Fisher House Madigan Army Medical Center, 9999 Wilson Avenue, Fort Lewis, WA 98433-5000. **C-253-964-9283,** Fax: C-253-968-3619. *Note: Appendix B has the definition of this facility. Fisher Houses are only available as lodging for families of patients receiving medical care at military and VA medical centers.*

AMENITIES: Snack and Soft Drink Vending Machines.

TML AVAILABILITY: Fairly good. Best, Oct-May.

CREDIT CARDS: Visa, MasterCard and American Express.

TRANSPORTATION: Off base shuttle/bus, C-253-581-8100; On base Car Rental, C-253-964-1331; On base taxi (Mon-Fri), C-253-967-8294, DSN-312-357-8294; Off base taxi, C-253-582-3000, C-253-472-3303.

DINING OPPORTUNITIES: Burger King, C-253-964-8998; Sparetime Cafe, C-253-964-3253 are within walking distance. American Lake (NCO Club), C-253-964-2555; Champs, C-253-964-0473; and O Club, C-253-964-0331 are within driving distance.

McChord Air Force Base (WA05R4)
62nd AW
Family Support Center
522 A Street
McChord AFB, WA 98438-1304

MAIN INSTALLATION TELEPHONE NUMBERS: C-253-982-1110, DSN-312-382-1110. Medical 911; Security Police 982-5777.

LOCATION: From I-5, take exit 125 east onto Bridgeport Way. One mile to Main Gate. Clearly marked. *USMRA: Page 101 (C-5), page 103 (B-7).* **NMC:** Tacoma, nine miles north.

RESERVATION INFORMATION: Evergreen Inn, Bldg 166, Main Street, P.O. Box 4118, McChord AFB, WA 98438-1109. **C-1-888-AFLODGE (1-888-235-6343),** For reservations only **C-1-800-847-3899. C-253-982-3591/2/3, DSN-312-382-3591/2/3,** Fax: DSN-312-982-3596, 24 hours daily. Call for reservations. Valid credit card required. Directions: From front gate on Main Street, go straight through the traffic light, lodging is the last building on the left side. Clearly marked. Check in at facility, check out 1100 hours.

VAQ Bedroom, private bath (108); shared bath (170). Microfridge, limited utensils, TV, housekeeping service, laundry facility, cribs, rollaways. SNCO Rooms: Bedroom, living area, private bath (11). Rates: single $17.50; double $24.75.

VOQ Bedroom, private bath (47). Mini-kitchens, microfridge, limited utensils, TV, housekeeping, laundry facility, cribs, rollaways. Rates: $20.

DV/VIP C-253-982-3591. O6+. One-bedroom suites, queen-size bed, private bath (21 O6+ and 2 CMS). Full kitchen, honor bar, TV/VCR, laundry facility, cribs, cots, living area, dining area. Microfridge, wet bar, living area. Rates: $25.

TML AVAILABILITY: Good, Nov-Feb. Difficult, Mar-Oct. Limited on family units.

CREDIT CARDS ACCEPTED: Visa, MasterCard and American Express.

TRANSPORTATION: On base shuttle/bus.

DINING OPPORTUNITIES: Burger King, C-253-582-1188; Bowling, C-253-982-5372; and Colocated Club, C-253-584-1371 are within walking distance.

Washington has lots to do: hiking, biking, canoeing, kayaking and skiing. Visit Tacoma attractions such as the Seattle Waterfront & Aquarium, Seattle Center, Pikes Place Market, Woodland Park Zoo, Ballard Locks & Fish Ladder and other national treasures such as Mt. Rainier National Park, Mount St. Helens and Snoqualmie Falls!

Pacific Beach Resort and Conference Center (WA16R4)

Everett Naval Station
113 N First Street
P.O. Box 0
Pacific Beach, WA 98571-1700

MAIN INSTALLATION TELEPHONE NUMBERS: C-360-276-4414 or 888-463-6697. Locator 276-4414; Medical 911; Security Police 911. *Ten-digit dialing required for local calls.*

LOCATION: From I-5 at Olympia, take exit 104 (Aberdeen/Port Angeles); west on US-8 and US-12 through Aberdeen to Hoquiam. Follow US-101 north approximately 4 miles to sign indicating Ocean Beaches; turn left and continue on Ocean Beach Road through Copalis Crossing, Carlisle and Aloha to Pacific Beach. Follow Main Street to entrance to Pacific Beach Resort and Conference Center. Watch for signs to office. *USMRA: Page 101 (A-4,5).* **NMC:** Aberdeen, 25 miles southeast. NMI: Fort Lewis, 115 miles northeast.

RESERVATION INFORMATION: Send information requests to: Pacific Beach Resort, P.O. Box 0, Pacific Beach, WA 98571-1700. **C-888-463-6697, C-360-276-4414,** Fax: C-360-276-4615, 0800-1600 hours. Check in 1600 hours, check out 1200 hours. Reservations made over the phone are confirmed when made. Make checks payable to: Pacific Beach. Cancellations must be received ten days prior (A $15 cancellation fee will be assessed). Notices received less than ten working days will be assessed one day's rental. Reservations not paid within ten working days are subject to cancellation. Reservation Priority: (one reservation per family) up to 90 days in advance for one week stay, up to 75 days for Active Duty, up to 60 days for retired and reserve, and up to 45 days for all others. Minimum two-night stay. *Note: A new Conference Center is now open.*

TML Motel, family (4) and studio units (25). Cabin, three- and four-bedroom (28); suites, one bedroom, sitting room, private bath (adults only) (6). Each cabin sleeps two people per bedroom. The suite and the studios can accommodate two adults. The family units sleep two adults and two children. All units have gas fireplaces and wood stoves. Crib linens not provided. Lodging can be reserved from one night in the suites, studios and family units and a minimum of two nights in the cabins. Maximum stay is two weeks. Extensions granted when space is available. Holiday weekends minimum of three nights (Fri-Mon). All other requests on a Space-A basis. *Note: Sponsor must accompany civilian guests during stay.* All military ID card holders welcome. *There are both pet and no-pet accommodations.* **See *Military Living's Military RV, Camping and Outdoor Recreation Around the World* for additional information and directions.**

TML AVAILABILITY: Fairly good. Best, winter.

CREDIT CARDS ACCEPTED: Visa, Master Card, American Express and Discover.

Below are the seasonal rates, per unit/per day. Specials are available 1 October -15 March, excluding holidays.

Type of Lodging	E1-E6 Peak	E7-O9 & DoD Civilians Peak
RV	$6	$14
Studios	$20	$35
Family	$25	$50
Type of Lodging	E1-E6	E7-O9 & DoD Civilians
Suites	$35	$60
*Three-Bdrm House	$40	$105
*Four-Bdrm House	$45	$105

*Add $15 for oceanfront accommodations and $5 for pet house rental Rates depend on rank, days of the week and season.

TRANSPORTATION: Car Rental.

DINING OPPORTUNITIES: Ocean Crest Resort Restaurant, C-1-800-684-8439 is within driving distance.

"May be the Navy's best kept vacation secret!" Social room with activities weekends off-season, and daily in spring, summer and fall. Bowling, exercise room, spa, restaurant and lounge, ball field, horseshoe pits, picnicking and whale watching platform, for what else? Watching whales!

Whidbey Island Naval Air Station (WA06R4)

260 West Pioneer Way
Oak Harbor, WA 98278-2500

MAIN INSTALLATION TELEPHONE NUMBERS: C-360-257-2211, DSN-312-820-0111. Locator 257-2211; Medical 257-9500; Security Police 257-3122. *Ten-digit dialing required for local calls.*

LOCATION: From I-5, exit 230, take WA-20 southwest to Whidbey Island, three miles west of WA-20 on Ault Field Road. *USMRA: Page 101 (C-2,3).* **NMC:** Seattle, 80 miles southeast.

RESERVATION INFORMATION: North Sound Combined Bachelor Housing and Whidbey Island Navy Lodge, NAS Whidbey Island N416, 3535 N Saratoga Street, Bldg 973, Oak Harbor, WA 98278-5200. **C-360-257-2529, DSN-312-820-2529,** Fax: C-360-257-5962, DSN-312-820-5962. WEB: www.navylifepnw.com Check in at facility after 1300 hours, check out 1100 hours. Directions: From Main Gate, continue on Langley Blvd, take left on Midway Street, McCormick Center is on corner of Midway and Saratoga. Government civilian employee billeting (on orders). Reservations will be held no later than 2300 hours on day of arrival. *Note: Navy funded TAD orders personnel make reservations through your local SATO Travel office. POV Government Air personnel, call 1-800-576-9327. Earned a five-star rating for Excellence in Bachelor Housing.*

TML McCormick Lodge. Bldgs 973, 2527. Bedroom, private bath. Refrigerator, CATV/VCR in room and lounge, telephone with voicemail, housekeeping service, laundry facility, snack vending, ice machine. Recently renovated. Rates: single occupancy $10, suite $16. Non-duty personnel are Space-A.

NAVY LODGE Navy Lodge. 2125 N Coral Sea Avenue, Oak Harbor, WA 98278-5000. **C-1-800-NAVY INN.** Lodge number is **C-360-675-0633,** Fax: C-360-675-1201, 0700-2300 hours. Directions: Take WA-20 to Whidbey Island, Oak Harbor, make a left onto Midway Blvd and a left onto Pioneer Way. Check in 1500-1800 hours, check out 1200 hours. Two-bedroom modular units, full private bath (23). Kitchen, refrigerator, stove, utensils, microwave, A/C, CATV/VCR, clock radio, video rental, hair dryer, housekeeping service, laundry facility, iron/ironing board, cribs, vending, playground. Handicap accessible. Rates: $59 per night. Maximum six per room. *No pets, but seeing eye dogs are allowed.*
Note: A new building with 50 rooms (2 handicap accessible) was built to compliment the Navy Lodge's 23 modular units. All new rooms have 2 queen-size beds with other navy lodge amenities, which include kitchenettes with flat top ranges and business class rooms. This Navy Lodge building is located at 760 Coral Sea Drive, Oak Harbor, WA 98278.

DV/VIP McCormick Lodge. CO Secretary, Bldg 973, 2527, **C-360-257-2037** or CBH manager, C-360-257-3205, O6+. Rates: $16.

TML AVAILABILITY: Best, winter. Difficult, weekends due to Reserve Training.

CREDIT CARDS ACCEPTED: Visa, MasterCard and American

Express. The Navy Lodge accepts Visa, MasterCard, American Express, Discover, and Diners.

TRANSPORTATION: Off Base shuttle/bus: Island Transit, C-360-678-7771; Car Rental: Budget; Diamond; Enterprise, C-360-675-6052; Jet City; Off base taxi: Fred's Taxi, C-360-675-1244; Harbor Taxi, C-360-675-1244; Whidbey Island Taxi Service, C-360-679-9330.

DINING OPPORTUNITIES: Eagles Loft, C-360-257-2715; Kegler's Kafe, C-360-257-1567; and McDonald's, C-360-675-3612 are within walking distance. China Harbor, C-360-679-1557; CPO Club, C-360-257-2891; For Pete's Sake, C-360-675-0132; Mi Pueblo, C-360-240-0813; and Kathi's Restaurant, C-360-240-1106 are within driving distance.

Whidbey Island can also be reached by ferry from Mukilteo (north of Seattle) to Clinton, in South Whidbey. Visit the hamlet of Langley then take a two-hour drive north to Oak Harbor and beautiful Puget Sound scenery.

WEST VIRGINIA

Camp Dawson Army Training Site (WV03R1)
240 Army Road
Kingwood, WV 26537-1092

MAIN INSTALLATION TELEPHONE NUMBERS: C-304-329-4334, DSN-312-623-4334. Locator 329-4334; Medical 329-1400; Post Security C-304-329-4301, DSN-312-623-4301, Police C-304-329-1611.

LOCATION: From I-68 to Morgantown exit (Route 7 southeast), turn left at traffic light. Follow Route 7 through Kingwood. At bottom of hill, cross bridge, make a left, then another immediate left (under bridge) to Camp Dawson. *USMRA: Page 46 (H-3).* **NMC:** Morgantown, 24 miles northwest.

RESERVATION INFORMATION: 240 Army Road, Kingwood, WV 26537-1092. **C-304-329-4420, DSN-312-623-4420,** Fax: C-304-329-4337, DSN-312-623-4337, 0630-1500 hours Sat-Thu, 0730-2200 hours Fri. E-mail: atswv@wv-arng.ngb.army.mil Duty may make reservations; others Space-A. Check in/out at billeting office (Bldg 301). After duty hours check in at Post Security, Bldg 100.

(BOQ/BEQ) Bldg 106. The Motel, bedroom (26). Refrigerator, TV in room and lounge, phone, housekeeping service, laundry facility, soft drink and snack vending, ice machine. Handicap accessible rooms available. Rates: $13.50 per person, each additional person $6.75, maximum $20 per family; PCS/TDY $12 per person, each additional person $6, maximum $18 per family. Maximum two per room. No pets.

(BOQ/BEQ) Bldg 301. Bedroom, private bath (12). Refrigerator, TV, phone, laundry facility, ice machine. Handicap accessible (6). Rates: $11.50 per person, each additional person $5.75, maximum $31 per family; PCS/TDY $10 per person, each additional person $5, maximum $27 per family. Maximum four per room. No pets.

(TML) Bldgs 302, 303, 304. Chalets, two bedrooms, two bathrooms, sleeps four (3). Kitchenette, refrigerator, complete utensils, TV, phone, housekeeping service. Rates: $15.50 per person, $7.75 each additional person, maximum $35 per family; PCS/TDY: $14 per person, $7 each additional person, maximum $32 per family. Maximum four per unit (five if sponsor is couple). No pets.

(Cottage) Bldg 104. Officers' Stone Cottage (1). Kitchenette, refrigerator, complete utensils, TV, phone, housekeeping service. Rates: $17.50 per person, $8.75 each additional person, maximum $66 per family; PCS/TDY $16 per person, $8 each additional person, maximum $60 per family. Maximum five per unit (six if sponsor is couple). No pets.

(DV/VIP) Bldg 101. E9, O6+. Cottages: three-bedroom, private bath (1); two-bedroom, private bath (1); one-bedroom, private bath (1). Kitchenette, refrigerator, complete utensils, TV in lounge, phone, housekeeping service, laundry facility. Rates: $23.50 per person, each additional person $11.75, maximum $88 per family; PCS/TDY $22 per person, each additional person $11, maximum $83 per family. Maximum five per unit (six if sponsor is couple). No pets.

AMENITIES: Exercise Room and Meeting/Conference Room.

TML AVAILABILITY: Fairly Good, Dec-Feb. Difficult, Mar-Nov.

CREDIT CARDS ACCEPTED: Visa, MasterCard, American Express and Diners.

TRANSPORTATION: Car Rentals: Hertz, C-304-842-4554; C-304-296-2331; AMS Rental, C-304-291-5867.

DINING OPPORTUNITIES: ATS Snack Bar, C-304-329-4383; Dairy Queen, C-304-329-0177; Hardee's C-304-329-1420; Heldreth Motel Restaurant & Lounge, C-304-329-1145; Mary's Restaurant, C-304-329-1160; Pizza Hut, C-304-329-0455; Preston Country Club, C-304-329-3520; Preston Country Inn, C-304-329-2220; and McDonald's are within driving distance.

While you are here, catch a sporting event live at West Virginia University!

Sugar Grove Naval Security Group Activity (WV04R1)
Bldg 63
Sugar Grove, WV 26815-9700

MAIN INSTALLATION TELEPHONE NUMBERS: C-304-249-6309, DSN-312-564-7276 ext 6309. Locator 249-6309; Medical 249-6381; Security Police 249-6310.

LOCATION: From I-81 in VA take Route 33 west from Harrisonburg, VA to Brandywine, WV. Turn left onto WV Route 21 five miles south to NSGA Sugar Grove on the right. *USMRA: Page 47 (I-6).* **NMC:** Harrisonburg, VA, 36 miles east.

RESERVATION INFORMATION: Bldg 26, Sugar Grove, WV 26815-9700. **C-304-249-6309, DSN-312-564-6309,** Fax: C-304-249-6316, 0730-1600 hours Mon-Fri. All ranks may make reservations. Check in at facility. After 1600 hours, check in at Community Center.

(Cottages) Rec Cottages. MWR Department, Bldg 26. Cottage: two-bedrooms, private bath, sofabed (6); apartments (2). Kitchenette, refrigerator, microwave, complete utensils, CATV, iron/ironing board, cots, BBQ. Modern structure, renovated. Handicap accessible (1). Rates: $45, each additional person $5. Maximum seven per cottage. No smoking. No pets.

AMENITIES: Exercise Room, Meeting/Conference Room, Mini Mart, Snack and Soft Drink Vending Machines.

TML AVAILABILITY: Good, Sep-Feb. Difficult, Mar-Aug.

CREDIT CARDS ACCEPTED: Visa, MasterCard, American Express and Discover.

TRANSPORTATION: None available.

DINING OPPORTUNITIES: The Mountainer Club, C-304-249-6362 is within walking distance. Fox's Pizza Den, C-304-249-5136; The Cabin Restaurant, C-304-249-5109; and Fat Boys Pork Palace, C-304-249-5591 is within driving distance.

New Market Civil War Battlefield and Museum, Massanutten and Season Resort, Grand Caverns, Shenandoah Caverns, Canaan Valley Resort and white water rafting are all within a short driving distance.

WISCONSIN

Fort McCoy (WI02R2)
DHC, Attn: AFRC-FM-HC
2168 South 8th Avenue
Fort McCoy, WI 54656-5161

MAIN INSTALLATION TELEPHONE NUMBERS: C-608-388-2222, DSN-312-280-2222. Locator 280-2222; Medical 280-3025; Security Police 280-2266.

LOCATION: From I-90/94, exit 143 west to WI-21 northeast to fort. Main Gate on north side of WI-21. *USMRA: Page 68 (C,D-7).* **NMC:** La Crosse, 35 miles east.

RESERVATION INFORMATION: AFRC-FM-HCC-HU, Bldg 2168, South 8th Avenue, Fort McCoy, WI 54656-6006. **C-608-388-2107, DSN-312-280-2107,** Fax: C-608-388-3946, DSN-312-280-3946, 24 hours daily.. WEB: www.mccoy.army.mil Directions: Turn left at Main Gate then left onto 8th Avenue. Check in at lodging 1400 hours, check out 1100 hours. Government civilian employee lodging.

TLQ Bedroom, shared bath (350); bedroom, private bath (70); one-bedroom (2) two-bedroom (5) and three-bedroom (1), private bath (four units are trailers). Kitchen, utensils, A/C, CATV, laundry facilities, cribs, cots ($3). Older structures, new trailers. Rates: $18-$30 for those on orders. All categories may make reservations.

Cabins Pine View Recreation Area. DPCA, 1439 South M Street, Attn: Pine View Recreation Area, Fort McCoy, WI 54656-5141, **C-608-388-3517, DSN-312-280-3517.** Directions: On post. Exit I-90 at Sparta to WI-21; eight miles northeast to Main Gate. Rec area off west Headquarters Road, one mile west of Post Headquarters. One-room cabins (2), one-bedroom duplex (2).

DV/VIP Protocol, Bldg 904, **C-608-388-3638.** O6+. 17 units, private bath, CATV. Rates: $30. Availability limited. Retirees and lower ranks Space-A.

TML AVAILABILITY: Fairly good, Jan-May and Sep-Dec. Difficult, other times.

CREDIT CARDS ACCEPTED: Visa, MasterCard, American Express and Discover.

TRANSPORTATION: On/Off base shuttle/bus, C-608-388-3616, DSN-312-280-3616; On/Off base Car Rental, C-608-269-7692, C-608-781-5678.

DINING OPPORTUNITIES: McCoy's, C-608-388-7673; and Rustic Inn, C-608-388-4968 are within walking distance. Club Oasis, C-608-269-2644; Mr. Ed's Tee Pee, C-608-372-0888; Perkin's, C-608-374-0550; and Primo's Express are within driving distance.

Mid December to February the installation ski hill has good cross country and downhill snow skiing. Visit the cheese factories, brewery, Amish shops and Cranberry Expo Museum. For Equipment rental, call C-ext 4498/3360. See *Military Living's Military RV, Camping and Outdoor Recreation Around the World* for more information and directions.

WYOMING

Francis E. Warren Air Force Base (WY01R4)
90 MSS/DPF
1105 Wyoming Avenue, Bldg 1200
Francis E. Warren AFB, WY 82005-2573

MAIN INSTALLATION TELEPHONE NUMBERS: C-307-773-1110, DSN-312-481-1110. Locator 773-1841 (military) 773-2081 (civilian); Medical 773-1847; Security Police 773-3501.

LOCATION: Off I-25, exit 11 west on Randall Avenue; Main Gate two miles north of I-80. Clearly marked. *USMRA: Page 102 (I-8).* **NMC:** Cheyenne, adjacent to city.

RESERVATION INFORMATION: Crow Creek Inn, 7103 Randall Avenue, Francis E. Warren AFB, WY 82005-2987. **C-1-888-AFLODGE (1-888-235-6343), C-307-773-1844, DSN-312-481-1844,** Fax: C-307-773-4450, DSN-312-481-4450, 24 hours daily. Check in 1600-1800 hours, credit card hold required. Check out 1100 hours. E-mail: laura.burchett@warren.af.mil All lodging rooms are non-smoking. Pets are not authorized in, on or around lodging facility. Regulations does not authorize pets to be kept in vehicles.

VQ Bldgs 21, 244. Rooms, some with private bath. Bldgs 44, 79, 129. Officers and civilians. One or two-bedroom suites, private bath, some with kitchen. All units have refrigerator, microwave, CATV, housekeeping service, laundry facility. Older structure, renovated. Rates: $21.50. Duty may make reservations any time; Space-A may make reservations 24 hours in advance.

TML Guest Lodging. Bldgs 1454, 238, 241. Two- or three-bedroom apartments. Kitchen, living room, CATV/VCR, housekeeping service, laundry facility, cribs, highchairs. Older structures, renovated. Rates: $29. PCS can make reservations.

DV/VIP Please call PAO, **C-307-773-2137/3052.** E9, GS/GM15 /O6+. Historic rooms and houses. Rates: $35-$40.50; O6+ $27 per person, $54 for two or more on duty/orders. Duty may make reservations any time; Space-A may make reservations 24 hours in advance.

TML AVAILABILITY: Good, except last two weeks of Jul (during Cheyenne Frontier Day Rodeo).

CREDIT CARDS ACCEPTED: Visa and MasterCard.

TRANSPORTATION: Car Rental: Avis, C-307-632-9371; Hertz, C-307-634-2131; On base taxi (official business only), C-307-773-1843; Off base taxi, Yellow Cab, C-307-635-5555.

DINING OPPORTUNITIES: Burger King, C-307-773-2399; Anthony's Pizza, C-307-773-3402; and Trails End Collocated Club, C-307-773-3048 is within walking distance. San Dong, C-307-634-6613; Chili's, C-307-635-1224; and Mcdonald's, C-307-632-1222 are within driving distance.

This base was once a frontier Army post and many of its buildings are on the National Historic Register. Cowboy and Indian lore abound, and nearby Colorado skiing draws many visitors. Visit Fort Collins' Old Town which is also nearby.

TRAVEL NOTES

Yellowstone Country Trailers (ID05R4)
c/o US Air Force Outdoor Recreation
366 SVS/SVRO
775 Pine Street, Bldg 2800
Mountain Home AFB, ID 83648-5125

MAIN INSTALLATION TELEPHONE NUMBERS: C-208-828-2111, DSN-312-728-1110. Locator 828-2111; Medical 911; Security Police 911.

LOCATION: Trailers are placed at commercial parks in and around Yellowstone National Park in Idaho and Wyoming. Directions to Mountain Home AFB: From Boise, take I-84 SE, 40 miles to Mountain Home exit, follow road through town to Airbase Road, ID-67 ten miles to Main Gate on left. USMRA: page 98 (C-9). NMI: Malmstrom AFB, MT, 254 miles north. **NMC:** Idaho Falls, 80 miles south.

RESERVATION INFORMATION: c/o US Air Force Outdoor Recreation, 366 SVS/SVRO, 655 Pine Street, Bldg 2800, Mountain Home AFB, ID 83648-5125. Reservations may also be made in person at Outdoor Recreation, Bldg 2800. **C-208-828-6333, DSN-312-728-6333.**

Reservations required, made up to two weeks prior in person or by phone. Accomodations must be paid in full at time of reservation with cash, check or credit card and cannot be made by mail.

Trailers Grant Village (6), Henry's Lake (1), Lion's Head Resort (4). Twenty-four foot travel trailers fully self-contained, sleep six, equipped with cooking and eating utensils. No smoking. Rates: $55. No pets.

TML AVAILABILITY: Memorial Day to 15 Sept (depending on occupancy and weather).

CREDIT CARDS ACCEPTED: Visa and MasterCard.

TRANSPORTATION: None available.

DINING OPPORTUNITIES: Numerous restaurants and snack bars at Henry's Lake and Lionshead.

Each location contains beautiful scenery plus rivers and lakes that are perfect for fishing.

UNITED STATES POSSESSIONS

GUAM

Andersen Air Force Base (GU01R8)
36th ABW/PA
Box 25, Unit 14003
APO AP 96513-4003

MAIN INSTALLATION TELEPHONE NUMBERS: C-671-366-1110, DSN-315-366-1110. Locator 351-1110; Medical 366-2978; Security Police 366-2913.

LOCATION: On the north end of the island, accessible from Marine Drive, which extends the entire length of the island of Guam. *USMRA: Page 130 (E,F-1,2)*. **NMC:** Agana, 15 miles south.

RESERVATION INFORMATION: Bldg 27006, 4th and Caroline Avenue, APO AE 96543-4004. **C-671-366-8144/8201, DSN-315-366-8144/8201,** Fax: C-671-366-6264, DSN-315-366-6264, 24 hours daily. Duty can make reservations any time; Space-A can make reservations 24 hours in advance. Check in 1400 hours, check out 1100 hours.

TLF Bldg 1656. PCS move or leave. Bedrooms, private bath, kitchenette (18). A/C, CATV, housekeeping service, laundry facility. Rates: $35.

VAQ Bldg 25003. One-bedroom, shared bath (120). Refrigerator, A/C, CATV, laundry facility. Rates: $17 per person.

VOQ Bldgs 27003, 27005. Bedroom, shared bath (30); private bath (16). Refrigerator, A/C, CATV, housekeeping service, laundry facility, ice machine. Rates: $18.50.

DV/VIP Protocol Office, 36 ABW, **C-(USA) 671-366-1320.** O6+, Retirees Space-A. Rates: suites (10) $25; houses (2) $30.

AMENITIES: Meeting/Conference Room and Business Center.

TML AVAILABILITY: Limited, year round.

CREDIT CARDS ACCEPTED: Visa and MasterCard.

TRANSPORTATION: Payless Car Rental, C-671-653-6945.

DINING OPPORTUNITIES: Anthony's Pizza, C-671-653-7149; Burger King, C-671-653-0782; Combined Club, C-671-366-1201; Robin Hood, C-671-653-7149 are within walking distance. AMC terminal, C-671-366-8283; Magellan Inn, C-671-366-3623; Palm Tree Golf Course, C-671-362-4654 are within driving distance.

Lots of sunshine, beaches, coral reefs, exciting WWII shipwrecks to explore for scuba enthusiasts. Hikers enjoy tropical mountains and jungles.

Guam Naval Computer & Telecommunications Area Master Station (GU05R8)
Bldg 198
PSC 455, Box 152
FPO AP 96540-1000

MAIN INSTALLATION TELEPHONE NUMBERS: C-671-355-1110, DSN-315-322-1110. Locator 355-1110; Medical 355-1110; Security Police 355-1110.

LOCATION: From Route 10A, right onto Route 1. Follow Route 1 until you see a Pizza Hut, take a left at the next traffic light onto Route 3. Take a left right before the McDonald's and you will see the front gate. *USMRA: Page 130 (E-2)*.

RESERVATION INFORMATION: BOQ/BEQ, FPO AP 96537-1800. **C-671-355-5793, DSN-315-355-5793,** Fax: C-671-355-5932. Hours 0700-2200. After hours check in through Quarterdeck.

BEQ E1-E4 double bedroom, shared bath (4); E5-E6 private bedroom, shared bath (10). Refrigerator, A/C, clock radio, iron/ironing board. Rate: $10 per person.

BOQ Bedroom, private bath (9). Refrigerator, A/C, CATV/VCR, clock radio, phone, housekeeping service, washer/dryer, iron/ironing board. Rates: $20, each additional guest $10.

DV/VIP C-671-355-5731/5749. BOQ. VIP Suites, double bedroom, private bath (2). Refrigerator, A/C, CATV/VCR, clock radio, phone, housekeeping service, washer/dryer, iron/ironing board. Rates: $25 per person, each additional guest $10.

AMENITIES: Exercise Room, Mini Mart, Snack Vending Machine and Soft Drink Machine.

TML AVAILABILITY: Fairly good. Best, Dec. Difficult, Jul-Aug.

CREDIT CARDS ACCEPTED: Visa, MasterCard and American Express.

TRANSPORTATION: Car Rental, Off base taxi.

DINING OPPORTUNITIES: Navy Exchange and the Galley C-671-355-5793 are within walking distance. McDonald's C-671-632-1006, Dominoes Pizza C-671-637-3030 and Reef Club are within driving distance.

Enjoy the many beaches, scuba diving, swimming, boating and sailing that are abundant in Guam.

Marianas U.S. Naval Forces (GU02R8)
Bldg 18
PSC 455, Box 152
FPO AP 96540-0051

MAIN INSTALLATION TELEPHONE NUMBERS: C-671-355-1110, DSN-315-322-1110. Locator 351-1110; Medical 344-9369; Security Police 333-2989.

LOCATION: South on Marine Drive on west side of island, clearly marked. *USMRA: Page 130 (C-3)*. **NMC:** Agana, 10 miles north.

RESERVATION INFORMATION: Combined BH, PSC 455, Box 150, FPO AP 96536-0051. **C-671-339-5259, DSN-315-339-5259,** Fax: C-671-339-6250, DSN-315-339-6250, 24 hours daily. Check in at facility after 1200 hours, check out 1200 hours. Government civilian employee billeting.

CBQ Bldgs 1, 7-16 Begonia Street; 1-8, 10, 38, 40 Lotus Circle; 1,3,5,7 Fern Street; 2, 4, 6, 8, 12, 22 Anthurium Street; 22, 24 South Columbus Avenue; 1-8, 10, 12-15, 19, 20, 23, 27 Carnation Street. All ranks, leave or official duty, Government civilian employees (stateside hire). Bedroom, private bath; suites, private bath (52). Refrigerator, coffee maker, A/C, CATV/VCR, housekeeping service, laundry facility, ice machine. Rates: E4 and below $10, E5-E6 $15, Officers $20. Duty can make reservations, others Space-A.

DV/VIP Flag Lt, C-671-339-5202. E7+/O5+/GS15+. Transient Madrid Houses. Bldgs 61, 63, 65, 67, 69, 71, 73. Two-bedroom, 1.5 private baths. Kitchen, refrigerator, coffee maker, A/C, CATV/VCR, phone, housekeeping service. Rates: $50 per night, each additional person $10.

TML AVAILABILITY: Fairly good. Best, December. Difficult, Jul-Aug.

CREDIT CARDS ACCEPTED: Visa, MasterCard, and American Express.

TRANSPORTATION: On base shuttle/bus; Off base shuttle/bus; Car Rental: Dollar and Hertz.

DINING OPPORTUNITIES: Exchange Food Court, McDonald's, Pizza Hut and Taco Bell are within walking distance. Hard Rock Cafe, Lone Star Steakhouse, Outback Steakhouse, and TGIF are within driving distance.

These quarters are within walking distance of all base support facilities. Scuba diving and other beach-related activities are popular.

PACIFIC ISLANDS

Bucholz Army Airfield (Kwjalein Atoll) (KW01R8) operates Kwjalein Lodge. C-805-355-3477, DSN-314-254-3477. Fax: C-805-355-3211, DSN-314-254-3211.

Wake Island Army Airfield (WK01R8)
Launch Center
Admin Office, Bldg 1502
Wake Island, HI 96898-5000

MAIN INSTALLATION TELEPHONE NUMBERS: C-808-424-2101, DSN-314-424-2101. Locator C-808-424-2101; Medical C-808-424-2455; Security Police C-808-424-2301.

LOCATION: A U.S. island in the Mid-Pacific, 2300 air miles west of Hawaii. **NMC:** Honolulu, 2300 miles southeast.

RESERVATION INFORMATION: Bldg 1502, Admin Office, Wake Island, HI 96898-5000. **C-808-424-2210, DSN-314-424-2210,** Fax: C-808-424-2190, DSN-314-424-2190, 0800-1700 hours, Mon-Sat. E-mail: chgacha@aloha.net Check in at facility during operation hours. Letter of approval from the base commander required to visit Wake Island.

TLQ Rooms and suites, refrigerator, housekeeping service, ice machine. Older structure recently renovated. Wood frame barracks, historic structure. Rates: $60. Active Duty on leave or official duty and NG/reserves on official duty can make reservations, others Space-A.

DV/VIP Refrigerator, housekeeping service, ice machine. Older structure recently renovated. Rates: $60.

TML AVAILABILITY: Limited.

CREDIT CARDS ACCEPTED: MasterCard, Visa, Discover and Government Credit Card.

TRANSPORTATION: Local contractor.

DINING OPPORTUNITIES: Mess Hall and Drifters Reef Bar are within walking distance.

PUERTO RICO

Borinquen Coast Guard Air Station (PR03R1)
Attn: Special Services
Aguadilla, PR 00604-9999

MAIN INSTALLATION TELEPHONE NUMBERS: C-787-890-8400. Medical C-787-890-8477; Security Police C-787-890-8472.

LOCATION: At the old Ramey Air Force Base, north of Aguadilla. Take PR-22/2 west from San Juan or north from Mayaguez to PR-110 north of CGAS. Main gate is at the end of Wing Road, just past 5th Street. *USMRA: Page 130 (B,C-2).* **NMC:** San Juan, 65 miles east.

RESERVATION INFORMATION: CGAS Borinquen MWR Office, P.O. Box 250520, Aguadilla, PR 00604. **C-787-890-8492,** Fax: 787-890-8493, 0930-1730 hours Mon-Fri. Reservations a must. PCS upon receipt of orders; Active Duty may reserve 45 days in advance; all others 30 days. Sponsor must make reservations (military widows make their own). Check in 1400 hours, check out 1100 hours. Directions: Straight on Wing Rd to La Plaza MWR. Located on second deck of La Plaza.

TML **Guesthouses/Cottages.** Five-bedroom house, private baths (1). A/C, shared living room and fully equipped kitchen area, CATV, washer/dryer. Rates: $25-$30 per room per night, $85-$105 for house per night. Three-bedroom houses, one bath (13), furnished. Kitchen, linens, CATV, A/C, washer/dryer, housekeeping service Mon-Fri. Non-smoking. Rates: $45-$70 per night. Maximum capacity six per unit. No pets.

Lighthouse Located behind Punta Borinquen Lighthouse. Two-bedroom apartment suites, furnished, private bath (2). Kitchen, CATV/VCR, A/C, washer/dryer, housekeeping service Mon-Fri. Rates: $55-$70 per day. Maximum capacity four per unit. No pets.

AMENITIES: Exercise Room, Mini Mart, Exchange and Package Store.

TML AVAILABILITY: Very limited. Best, Sep-May.

CREDIT CARDS ACCEPTED: Visa, MasterCard and Discover.

TRANSPORTATION: Car Rentals: Avis, C-787-890-3311; Budget C-787-890-1110.

DINING OPPORTUNITIES: Coast Guard Club (Wed & Fri 1700-2100 hours only), C-787-890-8490; and Ramey Pizza C-787-890-5544 are within walking distance. The Eclipse, C-787-890-0275; Golden Crown, C-787-890-5077; McDonald's and Wendy's are within driving distance.

Recreation gear available for rent, theater, swimming pool, picnic areas, several beaches surrounding area. Water sports, golf, horseback riding nearby. Contact MWR for information: C-787-890-8492.

Fort Buchanan (PR01R1)
US Army Puerto Rico
Attn: SOFB-PA-AL
Fort Buchanan, PR 00934-5007

MAIN INSTALLATION TELEPHONE NUMBERS: C-787-792-7977, DSN-313-740-3821. Medical 707-9117/3917; Security Police 707-3337.

LOCATION: From Luis Munoz Marin IAP toward San Juan, exit Caguas/Bayamon to PR-18, exit Bayamon right to PR-22, 1.5 miles to exit 5, fort on left. *USMRA: Page 130 (E-2).* **NMC:** San Juan, six miles southwest.

RESERVATION INFORMATION: Bldg 678, Depot Road, P.O. Box 34192, Fort Buchanan, PR 00934-0192. **C-787-792-7977, DSN-313-740-3821,** Fax: C-787-707-3939, DSN-313-740-3939, 24 hours, daily. WEB: www.buchanan.army.mil/mwr Check in at facility 1300 hours, check out 1100 hours. Directions: Go straight from Main Gate until the gas station; turn right. Follow road until traffic light; then turn left and immediately right. Pass bank and library; the next building is the lodge.

Army Lodging **El Caney Lodge.** Bldg 677. A new, state-of-the-art 75-unit guesthouse. Rooms have A/C, refrigerator, telephone, coffee maker, and TV. Larger rooms have kitchenette area with microwave. Cribs and rolling beds are available upon request. Laundry facilities available. Rates: $45-$85 daily, each additional person $5 per day. The new facility is conveniently located across from the commissary and exchange.

DV/VIP Protocol C-313-740-5047/5048, Bldg 1287 O6+. Reservations through Protocol Officer. Rates: $65, each additional person $15.

TML AVAILABILITY: Good, Nov-Apr. Difficult, Jun-Oct.

CREDIT CARDS ACCEPTED: Visa, MasterCard and American Express.

TRANSPORTATION: On base shuttle, C-787-707-3848/3255; Car Rental: Dollar, C-787-707-0188; Off base taxi, San Juan, C-787-722-2490; Metro, C-787-725-2870; Roehdale C-787-721-1900.

DINING OPPORTUNITIES: Community Club, C-787-792-7860 and Exchange, C-787-792-7047/7048 are within walking distance. Bowling Center, C-787-707-3272; Golf Club, C-787-707-3980/3852; and Special T's are within driving distance.

This is the capital of Puerto Rico. Visit El Morro Castle, Plaza las Americas Shopping Center, Paseo la Princessa, El Condado, local Bacardi Rum Distillers, and beautiful beaches. Post facilities include a golf course, tennis courts, water park, bowling alley, fitness center, exchange and commissary.

Roosevelt Roads Naval Station (PR02R1)
COMFAIR CARIB
PSC 1008, Box 3591
FPO AA 34051-3591

MAIN INSTALLATION TELEPHONE NUMBERS: C-787-865-2000, DSN-313-831-2000. Locator 865-2000; Medical 911; Security Police 911.

LOCATION: From Luis Munoz Marin IAP, San Juan left (east) onto PR-3 for 45 miles, sign on right indicating exit to Naval Station. *USMRA: Page 130 (F-2,3)*. **NMC:** San Juan, 50 miles northwest.

RESERVATION INFORMATION: Crossroads Inn. Combined Bachelor Quarters, Roosevelt Roads Naval Station, PSC 1008, Box 3032, FPO AA 34051-3032. Bldg 1209, C-787-865-4358, Fax: C-787-865-5377, 24 hours daily. Bldg 1209: From Gate 1, follow road for approximately two miles. Once you reach the stop sign, (taking the right fork), make a right turn. Keeping straight until the stop sign, make a left. Keep straight until you see the Anchor Inn Galley (on your right) turn right in front of Galley. Check in at billeting, check out 1100 hours. Government civilian employee billeting.

CBQ Bldg 725-728, 1688, 1707, 1708, 1709. Two-bedroom, private bath (8); three-bedroom, private bath (4). Refrigerator, microwave, limited utensils, A/C, TV/VCR, movies, phone, fax, housekeeping service, cots ($2). Modern structure. Handicap accessible. Rates: rooms BEQ $8; BOQ $14. Active Duty on orders, PCS/TAD/TDY have priority for reservations, others Space-A. Rates subject to change.

TML Guesthouse. C-787-865-4242. O7+. Two-bedroom houses (2). Kitchen, microwave, complete utensils, A/C, CATV/VCR, phone, housekeeping service, washer/dryer. Rates: $30, each additional person per night $10. Duty on orders can make reservations, others Space-A. *1-800-628-9446*

 **NAVY LODGE** Navy Lodge. PSC 1008, Box 3006, FPO AA 34051-3006. **C-1-800-NAVY-INN.** Lodge number is C-787-865-8282, Fax: C-787-865-8283, 24 hours daily. WEB: www.navy-nex.com Bedrooms, offering either two beds or one king bed, with private bath (120). Kitchenette, refrigerator, microwave, complete utensils, A/C, CATV/VCR, video rental, phone, hair dryer, newspaper, complimentary coffee, housekeeping service, coin washer/dryer, mini

mart, playground. No additional charge for rollaway beds, cribs, and highchairs. Interconnecting units for large families, handicap accessible (4). Rates: $57-$64. All categories can make reservations. Check in 1500-1800 hours, check out by 1200 hours. No pets.

DV/VIP CBQ. Bldgs 1688, 1707, 1709. O7+. One bedroom, private bath. Refrigerator, microwave, limited utensils, A/C, TV/VCR, movies, phone, fax, housekeeping service. Modern structure. Handicap accessible. Rates: BEQ VIP $20; BOQ VIP $30. Active Duty on orders, PCS/TAD/TDY have priority for reservations, others Space-A. Rates subject to change.

AMENITIES: Exercise Room, Soft Drink Machine, Snack Vending.

TML AVAILABILITY: Difficult.

CREDIT CARDS ACCEPTED: Visa, MasterCard and American Express. The Navy Lodge accepts Visa, MasterCard, American Express and Discover.

TRANSPORTATION: On base shuttle/bus; On base car rental: L&M Car Rental, C-787-865-4495; Off base car rental: Hertz C-787-885-3660, Avis C-787-885-0505, Thrifty C-787-860-2030; On base taxi C-787-865-7666; Off base taxi from base.

DINING OPPORTUNITIES: Galley and NEX Mall are located within walking distance. Chicken Jose's, McDonald's, Subway and Woody's Restaurant are within driving distance.

Don't miss El Yunque Rain Forest with its magnificent waterfalls, hiking trails, and restaurant.

Sabana Seca Naval Security Group Activity (PR04R1)
PSC 1009, Box 1
FPO AA 34053-1000

MAIN INSTALLATION TELEPHONE NUMBERS: C-787-261-8300. Locator 795-2255/2399; Medical 795-8755; Security Police 785-8310.

LOCATION: From Luis Munoz Marin IAP, take Route 26 west to Bayamon exit to PR-22 west to PR-886 north (Las Arenas exit) to base. Or take Interstate 22 west (toward Arecibo), get off exit La Arena. At the next intersection turn left; the base will be located on the left. *USMRA: Page 130 (D,E-2)*. **NMC:** San Juan, 14 miles east.

RESERVATION INFORMATION: Bravo Barracks, Bldg 21, PSC 1009, Box 1, Sabana Seca, PR 00952-5000. **C-787-261-8413.** Contact Quarterdeck after hours.

TML Very limited TML available. Extremely tight security; be prepared to show proper military ID and state your purpose of visiting the base. Plan to arrive only during daylight hours. This TML is not recommended for leisure travelers but is listed in the event of a need for lodging in the immediate area.

AMENITIES: Exercise Room.

TML AVAILABILITY: Very difficult.

CREDIT CARDS ACCEPTED: None.

TRANSPORTATION: None available.

DINING OPPORTUNITIES: Combined Club, C-787-261-8430; and Chicken Jose's, C-787-261-8429 are within walking distance.

Visit the great beaches, El Yunque Rain Forest, El Morro Fort and Casinos.

FOREIGN COUNTRIES

AUSTRALIA

The Naval and Military Club (AU05R8)

27 Little Collins Street
Melbourne, Victoria 3000
Australia
(Not U.S. Government Lodging)

MAIN INSTALLATION TELEPHONE NUMBERS: C-011-61-3-9650-4741. Medical (local physician 9650-4393); Security Police, Ambulance, Fire 000.

LOCATION: At the Paris end of Melbourne, just off Spring Street, at the "top end" of downtown. Parliament station is just around the corner. Melbourne's free City Circle trams service near the club. **NMC:** Melbourne, in city limits. NMI: RAAF Richmond, 730 km northeast.

RESERVATION INFORMATION: Address and telephone as above. Fax: C-011-61-3-9650-6529. E-mail: enquiries@nmclub.com.au WEB: www.nmclub.com.au Reservations may be made via mail, phone, fax, e-mail or web. Reception staffed 24 hours, 7 days. No limits on duration of stay. The club is happy to continue to offer bedroom accommodations and club facilities to male and female officers (Active Duty) and equivalent who are currently serving in all branches of the U.S. Armed Forces. **In addition we welcome all retired service personnel—regardless of whether they served as officers or not.** No dues required for short visits.

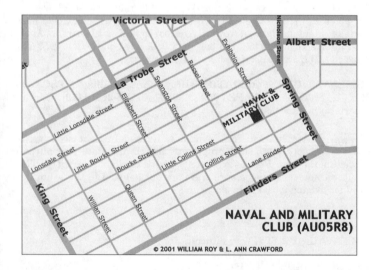

NAVAL AND MILITARY
CLUB (AU05R8)

© 2001 WILLIAM ROY & L. ANN CRAWFORD

TML Club and Hotel. Leave/vacation only. Single, double, and twin bedrooms (24). All units have private bath, TV, tea/coffee-making facilities, direct dial phone and mini bar. Morning newspaper and cooked breakfast included. Limited room service menu. Rates: AU$118.00 (U.S.$57.82 at press time).

AMENITIES: Gym, Squash Courts, Billiards/Snooker Tables, two bars and two dining rooms. Many historical relics and a very impressive display of paintings.

TML AVAILABILITY: Good, but early reservations recommended.

CREDIT CARDS ACCEPTED: American Express, Bankcard, Diners, MasterCard and Visa.

TRANSPORTATION: Airport "Skybus," tram, local taxi and hire limos.

DINING OPPORTUNITIES: The Streeton Room and city restaurants within walking distance.

Private Club established for Officers in 1881. Within walking distance of attractions, trams (street cars), subway, major shops, theaters and sporting venues. Book dinner in advance on the Colonial Tramcar Restaurant and eat while moving about the city. There are bus tours to see the Antarctic Penguins and Koalas in their natural habitat on Philips Island, 22 km south.

BAHRAIN

Bahrain Administrative Support Unit (BA01R9)

Southwest Asia (ASU SWA)
PSC 451, Box 95
FPO AE 09834-2800

MAIN INSTALLATION TELEPHONE NUMBERS: C-(USA) 011-973-724-000, DSN-318-439-4000. Locator C-973-724-000; Medical C-973-724-260; Security Police C-973-724-911.

LOCATION: The State of Bahrain is an island nation off the eastern coast of the Kingdom of Saudi Arabia in the Persian Gulf. A 24 km causeway connects the main island with Saudi Arabia. The administrative support unit is on the main island in the southeast section of Manama, Bahrain's capital city. From Muharraq and the airport, cross one of two causeways into Manama. Once across the causeway, head south on Route 37 (Al Fateh Highway) and into Al Juffayr, then continue south to the end of Route 37. At the end, turn left (east) to the support unit on the right side of the street. *EUSMRA: Page 12.* **NMC:** Dhahran, Saudi Arabia, 30 miles northwest.

RESERVATION INFORMATION: Combined Bachelor Housing PSC 451, FPO AE 09834-2800. **C-(USA) 011-973-724-716/762, DSN-318-439-4716, (BA) 318-439-4716,** Fax: C-(USA) 011-973-743-452 (BA) 318-439-3452, 24 hours daily. E-mail: cbh@nsa.bahrain.navy.mil Reservations accepted here. Directions: Main gate leads to parking lot; lodging is across from parking lot to the west side. Duty personnel only (PCS/TDY/TAD).

CBQ Bldg 264. Standard amenities: refrigerator, AC, CATV, housekeeping service, microwave, washer/dryer, ice machine. Rates: E1-O3 $6 per person per night; O4-O5 $8 per person per night. DV/VIP, O6+.One room only Rates: $12. Call for more information.

AMENITIES: Soft Drink Machine and Meeting/Conference Room.

TML AVAILABILITY: Very limited.

CREDIT CARDS ACCEPTED: Visa, MasterCard and American Express.

TRANSPORTATION: On/off base shuttle/bus, C-011-973-724-822; Car Rental: Avis, C-011-973-531-144; off base taxi, C-011-973-260-211.

DINING OPPORTUNITIES: MWR runs two restaurants on base and one sub/sandwich shop. Desert Dome, C-011-973-724-244; Jasmis, C-011-973-727-887; and Oasis Restaurant, C-011-973-724-204 are within walking distance. Fuddruckers, C-011-973-742-266; Kentucky Fried Chicken, C-011-973-713-777; and Pizza Hut, C-011-973-727-373 are within driving distance.

Bahrain is an island 24 km off the coast of Saudi Arabia. A causeway connects the main island with Saudi Arabia. The State of Bahrain requires a visa for all personnel entering the country.

BELGIUM

SHAPE/Chievres Air Base Community (BE01R7)

80th Area Support Group (NSSG)
CMR 45, Box 6675
APO AE 09708-5000

MAIN INSTALLATION TELEPHONE NUMBERS: C-(USA) 011-32-65-44-1110, (BE) 065-31-1110, DSN-314-361-1110 (Chievres Air Base—ask operator to connect you.) Locator 44-7111.

LOCATION: From Brussels take Autoroute 7 (E19) south for approximately 45 km toward Mons. Just north of Mons take exit 23 (Nimy-Maisieres) north onto Route 6 toward the town of Casteau. SHAPE is about 4 km north on the left (northwest) side of the road. Hotel Maisieres is located at the top of the hill directly across from SHAPE Headquarters building. (Mons is referred to as Bergen in the Northern (Flemish) Provinces and road signs in the north generally will only refer to Bergen.) *EUSMRA: Page 14 (C-1), page 16.* **NMC:** Mons, 5 km south. NMI: Chievres Air Base, 20 km southwest.

RESERVATION INFORMATION: Hotel Maisieres, 80th ASG (NSSG), CMR 451, APO AE 09708-5000. **Front Desk C-(USA) 011-32-65-73-93-00/99, DSN-314-366-7211; Reservations C-(USA) 011-32-65-73-192-71, DSN-314-366-6313.** Fax: Front Desk C-(USA) 011-32-65-72-42-56, DSN-314-366-7212; Reservations DSN-314-366-6313, 24 hours daily. E-mail: BrownJB@hq80asg.chievres.army.mil WEB: www.80asg.army.mil/community/housing.htm Space-A may check availability up to 24 hours prior to arrival.

TML **Hotel Maisieres.** Bedroom, private bath (70); *Bungalows for guests with pets* (19). Refrigerator, microwave, TV/VCR, phone, housekeeping service, laundry facility, cribs, cots, iron/ironing board. Rates: room $55, each additional person $5. *Note: Conversion of two guest rooms to accomodate physically challenged persons is in planning stages at this time.*

TML **SHAPE Inn.** Bldg 904, Room 108, PSC 79, Box 3, APO AE 09724-5000. **C-(USA) 011-32-65-44-4385,** Fax: C-011-32-65-44-5323. To reach NATO/SHAPE Headquarters, take the E-10 N from Paris or take the A-15/E-42 from Liege W to the Mons exit and follow signs. Chievres Air Base is located off BE-56, 17 km northwest of the village of Chievres. Officers and equivalent GS on official duty require reservations. Call for rates.

DVQ Suites (2). Reservations, C-(USA)011-32-65-73-192-41, DSN-314-361-5910/6313. O6+/E9. Rates: $75 per night, each additional person $5.

AMENITIES: Meeting/Conference Room, Indoor play area, Snack and Soft Drink Vending Machines, Computer Room with Internet/E-mail access for customers.

TML AVAILABILITY: Fairly good. Best, Oct-mid May.

CREDIT CARDS ACCEPTED: Visa, MasterCard, American Express, Discover and Diners.

TRANSPORTATION: On base shuttle/bus, C-(USA) 011-32-65-44-45-14, DSN-314-423-5414; Off base shuttle/bus, DSN-314-423-4571/4053; On base car rental (official business only), C-(USA) 011-32-65-44-45-14, DSN-314-423-5414; Off base Car Rental: Europcar, C-(USA) 011-32-65-72-30-35; Off base taxi, Taxi Willy C-(USA) 011-32-65-31-98-08.

DINING OPPORTUNITIES: International Club, C-011-32-65-44-51-29; O Club, C-011-32-65-44-41-33; Pizza Bowl, C-011-32-65-44-56-97; MacGregor's Market (located in hotel); and Sur Le Pouce C-011-32-65-72-39-50 are within walking distance. McDonald's and numerous varied cuisine restaurants are within driving distance in Mons and surrounding communities.

In Mons visit the Church of St. Waudru. "The Belfry" is accessible by elevator. Then visit the main square, town hall, and Van Gogh's house. To contact the Tourist Office, Grand-Place, 7000 Mons, call C-(BE) 065-33-55-80.

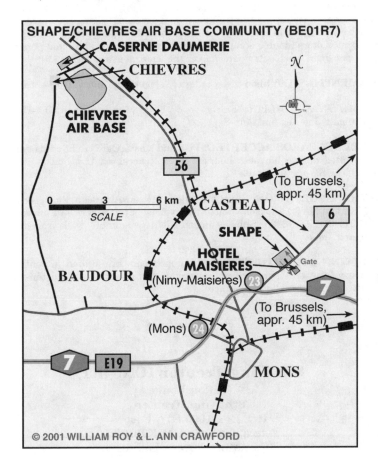

United States Embassy/ Tri-Mission Association (BE02R7)

c/o American Embassy
PSC 82 Box 002
APO AE 09710-5000
(U.S. State Department Billeting)

MAIN INSTALLATION TELEPHONE NUMBERS: C-(USA) 011-32-2-508-2481, DSN-314-365-9691. Medical 100; Security Police 101.

LOCATION: From the Brussels National Airport take the Autoroute 201 west toward Brussels and follow signs for the Ring 0 and exit at Leuven/Luik/Bergen. You are now on the Ring 0. Continue south on the Ring to southwest onto Autoroute 3 (E40), Continue on Autoroute 3 for approximately 2 km to exit 19 (Evere) and head north. At next traffic light, make a left onto Chaussee de Louvain (Leuvense Steenweg). Continue west on the Chaussee de Louvain, toward Central Brussels, for about 3 km to south on Blvd du Regent (Regent Laan) (cross Avenue des Arts before turning onto Blvd du Regent). The U.S. Embassy is approximately 0.5 km south on the right (west) side, 28 Blvd du Regent, 5th floor. *EUSMRA: Page 14 (C-1), page 15.* **NMC:** Brussels, in the city. NMI: NATO, 7 miles.

RESERVATION INFORMATION: 28 Blvd du Regent, c/o American Embassy, PSC 82 Box 002, APO AE 09724-5000. **C-(USA) 011-32-2-508-2481, DSN-314-365-9691,** Fax: C-(USA) 011-32-2-508-1626, 0900-1700 hours Mon-Fri. E-mail: delacruzks@state.gov or tmabrussels@state.gov WEB: militarytravelguide.com Check in at facility after 1300, check out 1000 hours. After duty hours report to American Embassy.

TML Apartments, private bath (12). Kitchen, refrigerator, microwave, utensils, CATV/VCR, housekeeping service (once a week), washer/dryer, cribs, fold-away beds. Apartments are two- and three-bedroom that sleep up to seven persons. Rates: Sponsoring employee and TDY personnel: 65 percent of per diem lodging rate; spouse and children over 12 years: 35 percent of per diem lodging rate; children under 12 years: 25 percent of per diem lodging rate; additional TDY personnel sharing same apt: 35 percent of per diem lodging rate; persons not on TDY but in company with person on TDY/per person: $5.00 per night; visitors (double occupancy): $85 per night, each additional person $5 per night, each extra person over the apartment's capacity $10.

AMENITIES: Gift Shop (need orders to shop there) and Video Rental.

TML AVAILABILITY: Fairly good. Best, Mar-June and Oct-Dec. Difficult, Jan-Feb and July-Sept.

CREDIT CARDS ACCEPTED: Visa and MasterCard credit cards only accepted during business hours. Personal checks on U.S. banks, cash USD or BF are acceptable.

TRANSPORTATION: Shuttle service between American Embassy to NSA and NATO. Carlson Wagonlit Travel Agency at American Embassy, C-011-32-2-508-2395. Subway (metro) is a two-minute walk from the apartments.

DINING OPPORTUNITIES: The apartments are located in central Brussels where there are many various restaurants within a ten- to fifteen-minute walking distance.

CANADA

8th Wing Trenton (CN04R1)
Yukon Lodge
8th Wing, Trenton
P.O. Box 1000 STN Forces
Astra, Ontario CN, K0K 3W0
(Canadian Forces Lodging)

MAIN INSTALLATION TELEPHONE NUMBERS: C-613-392-2811 (recording, then press 1, then 3402), DSN-312-827-7011, ext 3402. Locator 392-2811; Medical 392-3480; Security Police 392-3385.

LOCATION: From Toronto take CN-401 E approximately 100 miles, exit south on CN-33, 2 km to left on CN-2 and 1 km to CFB Trenton. May also be reached by crossing Canada/USA border on US-81 N to CN-401 W to CN-33 and directions as above. **NMC:** Toronto, 100 miles west.

RESERVATION INFORMATION: Bldg 142. **C-613-392-2811 ext 3402, DSN-312-827-7011, ext 3402,** Fax: C-613-965-7550. Write to: **Yukon Lodge,** 8th Wing Trenton, P.O. Box 1000 STN Forces, Astra, Ontario CN K0K 3W0. Directions: Take Glenn Miller Road south to Baker's Dozen. Turn left at light onto Hamilton Road. Straight ahead to fourth right at RCAF Road. Follow signs for RCAF Museum. Reservations accepted for leave personnel and their family members. Check in at Building 142 (Accommodations) just inside the main entry doors, room 115, for keys 24 hours daily. Check in 1400 hours, check out 1200 hours; late check out can be arranged.

(**TML**) Yukon Lodge. Bedrooms, one to three beds each, smoking or non-smoking, private and semi-private baths. Refrigerator, A/C, TV in room and lounge, phone, laundry facility, iron/ironing boards, cribs, ice machine. Older structure. Rates (subject to change): Can$12 adults (U.S.$7.63 at press time), Can$2 child (6-12) (U.S.$1.27 at press time). Verification of military/family member status required. Space-A lodging only. No pets.

(**DV/VIP**) Base Protocol, CFB Trenton, Astra, Ontario, CN K0K 1B0. Bldg 22. C-613-965-3379, DSN-312-827-3379. O6+. Limited number of accommodations.

AMENITIES: Mini Mart. Ice and Snack Vending Machine.

TML AVAILABILITY: Difficult. Best, Oct-May. Difficult, Jun-Sep.

CREDIT CARDS ACCEPTED: Visa, MasterCard, American Express and Interac (debit card).

TRANSPORTATION: Car Rental, C-613-392-3300; Off base taxi, C-613-392-3525.

DINING OPPORTUNITIES: Carney's, C-613-392-3385 is within walking distance. Kelsey's, C-613-392-7194; Trade Winds, C-613-392-8688; Harvey's, McDonald's and Suisse Chalet are within driving distance.

The Bay of Quinte Region is filled with wonderful fishing, camping, sailing and historical landmarks. Write to: Central Ontario Travel Association, P.O. Box 1566, Peterborough, Ontario K9J 7H7, or call C-1-800-461-1912 for more information.

9th Wing Gander (CN05R1)
Canadian Forces Base Gander
PO Box 6000
Gander, Newfoundland, Canada A1V 1X1
(Canadian Forces Lodging)

MAIN INSTALLATION TELEPHONE NUMBERS: C-709-256-1703 ext 107, DSN-312-622-3011 ext 107. Medical 651-2500, Security Police 800-709-7267.

LOCATION: Trans Canada Highway 1, exit north on Washington. Base is adjacent to Gander International Airport. Facility is next to Main Gate. **NMC:** St. John's, 300 km southeast.

RESERVATION INFORMATION: **C-709-256-1703 ext 212, DSN-312-622-3212.** Fax-709-256-1731, Mon-Fri 0800-1600 hours. After hours call C-709-256-1703 ext 209, DSN-622-3209.

(**TML**) Bldg 8. Room with single bed (17); room with two single beds (3). Units have sink and toilet, communal shower room. Refrigerator, microwave, coffee maker, CATV, laundry facilities, cots available. Housekeeping can be arranged for stays over 48 hours. Rates: Can$15 (U.S.$9.53 at press time).

(**TML**) Located in St. John's. 509-C Placentia Place, St. John's Canadian Forces Station. Reservations made through Gander. This facility is used primarily in support of dependents who must use St. John's for medical care. Space-A personnel may make use of it for R&R. Four-bedroom suite, two rooms with private bath and two with shared bath. King-size bed and couch in master bedroom, bunk and single beds in remaining rooms. Fully equipped kitchen, fully furnished, microwave, coffee pot, dining room, living room, sun room, CATV, laundry facility. Linen, toiletries and housekeeping are not provided. Linen can be arranged through Gander accommodations or you can bring your own. Facility overlooks Quidi Vidi Lake. Rates: Can$15 (U.S.$12.71 at press time) per bedroom used.

(**DV/VIP**) Bldg 86. E9, O4+. C-709-256-1703 ext 243. Suites (3). Bedroom with private bath. Sitting room, CATV/VCR, refrigerator, stocked honor bar, microwave, coffee maker, toaster, iron/ironing board, laundry facility, cots available. Housekeeping can be arranged for stays over 48 hours. Rate: Can$20 (U.S.$12.71 at press time).

AMENITIES: Meeting/Conference Rooms, Fitness Center. Ice, Snack and Soft Drink Vending Machines. Military Family Resource Center is within walking distance from the quarters and provides e-mail access to all guests.

TML AVAILABILITY: Good.

CREDIT CARDS ACCEPTED: None. All transactions must be on a Canadian dollars basis only.

TRANSPORTATION: Off base rental car and taxi.

DINING OPPORTUNITIES: Dining Hall on base; other food establishments approximately 2 km from base.

All lodgings have been recently renovated and are conveniently located close to local shopping. The town of Gander is located in central Newfoundland and provides an excellent base for exploration for this part of the province.

17th Wing Winnipeg (CN06R1)
P.O. Box 17000 STN Forces
Winnipeg, Manitoba CN R3J3Y5
(Canadian Forces Lodging)

MAIN INSTALLATION TELEPHONE NUMBERS: C-204-833-2500, DSN-312-257-2500.

LOCATION: From Perimeter Highway around Winnipeg, exit east on Portage Avenue. Proceed approximately 5 km to Whytewold Road and turn left (north). Follow to base. **NMC:** Winnipeg, approximately 9 km east.

RESERVATION INFORMATION: P.O. Box 17000 STN Forces, Winnipeg, Manitoba R3J 3Y5. **C-204-833-2500 ext 6416, DSN-312-257-6416** Fax: C-204-833-2661, DSN-312-257-2661. Mon-Fri 0700-1600 hours. E-mail: waccn@pangea.ca Directions: Follow Perimeter around city to Portage Avenue. East on Portage Avenue to Whytewold Road. Follow to base.

(TML) Bldg 79. Hotel bedrooms (90). Refrigerator, CATV, AC, cribs and cots available, housekeeping service, laundry facilities. Handicap accessible units. Rate: Can$25 (U.S.$15.89 at press time).

(DV/VIP) Bldg 79. O6+ Suites. Refrigerator, CATV, AC, cribs and cots available, housekeeping service, laundry facilities. Handicap accessible units. Rate: Can$40 (U.S.$25.42 at press time).

AMENITIES: Soft Drink Vending Machine.

TML AVAILABILITY: Good.

CREDIT CARDS ACCEPTED: None.

TRANSPORTATION: Taxis and Public Buses in Winnipeg.

DINING OPPORTUNITIES: Mess Hall within walking distance. Many restaurants and fast food establishments within driving distance.

CUBA

Guantanamo Bay Naval Station (CU01R1)
PSC 1005, Box 1
FPO AA 09593-0100

MAIN INSTALLATION TELEPHONE NUMBERS: C-(USA) 011-53-99-1110, DSN-313-723-3960 or DSN-313-564-4063. Locator 914; Medical 3200; Security Police 4105.

LOCATION: In the southeast corner of the Republic of Cuba. Guantanamo Bay Naval Station is accessible only by air travel. **NMC:** Miami, FL, 525 air miles northwest. *Note: All personnel not assigned must have the permission of the Commander to visit Guantanamo Bay Naval Station.*

RESERVATION INFORMATION: Attn: Billeting, PSC 1005, Box 53, FPO AE 09593-0137. **C-(USA) 011-53-99-2400, DSN-313-564-8877,** Fax: C-(USA) 011-53-99-2401, 24 hours daily. Check in at facility 1400, check out 1100 hours.

(BEQ) On Winward Point, Bldg 1670. E6 and below. Double beds, private bath (20). Refrigerator, microwave, A/C, CATV/VCR, housekeeping, common kitchen and laundry facility. Rates: $7 per person, second person $2.

(CBQ) On Winward Point, Bldg 2147. CPO/Officer Bedrooms, kitchen, living area (46). Refrigerator, microwave, A/C, CATV/VCR, housekeeping, exercise room, elevator and laundry facility. Rates: $12 per person, second person $3.

(CBQ) Leeward Bldg AV640. Officer bedrooms (20); enlisted rooms with double beds (14). Private bath, living area, kitchen, refrigerator, microwave, A/C, CATV/VCR, housekeeping, exercise room, laundry facility and drink vending machine. C-011-53-99-6272/6350 DSN-313-546-8877 ext 6272/6350; Fax: 011-53-99-6008.

(NAVY LODGE) Bldg. 2128. Navy Lodge. PSC 1005, Box 38, FPO AE 09593-0003. **C-1-800-NAVY-INN.** Lodge number is C-(USA) 011-53-99-3103, Fax: 011-53-99-3414, 0730-1700 hours Mon & Wed, 0700-1800 hours Tue, Thu, Fri, 0800-1630 hours Sat, Sun & holidays. Check in 1500-1800 hours, check out 1200 hours. Bedroom, two double beds, private bath (26). Kitchen, A/C, CATV/VCR, video rental, phone, housekeeping service, complimentary coffee in all rooms, coin laundry facility, cribs, cots, and ice machine. Rates: $41 per unit. No pets.

(DV/VIP) BOQ. Bldg 2147. O6+. Rates: $25. Reservations must be made through reservation desk. Chief VIP: Bldg 2147. C-011-53-99-2400/2907/2909, DSN-313-564-8877 ext 2400/2907/2909. Rates: E8-E9 $15.

AMENITIES: Exercise room and soft drink machine in Bldg 2147.

TML AVAILABILITY: Good most of the year except holidays.

CREDIT CARDS ACCEPTED: Visa, MasterCard and American Express. Navy Lodge accepts Visa, MasterCard, American Express, and Discover.

TRANSPORTATION: Car Rental, 011-53-99-4564; On base taxi, 011-53-99-62517; on base shuttle/bus available.

DINING OPPORTUNITIES: Bayview Club, ext 2304; Tiki Bar, Wind Jammer Cafe, Rusty Anchor and Jerk House are all within walking distance. General Galley, Hospital Galley, Baskin Robbins/Deli, Pizza Galley, ext 5233; are within driving distance.

CZECH REPUBLIC

Prague United States Embassy Apartments (CZ01R7)
Trziste 15, 118 01 Prague 1
Czech Republic

MAIN INSTALLATION TELEPHONE NUMBERS: C-011-420-2-5753-0663 ext 2096, Medical 155, Police 158.

LOCATION: On Trziste Street just west of Karmelitska Street in Mala Strana (Lesser Part), Prague. From Karlov Most (Charles Bridge) continue west on to Mosteka Street in Mala Strana. Make a left (south) on Karmelitska and a right (west) on Trziste. Located across from the U.S. Embassy and Schoenborn Palace. **NMC:** Prague, in city limits. **NMI:** Grafenwoehr Community, 185 km southwest.

RESERVATION INFORMATION: Attn: Mr. Karel Rinda, address and telephone as above. Fax: C-(USA) 011-420-2-5753-0920, E-mail: aepca@icom.cz Inquire about availability by phone, fax or e-mail. Major credit card required to make reservations. Actual payment must be in U.S. dollars, travelers checks or personal check. Check in 1400 hours, check out 1000 hours.

(TML) Luxury apartments, living room, bedroom, bath and well-equipped kitchen with appliances. Hair dryer, SATV/VCR, telephone and washer/dryer. Daily housekeeping service on weekdays. No elevator to second floor apartments. Rates: during season (Apr-Sep):

1 person $119, 2 persons $149, 3 or 4 persons $175; off season (Oct-Mar): 1 person $99, 2 persons $119, 3 or 4 persons $149. Special prices for long-term rentals. Free car parking, if needed.

AMENITIES: Privileges at the Embassy Commissary and Snack Bar granted to apartment guests.

TML AVAILABILITY: Year round.

CREDIT CARDS ACCEPTED: None.

TRANSPORTATION: Tram, metro, taxi.

DINING OPPORTUNITIES: Many great restaurants in the city, most with reasonable rates and most require advance reservations.

Great musical concerts, museums, St. Nicholas Cathedral (near U.S. Embassy).

DENMARK
(GREENLAND)

Thule Air Base (DN02R7)
12th SWS/CCF, Unit 82501
Bldg 100, Room 135
APO AE 09704-5000

Note: Base commander's permission is required to visit the base. Entry into the Thule Defense area will be approved for official U.S. Government business only.

MAIN INSTALLATION TELEPHONE NUMBERS: C-011-299-976-585, DSN-314-268-1110. Medical, ext 3409; Security Police, ext 3234/2335.

LOCATION: Thule AB is a remote site, located on the northwest coast of Greenland in the high Arctic, 800 miles south of the North Pole; 800 miles north of the Arctic circle; 2500 miles north of McGuire AFB, NJ; closer to Seattle, WA than New York City, NY by 5 miles. All flights arrive on base; there are no commercial airports. **NMC:** Nuuk, 1200 miles south.

RESERVATION INFORMATION: North Star Inn, Bldg 100, Thule Air Base, Unit 82501, APO AE 09704-5000. **C-011-299-976-585 ext 3276, DSN-314-268-1110 ext 3276,** Fax: C-011-299-976-585 ext 2270, DSN-314-268-1110 ext 2270, 0630-2130 Mon-Fri, 0630-1130 Sat, 1200-1700 Sun. A five-minute walk from the air terminal, base taxi at no charge, ext 2022.

VAQ/VOQ Bldg 100. Kitchenette, ice machine, housekeeping service, washer/dryer. Rates: single $21.50 per night. Duty can make reservations any time; Space-A can make reservations 24 hours in advance.

DV/VIP Bldg 708. O6+. Kitchenette, ice machine, housekeeping service, washer/dryer. Rates: single $35 per night. Duty can make reservations any time; Space-A can make reservations 24 hours in advance.

AMENITIES: Snack Vending Machine and Soft Drink Machine.

TML AVAILABILITY: Good.

CREDIT CARDS ACCEPTED: All except American Express.

TRANSPORTATION: On base shuttle/bus, C-011-299-50-636 ext 3284; On base taxi, C-011-299-50-636 ext 2022.

DINING OPPORTUNITIES: Dundas Dining Hall, ext 3251 is within walking distance; and Top of the World Club, ext 2418 is within driving distance.

FRANCE

Cercle National des Armées (FR01R7)
(National Officers' Club of the Armies)
Vice-President, Director of the Officers' Club
8 Place Saint-Augustin
75008 Paris, France
(Not U.S. Government Lodging)

Note: For Officers Only.

MAIN INSTALLATION TELEPHONE NUMBERS: C-011-33-1-4490-26-26, ask for Reservations or Front Desk. Fax: C-011-33-1-4522-17-75, Telegraph Address: "MILICERCLE-PARIS," Account Number 643-638; Medical 1-4723-8080; Security Police 1-4723-8080.

LOCATION: In Paris Center, from the Arc de Triomphe head east for about 1.8 km on the Avenue de Friedland and eventually the Avenue de Haussmann to a left (north) onto St. Augustin Place. The club is on the immediate right side of St. Augustin Place, across from the Church of St. Augustin. The nearest metro stop is the St. Augustin Place stop on Avenue de Haussmann, just south of the club. *EUSMRA: Page 21.* **NMC:** Paris, in city limits. NMI: Chievres Air Base, BE, 200 km northeast.

LODGING/RESERVATION OFFICE: The French Officers' Club is run by the Cercle National des Armées. It is not U.S. government lodging. The club kindly extends privileges on a space-available basis to officers of Allied Forces, (both active and retired, including their families). The hotel is open to members of the Officers' Club, their wives, children and parents accompanying them. Non-members must pay a temporary membership fee equal to 1/12 of the yearly membership fees of the Cercle National des Armées. The hotel is not open to other relatives or guests of members' families. As a rule the maximum length of stay in the hotel is eight days. After this time, the guest may be requested to leave the room within 24 hours of being notified. Officers must provide written proof stating the relation of family members accompanying them (ID cards/passports are adequate). To secure a room, it is best to write at least 20 days in advance by mail or fax indicating the exact date of arrival, type and cost of room, and length of stay. Call registration prior to mailing for complete information of rooms available. The administration cannot guarantee any specific price reductions or room number. Moreover, reservations made over the phone must be confirmed in writing with deposit (25 percent of total bill). Payment is required upon reply. Reserved rooms are held until 1700 hours unless the occupant has notified the hotel of his/her exact time of arrival in the evening. Those who have reserved rooms which remain unoccupied, and have failed to cancel their reservations at least 24 hours in advance, will be billed accordingly. If a guest plans to end his stay earlier than the date given at the time of reservation, he must notify the club 24 hours in advance. Check in after 1200 hours, check out 1100 hours. No pets.

RATES: Deluxe apartment (bedroom, living room and bath or shower) Fr 950 (U.S.$129.84 at press time); apartment (bedroom, living room and bath or shower) Fr 720 (U.S.$98.40 at press time); double room or two beds with bath or shower Fr 460 (U.S.$62.87 at press time); single room with bath or shower Fr 390 (U.S.$53.30 at press time). Extra bed Fr 100 (U.S.$13.67 at press time); cribs no charge. Continental breakfast served in room Fr 50 (U.S.$6.83 at press time). The above rates were effective 1 January 2001. Rates are subject to change at any time; however, rates are normally changed on the first day of each year. All rooms have TV, direct telephone line, A/C.

RESTAURANTS/CAFE-BAR: The Officers' Club has two restaurants. One is full service, coat and tie required; the other offers more casual dining. The club also has a bar which is open every day except for Sunday night and holidays.

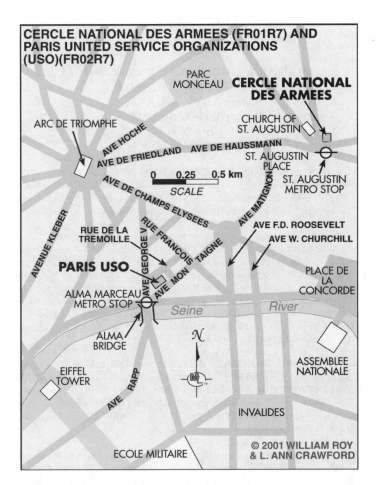

CERCLE NATIONAL DES ARMEES (FR01R7) AND PARIS UNITED SERVICE ORGANIZATIONS (USO)(FR02R7)

PARC MONCEAU

CERCLE NATIONAL DES ARMEES

ARC DE TRIOMPHE

CHURCH OF ST. AUGUSTIN

AVE HOCHE
AVE DE FRIEDLAND   AVE DE HAUSSMANN
ST. AUGUSTIN PLACE
AVE DE CHAMPS ELYSEES
ST. AUGUSTIN METRO STOP

0   0.25   0.5 km
SCALE

AVE MATIGNON

AVENUE KLEBER

RUE DE LA TREMOILLE
RUE FRANCOIS 1ER
AVE GEORGE V

AVE F.D. ROOSEVELT
AVE W. CHURCHILL

PARIS USO

AVE MONTAIGNE

PLACE DE LA CONCORDE

ALMA MARCEAU METRO STOP

ALMA BRIDGE

Seine   *River*

EIFFEL TOWER

AVE RAPP

𝒩

ASSEMBLEE NATIONALE

INVALIDES

ECOLE MILITAIRE

© 2001 WILLIAM ROY & L. ANN CRAWFORD

OTHER CLUB FACILITIES/SERVICES: The Club library is open every day, 1100-1200 hours and 1300-1700 hours, except Saturday, Sunday and holidays; the club also offers a separate reading room. The barbershop is open Monday through Friday 0900-1100 hours and 1200-1700 hours, closed Saturdays, Sundays and holidays. The fencing and exercise room is open daily 1600-2000 hours except Saturdays, Sundays and holidays (three fencing masters - one personal trainer). Theater and show ticket reservation service is available at the Reception Desk. Bulletin board service is available through the Reception Desk. Also, upon presentation of membership cards, members are given discounts on merchandise at numerous retail goods shops in Paris. Please inquire about membership at the Reception Desk.

Editor's Notes: The French Officers' Club has allowed the use of its facilities by American Active Duty and retired military officers, and their families for many years. Officers' widows have also written us about their stay in this beautiful hotel which is so conveniently located in Paris.

Quite a few impressive American "military" clubs can also assist their members in obtaining accommodations. These clubs offering reciprocal benefits are not a part of the U.S. military establishment, however. If you belong to an association or club which serves the military, ask if they can assist you in getting reservations.

There has been some inconsistency in whether or not some of our readers have been able to obtain reservations. The courtesy of extending accommodations has always been on a Space-A basis after the needs of their Armed Forces are met.

At times, our readers have received letters written in French which state that the club is not available to them. And, in that regard, we must say that the French Officers' Club is under no obligation to accept reservations from our United States officers. It is our belief, however, that some have been turned away simply because the hotel was full at the time of the reservation's request. When some of our readers have called us and told us this, we have often replied, "It must be April." Most hotels in Paris are booked solid during the pleasant months of April and May.

We suggest that if you are calling to inquire about reservations, that you call when it is late evening or early morning in Paris (six hours ahead of U.S. Eastern Standard Time). The desk is less busy at that time, and you

will probably find that the person answering the call speaks English and will gladly answer your questions. They may, however, advise you to contact the Reception Manager during the day for final reservations. If you speak French or know someone who does, who can compose a letter or fax for you, a written inquiry or fax might also work well.

If accommodations are not available to you at the time you desire, let the Paris USO (see info below this listing) help you find suitable accommodations at another civilian hotel. You may use the restaurants in the French Officers' Club even if not staying there. The club lounge is also a big $aver on drinks and is very pleasant.

La Fondation Furtado Heine, Villa des Officiers (FR03R7)
121 rue de France, 06000 Nice, France
(Not U.S. Government Lodging)

Note: For Officers Only.

MAIN INSTALLATION TELEPHONE NUMBERS: C-011-33-4-93-37-51-00, Fax: C-011-33-4-93-37-51-01.

LOCATION: This location is unique, situated along the famous Promenade des Anglais, in a 4000 square-meter garden facing the sea. The house was built two years before the French Revolution and was given to the Officers by Lady Furtado in 1895. If you come by car, you can park for a short time by 121 rue de France, retrieve your room keys, and then enter the park to unload your luggage (the gate is closed from 2200 hrs to 0800 hours daily). If you arrive by train, buses number 12 & 23 drop you off by the Villa at the "Groso" bus stop. If you arrive by plane, a shuttle from the airport takes you along the Promenade des Anglais. Get off at "Groso" stop. Parking: The Villa does not provide any parking. Nevertheless, an agreement with L'Elysee Palace, located 20 meters beyond the Villa, allows you to use the paying private parking of this hotel. **NMC:** Nice, in city limits. NMI: Camp Darby, IT, 350 km southeast.

RESERVATION INFORMATION: Address as above. Advance booking office: **C-011-33-4-93-37-51-00, (FR) 04-93-37-51-00,** Fax: C-011-33-4-93-37-51-01, (FR) Fax: 04-93-37-51-01. E-mail: furtado@wanadoo.fr WEB: perso.wanadoo.fr/furtado/ Reservations accepted via telephone 0800-1200 hours, daily.

TML **CLUB/HOTEL:** Thirty-six rooms including a lodge. Rooms are accessible by elevator and have bath or shower, WC, private telephone, TV and hair-dryer. The restaurant and living rooms have A/C. Important renovation work has been completed and you are hosted

La Fondation Furtado Heine, Villa des Officiers, Nice, France

Area Map Nice, France, La Fondation Furtado Heine

in a comfortable and modern building. Rates: Park-Side rooms: Double room, Fr 220-260; Single room, Fr 200, Lodge: twin beds, living room, Fr 330; Town-Side rooms: Double room, Fr 190-200; Extra bed Fr 50. There is a 20 percent discount on room prices in January and December, for a 10-day or more stay; Fr 10 per day will be added to room price for any stay less than one week. Breakfast, room delivered, Fr 25. Restaurant (evening only), Unique menu: Fr 60. **The club is allowed to receive only French Officers or Foreign Officers when they have a connection with the French Army (Armed Forces).** The ability to speak and/or write a little French is a plus.

TML AVAILABILITY: Good except holidays.

CREDIT CARDS ACCEPTED: Visa and MasterCard.

TRANSPORTATION: City bus, taxis, trains.

DINING OPPORTUNITIES: At the club, as well as many fine restaurants in Nice.

Beachfront, walking, jogging, swimming and great scenery. In the city of Nice.

United Service Organizations (USO)-Paris (FR02R7)
75008 PARIS USO
PSC 116
APO AE 09777-5000

MAIN INSTALLATION TELEPHONE NUMBERS: C-011-33-1-40-70-99-68, Fax: C-011-33-1-40-70-99-53. 0900-1700 hours Mon-Sat.

LOCATION: From the Arc de Triomphe head southeast on Ave des Champs Elysees for approximately 0.4 km to a right (south) onto Ave George V. Continue south on Ave George V for about 0.5 km to a left (northeast) onto Rue de la Tremoille. The USO is on right (southeast) side of the road at 20 Rue de la Tremoille. The nearest metro stop is the Alma Marceau metro stop at the corner of Ave George V and Ave Montaigne. *EUSMRA: Page 21.* **NMC:** Paris, in city limits. NMI: Chievres Air Base, BE, 200 km northeast.

SERVICES/FACILITIES: The Paris USO provides the following facilities/services: **Hotel Reservations,** Night Club Reservations, APO Letter Drop, Free Coffee in Lounge, Storage Lockers, Discount Tours, Souvenir Shop, Directions for Shopping/Free Fashion Shows and more!

Visit Military Living online at

www.militaryliving.com

GERMANY

Ansbach Community (DE60R7)
235th Base Support Battalion
Attn: AETV-WG-AJ-A
Katterbach Bldg 5817-A
Unit 28614
APO AE 09177-5000

MAIN INSTALLATION TELEPHONE NUMBERS: C-(USA) 011-49-981-183-113 (Ansbach), C-(USA) 011-49-9802-832-1110 (Katterbach), C-(DE) 0981-183-1110, 09802-832-1110, DSN-314-468-1110 (Ansbach), DSN-314-467-1110 (Katterbach). Locator DSN-314-467-2541/542.

LOCATION: From east-west Nuremberg-Heidelberg Autobahn 6 (E50), use exit 52 (Ansbach) north on Route 13 approximately 5.5 km through Ansbach to intersection with Route 14 (Nuremberger Strasse). Or use Autobahn exit 50 (Aurach) northeast on Route 14 approximately 1.9 km to intersection with Route 13. From intersection, continue east on Route 14 (Nuremberger Strasse) for approximately 5 km to entrances to Katterbach and Bismarck Kasernes. Franconian Inn is in Bldg 5908 at northeast side of Bismark Kaserne. *EUSMRA: Page 35 (C-1), page 40.* **NMC:** Nuremburg, 42 km northeast.

RESERVATION INFORMATION: Katterbach Office, Unit 28614, APO AE 09177-5000. **C-(USA) 011-49-9802-83-2812, (DE) 09802-83-1700, DSN-314-467-2812 or DSN-314-468-1700,** Fax: C-(USA) 011-49-9802-83-1707, Mon-Fri 0600-2200 hours, Sat, Sun and holidays 0900-1700. E-mail: franconian@XS7.mwr.army.mil Check in 1300 hours, check out 1000 hours, weekends 1200.

TLF **Franconian Inn, Bismarck Kaserne.** Bldg 5908. Single rooms, private bath, shared kitchenette (27); family rooms, living room, private bath, private kitchenette (5). Stove, refrigerator, microwave, toaster, coffee maker, utensils, TV/VCR, cribs, cots, housekeeping service, washer/dryer, soft drink/snack vending. Rates: first person $38, second person $15, each additional person $9. PCS in 60 days, PCS out 45 days, TDY 30 days. Space-A two weeks in advance.

DV/VIP 235th BSB, DSN-314-468-1700. O6+. Retirees Space-A.

TML AVAILABILITY: Good. Best in Feb-Apr, and Sep-Oct.

CREDIT CARDS ACCEPTED: Visa, MasterCard and American Express.

TRANSPORTATION: On base shuttle/bus; Off base taxi, 0981-5005.

DINING OPPORTUNITIES: Numerous restaurants are within driving distance in the Ansbach area.

Internationally famous for its yearly "Bach Week Ansbach," this Franconian capital also offers gourmet specialties, try "Schlotengeli," or "Pressack" with a cool Ansbach beer. Visit Orangerie Park at the "Hofgarten" afterwards.

Babenhausen Sub-Community (DE90R7)
Commander Area Support Team, CMR-462
APO AE 09089-5000

MAIN INSTALLATION TELEPHONE NUMBERS: C-(USA) 011-49-6073-38-113, (DE) 06073-38-113, DSN-314-348-1110. Locator C-6075-38-655.

LOCATION: Located between Darmstadt and Aschaffenburg. From Autobahn 3 (E42) use exit 57 (Stockstadt/Aschaffenburg West) south in the direction of Stockstadt on Route 469 approximately 3.1 km to Route 26. Go west on Route 26 approximately 6 km to Babenhausen Kaserne on southeast side of Babenhausen. Main gate is on south side of Route 26 (Aschaffenburger Strasse). Or, from Darmstadt, follow Route 26 northeast for approximately 25 km through Babenhausen to Babenhausen Kaserne. *EUSMRA: Page 32 (A-2), page 42.* **NMC:** Darmstadt, approximately 16 km southwest.

RESERVATION INFORMATION: Railgunner's Arms Guesthouse, Babenhausen Kaserne, Bldg 4502, APO AE 09089-5000. **C-(USA) 011-49-6073-38-655, (DE) 06073-72-880, DSN-314-348-3655,** E-mail: plenzn@233bsb.darmstadt.army.mil 0800-1700 hours Mon-Fri. Mail can be sent to the Patriot Inn Guesthouse. Check in at lodging office 0800-1700 hours, check out 1100 hours. After hours SDO, Bldg 4508. Government civilian employee billeting.

(Army Lodging) Guesthouse. Bldg 4502. Bedroom, hall bath (17); suites, private bath (2). Refrigerator, utensils (loan-closet kitchen packages), TV/VCR, clock radio, housekeeping service, washer/dryer, iron/ironing board, cribs, cots, ice machine. Modern building, renovated. Rates: sponsor $30, additional adult $10, children under 16 $5. PCS in/out have priority, all categories may make reservations.

(DV/VIP) Protocol Office, C-(USA) 011-49-6073-38-621. O1+/WO1. Retirees and lower ranks Space-A.

TML AVAILABILITY: Good.

CREDIT CARDS ACCEPTED: Visa, MasterCard and American Express.

TRANSPORTATION: On base shuttle/bus to Darmstadt and Aschaffenburg posts; Car Rental, GMT C-011-49-6151-60533; Off base taxi, C-011-49-6073-2500.

DINING OPPORTUNITIES: Burger King, C-011-49-6073-5873; Anthony's Pizza, C-011-49-6073-3433 and Baskin Robbins, C-011-49-6073-3433 are within walking distance. Pizzeria Little Italy, C-011-49-6073-4243; Chinese Restaurant-Lotos, C-011-49-6073-2461 and Taormina da Carmelo, C-011-49-6073-3252 are within driving distance.

Babenhausen traces its history to year 1236, and possibly even earlier. A walled city with castle, it was largely destroyed during the 30 Years War and Plague. The late 19th century crossing of two railway lines revitalized the town, and today it has a population of more than 15,000.

Bad Aibling Station (DE91R7)
Commander 407, HOC 718 MI
APO AE 09098-5000
Scheduled to close 30 September 2002

MAIN INSTALLATION TELEPHONE NUMBERS: C-(USA) 011-49-8061-38-3000, (DE) 08061-38-3000, DSN-314-441-1110. Locator DSN-314-441-3893.

LOCATION: From Munchen-Salzburg Autobahn 8 (E52), take exit 100 (Bad Aibling) north on secondary road 2089 (unmarked) approximately 3.2 km to intersection with Rosenheimer Strasse (secondary road 2078), then northwest 1 km to center of Bad Aibling. Follow signs "To Munchen" on Route 2078, which becomes Munchner Strasse approximately 0.9 km to intersection with Ebersberger Strasse. Turn right (northwest) on Ebersberger Strasse and drive approximately 1.7 km directly to Main Gate. *EUSMRA: Page 39 (A-2), page 42.* **NMC:** Munich, 49 km west.

RESERVATION INFORMATION: MWR Customer Service Center, Bldg 352, APO AE 09098-5000. **C-(USA) 011-49-8061-38-5778/3445, (DE) 08061-38-5778, DSN-314-441-3893,** Fax: C-(USA) 011-49-8061-38-5731, 0700-1700 hours Mon-Fri, 0800-1600 hours Sat-Sun. Duty, Reservists and NG on orders can make reservations, others Space-A. Check in 1400-2100 hours, check out 1000 hours. Government civilian employee billeting.

(TML) Visitors Quarters. Bldgs 359, 361. Bedroom, living room, private bath (24); Family suites, living room, private bath (2). Refrigerator, microwave, TV/VCR, clock radio, housekeeping service,

iron/ironing board. Community kitchen and laundry facility located in each building. Older structure. Rates: standard room $55.00, each extra adult $17.00 (breakfast voucher included). Children under 16 may stay for free.

(DV/VIP) Chief of Staff, Bldg 302, C-011-49-8061-38-5745, DSN-314-441-3827. O6+/GS15+. Visitors Quarters. Bldgs 359, 361. VIP suites (2). Refrigerator, microwave, TV/VCR, clock radio, housekeeping service, iron/ironing board. Community kitchen and laundry facility located in each building. Older structure. Rates: $75.00, each additional guest $17.00, with commander approval 18 years old and up. Children under 16 free.

TML AVAILABILITY: Very good. Best, Dec-Jan. Difficult, Feb-Nov.

CREDIT CARDS ACCEPTED: Visa and Mastercard.

TRANSPORTATION: None available.

DINING OPPORTUNITIES: Numerous restaurants are within driving distance.

Bad Aibling is a picturesque health resort near the Alpine mountains, excellent skiing opportunities are 20 minutes away in Austria. This location is only 50 miles from Salzburg on the crossroad to Italy and only 30 miles from historic Munich.

Bamberg Comunity (DE34R7)
279th Base Support Battalion
Bldg 7029, Unit 27535
APO AE 09139-5000

MAIN INSTALLATION TELEPHONE NUMBERS: C-(USA) 011-49-951-300-1110, (DE) 0951-300-1110, DSN-314-469-1110. Locator DSN-314-469-7777 (Schweinfurt).

LOCATION: Warner Barracks is located on the east side of Bamberg. From Autobahn 70 (E48), take exit 17 (Bamberg) south on Autobahn 73 past exit 3 to the Zollner Strasse exit. Go west on Zollner Strasse 1 km to Warner Barracks gate, on south side of street. *EUSMRA: Page 34 (C-2), page 45.* **NMC:** Nuremberg, approximately 50 km southeast. **NMI:** Wuerzburg, 81 km west.

RESERVATION INFORMATION: Bamberg Inn, Warner Barracks Kaserne, Guesthouse Office, Bldg 7678, APO AE 09139-5000. **C-(USA) 011-49-951-300-1700, (DE) 0951-300-1700, DSN-314-469-1700/8604,** Fax: C-(USA) 011-49-951-37957, E-mail: zamoraa@cmtymail.98asg.army.mil 0800-1730 hours Mon-Fri, 1030-1430 Sat-Sun. Other hours, Military Police, Bldg 7108. Located near Warner Club, Bldg 7070, across from Gates 3 and 8. WEB: 144.170.180.1 (click on Army Lodging), and bamberg.army.mil.com PCS, TDY and Space-A may make reservations. Check in at facility 1400 hours, check out 1000 hours. Government civilian employee billeting. *Bamberg Inn was winner of Lodging Operation of the Year Award in 1999.*

(Army Lodging) Bamberg Inn, Warner Barracks Kaserne. Bldg 7678, annex Bldg 7070, second floor of Warner Club, Zollnerstrasse. Bedrooms, shared baths (30). Refrigerator, coffee maker, TV/VCR, clock radio, housekeeping service (Mon-Fri), iron/ironing board, cribs, rollaways, vending room with microwaves, laundry facility. Older structure, renovated. Rates: standard, first person $40-$45, each additional person $5. No pets.

(DV/VIP) Deputy Community Commander, (USA) 011-49-951-300-1700. VIP Mini suites, private bath (O4+) (3); DV/VIP Suite (O6+) (2). Refrigerator, coffee maker, TV/VCR, clock radio, housekeeping service (Mon-Fri), iron/ironing board, cribs, rollaways, vending room with microwaves, laundry facility. Older structure, renovated. Rates: mini suites, first person $55-$60, each additional person $10; suite, first person $70-$85, each additional person $15. No pets.

AMENITIES: Snack and Soft Drink Vending Machine.

TML AVAILABILITY: Limited.

CREDIT CARDS ACCEPTED: Visa, MasterCard and American Express.

TRANSPORTATION: Off base shuttle/bus; Car Rental: C-0951-36501; Off base taxi, C-0951-15015.

DINING OPPORTUNITIES: Akropolis, C-0951-46234; M&M Diner, C-0951-35031; and Sub Shop, C-0951-37462/37996 are within walking distance. Dynasty, C-0951-131155; Rotisserie, C-0951-33201; and Volpino, C-0951-33718 are within driving distance.

Bamberg's streets are a Gothic tapestry, wander them and you'll find St. Michaels Church, the Old Town Hall, and a Baroque castle, the Concordia. Don't miss Little Venice.

Baumholder Comunity (DE03R7)
22nd BSB
Bldg 8746, Second Floor
Unit 23746, Box 2
APO AE 09034-5000

MAIN INSTALLATION TELEPHONE NUMBERS: C-(USA) 011-49-6783-6-1110, (DE) 06783-6-1110, DSN-314-485-1110. Locator 485-6446.

LOCATION: From Kaiserslautern, take Autobahn 6 (E50) west to exit 12, then take Autobahn 62 northwest toward Trier to north at exit 5 (Friesen). Continue north on this secondary road toward Baumholder for approximately 9 km to signs indicating Baumholder. For the Lagerhof Inn continue north on Berschweiler Strasse, past the Rolling Hills Golf Course and the Wetzel Housing Area on the left side of the street, to a left on Avenue B. Continue north on Avenue B for approximately 0.7 km to a right on Ivy Strasse. Continue straight to Lagerhof Inn located in Bldg 8076. *EUSMRA: Page 29 (B-3), page 46.* **NMC:** Kaiserslautern, 56 km southeast.

RESERVATION INFORMATION: Lagerhof Inn, Ivy Street, Bldg 8076, APO AE 09034-5000. **C-(USA) 011-49-6783-999300, (DE) 06783-999300, DSN-314-485-1700/7433,** Fax: C-(USA) 011-49-6783-999-3455, 0700-2200 hours Mon-Fri, 1000-1800 hours Sat-Sun, 1000-1600 hours Holidays, C ext 1700. Duty can make reservations; others Space-A. Check in 1300-2200 hours, check out 1100 hours. Government civilian employee billeting.

Army Lodging **Lagerhof Transient Billeting.** Bldg 8076. Bedroom, private bath (25); two-bedroom mini suite, private bath (3); Two room with private bath, kitchenette (15), two of these units are handicap accessible. DVQ houses: Doll House, two-bedroom, private bath (1); Chalet, one-bedroom, bath and kitchen (1). Community kitchen, refrigerator, limited utensils, TV in room and lounge, housekeeping service, laundry facility, cribs, cots, soft drink and snack vending machines. Older structure. Rates : $42-$69, each additional person $10. *Pets allowed,* $3 each daily, and one-time fumigation fee of $50.

DV/VIP Commander, C-(USA) 011-49-6783-6-6252/1500. O6/GS12+.

TML AVAILABILITY: Very good.

CREDIT CARDS ACCEPTED: Visa, MasterCard and American Express.

TRANSPORTATION: On base shuttle/bus, C-6783-6-1800/7273, DSN-485-1800/7273; On base taxi, C-6783-2133/2123, DSN-485-6100.

DINING OPPORTUNITIES: Bowling Alley, C-6783-6-6569, DSN-485-6569.

Visit nearby Idar Oberstein for precious gems and stones, Trier's Roman ruins, the castles and vineyards of the Mosel Valley.

Cassels House (DE15R7)
24 Trenchard Road
BSPO 40, Germany
(Not U.S. Government Lodging)

MAIN INSTALLATION TELEPHONE NUMBERS: C-011-49-2161-47-4234. Security Police ext 2222.

LOCATION: Approximately 40 km west of Dusseldorf on Route 52. Use the Monchen Gladbach exit. Follow signs south to Rheindahlem and JHQ (British HQ for their forces in Germany). JHQ is about 5 km before Rheindahlem.

RESERVATION INFORMATION: C-011-49-2161-47-4234, Fax: C-011-49-2161-47-3828, 24 hours daily. Eligibility: Open to Allied Forces I.D. Card holders (Active, Retired, Reserves). Check in after 1400 hours, check out 1000 hours.

TML: Double rooms with full board. CATV, coffee maker, housekeeping service, washer/dryer. Rates: single DM 67 (U.S.$30.40 at press time), double DM 53.5 (U.S.$24.29 at press time). Lodging is available without board, as well.

AMENITIES: Bar and lounge.

TML AVAILABILITY: Difficult during summer months.

CREDIT CARDS ACCEPTED: None.

TRANSPORTATION: Off base taxi services.

DINING OPPORTUNITIES: Dining room, local restaurants within walking and driving distance.

Chiemsee AFRC (DE08R7)
Unit 24604
APO AE 09098-5000

MAIN INSTALLATION TELEPHONE NUMBERS: Lake Hotel Front Desk C-(USA) 011-49-8051-8030. Please contact AFRC Europe's Vacation Planning Center to make reservations. (See Registration Information below for phone numbers.) E-mail: vacations@afrc.garmischarmy.mil WEB: www.AFRCEurope.com Locator DSN-314-440-355.

LOCATION: Located directly off Munich-Salzburg Autobahn 8 (E52). Take Autobahn 8 (E52) in direction of Salzburg, Austria. Take exit 107 (Felden). At traffic circle turn right and cross over Autobahn. Follow road, keeping right, to Lake Hotel (on northwest side of Autobahn). At southwest end of parking lot there is an underpass to Park Hotel and AFRC Campground on southeast side of Autobahn. Or, from Felden exit, take fourth right turn at traffic circle and follow road northeast to Park Hotel and AFRC Campground. *EUSMRA: Page 39 (B-2), page 50.* **NMC:** Munich, approximately 82 km northwest.

RESERVATION INFORMATION: Reservations accepted up to 365 days in advance with credit card number. The vacation planning center is open Mon-Fri 0700-1900 Central European Time (CET), six hours ahead of Eastern Standard Time (EST). Write to: AFRC Europe, Attn: Vacation Planning Center, Unit 24501, APO AE 09053-5000, or call **C-(USA) 011-49-8821-72981, (DE) 08821-72981, DSN-314-440-2575,** Fax: C-(USA) 011-49-8821-3942, (DE) 08821-3942. E-mail: vacation@afrc.garmisch.army.mil WEB: www.AFRCEurope.com

TML AFRC's Chiemsee Resort has two hotels and a full service campground.

ELIGIBILITY: Active Duty, retired, Reservists, DoD civilians serving in the European theater. See Garmisch listing for details.

FACILITIES: The POiNT Fitness Center, video game room, gift shop, tours office, Windjammer Bar and Lounge, recreational activity equipment rental (skis, snowboards, canoes, sailboats, in-line skates, etc.), campground, laundromat, playground, picnic area, conference/meeting room space, shoppette. New 'European Escapes' tours for retirees in summer.

RATES: Park Hotel, double occupancy, E1-E5 $57; E6-O3 and retired $67; O4-06 $72; 07+ $82. Lake Hotel, double, E1-E5 $61; E6-O3 $71; O4-O6 $76, O7+ $86. Small suite, all ranks, $105. Large suite, all ranks $115. Children 15 and under stay free in parent's room on existing bed space, with crib $3 daily, cot $6 daily. For more than two adults in one room, add $9 per adult per night. Some rooms handicap accessible. Prices effective 1 October 1999, but are subject to change.

TML AVAILABILITY: Good except Jun-Aug and Christmas/New Year periods.

CREDIT CARDS ACCEPTED: Visa, MasterCard, American Express, Discover.

TRANSPORTATION: Off base taxi: Winkler Taxi, C-011-49-8051-7213. Closest train station in Bernau approx. 2 km away.

DINING OPPORTUNITIES: The Lake Hotel Dining Room offers full-service dining each evening from 1730-2100. Reggie's Express cafeteria is open daily serving breakfast and lunch. In the nearby towns of Bernau and Prien, a wide variety of restaurants are available. Restaurants include: Alter Wirt, C-011-49-8051-89011; Gasthof Chiemsee, C-011-49-8051-7245; Kampen Wand, C-011-49-8051-89404 are within driving distance. Reggie's Express is within walking distance.

AFRC Chiemsee is situated on the shores of Bavaria's largest lake, Chiemsee. Enjoy water sports such as canoeing, paddleboats, sailing and windsurfing. At the nearby Chiemgauer Alps you can hike, hang glide and take in the panoramic scenery.

Darmstadt Community (DE37R7)
233rd Base Support Battalion
CFK, Bldg 4008
CMR 431
APO AE 09175-5000

MAIN INSTALLATION TELEPHONE NUMBERS: C-(USA) 011-49-6151-69-1110 or 011-49-6151-96430, (DE) 06151-69-1110, or 06151-96430, DSN-314-348-1110. Locator DSN-314-348-6229.

LOCATION: From Autobahn 5 North or South take exit 26 (Darmstadt) east onto Autobahn 672 which becomes Route 26 (Rhein Strasse). Continue east on Route 26 for approximately 4.5 km to south on Route 3 (Neckar Strasse/Heidelberger Land Strasse), then continue straight on Route 3 south for approximately 2.2 km to east on Landskron Strasse. Proceed on Landskron Strasse to a right onto Ludwigshoh Strasse and straight to the entrance to Cambrai Fritsch Kaserne. Cambrai Fritsch Kaserne PX is located in southwest corner of kaserne in Bldg 4033. For Jefferson Village continue south through Cambrai Fritsch Kaserne to village or return to Heidelberger Land Strasse and travel south for approximately 1 km to a left onto Cooper Strasse and straight to Jefferson Village entrance on right (south) side of street. The Patriot Inn is located in the southeast corner of Jefferson Village in Bldg 4091. It is the building with the red and white striped awning. *EUSMRA: Page 30 (C-4), page 51.* **NMC:** Darmstadt, 1.6 km north.

RESERVATION INFORMATION: Patriot Inn, Jefferson Village, CMR 431, Bldg 4091, Cambrai-Fritsch Kaserne, APO AE 09175-5000. **C-(USA) 011-49-6151-69-1700/7520 or C-011-49-6151-96430, DSN-314-348-1700/7520, Fax: C-(USA) 011-49-6151-964336, (DE) 06151-964336,** E-mail: plenzn@emtymail.26asg.army.mil 0730-2400 hours Mon-Fri, 1400-2200 Sat. Check in 1300 hours, check out 1100 hours. Call before 1800 hours for late check-in. Government civilian employee billeting.

Army Lodging **Patriot Inn**, Jefferson Village. Bldg 4091, Jefferson Village. Single rooms, shared bath (20); suites, private bath (35). Community kitchen, refrigerator, utensils, TV, housekeeping service, cribs, cots, lending closet, washer/dryer, ice machine. Older structure, remodeled. Rates: shared bath $40, suites $50

per night, each additional person $10, children under 16, $7. *Pets allowed;* daily pet fee $6 per night and fumigation $50/60. Duty and DoD civilians on orders can make reservations 30 days in advance. Space-A can make reservations 3 days in advance only. *New complimentary breakfast served Mon-Sat.*

DV/VIP VIP suites (2). Rates: single $60, each additional person $10.

TML AVAILABILITY: Good, Jan-Apr. Difficult, May-Dec.

CREDIT CARDS ACCEPTED: Visa, MasterCard and American Express.

TRANSPORTATION: On base shuttle/bus, C-011-49-6151-69-7403/6463; Car Rental: C-011-49-6151-69-6277 or Sixt Budget, C-011-49-6151-64200; Off base taxi, C-011-49-6151-19410. Off base streetcar also available.

DINING OPPORTUNITIES: Rod & Gun Club, C-011-49-6151-69-6402, recently moved to Stars and Stripes Compound, Griesheim; Happy Garden, C-011-49-6151-62406; and Haller Ranch, C-011-49-6151-56224 are within driving distance.

Downtown Darmstadt has a great "walkplatz" for shopping. Hike to the Odenwald from the railroad station, or tour the Mathildenhöhe, and the Kranichstein hunting palace on the city's outskirts. See the Russian Chapel built by Czar Nicholas II.

Friedberg Community (DE68R7)
Area Support Team
Bldg 3608, Unit 21105
APO AE 09074-5000

MAIN INSTALLATION TELEPHONE NUMBERS: C-(USA) 011-49-6031-81-1110, DSN-314-324-1110. Locator C-011-49-6031-81-3528/3465.

LOCATION: Approximately 33 km northeast of Frankfurt and 8.3 km east of the Frankfurt-Giessen Autobahn 5 (E451). From north or south on Autobahn 5 (E451), take exit 16 (Friedberg), then northeast on Route 455 (Homburger Strasse) 8 km to Route 3 (Frankfurter Strasse), then south on Route 3 (Frankfurter Strasse) approximately 0.7 km to Main Gate of Ray Barracks on east side of street. *EUSMRA: Page 30 (C-2), page 53.* **NMC:** Frankfurt, 33 km southeast.

RESERVATION INFORMATION: Friedberg Inn, Ray Barracks, Bldg 3643, APO AE 09074-5000. **C-(USA) 011-49-6031-73380, or C-011-49-6031-81-1700, DSN-314-324-1700,** Fax: C-(USA) 011-49-6031-7338333, E-mail: 284bsb.giessen.army.mil Reservations not accepted for leisure travelers, Space-A basis only.

Army Lodging Friedberg Guesthouse, Ray Barracks. Bldg 3643. Bedroom, private bath (3); bedroom, shared bath (24). Rates: $46 for room with private bath; $36 for room with shared bath; $15 each additional person.

DV/VIP Friedberg Inn, Ray Barracks. Bldg 3643. C-011-49-6031-81-3528/3465/3409. Bedroom (1). Rates: $55 for primary occupant, $15 each additional person.

TML AVAILABILITY: Good, Feb-May. Difficult, Jun-Jan.

CREDIT CARDS ACCEPTED: Visa, MasterCard and American Express.

TRANSPORTATION: Car Rental: Budget, C-011-49-6031-18709.

DINING OPPORTUNITIES: Anthony's Pizza, Burger King and Robin Hood are within walking distance. Mandarin Chinese Restaurant and Villa Calabria Italian Restaurant are within driving distance.

Visit the many historic structures, rich in medieval architecture. One of these is the Judische Bad which extends some 25 meters underground. Jewish women used the Bad, or bath, for

centuries. It is one of only four existing Hebrew baths in all of Germany.

Garmisch AFRC (DE10R7)
Vacation Planning Center
Unit 24501
APO AE 09053-5000

MAIN INSTALLATION TELEPHONE NUMBERS: Please contact AFRC Europe's Vacation Planning Center to make reservations. C-(USA) 011-49-8821-72981, (DE) 08821-72981, DSN-314-440-2575. E-mail: vacation@afrc.garmisch.army.mil WEB: www.afrceurope.com Medical 08821-2222; Security Police 08821-750-801.

LOCATION: From Munich take Autobahn 95 (E533) south approximately 75 km to the town of Oberau, where the Autobahn 95 ends and becomes Route 2. Continue on Route 2 south for approximately 15 km to the town of Farchant. From Farchant continue south on Route 2 to Partenkirchen or take Route 23 south, which continues into Garmisch. From northern Italy, east or west on Italian Autostrada 4 (E70) take Monte Balda exit (west of Verona) onto Italian Autostrada 22 (E45) north. Continue north on Autostrada 22 (which becomes Austrian Autobahn 13) through the Brenner Pass approximately 220 km to Innsbruck, Austria. At Innsbruck, take exit 3 west onto Austrian Autobahn 12 for 12 km to exit 87 (Zirl Ost). Take exit 87 north onto Austrian Route 177 (E533) (which becomes German Route 2). Stay on Route 2 north and west approximately 48 km directly to Garmish-Partenkirchen. For the Von Steuben Hotel from Farchant take Route 2 (E533) (Haupt Strasse) south for approximately 3 km to the hotel on the right side of the street. For the Patton Hotel from Farchant take Route 23 (Burg Strasse). Continue south on Burg Strasse until it changes into Promenade Strasse. Promenade Strasse (bear right) will then change into Zugspitz Strasse. Continue on Zugspitz Strasse for approximately 1 km until you pass an Esso Station on the right, then make the next left onto Osterfelder Strasse. The Patton Hotel is second building on right side of street. For the AFRC Travel Camp, follow the instructions to Patton Hotel, but stay on Zugspitz Strasse and continue until you reach Maximillian Strasse and turn right. Go over the bridge across Loisach River and enter the base. Turn left and follow the road taking the first right. The Travel Camp Store and check-in desk is just past the Trattoria da Marco. For the Haus Flora from the Patton Hotel take a right onto Zugspitze Strasse and continue straight for approximately 1 km to a left onto Promenade Strasse. Get in far left lane then take left onto Loisach Strasse then immediate right onto Fursten Strasse. Continue straight for approximately 0.3 km to left onto Lazarett Strasse, then continue to "T" intersection. You can go either left or right to entrances on either side of complex. *EUSMRA: Page 54.*

DESCRIPTION OF AREA: Located at the foot of the Zugspitze, Germany's highest mountain. With unforgettable Alpine scenery and a wide variety of sports activities at AFRC vacation area, Garmisch is one of the most popular Alpine resorts in Germany. AFRC offers two hotels and a modern travel camp with accommodations for up to 540 guests. A full range of support facilities are available.

RESERVATION INFORMATION: Reservations accepted up to 365 days in advance with credit card number. The Vacation Planning Center is open Mon-Fri 0700-1900 Central European Time (CET), six hours ahead of Eastern Standard Time (EST) Write to: AFRC Resorts in Europe, Attn: Vacation Planning Center, Unit 24501, APO AE 09053-5000 or contact **C-(USA) 011-49-8821-72981, (DE) 08821-72981, DSN-314-440-2575,** Fax: C-(USA) 011-49-8821-3942, (DE) C-08821-3942. E-mail: vacation@afrc.garmisch.army.mil WEB: www.afrceurope.com

TML General Patton Hotel, General Von Steuben Hotel and Haus Flora guesthouse. Room Rates: Double with bath E1-E5 $61, E6-O3, NF1-NF3, GS-10 and below, retired $71, O4-O6, NF4+, GS-11+ $76, O7+, NATO Forces and SES $86. Suites, large $115, small $105. Haus Flora Suites $125. Children 15 and under free in parent's room on existing bed space, add $3 for cribs daily, $6 for cots. More than two adult occupants, add $9 to double rate. Group rates available on request. Recreation prices in May. Special rates may be available during non-peak seasons: April and November. No pets.

An all-new 330-room AFRC hotel on Garmisch's Sheridan Barracks is under construction and is scheduled for completion as early as April 2004. This hotel will replace the two AFRC hotels in Garmisch and the two AFRC hotels in Chiemsee, which will be returned to the German goverment.

Cabins **Garmisch Travel Camp.** Vacation Cabins: Deluxe with master bedroom w/ double bed, loft with four single beds and full bathroom in cabin (4). Kitchenettes, microwave, linens, living room with TV/VCR. Housekeeping service not provided during stay. Maximum occupancy 6. Seven-day minimum. Rates: $945/week. Rustic, one double bed, one bunk bed and two single beds in loft (11). Living room with TV/VCR, refrigerator, and microwave. No indoor plumbing, but have use of the bathhouses (equipped with toilet, shower, and laundry area). Linens provided. Maximum occupancy 6 (4 adults max). Seven-day stay minimum. Rates: $399/week. Check in 1300 hours on Saturday, check out 1000 hours on Saturday. All cabins require advance deposit at time of booking, and all cancellations must be made 30 days prior to arrival date to avoid penalty.

SEASON OF OPERATION: Year round.

ELIGIBILITY: In general: U.S. military forces and family members assigned in the USEUCOM area (permanently or temporarily); reserve in training in Europe; U.S. DoD civilian employees working full time in USEUCOM and family members residing with them (Red Cross, USO, certain U.S. embassy personnel; U.S. citizen consultant and technical representatives; personnel with USAREUR ID Card AE Form 600-700); retired U.S. military personnel residing in or visiting Europe (Army, Navy, Marines and Air Force); PHS/NOAA not authorized; EUCOM Coast Guard; British Forces of the Rhein/Canadian Forces with family members residing with them stationed in Germany; certain NATO forces/liaison personnel authorized to purchase in commissary/exchange; those on official duty to AFRC or NATO/SHAPE School; unaccompanied widow(ers), and dependents retired with appropriate ID. Certain authorized guests, accompanied.

FACILITIES: Hausberg Recreation Lodge, winter and summer recreation equipment rental, convenience store, gift shops, tours office, conference/meeting center, bars and lounges, nine-hole golf course and clubhouse, laundromat, fitness center, game room, APO, Community Bank, beauty/barber shop, commissary, chapel, library, sports shop, Bavarian Shop, class VI (Package Store), Exchange, AAFES Bookmark, child care center, playground, hotel restaurants and bars, ski lodge, TV room and much more. *(Note: No U.S. medical support in Garmisch.)*

TML AVAILABILITY: Good except Jun-Aug and Christmas/New Year periods.

CREDIT CARDS ACCEPTED: Visa, MasterCard, American Express, Discover.

TRANSPORTATION: City bus; Car Rental: Sixt, C-011-49-8821-947825; Off base taxi: Bahnhofplatz C-011-49-8821-0171; Marienplatz, C-011-49-8821-2408/2409.

DINING OPPORTUNITIES: Both the Von Steuben and Patton Hotels serve breakfast and dinner. Bar food and snacks are available in the evenings in the bars and lounges. In the winter, the Hausberg Lodge serves lunch and in the summer the golf course clubhouse serves lunch. The town of Garmisch-Partenkirchen has a wide variety of restaurants.

Garmisch Community (DE62R7)
Commander Area Support Team
Unit 24515
APO AE 09053-5000

MAIN INSTALLATION TELEPHONE NUMBERS: C-(USA) 011-49-8821-750-113, DSN-314-440-1110. Locator DSN-314-440-7176.

LOCATION: Refer to Garmisch AFRC directions. Loisach Inn is across from the entrance to AFRC Travel Camp. *EUSMRA: Page 54.* **NMC:** Munich, 105 km northeast.

RESERVATION INFORMATION: Loisach Inn, Bldg 104, Room 334, Unit 24515, APO AE 09053-5000. **C-(USA) 011-49-8821-53396/750873, DSN-314-440-2876,** Fax: C-(USA) 011-49-8821-53401, 0630-2230 hours Mon-Fri, 0800-1700 hours Sat-Sun and holidays. E-mail: thomas. staples@cmtymail.6asg.army.mil Duty can make reservations thirty days in advance; PCS sixty days; all others Space-A seven days. **Space-A reservations can be bumped by official duty.** Check in at lodging office 1300-2230 hours Mon-Fri, 1300-1700 hours Sat-Sun, German and American holidays and after hours come to office at Sheridan Barracks. Check out 1000 hours, late check out request DSN-314-440-2873/76.

(**Army Lodging**) Loisach Inn. Bedroom, private bath (8); suite, private bath (4). Refrigerator, microwave, TV/VCR, housekeeping service, laundry facility, cribs ($4), cots ($4), ice machine. Rates: Duty, room, first person $45; suite, first person $60; others, room, first person $50; suite $65. each additional person $4. Maximum $58 per room; $81 suite. Maximum three per unit, four to five per suite. No pets

TML AVAILABILITY: Good, Mar-Apr and Sep-Oct (except during Oktoberfest). Difficult, May-Aug and Nov-Feb.

CREDIT CARDS ACCEPTED: Visa, MasterCard and American Express.

TRANSPORTATION: Off base bus; Off base taxi: Bahnhofplatz, C-011-49-8821-759495; Marienplatz, C-011-49-8821-2408/2409; Kurpark, C-011-49-8821-2343.

DINING OPPORTUNITIES: Rheinischerhof, C-011-49-8821-72024; Trattoria Da Marco, C-011-49-8821-59209; and U.S. Kantine, C-011-49-8821-750465 are within walking distance. AFRC Patton Hotel, C-011-49-8821-750695; La Lepanto, C-011-49-8821-57486; and Princess Garden, C-011-49-8821-73755 are within driving distance.

Geilenkirchen NATO Air Base (DE46R7)
470 Air Base Squadron/Family Support Center
APO AE 09104-5000

MAIN INSTALLATION TELEPHONE NUMBERS: C-011-49-2451-63-113, DSN-314-455-1110.

LOCATION: From Autobahn 44, take exit 6 (Aldenhoven) northwest Route 56 in the direction of Geilenkirchen for approximately 12 km to intersection with Route 221. Continue on Route 56/221 west approximately 2.8 km to an exit to secondary road to Teveren. Follow secondary road approximately 2.5 km southwest and then northwest around south side of Teveren directly to Main Gate of Geilenkirchen NATO Air Base. Alternatively, from Autobahn 46, take exit 4 to Route 221, then south approximately 6 km. toward Geilenkirchen. When Route 221 intersects with Route 56, continue southeast approximately 2.5 km to exit to secondary road toward town of Teveren. Follow secondary road southwest and then around south side of Teveren and then northwest directly to Main Gate of base. *EUSMRA: Page 29 (A-1), page 57.* **NMC:** Aachen, approximately 18 km south.

RESERVATION INFORMATION: Billeting, Bldg 141, 470 Air Base Squadron APO AE 09104-5000. **C-(USA) 011-49-2451-63-4962, (DE) 02451-63-4962.** Fax: C-(USA) 011-49-2451-63-4980, (DE) 02451-63-4980, 0815-1600 hours Mon-Thu, 0815-1500 hours Fri. Duty may make reservations any time; Space-A may inquire about availability 24 hours in advance. Directions from Main Gate: Follow the main road to the left, make the first left, the billeting office is on the left side of the street. Look for sign. Check in after 1300 hours at billeting, check out by 1000 hours. After hours key pick up is at Main Gate for confirmed reservations only.

(**VAQ**) Bldg 213. Single rooms, community bath (8). Small refrigerator in each room, kitchen and laundry facilities on each floor. Rates: DM 45 (U.S.$20.63 at press time).

(**VOQ**) Bldg 225. Single rooms, private bath (10). Small refrigerator in each room, kitchen and laundry facilities on each floor.

Rates: DM 60 (U.S.$27.51 at press time).

TML AVAILABILITY: Limited.

CREDIT CARDS ACCEPTED: None. Payment must be in German Marks.

TRANSPORTATION: Local taxi; Car Rental, C-011-49-2451-62-0741.

DINING OPPORTUNITIES: Sentry Club (E), Frisbee Club (NCO) and O Club are all within walking distance.

See the old watermills, palaces and castles that decorate the surrounding countryside. Located in central western Germany, this facility also offers easy access to both the Netherlands and Belgium.

Giessen Community (DE23R7)
284th BSB/ACS
Bldg 63, Unit 20911
APO AE 09169-5000

MAIN INSTALLATION TELEPHONE NUMBERS: C-(USA) 011-49-641-402-1110, (DE) 0641-402-1110, DSN-314-343-1110. Locator DSN-314-343-8307.

LOCATION: From Frankfurt, north on Autobahn 5 (E451) to exit 11 (Gambacher Kruez), then west on Autobahn 45 (E41) to exit 33 (Giessen Sudkreuz), then north on Autobahn 485 toward Linden and Giessen to exit 4 (Giessen Ursulem). Turn left (southeast) on Rudulf-Diesel Strasse (Route 49) and continue to Rodgener Strasse. Then turn left (east) on Rodgener Strasse and continue straight for approximately 0.4 km to entrance to Giessen Depot on north side of street and guesthouse on south side of street. *EUSMRA: Page 30 (C-1), page 59.* **NMC:** Giessen, in the city. NMI: Hanau, 70 km.

RESERVATION INFORMATION: Giessen Guesthouse, Giessen Depot, Bldg 63, 284th BSB-North-Unit 20911, APO AE 09169-5000. **C-(USA) 011-49-641-402-1700, (DE) 0641-402-1700, DSN-314-343-1700,** Fax: C-(USA) 011-49-641-42052. Directions: Opposite side of the road of the Giessen Main Depot; second building on the right. E-mail: stittc@284bsbexch.giessen.army.mil 0730-2000 hours Mon-Fri, 0900-1700 hours weekends and American and German holidays. Check in at facility 1300 hours, check out 1000 hours.

(**Army Lodging**) Giessen Guesthouse, Giessen Depot. Bldg 63/65, opposite Giessen Depot. DVQ-Suite (1); Bedroom suite, private bath (8); bedroom, private bath (5); bedroom, shared bath (8). Kitchenette, refrigerator, microwave, TV/VCR, housekeeping service, cribs, rollaways, laundry room, ice machine. Older structure, recently renovated (1997/98). Rates: DVQ-$45; suites or rooms with private bath $39; shared bath $25, each additional person $15. *Pets allowed;* $60/$50 non-returnable fumigation fee plus $6 per day, per pet. Personnel with Official Duty orders can make reservations, others are classed as Space-A (no reservations can be made).

(**DV/VIP**) Manager. DSN-314-343-7339/8434. O4+, civ GS13+. Determined by Manager.

AMENITIES: Snack Vending Machine and Soft Drink Machine.

TML AVAILABILITY: Good.

CREDIT CARDS ACCEPTED: Visa, MasterCard and American Express.

TRANSPORTATION: Car Rental: Budget C-011-49-641-493112, DSN-314-343-6162; Off base taxi, C-011-49-6033-2424/2611.

DINING OPPORTUNITIES: Alpine Club (Gsn Main Depot) DSN-314-343-7710, Capri Restaurant, C-011-49-641-41570 and Schnitzel Express, C-011-49-641-43602 are within walking distance. Burghof Neueh Bäue, C-011-49-641-34844; China Restaurant, C-011-49-641-32777; and Dach Cafe, Ludwigsplatz, C-011-641-76077 are within driving distance.

Grafenwoehr Community (DE11R7)

100th Area Support Group
Attn: AET TG-SB-DCA-ACS
Bldg 122, Unit 28130
APO AE 09114-5000

MAIN INSTALLATION TELEPHONE NUMBERS: C-(USA) 011-49-9641-83-1110, (DE) 09641-83-1110, DSN-314-475-1110. Locator-DSN-314-475-8371.

LOCATION: From Autobahn 9 (E51) north or south, exit 44 (Pegnitz/Grafenwoehr) east on Route 85 for 10 km to northeast on Route 470 for 26 km to south on Route 299 for 4 km through the village of Grafenwoehr to gate 1 of East Camp Grafenwoehr on Wilbur Road. Also accessible from the north-south Autobahn 93, exit 23 (Neiden) west to Route 470 for 18 km west to south on Route 299 for 4 km through the village of Grafenwoehr to gate 1 of East Camp Grafenwoehr on Wilbur Road. *EUSMRA: Page 36 (C-2), page 60.* **NMC:** Nuremberg, 91 km southwest. NMI: Vilseck, 24 km.

RESERVATION INFORMATION: Tower Inn, Training Area, Bldg 213, Argonne Avenue, APO AE 09114-5000 (located in Tower View Restaurant). **C-(USA) 011-49-9641-930103 or C-011-49-9641-83-1700, (DE) 09641-83-1700/6182, DSN-314-475-6182/1700,** Fax: C-011-49-9641-930930, 0600-2200 hours Mon-Fri, 0700-2000 hours Sat and Sun. After Duty hours see SDO 7th ATC Bldg 621, or call DSN-314-475-8302 for confirmed reservations or open rooms. E-mail: cmtymail@100asg.army.mil Check in 1300 hours, check out 1100 hours.

TML Total of 83 rooms located in nine buildings. Single and double rooms with private bath, family rooms. Kitchen, refrigerator, microwave, mini bar, TV/VCR, housekeeping service, washers/dryers, cribs, rollaways, soap, shampoo, lotion, deodorant, shaving cream and razor. Older structure renovated. Rates: private bath and living room $40, each additional person $6; private bath $36, each additional person $4. Reservations accepted 60 days prior for TDY and three days prior for visiting.

DV/VIP Bldg 209. Protocol Office, 7th Army Training Command. DSN-314-475-7145/6221. O6+. DVQ suites (3), toiletries. Rates $40, each additional occupant $6. Retirees and lower ranks Space-A.

TML AVAILABILITY: Best, Nov-Jan.

CREDIT CARDS ACCEPTED: Visa, MasterCard, American Express and Diners.

TRANSPORTATION: On base shuttle/bus, C-011-49-9641-83-1540/7664; Car Rental, C-011-49-9641-83-1503; Off base taxi, C-011-49-9641-83-2300/3661.

DINING OPPORTUNITIES: Tower View Restaurant; Burger King; and AAFES Food Mall are within walking distance. Various German Gasthauses are within driving distance.

Attractions available near Grafenwoehr include crystal, porcelain and nutcracker factories. Call Army Community Service for a list of local castles, churches and other sightseeing areas near the Grafenwoehr community, DSN-314-475-8317/6282.

Hanau Community (DE13R7)

414th Base Support Battalion
Unit 20193, Box 0003
APO AE 09165-0006

MAIN INSTALLATION TELEPHONE NUMBERS: C-(USA) 011-49-6181-88-1110, (DE) 06181-88-1110, DSN-314-322-1110. Locator C-6181-88-8965.

LOCATION: From Autobahn 66 take Exit 37 (Erlensee), then south on Route 8 for 2.2 km to intersection with Route 43 and Aschaffenburger Strasse (Route 8). Continue southeast on Aschaffenburger Strasse

(Route 8) for approximately 0.7 km to entrances to Pioneer Kaserne on north side of street. Continue less than 1 km to Inden Tannen and turn southward. *EUSMRA: Page 30 (C-3), page 62.* **NMC:** Frankfurt, 24 km west.

RESERVATION INFORMATION: 414th Guesthouses, Bldg 203, New Argonner Kaserne, APO AE 09165-6000. **C-(USA) 011-49-6181-88-1700/8357, 011-49-6181-9550, DSN-314-322-1700/8357,** Fax: C-(USA) 011-49-6181-955197/195, E-mail: rickse@414bsexch.hanau.army.mil 24 hours daily. Check in at billeting 1400 hours, check out 1000 hours. Reservations may be made 60 days in advance but are subject to prioritized placement guidelines, which are open to all valid ID card holders (restrictions may apply to civilian ID card holders). Space-A may make reservations three days in advance. Government civilian employee billeting.

Army Lodging Guesthouse. **Argonner Inn, Argonner Kaserne.** Bldg 203. Main reception desk for all lodgings here open 24 hours daily, except holidays. Intended for single persons or couples. Bedroom, private bath. TV/VCR, clock radio, telephone and small refrigerator. Rates: $39, each additional person $15. *Pets allowed.*

Army Lodging Guesthouse. **Pioneer Inn, Pioneer Housing.** Bldg 318 on Pioneer Kaserne in Hanau, just a few minutes from main reception desk. Intended for authorized families of three or more persons. Fully furnished apartments with kitchen, dining room, private bath, up to four bedrooms. Refrigerator, microwave, TV/VCR, clock radio and telephones. Laundry facilities located in building and playgrounds nearby. Rates: $39, each additional person $15. *Pets allowed.*

Army Lodging Guesthouse. **Copper Top Inn.** Bldg 1617 above Coleman Village in Gelnhausen, just 15 minutes from main office, operated as a satellite guesthouse. Registration and all transactions are completed at the Argonner Inn. These recently renovated units are the essence of a European gasthaus: quaint and comfortable. Double rooms (12); single rooms (3). Each room comes with a TV/VCR, clock radio, and refrigerator. This facility has a lounge, open daily and is preferred by many of our guests. The lounge includes snack bar, pool table, dart boards, video games and more. Military facilities are only minutes away. Rates: $39, each additional person $15. *Pets allowed.*

DV/VIP Bldg 204 on New Argonner Kaserne. Protocol DSN-314-322-9001. O6+/civilian equivalents. One-bedroom suites, king size bed, living room, private bath (2). Kitchenette, refrigerator, microwave, TV/VCR, clock radio and laundry facilities. No pets.

TML AVAILABILITY: Busiest season runs from Apr-Oct.

CREDIT CARDS ACCEPTED: Visa, MasterCard and American Express.

TRANSPORTATION: Car Rental: Budget C-(USA) 011-49-6181-57-1188. Taxi: Gates C-6181-2411 C-6181-19410. Local German buses and trains.

DINING OPPORTUNITIES: Anthony's, Burger King, Frank's Franks, Popeye's and Smiley's Bistro (at the Hessen Bowling Alley) are located on Wolfgang Kaserne within walking distance. Sunrise Grill, located on Old Argonner Kaserne is across the street from the guesthouse. Special T's (Robin Hood and Chicken Shack) and a Chinese restaurant are located on Pioneer Kaserne. Coppertop Lounge serves food in the evenings.

Highlights of the Hanau area include castles and open air markets. There are also special tributes to native sons the Grimm Brothers, authors of famous fairy tales. In Gelnhausen there are many historical buildings including a Rathaus built as a warehouse in 1333. The Marienkirche and Peterkirche are typical German churches. The Hexentrum was the scene of a ghastly trial during the execution of witches in the 16th century. Whatever brings you to the Hanau area, the friendly staff is eager to assist you and your family.

Heidelberg Community (DE33R7)
411th Base Support Battalion
Shopping Center, Bldg 3850
Unit 29245
APO AE 09102-5000

MAIN INSTALLATION TELEPHONE NUMBERS: C-(USA) 011-49-6221-17-1110, (DE) 06221-17-1110, DSN-314-370-1110. Locator 314-370-6883.

LOCATION: Located in mountains along the Neckar River, 90 km south of Frankfurt. For Patrick Henry Village take Autobahn 5 (E35) south from Frankfurt to exit 38 (Heidelberg) and onto Speyerer Strasse. Continue northeast on Speyerer Strasse toward Heidelberg for approximately 1 km to a left on Grasweg, then straight into Patrick Henry Village (or continue west on Speyerer Strasse for 0.4 km to entrance on north to South Lexington Avenue). For the U.S. Army Guesthouse in Patrick Henry Village continue straight on Grasweg then veer right onto North Lexington Avenue. Guesthouse (Bldg 4527) will be on the left side of the street. *EUSMRA: Page 31 (B-2; C-2,3), page 64, page 65.* NMC: Heidelberg, in the city.

RESERVATION INFORMATION: U.S. Army Guesthouse, Heidelberg, 411th BSB-Hospitality Management Group, APO AE 09102-5000. Reservations 24 hours, E-mail reservations accepted. **C-(USA) 011-49-17-6221-1700 or C-011-49-6221-795100/795402, (DE) 06221-795100, DSN-314-370-6941/7979,** Fax: C-(USA) 011-49-6221-795600. E-mail: scottjim@26asg.heidelberg.army.mil Check in at facility at 1300 hours, check out 1100 hours. Government civilian employee billeting.

Army Lodging U.S. Army Guesthouse. Bldg 4527. Bedroom, private bath (162). Community kitchen, refrigerator, TV/VCR, phone, housekeeping service, washer/dryer, cribs, cots ($4), sauna. "Key Quarter Apartments" with all amenities (40). Older structure, renovated. Handicap accessible, non-smoking rooms available. PCS reservations, 60 days ahead, TDY 14 days ahead, others Space-A, seven days ahead. Rates: standard room, $65; Key Quarter Apartments, $55 per day, two room family suites $75, second person $10. $/DM conversion available for in-house guests. *Pets allowed* with charge of $2 per day, plus one night's room fee.

DV/VIP SGS, HQ USAREUR, DSN-314-377-4500. O6/GS15+. Suites, private bath (21), (6) with kitchen. Sauna available in different building. Rates: $75, second person charges $10. Retirees and lower ranks Space-A.

AMENITIES: Exercise Room, Sauna.

TML AVAILABILITY: Good over Christmas holiday. Difficult all other times.

CREDIT CARDS ACCEPTED: Visa, MasterCard, American Express and Diners.

TRANSPORTATION: On/Off base shuttle/bus, Car Rental, Off Base Taxi, C-(USA) 011-49-6221-302030; and Airport Limousine, C-(USA) 011-49-6221-770077.

DINING OPPORTUNITIES: Anthony's Pizza, Burger King and Lexington Restaurant are within walking distance.

Visit famous University of Heidelberg, and its Students' Inns-Roten Ochsen (Red Ox) and Zum Sepp' are adjacent on the Hauptstrasse. The Castle above the city, and bridge across the Neckar River also should not be missed. Visit the Heidelberg Army Regional Medical Center (ARMC), Nachrichten Kaserne where R.J. was born and where General George Patton died.

Visit Military Living online at
www.militaryliving.com

Hohenfels Community (DE71R7)
282nd Base Support Battalion
Attn: AETTH-SB-ALS
Bldg 63, Unit 28216
APO AE 09173-5000

MAIN INSTALLATION TELEPHONE NUMBERS: C-(USA) 011-49-9472-83-1110, DSN-314-466-1110. Locator DSN-314-466-2035.

LOCATION: In southeast Germany, between Nuremberg and Regensburg. From the Neumarkt-Regensburg Autobahn 3 (E56), take exit 94 (Parsberg) north on secondary road approximately 8 km toward village of Grossbissendorf. Continue past Grossbissendorf east approximately 0.7 km to Hohenfels Training Area Gate 1 (Main Gate). Continue east approximately 2.2 km to Gate 3 on north side of village of Hohenfels. Follow signs Labeled Truppenubungsplatz. *EUSMRA: Page 36 (C-4), page 67.* NMC: Nuremberg, 53 km northwest.

RESERVATION INFORMATION: Sunrise Lodge, Bldg 63, APO AE 09173-5000. **C-(USA) 011-49-9472-950155/2 or C-(USA) 011-49-9472-83-1700, DSN-314-466-1700/2438,** Fax: C-(USA) 011-49-9472-950154, Mon-Fri 0600-2200 hours, Sat and Sun 0730-1630 hours. Reservations C-(USA) 1-800-462-7691, Fax: C-(USA) 011-49-69-699-6309. E-mail: sunriselodge@cmtymail.100asg.army.mil. Directions: Straight for approx. 500 meters, take first left, then first right. Continue another 100 meters, the parking lot is on the left.

Army Lodging Guesthouse. Bldgs 7, 1177. Suites (4); Rooms (10). Private baths, refrigerator, microwave, coffee maker, TV/VCR, phone, iron/ironing board, laundry facility. Rates: single room $30, suite $40; each additional person room $4, suite $6.

VOQ Bldgs 1172 and 1173. Suites, private bath (8). Refrigerator, microwave, coffee maker, TV/VCR, phone, iron/ironing board. Rates: $40, each additional person $6.

DV/VIP Bldg 6. O6+. Protocol C-011-49-9472-83-1600. Suites, private bath (6); Driver's (single) room (1). Refrigerator, microwave, coffee maker, TV/VCR, phone, iron/ironing board, ice machine, laundry room. Rates: Suites $60, each additional person $8; Driver's room $40, each additional person $6. Reservations through Protocol.

AMENITIES: Ice, Soft Drink and Snack Vending Machine.

TML AVAILABILITY: Good during Nov, training periods and holidays.

CREDIT CARDS ACCEPTED: Visa, MasterCard and American Express.

TRANSPORTATION: On/off base shuttle/bus, C-011-49-9472-83-2808, DSN-314-466-2808; Car Rental, C-011-49-9472-83-2051, DSN-314-466-2051.

DINING OPPORTUNITIES: Burger King, C-011-49-9472-83-4631; Cafeteria, C-011-49-9472-83-2734; and Hilltop Club, C-011-49-9472-83-2161 are within walking distance. Anthony's Pizza, C-011-49-9472-83-4631; and Herb's Kantine, C-011-49-9472-83-2683 are within driving distance.

Hohenfels is located in the mountains on the edge of a U.S. Army Training Area near the confluence of the Vils and Naab rivers.

Illesheim Community (DE72R7)
Area Support Team, CMR 416
Box F
APO AE 09140-5000

MAIN INSTALLATION TELEPHONE NUMBERS: C-(USA) 011-49-9841-83-113, DSN-314-467-1110. Locator DSN-314-467-4813

LOCATION: From Wuerzburg take Autobahn 7 (E70) south to exit 107

(Bad Windsheim) to Route 470 northeast in the direction of Bad Windsheim for 10 km to the village of Illesheim. In the village turn right (east) on secondary road approximately 0.6 km in the direction of village Urfersheim. Follow U.S. signs marked Storck Barracks to Main Gate on the right side of road. *EUSMRA: Page 34 (B-4), page 69.* **NMC:** Wuerzburg, approximately 46 km northwest.

RESERVATION INFORMATION: Illesheim Army Community Services, CMR 416, Box 1, Bldg 6624, APO AE 09140-5000. **C-011-49-9841-83-523, DSN-314-467-4523.** Fax: 011-49-9841-83-743. *Note: This facility is mainly used by permanent party personnel on duty; Space-A is extremely limited and never guaranteed. Call ahead.*

(BOQ) E7+ Bldg 6623. Single room (8), Suites (36). Fully furnished, kitchen, telephones, laundry facility.

TML AVAILABILITY: Extremely Limited.

TRANSPORTATION: Bus/Shuttle, C-(USA) 011-49-9841-83-757/800, DSN-314-468-7757/1800. Car Rental, Budget C-(USA) 011-49-9841-687610. Taxi, C-(USA) 011-49-9841-8827.

DINING OPPORTUNITIES: Restaurant C-(USA) 011-49-9841-83-674/567, DSN-314-467-4674/4567.

Kaiserslautern Community, Ramstein Air Base (DE30R7)
415th Base Support Battalion
Attn: AEUSG-K-ACS (Relo)
Unit 23152
APO AE 09227-5000

MAIN INSTALLATION TELEPHONE NUMBERS: C-(USA) 011-49-631-536-1110, DSN-314-489-1110, (DE) C-0631-536-1110. Locator C-(USA) 011-49-6371-47-6120, DSN-314-480-6120. (DE) C-06371-47-6120.

LOCATION: From the east-west Mannheim-Saarbrucken Autobahn 6 (E50), use exit 15 (Kaiserslautern West) south to Opel-Kreisel Strasse (Route L367). Approximately 1.2 km to intersection with Kaiser Strasse (Route L395) and Route 270. Turn east onto Route 270 and entrance to facility will be on the south side less than 1 km from intersection. *EUSMRA: Page 29 (C-4), page 70, page 77.* **NMC:** Kaiserslautern, 5 km northeast.

RESERVATION INFORMATION: Unit 3250, Box 500, Bldg 305, APO AE 09054-0500. **C-(USA) 011-49-6371-45-4920, DSN-314-480-4920, (DE) 06371-45-4920,** Fax: C-(USA) 011-49-6371-42589, DSN-314-480-7627, (DE) C-06371-42589, DSN-314-480-7627, 0730-2000 hours Mon-Fri, closed on U.S. holidays. E-mail: lodging.reservations@ramstein.af.mil Duty personnel may make reservations one year in advance; Space-A requests are taken only 24 hours in advance. Check in at Bldg 1002, check out 1100 hours. Government civilian employee billeting. *Note: See Ramstein Inns: North, South, Sembach and Landstuhl listing for more lodging. Building 305 on Ramstein AB manages all reservations for Kaiserslautern Community which includes Ramstein AB, Sembach AB, Vogelweh AS and Landstuhl Medical Center lodging facilities.*

(VOQ/VAQ) Ramstein Inn at Vogelweh, Bldg 1002, 1003, 1034. C-011-49-631-536-8910, DSN-314-489-8910, (DE) 0631-536-8910, Fax: C-011-49-631-7659, DSN-314-489-7659. Check in at Bldg 1002. Bedrooms, shared bath (98); bedrooms, private bath (35). Refrigerator, microwave, TV/VCR, phone, clock radio, housekeeping service, iron/ironing board. Laundry facility and ice machine in each building. Older structure. Rates: $18.50 per room.

(TLF) Bldg 1004. One-bedroom apartment, private bath (35). Kitchen, TV/VCR, radio, phone, iron/ironing board, and housekeeping service. Laundry facility in building. Newly renovated. Rates: $39 per unit.

(DV/VIP) POA Ramstein AB, C-(USA) 011-49-6371-47-6854. O6/GS15+. Suite (16). Microwave, TV/VCR, video rental, phone, clock radio, housekeeping service, laundry facility, iron/ironing board. Rates: one person $30, two people $43.50.

TML AVAILABILITY: Difficult. Best during winter months.

CREDIT CARDS ACCEPTED: Visa and MasterCard.

TRANSPORTATION: On base shuttle/bus/taxi, C-06371-47-5961; Off base shuttle/bus, C-06371-31-6670; Car Rental, C-06371-44202; Off base taxi, C-06371-50510/58626.

DINING OPPORTUNITIES: Various dining establishments on and off base. Dining information provided in Guest Book located in each room.

The city hall (Rathaus), is the highest in Germany. There is an elegant restaurant in the penthouse. Visit the Pfalztheater for opera, operetta, plays and ballet. Harry's gift shop, now limited to fine paintings, known around the world by military families, is at 5-11 Manheimer Strasse (C-(USA) 011-49-631-67081). TelePassport® Service is now available; call home in privacy/receive calls in your room.

Kitzingen Community (DE75R7)
417th Base Support Battalion
Harvey Barracks, Bldg 105
Unit 26137
APO AE 09031-5000

MAIN INSTALLATION TELEPHONE NUMBERS: C-(USA) 011-49-9321-305-113, DSN-314-355-113. Locator C-011-49-9321-305-509.

LOCATION: Take Autobahn 7 (E43) south from Frankfurt toward Wuerzburg. At the interchange with Autobahn 3 (E40), stay on Autobahn 7 south to exit 103 (Kitzingen). Take exit 103 east on Route 8 (Reppendorfer Strasse) toward Kitzingen for approximately 5 km to the gates to Marshall Heights on the right side of the street. The Shoppette is located in the southwest corner of Marshall Heights on Gabelsberger Strasse. For Harvey Barracks continue on Route 8 (will change from Reppendorfer Strasse to Hindenburgring) through the city and cross the Main River at Konrad Adenauer Brucke (Bridge). Once you cross the river take a right turn at a green and yellow "E Center." Follow the road around the curve to the end, then turn north on Staats Strasse 2271 and continue north approximately 1.5 km to the second set of traffic lights. Turn east on Staats Strasse 2272 and drive east approximately 0.9 km to a sign indicating the entrance to Woodland Inn Rod & Gun Club on the left side of the street. The Main Gate to Harvey Barracks is on the right side of Staats Strasse 2272 directly across from the Woodland Inn. *EUSMRA: Page 34 (A-3), page 71.* **NMC:** Wuerzburg, 17 km northwest.

RESERVATION INFORMATION: Woodland Inn Rod & Gun Club, 417th BSB, Unit 26124, Bldg 166, APO AE 09031-5000. **C-011-49-9321-31836, or C-011-49-9321-305-600, DSN-314-355-8311/8322,** Fax: C-(USA) 011-49-9321-31836, 0830-1600 hours Mon-Fri, Bar other hours. Duty can make reservations; others Space-A. Reservations recommended.

(Army Lodging) Kitzingen American Guesthouse, Harvey Barracks. C-011-49-9321-370-123, reservations C-011-49-09321-305-600. All ranks and civilians. Bedrooms, hall bath (10). Refrigerator, TV/VCR, phone, housekeeping service, laundry facility. Rates: all categories, sponsor $32-$36, each additional person $3, children under two stay for free.

(DV/VIP) Kitzingen American Guesthouse, Harvey Barracks. Separate VIP bedroom suite, private bath (1); two-bedroom VIP suite, private bath (1). Refrigerator, TV/VCR, phone, housekeeping service, laundry facility. Rates: $65, each additional person $6, children under two stay for free.

TML AVAILABILITY: Difficult. Best Dec-Jan.

CREDIT CARDS ACCEPTED: Visa, MasterCard; $50 minimum.

TRANSPORTATION: On/Off base shuttle bus, C-0931-305-744; Car Rental, C-011-49-9321-708475; Off base taxi, C-011-49-9321-8088; Train station (Bahnhof), C-011-49-9321-5100.

DINING OPPORTUNITIES: End Zone, C-011-49-9321-702609 is within driving distance.

The Woodland Inn was built in 1934 as a club for officers of the German Luftwaffe. The art and architecture is typical of the era, the setting is a Bavarian hunting lodge.

Landstuhl Medical Center (DE40R7)
80 SPTG, Unit 3220
Unit 3220, Box 410
APO AE 09094-5000

MAIN INSTALLATION TELEPHONE NUMBERS: C-(USA) 011-49-6371-86-1110, (DE) 06371-86-1110, DSN-314-486-1110. Locator C-011-49-6371-47-6120, DSN-314-480-6120, (DE) 06371-47-6120.

LOCATION: From Autobahn 6 (E50) use exit 13 (AS Landstuhl). Go south on L363 to intersection with L395/Saarbrucker Strasse/Kaiser Strasse. Go east and south to intersection with Ludwig Strasse to Luitpold Strasse, then southwest on Luitpold Strasse up steep hill to Gate 1. *EUSMRA: Page 77.* **NMC:** Kaiserslautern, 16 km northeast.

RESERVATION INFORMATION: Ramstein Inn-Landstuhl, Unit 3250, Box 500, Bldg 305, APO AE 09054-5000. **C-(USA) 011-49-6371-45-4920, DSN-314-480-4920, (DE) 06371-45-4920,** Fax: C-(USA) 011-49-6371-42589, DSN-314-480-7627, (DE) 06371-42589, DSN-314-480-7627, 0730-2000 hours Mon-Fri. Closed on U.S. holidays. E-mail: lodging.reservations@ramstein.af.mil Check in at facility, check out 1100 hours. Duty personnel may make reservations one year in advance; Space-A requests are taken only 24 hours in advance. Government civilian employee billeting. *The first overseas Fisher House opened at Landstuhl Medical Center on 18 June, 2001. Note: See Ramstein Inns: North, South, Vegelweh, and Sembach listing for more lodging. Building 305 on Ramstein AB manages all reservations for Kaiserslautern Community which includes Ramstein AB, Sembach AB, Vogelweh AS and Landstuhl Medical Center lodging facilities.*

VOQ/VAQ Ramstein Inn-Landstuhl. Bldgs 3751, 3752, 3753, 3754. C-011-49-6371-86-9070, (DE) 06371-86-9070. Check in at Bldg 3752. Bedroom, shared bath (168). Refrigerator, microwave, TV/VCR, radio, phone, housekeeping service, iron/ironing board. laundry facility in bldgs 3752, 3754, 3756. Older structure. Rates: $18.50 per room.

TLF Bldg 3756. Check in at Bldg 3752. One-bedroom apartment, private bath (34). Kitchen, TV/VCR, radio, phone, iron/ironing board, housekeeping service. Laundry facility in building. Newly renovated. Rates: $39 per unit.

DV/VIP Bldg 3754. O6/GS15+. Check in at Bldg 3752. Suite, private bath (13). Refrigerator, microwave, TV/VCR, radio, phone, iron/ironing board, and housekeeping service. Laundry facility and ice machine in building. Older structure. Rates: $30 per suite.

TML AVAILABILITY: Best during winter months.

CREDIT CARDS ACCEPTED: Visa and MasterCard.

TRANSPORTATION: On base shuttle/bus, C-6371-47-5961, DSN-314-480-5961; Off base shuttle/bus, C-011-49-631-316670; Car Rental, C-011-49-710-6219407; On base taxi, C-6371-50510; Off base taxi, C-06371-2700.

DINING OPPORTUNITIES: Various dining establishments on and off base. Dining information provided in Guest Book located in each room.

Visit the Marktplatz in Kaiserslautern for a traditional German farmer's market. Also, ask at USO Kaiserslautern for directions to local fests and sights—they have a wealth of information to share! TelePassport® Service is now available; call home in privacy/receive calls in your room.

Mannheim Community (DE43R7)
293rd Base Support Battalion
Sullivan Barracks, Bldg 253
Unit 29901, Box 25
APO AE 09086-5000

MAIN INSTALLATION TELEPHONE NUMBERS: C-(USA) 011-49-621-730-1110, (DE) 0621-730-1110, DSN-314-380-1110. Locator C-011-49-621-730-1500, DSN-314-380-1500.

LOCATION: Accessible from Autobahn A67 (E451) which intersects Autobahn A6 (E50). From Autobahn A6 (E50), use exit 26 (Veirnheimer Kreuz) to Route 38 westbound for approximately 1.2 km to northbound exit to Magdeburger Strasse. Go north on Magdeburger Strasse one block to left on Birkenauer Strasse. Continue straight on Birkenauer Strasse to entrances to Benjamin Franklin Village, Funari Barracks and Sullivan Barracks. For the Franklin Guesthouse, same directions as above except once you take a left from Magdeburger Strasse onto Birkenauer Strasse take an immediate left onto Fürtherstrasse. The Franklin Guesthouse is on the right side of Further Strasse. *EUSMRA: Page 31 (B-2), page 73, page 74.* **NMC:** Mannheim, 13 km southwest.

RESERVATION INFORMATION: Unit 29901, Box 3, Bldg 312, Benjamin Franklin Village Housing Area, Fürtherstrasse, APO AE 09086-5000. 0600-2400 hours. **C-(USA) 011-49-621-730-9218/1700, (DE) 0621-730-9218/1700, DSN-314-380-1700/9218,** Fax: C-011-49-621-738607, C-(DE) 0621-738607, E-mail: frankling@cmtymail.26asg.army.mil Mon-Fri 0600-2400 hours, Sat-Sun and holidays, 0800-2400 hours, closed Christmas and New Years. Duty may make reservations; others Space-A. Check in 1400 hours, check out 1100 hours.

Army Lodging **Franklin Guesthouse, Benjamin Franklin Housing.** Bldg 312, Fürtherstrasse. Two-bedroom, private bath (39). Kitchenette, CATV, laundry facility, housekeeping service, cribs, cots, ice machine. Older structure, renovated. Rates: single $55, each additional person $10. No pets.

TLF Sub-standard quarters (previously maids quarters) on the fourth floor of family apartment buildings. There are three-, four-, and five-bedroom units. Rates: $55 per day regardless of size. *Pets allowed.*

DV/VIP Franklin House. Bldg 312, Benjamin Franklin Village Housing Area, Fürtherstrasse. C-(USA) 011-49-621-730-6118/6547/1700. Suites, private bath (3). Kitchenette, honor bar, CATV, washer/dryer, housekeeping service, cribs, cots, ice machine. Older structure, renovated. Rates: suites $65, each additional person $10. No pets.

The Franklin House at Mannheim, Germany is conveniently located on the installation.

TML AVAILABILITY: Good, Dec-Jun. Difficult, May-Sep.

CREDIT CARDS ACCEPTED: Visa, MasterCard, American Express and Diners.

TRANSPORTATION: Car Rental: Budget C-0621-734155.

DINING OPPORTUNITIES: Burger King and Strike Zone are within walking distance.

Visit the National Theater (wonderful sounds), Observatory and Mannheim Castle. A good area for a Volksmarch.

Oberammergau Community (DE36R7)
NATO Community Club,
Hotel & Restaurant
Am Anger 3, 82487 Oberammergau, Germany
(Not U.S. Government Lodging)

MAIN INSTALLATION TELEPHONE NUMBERS: C-(USA) 011-49-8822-916-0. Medical 19222, Security Police 110.

LOCATION: From Munich, south on Autobahn 95 (E533) to Route 2 to Oberau, then northwest on Route 23 and follow signs to direction of Oberammergau. After 6 km, go through Ettal, and after another 4 km, take the first exit to Oberammergau. Take first right onto Am Rainenbichl, go 1 km to Main Gate of NATO School (SHAPE) on the right. For the NATO Community Club continue on Am Rainenbichl, which changes into Aufacker Strasse, past the NATO School and take first right onto Am Anger. Club is on left side. *EUSMRA: Page 38 (A-4), page 76.* **NMC:** Garmisch-Partenkirchen, 20 km south.

RESERVATION INFORMATION: NATO Community Club, Am Anger 3, 82487 Oberammergau, Germany. **C-(USA) 011-49-8822-9160,** Fax: C-(USA) 011-49-8822-916-252/279, 0730-2000 hours Mon-Tue and Thu-Fri, 0700-1400 hours Wed, 0730-1030 hours and 1500-2000 hours Sat, and 0730-2300 hours Sun. E-mail: ncc.reception@t-online.de WEB: www.hotel-oberammergau.de/ncc Reservations accepted; direct request is also possible, space allowing. Check in at facility.

(TML) Private standard class hotel. Bldg 763. Bedrooms, private bath (65). Refrigerator, TV, telephone, housekeeping service, laundry facility, cribs, cots. Modern structure. Rates: DM 70 first occupant in room per night, DM 55 each additional person, DM 10 for a rollaway bed; TDY DM 5,00 less. Maximum four per room. All rates include Breakfast Buffet at NCC restaurant.

AMENITIES: Ice and Soft Drink Vending Machines, Bar, Dining Room.

TML AVAILABILITY: Good, year round.

CREDIT CARDS ACCEPTED: Visa, Euro, EC. Other options: U.S. cash, travelers checks and personal checks; DM and Euro cash, travelers checks, U.S. dollars, DM and Eurocheques.

TRANSPORTATION: Off base shuttle/bus, C-011-49-8821-948274 (Garmisch); Car Rental, C-011-49-8821-7209 (Garmisch); Off base taxi, C-011-49-8822-94440 or 94294.

DINING OPPORTUNITIES: The NCC restaurant is open for breakfast, 1130-1330 hours Mon-Fri for lunch and 1730-2100 hours Sun-Fri for dinner. La Grappa, C-011-49-8822-6772; Larchenhügel, C-011-49-8822-92000 are within walking distance. ZUR Rose, C-011-49-8822-4706; and numerous other restaurants available in Oberammergau.

Visit the famous King Ludwig II castles, Neuwschwanstein and Linderhof or traditional Wies-Church in nearer surrounding Oberammergau. Oberammergau offers to all visitors a traditional village with the famous Passion Play and world-famous woodcarvings. Take your family for a day to Wellenberg Alpenbad Swimming Pool and Sport Center. Enjoy mountain climbing, tours through one of the most beautiful areas of Southern Bavaria.

Ramstein Air Base (DE24R7)
86th MSS/DPF
Unit 3220, Box 410
APO AE 09094-5000

MAIN INSTALLATION TELEPHONE NUMBERS: C-(USA) 011-49-6371-47-113, (DE) 06371-45-1110, DSN-314-480-1110. Locator 06371-45-6120.

LOCATION: North of Mannheim-Saarbrucken Autobahn A-6 (E-50). From Autobahn A-6 (E-50), take exit 13 (Landstuhl) and go north on L363 toward Ramstein-Miesenback for approximately 1 km. Exit right on Ramstein Flugplatz access road and continue northeast approximately 2.1 km to West Gate. Also, from Autobahn A-6 (E-50), take exit 14 (Kaiserslautern-Einiedlerhof) north of Jacob Pfeiffer Strasse/K25, immediately turn left on Ramstein Flugplatz access road and follow for approximately 3.6 km to East Gate. *Note: Entry to base requires a visitor's pass. Passes can be obtained at the Visitor Control Centers, 0600-1600 hours Mon-Fri, located on the right just prior to the gates. After hours the passes are available at the gates. EUSMRA: Page 29 (B-4), page 77.* **NMC:** Kaiserslautern, 12 miles east.

RESERVATION INFORMATION: Ramstein Inn North and South, 86 SVS/SVML, Bldg 305, Washington Avenue, Unit 3250, Box 500, APO AE 09054-5000. **C-(USA) 011-49-6371-45-4920/47-4920, (DE) 06371-45-4920/47-4920, DSN-314-480-4920,** Fax: C-(USA) 011-49-6371-42589, DSN-314-480-7627, (DE) 06371-42589. DSN-314-480-7627, 0730-2000 hours Mon-Fri. Closed on U.S. holidays. E-mail: lodging.reservations @ramstein.af.mil Duty personnel may make reservations up to one year in advance; Space-A requests are taken only 24 hours in advance. Check in at facility, check out 1100 hours. Government civilian employee billeting. *Note: See Ramstein Inns: Vogelweh, Sembach and Landstuhl listing for more lodging. Building 305 on Ramstein AB manages all reservations for Kaiserslautern Community which includes Ramstein AB, Sembach AB, Vogelweh and Landstuhl lodging facilities.*

(VOQ) Ramstein Inn North. Bldg 304, 305, 306. C-(USA) 011-49-6371-45-4900, DSN-314-480-4900. Check in at Bldg 305. Bedroom, shared bath (172); bedroom, private bath (9). Refrigerator, microwave, TV/VCR, radio, phone, iron/ironing board, housekeeping service. Laundry facilities in each building. Older structure. Rates: $18.50 per room.

(TLF) Ramstein Inn North. Bldgs 310, 908. Check in at Bldg 305. Bldg 908: One-bedroom apartment, private bath (40); Bldg 310: Two-bedroom apartment, private bath (30). All units have kitchen, TV/VCR, radio, phone, iron/ironing board, housekeeping service. Washer/dryer and dishwasher in each apartment in Bldg 310 and in common area in Bldg 908. Bldg 310 newly built in 2000. Rates: $39 per unit.

(VAQ) Ramstein Inn South. Bldg 2408, 2409. **C-(USA) 011-49-6371-45-4940, DSN-314-480-4940,** Fax: C-(USA) 011-49-6371-45-5800, DSN-314-480-5800, 24 hours daily. Enlisted. Check in at Bldg 2408. Single rooms, shared bath (152). Refrigerator, microwave, TV/VCR, radio, phone, iron/ironing board, housekeeping service. Laundry facilities in each building. Older structure. Rates: $18.50 per room.

(DV/VIP) Ramstein Inn North. O6/GS15+. Bldgs 304 and 306. Check in at Bldg 305. Suites with private bath (20). Refrigerator, microwave, TV/VCR, radio, telephone iron/ironing board, housekeeping service. Laundry facilities in each building. Older structure. Rates: $30 per suite.

(DV/VIP) Ramstein Inn South. Bldg 2408. E9. Suites with private bath (10). Refrigerator, microwave, TV/VCR, radio, phone, iron/ironing board, laundry facility, housekeeping service. Older structure. Rates: $29 per suite.

DV/VIP General Cannon Hotel. Bldg 1018. O6/GS15+. Reservations through USAFE Protocol. **C-011-49-6371-45-7558, DSN-314-480-7558,** (DE) 06371-45-7558, DSN-480-7558; Fax: C-011-49-6371-45-7109, DSN-314-480-7109, (DE) 06371-45-7109. Separate bedroom suites, private bath (12). Refrigerator, TV/VCR, radio, telephone, iron/ironing board, housekeeping service, laundry facilities. Modern structure. Rates: $30 per suite.

AMENITIES: Ice Machines.

TML AVAILABILITY: Best during winter months.

CREDIT CARDS ACCEPTED: Visa and MasterCard.

TRANSPORTATION: On base shuttle/bus/taxi, C-011-49-6371-45-5961/6961; Off base shuttle/bus, C-011-49-631-316670; Car Rental, C-011-49-6371-43971; Off base taxi, C-011-49-6371-50510/58626.

DINING OPPORTUNITIES: Various dining establishments on and off base. Dining information provided in Guest Book located in each room.

Small villages surround Ramstein; it's fun to just drive through them. People here are friendly and helpful and many speak English. Kaiserslautern and Landstuhl are nearby.

Rhein-Main Air Base (DE16R7)
469 ABG/DPF
Bldg 347, Room 30
Unit 7405, Box 15
APO AE 09050-5000

MAIN INSTALLATION TELEPHONE NUMBERS: C-(USA) 011-49-69-699-1110, (DE) 069-699-1110, DSN-314-330-1110. Locator 7691/7348.

LOCATION: Adjacent to the Frankfurt International Airport (Flughafen Frankfurt/Main). From Autobahn 5 (E451) north or south, take exit 23 (Anschlussstelle-Zeppelinheim) west. Continue straight west to the Rhein-Main Air Base Main Gate. For Gateway Gardens from the Rhein-Main Air Base Main Gate, take an immediate right (north) on Ellis Road. Continue straight north for approximately 2.5 km to front gate of Gateway Gardens (will pass under Autobahn 3 just before gate). For Gateway Inn take the first left onto Hewell Road. Continue straight to the end of Hewell Road and to the Gateway Inn on the left side of the street. *EUSMRA: Page 30 (B-3), page 80.* **NMC:** Frankfurt, 16 km north.

RESERVATION INFORMATION: Gateway Inn, Bldg 600, APO AE 09050-5000. **C-(USA) 011-49-69-699-7265/6, (DE) 069-699-4630, DSN-314-330-6843/7265,** (for reservations) daily, **C-(USA) 011-49-69-699-7265** (front desk). Fax: C-(USA) 011-49-69-699-7440, DSN-314-330-7440, 24 hours daily. E-mail: reservations@rheinmain.af.mil Duty may make reservations any time; Space-A may make reservations 24 hours in advance. Check in at front desk, check out 1000 hours. Advanced payment is required of all guests. Government civilian employee billeting on official duty.
Note: A copy of all official orders, if applicable, must be faxed.

TLF Bldg 634. Family unit: two bedroom, private bath (6); three bedroom, private bath (6). Kitchen, refrigerator, microwave, TV/VCR, housekeeping service, washer/dryer, cribs, ice machine, living room, dining room, picnic area, playground. Non-smoking. Rates: $39 per night per family. Priority to families PCS to Rhein-Main AB. No pets.

VAQ Bldg 343. Two single occupants per room, shared bath. Refrigerator, microwave, TV/VCR. Non-smoking. Rates: $18.50 per bed.

VQ Gateway Inn. Bldg 600. Bedroom with one double bed and shared bath (126), bedroom with one double bed equipped for handicap with shared bath (2), bedroom with double bed, sitting room and private bath (15). Refrigerator, microwave, TV, housekeeping service, washer/dryer, cribs, ice machine, picnic area, playground. Non-smoking.

Rates: $18.50 single. Space-A rooms are available after 1800 hours daily. No pets.

DV/VIP Gateway Inn. Bldg 600. DV bedroom, queen size bed, private bath (5), living room. Refrigerator, microwave, honor bar, TV/VCR, housekeeping service, washer/dryer, cribs, ice machine, picnic area, playground. Non-smoking. Rates: $30. No pets.

TML AVAILABILITY: Good, Dec-Feb. Difficult, other times.

CREDIT CARDS ACCEPTED: Visa and MasterCard.

TRANSPORTATION: On base shuttle/bus; On base taxi C-011-49-69-699-23404; Hertz Rent-a-Car C-011-49-69-699-2188; Budget Rent-a-Car C-011-49-69-699-591624.

DINING OPPORTUNITIES: Rocket Bowling Center IFF Snack Bar, C-011-49-69-699-7219; Rocket Sports Lounge, C-011-49-69-699-7727; Gateway Cafe, C-011-49-69-699-7311; and Zeppelinhaus, C-011-49-69-699-7120 are located on base.

Rhein-Main is scheduled to be turned over to the government of Germany by the end of 2005. USAFE operations will relocate to Ramstein and Spangdahlem Air Bases, Germany.

Don't miss Frankfurt's famous Fairgrounds (Messa), for exhibits of all types, and the Frankfurt Zoo. The southern part of the city is a forest with deer, hiking and bicycling paths. Watch for special seasonal "fests."

Schweinfurt Community (DE48R7)
280th Base Support Battalion
Ledward, Bldg 242
CMR 457
APO AE 09033-5000

MAIN INSTALLATION TELEPHONE NUMBERS: C-(USA) 011-49-9721-96-113, (DE) 09721-96-113, DSN-314-354-1110, ask for Schweinfurt. Locator 354-6748.

LOCATION: Located approximately 12 km east of the Kassel-Wuerzburg Autobahn A7 (E45) and two km north of the east-west Wuerzburg-Bitburg Autobahn A70 (E48). From east or west on Autobahn A70 (E48), take the Schweinfurt/Bergrheinfield exit (exit 4). Go north on Route 26 for 3 km to merge with Route 286. Continue north 1.75 km to Route 303, then west on Route 303 (Niederwerner Strasse) for 1.4 km to main entrance of Ledford Barracks (Kaserne) on north side of street. From main entrance of Ledford Barracks, go west on Route 303 (Niederwerner Strasse) for 4.2 km to main entrance of Conn Barracks on south side of street. Also, from Autobahn A70 (E48), use Schweinfurt exit (exit 5) to Route 216 north to merge with Route 26, then north to Route 303 and west to Ledward and Conn Barracks. *EUSMRA: Page 34 (A-2), page 81.* **NMC:** Schweinfurt, in the city.

RESERVATION INFORMATION: Bradley Inn, Guesthouse, Bldg 89, 280th Support Battalion, APO AE 09033-5000. **C-(USA) 011-49-9721-96-1700/7940, (DE) 09721-96-1700/7940, DSN-314-354-1700,** Fax: C-(USA) 011-49-9721-79-4145/4101, 24 hours daily. After hours contact Bldg 206, Ledward Barracks, COC Office (in case of emergency closing). E-mail: 280guest@xs1.mwr.army.mil Duty may make reservations; others Space-A. Check in at facility between 1300-1800 hours Mon-Fri, check out 1000 hours. Government civilian employee billeting.

Army Lodging Bradley Inn. Bldg 89, Conn Barracks. Large-family room units, private bath (20); small-family room units, private bath (14); single rooms, private bath (6); bedroom, queen bed, private bath (2); bedroom, two single beds, private bath (8). Community kitchens, utensils, housekeeping service, laundry facilities, cribs, cots, snack vending. Older structure, renovated. Rates: large family room $55, each additional person $5; small family room $49, each additional person $5; single room $30; bedroom, queen or two single beds $35, each additional person $5.

TML Askren Manors, Bldg 540, 541. Three bedroom apartment, with private bath, fully equipped kitchen and dining area (6). Rates: Single occupancy $90; each additional family member $5. *Pets allowed.*

DV/VIP Chief, Business Operations, Bldg 206, C-(USA) 011-49-9721-803834, DSN-312-354-6715. O3/GS13+. Bradley Inn. DV/VIP suites, private bath (2). Kitchen, utensils, housekeeping service, laundry facility, cribs, cots, snack vending. Older structure, renovated. Rates: suites, single occupancy $98, each additional family member $5.

TML AVAILABILITY: Good, all year.

TRANSPORTATION: On base shuttle/bus C-011-49-9721-968386; Taxi C-011-49-9721-16060; Car rental and mass transit available.

CREDIT CARDS ACCEPTED: Visa, MasterCard and American Express.

DINING OPPORTUNITIES: NCO Club, C-011-49-9721-88048/803201 (dinner only); Burger King C-011-49-9721-804346; and Popeye's C-011-49-9721-87553 are within walking distance.

Wednesday and Saturday morning, and Tuesday and Friday afternoon, the Schweinfurt Marktplatz hums with activity. Don't miss a colorful sight. Then stroll down to the Stadtpark and the Tiergehege near the Main River. Schweinfurt is only 1.5 hours from Frankfurt International Airport. Travel to and from airport may be coordinated upon request.

Sembach Air Base Annex, Ramstein AB (DE18R7)
86 MSS/DPF
Unit 3220, Box 410
APO AE 09094-5000

MAIN INSTALLATION TELEPHONE NUMBERS: C-(USA) 011-49-6302-67-1110/113, DSN-314-486-1110/113, (DE) 06302-67-1110. Locator C-011-49-6371-47-6120, DSN-480-6120.

LOCATION: From the Mannheim-Saarbrucken Autobahn A6 (E50) E or W, take exit 16 (AS Kaiserslautern Ost) to Route 40 N toward Bad Kreuznach. Go north for approximately 7.5 km to Sembach. Turn right at the first road past the Sembach flight line. Continue for 1.75 km, then turn north for 0.8 km on road leading directly to Sembach Annex Main Gate. Also from Autobahn A6 (E50) E or W, take exit 17 (Enkenbacl-Alsenborn) to Route 48 N toward Bad Kreuznach for approximately 9 km. Turn left on road leading to Sembach for 1.75 km, then turn right on road leading to Main Gate. *EUSMRA: Page 29 (C-4), page 82.* **NMC:** Kaiserslautern, 9 miles west.

RESERVATION INFORMATION: Sembach Annex, 86 SVS/SVML, Unit 3250, Box 500, Bldg 305, APO AE 09054-5000. **C-(USA) 011-49-6371-45-4920, DSN-314-480-4920, (DE) 06371-45-4920, DSN-480-4920,** Fax: C-(USA) 011-49-6371-42589, DSN-314-480-7627, (DE) 06371-42589, DSN-314-480-7627, 0730-2000 hours Mon-Fri. Closed on U.S. holidays. E-mail: lodging.reservations@ramstein.af.mil Check in at facility, check out 1100 hours daily. Government civilian employee billeting. Duty reservations accepted up to one year in advance; Space-A may make reservations 24 hours in advance. *Note: See Ramstein Inns: North, South, Vegelweh, and Landstuhl listing for more lodging. Building 305 on Ramstein AB manages all reservations for Kaiserslautern Community which includes Ramstein AB, Sembach AB, Vogelweh and Landstuhl lodging facilities.*

VOQ/VAQ Ramstein Inn-Sembach. Bldg 216. **C-(USA) 011-49-6302-67-7588/8510, DSN-314-496-7588/8510,** Fax: C-(USA) 011-49-6302-4948. Check in at Bldg 216. Bedroom, shared bath (102). Refrigerator, microwave, TV/VCR, radio, phone, iron/ironing board and housekeeping service. Washer/dryer and ice machine in each building. Older structure. Rates: rooms $19.50 for first person, $27 with spouse.

DV/VIP Ramstein Inn-Sembach. Bldg 110. O6/GS15+. Check in at Bldg 216. Suites with private bath (15). Refrigerator, microwave, TV/VCR, radio, phone, iron/ironing board, housekeeping service, washer/dryer and ice machine. Older structure. Rates: single $28, double $41.

TML AVAILABILITY: Poor due to Reservist/National Guard use for various contingencies.

CREDIT CARDS ACCEPTED: Visa and MasterCard.

TRANSPORTATION: On base shuttle/bus/taxi, DSN-314-480-5961; Off base shuttle/bus, C-011-49-631-316670; Car Rental, C-011-49-710-6219407; Off base taxi, 06371-50510/58626/67023.

DINING OPPORTUNITIES: Various dining establishments on and off base. Dining information provided in Guest Book located in each room.

Sembach has been greatly reduced in size. The runway is closed and there is limited base support but Ramstein AB is within easy reach. Keep updated with Military Living's *R&R Travel News*®. The city hall (Rathaus), is the highest in Germany. There is an elegant restaurant in the penthouse. Visit the Pfalztheater for opera, operetta, plays and ballet. TelePassport® Service is now available; call home in privacy/receive calls in your room.

Spangdahlem Air Base (DE19R7)
Family Support Center
52 MSS/DPF
Unit 3655, Box 65
APO AE 09126-5000

MAIN INSTALLATION TELEPHONE NUMBERS: C-(USA) 011-49-6565-95-1110, (DE) 06565-95-1110, DSN-314-452-1110. Locator 452-7227.

LOCATION: From Autobahn 1 (E44) north or south take exit 125 onto national Route 50 west toward Wittlich and Bitburg. Continue west on Route 50 through the town of Binsfield for approximately 24 km to secondary road north toward town of Spangdahlem for approximately 1 km to base entrance on right (east side of road.). Clearly marked. *EUSMRA: Page 27 (C-1), page 83.* **NMC:** Trier, 34 km southwest. *Note: Use caution as you drive through the Spangdahlem-Bitburg area, there are many no passing zones which German and U.S. Military police enforce with high fines and other punishment.*

RESERVATION INFORMATION: Eifel Arms Inn, Unit 3670, Box 170, Bldg 38, APO AE 09126-5000. **C-(USA) 011-49-6565-95-6525, DSN-314-452-6504, (DE) 06565-95-6504,** Fax: C-011-49-6565-95-6530, DSN-314-452-0530, 24 hours daily. E-mail: 52svs.svmllodge@spangdahlem.af.mil Duty may make reservations any time; Space-A may make reservations 24 hours in advance. Directions from Main Gate: Turn right at intersection, go past the gas station and turn left, then turn left again. Bldg 38 is on the left. Check in at facility 1400 hours, check out 1100 hours. No government civilian employee billeting. *Winner of 2002 Inkeeper Award, small category; named best in Air Force for small facilities.*

TLF Facility is located 12 miles from the base, Eifel West (Bitburg). Check in at either location. Two-bedroom and three-bedroom units with private bath. Full kitchen, CATV, housekeeping service. Modern structure. Rates $39 per unit. No pets.

VQ Bldg 38, Spangdahlem AB. 102 units with private bath. Kitchenette, microwave, CATV, housekeeping service, laundry facility, ice machine, exercise room. Rates: single $18.50, with spouse $27.75. No pets.

DV/VIP Business Suites. Bldg 38. Reservations for six of the suites are made through base protocol, C-(USA) 011-49-6565-95-6057, DSN-314-452-6057. Reservations for remaining eight suites are made by contacting lodging reservation, C-011-49-6565-95-6504, DSN-314-452-6504. Suites, private bath (14). Kitchenette, microwave, CATV, housekeeping service, laundry facility, ice machine, exercise room. Rates: single $30, with spouse $43.50. No pets.

AMENITIES: Exercise Room, Meeting/Conference Room, Internet/E-mail access for all units.

TML AVAILABILITY: Limited all year. Best, Nov-Dec.

CREDIT CARDS ACCEPTED: Visa and MasterCard.

TRANSPORTATION: On base shuttle; Hertz Car Rental, C-011-49-6565-95-6629, DSN-314-452-6629; Taxi Service C-011-49-6565-95-1010. Transportation from Frankfurt and Rhein-Main is the White Swan C-011-49-6565-95-6661, DSN-314-452-6661 or call about our shuttle service C-011-49-6565-95-6645, DSN-314-452-6645.

DINING OPPORTUNITIES: Mom's, C-011-49-6565-4619 is within walking distance of Bldg 38. Zum Edelweiss, C-011-49-6561-3033 is within walking distance of TLF. Waldhaus Eifel, C-011-49-6565-2101; and Zum Alten Brauhaus, C-6565-2057 are within driving distance.

Trier lies where the Saar and Mosel rivers meet, and is Germany's oldest city, dating from the second century. Don't miss lunch in the shadow of the Porta Nigra, and a stroll past renaissance half-timbered houses in the Hauptmarkt.

Stuttgart Community (DE20R7)
6th Area Support Group
Army Community Services
Unit 30401, Box 4010
APO AE 09107-5000

MAIN INSTALLATION TELEPHONE NUMBERS: C-(USA) 011-49-711-680-1110, (DE) 0711-680-1110, DSN-314-430-1110 (Stuttgart Patch Barracks); C-011-49-711-680-1110, DSN-314-421-1110, (DE) 0711-680-1110 (Stuttgart Kelley Barracks); C-011-49-711-819-1110, DSN-314-420-1110, (DE) 0711-819-1110 (Stuttgart Robinson Barracks). Locator 113.

LOCATION: Kelley Barracks: Located south of Stuttgart. From Karlsruhe-Munich Autobahn A8 (E52) take exit 52 or 52B (Stuttgart Degerloch) north on Route 27 for 2.2 km to Stadbezirk-Mohringen exit to Plienger Strasse. Go east on Plienger Strasse for 1.2 km to main entrance. **NMC:** Stuttgart, 4 km north. **Panzer Kaserne:** From Karlsruhe-Munich Autobahn A8 (E52) take exit 51 (Autobahnkreuz Stuttgart) south on Autobahn A81 (E41) for approximately 3.2 km toward Boblingen. Take exit 22 (Boblingen Ost) and go southwest approximately 1 km to intersection with Fredrick Gertlacher Strasse which becomes Panzer Strasse (Route K1057). Turn left on Panzer Strasse (Route K1057) and go approximately 1.3 km, up a hill, to entrance. **NMC:** Stuttgart 15 km northeast. **Patch Barracks:** Located northwest of Vaihingen. From Karlsruhe-Munich Autobahn A81 (E52), take exit 51 (Autobahnkreuz Stuttgart) north on Autobahn A831 for approximately 1.7 km to Stuttgart-Vaihingen exit to Hauptstrasse. Follow for approximately 0.6 km west to entrance. **NMC:** Stuttgart, 6 km northeast. **Robinson Barracks:** Located in north Stuttgart. From Karlsruhe-Munich Autobahn A81 (E52), take exit 52 or 52B (Stuttgart-Degerloch) north to Route 27. Follow Route 27 north for approximately 13 km through Stuttgart (in the tunnel, keep right and follow sign to Heilbrosen Strasse). Continue on Route 27 to Auerbachstrasse. (The landmark is the tall round Bosch Tower.) Turn north on Auerbachstrasse and follow for two km to entrance. Also, from Autobahn A81 (E41), take exit 17 (Stuttgart-Zuffeauren) southeast on Route 10 for approximately 7.5 km to intersection with Auerbachstrasse. (The landmark is the tall round Bosch Tower.) Turn north on Auerbachstrasse and follow for 2 km to entrance. *EUSMRA: Page 33 (A-4), page 84, page 85.* **NMC:** Stuttgart, in the city.

RESERVATION INFORMATION: Swabian Inn, Bldg 2506, Patch Barracks, Unit 30401, Box 4010, APO AE 09131-5000. **C-(USA) 011-49-711-67840, (DE) 0711-67840, DSN-314-430-7181/4137,** Fax: C-(USA) 011-49-711-67-4199, 24 hours daily. E-mail: korbr@6asg,army.mil Check in at facility, check out 1000 hours.

(VOQ) **Swabian Inn, Patch Barracks.** Bldg 2506, 2508 Patch Barracks. Bedroom, shared bath (122); suites (4). Refrigerator, microwave, TV/VCR, housekeeping service, laundry facility, cribs, cots, ice machine, full kitchen on each floor. Older structure, renovated. Rates: Duty $35-$40, others $40-$45; suites $53.50, each additional person $4. Maximum capacity/charge depends on lodging and number in party. Duty can make reservations anytime; others Space-A can make reservations seven days in advance.

(TML) **Hilltop Hotel, Robinson Barracks. Renovation completed in early 1998.** Bldg 169, CMR 447, Box 36, APO AE 09154-5000, **C-(USA) 011-49-711-896-5270, (DE) 0711-896-5270, DSN-314-420-7193,** Fax: C-011-49-711-896-52-7199. E-mail: hilltop.hotel@6asg.army.mil Check in 1400 hours, check out 1000 hours. Bedroom, queen size bed, two single beds in connecting room, private bath (64; 1 is handicap accessible). Community kitchenette, refrigerator, microwave, CATV/VCR, phone, clock radio, safe, housekeeping service, washer/dryer, iron/ironing board, fitness center with sauna in basement. Snacks sold 24 hours daily at Front Desk. Rates: standard rooms $45-$50, each additional person $4; suites $52, each additional person $4. Maximum three per room.

(TML) Panzer Kaserne, Panzer Community Club. Bldg 2916. C-(USA) 011-49-7031-115-401, DSN-314-420-2694; Room (11) with bath and VIP suite (1). Kelley Barracks, Kelley Community Club, Bldg 3308, C-(USA) 011-49-711-729-2811/568, DSN-314-421-2811/568, Fax: C-011-49-711-726-1343. Room (11) with bath and VIP suite (2), TV, telephone, and refrigerator. E-mail: strobele@6asg.army.mil Rooms and suites available. Rates: single $35, suite $85, each additional person $15. Call lodging office above for more information.

Note: The New Kelley Hotel opened its doors to the public on 1 August 2001. Call C-011-49-711-729-2815 (USA) or Fax: C-011-49-711-907-261-124(USA) or email: kelley.hotel@6asg.army.mil for details. Panzer Kaserne has been undergoing renovation.

(DV/VIP) HQ USEUCOM, Patch Barracks, Unit 30400, APO AE 09131-5000. C-(USA) 011-49-711-680-4186, DSN-314-430-4186. O6/GS15+. Separate bedroom VIP suites, private bath (7). Refrigerator, microwave, TV/VCR, housekeeping service, washer/dryer, cribs, cots, ice machine, full kitchen on each floor. Older structure, renovated. Rates: $60-$65, each additional person $4. Maximum capacity/charge depends on lodging and number in party. Duty can make reservations; others Space-A.

(DV/VIP) **Hilltop Hotel, Robinson Barracks.** Bldg 169, CMR 447, Box 36, APO AE 09154-5000. VIP Suites (4). Bedroom, queen-size bed, living room with sofabed, private bath. Community kitchenette, refrigerator, microwave, mini bar, CATV/VCR, phone, clock radio, safe, housekeeping service, washer/dryer, iron/ironing board, fitness center with sauna in basement. Snacks sold 24 hours daily at Front Desk. Rates:$60-$65 per night, each additional person $4. Maximum three per room. No pets.

TML AVAILABILITY: Swabian Inn: Good, Dec-Mar. Difficult, May-Aug.

CREDIT CARDS ACCEPTED: Swabian Inn: Visa, MasterCard, American Express and Diners. Hilltop Hotel: Visa, MasterCard and American Express.

TRANSPORTATION: Panzer Kaserne Budget Rental Car C-011-49-711-680-7275; Kelley Barracks Shuttle/Bus C-011-49-711-729-2454. Taxi at gates.

DINING OPPORTUNITIES: Alten Pfefferer, C-011-49-711-541339/40; Aussichtsrecih, C-011-49-711-851424; and Distelfarm, C-011-49-711-851782 are within walking distance of Hilltop Hotel. Hundrfreunde Vereinsheim, C-011-49-711-851963 is within driving distance.

Starting the end of April the Stuttgarter Frülingsfest, with carnival attractions and beer tents is a must for visitors. Also don't miss the Cannstatter Volksfest in Bad Cannstatt at the end of September.

Vilseck Community (DE85R7)
Attn: AE TTV-SB-DCA-ACS-RAM
409th Base Support Battalion
Unit 28038
APO AE 09112-5000

MAIN INSTALLATION TELEPHONE NUMBERS: C-(USA) 011-49-9662-83-1110, (DE) 09662-83-1110, DSN-314-476-1110. Locator 113.

LOCATION: From Nuremberg take Autobahn 6 (E50) east toward Amberg. Use exit 65 (Amberg West) and go northeast on Route 299 approximately 7 km to Amberg. Watch for signs to Vilseck. Stay on Route 299 through Amberg (crossing Routes 85 and 14) approximately 16 km to Grossschonbrunn, then turn northwest on secondary road approximately 7 km to village of Vilseck. From Vilseck continue northwest approximately 2 km to village of Sorghof, then north approximately 2 km to Main Gate of Rose Barracks. (Follow signs.) Alternatively, from intersection of Route 299 and Route 14 (north of Amberg), continue northeast on Route 299 approximately 10 km to village of Friehung, then west approximately 9 km on road to Vilseck and village of Sorghof. Turn north at Sorghof and go north approximately 2 km to Main Gate of Rose Barracks. *EUSMRA: Page 36 (C-2), page 87.* **NMC:** Nuremberg, 40 miles northwest.

RESERVATION INFORMATION: Kristall Inn, 409th BSB, Rose Barracks, Vilseck, Bldg 275, APO AE 09112-5000. **C-(USA) 011-49-9662-83-441104 or C-011-49-9662-83-2555/1700, (DE) 09662-441104 or 09662-83-2555/1700, DSN-314-476-2555/1700,** Fax: C-(USA) 011-49-9662-441140. E-mail: Kristall.Inn@cmtymail.100asg.army.mil Directions: From Main Gate, turn right at 6th traffic light, take first left to building 275, 0700-2300 hours. Check in at facility, check out 1100 hours. Government civilian employee lodging.

(TLQ) Kristall Inn, Rose Barracks. Bldgs: 275 (reception desk). Rooms, private bath (233). Refrigerator, microwave, coffee maker, ceiling fans, phone (with answering machine, wake-up service and PC connection), TV/VCR, hair dryer, housekeeping service (daily), washer/dryer, irons/ironing boards, cribs, rollaways, ice making machine, complimentary coffee and movies. Modern structure, renovated. Rates: sponsor $30, each additional person $4. *Pets allowed (PCS),* fee $3 per day (final cleaning and spraying: one additional room charge). Room rates are subject to change.

(TML) Big Mike Travel Camp. C-(USA) 011-49-9662-83-2563, DE-09662-83-2563. Directions: Easily found on base via signs. Check in is at Outdoor Recreation, Bldg 2236, which is on the right on the way to the camp. Two-bedroom apartments (2) and three-bedroom apartments (2), furnished, living room, kitchen, utensils. Rates: $60-$70. See *Military Living's Military RV, Camping and Outdoor Recreation Around the World* for additional information and directions.

AMENITIES: Meeting/Conference Room, Snack Vending Machine, Soft Drink Machine.

TML AVAILABILITY: Good. Best in winter, difficult Aug/Sep.

CREDIT CARDS ACCEPTED: Visa, MasterCard and American Express.

TRANSPORTATION: Budget Car Rental, C-011-49-9662-40289; Off base taxi, C-011-49-9662-300/6454/7604/7711.

DINING OPPORTUNITIES: Burger King, Cafeteria, Foodmall, Tumbleweed Restaurant (TexMex) and Greek Restaurant are located within walking distance. Many off-post restaurants with German, Italian, Greek and Oriental food are within driving distance.

Vilseck is near Grafenwoehr. Army Community Service (DSN-314-476-2650/2733) has a wonderful list of points of interest in the area put together by the Oberpfalz area women's clubs.

Wiesbaden Community (DE27R7)
221st Base Support Battalion
Unit 29623
APO AE 09096-5000

MAIN INSTALLATION TELEPHONE NUMBERS: C-(USA) 011-49-611-705-1110, (DE) 0611-705-1110, DSN-314-337/338-1110. Locator 011-49-611-705-5055.

LOCATION: Accessible from Autobahn 3 (E35) and Autobahn 5 (E451) which connect to Autobahn 66 (East/Army Airfield) (Center Map). From east-west Autobahn 66 take exit 6 (Wiesbaden-Erbenheim) to Route 455 north. Route 455 leads into Berliner Strasse. Go north on Route 455 (Berliner Strasse) approximately 3.7 km to Gustav-Stresemann Ring/New York Strasse. Stay on Berliner Strasse and follow signs to "STADMITTE KURHOUSE/CASINO." Berliner Strasse changes to Frankfurter Strasse. Continue on Frankfurter Strasse approximately 0.7 km. The American Arms Hotel will be on the left. *EUSMRA: Page 30 (A-3; B-3,4), page 88.* **NMC:** Wiesbaden, in the city.

RESERVATION INFORMATION: Wiesbaden Conference Center, American Arms Hotel, 221st Base Support Battalion, 17 Frankfurterstrasse, APO AE 09096-5000. **C- (USA) 011-49-611-343136/343664, (DE) 0611-343664, DSN-314-337-7493/7212,** Fax: C-(USA) 011-49-611-304522, 24 hours daily. WEB: www.wiesbaden.army.mil E-mail: conf@221bsb. wiesbaden.army.mil or reserve@221bsb.wiesbaden.army.mil Duty may make reservations. For unofficial reservations by stateside arrivals and individuals on R&R during deployment downrange, reservations may be made no earlier than 7 days prior to check-in date. For all other unofficial visitors, reservations may be made 365 days in advance, but only for Fri, Sat and Sun nights. Reservations will not be made for persons wanting to stay Mon-Thu. Rooms are available Mon-Thurs on a Space-A/walk-in basis after 1800 hours and may be extended (if rooms are available) by the reservations office. Room extensions should be performed and executed daily before check-out time (1100 hours) for those staying Mon-Thurs on a Space-A basis. All unofficial weekend reservations are subject to cancellation based on official travel requirements. Persons who have booked a reservation, but will be bumped due to official business travelers will be notified no later than 24 hours prior to arrival date. Reservations will only be guaranteed when a valid credit card is offered, and guaranteed reservations are subject to cancellation as stated above. Check in after 1400 hours at front desk, check out 1100 hours. Billeting for government civilian employees on orders.

(TML) American Arms Hotel. 17 Frankfurterstrasse. Suites, private bath, living room bedroom, mini-bar refrigerator, coffee maker and TV (95); Bedroom, standard room, shared bath (101). Refrigerator, TV/VCR, phone, housekeeping service, laundry facility, cribs, cots. Modern structure, renovated. Rates: Official Visitors standard room, single $49, double $27(each person), each additional person $5; suite, $65, each additional person $5; Ambassador suite (0-7+ or civilian equivalent), $75, each additional person $5. Rates: Unofficial Vistors standard room, single $54, each additional person $5; suite, $70, each additional person $5; Ambassador suite (0-7+ or civilian equivalent), $80, each additional person $5.

(DV/VIP) Contact the Conference Sales Office of the American Arms Hotel at C-(USA) 011-49-611-343350, (DE) 0611-343350 DSN-314-338-7496, O5+/GS14+. DV/VIP suite (1). Refrigerator, TV/VCR, phone, housekeeping service, laundry facility, cribs, cots. Modern structure, renovated. Rates: $69.50, each additional person (over age 11) $25, (age 5-11) $15, (under age 5) $10.

AMENITIES: Newly Renovated Lobby, Weinstube, ATM Machine, small Exchange, Beauty Salon, Fitness Room, Meeting/Conference Room, Dry Cleaning Service, and Video Rental. Ice, Soft drink and Snack Vending Machine.

TML AVAILABILITY: Weekends usually good.

CREDIT CARDS ACCEPTED: Visa, MasterCard, American Express and Diners.

TRANSPORTATION: On/Off base shuttle/bus, C-06134-604492, DSN-314-337-6898; Car Rental, C-0611-713031; Off base taxi, C-0611-333333/444444.

DINING OPPORTUNITIES: Restaurant and bar on premises.

The American Arms Hotel is conveniently located in historic downtown Wiesbaden. In addition to other amenities, it also has 24-hour slot machines. Hainerberg Shopping Center is three blocks away from lodging and is "shop till you drop" country! In the center of Wiesbaden, you are also within walking distance of wonderful architectural and cultural treasures (Wiesbaden had little damage during WWII).

Wuerzburg Community (DE21R7)
417th Base Support Battalion
Leighton Barracks, Bldg 26
Unit 26137
APO AE 09031-5000

MAIN INSTALLATION TELEPHONE NUMBERS: C-(USA) 011-49-931-889-1110, (DE) 0931-889-1110, DSN-314-350-1110. Locator 350-4224.

LOCATION: From east-west Autobahn 3, take exit 70 (Wuerzburg-Heidingfeld) north toward Wuerzburg on Route 19 for approximately 4.3 km to Rottendorfer Strasse. Turn right on Rottendorfer Strasse in the direction of Gerbrunn and Frauenland and go east for approximately 1.1 km directly to Main Gate of Leighton Barracks. *EUSMRA: Page 34 (A-3), page 90.* **NMC:** Wuerzburg, 1 km west.

RESERVATION INFORMATION: American Guesthouse, Leighton Barracks, Bldg 2,3,5. APO AE 09036-5000. **C-(USA) 011-49-931-70582-0 or C-011-49-931-889-1700/6648, (DE) 0931-70582-0 or 0931-889-1700/6648, DSN-314-350-1700/6648,** Fax: C(USA)-011-49-931-705-8257, 24 hours daily. E-mail: wurzgh@xs1.mwr.army.mil WEB: www.98asg.wuerzburg.army.mil Check in 1200 hours, check out 1000 hours. Government civilian employee billeting.

(Army Lodging) American Guesthouse, Leighton Barracks. Bldg 2, 3, 5. Bedrooms, shared bath (40), mini suites (2), *pet friendly rooms* (6). Refrigerator, microwave, coffee maker, CATV/VCR, hair dryer, housekeeping service, laundry facility, iron/ironing board. Older structure. Rooms refurbished in 1996. Rates: room $32-$50, each additional person $3. Duty can make reservations thirty days in advance, others Space-A 24 hours in advance.

(DV/VIP) SGS, Protocol, Bldg 6, C-(USA) 011-49-931-889-6747. O6/GS15+. American Guesthouse. Two-bedroom suite (2). Rates: $60. Retirees Space-A.

AMENITIES: Mini Mart. Ice, Snack and Soft Drink Vending Machine.

TML AVAILABILITY: Good, Nov-Jan. Difficult, other times.

CREDIT CARDS ACCEPTED: Visa, MasterCard and American Express.

TRANSPORTATION: Shuttle/Bus C-011-49-931-889-7139; Budget Car Rental, C-011-49-931-708475.

DINING OPPORTUNITIES: Top of Maine Club, C-011-49-931-889-6305; and AAFES Food Court are located within walking distance.

Highlights: 1st Infantry Division Museum. Located within walking distance of 67th Combat Hospital, Commissary, the largest Post Exchange in Europe. The annual Mozart Festival in summer, the Marienberg Castle, about 45 minutes from the old walled city of Rothenburg.

More Safety • Save Money • Enjoy Military Camaraderie
Travel on less per day . . . the military way!
Your military ID card is your passport to savings and safety.

HONDURAS

Soto Cano Air Base (HO01R3)
Attn: Billeting, PSC 42, Unit 5720
APO AA 34042-5000

MAIN INSTALLATION TELEPHONE NUMBERS: C-(USA) 011-504-237-88-33, DSN-313-449-4000.

LOCATION: From Tegucigalpa take highway northwest to Comayagua, after about 24 miles you will see the signs for Soto Cano AB. Comayagua is eight miles further.

RESERVATION INFORMATION: Attn: Billeting, PSC 42, Unit 5720 APO AA 34042-5000 **C-(USA) 011-504-237-88-33, DSN-313-449-4000.** Fax:C-(USA) 011-504-237-88-33 ext 4599.

(TML) Air Force and Army BQ's. Substandard conditions. Temporary wooden units; permanent metal barracks. Beds, community bath, A/C, TV/VCR, refrigerators, microwaves, laundry facility. Rates: No charge. *Note: Be advised, this is a combat training area with few support facilities. This TML is not recommended for leisure travelers but is listed in the event of a need for lodging in the immediate area.*

TRANSPORTATION: Commercial bus. Taxi to Tegucigalpa (inexpensive). Government shuttle bus is free.

DINING OPPORTUNITIES: Dining for Duty only within walking distance. Three clubs on base. No BX access for transients.

HONG KONG

Hong Kong Community (HK02R8)
Officer in Charge, USN Contracting Department
Fenwick Pier, Hong Kong, China
(China Special Adminstrative Region)
FPO AP 96659-2200
(Not U.S. Government Lodging)

MAIN INSTALLATION TELEPHONE NUMBERS: C-(USA) 011-852-2-861-0063 (USN Contracting Department).

LOCATION: Fenwick Pier is on Lung King Street, Wanchai District, Hong Kong. It is located off Convention Avenue across from the Hong Kong Academy for Performing Arts. There are MTR (Underground Rail) entrances nearby on Hardcourt Road. **NMC:** Hong Kong, in city limits.

RESERVATION INFORMATION: Mariners' Club, 11 Middle Road, Kowloon, FPO AP 96521-5000. **C-(USA) 011-852-2-368-8261, (HK) 2368-8261,** Fax: C-(USA) 011-852-2-366-0928. E-mail: mariners@netvigator.com Directions: In Kowloon, from Salisbury Road E of W to north at New World Centre then one block to Middle Road and club. Four blocks west to Starr Ferry Pier. Club is operated by the Mission to Seafarers, an Anglican missionary society which provides churches, clubs and chaplains in two hundred of the world's largest ports. Reservations can be made via email without a deposit. All credit cards are accepted.

(TML) Facility includes in-suite family rooms, bedroom, private bath. TV, laundry service, bar, dining, darts, video/laser films, pool and Ten Pin Bowling Alley. Rates: Single room $31-$38; Single room with shower $48-$55; Double room $47-$53; Double room (Ensuite) $57-$67. All prices include complimentary breakfast. *Note: This site has plans for renovations stated for mid 2002; call in advance to verify that lodging is available.*

Author's Note: This is not a military installation, but a Seafarer's Club primarily for the use of Merchant Seaman, however they do welcome the Allied Armed Forces. These facilities are operated by the Mission to Seamen, an Anglican missionary society. Be sure to visit all the sights in Hong Kong.

ICELAND

Keflavik NATO Base (IC01R7)
Family Service Center Keflavik
Bldg 2351
PSC 1003, Box 45
FPO AE 09728-0345

MAIN INSTALLATION TELEPHONE NUMBERS: C-(USA) 011-354-425-2000, (IC) 425-0111, DSN-(USA) 314-450-0111 (Europe) DSN-314-228-0111. Locator ext 2100; Medical ext 3300; Security Police ext 2211.

LOCATION: Keflavik International Airport (IAP) shares landing facilities with the Keflavik (US/NATO) Naval Station. From Reykjavik take Route 41 southwest 41 km following the signs for the town of Keflavik. The highway splits; the right fork is Route 45 and the left fork is Route 44. Take the right fork Route 45 for 4 km to a west exit to the Main Gate on the west side of Route 45. Clearly marked. *EUSMRA: Page 94 (A-3), page 95.* **NMC:** Reykjavik, 57 km northeast.

RESERVATION INFORMATION: Bldg 761, PSC 1003, Box 34, FPO AE 09728-0334. **C-(USA) 011-354-425-4333, (IC) 425-4333, DSN-(USA) 314-450-4333.** Fax: C-011-354-425-2511, DSN-314-450-2511, 24 hours daily. E-mail: billeting.booking@naskef.navy.mil WEB: naskef.navy.mil/Departments/Billeting/cbq.htm Sponsors for duty personnel can make reservations; others Space-A. Check in at billeting, check out 1000 hours. Government civilian employee billeting. *Awarded the Cinclant Fleet Five Star Accreditation for year 2000 for Berthing Excellence.*

(CBQ) Bldgs 634, 636. Bedroom, shared bath. Bldgs 639, 761, Bedroom, private bath, kitchen. All rooms refrigerator, CATV, free video rental, housekeeping service, laundry facility, computers with internet access in lobby. Rates: single $15, double $13. USN personnel should utilize local SATO office for official travel.

(NAVY LODGE) Navy Lodge, Bldg 786. US Navy Exchange, Naval Station, PSC 1003, Box 10, FPO AE 09728-0310. **C-1-800-NAVY-INN.** Lodge number is C-(USA) 011-354-425-2210, (IC) 425-2000 ext 7594/2210, Fax: C-(USA) 011-354-425-2091. Located 0.4 km inside Main Gate. Adjacent to air passenger terminal. 27 units. One- and two-bedroom units, private bath. Family room with complete laundry and kitchen (1). All family rooms come with microwave oven. Refrigerator, coffee maker, CATV/VCR, video rental, TV in lounge, housekeeping service, coin laundry facility, cribs, cots, ice machine. Newly renovated structure. Rates: single room w/ one double bed $55; family room w/ two double beds $66; family room w/ two double beds and kitchen $78; small apartment $66; suite $96. Maximum six persons. All categories can make reservations. No pets. Trivia: Reykjavik McDonald's takes credit cards.

(DV/VIP) Commander, C-(USA) 011-354-425-4414. O5+. Retirees Space-A.

AMENITIES: Exercise Room, Mini Mart. Ice, Snack and Soft Drink Vending Machine.

TML AVAILABILITY: Fair, winter; poor, summer. The Navy Lodge good, winter; difficult, Apr-Aug.

CREDIT CARDS ACCEPTED: Visa, MasterCard, and American Express.

TRANSPORTATION: On base shuttle/bus, C-011-354-425-2259; Off base shuttle/bus, C-011-354-421-1555; Car Rental, C-011-354-421-3357; On base taxi, C-011-354-425-4141/2525; Off base taxi, C-011-354-421-1515.

DINING OPPORTUNITIES: Parcheezi's, C-011-354-425-6126; Three Flags Club, C-011-354-425-7004; and Wendy's, C-011-354-425-2722 are within walking distance. Glodin, C-011-354-421-1777; Olsen Olsen, C-011-354-421-4457; and Rain, C-011-354-421-4601 are within driving distance.

Into summer skiing? Visit the Kerlingarfjoll area. Fishing? July and August are best for brown trout, char and salmon. Also try sightseeing.

ITALY

Admiral Carney Park (IT03R7)
PSC 810, Box 13
FPO AE 09619-1013

MAIN INSTALLATION TELEPHONE NUMBERS: C-(USA) 011-39-081-724-1110, (IT) 081-724-1110. Locator 724-5547.

LOCATION: On the west coast of Italy in Admiral Carney Park. From Autostrada 2 to the Tangenziale toll route exit, head west on the Tangenziale for approximately 20 km to the Via Campana exit, then north on Via Campana. At the end of the traffic circle complete a 3/4th turn, then head west. Follow signs to park. *EUSMRA: Page 108.* **NMC:** Naples, 20 km south. NMI: Naples, Naval Support Activity, 10 km southwest.

RESERVATION INFORMATION: Admiral Carney Park, Attn: MWR, PSC 817, Box 09, FPO, AE 09622-5000. **C-(USA) 011-39-081-526-3396/1579, (IT) 081-526-3396/1579,** Fax: C-(USA) 011-39-081-526-4813. Reservations required up to 90 days in advance. Check in at facility 1300 hours, check out 1030 hours.

(Cabins) The 54-acre recreational and sports complex is contained within the walls of a crater. Bedroom cabins (9); two-bedroom cabins (11). Kitchenette, refrigerator, grill and picnic area. Bath house and laundromat separate, no utensils or towels. Rates: $35-$45 per night per cabin, weekly rates available. Maximum four to six per cabin. No pets.

AMENITIES: Mini Mart (summer only), Snack and Soft Drink Vending Machine.

TML AVAILABILITY: Good, winter. Difficult, summer.

CREDIT CARDS ACCEPTED: Visa, MasterCard and American Express.

TRANSPORTATION: On base shuttle/bus (summer only); Car Rental.

DINING OPPORTUNITIES: Crater Cafe, Golf Course and Le Palme are within walking distance. Crater Cantina, Da Ciufflello, Il Brontolone, burgers and pizza are within driving distance.

Visit historic Pompeii, Herculanum, the popular beaches on Capri, and Ischia. In Naples the National Museum, the Art Gallery of Capodimonte are nearby. This is a full rec park—for more details see *Military RV, Camping and Outdoor Recreation Around The World*.

Aviano Air Base (IT04R7)
31st MSS/DPF
Unit 6125, Box 260
APO AE 09601-5260

MAIN INSTALLATION TELEPHONE NUMBERS: C-(USA) 011-39-0434-66-7110, (IT) 0434-66-7110, DSN-314-632-1110. Locator 113.

LOCATION: From the vicinity of Mestre and Venezia take Autostrada 4 (E70) northeast approximately 60 km to Portogruaro exit north onto

Autostrada A28. Go northwest on Autostrada 28 approximately 10 km to Cimpello exit, then north 6 km to the intersection with Route SS 13. (Follow the Autostrada 28 exit extension north to traffic circle at intersection with Route SS 13.) At traffic circle, go west on Route SS 13 and follow signs toward Sacile and Pordenone. Turn right (north) onto Route SS 251 at the traffic light at the intersection (with a VW/Audi dealer on right) toward Maniago. After 1 km, fork left onto secondary road at Aviano sign across from Italian military base. Continue straight past town of Roveredo in Piano for 7 km. Entrance to Aviano Air Base is on the left (west) side of road, marked by a flashing yellow light. For the Aviano Air Base Support Areas, continue straight past Area F and the flightline into the City of Aviano. Lodging and support facilities are well marked in Areas 1 and 2. *EUSMRA: Page 98 (C-1), page 104.* **NMC:** Pordenone, 13 km south.

RESERVATION INFORMATION: 31 SVS/SVML, Bldg 256, Pedemonte Street, APO AE 09601-2245. **C-(USA) 011-39-0434-66-5722/5041, (IT) 0434-66-5722/5041,** Fax: C-(USA) 011-39-0434-66-5581, DSN-314-632-5581, 24 hours daily. E-mail: lodging@aviano.af.mil WEB: www.aviano.af.mil Active Duty, Retirees, Reservists, NG, DoD civilian employee billeting. Duty can make reservations anytime; Retirees and leave can make reservations 24 hours in advance. Check in at facility, check out 1100 hours. *Note: As part of the Aviano 2000 Plan, new lodging will be constructed which will include 71 VQ Suites, 3 VQ Suites, 6 DV Suites and 100 TLF units. Handicap access rooms will also be available. As a result, temporary military lodging at press time is extremely limited.*

(VOQ/VAQ) Bldgs 273, 274, 255. VAQ rooms, shared bath (12); VOQ rooms, private bath (5). Family members OK. No TLF. Rates: single $19.50 per night. Families are currently placed off-base. This will change when new facilities come up.

(DV/VIP) PAO, CCP. Bldg 1360, Room 4, C-(USA) 011-39-0434-667-4704/5/6, DSN-314-632-4704/5/6. E9, O6+. Bldg 273 Enlisted Suite, private bath (2). Rate: $29 single per night. Bldg 255 Officer Suite, private bath (1). Rate: single $30 per night. Family members OK. No TLF.

TML AVAILABILITY: Extremely Limited.

CREDIT CARDS ACCEPTED: Visa and MasterCard.

TRANSPORTATION: On/Off base shuttle/bus, C-011-39-0434-66-7666; Car Rental: Eurocar, C-011-39-0434-66-8719; On base car rental; On base taxi, C-011-39-0434-66-7666; Off base taxi, C-011-39-0337-545480/ 651019.

DINING OPPORTUNITIES: Aviano Inn, C-011-39-0434-65-1050; Da Bepi, C-011-39-0434-65-1024; Da Marios, C-011-39-0434-65-2138; Da Tussi, C-011-39-0434-65-1930; La Passeggiata, C-011-39-0434-65-1259; San Giorgio, C-011-39-0434-65-1482; Stradella, C-011-39-0434-65-1108; and Western House, C-011-39-0434-65-1851 are within driving distance.

Don't miss the Castello di Aviano, Aviano's castle ruins. Pordenone (12.8 km south) for shopping, strolling and cappuccino. Many other sights are nearby.

Camp Darby (Livorno) (IT10R7)
Livorno AST
Attn: AESE-BSL-CS
Unit 31301, Box 55
APO AE 09613-5000

MAIN INSTALLATION TELEPHONE NUMBERS: C-(USA) 011-39-050-54-7111, (IT) 050-54-7111, DSN-314-633-7111. Locator 113.

LOCATION: Between Livorno and Pisa on Italy's northwestern coast. From Autostrada 12 (E80) take Pisa Centro exit just south of Pisa. After the toll station follow signs marked Livorno, bear left at the yield sign and turn right onto the SS 1 "Aurelia" Road. After approximately 6.2 km, make a right turn on the first paved road after the "AGIP" gas station. This road passes over a canal, the Main Gate is on the left (west) side of Via Vecchia Livornese. The Sea Pines Camp and Lodge Office is located

in Bldg 678 in the northern section of Camp Darby. *EUSMRA: Page 99 (A-2), page 106.* **NMC:** Pisa, 9 km north.

RESERVATION INFORMATION: Camp Darby Lodging Unit, 31301 Box 60, APO AE 09613-5000. **C-(USA) 011-39-050-54-7225, (IT) 050-54-7225, DSN-314-633-7448/7225/7221,** Fax: C-(USA) 011-39-050-54-7758, (IT) 050-54-7758, DSN-314-633-7758, 0700-2300 hours (winter), 24 hours daily (Memorial Day to Labor Day). WEB http://www.livorno.army.mil Reservations made by fax and/or e-mail must be confirmed by phone. Check in at Bldg 678.

(TML) **Sea Pines Lodge Camp and Lodge.** Bldg 832-838. Old facility. Room, private bath (24). Double bed, single bed and sofa bed, sleeps four. Small refrigerator, SATV/VCR, in room telephone service, housekeeping service, cribs available ($3 per night). Rates: begin at $27. New facility. Room, private bath (14). Two single beds and one sofa bed, sleeps three. Rates: begin at $60. Game room and swimming pool in season. All categories may make reservations for summer beginning 1 Feb. No pets allowed in new facitlity or on beaches. **All guests during peak season have free entry to the American Beach while staying at Camp Darby Lodging.**

(TML) Guesthouse. **Casa Toscana.** Bldg 202. Check in 1400 hours at Bldg 678, check out 1000 hours. Rooms, apartments. Types of accommodations cannot be guaranteed. TV/VCR, A/C, housekeeping service, cribs. PCS in/out, TDY and Space-A. Active, retired, U.S. civilian employees and NATO ID card holders. *Note: Casa Toscana is currently closed for renovation.*

(DV/VIP) O6/GS13+. DV/VIP rooms available. TDY, Retirees Space-A.

TML AVAILABILITY: Best, Labor Day to Spring Break/Easter. Difficult, Spring Break/Easter to Labor Day.

CREDIT CARDS ACCEPTED: Visa, American Express and Discover. *Note: Local currency, Eurocheks and MasterCard are NOT accepted.*

TRANSPORTATION: On/Off base shuttle/bus C-011-39-650-54-8160; Car Rental: Europcar, C-(USA) 011-39-050-54-7395, DSN-314-633-7395, Fax: C-(USA) 011-39-050-54-4817; Taxis are not allowed on post.

DINING OPPORTUNITIES: Darby Combined Club, within driving distance on post, serves evening meals. Mensa open for lunch at 1130-1400 hours, Americans can eat from 1230-1400 hours Mon-Fri. Greek Place (next to bowling center) 1200-2100 hours Sun-Sat. AAFES Burger Bar (next to PX) open 0700-1800 hours Mon-Fri , 0800-1700 hours Sat, 0900-1600 hours Sun. There are several restaurants within driving distance in Tirrenia, Marina di Pisa, Pisa and Livorno.

Located in the choice Tuscany region of Italy, one hour from Florence. Camp Darby has its own stretch of Mediterranean beach at the resort town of Tirrenia (4.5 km). The famous Leaning Tower of Pisa is 9.6 km north. Take advantage of the Information, Tours & Registration (ITR) Office.

Capodichino Airport (Naples) (IT17R7)
PSC 817, Box 3
FPO AE 09622-1200

MAIN INSTALLATION TELEPHONE NUMBERS: C-(USA) 011-39-081-568-1110, (IT) 081-568-1110, DSN-314-626-1110. Locator 081-724-1110.

LOCATION: On the Gulf of Naples. From Autostrada 2 (E45) north or south to Naples to the Tangenziale toll route exit, then continue west on the Tangenziale toll route approximately 2 km toward downtown Naples. The entrance to Capodichino Airport is on the right side of the street. Look for signs to U.S. Navy Facility. **NMC:** Naples, 4.8 km southeast.

RESERVATION INFORMATION: Bldg 453, PSC 817, Box 7, FPO AE 09622. **C-(USA) 011-39-081-568-5250, (IT) 081-568-5250, DSN-314-568-5250,** Fax: C-(USA) 011-39-081-568-4842, DSN-314-626-4842.

TML **Capo Inn.** Located 0.25 miles from Main Gate. Single rooms, private bath. Refrigerator, TV/VCR, housekeeping service, laundry facility, microwave. Rates: $22, $28, $47.50 depending on room size. Navy funded personnel $22 per person up to $59. Non-Duty stay Space-A. No children.

AMENITIES: Ice, Snack and Soft Drink Vending Machine.

TML AVAILABILITY: May-Sep, difficult. Best, winter.

CREDIT CARDS ACCEPTED: Visa and MasterCard.

TRANSPORTATION: Off base shuttle/bus; Car Rentals: Avis, C-011-39-081-780-5790; Eurocar, C-011-39-081-780-5643; Hertz, C-011-39-081-568-5228; Taxi C-011-39-081-560-6060.

DINING OPPORTUNITIES: Ciao Hall, C-011-39-081-568-5502; Blue Parrot Club C-011-39-081-568-5348 are within walking distance.

La Maddalena Naval Support Activity (Sardinia) (IT13R7)
Commanding Officer
PSC 816, Box 1795
FPO AE 09612-0051

MAIN INSTALLATION TELEPHONE NUMBERS: C-(USA) 011-39-0789-798-1110, (IT) 0789-798-1110, DSN-314-623-1110. Locator 0789-798-244.

LOCATION: On the island of La Maddalena, approximately 5 km off the northern tip of the island of Sardenia. Driving directions: Take Route 125 north from Olbia 35 km to Palau. At the Palau Pier, purchase ferry ticket on the pier, before boarding car/passenger ferry for 15-minute ride to the ferry landing in the town of La Maddalena. From the La Maddalena ferry landing go northeast approximately 0.4 km to the intersection of Via C. Duilio and Via Principe. Main gate and pedestrian gate to Mordini Compound, housing main NSA facilities, are on the north side of Via Principe. The Paradiso Complex is approximately 2.5 km northwest of the La Maddalena ferry landing; follow signs to the installation. *EUSMRA: Page 100 (B-2), page 106.* **NMC:** Olbia, 45 km southeast.

RESERVATION INFORMATION: Calabro Hall, Paradiso Complex, PSC 816, Box 1795, FPO AE 09612-0006. **C-(USA) 011-39-0789-798-297/416/417/418/419, (IT) 0789-798-297/416/417/418/419, DSN-314-623-8297/416/417/418/419,** Fax: C-(USA) 011-39-0789-798-249, (IT) 0789-798-249, DSN-314-623-8249, 24 hours daily. Check in at facility, check out any time. *Note: No TML available for personnel on leave or temporary duty. PCS facilities only.*

BEQ Paradiso Complex (71) and Santo Stefano (36). Bldg 300. PCS personnel only. Bedroom, one bed, shared bath (10); bedroom, one bed, shared bath (51); two-bedroom, private bath (5). Refrigerator, microwave, A/C, housekeeping service, washer/dryer, soft drink and snack vending, ice machine. Modern structure. Rates: no charge. Maximum two per room.

DV/VIP Write to: Supply Officer, NSA La Maddalena, FPO AE 09612. Bldg 13. Bedroom, two beds, private bath (1). Kitchenette, limited utensils, TV, housekeeping service, washer/dryer, ice machine, small NEX/Commissary, swimming pool, gazebo with barbeque patio. Rates: no charge. Officers and GS on official orders. Reservations required. No pets.

AMENITIES: Exercise Room and Meeting/Conference Room.

TML AVAILABILITY: Extremely difficult, especially in summer.

CREDIT CARDS ACCEPTED: Visa.

TRANSPORTATION: Off base shuttle/bus; Car Rental; Off base taxi.

DINING OPPORTUNITIES: Dining facilities on base.

A very historical area. Hotel rooms are limited during the summer months due to the large number of tourists.

Naples Naval Support Activity (IT05R7)
PSC 810, Box 53
FPO AE 09619-1053

MAIN INSTALLATION TELEPHONE NUMBERS: C-(USA) 011-39-081-724-1110, (IT) 081-724-1110, DSN-314-625-1110. Locator 081-724-4556.

LOCATION: In Naples Agnano District, from Autostrada 2 (E45) to Tangenziale toll route exit, then continue west on Tangenziale through the city of Naples to south at the Agnano/Terme exit. Pay the toll and make a left (south), then continue south to the first traffic light then make a right (west). Naples NSA is located 1 km ahead on the right. *EUSMRA: Page 101 (B-3), page 108.* **NMC:** Naples, in the city.

RESERVATION INFORMATION: C-(USA) 011-39-081-509-7120, (IT) 081-509-7120/21/22/23, Fax: C-(USA) 011-39-081-509-7124, (IT) 081-509-7124, 24 hours daily. PCS have priority; others may make reservations.

NAVY LODGE Navy Lodge, PSC 810 Box 30, FPO AE 09619-0003. **C-1-800-NAVY-INN.** Lodge number is C-(USA) 1-800-NAVY-INN, (IT) 800-87-0740 (toll free Italy); C-011-39-081-811-6289 (NAVY), (IT) 081-811-6289, Fax: C-011-39-081-811-6660, (IT) 081-811-6660, DSN-314-629-6660 24 hours daily. E-mail: navy_lodge-naples@nexnet.navy.mil Air-conditioned units with private bath (96) (Family accomodation and Business-class rooms). Amenities include newspaper, free base calls, fax/copy services, eight-channel AFN, VCR, children's playground, conference room, electronic locks, vending, hair dryer, iron/ironing board, laundy facilities. Free shuttle bus (Mon-Sat) to the Pinetamare NEXmart located approximately one mile from the Lodge. Services provided within the Lodge are a snack bar, movie theater, slot machine room, beauty salon, fax service, parking garage, play area for children, video rental, and conference room. Nearby: Naval Support Activity, 30.4 km. Rates: Based on number of occupants/fluctuating per diem (i.e. around $63 single occupancy, $97 double occupancy, $125 triple occupancy). No pets, kennel available. *Note: Navy Lodge at Pinetamare closed in 2002.*

TML AVAILABILITY: May-Sep, difficult. Best, winter.

CREDIT CARDS ACCEPTED: Visa, MasterCard, American Express and Discover.

TRANSPORTATION: On base shuttle/bus; Off base shuttle/bus, C-011-39-081-509-7120.

DINING OPPORTUNITIES: Restaurants and coffee shops within walking distance.

Sigonella Naval Air Station (IT01R7)
Attn: Family Service Center
PSC 824, Box 2650
FPO AE 09627-2650

MAIN INSTALLATION TELEPHONE NUMBERS: C-(USA) 011-39-095-86-1110, C-(IT) 095-86-1111, DSN-314-624-1110. Locator 113; Medical 911; Security Police 911.

LOCATION: Located on the east side of the island of Sicily. From Catania-Palermo Autostrada 19, exit at Motta S. Anastasia south to Route 192, then east approximately 1.7 km on Route 192 to NAS I Main Gate on south side of road. For NAS II, continue east on Route 192 to intersection with Route 417, then southwest on Route 417 approximately 10 km to NAS II Main Gate on southeast side of road. *EUSMRA: Page 103 (B-3), page 109.* **NMC:** Catania, 13 km northeast.

Visit Military Living online at
www.militaryliving.com

RESERVATION INFORMATION: Supply Officer, Attn: Bachelor Housing Director, PSC 812, Box 3230, FPO AE 09627-3230. **C-(USA) 011-39-095-86-2300/6830/6508, (IT) 095-86-2300/6830/6508, DSN-314-624-2300/6830,** Fax: C-(USA) 011-39-095-86-6143, DSN-314-624-6143, 24 hours daily. E-mail: alongo@nassig.sicily.navy.mil Official orders can make reservations; others Space-A. Directions: After entering NAS II Gate, make left turn and go approximately one mile. BOQ is on right. Check in at facility, check out 1000 hours. Government civilian employee billeting.

(BEQ) Bedroom, some shared rooms, private bath. A/C, TV/VCR, housekeeping service, laundry facility, ice machine. Rates: E1-E6 $9-$11; E7-E9 $11-$14 per day.

(BOQ) C-(USA) 011-39-095-86-2300. Bedroom, private bath (24). A/C, TV/VCR, housekeeping service, laundry facility, ice machine, gymnasium, fitness center, bar, alcohol free/non-smoking club. Older structure. Rates: $14-$18. Maximum three per unit.

(NAVY LODGE) Navy Lodge, Bldg 313, NAS I. PSC 824 Box 2620, FPO AE 09627-2620. **C-1-800-NAVY-INN.** Lodge number is C-(USA) 011-39-095-56-4082, (IT) 095-56-4082, DSN-314-624-4082, Fax: C-(USA) 011-39-095-56-7130, (IT) 095-56-7130, 24 hours daily. Bedroom, two extra-long double beds, private bath (52). Kitchenette, microwave, utensils, A/C, CATV/VCR, video rental, phone, Fax/Copy service, clock radio, hair dryer, laundry facility, iron/ironing board, cribs, rollaways, highchairs, soft drink and snack vending, playground, barbecue grills/tools, complimentary coffee in lobby. Handicap accessible, interconnecting and non-smoking rooms available. Rates: $65 per night. All categories can make reservations. No pets.

(DV/VIP) Protocol, Bldg 632, C-(USA) 011-39-095-86-2300. O6+. BOQ. Separate bedroom, living room suites, private bath (16). Honor bar, TV/VCR. Rates: $25 per person. Retirees Space-A. No dependents under age 15.

TML AVAILABILITY: *All transient rooms have very limited availability through 2000-2002 due to major BQ renovations.* Most difficult, May-Sep.

CREDIT CARDS ACCEPTED: MasterCard. The Navy Lodge accepts Visa, MasterCard and American Express.

TRANSPORTATION: On base shuttle/bus, C-011-39-095-86-5248/5255; Car Rental: Eurocar, C-011-39-095-86-5468/5982; On base taxi, C-011-39-095-56-4201/2.

DINING OPPORTUNITIES: Enlisted Dining Facility, C-011-39-095-624-5738; and Pizza Villa, C-011-39-095-624-5245 are within walking distance. Mama Elios, C-011-39-095-713-0137; Sigo Pub; Paradise Restaurante; and Valentino's Restaurante are within driving distance.

Mount Etna, Taormina, Enna, ancient Greek city of Agrigento, beaches, local markets, wonderful Italian cuisine, and old world charm of Sicily at its best.

Vicenza Community (IT06R7)
22nd Area Support Group
Unit 31401, Box 80
APO AE 09630-5000

MAIN INSTALLATION TELEPHONE NUMBERS: C-(USA) 011-39-0444-51-1110, (IT) 0444-51-1110, DSN-314-634-1110. Locator C-011-39-0444-51-7430.

LOCATION: Three km east of the center of Vicenza. Approximately 3.5 km north of the Autostrada 4/E70 east-west and west of the Autostrada 31 north-south. Take the Vicenza east exit from the Autostrada 4/E70 on Viale Della Serenissima northwest to Viale Camisano and west to Viale Della Pace. The installation is on the north side of Viale Della Pace. The Main

Gate is on Viale Della Pace and enters the installation on Olson Avenue. From Autostrada 31 take the Vicenza Nord exit to Raccordo southwest to Strada Comunale Di Ospedaletto south to a west on Strada Di Bertesina to a southeast on Via Aldo Moro to a west on Viale Della Pace and the installation on the north side of the street. The installation is approximately 5 km southwest of the Vicenza Nord exit from Autostrada 31. *EUSMRA: Page 98 (B-2), page 111.* **NMC:** Vicenza, in city limits.

RESERVATION INFORMATION: Headquarters, 22nd ASG, Attn: Ederle Inn, Unit 31401, Box 80, APO AE 09630-5000. **C-(USA) 011-39-0444-51-8034/35, (IT) 0444-51-8034/35, DSN-314-634-8034/35,** Fax: C-011-39-0444-51-5380, 24 hours daily. E-mail: ederleinn@22asg.vicenza.army.mil WEB: www.setaf.army.mil/mwr/mwr/ederle.htm Check in 1500 hours, check out 1100 hours. Directions from Main Gate: Go straight to the end of the street. Government civilian employee billeting.

(DV) Lodging, Bldg 345. Official duty, PCS in/out and MTDY, TDY, ID card holders, and leave Space-A. Three bedroom apartments (15); Guestrooms with queen size bed (102). Kitchenette, microfridge, microwave, utensils, A/C, TV/VCR, laundry facility, housekeeping service, cribs. Modern structure, remodeled. Interconnecting units, handicap accessible. Rates: Lodging PCS/TDY $55, additional person $5; DVQ PCS/TDY $65, additional person $5; Space-A $65, additional person $5; DVQ Space-A $70, additional person $5. *Limited pet space.*

(DV/VIP) Protocol, HQ SETAF, Bldg 1, C-011-39-0444-51-7712, DSN-314-634-7712. O6/GS15+. Retirees Space-A.

AMENITIES: Meeting/Conference Room, Snack and Soft Drink Vending Machine, Internet/E-mail access for all customers.

TML AVAILABILITY: Good, Oct-Nov. Difficult, May-Sep.

CREDIT CARDS ACCEPTED: Visa, American Express and Discover.

TRANSPORTATION: Car Rental: Eurocar, C-011-39-0444-505916; Avis C-011-39-0444-321622; Off base taxi: Radio Taxi, C-011-39-0444-920600; Off base shuttle bus, C-011-39-0444-223111.

DINING OPPORTUNITIES: Club Pizza, C-011-39-0444-51-7685 and Magic Dimitri, DSN-314-634-7013 are within walking distance. Il Fauno, C-011-39-0444-301960 and Verchio Trattoria, C-011-39-0444-580999 are within driving distance.

Verona, the city of Romeo and Juliet, is rich in monuments of every period and a modern and hospitable city. Don't miss the Roman Arena, which is still an active entertainment site. Venice, Florence, Pisa and many others are close.

JAPAN

Atsugi Naval Air Facility (JA14R8)
Bldg 949, First Floor
PSC 477, Box 9
FPO AP 96306-1209

MAIN INSTALLATION TELEPHONE NUMBERS: C-(USA) 011-81-6160-64-1110, DSN-315-264-1110, (JA) 0467-78-5015 ext 264-1110. Locator 264-1111.

LOCATION: In central Japan off Tokyo Bay. Yokohama is 23 km east and Tokyo is 45 km northeast. From Narita Airport, use bus or train service-information provided by the Northwest Military Counter at the airport. Camp Zama is eight km north. The Tokyo Expressway is three km south of Atsugi and the Sagamiohtsuka Station for light rail to Yokohama is outside the Main Gate. **NMC:** Tokyo, 45 km northeast.

RESERVATION INFORMATION: BOH Bldg 482; **C-(USA)-011-81-6160-64-3696, (JA) 6160-64-3696, DSN-315-264-3696,** Fax: 011-81-6160-64-3256, 24 hours daily. E-mail: yamatsuo@atsugi.navy.mil, mabinkle@atsugi.navy.mil or jvlucero@atsugi.navy.mil **BEH** Bldg 1290, **C-(USA)-011-81-6160-64-3698, (JA) 6160-64-3698, DSN-315-264-3698,** Fax: 011-81-6160-64-3256, 24 hours daily. E-mail: yamatsuo@atsugi.navy.mil, mabinkle@atsugi.navy.mil or a-cortezano@atsugi.navy.mil Active Duty, Reservists and NG on orders may make reservations; others Space-A. Reservations can be made/confirmed by e-mail, fax or phone. Check in at appropriate billeting, check out 1200 hours. Overnight guests are not permitted, unless they are dependents of a valid military/civilian ID card holder and registered at check-in. DoD civilian employee billeting. *Winner of the 1997 and 1999 Admiral Elmo R. Zumwalt Award for Excellence in Bachelor Housing.*

(BEQ) Bldg 979. Bedroom, single bed, two beds per room, private bath (E1-E4) (54). Bedroom, single bed, private bath (E5-E6). Bedroom, double bed, private bath (E7-E9) (51). Central kitchen, refrigerator, microwave, coffee maker, TV/VCR, closed circuit movie channel, housekeeping service, laundry facilities, iron/ironing board, toiletries, large screen TV in lounge, pool and ping pong tables, outdoor BBQ shelter. Rates: E7+ $8, each additional person $2; E1-E6, $3.

(BEQ) Bldgs 985, 988. E1-E6. Bedroom, shared bath (411). Refrigerator, microwave, coffee maker, TV/VCR, closed circuit movie channel, iron/ironing board, laundry facilities, pool and ping pong tables, large screen TV in lounge, outdoor BBQ shelter. Recently renovated.

(BEQ) Bldgs 980-982. E1-E6. Bedroom, shared bath (80). Refrigerator, microwave, TV/VCR, closed circuit movie channel, housekeeping service, iron/ironing board, toiletries, large screen TV in lounge, outdoor BBQ shelter. Recently renovated.

(BEQ) Bldg 1290. E1-E6. Bedroom with two single beds, shared bath (E1-E4) (117); Bedroom with one single bed, shared bath (E5-E6) (149). Refrigerator, microwave, coffee maker, TV/VCR, housekeeping service, laundry facilites, iron/ironing board, toiletries. Large screen TV in lounge, internet access in lobby, pool, ping pong tables, and outdoor BBQ shelter. Rates: E1-E4 $4; E5-E6 $6.

(BEQ) Bldg 484. E7-E9. Separate bedroom, double bed, private bath (20). Kitchenette, toaster, coffee maker, microwave, complete utensils, TV/VCR, closed circuit movie channel, housekeeping service, laundry facilities, iron/ironing board, toiletries large screen TV in lounge, sauna, pool table, outdoor BBQ shelter. Rates: E7+ $10, each additional person $2. Used to billet permanent party and transient Enlisted on orders.

(BOQ) Bldgs 480, 482, 483. Leave or official duty and civilian employees on orders. Separate bedroom, double bed, private bath (269). Kitchenette, coffee maker, toaster, microwave, complete utensils, TV/VCR, closed circuit movie channel, video checkout, hair dryer, housekeeping service, laundry facilities, iron/ironing board, toiletries, ping pong table, large screen TV in lounge, outdoor BBQ shelter. Recently renovated rooms. Rates: $10, each additional person $2; VIP rooms (O6) (6) $12, each additional person $2; Guest Quarters (O7+) (2) $25, each additional person $5. No pets; kennels at Camp Zama (15 minutes by car) and Kamiseya NSF.

(NAVY LODGE) Navy Lodge. Bldg 946, PSC 477, Box 10, FPO AP 96306-0003. **C-1-800-NAVY-INN.** Lodge number is C-(USA) 011-81-6160-64-6880/1/2/3, DSN-315-264-6880/1/2/3, (JA) 6160-64-6880/1/2/3, Fax: C-(USA) 011-81-6160-64-6882, DSN-315-264-6882, (JA) 0467-70-3243, 24 hours daily. All ranks. Check in 1500 hours, check out 1200 hours. Bedroom, two queen size beds, private bath, no kitchen (30); Bedroom, two queen size beds, private bath, kitchen, complete utensils (58). Refrigerator, CATV/VCR, video rental, housekeeping service, laundry facility, cribs. Modern structure. Handicap accessible. Rates (change yearly): without kitchen $45, with full kitchen $53. Maximum five per unit. All categories can make reservations. No pets, kennels at Camp Zama and Kamiseya NSF.

(DV/VIP) Commanding Officer's Office, C-(USA) 011-81-6160-64-3104, DSN-315-264-3104 or E-mail: mabinkle@atsugi.navy.mil O6+. Others Space-A. Off-base hotels located in front of Main Gate.

AMENITIES: Ice, Snack and Soft Drink Vending Machines.

TML AVAILABILITY: Difficult, best when CVW-5 is deployed, worst when in port or in the local area.

CREDIT CARDS ACCEPTED: Visa. The Navy Lodge accepts Visa, MasterCard and American Express.

TRANSPORTATION: On base shuttle/bus available Mon-Fri C-6160-64-3562; Transportation for offical business on base is available, call DSN-315-264-3900; Taxi, C-(USA) 011-81-462-77-0100; Car Rental C-011-81-6160-64-6230.

DINING OPPORTUNITIES: Smokey's BBQ, Blue Water Grill, Parchezzi's Pizza and Subs and 19th Hole Restaurant are all within walking distance. Exchange food court also offers several fast food choices.

Book a one day tour of Tokyo through MWR at Atsugi, or just ask the friendly Navy Lodge people to provide you with maps, directions and info, but don't miss seeing as much as you can of this marvelous city!

Camp S.D. Butler Marine Corps Base (JA07R8)
Unit 35026
PSC 557, Box 935
FPO AP 96373-5023

Note: Direct dialing from the U.S. to Okinawa 011-81-6117+ last six digit extension number Example: MCB locator service 645-7218, from the U.S. 011-81-6117-45-7218

MAIN INSTALLATION TELEPHONE NUMBERS: C-(USA) 011-81-98-892-1110 or 011-81-6117-40-1110, (JA) 098-892-1110, DSN-315-640-1110. Locator 645-7218 (USMC); 632-7653 (USN); 644-4300 (USA); 634-3374 (USAF).

LOCATION: Six km south of Okinawa City on JA-330 at Camp Foster three km north of Futenma. **NMC:** Naha, 10 km south.

RESERVATION INFORMATION: Transient Billeting Fund, PSC 557, Box 935, FPO AP 96373-5023. **C-(USA) 011-81-98-892-2455, (JA) 098-892-2191, DSN-315-635-2191,** Fax: C-(USA) 011-81-6117-45-7549, DSN-315-645-7549, 0700-1630 hours. Other hours, Bldg 1, OD, DSN-315-635-7218/2644. Check in at facility, check out 1200 hours. Government civilian employee billeting. *Note: Camp Butler, which is located on Camp Foster, is the headquarters for the camps listed below. For information on lodging contact the Transient Billeting Fund at the above number or call the individual camp's lodging facilities.*

(TML) Camp Courtney Lodging. Courtney Lodge, Bldg 2540. All categories, **C-(USA) 011-81-6117-22-9578, DSN-315-622-9578,** 0800-1700 hours Mon-Fri. Suites, private bath (16). Kitchenette, refrigerator, A/C, CATV in room and lounge, housekeeping service, coin washer/dryer, cribs, cots. and vending at front desk. .5 km to front gate and 7-day store, 2 km to commissary and exchange. Modern structure. Rates: $30 per unit, each additional person $5. **CBOQ. C-011-81-98-622-9602,** call CBOQ for more information. Check in at facility, check out at 1200. No pets. **Camp Location: Located on east coast of Okinawa at the intersection of JA-24 (N and S) and JA-8 (E and W). NMC: Naha, 25 km south.**

(TML) Camp Foster Lodging, WESTPAC Inn. **C-(USA) 011-81-6117-45-2191, DSN-315-645-2455/2191,** Fax: C-(USA) 011-81-6117-45-7549, DSN-315-645-7549, 0730-1630 hours daily. Futenma, C-(USA) 011-81-92-2112, (VOQ). Separate bedroom, living room, private bath (20); (Futenma) bedroom, private bath (10); separate bedroom,

private bath (2); suites, private bath (2). Maximum two per suite, two per room. Kitchen, A/C, TV/VCR, housekeeping service, laundry facility. Older structure, renovated. Rates: $29/night for two people. Duty can make reservations; others Space-A. **CBOQ. C-011-81-98-645-7558,** call CBOQ for more information. Check in at facility, check out 1200 hours. No pets. **Camp Location: On west coast of Okinawa, 7 km south of Kadena AB. JA-3330 N and S bisects the base, JA-58 is on the west side of the base and also JA-8 passes through the base north and south. NMC: Naha, 10 km south.**
Note: New Kuwae Lodge, replacing this facility,opened on 1 May 2002.

(TML) **Camp Hansen Lodging. Hansen Lodge,** Bldg 2540. **C-(USA) 011-81-6117-23-4511, DSN-315-623-4511,** 24 hours daily. Same as Courtney except bedroom, shared bath (18). Microwave and refrigerator in room. Rates: $10 per room, $5 each additional person. Maximum two per room. Reservations accepted. **BOQ/BEQ. C-011-81-98-623-4711 (BOQ), C-011-81-98-623-7159 (BEQ),** call BOQ/BEQ for more information. Check in at facility, check out 1200 hours. No pets. **Camp Location: Located in the center on Okinawa off JA-13 N or S. NMC: Naha, 45 km south.**

(TML) **Camp Lester Lodging. Kuwae Lodge,** Bldg 400. **C-(USA) 011-81-6117-45-9102/9201, DSN-315-645-9102/9201,** 24 hours daily. Rooms with kitchenette (165). Laundry facility, playroom, playgrounds, tennis courts, game room, BBQ area, snack bar and vending. Rates: Duty $75 single room, $150 three adjoining rooms; Space-A $42 single room, $105 three adjoining rooms. Adjacent to park. Within driving distance of commissary and exchange. Free shuttle bus service. Check in 1500 hours at facility, check out at 1100. Reservations: Duty may make reservations one year in advance; Space-A 30 days in advance. No pets. **Camp Location: Located .5 km from Main Gate on northeast side of Okinawa off JA-58. NMC: Naha, 13 km south near Sunset Beach/American Town.**

(BOQ/BEQ) **Futenma MCAS Lodging.** C-011-81-98-636-3443 (BOQ), C-011-81-98-636-3748 (BEQ), call BOQ/BEQ for more information. **Camp Location: Located in southern Okinawa three km south of Camp Foster. NMC: Naha, 10 km south.**

(BOQ/BEQ) **Camp Schwab Lodging,** C-011-81-98-625-2738 (BOQ), C-011-81-98-625-2230 (BEQ). **Camp Location: Located on east coast of Okinawa 58 km north of Camp Foster. NMC: Naha, 70 km south.**

(CBOQ) **Camp Kinser Lodging,** C-011-81-98-637-3748, call CBOQ for more information. **Camp Location: Located on southwestern coast of Okinawa on Highway-58. NMC: Naha, 8 km south.**

(DV/VIP) **Day House, Awase House.** Bldgs 4205, 4515. Kitchen, TV/VCR. Rates: $30.

(DV/VIP) Protocol Office, Bldg 1, Camp SD Butler MCB, C-(USA) 011-81-98-892-7274/2901, DSN-315-645-7274/2901. Protocol Office, Bldg 4225, III MEF, Camp Courtney, C-(USA) 011-81-98-2972-7749, DSN-315-645-7749.

TML AVAILABILITY: Good. Best, Aug-Mar. More difficult, other times.

CREDIT CARDS ACCEPTED: American Express (for TAD/TDY personnel only).

TRANSPORTATION: Camp-to-Camp Shuttle (Mon-Fri); Off base shuttle/bus: Ryukyu Bus System, C-098-863-3636; Car Rental: AAFES, C-011-81-98-633-0007; Papasan Rental Car, C-98-939-7930; Coral Isle Motors Co., C-98-936-7287; On base taxi: AAFES, C-011-81-98-633-1404/1405/1406/1407. Off base taxi, C-098-937-2467.

DINING OPPORTUNITIES: Each of the camps has separate dining facilities and restaurants. **Camp Courtney:** Anthony's Pizza, Chicken & Sub Shop and Tengan Restaurant. **Camp Foster:** Anthony's Pizza; Burger King; and Seamen's Club, C-098-857-1753. **Futenma MCAS:** Frank's Franks; O Club, C-011-81-98-636-4051; and SNCO Club, C-011-81-98-636-3246. **Camp Hansen:** Burger King, C-011-81-98-623-5033; EM Club, C-011-81-98-623-4969; and SNCO Club, C-011-81-98-623-4575/4926. **Camp Kinser:** Anthony's Pizza; Burger King; and Kinser Restaurant, C-011-81-98-637-2138. **Camp Lester:** Frank's Franks and Hospital Snack Bar. **Camp Schwab:** Adventurer Cafeteria, C-011-81-98-625-3837; Beach Snack Bar; and Frank's Franks, C-011-81-98-625-3837.

Don't miss seeing Nakagusuku Castle, left over from Okinawa's feudal period, and the Nakamura House, which displays Okinawan lifestyle of yesteryear. Check with the USO for locations and possible tours.

Camp Zama (JA06R8)
17th Area Support Group
Attn: APAJ-GH-CA-L
Unit 45006
APO AP 96343-5006

MAIN INSTALLATION TELEPHONE NUMBERS: C-(USA) 011-81-3117-63-1110, (JA) 03117-63-1110, DSN-315-263-1110. Locator C-011-81-462-51-1521, DSN-315-263-5344.

LOCATION: Forty-two km southwest of Tokyo or 23 km west of Yokohama. Excellent rail service. Sobudai-Mae train station outside gate 4. **NMC:** Tokyo, 42 km north.

RESERVATION INFORMATION: 17th ASG, Attn: APAJ-GH-CA-L (Lodging), Bldg 563, Sand Street, APO AP 96343-5006. **C-(USA) 011-81-3117-63-3830/4474, DSN-315-263-3830/4474,** Fax: C-(USA) 011-81-3117-63-3598, DSN-315-263-3598, 24 hours daily, Business office 0800-1645. Duty can make reservations; others Space-A. Directions from Main Gate: Veer left and go around traffic circle. Take third road off of traffic circle. Go straight. Bldg 563 is the fourth building on the right. Zama Lodging sign is in front of building. Check in 1500 hours, check out 1200 hours. Handicap accessible units available. No pets, boarding at vet clinic. *Note: Camp Zama also operates award-winning Kure Lodge as part of its lodging facilities. Call C-011-81-6117-56-2539(USA) or email: reservations.kure@ zama.army.mil for details.*

(Army Lodging) Family Quarters. Bldg 552. PCS in/out, or official duty. Separate bedroom, private bath (56). Kitchenette, complete utensils, A/C, TV/VCR, housekeeping service, washer/dryer, amenities. New structure, furnishings 1992. Handicap accessible first floor. Rates (all rooms): sponsor $30.

(Army Lodging) Family Quarters. Bldg 780. PCS in/out or official duty. Single bedroom, hall bath (5); two-bedroom, hall bath (14); three-bedroom, private bath (2). Community kitchen, refrigerator, microwave, complete utensils, A/C, TV/VCR, housekeeping service, laundry facility. Older structure, due to be refurbished in 2001. Rates: sponsor $10-50.

(VEQ) Bldg 580. Bedroom, community bath (29). Community kitchen, refrigerator, microwave, A/C, TV/VCR, housekeeping service, amenities, laundry facility. Rates: sponsor $10-$15.

(VOQ) Bldg 742. Bedroom, private bath (38). Refrigerator, microwave, A/C, TV/VCR, housekeeping service, laundry facility. Modern structure. Rates: sponsor $25.

(DVQ) Bldg 550. O6/GS14/NF5+. Separate bedroom, private bath (12). Refrigerator, microwave, stocked bar, amenities, A/C, TV/VCR, housekeeping service, laundry facility. Rates: sponsor $35.

(DV/VIP) USARJ Protocol Office, Bldg 101. C-(USA) 011-81-3117-63-3830, DSN-315-263-3830. O6/GS14+. Retirees Space-A.

AMENITIES: Ice, Snack and Soft Drink Vending Machine.

TML AVAILABILITY: Good, Jul-Aug difficult.

CREDIT CARDS ACCEPTED: Visa, MasterCard and American Express.

TRANSPORTATION: All facilities within walking distance.

DINING OPPORTUNITIES: Burger King, Anthony's Pizza and Combined Club are within walking distance.

Check with the ITT office on base for local tours, such as trips to Disneyland, Kamakura, Hakone, Mount Fuji, Kyoto, Nikko and Seto.

Iwakuni Marine Corps Air Station (JA12R8)
Bldg 210, Room 201
PSC 561, Box 1861
FPO AP 96310-1861

MAIN INSTALLATION TELEPHONE NUMBERS: C-(USA) 011-81-6117-53-1110, (JA) 0827-21-1110, DSN-315-253-1110. Locator C-011-81-6117-53-1110.

LOCATION: Facing the Seto Inland Sea on the south portion of the island of Honshu, 730 km southwest of Tokyo, 16 km off Sanyo Expressway. From north or south, take Route 2 off the expressway toward downtown Iwakuni. Take Route 188, then Route 189 to the Main Gate. May also be reached by Shinkansen (Bullet Train) at Shin-Iwakuni stop or by local train at Iwakuni train station stop from Fukuoka, Osaka or Hiroshima. Take a taxi to base from the local train for about 1,000 Yen and from the Shinkansen for about 4,000-5,000 Yen. Taxi service requires payment in Yen not U.S. dollars. **NMC:** Hiroshima, 41 km north.

RESERVATION INFORMATION: Kintai Inn, Bldg 606 MCCS, Attn: Bachelor Housing, PSC 561, Box 1867, FPO AP 96310-0027. **C-(USA) 011-81-6117-53-3181 (BHD) or 011-81-6117-53-3221 (TLF), (JA) 0827-21-4171 ext 3221, DSN-315-253-3221,** Fax: DSN-315-253-6655, 24 hours daily. Check in at Bldg 606, check out 1000 hours for TLF, 1200 hours for BH. Government civilian employee billeting.

(TML) Transient Billeting. Bldgs 204, 606, 1189, 1368, 1388. C-ext 3181. Bedroom, private bath (Enlisted) (73); separate bedroom, private bath (SNCOs and Officers) (51); two-bedroom, private bath (DG-Shogun House) (1); Kitchenette (Bldg 606), refrigerator, utensils, A/C, TV, housekeeping service, ice machine. Modern structure. Some facilities handicap accessible. Rates: Officers $15, SNCOs $12, E5 and below $10. Duty can make reservations, others Space-A.

(TML) Lodging facilities. Bldg 444, 1188, 5 km from gate. Single room, private bath, kitchenette (24); two room suites, private bath, kitchenette (24). 1.2 km from commissary, exchange, seven day store and clubs. Rates: $35-$45 for one or two persons, each additional person $2. PCS on station, command sponsored accompanied (Priority 1A); PCS off station, command sponsored (Priority 1B); all others Space-A.

(DV/VIP) DGR, Bldgs 511, 606. Protocol, C-011-81-6117-53-4211, DSN-315-258-4211.

TML AVAILABILITY: Good.

CREDIT CARDS ACCEPTED: Visa, MasterCard and American Express.

TRANSPORTATION: On base shuttle/bus: C-011-81-6117-53-3944, DSN-315-253-3944; Car Rental, C-011-81-6117-53-4245, DSN-315-253-4245; Flight Crew taxi, C-011-81-6117-53-3063, DSN-315-253-3063; Off base taxi, C-011-81-0827-21-1111.

DINING OPPORTUNITIES: Cross Roads Food Court, C-011-81-6117-53-4108; Eagle's Nest, C-011-81-6117-53-4778; Enlisted Club, C-011-81-6117-53-3406; SNCO Club, C-011-81-6117-53-3363/5798; and Officers' Club, C-011-81-6117-53-3111 are within walking distance. Kinnan Steak House (Route 189 outside Main Gate), C-011-81-827-22-8130; McDonald's (Route 2), C-011-81-827-23-5991 (US $ accepted); and Monami (Route 188, downtown) are within driving distance.

See the famous Kintai Bridge, and view the Iwakuni Castle Ropeway. Hiroshima is 50 minutes by train, and visitors should see the Peace Memorial Park, Atomic Bomb Memorial Dome, and reconstructed Hiroshima Castle. Also nearby is Miyajima Island, one of Japan's "Three Most Beautiful Spots" with its historic "O-Torii" (Grand Gate) standing 200 meters on the sea front. Don't miss the cherry blossoms in bloom, March to April.

Kadena Air Base (JA08R8)
18 MSS/DPF
Bldg 99
Unit 5134, Box 80
APO AP 96368-5134

MAIN INSTALLATION TELEPHONE NUMBERS: C-(USA) 011-81-6117-34-1111, (JA) 06117-34-1111, DSN-315-632-1110. Locator 632-1110.

LOCATION: Located on the west side of Okinawa. Take JA-58 N from Naha to Kadena's Gate 1 on the right, immediately north of USMC Camp Lester. **NMC:** Naha, 18 km south.

RESERVATION INFORMATION: Shogun Inn, Bldg 332, Beeson Avenue, Unit 5135, Box 10, APO AP 96368-5134. **C-(USA) 011-81-6117-32-1100/1101/1010/1050, DSN-315-632-1100/1101/1010/1050,** Fax: C-011-81-611-732-1740, DSN-315-632-1740, 24 hours daily. Duty may make reservations any time; Space-A may make reservations 24 hours in advance. Check in 1500 hours at billeting, check out 1000 hours.

(TLF) Family Quarters. Bldgs 322, 437, 507. Apartments (122). Kitchen, refrigerator, complete utensils, A/C, TV/VCR, housekeeping service, washer/dryer, cribs, rollaways. Modern structure. Handicap accessible. Rates: $35 per unit. Maximum six persons per unit. No pets.

(VAQ) Bldgs 317, 332, 504, 506, 509, 510. Bedroom, private bath (124); shared bedrooms, semi-private bath (60). Refrigerator, A/C, TV/VCR, housekeeping service, laundry facility. Rates: $17 per person per night. Maximum two per unit. No pets.

(VOQ) Bldgs 304, 306, 314, 316, 318, 502, 508. Bedroom, private bath (109); separate bedroom, semi-private bath (20). Refrigerator, A/C, TV/VCR, housekeeping service, laundry facility. Rates: $18.50 per person per night. Maximum two persons. No pets.

(DVQ) Bldgs 78, 85, 86, 315, 2024. O6+. Bedroom, living area private bath (24); two-bedroom, private bath, living area, dining area (2); bedroom, private bath, living area, dining area (1). Kitchen, complete utensils, A/C, TV/VCR, housekeeping service, laundry facility. Rates: $25 per person per night. DV Houses: $30 per person per night. No pets.

(DV/VIP) Protocol Office, Bldg 10, DSN-315-634-0106/1808. O6+.

AMENITIES: Exercise Room and Mini Mart.

TML AVAILABILITY: Good, Dec-Jan. Difficult, spring and summer.

CREDIT CARDS ACCEPTED: Visa, MasterCard, and Government Travel Card.

TRANSPORTATION: Airport shuttle/bus, C-011-81-611-634-1549/2465; Car Rental, C-011-81-611-733-0007; On base taxi, C-011-81-6117-34-3030 (gov), AAFES taxi C-06117-34-2467.

DINING OPPORTUNITIES: Dragons Chinese Food, C-011-81-611-933-6236; Genghis Khan, C-011-81-611-936-8567; Myondon, C-011-81-611-926-1388; Italian Restaurant C-011-81-6117-33-4502; New York Restaurant, C-011-81-611-937-3658; Obbligato's, C-011-81-611-926-1388; and Pizza Inn, C-011-81-611-936-9441 are within driving distance.

This is the crossroads of the Pacific, and a great Space-A departure point, but don't miss seeing the Children's Park Zoo in Okinawa City, the Ryukyuan Village and Takoyama Habu Center. Near Nenoko see the Shell House, visited by shell collectors.

Misawa Air Base (JA03R8)
35th FW/CP
Bldg 1026
Unit 5009
APO AP 96319-5009

MAIN INSTALLATION TELEPHONE NUMBERS: C-(USA) 011-81-3117-66-1110, (JA) 0176-53-5181, DSN-315-226-1110. Locator C-011-81-3117-66-4590.

LOCATION: On the northeast portion of the Island of Honshu, 648 km north of Tokyo. **NMC:** Hachinohe City, 28 km southeast.

RESERVATION INFORMATION: Misawa Inn, 35 SVS/SVML, Unit 5019, APO AP 96319-5019. **C-(USA) 011-81-3117-62-1100 ext 3526, (JA) 0176-53-5181 ext 1100, DSN-315-222-1100,** Fax: C-(USA) 011-81-3117-66-2165, DSN-315-226-2165, 24 hours daily. Duty may make reservations any time; Space-A may make reservations 24 hours in advance. Check in at 1400, check out 1200 hours.

BOQ/BEQ Misawa Naval Air Facility. C-(USA) 011-81-3117-66-3131/4483, Fax: C-(USA) 011-81-3117-66-9312. BOQ, Bedroom, private bath, mini music system (122); BEQ, E1-E4 double room, shared bath; E5+ single, private bath, refrigerator, microwave, clock radio, iron/ironing board (325). Rates: Enlisted $4, Officers $8. *Winner of the 1997 Admiral Elmo R. Zumwalt Award for Excellence in Bachelor Housing.*

TLF Bldg 670. Single family units (40). Private bath, living room, kitchen, utensils. Rates: $35 per unit.

VQ Bldg 669. Bedroom, private bath (32). Prime Knight Aircrew Quarters, bedroom, private bath (10). Refrigerator, TV/VCR, housekeeping service, laundry facility, ice machine. Rates: $17 per person.

VQ Bldgs 662, 664. Bedroom, private bath (71). Kitchen, refrigerator, microwave, utensils, TV/VCR, housekeeping service, laundry facility. Rates: $18.50 per person.

DV/VIP 35th FW/CCP. C-(USA) 011-81-3117-66-4804 (Mon-Fri). Bedroom, private bath, suites (4). Kitchen, refrigerator, utensils, A/C, TV/VCR, housekeeping service. Rates: $18.50-$30.

AMENITIES: Exercise Room, Meeting/Conference Room, Snack Vending Machine and Soft Drink Machine.

TML AVAILABILITY: Dec-Mar.

CREDIT CARDS ACCEPTED: Visa, MasterCard. Official Duty travelers are required to use their government Travel Card to pay for their lodging room fees.

TRANSPORTATION: On base shuttle/bus, ext 226-3328; Car Rental, ext 226-7222; On/Off base taxi, ext 222-5438/9.

DINING OPPORTUNITIES: Anthony's Pizza, C-011-81-176-53-5000; Burger King, C-011-81-176-53-5905; and Popeye's Chicken, C-011-81-176-53-7772 are within walking distance. Noodle House Manumiya, C-011-81-176-57-0383; Restaurant Miyaki, C-011-81-176-53-2860; and Swan, C-011-81-176-53-2994 are within driving distance.

Enjoy the excellent eating establishments in downtown Misawa, and try a hot bath at Komakis. Explore the Komaki Onsen, Komaki Grand and the Second Grand Hotels. Get hints from Services (Bldg 1044) for trips farther afield.

The New Sanno U.S. Forces Center (JA01R8)
Unit 45003
APO AP 96337-5003

MAIN INSTALLATION TELEPHONE NUMBERS: C-(USA) 011-81-3-3440-7871, (JA) 03-3440-7871. DSN-315-229-8111. Locator 03-3440-7871; Security Police 03-3440-7871. WEB: www.thenewsanno.com/ E-mail: room_rsv@thenewsanno.com

LOCATION: At 4-12-20 Minami Azabu, Minato-ku, Tokyo 106-0047, a five-minute walk from nearest subway station, Hiroo (Hibiya line). **NMC:** Tokyo, in city limits. NMI: Tokyo Administrative Facility/Hardy Barracks, two km.

DESCRIPTION: Located in a quiet residential area not far from downtown Tokyo, only a five-minute walk from the nearest subway station, Hiroo. Offers guests commercial hotel quality, newly renovated accommodations and food service at affordable prices. Each of 149 guest rooms features private bath or shower, and central heating and air conditioning. TV with remote, VCR, refrigerator, iron/ironing board, hair dryers, coffee maker, computer hookup. Video rentals are available. Two traditional Japanese-style suites for guests to enjoy the full flavor of the Orient.

A family dining room, Japanese-style restaurant, fine dining restaurant, sandwich shop and lounge are available to guests of The New Sanno. Entertainment and special events are scheduled on a regular basis in The New Sanno's main ballroom with banquet facilities can seat up to 500 guests. Also four themed function rooms with banquet facilities and audio visual equipment can hold from 8-35 people.

There is a rooftop pool (seasonal), an exercise room and video game room, first- and second-floor arcades with a Navy Exchange, bookstore, convenience store and concessionaires. An APO, military banking facility, pack-and-wrap service, barber shop, beauty salon, flower shop and laundry and dry cleaning, plus public restrooms (handicap accessible) on the lobby level, and other American-style conveniences make The New Sanno a meeting place for military personnel and their families touring Tokyo. *Note: A new recreational area is under construction, which will be completed May 2001. The area will consist of an indoor swimming pool, and fully equipped work-out room with jacuzzi and sauna. This facility will be open year round.*

Tours, theater, concert and sporting event tickets are available through the Information and Tours Desk. They can also book airline reservations, C-03-3440-7871 ext 7200. If you are arriving at Narita International Airport, an economical airport express bus is available to The New Sanno's front door. Daily buses run to and from Yokota Air Base (schedule available at AMC terminal). The New Sanno is a Joint Services, all ranks facility managed by the U.S. Navy as Executive Agent.

Room Rates for the New Sanno U.S. Forces Center

Room Type	No.	I*	II*	III*	IV*
Single (Queen bed)	39	$29	$38	$44	$63
Double (Queen + sofa)	75	$40	$47	$55	$77
King Suite (King + sofa)	17	$56	$61	$68	$95
Twin Suite (2 twins + sofa)	3	$56	$61	$68	$95
Family Suite (sgl rm + bunk)	2	$56	$61	$76	$100
Japanese Suite (3 futons)	2	$70	$76	$84	$111

***I:** E1-E5; **II:** E6-O3, WO1-WO4; **III:** O4-O10; **IV:** retired/non-DoD. I, II and III include comparable DoD Civilian grades. II includes DAVs, Unremarried Widows and Orphans (all with DD1173).

ALL RATES SUBJECT TO CHANGE.

RESERVATIONS: Reservations may be made up to 365 days in advance, recommended at least 45 days in advance with one night's deposit for each room reserved. Deposits by check, money order, American Express, Diners, MasterCard, Visa. Address: The New Sanno

Hotel, APO AP 96337-5003, Attn: Reservations. **C-(USA) 011-81-3-3440-7871 ext 7121, (JA) 03-3440-7871 ext 7121, DSN-315-229-7121,** Fax: C-(USA) 011-81-3-3440-7824, DSN-315-229-7102; E-mail: room_rsv@thenewsanno.com

SEASON OF OPERATION: Year round.

CREDIT CARDS ACCEPTED: American Express, Diners, MasterCard, Visa.

ELIGIBILITY: Active Duty, retired, U.S. Embassy Tokyo, Reserves, DoD and other SOFA recognized Federal Civilian Employees on official orders to or through Japan.

RESTRICTIONS: No pets.

Okuma Joint Services Rec Facility (Okinawa) (JA09R8)
Schilling Community Activities Center
Okuma Reservation
18th SVS/SVMR
Unit 5135, Box 10
APO AP 96368-5135

MAIN INSTALLATION TELEPHONE NUMBERS: C-(USA) 011-81-980-41-5164 (JA) 0980-41-5164, DSN-315-634-1110. Locator 0980-41-5164.

LOCATION: Off base. On Okinawa, take Highway 58 north from Kadena AB approximately 42 km. Turn left just before Hetona. NMI: Kadena AB, 42 km southwest. **NMC:** Naha, JA 75 km south.

RESERVATION INFORMATION: Schilling Community Activities Center, 18 SVS/SVMR, Unit 5135, Box 10, APO AP 96368-5135. Duty, retired, DoD civilians assigned overseas. May make reservations up to 90 days in advance, **C-(USA) 011-81-6117-34-4322, (JA) 098938-1110 ext 634-4322, DSN-315-634-4322,** Fax: C-(USA) 011-81-98-041-5165, (JA) 098-041-5165. 0800-1700 hours Mon-Fri (summer), Wed-Mon (winter). Reception Center Bldg 116. Check in 1500 hours, check out 1100 hours. Operates year round. No pets. No glass.

TML Rec Cabanas. Bedroom, two double beds, shared bath, (30); bedroom, two double beds, private bath (10); bedrooms, double bed, private bath, dry bar, couples only (12); suites, four double beds, private bath (9); VIP suite (1). Refrigerator, microwave, utensils, A/C, TV/VCR, housekeeping service, cribs ($3), rollaways ($3). Rates: $25-$55. All categories can make reservations.

DV/VIP 18th Wing/Protocol, Bldg 10, Kadena AB, Okinawa, DSN-315-634-0106. O6+. Retirees and lower ranks Space-A.

AMENITIES: Meeting/Conference Room and Mini Mart. Recreation and boat rentals available (certification by a sanctioned organization or qualification test by instructor required to rent sailboat, wind surfing and diving equipment).

TML AVAILABILITY: Good, Nov-Feb. Difficult, other times.

CREDIT CARDS ACCEPTED: Visa and MasterCard.

TRANSPORTATION: Off base shuttle/bus; Car Rental; Off base taxi.

DINING OPPORTUNITIES: Restaurant/Lounge is within walking distance.

Great beach rec area. For full details and camping opportunities, see Military Living's *Military RV, Camping and Outdoor Recreation Around The World*.

Sasebo Fleet Activities (JA15R8)
Bldg 310
PSC 476, Box 1100
FPO AP 96322-1100

MAIN INSTALLATION TELEPHONE NUMBERS: C-(USA) 011-81-956-24-6111, (JA) 0956-24-6111, DSN-315-252-1110. Locator C-011-81-956-24-6111.

LOCATION: From either Nagasaki or Fukuoka. take the Nishi-Kyushu Expressway to Sasebo exit (both in Japanese and English). Follow Route JA-35 to downtown Sasebo, to left on International Drive to Main Gate. Far southwestern Japan, on the Korean Strait, **NMC:** Fukuoka, 80 km northeast.

RESERVATION INFORMATION: Attn: CBH Officer, U.S. Fleet Activities, Sasebo, PSC 476, Box 20, FPO AP 96322-0004. **C-(USA) 011-81-956-24-6111 (BOQ ext 3794) (BEQ ext 3413), (JA) 095624-6111 (BOQ ext 3794) (BEQ ext 3413), DSN-315-252-3794 (BOQ), DSN-315-252-3413 (BEQ),** Fax: C-(USA) 011-81-956-24-6111 (BOQ ext 3530) (BEQ ext 2414), DSN-315-252-3530 (BOQ), DSN-315-252-2414 (BEQ), 24 hours daily. Active Duty PCS and TAD/TDY (civilians below GS7) on orders to FLEACT Sasebo may make reservations up to 45 days in advance; all others Space-A. Reservations for official duty from CONUS, call C-1-800-576-9327. Reservations for official duty from Hawaii and Pacific area, call above BOQ/BEQ numbers. Check in at BOQ/BEQ office after 1200 hours, check out 1200 hours. Government civilian employee billeting.

BEH Bldgs 1604, 63. Shared bedrooms, private bath (74). Refrigerator, microwave, TV/VCR in room and lounge, phone, laundry facility. Modern structure. Rates: $6 per person per unit. Maximum two per unit. No pets.

BOH Bldgs 1455, 1603. Bedrooms (60). Kitchenette, refrigerator, microwave, utensils, TV/VCR in room and lounge, housekeeping service, laundry facility, cribs. Modern structure. Rates: $12-$30 per person per unit. Maximum two per unit.

NAVY LODGE Navy Lodge, Bldg 1602 Attn: US Fleet Activities Sasebo, PSC 476, Box 30, FPO AP 96322-0030. Lodge number is C-(USA) 011-81-956-24-0322/0223, (JA) 0956-24-0322, DSN-315-252-3608, Fax: C-(USA) 011-81-956-24-0173, (JA) 0956-24-0173, DSN-315-252-3605, 24 hours daily. Check in 1500-1800 hours, check out 1200 hours. Bedroom, two queen beds, private bath, handicap accessible (58). Elevator, kitchenette, microwave, stove, refrigerator, utensils, A/C, CATV/VCR, video rental, phone, fax and copy service, hair dryer, clock radio, housekeeping service, coin laundry facility, iron/ironing board, cribs, rollaways, mini mart, picnic grounds, playground, coffee service in lobby. Near Harborview Club, O Club, Liberty Grill, Base Galley, Swimming Pool, Bowling Alley. NEX is 10-minute walk. Located on base shuttle route. Modern structure. Rates: $53. All categories can make reservations. No pets. Newly remodeled and expanded early 1999.

DV/VIP Commander, Fleet Activities Sasebo, Attn: Protocol Officer, PSC 476, Box 1, FPO AP 96322-1100. BOQ/BEQ. Bldg 80, C-(USA) 011-81-956-24-3401. E9, O6+.

AMENITIES: Ice, Snack and Soft Drink Vending Machines.

TML AVAILABILITY: Fairly good, Apr-Aug. Difficult, Sep-Dec.

CREDIT CARDS ACCEPTED: American Express. The Navy Lodge accepts Visa, MasterCard, American Express, Discover and Diners.

TRANSPORTATION: Car Rental: C-011-81-956-24-6111 ext 3609, DSN-315-252-3609; On/off base taxi, C-011-81-956-24-4136, Free Shuttle from Fukuoka to Sasebo at 1100, 1700, 2015 and 2230 hours daily.

DINING OPPORTUNITIES: Harborview Club, C-ext 3967, DSN-315-252-3967/6; Liberty Grill, C-ext 3622, DSN-315-252-3622; NEX Food Court, C-ext 3476, DSN-315-252-3476 are within walking distance of

Navy Lodge. McDonald's, C-011-81-956-26-0078; and Mr. Doughnut are within driving distance.

Mount Yumihari has an excellent view. Take a 99 Islands boat cruise, from nearby Kashimae Pier (15 minutes from base by car). Hachiman Shrine is a 20-minute walk from base. Nagasaki and Fukuoka are one-hour drives. Don't miss the Fukagawa/Noritake Chinaware Factory, the finest bone china in the world! Don't forget to see Huis Ten Bosch and Holland Village.

Tama Hills Recreation Area (JA10R8)
374 SPTG/SVBL
Unit 5119
APO AP 96328-5119

MAIN INSTALLATION TELEPHONE NUMBERS: C-(USA) 011-81-423-77-1110, (JA) 042-377-1110, DSN-315-224-1110. Locator 225-1110.

LOCATION: Fifteen miles southeast of Yokota AB. **NMC:** Tokyo, 25 miles west. **NMI:** Yokota AB, 15 miles northwest.

RESERVATION INFORMATION: 374 SPTG/SVBL, Unit 5119, APO AP 96328-5119. **C-(USA) 011-81-423-77-7009, (JA) 042-377-7009, DSN-315-224-3421/3422,** Fax: C (USA)-011-81-423-78-8446, (JA) 0423-78-8446, 24 hours daily. Reservations recommended taken 90 days in advance for Yokota AB residents, 60 days for all others. Credit card guarantee required for first night's stay. Check in at facility after 1500 hours, check out 1100 hours. Directions: One mile from JR Nambu-Line Minami-Tama train station.

TML Rec Lodge and cabins. Single rooms (9); Twin suites (3); King suites (4); DV suite (1); Handicap room (1). Suite cabins with loft, kitchenette, and hot tub (10); Private four-bedroom lodge with kitchen, fireplace, and hot tub (1). All rooms and cabins with private baths or showers. Refrigerator, microwave, A/C, TV/VCR, housekeeping service, laundry facility (in main lodge), hairdryer, cribs, iron/ironing board, coffee maker, and rollaways available upon request. BBQ grill and picnic tables in cabins. Rates: $30-$150. *Pets allowed in selected cabins only.*

AMENITIES: Exercise Room, Meeting/Conference Room and Mini Mart, Ice, Snack and Soft Drink Vending Machine. Dining room, lounge, video rentals, game room, outdoor recreation equipment rental, mountain bikes, tennis court, basketball court, archery range, miniature golf course, softball field, playground, horseback riding stables, paintball field, campsites, picnic areas, hiking trails, mountain bike trail and 18-hole golf course.

TML AVAILABILITY: Year round. Good, Oct-Mar. Difficult, weekends and other times.

CREDIT CARDS ACCEPTED: Visa, MasterCard and AF Club Card.

TRANSPORTATION: Bus once a day en route to and from Yokota AB and the New Sanno Hotel in Tokyo. Off base taxi and train.

DINING OPPORTUNITIES: Tama Lodge Kiji Dining Room: Full-service dining room open daily for breakfast, lunch, and dinner; Tama Hills Golf Course Tee House Restaurant: Self service dining room, open Tue-Sun for breakfast and lunch; Tama Lodge Hillcrest Lounge: Bar snacks, alcoholic and non-alcoholic beverages, open daily.

This is a 500-acre retreat west of Tokyo. It's a quiet getaway offering many facilities, such as a golf course and horse stables. See Military Living's *Military RV, Camping and Outdoor Recreation Around The World* for more details.

Tokyo Administration Facility (JA02R8)
Akasaka Press Center (Hardy Barracks)
Bldg 1, Room 211
APO AP 96337-5002

MAIN INSTALLATION TELEPHONE NUMBERS: C-(USA) 011-81-3117-29-1110 (JA) 03117-29-1110, DSN-315-229-3270/3345. Locator 03117-29-1110.

LOCATION: At 7-23-17 Roppongi, Minato-ku, Tokyo. Near Imperial Palace and three km by taxi from New Sanno Hotel. Nogizaka subway station, left out of exit 5. **NMC:** Tokyo, in the city.

RESERVATION INFORMATION: Hardy Barracks, Bldg 1, Room 211, APO AP 96337-5002. **C-(USA) 011-81-3117-29-3270, (JA) 03117-29-3270,** Fax: C-011-81-3117-29-3271, DSN-315-229-3270, 0730-2230 daily. Reservations may be made up to 180 days in advance by phone or in person for Space-A. Check in at facility 1500 hours, check out 1200 hours. Government civilian employee billeting.

VOQ/VEQ Separate bedroom suites (19); bedroom, private bath (2). Community kitchen, refrigerator, coffee maker, A/C, TV/VCR, housekeeping service, laundry facility, cribs, travel kit. Remodeled Jan 2000. Rates: room double occupancy $25; suites double occupancy $30. No Pets. *Note: Tokyo city bus 97 runs between the New Sanno Hotel and Hardy Barracks.*

TML AVAILABILITY: Good. Best months Jan-Mar.

CREDIT CARDS ACCEPTED: Visa, MasterCard and American Express.

TRANSPORTATION: Off base shuttle/bus; Car Rental; Off base taxi.

DINING OPPORTUNITIES: Numerous fine restaurants are within walking and driving distance in Tokyo.

Check with the New Sanno Hotel for guided tours or just pick up some city maps. Then visit the Ginza, Kabuki theater, Akasaka/Roppongi (the entertainment district), Ueno Park, Zoo and shopping are musts.

White Beach Recreation Services (JA13R8)
Commander, Fleet Activities Okinawa
PSC 480, MWR Department
FPO AP 96370-1150

MAIN INSTALLATION TELEPHONE NUMBERS: C-011-81-6117-34-1110, C-(JA) 098-892-5111, DSN-315-634-1110. Locator 645-7218 (USMC); 632-7653 (USN); 644-4300 (USA); 634-3374 (USAF).

LOCATION: On the east side of island on the Katsuren Peninsula in Buckner Bay. From JA-24 north of Okinawa City, turn east to JA-329 to JA-8 to White Beach. **NMC:** Naha, 20 km south.

RESERVATION INFORMATION: Commander, Fleet Activities Okinawa, PSC 480, MWR Department, FPO AP 96370-0057, **C-(USA) 011-81-634-6952/6954, DSN-315-634-6952/6954/6342.** Fax: C-011-81-6117-32-4501, DSN-315-634-6918, 0700-1530 hours. E-mail: mwr.reservations@kadena.af.mil WEB: www.cfao.navy.mil/navymwr/navymwr.htm Reservations required with full payment up to 10 days in advance. See *Military Living's Military RV, Camping and Outdoor Recreation Around the World* for additional information and directions.

Have **YOU** seen this dog? If not, visit **www.militaryliving.com** and read all about Tootie, a military dependent dog. There are letters from other military pets, as well as lots of helpful pet-related travel information!

(TML) **White Beach Recreation Services.** Camper Trailers (42) Rates: $15-$30. Duplex cabins (2) Rates: $40-$50. Suites (2) Rates:$40-$50 Studio cabins (2) Rates: $30-$50. Log cabins (4) Rates:$30-$50. Rates vary depending on rank.

TML AVAILABILITY: Difficult.

CREDIT CARDS ACCEPTED: Visa, MasterCard and Discover.

TRANSPORTATION: On base taxi, MWR taxi service, C-642-2266; Off base taxi, MWR taxi service, C-642-2266.

DINING OPPORTUNITIES: Ocean Cliff Club, C-642-2311; and Port of Call Club, C-642-2345 are within walking distance.

Yokosuka Fleet Activities (JA05R8)
PSC 473, Box 1
FPO AP 96349-1110

MAIN INSTALLATION TELEPHONE NUMBERS: C-(USA) 011-81-468-21-1911, (JA) 0468-21-1911, DSN-315-243-1110. Locator 113.

LOCATION: About 38 km south of Tokyo and 41 km north of Yokohama. **NMC:** Tokyo, 41 km north. Excellent train service.

RESERVATION INFORMATION: Combined BQ, PSC 473, Box 40, FPO AP 96349-1110. **C-(USA) 011-81-6160-43-7317/5685, DSN-315-243-7317,** Fax: C-(USA) 011-81-6160-438-990, DSN-315-243-8990. 24 hours daily. E-mail: c932@cfay-emh.yoko.mrms.navy.mil Check in at facility after 1200 hours, check out before 1200 hours. Government civilian employee and military billeting. *Winner of the 1997 and 1999 Admiral Elmo R. Zumwalt Award for Excellence in Bachelor Housing and the 3rd Pineapple Award for Quality Guest Service.*

(BEQ) Bldgs 1492, 1393. Bedroom, two beds, private bath (232). Refrigerator, A/C, TV/VCR in room and lounge, housekeeping service, laundry facility, iron/ironing board. Modern structure. Rates: Bldg 1492 $6 per person. Bldg 1393 $6 per person. Maximum two per room. Duty can make reservations, others Space-A.

(BOQ) Bldgs 1556, 1723. Bedroom, private bath (95). Kitchen, A/C, TV in room and lounge, housekeeping service, laundry facility, barber shop. Modern structure. Rates: $12 per person. Duty can make reservations, others Space-A.

(CPOQ) Bldg 1475. E7-E9. Bedroom, private bath (26). Community kitchen, refrigerator, A/C, TV/VCR, housekeeping service, laundry facility, iron/ironing board, ice machine. Modern structure. Rates: $8 per person. Duty can make reservations, others Space-A. Note: all beds are singles.

(TML) Nasu Lodge. 160 km north of Tokyo. Rec Service Office, C-(USA) 011-81-6160-43-911 ext 5613/7306. Two-story wood-frame building accommodates up to 26 persons. Japanese style floor and bath. Kitchen and lodging requirements. Reservations taken one month in advance.

(NAVY LODGE) Navy Lodge. Bldg J-100, J-200, PSC 473, Box 70, FPO AP 96349-0003. **C-1-800-NAVY-INN.** Lodging number is C-(USA) 011-81-6160-43-6708, (JA) 0-468-27-0080, DSN-315-243-6708, Fax: C-(USA) 011-81-6160-43-8980, DSN-315-241-2381, 24 hours daily. WEB: www.navy-nex.com Two queen size beds, kitchenette, microwave, toaster, private bath (98). One queen size bed, kitchenette, microwave, toaster, private bath, handicap accessible (4). Two double beds, kitchenette, microwave, toaster, private bath (8). One double bed, microfridge, private bath (5). One double bed, sofabed, microfridge, private bath (50). A/C, CATV/VCR, video rental, clock, hair dryer, coin laundry facility, cribs, iron/ironing boards, ice machine, lounge, dining table, futons, mini mart, picnic grounds, playground, restaurant, coffee. Rates: $45, kitchen units $53. *Pets kept overnight in lounge until kennel opens.*

(DV/VIP) Protocol Office, C-(USA) 011-81-6160-43-5685, DSN-315-243-7317, Bldg 1471. O7+. Bedroom, single bed, private bath, refrigerator, A/C, TV/VCR, housekeeping service, laundry facility, iron/ironing board, ice machine. Modern structure. Rates: $6. Duty can make reservations, others Space-A. Available at BOQ: VIP suite $20; Togo Room (O7+) $25.

AMENITIES: Snack and Soft Drink Vending Machine.

TML AVAILABILITY: Good. Somewhat difficult, Jun-Sep.

CREDIT CARDS ACCEPTED: Visa, American Express and Government Visa. The Navy Lodge accepts Visa, MasterCard, American Express and Discover.

TRANSPORTATION: On base taxi, C-011-81-6160-43-4444, DSN-315-243-4444/4511; Off base taxi, C-011-81-6160-43-4444.

DINING OPPORTUNITIES: Sumo Restaurant located in Navy Lodge and Seaside Club, C-011-81-6160-43-5625 is within walking distance of Navy Lodge (within driving distance of other facilities). Commodore Perry General Mess, C-011-81-6160-43-5741; and O Club, C-011-81-6160-43-5930/5002 are within walking distance of other facilities. CPO Club, C-011-81-6160-43-5506; and E Club, C-011-81-6160-43-5951 are within driving distance of other facilities.

Located close to Tokyo, near many historic Japanese shrines, beautiful beaches, a 10-minute walk to a shopping mall, and two hours from Disneyland Tokyo, Yokosuka boasts "the best MWR facility in the Pacific."

Yokota Air Base (JA04R8)
374th MSS/DPF
Unit 5123
APO AP 96328-5123

MAIN INSTALLATION TELEPHONE NUMBERS: C-(USA) 011-81-3117-52-1110 (JA) 03117-52-2511, DSN-315-225-1110. Locator 225-8390.

LOCATION: Take JA-16 S from Tokyo. AB is two km west of Fussa. Clearly marked. **NMC:** Tokyo, 57 km northeast.

RESERVATION INFORMATION: Kanto Lodge, Bldg 10, Airlift Avenue and 1st Street, 374 SPTG/SVML, PCS 78, Unit 5119, APO AP 96328-5119. **C-(USA) 011-81-3117-55-7712/754-2002, C-(JA) 042-552-2510 ext 4-2000, DSN-315-224-2002,** Fax: C-(USA) 011-81-311-7553499, DSN-315-225-3499, 24 hours daily. Duty can make reservations any time; Space-A can make reservations 72 hours in advance. No pets allowed in any lodging facilities. Check in 1200 hours at lodging, check out 1000 hours. Government lodging. *Note: A new 125 unit TLF is due to open in July 2001.*

(TLF) Bldg 4304 ext 5-7712. One family unit per suite, three bedrooms, two baths. Kitchen and living room, utensils, A/C, TV in each bedroom and living room, housekeeping service, cribs available, laundry facilities. Modern structure. Rates: $35.00 per unit. Limited pet care available on base.

(VAQ) Bldgs 690 and 10. Bldg 690, bedroom, common bath (24). Bldg 10, four individual units per suite, shared bath between two units, shared kitchen and living room, utensils, TV in every unit, housekeeping service, and laundry facilities. Rates: $21.00 per person.

(VQ) Bldgs 120, 131 and 133. C ext 5-9270. Bedroom, private bath (182). Refrigerator, A/C, TV, housekeeping service, laundry facilities. Modern structure. Rates: $22.50 per unit.

(DV/VIP) Contact 374th AW/CSP, C-(USA) 011-81-311-755-3748, DSN-315-225-3748. Bldg 32. C-ext 5-9270. O6+ (Mon and Fri). Suite, bedroom, private bath (1). Refrigerator, A/C, TV, housekeeping service, laundry facility. Older structure. Rates: $18.50.

TML AVAILABILITY: Good.

CREDIT CARDS ACCEPTED: Visa and MasterCard.

TRANSPORTATION: On base shuttle/bus, C-011-81-311-755-9121; Off base taxi, Keio Taxi, C-(JA) 553-9966.

DINING OPPORTUNITIES: O Club C-011-81-311-755-8520; Outback, C-011-81-311-755-7341; Yokota Burger, C-011-81-311-757-8839 are within walking distance. Firehouse Deli, C-011-81-311-755-7474; Main Street USA, C-011-81-311-755-8669; Popeye's Chicken, C-011-81-311-755-7615 are within driving distance.

KOREA

Camp Carroll (RK12R8)
c/o Unit 15494, Box 2093
20th Support Group
APO AE 96260-5000

MAIN INSTALLATION TELEPHONE NUMBERS: C-(USA) 011-82-545-970-1110, DSN-315-765-1110.

LOCATION: In the center of the Nak Tong River Valley, east of the river. **NMC:** Taegu, 35 km northeast.

RESERVATION INFORMATION: C-(USA) 011-82-545-970-7823. Call for more information. Fax: 011-82-545-970-8058. E-mail: buchanangf@usfk.korea.army.mil

TML Room (43). Rates: single $20, double $28.

AMENITIES: Snack and Soft Drink Vending Machine.

TML AVAILABILITY: Good year round.

CREDIT CARDS ACCEPTED: Visa, MasterCard and American Express.

TRANSPORTATION: Shuttle bus to Camp Henry (0700-2000 hours daily).

DINING OPPORTUNITIES: Anthony's Pizza 765-7544; Burger King, 767-7537; Special T's 765-7780; and Combined Club all on camp.

Visit Kuimi Industrial Complex.

Camp Casey (RK01R8)
Attn: EANC-AI-CFA-ACS
Unit 15543
APO AP 96224-0453

MAIN INSTALLATION TELEPHONE NUMBERS: C-(USA) 011-82-31-869-1110, (RK) 031-869-1110, DSN-315-730-1110.

LOCATION: Located in northwestern South Korea. Take RK-3 north from Seoul for 40 km to Tongduchon and follow signs to Camp Casey Gate 2, east of RK-3. **NMC:** Tongduchon, 2 km south.

RESERVATION INFORMATION: Casey Lodge, Bldg 2626, APO AP 96224-0453. **C-(USA) 011-82-31-869-4247, (RK) 031-869-4247 DSN-315-730-4247,** Fax: C-(USA) 011-82-31-869-4247, DSN-315-730-4247. E-mail: kimykwang@usfk.korea.army.mil. WEB: www-areal.korea.army.mil PCS/TDY may make reservations six months in advance, 30 days for TDY/Leave/Pass personnel. *Note: A $6.039 million Guesthouse was approved in the DoD Fiscal Year 2001 NAF Construction Program.*

TML Bldg 2626. Standard room has four twin beds; Deluxe room has a queen bed/pull-out sofa and a twin bed, all rooms have

private bath, CATV, microwave, refrigerator, laundry facilitiy. Vending machine. Rates: standard room $35/person all ranks, every travel status. Each additional person $5.

TML AVAILABILITY: Good. Best, Nov-Dec. Difficult, Dec-Feb, June-Sep.

CREDIT CARDS ACCEPTED: Visa, MasterCard, and American Express.

TRANSPORTATION: On base shuttle/bus, C-011-82-351-730-4259; Off base shuttle/bus; On base taxi: AAFES, C-011-82-351-730-2851/2853; Off base taxi.

DINING OPPORTUNITIES: Primo's Express, PX Food Court and Indianhead Golf Clubhouse are within walking distance. Reggie's Beverage Company, Warriors Club and Borderline Cafe are within driving distance.

Camp Henry (RK02R8)
20th Support Group
Unit 15494, Box 2093
APO AP 96218-0565

MAIN INSTALLATION TELEPHONE NUMBERS: C-(USA) 011-82-53-470-1110, (RK) 53-470-1110, DSN-315-768-1110. Locator, C-011-82-53-470-7495.

LOCATION: Located in the city of Taegu west of the Shinehon River. Five blocks south of Taegu City Hall. Camp George is two blocks west and Camp Walker is three blocks southwest. Many of the streets do not have signs. Taegu is south off of the RK-1 Expressway. **NMC:** Taegu, in city limits.

RESERVATION INFORMATION: Bldg 1712. Billeting Office, Lodging Division, DCA, 20th Area Support Group, Unit 15494, APO AP 96218-0565. **C-(USA) 011-82-53-470-7459, DSN-315-768-8171,** Fax: C-(USA) 011-82-53-470-8171, DSN-315-768-8171, 24 hours daily.

VOQ Camp Henry. Bldg 1712. E1-O6, TDY and PCS personnel. One-bedroom, private bath (28). Kitchenette, refrigerator, microwave, AC, TV in room and lounge, housekeeping service, laundry facility. Rates: first person $45, each additional person $5. TDY and PCS have priority. Reservations can be made 30 days in advance. No pets.

DVQ Camp Walker. Bldg S-264. C-(USA) 011-82-53-470-8949, DSN-315-764-4115/4293. O5+, TDY or PCS. Queen size bed, private bath (3); Twin bed, private bath (2). Kitchenette, refrigerator, microwave, AC, TV in room and lounge, housekeeping service. Rates: first person $55, each additional person $10. TDY, PCS and reserves. *Note: A $7.775 million Guesthouse was approved in the DoD Fiscal Year 2001 NAF Construction Program.*

DV/VIP Camp Walker. Protocol DSN-315-768-8949. Bldg 563, 565. O6+. Bedroom, private bath (10). Kitchenette, refrigerator, microwave, AC, TV in room and lounge, phone, housekeeping service. Rates: single $43, double $53. Maximum two per room.

AMENITIES: Soft Drink Machine and Internet/E-mail access for all customers.

TML AVAILABILITY: Very good. Best, Nov-Dec. Difficult, May-Oct.

CREDIT CARDS ACCEPTED: Visa and MasterCard.

TRANSPORTATION: On/Off base shuttle/bus, C-011-82-53-470-7936, DSN-315-768-7936; Car Rental, C-011-82-53-470-6174, DSN-315-768-6174; On/Off base taxi, C-011-82-53-470-8623, DSN-315-768-8623.

DINING OPPORTUNITIES: Henry Place, C-011-82-53-470-7300 and Snack Bar, C-011-82-53-470-8901 are within walking distance. Jin Yang, C-011-82-53-472-3928; Sin Hung, C-011-82-53-476-0953; Pak Ga Ne, C-011-82-53-476-0017; Gun Dul Ba Wi, C-011-82-53-471-1500; Taegu Garden, C-011-82-53-471-9911; Su Sung, C-011-82-53-763-7311; Burger King, C-011-82-53-764-4876 and Ever Green, C-011-82-53-764-4060 are within driving distance.

Camp Hialeah (RK10R8)
20th Support Group
ACS, Unit 15181
APO AP 96259-0270

MAIN INSTALLATION TELEPHONE NUMBERS: C-(USA) 011-82-51-801-1110, (RK) 051-801-1110, DSN-315-763-1110. Locator 051-801-1110.

LOCATION: Camp Hialeah is located 162 km south of Taegu and about 18 km north of Pusan (second largest city in Korea). Exit from the Seoul-Pusan RK-1 Expressway, follow signs to Camp Hialeah (10 km from north/south expressway). There is a subway stop 10 minutes (walking) from Camp Hialeah. **NMC:** Pusan, 13 km south.

RESERVATION INFORMATION: Housing Division, DPW, 20th Support Group, Bldg 508, Unit 15181, ACS, APO AP 96259-0270. **C-011-82-51-801-3668, DSN-315-763-3668,** Fax: C-011-82-51-801-7559, DSN-315-763-7559, 0700-2100 hours. Directions: Enter through gate. Take first left at intersection. Proceed 100 yards, on the left building 508.

(VOQ) Bldg 508. Bedroom with private bath and kitchenette (29); bedroom with shared bath and kitchenette (27). Rates: $25-$60.

AMENITIES: Exercise Room, Meeting/Conference Room, Snack Vending Machine and Soft Drink Machine.

TML AVAILABILITY: Good. Best, Nov-Dec. Difficult, May-Oct.

CREDIT CARDS ACCEPTED: Visa and MasterCard.

TRANSPORTATION: Off base shuttle/bus, Camp Hialeah to Camp Henry MTWFS dep 0630 return 1400; Off base taxi; City bus and subways are accessible and inexpensive.

DINING OPPORTUNITIES: Anthony's Pizza and Snack Bar, C-051-801-3753; Katusa Snack Bar, C-051-801-3032; and Restaurant Pub, C-051-801-3900 are located within walking distance. Lotte Hotel, C-051-810-5200; and Somyon Circle are located within driving distance.

Camp Humphreys (RK08R8)
23rd Support Group
Attn: EANC-HG-PCA-ACS
Bldg T343, Unit 15228
APO AP 96271-0716

MAIN INSTALLATION TELEPHONE NUMBERS: C-(USA) 011-82-333-690-1110, (RK) 0333-690-1110, DSN-315-753-1110. Locator C-0333-690-6222.

LOCATION: Located 80 km south of Seoul via RK-1 Expressway, take Pyongtaek exit south approximately 13 km. The camp is off of Hwy 38. **NMC:** Pyongtaek, 13 km north.

RESERVATION INFORMATION: Housing Division, DPW, USASA Area III, Unit 15716, Bldg S-247 APO AP 96271-0716. **C-(USA) 011-82-333-690-7355/7269, DSN-315-753-7355/7269,** Fax: C-(USA) 011-82-333-690-7357, DSN-315-753-7357, 0800-1700 hours Mon-Fri, 0800-1200 hours Sat. After hours report to EOC, Bldg 251. Duty can make reservations; all others Space-A. Check in at billeting, check out 1200 hours. *Note: Construction of a new 80-room TLF is underway.*

(BEQ) Bldgs 727, 728. Bedroom, private bath; bedroom, hall bath. Refrigerator, microwave, CATV/VCR, coffee maker, ironing/board, alarm clock, housekeeping service, laundry facilities. Rates: $34, additional occupant $5. Maximum two people.

(BOQ) Bldgs 203, 206, 254. Bedroom, private bath. Refrigerator, microwave, CATV/VCR, coffee maker, ironing/board, alarm clock, housekeeping service, laundry facilities (Bldg 206). Rates: $34, additional occupant $5. Maximum two people.

(DV/VIP) Bedroom, private bath. Shared kitchen, refrigerator, microwave, CATV/VCR, coffee maker, ironing/board, alarm clock, housekeeping service, laundry facilities. Rates: $38, additional occupant $5. Maximum two people.

TML AVAILABILITY: Fairly good. Difficult, Dec-Feb.

TRANSPORTATION: On base taxi, Bldg T-128, DSN-315-753-3414. Pyongtack Train Station, Myumg Jim Bus Terminal, Bldg T-128, DSN-315-753-7353.

DINING OPPORTUNITIES: Leaders Lounge, DSN-315-753-8177.

Don't miss seeing the Secret Garden and Puyong Pavilion in Seoul.

Camp Page (RK03R8)
SSD USAG
Area 1 Sub-Post
APO AP 96208-0252

MAIN INSTALLATION TELEPHONE NUMBERS: C-(USA) 011-82-32-259-1110, (RK) 03-259-1110, DSN-315-721-1110. Locator 315-721-5820.

LOCATION: From Seoul, take Highway 46 NE into Chunchon City. **NMC:** Chunchon City, in city limits.

RESERVATION INFORMATION: SSD USAG, Bldg T-452, APO AP 96208-0252. **C-(USA) 011-82-33-259-5331, DSN-315-721-5331/5691.** Hours of operation: 0800-1700, Mon-Fri. Reservations through Installation Commander's Office, C-(USA) 011-82-33-259-5316, DSN-315-721-5316.

(BEQ) Bldgs S-1416. E1-E7. Bedroom, private bath (48). Refrigerator. Rates: Primarily used by permanent party members, with private bath $3 per two nights.

(BOQ) Bldgs S-1304, S-1305, S-1306, S-1307. Officers and E1-E9. Combination of single shared bedrooms, and single private bedrooms, private bath (48). Kitchenette, refrigerator. Rates: Primarily used by permanent party members; with private bath $3 per two nights; with DVQ $5 per two nights.

TML AVAILABILITY: Good. Best, December. Difficult, June.

TRANSPORTATION: On base shuttle/bus, DSN-315-721-5453.

DINING OPPORTUNITIES: Community Club, DSN-315-721-5164.

Cheju-do Recreation Center (Camp McNabb) (RK13R8)
Unit 15031
APO AP 96220-0123

MAIN INSTALLATION TELEPHONE NUMBERS: C-011-82-64-792-5698, DSN-315-763-3330, Fax: C-011-82-51-801-3305, DSN-315-763-3305.

LOCATION: Sub-tropical island off the south coast of Korea. Cheju is located 25 miles southwest from Cheju City, next to Mosulpo town. Cheju is a one-hour flight from Seoul.

RESERVATION INFORMATION: Unit 15031, APO AP 96220-0123. **C-011-82-53-470-4003,** DSN-315-764-4403, Fax: C-011-82-64-94-2672. WEB: www.19thtaacom.korea.army.mil

(TLF) Guestrooms. Standard room with one double bed and one sofa sleeper or day bed (16); deluxe rooms with two double beds, two sleeper sofas, kitchenette, living area (2) and family suites with two double beds, two sleeper sofas (3); open bay with 25 bunk beds (1). Refrigerator, microwave, CATV/VCR, phone. Rates: standard $40; deluxe $75; family suite $60; open bay $10.

AMENITIES: Swimming pool, tennis courts, fitness center/gym, laundromat, shoppette, outdoor picnic areas, package tours.

TML AVAILABILITY: Peak season 26 May to 30 November.

CREDIT CARDS ACCEPTED: Visa, MasterCard and American Express.

TRANSPORTATION: Airport to Recreation Area transportation/ shuttle, Off-base Car Rental.

DINING OPPORTUNITIES: AAFES All-American Eatery and the Islander Club are within walking distance.

Located less than sixty miles south of the Korean Peninsula, the facility is located on the south side of the island of Cheju. The history of Cheju Island dates back more than two thousand years. Palm trees, waterfalls and a stunning coast line make up the beauty of this magical island.

Chinhae Fleet Activities (RK06R8)
Bldg 714, PSC 479, Code 01R
FPO AP 96269-1100

MAIN INSTALLATION TELEPHONE NUMBERS: C-(USA) 011-82-555-40-5110, (RK) 0555-40-5110 DSN-315-762-5110; Chinhae OOD DSN-315-762-5110.

LOCATION: On the east coast of Korea, south of Pusan. Take the Seoul-Pusan Expressway 1 to Pusan, exit and continue along the coast for 40 km southwest on Masan Bay. Follow main road into city, pass statue of Chinhae Admiral Yi to Chinhae Naval Facility four blocks on right.

RESERVATION INFORMATION: Combined Bachelor Housing, PSC 479 FPO AP 96269-1100. **C-(USA) 011-82-55-540-5336, DSN-315-762-5336.** Mon-Fri 0730-1700 hours. After hours OOD: C-(USA) 011-82-55-540-5110, DSN-315-762-5110. WEB: www.cfac-100.korea.army.mil Duty may make reservations; others Space-A.

BOQ/BEQ BOQ Bldg 794, BEQ Bldg 704. BOQ one bedroom, private bath, kitchenette, laundry facility, electric range, phone lines, sofa bed. BEQ bedroom, shared bath. All units refrigerator, microwave, CATV/VCR, central heating, A/C, housekeeping service and non smoking. Rates: BOQ $23 per night, add a guest $5.75; BEQ $10.

DV/VIP Pilot and Chart House: one bedroom, private bath, kitchenette, refrigerator, housekeeping service, CATV/VCR, microwave oven, washer/dryer, electric range, phone lines, sofa bed, central heating and AC. Non-smoking. Rates: $28 per person, added guest $7.

TML AVAILABILITY: Very limited.

CREDIT CARDS ACCEPTED: Visa and MasterCard.

TRANSPORTATION: Off base taxi.

DINING OPPORTUNITIES: General Mess, C-762-5283; C1 Restaurant, C-762-5350; Morning Calm Cafe, C-762-5358.

If you are lucky enough to be in Chinhae in April, you may see the city covered in cherry blossoms. There will be folk dances, and you may visit fascinating street markets, as well as participate many other exciting activities. This is a very interesting port city.

Dragon Hill Lodge (RK09R8)
Unit 15335
APO AP 96205-0427

MAIN INSTALLATION TELEPHONE NUMBERS: C-(USA) 011-82-2-790-0016, (RK) 02-790-0016, DSN-315-738-2222 (ask for front desk). Locator 724-6830.

LOCATION: Located on South Post, Yongsan, in Seoul. From Kimpo International Airport, enter the Olympic Stadium Expressway 88 for approximately 24 km, then take the Panpo Bridge exit and cross the bridge. Look for the Crown Hotel on the right side as you come off the bridge. Stay on the right side of the road and do not go underground where the road splits. Go to the major intersection and turn left (one mile from bridge), enter the second gate on the left side (Gate 10) and proceed to the Lodge. **NMC:** Seoul, in the city.

RESERVATION INFORMATION: Hotel Reservations, Yongsan, South Post, Unit 15335, APO AP 96205-0427. Check in at front desk. **C-(USA) 011-82-2-790-0016, (RK) 790-0016, DSN-315-738-2222** (ask for front desk)**,** Fax: C-(USA) 011-82-2-790-1576 (RK) 792-1576. E-mail: reservations@dh1.korea.army.mil All categories can make reservations. Priority travel status are PCS/LP and TDY respectively. ***Note: A $14 million expansion was completed in the year 2000. Ninety-five guest rooms were added.***

ELIGIBILITY: Active Duty, retired military, dependents, DoD civilians and all foreign non-Korean military with orders to USFK. All must present either DD form 1173 or DD form 2.

TML **Dragon Hill Lodge.** 394 guestrooms. All rooms have a queen size bed, double sofa bed, private bath. Kitchenette, refrigerator, microwave, coffee maker, utensils. Smoking and non-smoking rooms available. Handicap accessible rooms (partial ambulatory). Rates: (based on SINGLE occupancy ONLY) PCS, all ranks $92.95; LP/Pass: PVT-SGT, $45; SSG-CSM, W01-CW3, 2LT-Cpt, $55; CW4, MAJ-COL, DOD Civ, Ret Mil, BG-GEN, SES, $65; TDY, all ranks $140. Pets can be boarded at the veterinary clinic near Gate 17, South Post.

AMENITITIES: Lounges, Fitness Club with Pool, Internet Cafe.

TML AVAILABILITY: Good. Best, Oct-May.

CREDIT CARDS ACCEPTED: Visa, MasterCard, American Express and Diners.

TRANSPORTATION: Off base shuttle/bus; Car Rental; Off base taxi.

DINING OPPORTUNITIES: Four restaurants at lodge. Primo's Pizza, Bentleys Pub, Deli/Bakery, Greenstreet Restaurant (breakfast, lunch, dinner, Sunday brunch), Oasis Bar and Grill/Mexican restaurant, Sables Restaurant and Whispers Lounge are within driving distance.

See Myong-Dong, Korea House, Duksoo Palace. The National Museum and Folk Museum on Kyongbok Palace grounds acquaint visitors with Korean culture.

Kunsan Air Base (RK05R8)
8th FW/PA
Bldg 753, Unit 2102
APO AP 96264-2102

MAIN INSTALLATION TELEPHONE NUMBERS: C-(USA) 011-82-654-470-1110, (RK) 0654-470-1110, DSN-315-782-1110. Locator 315-782-4604.

LOCATION: On the west central coast of the Republic of Korea. Exit from Seoul-Pusan Expressway 1, directions to AB clearly marked. **NMC:** Kunsan City, 10 km north.

RESERVATION INFORMATION: Kunsan Lodging, Bldg 392, Unit 2105, APO AP 96264-2101. **C-(USA) 011-82-654-470-4604, (RK) 0654-470-4604, DSN-315-782-4604/4743,** Fax: C-(USA) 011-82-654-472-5275, 24 hours daily. Duty can make reservations any time; Space-A can make reservations 24 hours in advance. Check in at billeting, check out 1200 hours.

VQ Bldg 391. C-ext 4604. VAQ and VOQ shared bath. Refrigerator, A/C, TV, housekeeping service, laundry facility. Older structure. Rates: VAQ $17; VOQ $18.50; Small DVQ $25; Large DVQ $30.

TML AVAILABILITY: Limited.

CREDIT CARDS ACCEPTED: Visa and MasterCard.

TRANSPORTATION: On base shuttle/bus, C-011-82-654-470-4597; On base taxi, C-011-82-654-470-4318; Off base taxi, C-011-82-654-470-4537.

DINING OPPORTUNITIES: Jet Stream, C-011-82-654-470-4736; Loring Club, C-011-82-654-470-4312; and Oriental House, C-011-82-654-470-4100 are within walking distance.

Kunsan is a deep water port on the Yellow Western Sea, and a major fishing port. The mountainous areas of Korea are dotted with temples and shrines of both Japanese and Korean influence and are set in magnificent natural scenery.

Osan Air Base (RK04R8)
51st FW/PA
Bldg 769, Unit 2097
APO AP 96278-2097

MAIN INSTALLATION TELEPHONE NUMBERS: C-(USA) 011-82-333-661-4110/1110, (RK) 333-661-4110, DSN-315-784-4110. Locator 784-1841; Medical 911; Security Police 911.

LOCATION: Exit the Seoul-Pusan Expressway 1, 62 km south of Seoul. Directions to Osan AB clearly marked. AB is west of the expressway adjacent to Songtan City. **NMC:** Seoul, 62 km north.

RESERVATION INFORMATION: Osan Inn, Bldg 771, 51 SVS/SVML, Unit 2065, APO AP 96278-2065. **C-(USA) 011-82-31-661-1844/4597, DSN-315-784-1844/4597,** Fax: C-(USA) 011-82-31-661-4872, DSN-315-784-4872, 24 hours daily. Duty may make reservations any time; Space-A can make reservations 24 hours in advance. Check in at billeting 1500 hours, check out 1200 hours. Government civilian employee billeting.

TLF Bldg 1007. Separate bedroom, sleeps five, private bath (17). Kitchen, A/C, TV, housekeeping service, laundry facility, cribs. Modern structure. Rates: $35 per unit; DVQs $25. Maximum five per unit.
Note: New VQ for transient personnel opened February 2003 in Bldg 772. A/C, TV, housekeeping service, laundry facility. Rates: $22.50 per person.

VOQ/VAQ Bldgs 745, 746. Bedroom, two beds, common bath (258). Community kitchen, refrigerator, limited utensils, A/C, TV, housekeeping service, laundry facility. Modern structure. Rates: VAQ $17, VOQ $18.50.

VOQ Bldgs 1001, 1093, 1094. Bedroom, private bath (65). Kitchen, limited utensils, A/C, TV, housekeeping service, laundry facility, cribs. Modern structure. Rates: $18.50.

DV/VIP Protocol Officer, 7th AF, C-(USA) 011-82-333-661-6020. On Hill 180. O6+. Bedroom, private and semi-private baths (20); separate bedroom suite, private bath (1). Refrigerator, A/C, TV, housekeeping service, cribs, cots, laundry facility. Modern structure. Rates: $25.

AMENITIES: Meeting/Conference Room.

TML AVAILABILITY: Best, Nov-Feb. Difficult, other times.

CREDIT CARDS ACCEPTED: Visa, MasterCard and Services Club Card.

TRANSPORTATION: On base taxi, C-784-4121/4122/4123.

DINING OPPORTUNITIES: NCO Club and O Club are within driving distance.

Don't miss seeing Duksoo Palace (home of the National Museum), Kyonbok and Changduk Palaces, and the Secret Garden and Puyong Pavilion in Seoul.

Yongsan Army Garrison (RK07R8)
34th Support Group
Bldg 4260, South Post
APO AP 96205-0177

MAIN INSTALLATION TELEPHONE NUMBERS: C-(USA) 011-82-2-7918-7999, (RK) 2-07918-7999, DSN-315-723-1110. Locator 2-7912-87404 (Must have individual SSAN to locate).

LOCATION: Located in the Yongsan district of Seoul on the north side of the Han River, 32 km from Kimpo Airport. Bounded on the west by Han-Gang Street, on the north by Hann-Am Street, on the east by Sogong Street and on the south by unnamed street one block north of Gang-Byeon Street. **NMC:** Seoul, in the city.

RESERVATION INFORMATION: Sports Billeting, BOD, DCA, 34th SPT GP, APO, AP 96205-0177. **C-(USA) 011-82-2-7914-8830/8810, (RK) 2-07914-8830, DSN-315-724-8830/8810,** Fax: DSN-315-738-7501, 0900-1800 hours. Directions: Come to Gate 5, go straight about 0.5 mile and pass Trent Gym on left side. Continue up hill to lodging office, Bldg 1041. Check in at facility, check out 1200 hours. No government civilian employee billeting.

Army Lodging Sports Billeting, Bldg 1041. Twelve rooms, each with two single beds. Rate: $20 per bed. Refrigerator, A/C, CATV, VCR, microwave. Handicap accessible units available. Meeting room, washer/dryer, vending machines available. Renovated in 1998.

VEQ Bldg 4110. C-(USA) 011-82-2-7918-2222. E1-E6. 413 total units: separate bedroom, common bath (29). Community kitchen, refrigerator, A/C, TV, housekeeping service, washer/dryer. Modern structure. Rates: $4 per room. Duty can make reservations, others Space-A.

VOQ Bldgs 8102, 8103, 8104. Officers all ranks; E7-E9 official duty only. C-(USA) 011-82-2-7918-4249. 571 total units: separate bedroom suites, private bath (3); two-bedroom, shared bath (1). Refrigerator, A/C, TV, housekeeping service, cribs, washer/dryer. Modern structure. Rates: $15 per person, maximum $20 per family. Duty can make reservations, others Space-A.

DVQ Bldgs 3723, 4436, 4464, 4468. C-EX-7913-3315. O7+ or civilian equivalent. Separate bedroom, private bath. Community kitchen, kitchenette, complete utensils, TV, A/C, housekeeping service, cribs. Modern structure. Rates: sponsor $25, adults $12.50, children $5. Duty can make reservations, others Space-A.

DV/VIP Sec Joint Staff, Protocol Branch, SJS-P, HHC, EUSA, Bldg 2472. C-(USA) 011-82-2-7913-3315, DSN-315-723-3315. O7+, civilian equivalent. Lower ranks Space-A.

AMENITIES: Exercise Room, Mini Mart, Snack Vending Machine and Soft Drink Machine.

TML AVAILABILITY: Good, but reserve early.

CREDIT CARDS ACCEPTED: Visa, MasterCard and American Express.

TRANSPORTATION: On base shuttle/bus, C-011-82-2-7913-7152, DSN-315-723-7152; On base car rental; On base taxi, C-011-82-2-7738-7348, DSN-315-738-5113/5415.

DINING OPPORTUNITIES: Shoppette dining facility C-011-82-2-7736-5113/4/5; Commiskey's Club, C-011-82-2-7736-3968/3971; Main Post Club, C-011-82-2-7723-5696/8785; and Oriental Gardens, C-011-82-2-7738-5146/4094 are within driving distance.

NETHERLANDS

Schinnen Community
(NATO HQ AFNORTH) (NT02R7)
254th Base Support Battalion
Brunssum International Inn
Lodging Office, Bldg H701
APO AE 09703-5000
(This is not U.S. Government Lodging.)

MAIN INSTALLATION TELEPHONE NUMBERS: C-(USA) 011-31-45-526-2222, (NT) 045-526-2222, DSN-314-360-7113. Locator 045-526-2222; Medical (local hospital)-045-527-9999; Security Police 045-526-2000.

LOCATION: In southeast corner of the Netherlands. HQ AFNORTH/Hendrik Camp is located just south of downtown Brunssum, 6 km east of Schinnen. From Autobahn 76 (E314) northwest from Germany take exit 5 (Nuth) northeast onto N276 (Randweg-Petersweg) through the village of Hoensbroek. Continue on N276 until it runs straight into N299 (Emmaweg) (N276 veers off to the northwest just before Brunssum. Do not follow the road to the northwest. Continue straight onto N299.) When on N299, proceed straight for approximately 3 km to a right (south) onto Aker Straat, then to Main Gate on the left (east) side of road. Look for signs. *EUSMRA: Page 113 (B-3), page 114.* NMC: Heerlen, 16 km southwest.

RESERVATION INFORMATION: International Inn (Eisenhower House Hotel), Bldg H701, APO AE 09703-5000. **C-(USA) 011-31-45-564-6200/526-3188, (NT) 045-564-6200/526-3188, DSN-314-360-3188,** Fax: C-(USA) 011-31-45-564-6209. 0800-2000 hours duty days. WEB: geocities.com/internationalinn E-mail: international.inn@planet.nl Check in 1400 hours, check out 1000 hours.

TML General Eisenhower House Hotel. Regular room, private bath (10); suite room (10). Breakfast included. Rates: room single occupancy is 70 guilders (U.S.$28.21 at press time, double occupancy 105 guilders (U.S.$42.32 at press time); Suite single occupancy 125 guilders (U.S.$50.38 at press time), double occupancy 187.50 guilders (U.S.$75.57 at press time). Extra bed 17 guilders (U.S.$6.85 at press time). No pets. Support facilities at Schinnen Community, 254th Base Support Battalion, 16 km. This is NATO Allied and not U.S. government billeting. Brunssum AFNORTH NATO Exchange available to U.S. Forces. Coordination can be made through the International Inn for various trips/tours, horseback riding, swimming pool trips, mountain biking, golf, go-carting.

DV/VIP Bldg H-701, C-04493-7-331. O6+. Bedroom, private bath, living room (2). Rates: Single occupancy 150 guilders (U.S.$60.45 at press time), double occupancy 225 guilders (U.S.$90.68 at press time). Extra bed 17 guilders (U.S.$6.85 at press time). No pets.

TML AVAILABILITY: Limited.

CREDIT CARDS ACCEPTED: MasterCard and Euro Card.

TRANSPORTATION: Car Rental, C-011-31-45-526-2304; Off base taxi, C-011-31-45-525-7777.

DINING OPPORTUNITIES: International Inn, C-011-31-45-564-6200. Lunch: 1200-1400 hours Mon-Fri , 1200-1400 hours Sun ; Dinner Bistro 1800-2200 hours Mon-Fri .

PORTUGAL

Lajes Field Air Base (Azores) (PO01R7)
65th MSS/DPF Unit 6856
Unit 6856
APO AE 09720-5000

MAIN INSTALLATION TELEPHONE NUMBERS: C-(USA) 011-351-2-95-540-100 ext 25178, (Europe) 245-5178, DSN-314-535-5178/1110 (CONUS direct). Locator 113.

LOCATION: Located on Ilha Terceira (Terciera Island), Azores, Portugal. The island is 32.5 km wide and 19.5 km long. Base is on the northeast corner of the island and is 3.25 km northwest of the town of Vila da Praia da Vitoria. The field is adjacent to and northeast of highway 1-1 (Mason Highway). The Main Gate can be accessed from Praia or Lajes. If arriving by military air, you will be processed through the AMC Passenger Terminal, Bldg T-612. *EUSMRA: Page 118 (B-3), page 119.* NMC: Lisbon, 850 miles east.

RESERVATION INFORMATION: Mid-Atlantic Lodge, 65 MSS/DPF, Unit 6856, APO AE 09720-8010. **C-(USA) 011-351-295-57-4138/24146, DSN-(USA) 314-535-4138, DSN-(Europe) 314-245-3426,** Fax: C-(USA) 011-351-295-57-3426, DSN-(USA) 314-535-3426, (Europe) 245-3426. E-mail: fsc@lajes.af.mil TDY, PCS can make reservations any time; Space-A can make reservations 24 hours in advance. Check in at facility 24 hours daily, check out 1200 hours. Government civilian employee billeting. ***Note: Kennel available on base (fee).***

TLF Bldg T-306. Bedroom apartments, living room, private bath (30). Kitchenette, refrigerator, microwave, TV, laundry facility, cribs, cots, housekeeping service. Modern structure. Handicap accessible. Gift Shop in Guest Reception Center open 24 hours daily. Rates: $27 per unit. Maximum five per room.

VOQ/VAQ VAQ open bay bath. VOQ private and shared bath. Rates: VAQ $15.50; VOQ $18.

DV/VIP Contact lodging office. O6+. $27.50 per night.

AMENITIES: Meeting/Conference Room, Snack and Soft Drink Vending Machine and Internet/E-mail access for all customers.

TML AVAILABILITY: Best, Nov-Apr. Difficult, May-Oct.

CREDIT CARDS ACCEPTED: Visa and MasterCard.

TRANSPORTATION: On base shuttle/bus, C-ext 23151; On base taxi C-ext 23400; Off base taxi, C-ext 52654.

DINING OPPORTUNITIES: Bowling Center, ext 26169 is within walking distance. Pizza Place and Round House are within driving distance, just outside of gate.

Bullfights, beaches, camping, hiking, fishing, scuba diving, sightseeing, great restaurants, picnic nature walks, culture and romance.

SAUDI ARABIA

Dhahran Community (SA01R9). Located in eastern Saudi Arabia on the Persian Gulf coast near the island nation of Bahrain. Ophelia Sericklin, USMTM Dhahran, Unit 61300 Box 2, Attn: L6D, APO AE 09858-5000. Main installation numbers: **C-(USA) 011-966-3-899-1119 ext 431-4018, DSN-318-435-7081/2,** Fax: C-(USA) 011-966-3-899-1119 ext 431-4019. Rates: $12-$15. *EUSMRA: Page 122.* **Riyadh Community (SA03R9).** Located in central Saudi Arabia in the capital city of Riyadh. Attn: Billeting, USMTM, AFX, AMEM B, Unit 61307, APO AE 09803-1307. Main installation numbers: **C-(USA) 011-966-1-435-7837,** DSN-318-435-1110. *EUSMRA: Page 122.* **Note: Only personnel on orders or with country (VISA) approval may travel to Saudi Arabia.**

SINGAPORE

Sembawang Community (SI01R1)
497th Combat Training Squadron
PSC 470, Box 3018
FPO AP 96534-5000

MAIN INSTALLATION TELEPHONE NUMBERS: C-011-65-750-2421. Medical, C-011-65-257-4233; Security Police 999.

LOCATION: The United States Navy and United States Air Force elements in Singapore are located in the Sembawang area of Singapore and at the RSAF Paya Lebar. The Sembawang area is located in the north central section of the island of Singapore on the Straights of Johore. It is approximately 19 km north of the city (center) of Singapore. Take the North-South MRT (subway) line north to the Yishum Station then a taxi to Sembawang. You can take a taxi direct for about $15 Singapore. There is also bus service about every 12 minutes: Buses #160, Victoria Street; #161, Shenton Way, downtown; #164, New Bridge Road, Chinatown; and #167, New Bride Road, downtown. The RSAF Paya Lebar is located on Airport Road off Paya Lebar Road.

RESERVATION INFORMATION: Sling Inn, 247 Bermuda Road, FPO AP 96534-5000. **C-(USA) 011-65-257-0256,** Fax: C-011-65-257-9597, 24 hours daily. Directions: From Changi International Airport & Paya Lebar Airport (main terminal) take TPE (Expressway) exit at Yishun Avenue 2, right on Sembawang Road, left on Admiralty Road, left on Ottawa Road, right on Bermuda Road. *Note: Due to ongoing renovations of all TLFs at this site, Space-A is currently unavailable.*

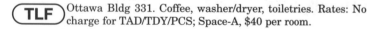

TLF Bldgs 293, 295, 297, 299 Durban; 235, 323, 325, 329 Ottawa. Coffee, washer/dryer, toiletries. Rates: No charge for TAD/TDY/PCS; Space-A, $40 per room. Call for more information.

TLF Ottawa Bldg 331. Coffee, washer/dryer, toiletries. Rates: No charge for TAD/TDY/PCS; Space-A, $40 per room.

DV/VIP Ottawa Bldg 327. Two flats available. Mini bar, coffee, toiletries. Rates: No charge for TAD/TDY/PCS; Space-A, $40 per room.

AMENITIES: Exercise Room, Mini Mart and Soft Drink Machine.

TML AVAILABILITY: Extremely Limited.

CREDIT CARDS ACCEPTED: None, cash only.

TRANSPORTATION: Off base taxi, C-011-65-552-1111, C-011-65-552-2222.

DINING OPPORTUNITIES: Eagle Club, C-011-65-755-1476 is within walking distance from Durban Road and driving distance from Ottawa Road. Terror Club, C-011-65-759-3694 is within driving distance.

SPAIN

Moron Air Base (SP01R7)
496th Air Base Squadron
Unit 6585
APO AE 09643-6585
(This is a contingency base.)

MAIN INSTALLATION TELEPHONE NUMBERS: C-(USA) 011-34-95-584-8111, (SP) 095-584-8111, DSN-314-722-1110. Locator 95-584-8111; Medical 8068; Security Police 8132.

LOCATION: Southeast of Sevilla. Take Autopista (Autobahn) (Sevilla-Osuna) A92 east or west. Use exit 39 (El Arahal), approximately 42 km southeast of Sevilla) south to Route SE 432. Go south on Route SE 432 approximately 11 km to Route A360. Turn northwest on Route A360 approximately 1.8 km to Main Gate on north side of road. (Moron Air Base is on west side of Route SE 432.) *EUSMRA: Page 123 (C-1), page 124.* **NMC:** Sevilla, 65 km northwest.

RESERVATION INFORMATION: Hotel Frontera, Attn: 496 ABS/SVCH, Bldg P-303, 1st Street, APO AE 09643-6585. **C-(USA) 011-34-95-584-8098, (SP) 095-584-8098, DSN-314-722-8098,** Fax: C-(USA) 011-34-95-584-8009, DSN-314-722-8009, 24 hours daily. E-mail: hotel.frontera@moron.af.mil Duty can make reservations any time; Space-A can make reservations 24 hours in advance. Check in at Bldg 303, 1st Street, check out 1200 hours. Government civilian employee lodging. **ATTENTION: AD not assigned in Spain, retired personnel, widows(ers), government civilian employees not assigned in Spain, dependents of all groups, are not permitted to purchase any articles free of Spanish taxes on any military installation, i.e,. Foodland. Military ID card holder visitors to Spain are permitted to make purchases in open messes, lodging and NEX Mart. Also, personnel arriving by military air at Rota NAS are advised to contact security or passenger service for immigration clearance. *This notice applies to other Spanish listings.***

VOQ/VAQ Hotel Frontera. Bldg P-303. Separate bedroom, shared bath (55). Community kitchen, refrigerator, mini bar, A/C, TV/VCR, housekeeping service, laundry facility. Modern structure. Rates: single occupance $19.50, double occupancy $27.75. Maximum two plus one crib per unit.

DV/VIP Lodging, C-and DSN- ext 8098 or 8172. Determined by Commander. VOQ/VAQ. Hotel Frontera. Bldg 303. DV suites, private bath. Community kitchen, refrigerator, microwave, mini bar, A/C, TV/VCR, housekeeping service, laundry facility. Modern structure. Rates: single occupancy $30.50, double occupancy $43.50. Maximum two plus one crib per unit.

AMENITIES: Meeting/Conference Room, Mini Mart.

TML AVAILABILITY: Good Nov-Mar, fairly good Apr-Oct.

CREDIT CARDS ACCEPTED: Visa.

TRANSPORTATION: On Base Shuttle/Bus, C-011-34-95-584-8063, DSN-314-722-8063; On base taxi, C-011-34-95-584-8063, DSN-314-722-8063.

DINING OPPORTUNITIES: Dining Facility, Bldg 115, C-011-34-95-584-8392, DSN-314-722-8392 is within walking distance.

Soak up the light and landscape of Sevilla along the Guadalquivir (Great River), and then visit the Cathedral (third largest in the world) and the Giralda Tower. Don't miss the gardens of the Alcazar and the many others in the city.

Rota Naval Station (SP02R7)
Navy Family Service Center
PSC 819, Box 57
FPO AE 09645-5500

MAIN INSTALLATION TELEPHONE NUMBERS: C-(USA) 011-34-956-82-1110, (From Spain but outside the province of Cadiz dial 956-82-1110), DSN-314-727-1110. Locator 1110.

LOCATION: On Spain's Atlantic Coast (South of Portugal), Costa De La Luz, accessible from Autopista A4(E5) (Sevilla-Cadiz). From Sevilla, take Autopista A4 (E5) south approximately 104 km to exit 6. Take exit 6 northwest at El Puerto de Santa Maria, then northwest approximately 9.5 km to intersection with Route CA 603 (toward San Marcos), then west approximately 9.2 km to Puerto Gate. Watch for signs to "Base Naval." Main gate (Rota Gate) and visitor center is at northeast side of City of Rota. *EUSMRA: Page 123 (A-3), page 125.* **NMC:** Cadiz, 36 km south.

RESERVATION INFORMATION: Gateway Inn, Bldg 35, PSC 819, Box 5, FPO AE 09645-1600. **C-(USA) 011-34-956-82-1871/1752, (SP) 0956-82-1871/1752, DSN-314-727-1871/1752,** Fax: C-(USA) 011-34-956-82-1754, DSN-314-727-1754 hours: BOH 0600-2200 Mon-Sun. E-mail: AlegreJ@navsta.rota.navy.mil. WEB: www.rota.navy.mil Duty can make reservations; others Space-A. Air Terminal 24 hours daily. Directions to Air Terminal on base: Come through Rota gate. Go straight passing 2 lights. Go to end of road and building is on the right. Check in at air terminal, check out 1200 hours. Directions: BOH, Bldg 39: from Main Gate (3rd Street), turn right on Flor Street, past hospital. Turn left on 4th Street and then right on BOH main entrance.

(BEH) Bldgs 31, 33, 35. C-(USA) 011-34-956-82-1871. Bedroom, private bath and all amenities. Rates: $12 per night, each additional person $4, maximum two guests.

(BOH) Bldg 39. C-(USA) 011-34-956-82-1871. E7+ and civilian equivalents. Bedroom with private bath and all amenities. Rates: $18 per person. Each additional person $4 with a maximum of two guests.

(NAVY LODGE) Navy Lodge. Naval Station, PSC 819, Box 17, FPO AE 09645-0003. **C-1-800-NAVY-INN.** C-(USA) 011-34-956-82-2643, (SP) 956-82-2643, DSN-314-727-2643, Fax: C-(USA) 011-34-956-82-2078, DSN-314-727-2078, 24 hours daily. Check in 1500-1800 hours, check out 1200 hours. Bldg 1674-1683, 1974A, Bedroom, private bath (48). Kitchen, microwave, utensils, A/C, CATV/VCR, housekeeping service, coin laundry facility, cribs, cots, TV lounge. Modern structure. Rates: $57. Maximum five per unit. All categories can make reservations; Reservists on official duty. No pets. *Winner of 1999 American Hotel & Motel Association Educational Institute's Performance Plus Gold Award.*

(DV/VIP) Protocol Office. Bldg 1, 2nd floor, C-(USA) 011-34-956-82-2795/2440. BOH. Bldg 39. DV and VIP suites have full amenities. Bldg 226 Chief Petty Officer DV suites have full amenities. Rates: $25. Each additional person $4 per night with a maximum of two guests. For CPO DV suites, call the Command Master Chief at DSN-314-727-2444.

AMENITIES: Exercise Room, Meeting/Conference Room, Business Center, Snack and Soft Drink Vending Machine.

TML AVAILABILITY: All bachelor housing undergoing renovation, expected completion date early 2003. *During renovation, Space-A rooms extremely limited, especially May-Sep.* Ask on base for local, off base accommodations.

CREDIT CARDS ACCEPTED: Visa, MasterCard and American Express. The Navy Lodge accepts Visa, MasterCard, American Express and Discover.

TRANSPORTATION: On base shuttle/bus, ext 2563/2564, Off base taxi 2929; Car Rental, C-011-34-956-82-2675/3234, DSN-314-727-2675/3234;

On base taxi (official business only), ext 2244/ 2403; Off base taxi, C-011-34-956-822929.

DINING OPPORTUNITIES: Champions, ext 2433; Gateway Galley, ext 1654; Pizza Villa, ext 3212; and Reflections, ext 2851 are within walking distance.

Gate security is strict (administered by Spanish Military Police). Commissary and NEX unavailable to Retirees. Call ITT C-956-82-3103, DSN-314-427-3101 for local tour information.

TURKEY

Incirlik Air Base (TU03R9)
39th Wing
Relocation Assistance Program
Unit 8790, Box 175
APO AE 09824-0175

MAIN INSTALLATION TELEPHONE NUMBERS: C-(USA) 011-90-322-316-1110, (TU) 0322-316-1110, DSN-314-676-1110. Locator 6289.

LOCATION: Take Motorway O-52 (E-90) east or west toward Adana. Use exit 1 (Adana Kuzey) southeast approximately 4.5 km to Route 400, then east approximately 5 km through Adana to intersection with Route 815. Continue east on Route 400 approximately 5 km to exit marked Incirlik Air Base, which will be on left (north) side of Route 400. The Main Gate is approximately 0.8 km northeast of Route 400. Alternatively, from Motorway O-52 (E-90), use exit 1 (Adana Dogu) southwest approximately 3.8 km toward Adana to Route 815, then southwest on Route 815 approximately 5 km to Route 400. Go left (east) on Route 400 approximately 5 km to exit marked Incirlik Air Base on left (north) side of road. *EUSMRA: Page 127 (C-4), page 129.* **NMC:** Adana, 4.8 km west.

RESERVATION INFORMATION: Hodja Inn, Bldg 1081, 7th Street, APO AE 09824-5165. **C-(USA) 011-90-322-316-6786, (TU) 0322-316-6786. DSN-314-676-6786,** Fax: C-(USA) 011-90-322-316-9353/9341, DSN-314-676-9353/9341, 24 hours daily. E-mail: lisa.mayor@incirlik.af.mil WEB: www.incirlik.af.mil Duty can make reservations any time; Space-A reservations not accepted due to Force Protection Issues. Check in at facility 1400 hours, check out 1200 hours.

(TLF) Bldg 1066. Separate bedroom, living room, dining room, private bath (50). Kitchen, microwave, complete utensils, A/C, TV/VCR in room and lounge, clock radio, housekeeping service, washer/dryer, iron, cribs, cots, ice machine. Modern structure. Rates: $39 per unit.

(TLF) Bldgs 1075-1077. Two-bedroom, private bath (30). Kitchen, complete utensils, washer/dryer, iron, cribs, cots, ice machine, living room, dining room. Modern structure. Rates: $39 per unit.

(VQ) Bldgs 1080, 1082, 934, 936. Bedroom, shared bath. Refrigerator, A/C, TV in room and lounge, housekeeping service, laundry facility (1080/82). Modern structure (1080/82). Rates: $18.50 per person.

(VQ) Bldg 952. Official duty. Bedroom, shared bath. Refrigerator, A/C, TV/VCR in room and lounge, housekeeping service, laundry facility. Older structure, renovated. Rates: $18.50 per person.

(DV/VIP) Protocol Office, 39 WG/CC, C-(USA) 011-90-322-316-8352, DSN-314-676-8352. Bldg 1072/82. O6+. Separate bedroom suites, private bath (16); bedroom, private bath. Kitchen, honor bar, limited utensils, A/C, TV, housekeeping service, laundry facility, ice machine. Older structure. Rates: $30 per person.

AMENITIES: Exercise Room, Meeting/Conference Room, Snack and Soft Drink Vending Machine.

TML AVAILABILITY: Very Limited.

CREDIT CARDS ACCEPTED: Visa and MasterCard.

TRANSPORTATION: On base shuttle/bus C-322-316-6756; Off base car rental; On/Off base taxi, DSN-314-676-6461.

DINING OPPORTUNITIES: Numerous restaurants are within driving distance in Adana.

Historic sites near Adana include Misis (Roman), Yilanlikale (Castle of Snakes), Karatepe (Hittite) and Payas (16th Century and Alexander the Great). There's much more to see and do.

Izmir Community/Air Station (TU04R9)
425th Air Base Squadron/DPF
Unit 6870, Box 50
APO AE 09821-5000

MAIN INSTALLATION TELEPHONE NUMBERS: C-(USA) 011-90-232-484-5360/1110, DSN-314-675-1110 ext 3379/3366, Fax: C-(USA) 011-90-232-489-4089, DSN-314-675-3368. Locator 3431.

LOCATION: On Turkey's west coast along the Aegean Sea, 240 km south of the Dardanelles, the strait that divides Europe and Asia. From Izmir take Route 550 (E87) northwest for about 20 km to west at exit 3 onto Route 35-76 at the town of Cigli. The air base is on the right (north) side of the street. Look for signs. Izmir Community/Air Station support facilities are in separate buildings south and west of Kultur Park. For the Grand Hotel Mercure from Kultur Park, head west at Montro Circle on Sehit Nevresbey Bulvari approximately 0.8 km to Ataturk Circle. Turn left on the circle directly to hotel on the left (south) side of the street. *EUSMRA: Page 126 (A,B-3), page 130.* **NMC:** Izmir, in the city.

RESERVATION INFORMATION: Grand Hotel Mercure, Izmir, Lobby, APO AE 09821-5000. **C-(USA) 011-90-232-489-4090, DSN-314-675-3379,** Fax: C-011-90-232-489-4089, DSN-314-675-3668, 0700-2300 hours. Billeting office, in lobby of hotel, is the 24-hour check in point. Duty can make reservations any time; Space-A can make reservations 24 hours in advance. Check in at facility, check out 1200 hours. Government civilian employee billeting.

TLF **Grand Hotel Mercure, Izmir.** Bedroom, private bath (63). Refrigerator, A/C, TV in room and lounge, housekeeping service, laundry facility, cribs, cots, ice machine, swimming pool. (The 63 rooms are leased in a Five-Star commercial hotel.) Handicap accessible. Rates: single $75, double $95. Maximum three per unit. No pets.

DV/VIP Protocol Office, 425 ABS/CCE, Facility 48, Room 603. DSN-314-675-1110 ext 3341. O6+/E9.

AMENITIES: Exercise Room and Meeting/Conference Room, a new 100,000 sq. ft. community center housing various support facilities such as medical and dental clinics, family support center, child development center, and recreational facilities such as fitness center, teen center.

TML AVAILABILITY: Limited, better May-Oct.

CREDIT CARDS ACCEPTED: Visa, MasterCard, American Express and Diners.

TRANSPORTATION: City shuttle/bus; Car Rental. Travel Office C-232-489-5360 ext 3405/3689.

DINING OPPORTUNITIES: Burger King, Domino's, McDonald's and Pizza Hut are within walking distance.

Visit the tours desk, MWR for one day, overnight and multi-day excursions to Ephesus, Pergamon, Pamukkale, Aphrodisias, Istanbul and the Greek Islands. East and west meet here; don't miss the fascinating consequences!

UNITED KINGDOM

RAF Alconbury (UK01R7)
423rd Air Base Squadron/SVML
Unit 5570, Box 75
APO AE 09470-7075

MAIN INSTALLATION TELEPHONE NUMBERS: C-(USA) 011-44-1480-82-3000, (UK) 01480-82-3000, DSN-314-268-3000. Locator DSN-268-2565.

LOCATION: Located 75 km north from the outskirts of London and 3.5 km northwest of Huntingdon. Take Route A1 north or south to the exit marked "Huntingdon," just north of the town of Alconbury, to Route A14 southeast, then take the immediate exit marked "RAF Alconbury-The Stukeleys" onto Ermine Street. Main Gate is across from Little Stukeley approximately 2.5 km southeast on the northeast side of Ermine Street. *EUSMRA: Page 134 (A-1), page 135.* **NMC:** Cambridge, approximately 30 km southeast.

RESERVATION INFORMATION: Britannia Inn, 423rd SVS/SVML, Bldg 639, Texas Street, APO AE 09470-5000. **C-(USA) 011-44-1480-82-6086, DSN-(USA) 314-268-6086, (UK) 01480-82-6086,** Fax: C-(USA) 011-44-1480-82-3001, DSN-(USA) 314-268-3001, 24 hours daily. Email: 423abs.svml@molesworth.af.mil. Duty can make reservations any time; Space-A can make reservations up to thirty days in advance and stay up to thirty days, space permitting. Check in at facility 1400 hours, check out 1000 hours.

TML TLF also available. Bldg 628. Suite, private bath (20). Refrigerator/freezer, microwave, stove, utensils, TV/VCR, phone, laundry facility. Rates: $39 per unit.

VOQ/VAQ Bldg 675. Bedroom, shared bath (VAQ) (86); bedroom, private bath (VOQ) (25). Refrigerator/freezer, microwave, CATV/VCR, housekeeping service, washer/dryer, games room. Modern structure. Rates: $24.50 per room.

VOQ Bldgs 639, 640. Bedroom, living room, private bath. Refrigerator/freezer, microwave, TV/VCR, phone, housekeeping service, laundry facility, cribs. Modern structure, newly renovated. Rates: $18.50 per room.

DV/VIP Bldg 640. E9, O6+. DV suites, private bath (6), General Officer Suite (1). refrigerator/freezer, microwave, TV/VCR, phone, housekeeping service, laundry facility. Rates: $30 for DV; $33 for General Officer Suite. Duty can make reservations any time.

AMENITIES: Conference Room (25 people), Business Center, Snacks and Drinks available at front desk.

TML AVAILABILITY: Good, Oct-Jan. Difficult, other times.

CREDIT CARDS ACCEPTED: Visa and MasterCard.

TRANSPORTATION: On base shuttle/bus; Off base shuttle/bus, C-011-44-1480-82-3950/3965, DSN-314-268-3950/3965; Car Rental: AAFES, C-011-44-1480-45-9191; Off base taxi, C-011-44-1480-41-3222/2444/42-5111.

DINING OPPORTUNITIES: Burger King, C-011-44-1480-82-3041; Food Court, C-011-44-1480-82-3411/3426; and Stukley Inn Combined Club, C-011-44-1480-82-3382 are located within walking distance. McDonald's, C-011-44-1480-43-6878; The Olde Mill, C-011-44-1482-45-9758; and Three Horseshoes, C-011-44-1480-45-3583 are within driving distance.

East Anglia, Essex, Suffolk and Norfolk are full of historical sights. Start with the village of Little Stukeley (interesting church with carvings), and pass on to Huntingdon, where Romans first settled. You will need a warm coat in the winter and a light coat or jacket for summer. There is rarely a time of year when a raincoat or umbrella will not come in handy.

RAF Croughton (UK09R7)
422nd Air Base Squadron
Unit 5855
APO AE 09494-5000

MAIN INSTALLATION TELEPHONE NUMBERS: C-011-44-1280-70-1110, DSN-314-236-1110. Locator C-01280-70-8000, DSN-314-236-8000.

LOCATION: From London take Motorway M40 west toward Oxford, then stay on Motorway M40 past Oxford (exit 7) for approximately 21 km to exit 10 and north onto Route A43. Continue north on Route A43 toward Northampton for 6 km to a west exit onto Route B4031. Go west toward the village of Croughton for approximately 2 km. The Main Gate is on the left (south) side of Route B4031. Watch for signs. *EUSMRA: Page 133 (C-1,2), page 136.* **NMC:** Oxford, 26 km south.

RESERVATION INFORMATION: Shepherd's Rest Inn, Bldg 33, RAF Croughton, APO AE 09494-5000. **C-011-44-1280-708-394, DSN-314-236-8394,** Fax: C-011-44-1280-708-414, DSN-314-236-8414, 0700-1700 hours Mon-Fri, 0800-1300 hours Sat-Sun, closed Thanksgiving, Christmas and New Year's Day. E-mail: lodging@croughton.af.mil Duty can make reservations any time; Space-A can make reservations 24 hours in advance. Directions from Main Gate: Go approximately 0.4 km up the hill. Road takes a sharp left turn, turn left immediately afterwards.

TLF Bldgs 2, 4, 6, 8, 10-12, Andrews Street. Active Duty, Retirees, government contractors on orders and civilian government employees. Two-bedroom townhouses (6), master bedroom, double bed; bedroom, two twin beds; sofabed in living room. Kitchen, washer/dryer. Rates: $39 per unit.

VOQ Bldg 22. Active Duty, Retirees, government contractors on orders and civilian government employees. Bedroom, double bed, shared bath (10); bedroom, double bed, private bath (4); bedroom, double bed, handicap accessible, private bath (1). Central kitchen, laundry facilities. Rates: $18.50 per unit.

DV/VIP Bldg 22. Active Duty or Retirees. Bedroom, double bed, shower and full bath (1). Living room area. Rates: $30 per unit.

AMENITIES: Meeting/Conference Room.

TML AVAILABILITY: Limited, especially in summer.

CREDIT CARDS ACCEPTED: Visa and MasterCard.

TRANSPORTATION: Off base shuttle/bus; Car Rental, C-011-44-1280-705-959.

DINING OPPORTUNITIES: BlackBird Pub is within walking distance. Cartwright Arms is within driving distance.

Local places of interest include Blenheim Palace, which boasts a rich heritage and lovely landscaped gardens; and the internationally famous Ashmoleum Museum in Oxford. Warwick, 72 km away, has the oldest inhabited medieval castle in England, a doll museum, St. Mary's church, and Madame Tussaud's Waxworks exhibit.

Diego Garcia Atoll, US Navy Support Facility (UK01R9)
PSC 466, Box 8
FPO AP 96595-0008

MAIN INSTALLATION TELEPHONE NUMBERS: C-011-246-370-2000, DSN-315-370-2000. Locator 4830; Medical 4748; Security Police 95.

LOCATION: In the Chagos Archipelago, approximately 1,600 km off the southern tip of India in the Indian Ocean. **NMC:** Colombo, Sri Lanka, 1,460 air km northeast.

RESERVATION INFORMATION: NSF Billeting, FPO AP 96595-0031. Office located 4.8 km north of island airport across from base swimming pool. **C-011-246-370-4830, DSN-315-370-4830,** Fax: C-011-246-370-3972, 24 hours daily. Check in at billeting, check out 1200 hours.

TML BOQ/BEQ/DV/VIP. Located downtown within walking distance of billeting office. Active Duty/contractors on official business only. Shared room, private bath (150). Refrigerator, TV in lounge and rooms, housekeeping service, washer/dryer, ice machine. Rates: enlisted $4; officers $8; senior officers (flag grade) $10.

DV/VIP DSN-315-370-4415. O6+. Bob Hope Suite and Donovan Suite, two-bedroom suite with dining area.

AMENITIES: Exercise Room, Meeting/Conference Room and Mini Mart.

TML AVAILABILITY: Not Available.

CREDIT CARDS ACCEPTED: Visa.

TRANSPORTATION: On base shuttle/bus/taxi, C-370-2770/2771.

DINING OPPORTUNITIES: Dining Hall, ext 2737; Diego Burger II, ext 2816; E Club, ext 2810; NCO/CPO Club, ext 2807; O Club, ext 2813; Peacekeeper Inn, ext 2810; and Seamen's Club, ext 2878 are within driving distance.

ALL PERSONNEL MUST APPLY FOR "AREA CLEARANCE" A MINIMUM OF 30 DAYS PRIOR TO TRAVEL TO DIEGO GARCIA. ACCESS IS AVAILABLE ONLY VIA AMC OUT OF BALTIMORE, MD OR YOKOTA, JAPAN. SPACE-A PASSENGERS MUST BE STATIONED AT OR EMPLOYED AT DIEGO GARCIA IN ORDER TO FLY INTO, OUT OF OR THROUGH DIEGO GARCIA; NO FAMILIES ARE PERMITTED ON THE ISLAND—NO EXCEPTIONS.

Attractions include East Pointe Plantation, deep sea fishing and snorkeling.

RAF Fairford (UK11R7)
Stirling House
424th Air Base Squadron/SVML
APO AE 09456-5000
(This is a contingency base.)

MAIN INSTALLATION TELEPHONE NUMBERS: C-011-44-1285-71400, DSN-314-247-4000. Locator C-01285-71-4200; Medical DSN-314-247-4320; Security Police C-01285-71-4477.

LOCATION: Approximately 95 km west of central London and 33 km northwest of Swindon. From London take the Motorway M4 to Swindon to exit 15 north onto Route A419. Continue northwest on Route A419 for approximately 27 km to Cirencester, then exit east onto Route A417. Stay on Route A417 for about 12 km to the village of Fairford. Once in the village, turn right on the road marked Whelford. The base is approximately 0.8 km southeast on both sides of Whelford Road. *EUSMRA: Page 133 (B-2), page 137.* **NMC:** Oxford, 29 km east.

RESERVATION INFORMATION: Gloucestershire, Bldg 551, 424 ABS/SVL, APO AE 09456-5000. **C-(USA) 011-44-1285-716-100, (UK) 01285-716-100,** DSN-314-247-4272, Fax: C-(USA) 011-44-1285-714-886, DSN-314-247-4886. Due to being in care-taker status, call ahead to check availability for Space-A. 0700-1800 hours, Mon-Fri. 0800-1400 hours Sat-Sun. Duty can make reservations any time; Space-A can make reservations 72 hours in advance. Check in 1300 hours, check out 1100 hours. After duty hours, keys are left at Main Gate for late check in. Government civilian employee billeting.

TLF Bldg 551. Bedroom, private bath (8). Refrigerator, TV/VCR in room and lounge, housekeeping service, laundry facility, cribs, cots, highchairs. Modern structure. Rates: $39.

VQ Bldg 551. Bedroom, private bath (51). Refrigerator, TV/VCR, housekeeping service, laundry facility. Modern structure. Rates: $18.50.

DV/VIP VQ. Bldg 551. E9, O6+. Call Protocol, DSN-314-247-6100 for reservations. Suites, private bath (5); mini suite (1). Rates: $30. Duty may make reservations any time; Space-A may make reservations thirty days in advance through Protocol.

TML AVAILABILITY: Fairly good. Best Nov-Mar. Difficult other times.

CREDIT CARDS ACCEPTED: Visa and MasterCard.

TRANSPORTATION: Off base taxi, C-01285-713-937.

DINING OPPORTUNITIES: Bowling Center, DSN-314-247-4444; and Bull Hotel, C-01285-712-535 are within walking distance.

The Cotswolds is one of the most beautiful parts of England. Fairford boasts a 15th century church with magnificent stained glass windows. Cirencester, 16 km west, offers shops and services, a sports center and the Cornium Museum.

RAF Lakenheath (UK07R7)
48th MSS/DPF
Unit 5200, Box 105
APO AE 09464-0105

MAIN INSTALLATION TELEPHONE NUMBERS: C-(USA) 011-44-1638-52-1110, (UK) 01638-52-1110, DSN-314-226-1110. Locator C-(USA) 011-44-1638-52-3749.

LOCATION: From London, head north on Motorway M11 toward Cambridge. When approximately 15 km south of Cambridge, take exit 9 (Great Chesterford) northeast to Route A11. Continue on Route A11 (which joins with Route A14), past Newmarket. Stay on Route A11 to the village of Barton Mills and the exit for Route A1065. Head north on Route A1065 for approximately 9 km to the Brandon Gate entrance on the left (west) side of Route A1065. *EUSMRA: Page 134 (B-1), page 137, page 138, page 142.* **NMC:** Cambridge, 48 km south. NMI: RAF Mildenhall, 10 km south.

RESERVATION INFORMATION: Liberty Lodge, Bldg 955, 48 SVS/SVML, Unit 5185, Box 70, APO AE 09464-0105. **C-(USA) 011-44-1638-52-6700/6713, (UK) 0638-52-6700/6713, DSN-314-226-6700/6713,** Fax: C-(USA) 011-44-1638-52-6717, DSN-314-226-6717, 24 hours daily. E-mail: liberty.lodge@lakenheath.af.mil Duty may make reservations any time; Space-A may make reservations 24 hours in advance. Directions: Through round-about, second left brings you to bldg. 955. Check in at facility 1500 hours, check out 1100 hours.

TLF Bldgs 981-983, 985. Small units sleep three; medium units sleep four to five; large units sleep five to seven. Full kitchen, complete utensils, TV/VCR, refrigerator, microwave, housekeeping service, laundry facility, cribs, cots. Rates: $39 per unit. No smoking, no pets.

VAQ Bldgs 955, 957. Shared bedroom, shared bath (E1-E6) (46). Complete utensils, TV/VCR, refrigerator, microwave, housekeeping service, laundry facility, cribs, cots. Rates: $18.50. Maximum two per room. No smoking, no pets.

VQ Bldg 978, 980. Bedroom, private bath (80). Shared kitchen, complete utensils, TV/VCR, refrigerator, microwave, housekeeping service, laundry facility, cribs, cots. Rates: single $18.50. Maximum two per unit. No smoking, no pets.

DV/VIP 48 FW/Protocol. Bldgs 956, 1156. C-011-44-1638-52-2444, DSN-314-226-2444. O6+/E9. Separate bedroom, private bath, Enlisted (4); Officer (7). Kitchenette, private sitting area, TV, housekeeping service, laundry facility, cots. Older structure. Rates: Officier $30; Enlisted $29. Duty can make reservations any time; no Space-A reservations. No smoking, no pets and no children under 13 allowed in suites.

AMENITIES: Meeting/Conference Room.

TML AVAILABILITY: Very limited.

CREDIT CARDS ACCEPTED: Visa and MasterCard.

TRANSPORTATION: On base shuttle/bus; Car Rental, C-011-44-1638-52-3050, DSN-314-226-3050; Off base taxi, C-011-44-1638-52-2306, DSN-314-226-2306.

DINING OPPORTUNITIES: Liberty Club (Enlisted), C-011-44-1638-52-3869; and O Club, C-011-44-1638-52-2535 are within walking distance.

Don't miss seeing Cambridge University, which attracts thousands of tourists each year. Visit the ITT Office for information on the many attractions of London. Lakenheath is the largest U.S. Air Force operated facility in England. Shuttle bus to Mildenhall departs 50 minutes after the hour 0650-1450.

Menwith Hill Station (UK22R7)
Community Support Center
PSC 45, Bldg 26
APO AE 09468-5000

MAIN INSTALLATION TELEPHONE NUMBERS: C-(USA) 011-44-1423-777-1110/113, DSN-314-262-1110/113. Command C-(USA)011-44-1423-777-730, DSN-314-262-7730; Medical Clinic C-011-44-1423-777-885, DSN-314-262-7885, Security Police C-011-44-1423-777-825, DSN-314-262-7825.

LOCATION: In Yorkshire Dales, UK, about 350 km northwest of London. From London take Motorway M1 north approximately 335 km to Leeds. Follow signs through Leeds to Route A61. From Leeds take Route A61 north 21 km to Harrogate and exit west onto Route A59. Continue on A59 for about 9 km to north on Route B6451 approximately 1.5 km to installation on the right (east) side of the road. *EUSMRA: Page 132 (B-3), page 141.* **NMC:** Harrogate, 9 km.

RESERVATION INFORMATION: PSC 45, APO AE 09468 **C-(USA) 011-44-1423-77-7895, DSN-314-262-7895,** Fax: 011-44-1423-77-1556, 0800-1600 hours Mon-Fri. After hours information and key pick up call club bar C-(USA) 011-44-1423-77-7895.

TML Bedroom, private bath. Refrigerator, microwave, CATV/VCR, housekeeping service, laundry facilities. Rates: standard room (2) $39, each additional person over age 13 $17; two-room suite (6) $45, each additional person over age 13 $19.

AMENITIES: Snack and Soft Drink Vending Machine.

TML AVAILABILITY: Extremely limited.

CREDIT CARDS ACCEPTED: Visa and MasterCard.

TRANSPORTATION: Off base taxi, Blue Line C-(USA) 011-44-1423-530830; Car Rental, Budget C-(USA) 011-44-1423-770065/507995.

DINING OPPORTUNITIES: Cafeteria, Strike Zone, Club (Mon-Fri) all within walking distance. Many pubs and restuarants in area.

RAF Mildenhall (UK08R7)
100 MSS/DPF
Bldg 460
Unit 4925, Box 280
APO AE 09459-5280

MAIN INSTALLATION TELEPHONE NUMBERS: C-(USA) 011-44-1-638-54-1110/3000, (UK) 01638-54-1110/3000 DSN-314-238-1110/3000. Locator DSN-314-238-2669.

LOCATION: From London, head north on Motorway M11 toward Cambridge, then approximately 15 km south of Cambridge, take exit 9 (Great Chesterford) northeast onto Route A11. Continue on Route A11 (which joins with Route A14) past Newmarket. Stay on Route A11 to the village of Barton Mills and the exit for Route A1101. Continue northwest on Route A1101 for 4 km through the village of Mildenhall to Beck Row Village, the base is on the left side of the road. Follow red and white signs to gate. As you enter Gate 1, O Club and lodging office on right. *EUSMRA: Page 134 (B-1), page 137, page 138, page 142.* **NMC:** Cambridge, 49 km southwest.

RESERVATION INFORMATION: Gateway Inn, Bldg 459, APO AE 09459-5000. **C-(USA)** 011-44-1-638-54-2655/3093/6001, **DSN-314-238-2655/3093/6001, (UK)** 01638-54-2655/2965, Fax: C-(USA) 011-44-1-638-54-3688, DSN-314-238-3688. 24 hours daily. E-mail: lodgemh2@mildenhall.af.mil Duty may make reservations any time; Space-A may make reservations 24 hours in advance. Check in at facility 1500-1800 hours, check out 1100 hours. WEB: www.mildenhall.af.mil

(TML) Gateway Inn. Bldg 459.

(TLF) Bldg 104. Bedroom apartment, private bath (40). Kitchen, microwave, complete utensils, CATV/VCR, complimentary video rental, housekeeping service, laundry facility, cribs. Modern structure. Rates: $12-$35. Maximum four per room.

(VAQ) 200 and 400 area. Shared room, open bay restroom, some bedrooms, private bath (46). CATV, housekeeping service, laundry facility. Rates: single occupancy $19.50, double occupancy $27.75.

(VOQ) 200 and 400 area. Bedroom, private bath (42). CATV, housekeeping service, laundry facility. Rates: single occupancy $19.50, double occupancy $27.75.

(DV/VIP) Protocol Office, 3rd AF, Bldg 239. C-(USA) 011-44-1-638-54-2777/5432, DSN-314-238-2777/5432. O7+. Bedroom suites, private bath (3). Rates: Enlisted DVQ, $29 single occupancy, $42 double occupancy; Officer DVQ, $30 single occupancy, $43.50 double occupancy.

TML AVAILABILITY: Extremely limited. Best, Nov-Dec.

CREDIT CARDS ACCEPTED: Visa and MasterCard.

TRANSPORTATION: On base shuttle; Car Rental.

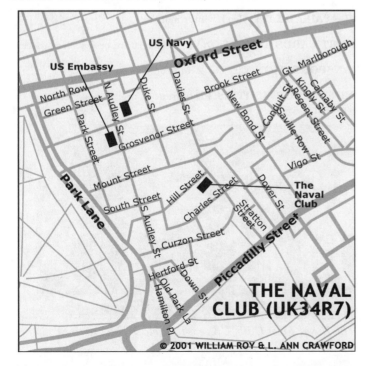

THE NAVAL CLUB (UK34R7)

© 2001 WILLIAM ROY & L. ANN CRAWFORD

DINING OPPORTUNITIES: Fen Tiger Cafe in Pax Term Bldg 598, C-011-44-1-638-54-4565, DSN-314-238-4565. Dining Hall Bldg 436, C-011-44-1-638-54-2689, DSN-314-238-2689. Galaxy Club Complex Bldg 449, C-011-44-1-638-54-2683, DSN-314-238-2683- food facilities include American Cafe; Marauder Sports Lounge C-011-44-1-683-54-2323, DSN-314-238-2323; O Club C-011-44-1-638-54-2606, DSN-314-238-2606. Popo Loco's and New York Pizza Deli. Bowling Center Bldg 400, C-011-44-1-638-54-2348, DSN-314-238-2348, Tiffnay's Cafe (lunch), 0600-1400 daily.

Shopping and antique hunting is popular in the area. Discover the story of Mildenhall Treasure in the Mildenhall Museum on High Street. Most active Space-A airport in the UK. Daily Bus to RAF Lakenheath and AMC Terminal.

THE NAVAL CLUB

The Naval Club (UK35R7)
38 Hill Street, Mayfair
London W1J5NS
United Kingdom
(Not U.S. Government Lodging)

MAIN INSTALLATION TELEPHONE NUMBERS: C-(USA) 011-44-20-7493-7672, (UK) 020-7493-7672.

LOCATION: Ideally placed between Park Lane and Berkeley Square. Five minutes walk from U.S. Embassy and London (U.S.) Naval Activities in Grosvenor Square. Easy distance for shopping areas of Knightsbridge and Oxford Street, and close to West End Theaters. Nearest Underground Station-Green Park. **NMC:** London, in city limits. **NMI:** London Naval Activities.

RESERVATION INFORMATION: Address and telephone as above. Fax: C-(USA)-011-44-20-7629-7995 E-mail: reservations@navalclub.co.uk. This is a member-only club. Originally founded for Officers of the Royal Naval Volunteer Reserve, the club is now open to all Naval Officers and others with an interest in maritime affairs or connections with the sea.

(TML) Officers' Club. Fifteen double/twin rooms and thirteen single rooms. Full English breakfast included. Facilities include dining room, bar, private meeting and function rooms. Rates: £55-£115 per night (U.S.$78.50-$164.12 at press time). Special weekend rates available.

TML AVAILABILITY: Varies throughout the year depending on what's on in London. Early booking advisable especially for double/twin rooms.

CREDIT CARDS ACCEPTED: All major cards accepted except American Express.

TRANSPORTATION: Taxis available outside front door. All rail and underground networks within easy walking distance. Fast public transport links to both Heathrow and Gatwick airports. Further details held at reception.

DINING OPPORTUNITIES: The Club Dining Room, with a first class standard, is open for lunch and dinner (Mon-Fri). There is a large selection of pubs and restaurants within walking distance.

In the heart of Mayfair, the most exclusive area of London, the Naval Club is housed in a listed building, once the residence of Prime Minister William Pitt, dating from the mid-1700s. The Louis XVI style dining room and main staircase are particularly impressive.

Portsmouth Royal Sailors' Home Club (UK10R7)
Queen Street
Portsmouth Hampshire
PO1 3HS
United Kingdom 01705 824231
(Not U.S. Government Lodging)

MAIN INSTALLATION TELEPHONE NUMBERS: C-(USA) 011-44-23-92-824231. Security Police 92-839333.

LOCATION: Located near the Portsmouth H.M. Naval Base. From London take the A3 southwest for approximately 70 km to west on the A27 and then to exit 12 south onto the M275 toward Portsmouth. From the M275 exit south on Marketway to Alfred Road and finally Queen Street west. Continue west on Queen Street for approximately 0.6 km to the club on the south (left) side of the street, across from the Heritage Car Park. Follow signs to Portsmouth H.M. Naval Base and the club. *EUSMRA: Page 133 (C-4), page 143.* **NMC:** Portsmouth, in city limits. NMI: RAF Fairford, 130 km northwest.

RESERVATION INFORMATION: Address and telephone as above. Fax: C-(USA) 011-44-23-92293496, 24 hours daily. E-mail: sailors@homeclub.fsnet.co.uk WEB: www.homeclub.fsnet.co.uk

TML Residency Club. This club has Twin/Double/Single/Family rooms (130), all with in-suite bathroom, TV, tea/coffee making facilities. Some rooms handicap accessible. Rates: twin/double £57 (U.S.$81.35 at press time), single £29 (U.S.$41.39 at press time), includes breakfast. Choice of bars, restaurant offering carvery style menu, fully equipped leisure center with swimming pool, darts, table tennis, skittles alley. Payment in cash or credit card.

AMENITIES: Ballroom Banqueting Facilities, Conference Rooms, Cafe for hot and cold snacks.

TML AVAILABILITY: Good all year.

CREDIT CARDS ACCEPTED: Visa and MasterCard.

TRANSPORTATION: Shuttle/bus, Car Rental and Train Station are a two-minute walk from club. Taxi phone line at club.

DINING OPPORTUNITIES: Horatio's Restaurant on club premises. A number of public houses are within walking distance, and numerous restaurants and pubs are within driving distance.

Visit Nelson's flagship HMS Victory, Henry VIII's favorite warship Mary Rose, the first iron-clad warship in the world, HMS Warrior and D-Day Museum.

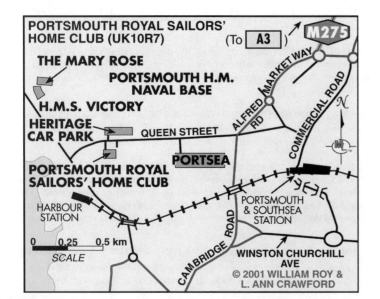

Royal Fleet Club (UK14R7)
9-12 Morice Square
Devonport, Plymouth,
Devon PL1 4PG, United Kingdom
(Not U.S. Government Lodging)

MAIN INSTALLATION TELEPHONE NUMBERS: C-(USA) 011-44-1752-562723.

LOCATION: From the Exeter direction, take Route A38 west and exit at the Marsh Hills flyover (overpass). Descend to the lower level and turn left at Route A374 and drive in the direction of Plymouth City Centre. Stay on Route A374 along the Embankment, Royal Parade and Union Street, cross the Stonehouse Bridge and approximately 0.8 km turn left (first road past traffic lights) onto St. Aubyn Road. The club will be on the right (north) side of St. Aubyn Road. *EUSMRA: Page 131 (C-3), page 144.* **NMC:** Plymouth, 0.5 km. NMI: St. Mawgan Joint Maritime Facility, 70 km northwest.

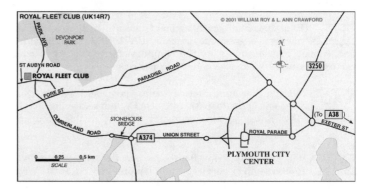

RESERVATION INFORMATION: Address and telephone as above. Fax: C-(USA) 011-44-1752-550725, 24 hours daily. Reservations required.

TML Servicemen's Club and Hotel. Bedroom, private bath (60). TV in rooms and lounge, housekeeping service, cribs, cots. Modern structure, renovated. Rates: £25 single (US$35.68 at press time), £50 double (US$71.35 at press time), £10 per child toddler to age 16 (US$14.27 at press time), no charge for infants. Includes breakfast. Maximum four per room. No pets.

AMENITIES: Meeting/Conference Room. Ice Machine.

TML AVAILABILITY: Good, winter months.

CREDIT CARDS ACCEPTED: Visa, MasterCard or travelers checks.

TRANSPORTATION: City bus located outside gate.

DINING OPPORTUNITIES: Restaurant on premises serves breakfast and dinner.

The Royal Fleet Club, UK is a first-class hotel with excellent club facilities.

The Royal Scots Club (UK36R7)
30 Abercromby Place
Edinburgh City, Scotland
EH3 6QE United Kingdom
(Not U.S. Government Lodging)

MAIN INSTALLATION TELEPHONE NUMBERS: C-(USA) 011-44-131-556-4270.

LOCATION: One block north of Queen Street and three blocks north of Princes Street, cross street is Dundas Street, in the heart of Edinburgh New Town. **NMC:** Edinburgh, in city limits. NMI: RAF Menwith Hill, approximately 240 km southeast.

RESERVATION INFORMATION: Attn: Advance Booking Office, address and telephone as above. Fax: C-(USA) 011-44-131-558-3769, 24 hours. E-mail: royscotsclub@sol.co.uk WEB: www.scotsclub.co.uk This is a Members Club that welcomes allied military personnel (all ranks) and U.S. DoD Civilians for overnight accommodations. Membership is not necessary for short stays.

TML **Club and Hotel.** Twenty ensuite bedrooms. All rooms fully refurbished in the last three years. TV, microwave, toiletries, hair dryer, housekeeping service, cribs, cots. Double and twin rooms £140 (U.S.$205.58 at press time). Single rooms £115 (U.S. $168.87 at press time). Rates include service, tax and English Breakfast.

AMENITIES: Exercise Room, Meeting/Conference Rooms, Business Center, Ice Machine, Internet/E-mail access for customers.

TML AVAILABILITY: Good, but book early.

CREDIT CARDS ACCEPTED: American Express, MasterCard, Visa and Diners.

TRANSPORTATION: Taxi at door, City Buses. British Rail and Air Service in UK and internationally.

DINING OPPORTUNITIES: In Club Restaurant, open for breakfast, lunch, high tea and dinner daily. Also many restaurants and pubs in the city.

Castle and Princes Street Gardens, High Street and period town homes.

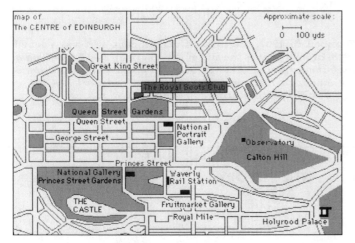

St. Mawgan Joint Maritime Facility (UK25R7)
PSC 804 Box 1
FPO AE 09409-1001

MAIN INSTALLATION TELEPHONE NUMBERS: C-011-44-1637-85-1110, DSN-314-234-1110. Locator DSN-314-234-3464. Medical 999, Security Police 999.

LOCATION: From Plymouth, take Route A38 west for approximately 40 km to intersection with Route A30 near Bodmin. Continue west on Route A30 for approximately 15 km to west (right) onto Route A3059 toward Newquay. The facility is approximately 10 km west on the right (north) side of the road. Look for signs. *EUSMRA: Page 131 (B-3), page 145.* **NMC:** Plymouth, 60 km east.

RESERVATION INFORMATION: Lodging Office located at ITT Office. MWR Department, Joint Maritime Facility St. Mawgan, PSC 804, Box 8, FPO AE 09409-5000. **C-011-44-1637-85-3541/3597, DSN-314-234-3541/3597,** Fax: C-011-44-1637-85-3488.

TLF Two-bedroom furnished townhouses, sleep four (6); three-bedroom furnished townhouse, sleeps five (1). Refrigerator/freezer, stove, microwave, coffee maker, utensils, TV/VCR, washer/dryer. Rates: $56-$64 daily.

AMENITIES: Exercise Room and Mini Mart.

TML AVAILABILITY: Available year round.

CREDIT CARDS ACCEPTED: Visa, MasterCard and American Express.

TRANSPORTATION: Car Rental, C-011-44-1637-85-3559, DSN-314-234-3559; Off base taxi: Carminow, C-011-44-1637-85-0000.

DINING OPPORTUNITIES: Many pubs and restaurants nearby.

This is the perfect base for exploring the English countryside. Cornwall has several famous attractions including Tintagel Castle (the legendary birthplace of King Arthur), Lanhydrock House, featured in Disney's Three Musketeers, and dozens of golf courses. Installation and beach within thirty-minute drive. Vehicle is essential.

Union Jack Club (UK16R7)
Sandell Street, Waterloo
London, SE1 8UJ, United Kingdom
(Not U.S. Government Lodging)

MAIN INSTALLATION TELEPHONE NUMBERS: C-(USA) 011-44-20-7928-6401, (UK) 020-7928-6401.

LOCATION: In central London, opposite Waterloo Station (train and subway). From the south bank of the Thames River go southeast on Waterloo Road to east on Sandell Street across from Waterloo Station. The club is on the south side of the street in the first block. Look for the high rise brick building. *EUSMRA: Page 134 (A,B-3), page 140.* **NMC:** London, in city limits. NMI: London Naval Activities.

RESERVATION INFORMATION: Address as above. Advance Booking Office **C-(USA) 011-44-20-7928-4814, (UK) 020-7928-4814,** 0830-1700 hours Mon-Fri, 0900-1400 Sat. Fax: C-(USA) 011-44-20-7620-0565, 24 hours. E-mail: abo@ujclub.co.uk WEB: www.ujclub.co.uk Reservations accepted by phone, e-mail or by booking form on web site. *Allied Forces are welcome and granted Temporary Honorary Membership, 24 hours.* Check in 1300 hours, check out 1000 hours.

TML **Club and Hotel.** Leave/vacation only. 330 bedrooms, 164 include own bath/shower, water closet, TV, telephone. thirty-year old structure, continually being renovated. Rates: single £30.10-£42.70 (U.S.$42.96-$60.95 at press time), double £75.50-£77.50 (U.S.$107.76-$138.16 at press time), family room £96.80-£99 (U.S.$138.16-$141.30 at press time), children age 3-12 occupying single/twin bedded room £11.80-£17 (U.S.$16.84-$24.26 at press time) depending on room. Handicap accessible facilities throughout the facility. Meals paid for when taken. All charges include VAT (Value added tax). 10 percent discount for seven days booking or more, deposit of one night when booking, refundable if canceled 48 hours in advance of arrival.

OTHER: Used by over 5,000 American Service men and women in 2000, will provide rates and other information on request. Reciprocal

UNION JACK CLUB (UK16R7)

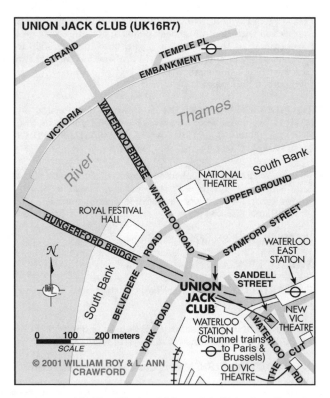

arrangements with The Marines' Memorial Club, San Francisco, CA. **Active and Reserves equally welcome.**

Author's Note: This is a private club and is not government/military billeting.

AMENITIES: Cyber Station, Souvenir Shop, Snooker/Billiards, Reading Room, Writing Room, Library, Conference Rooms, Snack and Soft Drink Vending Machines, Launderette. Afternoon tea in the Bar Lounge or on the patio. Local gym available to all residents at discounted rates.

TML AVAILABILITY: Good, but book early.

CREDIT CARDS ACCEPTED: All cards accepted. Checks accepted when supported by Check Card.

TRANSPORTATION: Subway; Shuttle/bus; Taxi. Good train links to all airports serving London, also a shuttle bus to London (Heathrow) given 24 hours booking.

DINING OPPORTUNITIES: Restaurant in club with extensive menu and wine list. Various restaurants, bistros and "character" pubs locally and in West End of London.

A ten minute walk takes you to the British Airways London Eye—the new 450-foot tall ferris wheel giving marvelous views of London, the Old Vic and the New Vic theaters, the new IMAX cinema, Shakespear's Globe Theater, the West End, Theaterland, and the EuroStar International trains to Paris, Brussels, and Lille. All of London is easily accessible by bus, train, river boat on the Thames and the famous London Black Cab.

Victory Services Club (UK17R7)

63/79 Seymour Street
London W2 2HF, United Kingdom
(Not U.S. Government Lodging)

MAIN INSTALLATION TELEPHONE NUMBERS: C-(USA) 011-44-207-723-4474, (UK) 0207-723-4474. Medical 207-3338; Security Police 321-9652.

LOCATION: Located north of Hyde Park and Kensington Gardens. Two

short blocks from the Marble Arch Underground Station (Central Line) on Oxford Street. From the Marble Arch Underground at Oxford Street, walk west on Oxford Street one block to Edgware Road then northwest to Seymour Street, then west to the club on the south side of Seymour Street. Flying to London: From Heathrow IAP take underground (Piccadilly Line) east to Holborn Station and change to a westbound train on the Central Line to Marble Arch (one hour). Also frequent bus service to Oxford Street (50 minutes). From Gatwick IAP take train to London Victoria Station (30 minutes) and taxi to the club (10 minutes). EUSMRA: Page 134 (A-3), page 141. **NMC:** London, in city limits. NMI: London Naval Activities.

RESERVATION INFORMATION: Address and telephone as above. Fax: C-(USA) 011-44-207-402-9496, 24 hours daily. E-mail: res@vsc.co.uk WEB: www.vsc.co.uk **This is a members-only club.** The following are eligible to join. A) serving and ex-service personnel of all ranks of the Armed Forces of the Crown, including those of the Commonwealth and members of NATO Forces; B) spouses of members of the club; C) widows(ers) of ex-service personnel. The U.S. Coast Guard does not qualify. **The membership year is from 1 April and 31 March. Membership Fees: Single £14** (U.S.$19.98 at press time)**, Joint husband and wife £23** (U.S.$32.83 at press time) **annually.** Write, fax or e-mail to the club for an application and further details. **Serving personnel are not required to pay membership fees.** All categories may make reservations.

(TML) **Club and Hotel.** Bedroom accommodations for 300 members with 89 twin/double bedrooms and 8 single rooms with private bath. 22 twin/double and 113 single rooms with shared bath. Rates: twin rooms £53 (U.S.$75.65 at press time); single rooms from £26.50 (U.S.$37.83 at press time). Twin rooms with private bath available at £74 (U.S.$105.62 at press time); single with private bath £37 (U.S.$52.81 at press time).

AMENITIES: Modern Buttery, Grill Room, Bar Lounge, Television Rooms and Library.

TML AVAILABILITY: Good, but book early.

CREDIT CARDS ACCEPTED: Visa and MasterCard. Checks accepted when supported by a Check Card.

TRANSPORTATION: Off base shuttle/bus, C-011-44-1293-532244; Car Rental (Hertz), C-011-44-207-402-4242; Off Base taxi, C-011-44-207-286-0286.

DINING OPPORTUNITIES: Many dining facilities located within a short walk.

Founded in 1907, the present magnificent site was opened in 1948. In WWII it was the site of the *American Red Cross Columbia Club-the largest in Great Britain. Within easy walking distance to the American Embassy and U.S. Navy Headquarters (Grosvenor Square), Mayfair and Oxford Street areas.*

VICTORY SERVICES CLUB (UK17R7)

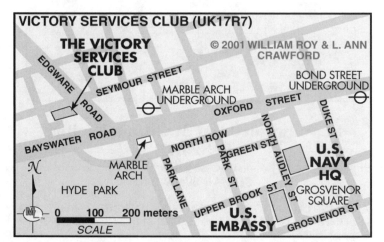

APPENDIX A

GENERAL ABBREVIATIONS USED IN THIS BOOK

The general abbreviations used in this book are listed below. Commonly understood abbreviations (e.g., Mon-Fri for Monday through Friday) and standard abbreviations found in addresses have not been included in order to save space.

A

AAF-Army Airfield
AAFES-Army & Air Force Exchange Service
AB-Air Base
A/C-Air Conditioning
ACS-Army Community Services
AD-Active Duty
ADT-Active Duty for Training
AE-Army Europe
AF-Air Force
AFAF-Air Force Auxiliary Field
AFB-Air Force Base
AFNORTH-Allied Forces Northern Europe
AFRC-Armed Forces Recreation Center
AFRES-Air Force Reserve
AFS-Air Force Station
APG-Army Proving Ground
AIRVAC-Air Evacuation
AMC-Army Medical Center
AMC-Air Mobility Command
ANG-Air National Guard
ANGB-Air National Guard Base
AP-Army Pacific
APO-Army Post Office
ARB-Air Reserve Base
AST-Area Support Team
ATM-Automatic Teller Machine
Attn-Attention

B

BAQ-Bachelor Airmen's quarters
BBQ-Barbecue
BEH-Bachelor Enlisted Housing
BEQ-Bachelor Enlisted Quarters
Bldg-Building
BOH-Bachelor Officers' Housing
BOQ-Bachelor Officers' Quarters
BQ-Bachelor Quarters
BSB-Base Support Battalion
BX-Base Exchange

C

C-Commercial phone number
CATV-Cable television
CBH-Combined Bachelors Housing
CBQ-Combined Bachelors Quarters
CG-Coast Guard
CGAS-Coast Guard Air Station
CGES-Coast Guard Exchange Service
CGG-Coast Guard Group
CGISC-Coast Guard Integrated Support Command
CGSC-Coast Guard Support Command
CGTC-Coast Guard Training Center
CIV-Civilian
CMSgt-Chief Master Sergeant
CO-Commanding Officer
Comm-Commercial
CONUS-Continental United States
CPO-Chief Petty Officer
CPOQ-Chief Petty Officer Quarters
CSM-Command Sergeant Major
CWO-Chief Warrant Officer

D

DAV-Disabled American Veterans
DD-Defense Department
DGQ-Distinguished Guest Quarters
DM-Deutsche Mark
DoD-Department of Defense
DoT-Department of Transportation
DSN-Defense Switched Network
DV-Distinguished Visitor
DVOQ-Distinguished Visiting Officers' Quarters
DVQ-Distinguished Visitor Quarters

E

EFQ-Enlisted Family Quarters
EML-Environmental Morale Leave
EUSMRA-European U.S. Military Road Atlas
Ext-Extension

F

Fax-Telefax number
FPO-Fleet Post Office

G

GH-Guest House
Gov-Government
GS-General Schedule

H

HBO-Home Box Office
HP-Homepage
HQ-Headquarters

I

IAP-International Airport
ID-Identification
ITR-Information, Ticketing and Registration
ITT-Information, Tickets and Tours

J

JRB-Joint Reserve Base

M

MCB-Marine Corps Base
MCAS-Marine Corps Air Station
MCLB-Marine Corps Logistics Base
MCPO-Master Chief Petty Officer
MCRD-Marine Corps Recruit Depot
Mil-Military
MP-Military Police
MWR-Morale, Welfare and Recreation

N

NAF-Naval Air Facility
NAF-Non Appropriated Funds
NAS-Naval Air Station

NAWC-Naval Air Warfare Center
NAWS-Naval Air Warfare Station
NB-Naval Base
NCBC-Naval Construction Battalion Center
NCO-Noncommissioned Officer
NETC-Naval Education Training Center
NEX-Navy Exchange
NG-National Guard
NMC-Nearest Major City
NMI-Nearest Major Installation
NOAA-National Oceanic & Atmospheric Administration
NS-Naval Shipyard
NS-Naval Station
NSA-Naval Support Activity
NSB-Naval Submarine Base
NSCS-Navy Supply Corps School
NSGA-Naval Security Group Activity
NSWC-Naval Surface Weapons Center
NTC-Naval Training Center
NTTC-Naval Technical Training Center
NWS-Naval Weapons Station

O

O'Club-Officers' Club
OD-Officer of the Day
OOD-Officer of the Day

P

PAO-Public Affairs Office
PCS-Permanent Change of Station
PG-Proving Ground
PHS-Public Health Service
PMO-Provost Marshall's Office
PX-Post Exchange

R

RAAF-Royal Australian Air Force
RAF-Royal Air Force
RSAF-Royal Singapore Air Force

S

SATO-Scheduled Airlines Ticket Office
SCPO-Senior Chief Petty Officer
SDO-Staff Duty Officer
SES-Senior Executive Service
SNCO-Senior Noncommissioned Officer
SNCOQ-Senior Noncommissioned Officers' Quarters
SOFA-Status of Forces Agreement
Space-A-Space Available

T

TAD-Temporary Attached Duty
TAQ-Temporary Airmen's Quarters
TDY-Temporary Duty
TEQ-Temporary Enlisted Quarters
TFQ-Temporary Family Quarters
TLA-Temporary Lodging Allowance
TLF-Transient Lodging Facility

TLQ-Temporary Living Quarters
TML-Temporary Military Lodging
TOQ-Transient Officers' Quarters
TQ-Temporary Quarters
TV-Television
TVEQ-Temporary Visiting Enlisted Quarters
TVOQ-Temporary Visiting Officers' Quarters
TVQ-Temporary Visiting Quarters

U

UPH-Unaccompanied Personnel Housing
USAF-United States Air Force
USCG-United States Coast Guard

USEUCOM-U.S. European Command
USMC-United States Marine Corps
USMRA-United States Military Road Atlas
USN-United States Navy
USPHS-United States Public Health Service
USS-United States Ship

V

VA-Veterans' Administration
VAQ-Visiting Airman's Quarters
VAT-Value Added Tax
VCP-Video Cassette Player
VCR-Video Cassette Recorder

VEQ-Visiting Enlisted Quarters
VFQ-Visiting Female Quarters
VHA-Variable Housing Allowance
VIP-Very Important Person
VOQ-Visiting Officer Quarters
VQ-Visiting Quarters, all ranks

W

WG-Wing
WO-Warrant Officer

GENERAL LODGING TERMS/ICONS USED IN THIS BOOK

(Army Lodge)

(Army Lodging)

(BEH) Bachelor Enlisted Housing

(BEQ) Bachelor Enlisted Quarters

(BOH) Bachelor Officer Housing

(BOQ) Bachelor Officer Quarters

(BQ) Bachelor Quarters

(Cabins)

(CBH) Combined Bachelor Housing

(CBOQ) Combined Bachelor Officer Quarters

(CBQ) Combined Bachelor Quarters

(Cottage)

(CPOQ) Combined Petty Officer Quarters

(DVAQ) Distinguished Visiting Airmen Quarters

(DV) Distinguished Visitor

(VIP) Very Important Person Quarters

(DVOQ) Distinguished Visiting Officer Quarters

(DVQ) Distinguished Visitor Quarters

(Fisher House)

(Guesthouse)

(Lighthouse)

(Lodge)

(Mobile Home)

(NAVY LODGE)

(RV Park) Recreational Vehicle Park

(SEBQ) Senior Enlisted Bachelor Quarters

(TFQ) Temporary Family Quarters

(TAQ) Temporary Airmen Quarters

(TDY) Temporary Duty

(TEQ) Temporary Enlisted Quarters

(TLF) Temporary Lodging Facility

(TLQ) Temporary Lodging Quarters

(TOQ) Temporary Officer Quarters

(TML) Temporary Military Lodging

(TQ) Temporary Quarters

(Trailers)

(VAQ) Visiting Airmen Quarters

(VEQ) Visiting Enlisted Quarters

(VOQ) Visiting Officer Quarters

(VQ) Visitor Quarters

APPENDIX B

Temporary Military Lodging (TML) Questions and Answers

Editor's Note: The answers below are based on information available to us at press time. Due to the fact that there is not a detailed operational uniform DoD/DoT temporary military lodging policy, the reader will find that operational policies differ between and among the Uniformed Services and in some cases also differ from installation to installation within a Uniformed Service. Also policies differ between Continental United States (CONUS) and overseas (U.S. possessions and foreign countries) and among the various types of temporary military lodging. For these reasons among others, these general answers must be accepted only as guides--not absolute rules. Specific questions should be directed to each individual installation at the time of your visit. Policies do often change.

1. What types of lodging are available on military installations? There are numerous types of lodging available on military installations. They range from very modern, modular-construction, complete housekeeping units which will sleep a family of five, with all amenities found in a good motel (plus a furnished kitchenette) such as is found in Navy Lodges, to the old faithful guest houses (now titled "Army Lodging" at Army installations)—in most cases relics of World War II, which are often barracks-type buildings. Some may have been improved while others are definitely substandard. Some are the modern low-rise to high-rise hotel types such as the Shades of Green on Walt Disney World Resort, Florida; Hale Koa Hotel AFRC, Hawaii; The New Sanno U.S. Forces Center, Japan and the Dragon Hill Lodge, Korea. There is also the modern motel-type lodging such as the Inn at Schofield Barracks, Hawaii, and motel chain operations at Fort Bliss, Texas. Somewhere in between, you will find Very Important Enlisted Quarters (VEQ) and Very Important Officer Quarters (VOQ) type accommodations that usually consist of private rooms with a shared bath between rooms. Also, there are the Distinguished Visitors (DV) and Very Important Persons (VIP) facilities which have in most cases a bedroom, sitting room and kitchen/dining facility. If you are the "picky" type, we suggest you take a look before signing in, if possible, or talk with the lodging management.

2. Were the units mentioned above constructed with tax dollars? According to information given Military Living Publications, the answer on most of the lodging is an emphatic "NO." The newer construction was built from non-appropriated funds or grants from welfare funds, generated from profits from military exchanges, etc. The exception to this is in cases where old unused family housing, initially built with appropriated funds, has been converted into temporary military lodging facilities. Also, TML is frequently available in bachelor officers', NCO and enlisted grade quarters which have been constructed with appropriated funds.

3. What does space-available (Space-A) mean? The purpose of having lodging on military installations is to accommodate duty personnel and those arriving or departing an installation on Temporary Duty orders (TDY), Temporary Attached Duty (TAD) or Permanent Change of Station (PCS) orders. Those on orders generally have first priority on all lodging. After these needs have been met, if there is any space left over, leave personnel (including retirees, reservists and their families) may utilize the facilities on a Space-A basis. During the summer months, Space-A lodging may be more difficult to obtain than during the spring, fall and winter.

4. How about advance reservations? While most installations will accept reservations from those on duty; leave, reservist and retired travelers will generally find that they cannot make reservations in advance but are accepted on a Space-A basis on arrival at the billeting office. The USAF is an important exception as they will provide reservations 24 hours in advance of arrival for a stay of up to three days. Also, Navy Lodges do accept reservations from all categories. As we are listing the lodging of five Uniformed Services (USA, USN, USMC, USCG and USAF) in this book, the rules may vary greatly from installation to installation. Please check each listing in this book or call in advance to check on specific policies on making reservations at the time of your trip. You may be surprised and find that the place you want to visit will accept your reservation.

5. Can retirees use military lodging? Definitely! Usually on the same Space-A basis as active duty on leave. Retirees will also find that they are welcome to use the lodging on most installations overseas, even though they may be restricted from using the commissary and exchange in most overseas areas due to the local Status of Forces Agreement (SOFA). The rules are different for the use of support facilities in each

foreign country. Complete details on "Support Authorized United States Uniformed Services Personnel and Their Dependent Family Members Visiting Foreign Countries" are in Appendix E in this book.

6. Are Reservists eligible for TML? Many favorable changes have occurred for Reservists as a result of the DoD "One Force Policy." Reservists now have the same eligibility for TML as Active Duty personnel. There is one notable exception in that Reservists cannot use TML in foreign countries or facilities in foreign countries where their use is not provided for in the SOFA, i.e., Reservists are not permitted to use the AFRCs in Germany and The New Sanno U.S. Forces Center in Japan. See Appendix C, "National Guard and Reserve Components Personnel Are Eligible For Temporary Military Lodging."

7. Your book often refers to Defense Switched Network (DSN) telephone/telefax numbers. What are they? The Defense Switched Network numbers are military telephone/telefax numbers which are to be used only by those on official business. Such numbers can normally be dialed only from a military installation and are monitored to ensure their use is not violated. As many of our readers use military lodging and other facilities while traveling on duty, and many government offices use our book as a reference guide, we publish the DSN numbers, when available, as a service to them. The DSN requires area codes to facilitate dialing to and through different areas of the DSN system. In the DSN system these area codes are called "Area Voice Codes" which are Alaska=317; Caribbean=313; CONUS=312; Europe=314, Pacific=315 and Southwest Asia=318.

8. What is DV/VIP lodging? It is lodging for distinguished official visitors. Some installations will have a few rooms or a small guest house available for them. If these facilities are not being used by official visitors, many installations will often extend the courtesy of their use to qualified active duty and reservist personnel on leave status or retirees on a day-to-day Space-A basis. Most military installations we surveyed referred to DV/VIP as pay grades 06 and above of all Services. Just a few lodging facilities included lower officer grades (05) and senior NCO (E-8/9) in this category. The Marine Corps calls their distinguished visitors lodging, Distinguished Guest Quarters (DGQ). Since 1977, we have noted that many more Air Force bases are providing DV/VIP lodging for their senior NCOs. Personnel in the DV/VIP category should check our listings in this book for more complete information and inquire at each installation upon arrival. Distinguished visitors will usually find that it is best to make advance reservations through the Protocol Office or Visitor's Bureau of the installation concerned. In some cases, the billeting office has authority to place personnel in the DV/VIP lodging and coordinate the visit for the traveler.

9. My husband is enlisted. What chance do we have at staying in military lodging? Better than ever. In the past few years, concentrated efforts have been made to provide more temporary lodging for enlisted members. Please notice in our listing the numerous references to quarters for all ranks. In the newer Air Force Transient Living Quarters, Navy Lodges, and Army Lodging, rank has absolutely no privileges. All ranks are accommodated on an equal basis. Policies may vary on other types of lodging. At some facilities, enlisted have priority.

10. May 100% DAV use TML? Most military lodging units accept 100% DAV (Disabled American Veterans) on a Space-A basis if it is possible. In fact the Hale Koa Hotel, AFRC specifically mentions 100% DAV in their brochure as being eligible. One problem that 100% DAV have encountered has been caused by the color of their ID Card (DD-1173). It is the same color (buff or butterscotch) as carried by family members. Many times 100% DAV are turned away from facilities which require family members to be accompanied by their sponsor. The "ID card-checking authority" assumes this 100% DAV is not a military member but a "dependent" or family member. The DoD is now issuing a new card, DD Form 2765, Uniformed Services Identification and Privilege Card to 100% DAVs in lieu of the older DD Form 1173. The new card is issued to sponsors, other than active duty military members, who are entitled to uniformed services benefits and privileges. Editor's Note: This new card, DD Form 2765 does not change the fact that 100% DAVs are not entitled to fly Space-A air on DoD aircraft. They may fly Space-A on DoT (U.S. Coast Guard) aircraft.

11. How about Navy-Bachelor Quarters (BQ)? We are told that a few Bachelor Enlisted Quarters (BEQ) locations are unsuitable facilities for family members--central baths (latrines), etc. However, most Bachelor Enlisted Quarters (BEQ) have suitable facilities. Also, Bachelor Officers' Quarters (BOQ) are almost always suitable. They will generally accept family members accompanying their sponsor. Rules can vary from installation to installation. If a Navy Lodge is not available, always ask about the possible use of BEQ/BOQ.

12. What about widows, widowers, and unaccompanied dependents? The news gets better each time we report in our new TML book. Dependents of active duty personnel who are involved in a PCS move may now use TML and make reservations at the installation they are leaving and at the new one to which they are assigned. They may also use TML en route on a Space-A basis. This includes TML in TLF and in VEQ or VOQ.

Unaccompanied dependents of service members on leave and also widow/ers of service members may use TML on a Space-A basis in VEQ or VOQ if this policy has been approved by the base commander. Therefore, this may NOT be in effect at all Air Force installations. This does not include the use of TLF.

Uniformed Services other than the USAF generally have always allowed unaccompanied service family members to use TML on a Space-A basis. This, of course, has and will continue to differ from installation to installation. Navy Lodges, however, welcome dependent children, and non-ID card holders when accompanied by a parent or guardian authorized to utilize Navy Lodges.

13. What's a Fisher House? Overview: A Fisher House is "a home away from home" for families of patients receiving medical care at major military and VA medical centers. The houses are normally located within walking distance of the treatment facility or have transportation available. There are 26 Fisher Houses located on 16 military installations and 4 VA medical centers, including 5 in design and planning.

Description: Fisher Houses are comfortably furnished homes donated by Zachary and Elizabeth M. Fisher of New York. Each house is designed to provide eight suites, two of which are handicap accessible. The houses can accommodate up to 16 family members. They feature a common kitchen, laundry facilities, spacious dining room and an inviting living room and library, and toys for children. A Fisher House is a temporary residence and is not a treatment facility, hospice or counseling center.

Responsibilities: Fisher Houses are give to the U.S. Government as gifts from Mr. and Mrs. Fisher. The military service secretaries and the Secretary of Veterans Affairs are responsible for the operation and maintenance of the homes. The Fisher House Foundation, Inc., a not-for-profit organization, assists in the coordination of private support and encourages public support for the homes.

Eligibility and Cost: Criteria established locally by hospital or installation commanders. Cost varies by location. The average charge for lodging is $10 per family per day. Several of the houses offer free lodging.

Editor's Note: Families may stay while visiting patients requiring treatment, and are referred by physicians or social workers based on a variety of priorities. Generally priorities are lack of family in the immediate area, severity of illness and financial need. Different hospitals may have varying criteria. The Fisher Houses addresses and telephone numbers are contained in each listing in this book which has one or more Fisher Houses.

Directory of Zachary & Elizabeth M. Fisher Houses

CALIFORNIA
David Grant USAF Medical Center
100 Bodin Circle
Travis AFB, CA 94535-5000
C-707-423-7551, fax C-707-423-7552

San Diego Naval Medical Center
38400 Bob Wilson Drive
Building 46
San Diego, CA 92134-5000
C-619-532-9055, fax C-619-532-5216

COLORADO
Denver VA Medical Center
1055 Clermont Street
Denver, CO 80220-3873
C-303-364-2817, fax C-303-393-4679

DISTRICT OF COLUMBIA
Walter Reed Army Medical Center I & II
6825 Georgia Avenue, NW
Washington, D.C.
20307-5001
C-301-295-7374, fax C-301-295-8012
Fisher House II: C-202-356-7564 ext 10

FLORIDA
West Palm Beach VA Medical Center
7305 N. Military Trail-Route 136
W. Palm Beach, FL 33410-5000
C-561-882-7180, fax C-561-882-6565

GEORGIA
Dwight David Eisenhower
Army Medical Center
Fisher House Road, Bldg 280
Ft. Gordon, GA 30905-5000
C-706-787-7100, fax C-706-787-5106

HAWAII
Tripler Army Medical Center
315 Krukowski Road
Honolulu, HI 96819-5000
C-808-433-1291 ext 28, fax C-808-433-3619

MARYLAND
Malcolm Grow Medical Center
1076 West Perimeter Road

Andrews AFB, MD 20762-5000
C-301-981-1243, fax C-301-981-7629

National Naval Medical Center I & II
24 Stokes Road
Bethesda, MD 20814-5002
C-301-295-5074, fax C-301-295-5632

MINNESOTA
Minneapolis VA Medical Center
One Veterans Drive
Minneapolis, MN 55417-5000
C-612-725-2106, fax C-612-725-2016

MISSISSIPPI
Keesler Medical Center
509 Fisher Street
Keesler AFB,
MS 39534-2599
C-228-377-8264, fax C-228-377-7691

NEW YORK
Stratton VA Medical Center
113 Holland Avenue
Albany, NY 12208-5000
C-518-626-6919, fax C-518-626-5452

NORTH CAROLINA
Womack Army Medical Center
12 Bassett Street
Fort Bragg, NC 28307-5000
C-910-432-1486, fax C-910-432-3825

OHIO
Cincinnati VA Medical Center
3200 Vine Street
Cincinnati, OH 45220-5000
C-513-475-6571, fax C-513-487-6661

United States Air Force
Medical Center I & II
415 Schlatter Drive
Wright-Patterson AFB, OH 45433-5000
C-937-257-0855, fax C-937-656-2150

TEXAS
Brooke Army Medical Center I & II
3623 George C. Beach Road

Fort Sam Houston, TX 78234-5000
C-210-225-4855 ext. 101, fax C-210-270-2560

Darnall Army Community Hospital
36000 Darnall Loop
Fort Hood, TX 76544-4752
C-254-286-7927, fax C-254-286-7929

Wilford Hall Medical Center I, II & III
2580 Luke Blvd, Bldg 3810
Lackland AFB, TX 78236-5000
C-210-292-3000, fax C-210-292-3031

William Beaumont Army Medical Center
5005 North Piedras Street
El Paso, TX 79920-5001
C-915-569-1860, fax C-915-569-1862

VIRGINIA
Portsmouth Naval Medical Center I
313 Green Street
Portsmouth, Virginia 23724-5001
C-757-399-5461

Portsmouth Naval Medical Center II
853 Fisher Drive, Bldg 287
Portsmouth, VA 23708-5000
C-757-953-6889, fax C-757-953-7174

WASHINGTON
Madigan Army Medical Center
9999 Wilson Avenue
Fort Lewis, WA 98433-5000
C-253-964-9283, fax C-253-968-3619

GERMANY
Fisher House
U.S. Hospital Landstuhl
66849 Landstuhl/Kirchberg
C-011-49-6371-6183311

IN PLANNING OR DESIGN
Fisher House II, Tripler Army Medical Center, Hawaii (Due to open in 2003)
Bay Pines VA Medical Center, Florida (Due to open in June 2002)
Regional Medical Center, Landstuhl, Germany (Second one due to open Nov 2002)

APPENDIX C

Billeting Regulations and Policies

Department of Defense Instructions

The Department of Defense (DoD) has issued several instructions which outline for the Military Departments the general guidance for the organization, operation, management and reporting for broad categories of Temporary Military Lodging (TML). Applicable references include: DoD Directive 4165.63, *DoD Housing,* dated 20 July 1989, DoD Instruction 1100.16, *Equal Opportunity in Off-Base Housing,* dated 14 August 1989, DoD Manual 4165.63-M, *DoD Housing Management,* dated 30 September 1993, DoD Instruction 1015.10, *Programs for Military Morale, Welfare and Recreation (MWR),* dated 3 November 1995 reissued with Change 1 dated 31 October 1996, and DoD Instruction 1015.12, *Lodging Program Resource Management,* dated 30 October 1996. The Military Departments within the Department of Defense and the United States Coast Guard within the Department of Transportation have issued more specific policy and procedures directives covering the organization, management, and reporting for their respective categories of TML. These Military Department directives are not identical or uniform in their content. As a special service to our readers, we have synthesized each Military Department directive and Navy Lodge policy below. In each case we have selected the items from the directives which we believe will provide the greatest benefit to our readers. We have provided the reference for each directive and the reader may request to see the complete directive at the respective Military Department lodging facilities or at their personnel offices.

Members of all U.S. Uniformed Services, Active Duty, Reservists, Retirees, 100% DAV, and authorized family members generally can use lodging of all services described in this book, with some exceptions. For specific information, contact the facilities you plan to visit.

Army Lodging Management

Army Regulation AR 210-50, *Housing Management,* dated 26 February 1999, provides guidance on the management and operation of the Army's family, unaccompanied personnel and guest housing programs. This regulation is applicable to the active Army, Army National Guard and Army Reserve, with some exceptions. Army Regulation AR 215-1, *Morale, Welfare and Recreation Activities and Non-Appropriated Fund Entities,* dated 25 October 1998 provides guidance on the operation and utilization of Guest Houses (GH), Recreational Housing (cabins, cottages and fixed trailers), Armed Forces Recreational Centers (AFRC), and hotels/motels operated by MWR as non-appropriated fund activities. U.S. Army Community and Family Support Center memorandum CFSC-AL, *Lodging Fund Transition Guidance,* dated 1 June 2000 supplemented by CFSC-AL memorandum, *Lodging Fund Supplemental Guidance,* dated 15 September 2000, promulgated guidance and procedures for the consolidation of all installation transient lodging (temporary duty (TDY) billeting and guest houses (GH)) into a single, separate installation lodging fund. In November 1997, a Joint Federal Travel Regulation (JFTR) revision specifically classified Permanent Change of Station (PCS) travel as official travel and guest houses as official government lodging facilities. DoD Instruction DODI 1015.12, *Lodging Program Resource Management,* dated 30 October 1996, and DoD Instruction DODI 1015.10, *Programs for Military Morale, Welfare and Recreation (MWR),* dated 3 November 1995, administratively reissued, incorporating change 1, dated 31 October 1996, provide additional guidance. Surcharges for non-duty travel are authorized to be collected.

The primary consideration in the management of Army lodging activities is to promote the use of housing assets to ensure that available housing is used for its intended purpose, and meets the housing needs of authorized personnel in the performance of their duties.

Army Lodging Activities include the following:

(1) Army Lodging Facilities:
　　(a) Unaccompanied Personnel Housing (UPH) Temporary Duty (TDY). This includes all visiting officer quarters (VOQ), visiting enlisted quarters (VEQ), and distinguished visitor quarters (DVQ)

　　(b) Guest Houses (GH) (Army Lodging)
(2) Unaccompanied Personnel Housing (UPH) Private Party (PP) (limited services only)
　　(a) Officers Quarters (OQ)
　　(b) Senior Officers Quarters (SOQ)
　　(c) Enlisted Quarters (EQ)
　　(d) Senior Enlisted Quarters (SEQ)

Authority to Occupy Transient Facilities:

A. Personnel authorized to occupy UPH (TDY) housing

1. The following personnel are authorized to occupy UPH(TDY) and receive confirmed reservations:
　　(a) TDY military and TDY DoD civilians
　　(b) PCS military personnel, with or without family members, or family members alone, when GH or permanent housing is not immediately available
　　(c) U.S. and foreign guests of the Military Services, and guests of the Armed Forces as determined by the installation commander. Payment of the Service Charge is required
　　(d) USAR, ARNG, and Reserve Officers Training Corps (ROTC) personnel on active duty for training (ADT), active duty for special work (ADSW), or performing annual training (AT) as individuals and scheduled inactive duty training (IDT)
　　(e) TDY foreign nationals or foreign military trainees engaged in or sponsored by military assistance or similar programs
　　(f) Military family members on medical TDY orders
2. When space is available, the following personnel may occupy UPH(TDY):
　　(a) Reserve Component (RC) personnel not otherwise addressed in 1(d) above (including personnel not under orders, paid retirees, gray area retirees, military personnel on leave, military personnel granted permissive TDY, family members and guests of military personnel assigned to the installation if GH space is not available
　　(b) Nonmilitary uniformed personnel of the U.S. Public Health Service (USPHS) and the National Oceanic and Atmospheric Administration (NOAA), U.S. Coast Guard personnel, and foreign military personnel, when authorized by the installation commander
3. Personnel eligible for UPH(TDY) on a confirmed reservation basis will compete on an equal basis for UPH(TDY).
4. Personnel eligible for UPH(TDY) on a space-available basis will compete on an equal basis for UPH(TDY).
5. Soldiers in promotable status may be assigned to housing of the next higher grade upon presenting proof of pending promotion.
6. Except for active duty military personnel on leave and retired military personnel, at the discretion of the installation commander, personnel who occupy UPH(TDY) on a space-available basis will pay the fair market rental rate. However, RC personnel not addressed in 2(a) above, who use UPH(TDY) on a space-available basis when GH is not available, may be charged a service charge, instead of a rental rate, if their status is the same as other soldiers paying service charges.

B. Personnel authorized to occupy Guest House (GH) (Army Lodging) facilities

1. The following personnel may occupy GH facilities and request a confirmed reservation:
　　(a) PCS soldiers and their family members or family members alone who are temporarily without permanent housing
　　(b) PCS DoD civilian personnel with or without family members or family members alone who are in overseas and foreign locations and are temporarily without permanent housing
　　(c) Official guests of the installation as determined by the installation commander
　　(d) Active and retired military personnel and family members undergoing outpatient treatment at a medical facility and who must stay overnight

(e) Official guests of the installation as determined by the installation commander

(f) Soldiers or their family members when visiting the installation incident to internment of the soldier or family members

2. When space is available, the following personnel may occupy GH facilities:

(a) TDY soldiers and TDY DoD civilian personnel when UPS(TDY) facilities are not available

(b) All RC personnel (including members not under orders, paid retirees, and gray area retirees), not otherwise addressed above

(c) Active duty retirees, with or without family members

(d) Members of the U.S. Coast Guard (USCG), U.S. Public Health Service (USPHS), and National Oceanic and Atmospheric Administration (NOAA)

(e) PCS DoD civilians with or without family members, family members alone, and relatives and guests of soldiers assigned to the installation

3. Personnel eligible for GH on a confirmed reservation basis may compete on an equal basis or the installation commander may establish priorities within the categories listed in item 1 above to meet the needs of the installation.

4. Personnel eligible for GH on a space-available basis may compete on an equal basis.

5. RC personnel shall be accommodated in GH on the same basis as soldiers on active duty.

C. Medal of Honor (MOH) recipients

MOH recipients of all services are authorized Army lodging facilities at the discretion of the installation commander. Active duty, retired, and discharged (without retirement) MOH recipients may receive priority placement and confirmed reservations in UPH(TDY) or GH facilities. A DVQ may be assigned regardless of military pay grade. The established service fee applies.

Reservation System:

A. Army Centralized Reservation Center

In 1994 the Army established the Army Central Reservations Center (ACRC) located in Huntsville, AL, which is continually being expanded and improved. Official duty travelers to Army facilities are encouraged to utilize the ACRC toll-free access number 1-800-GO-ARMY-1 (1-800-462-7691). Travelers can reach ACRC from outside CONUS (OCONUS) by dialing DSN-312-897-2790. (Please see the section on Army Lodging Reservations on page vii at the front of this book.) Travelers may call each lodging facility directly, using the telephone numbers listed in this book . ACRC does not make reservations at Fisher Houses, Armed Forces Recreation Centers, or MWR Recreational Housing.

B. Reservations Systems at Individual UPH (TDY) Housing Facilities

Billeting offices have established reservation systems which will enable TDY travelers to confirm reservations at least 15 days prior to actual travel. A reservation confirmation number will be provided to the traveler. Reservations normally are not held beyond 1800 hours unless the TDY traveler notifies the Billeting/Lodging Office of late arrival and makes arrangements to guarantee payment with a credit card. It is possible to make reservations for use by Space-A travelers at some facilities, however this varies both seasonally and from post to post depending on changing demands to accommodate official duty travelers. Many facilities do not make reservations for Space-A travelers, but make available rooms which are released at 1800 hours or other specified time on a first-come basis.

C. Guest House (GH) (Army Lodging) Facilities

Reservations for official duty travelers are accepted on a first-come basis without regard to rank, race, color, religion, gender, national origin or handicap. Official duty reservations normally may be accepted up to 30 days in advance of requested date. Confirmation should be provided as early as possible.

Reservations are not held beyond 1800 hours unless the billeting office is notified of late arrival. The normal duration of occupancy for all lodging categories is 30 days unless a hardship extension is approved by the installation commander.

D. Armed Forces Recreation Centers and MWR Recreational Housing

Reservations for Armed Forces Recreation Centers and Army MWR Recreational Housing must be made directly with each facility. ACRC does not make these reservations. Please see individual listings in this book for details concerning eligibility and reservations.

Navy Temporary Lodging Facilities

The Navy operates Bachelor Housing (BH) and Navy Lodges as Temporary Lodging Facilities (TLF). Bachelor Housing facilities are operated for both permanent party (PP) and TDY/TAD personnel. The Navy Lodge program is administered by the Navy Exchange Service and provides Temporary Lodging Facilities for a wide category of personnel (See below).

OPNAV Instruction 11103.1B, *Policies and Procedures Governing Bachelor Housing,* dated 20 March 1997, promulgates policy and provides Navy-wide guidance regarding the operation of Navy bachelor housing, including, among other things, the utilization and occupancy of BQ and the related management of this program. The instruction applies to all Navy activities, commands, and installations worldwide which operate bachelor housing. Bachelor Housing includes Bachelor Enlisted Housing, Bachelor Officers' Housing and Distinguished Visitor Housing. The Commander, Navy Facilities Engineering Command (COMNAVFAC ENGCOM) (Code 50) is the Program Manager for all Navy Bachelor Housing.

The policy outlined in the above instruction applies to the following quarters:

1-Bachelor Enlisted Quarters (BEQ). 2-Bachelor Officers' Quarters (BOQ). 3-Bachelor Civilian Quarters (BCQ). 4-Recruit Training Quarters (RTQ). 5-Reserve Component Quarters (RCQ). 6-Quarters for duty personnel. 7-Discipline and legal hold quarters. 8-Medical holding units. 9-Ashore Quarters for Afloat Staffs. 10-United States Marine Corps Barracks. 11-Leased or Contract Quarters. 12-Temporary Lodging Facilities (TLF). 13-Transient Visiting Officers Quarters (TVOQ). 14-Transient Personnel Unit Quarters (TPU).

Eligibility to Reside in Transient Spaces

OPNAV Instruction 11103.1B dated 20 March 1997 states that the following personnel are authorized to reside in transient spaces:

A. Active Duty Military

(1) On temporary duty (TDY) orders to the host command/installation will be berthed (billeted) on a transient space-required basis

(2) On PCS orders to the host or tenant activities supported by a host/tenant agreement, when permanent housing is not immediately available, will be berthed (billeted) on a transient protected status basis for up to 30 days.

(3) On deployed units and eligible for per diem (e.g., patrol squadrons, construction battalion units (CBU, etc.), and supported by a host/tenant agreement, will be berthed (billeted) on a space-required basis.

(4) All crews of ships, including GBs, are berthed (billeted) on a transient space-required basis when the ship is declared uninhabitable.

(5) Midshipman and officer candidates in training, will be berthed (billeted)on a transient space-required basis. Midshipmen and officer candidates on leave or liberty will be berthed (billeted)on a space-available basis.

(6) Air Mobility Command (AMC) aircrews at activities traversed by AMC aircraft during regularly scheduled missions, will be berthed (billeted) on a transient space-required basis, in accordance with a Navy-AMC agreement.

(7) Activities which, by agreement, provide support to AMC aircrews on an "as needed" basis will be berthed (billeted) on a transient space-required basis.

(8) Active duty military on leave or liberty will be berthed (billeted) on a space-available basis.

B. Reserve Personnel

(1) Categories of Reserve Duty

(a) Inactive Duty Training (IDT) - involves the duty of reservists at a training site, who are not under separate temporary duty orders, and who live outside of a 50-mile radius of the training site. These are mostly weekend reservists who reside beyond a reasonable commuting distance (50 miles) of their training site. IDI personnel when on an advanced reservation list, will be housed transient space-required; otherwise, space-available.

(b) Inactive Duty Training Travel (IDTT) - involves temporary duty at a training site other than the normal drill site with directed travel under funded orders. IDTT personnel, when on advanced reservations list will be housed transient space-required; otherwise, space-available.

(c) Active Duty for Training (ADT) - usually a two-week period of active duty under orders. Members on ADT orders will be berthed (billeted) on a transient space-required basis.

(d) Annual Training (AT) - normally a two-week training period under funded orders. Members on AT will be berthed (billeted) on a transient space-required basis.

(2) Reservists residing within a 50-mile radius of the installation will be berthed (billeted) on a space-available basis.

(3) Reservists not under orders, paid retirees and gray area retirees may occupy Transient Facilities on a space-available basis.

C. Other Government Agencies

U.S. Coast Guard personnel, civilian employees of the U.S. Public Health Service, and the National Oceanic and Atmospheric Administration will be berthed (billeted) on a space-available basis if supported by a host/tenant agreement.

D. Family Members (Dependents)

(1) When the sponsor is under PCS orders and when the Navy Lodge or permanent housing (i.e., military family housing or civilian housing) are not immediately available, dependent family members may be berthed (billeted) on a transient protected-status basis for no more than 10 days if appropriate Bachelor Housing space is available (private room with private bath). They will be berthed (billeted) on a space-available basis thereafter.

(2) When the sponsor is on medical temporary duty, family members may be berthed (billeted) on a transient-protected basis, provided appropriate Bachelor Housing space is available (private room with private bath).

E. Civilians

(1) Space Required. The following civilian personnel will be berthed (billeted) on a space-required basis when on temporary duty orders to an installation:

(a) DoD civilian employees (Time limits apply.)
(b) Non-appropriated fund personnel
(c) Red Cross workers
(d) USO professional and staff personnel
(e) Navy-Marine Corps Relief Society Personnel
(f) Contractors, when lodging expenses are paid by the Navy
(g) Non-DoD civilian employees, not noted above, who contribute to naval mission accomplishment, with the approval from the host command's major claimant

(2) Space Available. The following civilian personnel will be berthed on a space-available basis:

(a) Navy Wives Club officers on official business
(b) Navy command ombudsman on invitational travel orders
(c) Navy-sponsored youth groups (as defined by the Navy Recruiting Command)
(d) Law enforcement officials on official business

F. Retired Personnel

Retirees, with or without family members, will be berthed (billeted) on a space-available basis. Appropriate Bachelor Housing facilities (private room with private bath) must be available to accommodate retirees with family members.

G. Foreign Military Personnel

Foreign military members in the Personnel Exchange Program (PEP), International Military Education Exchange (IMET) Program, or Foreign Military Training (FMT) program, or when on official orders will be berthed (billeted) at the same criteria as their U.S. military counterparts. When on leave or liberty, members of the PEP, MET, or FMT will be berthed (billeted) on a space-available basis.

H. Medal of Honor Recipients

Medal of Honor Recipients may be housed in Distinguished Visiting Officer Housing at the discretion of the host commander, unless prohibited by international agreement.

Policy on Priority of Assignment to Bachelor Housing

The following is the priority list for assignment to Bachelor Housing:
(1) Military necessity
(2) Recruits
(3) "A" School students
(4) Transients
(5) E1-E6 Rotations
(6) E1-E4 Permanent Party
(7) E5-E6 Permanent Party
(8) E7-E9 Permanent Party
(9) Space-Available Geographic Bachelors
(10) Officers Permanent Party.
(11) Space-Available Transients
(a) Active duty military
(b) Reservists
(c) Retirees

Navy Lodges

Navy Lodge Mission. The Navy Lodge mission is to provide reasonably priced quality lodging facilities to authorized guests.

Categories of Personnel Eligible to Make Reservations
Reservations may be made in advance as follows:

Category	Advance Reservations
Active Duty PCS with family	Anytime
Active Duty on TDY/TAD orders	Anytime
Active Duty on leave, Rest and Recreation (R&R), Widow/ers and dependents of Active Duty Military Personnel	60 days
Reservists	60 days
Retirees, Widows/Widowers/Dependents of Retired Military Personnel, Retired Reservists	30 days
Foreign Military	30 days
DoD and DN Civilians (on orders), DoD and DN (not on orders, but with Navy Exchange Privileges), U.S. Public Health Service (USPHS) (on orders), American Red Cross (on orders)	30 days
Medical inpatients and family of seriously ill	Anytime
Medical outpatients	60 days
Employees, active and retired, of Exchange systems	30 days

Note: Official guests and visitors of the command may stay at Navy Lodges, but must be checked in by their sponsors. Family members and guests of military personnel may stay at Navy Lodges provided the military members is present at check-in.

Reservations

Please see Central Reservations System on page viii at the front of the book. Call 1-800-NAVY INN (1-800-628-9466) to make a reservation, or you may call the lodge directly at the numbers found in each Navy Lodge listing in this book. As of press time, overseas Navy Lodges must be called directly except for Keflavik, Iceland and Rota, Spain. Reservations are held until 1800 hours at most Navy Lodges. You may guarantee your reservation for late arrival with either a major credit card or an advance cash deposit (one night's lodging) sent directly to the lodge. You will be given a confirmation number at the time the reservation is made. The reservations clerk also will inform you that unless you call and cancel your reservation prior to 1800 hours (the time zone where the Navy Lodge is located) you will be charged for one night's lodging. Call 1-800-NAVY-INN (1-800-628-9466) prior to the day of arrival or call the Lodge directly on the day of arrival prior to the local check-in time (1800 hours Lodge local time) to cancel your reservation.

Credit Cards: Navy Lodges accept Visa, MasterCard, American Express, and Diner's Club credit cards.

Check-in Time: Check-in time at most Lodges is between 1500-1800 hours. Please call 1-800 NAVY INN (1-800-628-9466)for more information. Early arrivals will be accommodated according to room availability.

Check-out Time: Check-out time at all Navy Lodges is 1200 noon.

Is My Pet Allowed? Unfortunately for pet owners, pets are not allowed in the Navy Lodges. Please ask for local kennel information at the time of your reservation.

Navy Lodge Renovations: In an effort to provide Navy Lodge guests with comfortable accommodations, the Navy Lodge system renovates all Navy Lodge guest rooms on a continuing schedule. Each guest room is scheduled for renovations on a five-year cycle.

MWR Recreational Housing

Call the individual facility to determine reservations policy and eligibility.

Marine Corps Housing Management

The following has been extracted from MCO P11000.22, Marine Corps Housing Management Manual, dated 14 February 1991, with change 1 dated 10 February 1992 and change 2 dated 1 June 1992.

Transient Quarters Management

Transient quarters are operated primarily to provide a service to duty transient personnel and TAD students. Adequate quarters shall be set aside to accommodate TAD transient personnel. When designated transient quarters are fully occupied, transients may voluntarily occupy permanent party quarters.

1. The following personnel are entitled to designated TAD transient quarters on a confirmed reservation basis:

(a) Military personnel and DoD civilians on TAD orders.

(b) American Red Cross and Navy Relief Society on official business

(c) U.S. and Foreign civilians traveling as guest of Armed Forces

(d) Reserve personnel in TAD status, unit training status, and annual trainees on individual orders

(e) TAD foreign nationals or foreign military trainees engaged in or sponsored by military assistance or similar training programs unless prohibited by a Status of Forces Agreement (SOFA)

(f) Family members on medical TAD orders

(g) Military personnel with or without family members, arriving or departing for overseas installations on PCS when TLF or permanent housing is not immediately available

(h) Official guests of the activity commander

2. The following personnel may occupy designated transient quarters on a space-available basis:

(a) Retirees, military personnel on leave, family members, or guests of military personnel assigned to the activity if TLF space is not available

(b) DoD civilian employees and their families arriving or departing incident to PCS when TLFs are not available

(c) Guests of the activity commander

Non-duty transients shall be advised at the time of registration that occupancy is strictly on a day-to-day, space-available basis and that they must vacate not later than the following day if the quarters are required for duty transients.

Distinguished Guest Quarters (DGQ) are also available to accommodate the frequent travel of high ranking officials, both civilian and military. DGQs are under the control of the installation commander.

In the case of Marine Corps Inns and recreational housing operated by MCCS (MWR), call the individual facility to determine eligibility (similar to other USMC TML facilities) and reservations policy. Also see the listing for the facility in this book.

Coast Guard Temporary Guest Housing Facility Policies

The following information has been derived from Commandant Publication P1710.15 dated May 21 1999 (updated December 15, 1999), Coast Guard Recreation Areas and Temporary Guest Housing Facilities Guide.

Many large Coast Guard installations have developed guest housing (GH) in response to the need for temporary lodging for Coast Guard active duty members and their families. In addition, some Coast Guard installations operate outdoor recreation areas with recreational housing to respond to the increased interest in outdoor recreational activities as part of their Morale, Well-Being and Recreation (MWR) program. These facilities are under the auspices of the Coast Guard Exchange System (CGES) through the Coast Guard Morale, Well-Being and Recreation (MWR) Program. Since each Coast Guard installation manages its own GH and/or recreational housing, each installation has its own rules and regulations regarding usage.

Guest housing was developed mainly for use by active duty Coast Guard members and their families traveling under PCS orders; however, Coast Guard personnel in other than PCS status and members of the other uniformed services, including retirees, are allowed to use some Coast Guard guest housing facilities on a space-available basis. COMDT INST M1710.13, *Coast Guard Morale, Well-Being and Recreation (MWR) Manual,* dated 6 September 2000 states that recreational lodging and temporary lodging facilities are classified as MWR Category C activities. **Chapter 3 of the manual lists the following persons as having "unlimited patronage for all MWR programs."** (These authorizations do not apply to military exchanges, facilities, and programs operated principally by the Coast Guard Exchange System (CGES.)

1. All active duty Coast Guard personnel and their dependents

2. All members of the other U.S. Armed Forces and their dependents

3. Members of the ready reserve, reserves in training, members of the National Guard, and their dependents

4. Military Cadets of Service academies and their families

5. Commissioned Corps of the U.S. Public Health Service (USPHS)and their dependents

6. Commissioned Corps of the National Oceanic and Atmospheric Administration (NOAA) on active duty

7. Armed Forces retirees from Active Duty and their dependents

8. Armed Forces retirees from reserves with/or without pay and their dependents

9. Honorably discharged veterans with 100 percent service-connected disability and their dependents

10. Medal of Honor recipients and their dependents

11. Un-remarried surviving spouses and their dependents (with military ID cards) of military personnel who died while on active duty or while in retired status

12. Un-remarried former spouses who were married to a military member for at least 20 years while the military member was on active duty in the armed forces, and their dependents

13. Orphans of a military member, when not adopted by new parents, under 21 years old (or over if they are incapable of supporting themselves, or 23 years old if they are in full time study)

14. Department of Transportation (DoT) civilian employees

In that each Coast Guard facility commander manages recreational housing and temporary lodging assigned to that facility, it is always advisable to call the facility you wish to visit to determine your eligibility and the facility's reservation policy. Remember, the United States Coast Guard is a Department of Transportation organization, not Department of Defense. Much of this essential information is included in each Coast Guard listing in this book.

Air Force Lodging Program

Policy Guidance

Air Force Instruction 34-246, Air Force Lodging Program, dated 1 May 1999, provides general lodging operating information, management requirements, and specific performance standards. It also provides standard operating procedures, where appropriate, to ensure consistent services to lodging guests Air Force-wide. Air Force Directive 34-6, Air Force Lodging, dated 22 July 1993 provides additional broad policy guidance on Air Force lodging facilities which generally include Visiting Officer Quarters (VOQ), Visiting Airmen Quarters (VAQ) and Temporary Lodging Facilities (TLF).

Air Force Lodging Facilities

Air Force lodging includes the following:

(a) Visiting Quarters (VQ) which include Visiting Officer Quarters (VOQ) and Visiting Airmen Quarters (VAQ)

(b) Distinguished Visitor Quarters (DVQ). Installation commanders may designate DV lodging, both officer and enlisted, within the VQ. Individual base commanders develop local operating instruction governing the management of DVQ reservations. If the Protocol Officer manages DVQ reservations, unused rooms should be released to the Lodging office for use by other travelers by 1600 each day to maximize the use of base lodging.

(c) Temporary Lodging Facilities (TLF)

Eligibility to Use Air Force Lodging Visiting Quarters (VAQ, VOQ, DVQ):

Priority 1: (Not listed in priority sequence)

(a) Military or DoD civilian TDY to the installation

(b) Military on permissive TDY

(c) Active duty military on emergency leave

(d) Aircraft passenger (including family members) on official orders or emergency leave at actual ports of embarkation

(e) Family member on medical TDY orders

(f) Military or civilian using military aircraft in TDY or PCS status who, for reasons beyond his or her control, remains oversight (RON) at a location other than TDY or PCS location

(g) Contract personnel traveling on official government orders TDY to the installation

(h) Guest of the installation, as determined by the installation commander

(i) Unaccompanied military entitled to permanent quarters, but temporarily without permanent housing due to PCS

(j) Unaccompanied civilian (OCONUS only) entitled to permanent quarters, but temporarily without permanent housing due to PCS

(k) Military and civilian personnel and family members, or family member alone, when in a PCS status (Civilians and/or their family members are Priority 1 when in PCS status overseas. In CONUS they are Priority 2 for government lodging.)

(l) Individual Mobilization Augmentee (IMA) members on annual tours, school tours, special tours of active duty, or inactive duty training, in a per diem or non-per diem status.

(m) Unit-assigned Reserve personnel on annual tours, school tours, special tours of active duty, in a per diem or non-per diem status

(n) Unit-assigned Reserve personnel in an inactive duty for training (DT) status away from unit of assignment

(o) Unit-assigned Reserve personnel on an inactive duty for training (IDT) status at unit of assignment

(p) National Guard personnel on annual tours, school tours, special tours of active duty, in a per diem status

(q) Guard personnel in an inactive duty for training (IDT) status

(r) Military Academy and Reserve Officer Training Corps (ROTC) cadet traveling on official orders

(s) Applicant for an Air Force commission under Air Force Instruction 36-2001, *Officer Training Program Examining Centers (OPTEC),* dated 14 September 1998

(t) TDY foreign military or civilian sponsored through U.S. security assistance programs

(u) Individuals or groups housed for humanitarian reasons, such as natural disasters or adverse weather conditions, when no private or commercial lodging is available and approved by the installation commander

Priority 2:

(a) Military and civilian personnel TDY to a nearby location who desire on-base quarters

(b) Family member accompanying official TDY personnel

(c) Friends/relatives of an active duty patient in a DoD medical facility (or when referred to a civilian medical facility by DoD medical authorities when TLF are not available

(d) Relative or guest of military member assigned to the installation

(e) Military retiree (to include Guard and Reserve) and their accompanying family members

(f) Active duty member and/or his/her family member on leave or PCS en route

(g) Senior Executive Service (SES) and their dependents on leave

(h) U.S. civilian and his/her family members on environmental and morale leave (EML) orders from overseas duty assignment, only if TLFs are not immediately available

(i) Guard and Reserve personnel (in non-duty status possessing valid ID card) and his/her family members

(j) Space-Available passengers aboard military aircraft delayed short of destination, or passengers arriving at ports for Space-Available travel on departing military flights

(k) ROTC cadets, Civil Air Patrol organizations, and youth groups, when approved by the installation commander

(l) Family member (18 years or older, with valid ID card) of deceased military member

(m) Family member (18 years or older, with valid ID card) unaccompanied by their active duty or retired military sponsor

(n) Transient family members (18 years or older, with valid ID card) of DoD Command-sponsored civilian overseas

(o) Nonmilitary uniformed personnel of the U.S. Public Health Service (USPHS), National Oceanic and Atmospheric Administration (NOAA), U.S. Coast Guard, and foreign military personnel when authorized by the installation commander

(p) Persons separated under the "Transition Assistance Management Program (TAMP)

Eligibility to Use Temporary Lodging Facility (TLF):

Priority 1:

(a) Active Duty military or Active Duty Guard Reserve with one or more family members on PCS orders, in or out (Does not apply to en route locations.)

(b) Displaced military family housing occupant (due to emergency conditions)

(c) Active duty military or Active Guard Reserve member on permissive TDY or on leave to house hunt in connection with PCS, retirement, or separation

(d) Friends and relatives of an active duty patient in a DoD medical facility (or in a civilian medical facility when referred there by DoD medical authorities)

(e) Outpatient of a civilian or military hospital if referred by an Air Force hospital

(f) Guests of the installation as determined by the installation commander

(g) PCS DoD civilian personnel with family members or family members alone (18 years or older) outside CONUS, incident to PCS, separation, retirement, when eligible for living quarters allowance (LQA)

(h) Military member TDY (and accompanying family members) enroute to PCS location

Priority 2:

(a) Military member and family members on leave or delayed en route

(b) Military and DoD personnel on TDY when VQ is fully occupied

(c) Retired military member and his/her family members

(d) DoD civilians and family members on leave

(e) Unaccompanied personnel incident to PCS if either VQ or permanent party housing is available

(f) DoD civilians accompanied by family members incident to PCS in the CONUS

(g) Guard and Reserve personnel (in a non-duty status possessing a valid ID card) with his/her family members

(h) Non-military uniformed personnel of the U.S. Public Health Service (UPHS), National Oceanic and Atmospheric Administration (NOAA), foreign military personnel, and U.S. Coast Guard, when authorized by the installation commander

(i) Relative or guest of military member assigned to the installation

Reservations

Air Force Lodging operates a centralized reservations system utilizing a toll-free number, 1-888-AF LODGE (1-888-235-6343), to assist both official duty travelers and Space-A guests. (Note: If you are traveling with children, please inform the clerk when making reservations, so that the best arrangements may be made. There may be some restrictions on staying in a BOQ if you have a small child, and you may be better served in a TLF.) Please see a detailed description of the Air Force Central Reservations System at the beginning of this book.

Visiting Quarters (VQ) Reservations

Air Force Lodging accepts reservations for Priority 1 travelers 24 hours a day, 7 days a week on a first-come, first-served basis without regard to rank or listing within Priority 1.

TLF Reservations

Reservation requests must include expected date and time of arrival. PCS status guests must present PCS orders or the special order number, date and issuing headquarters before or at the time of registration. Personnel visiting hospital patients must give the patient's name with the reservation request. Personnel traveling for the purpose of house hunting must show a copy of the leave authorization verifying permissive TDY status, or a copy of PCS, retirement or separation orders; or the special order number, date and issuing headquarters, either before or at the time of registration.

If Priority 1 guests occupy all TLFs, and other Priority 1 personnel desire TLFs, the lodging manager keeps the requests on a standby basis for a reasonable time, pending cancellation of reservations or early departure of guests. Lodging fills vacancies from these Standby Priority 1 reservations on a first-come, first-served basis, before assigning personnel from Priority 2. The maximum stay in a TLF by Priority 1 personnel normally is 30 days; however, this may be adjusted/reduced by the Lodging Manager depending on circumstances. Requests for extension beyond 30 days must be approved by the installation commander.

Guaranteed and Non-Guaranteed Reservations

If a guest makes a reservation with a valid credit card, or provides prepayment with cash or check for the first night's stay, the reservation is considered "guaranteed" and a room must be saved for that guest. If the guest does not arrive by 0500 hours the following day, or has not been heard from, the reservation is to be cancelled and the room is to be made available to other guests. "Non-guaranteed" reservations are to be held

until 1800 hours; if the guest does not arrive by 1800 hours and has not informed lodging that he/she will be arriving later, the reservation may be cancelled and the room made available to other guests.

Space-Available Reservations

Lodging will accept and confirm reservations for Priority 2 (space-available) guests up to 24 hours in advance of their arrival date, for up to three nights, space permitting. Priority 1 customers will not "bump" Priority 2 customers with confirmed reservations, nor will they bump them once they have been assigned quarters for a specific period of time. (Installation commanders may establish a policy limiting the number of days a Space-A guest can stay in on-base lodging to no more that 30 days a year.) Space-A guests requesting lodging should be assigned to uncommitted (not occupied reserved) lodging rooms upon arrival. Space-A guests must not be placed on a waiting list unless all rooms are occupied or specifically reserved. If all rooms are committed, lodging may establish a waiting list (first-come, first-served) until 1800 hours. After 1800 hours, lodging assigns all vacant rooms resulting from no-shows of Priority 1 and 2 personnel with non-guaranteed hold reservations to remaining Space-A guests on a first-come, first-served basis.

Reservation No-Shows

If a guest with an on-base "guaranteed" reservation fails to show by 0500 hours (the day following the scheduled arrival date) without cancelling the reservation, lodging may charge a one-night service charge. Lodging will inform guests of the cancellation policy when the reservation is made.

Recreational Housing

Reservations for Air Force recreational housing cannot be made through the Central Reservation System or through base lodging offices. Please refer to the individual listings in this book and contact the recreational housing facility directly to make reservations and to clarify your eligibility.

Armed Forces Recreation Centers (AFRC)

Expanded patronage policy in DoD Instruction 1015.10 allows currently employed and retired DoD civilians (both appropriated and non-appropriated fund) patronage of the AFRCs where not prohibited by Status of Forces Agreements (SOFAs). As a result of this expanded patronage policy, currently employed and retired DoD civilians can utilize prime resort AFRCs in Orlando, FL (Shades of Green); Honolulu, HI (Hale Koa Hotel); and Seoul, Korea (Dragon Hill Lodge). The SOFA precludes DoD civilian patronage at AFRC-Europe (Garmisch and Chiemsee, Germany) unless the DoD civilian employee is stationed outside the United States.

Reserve Component personnel use of AFRC lodging facilities is not authorized unless provided for in the Status of Forces Treaty for the country. Examples are the AFRCs in Germany and the New Sanno U.S. Forces Center in Japan which are not authorized. Reserve Component personnel **are** authorized to utilize AFRC lodging in CONUS, Hawaii and Korea. Please see the more complete patronage list in each AFRC listing in this book.

Please check the individual listings in this book and call the individual facility you would like to use to find out what restrictions currently are in effect and to verify your eligibility.

More Safety • Save Money
Enjoy Military Camaraderie

Travel on less per day . . . the military way!
Your military ID card is your passport to savings and safety.

APPENDIX D

TELEPHONE INFORMATION

A Few Words About Telephone Systems in Germany

Each of the commercial/civilian telephone numbers at the top of all listings in Germany follow the same pattern. When dialing from the USA, the first set of digits is the international access, 011, the second set of digits is the country code (49 in Germany), and the third set of digits is the city code (631 - Kaiserslautern). The fourth set of digits is the local area civilian prefix. The next set of digits is the civilian-to-military conversion code. The last set of digits is the line number/extension (or a set of Xs indicating line number/extension). Telephone calls originating on civilian instruments and terminating on military instruments require the conversion code. Telephone calls originating and terminating on civilian instruments do not require the conversion code. Commercial-to-commercial or commercial-to-military telephone calls originating and terminating in the same local area do not generally require the use of the civilian prefix. Also, local area civilian prefixes all begin with a "0." The "0" is only used in-country. Drop the "0" if dialing from outside the country except for Italy where the zero is retained.

CIVILIAN EMERGENCY NUMBERS
(Limited to Countries having Temporary Military Lodging)
(From Civilian Phone)

COUNTRY	FIRE	MEDICAL	POLICE
Australia	000	000	000
Belgium	100	100	101
Canada	911	911	911
France	18	15	17
Germany	112	110	110
Honduras	0	0	0
Iceland	112	112	112
Italy	115	118	112
Japan	119	119	110
Korea	119	119	112
Netherlands	112	112	112
Portugal (Azores)	112/115112/115	112/115	
Singapore	995	995	999
Spain	080	061	091
Turkey	110	112	155
United Kingdom	112/999112/999	112/999	

WORLDWIDE AREA VOICE CODES FOR THE DEFENSE SWITCHED NETWORK (DSN) TELEPHONE SYSTEM

ALASKA - 317
CANADA-312
CARIBBEAN - 313
CONTINENTAL UNITED STATES
(CONUS) -312
EUROPE - 314
PACIFIC - 315
SOUTHWEST ASIA-318

NOTE: The United States Army, Europe Telephone Directories list "Civilian to Military prefixes," "Telephone Exchange DSN prefixes" and "Numerical Military Dial prefixes" all of which are too numerous to list here!

NOTE: * The Direct Distance Dial (DDD) system (also known as the Military system) has been replaced with the Defense Switched Network.

STANDARD EMERGENCY & SERVICE NUMBERS FROM ALL DEFENSE SWITCHED NETWORK EUROPE TELEPHONE (DSN)

DSN EMERGENCY NUMBER
Ambulance/Hospital/Clinic-116
Engineer-115
Fire-117
Military Police-114

MILITARY SERVICE NUMBER
Operator-0 or 1110
CONUS DSN-312
Booking-112
Information-113
Civilian Access-133
AFN-TV Trouble-113
Telephone Repair-119

APPENDIX E

Support Authorized United States Uniformed Services Personnel and Their Dependent Family Members Visiting Foreign Countries

INTRODUCTION: Almost every day at Military Living Publications, concerned military travelers ask the generic question: **What support facilities and/or services am I entitled to while traveling on leave/vacation in foreign countries?**

First, we determine if the country in question has United States military forces and accompanying support facilities and services.

Second is the task of determining the scope of U.S. military administrative and logistical support; health and welfare service; and rest and recreational facilities and services that are available in the country. There are wide ranges of support in and between countries, depending upon the requirements of the forces stationed in each country.

Third, and most importantly, is the task of determining, under the Status of Forces Agreement (SOFA) or other bilateral agreement between the United States and the foreign country, the support that is authorized to visiting/leave status Uniformed Services Personnel and their dependent family members.

CATEGORIES OF PERSONNEL: Most SOFA and other bilateral agreements group Uniformed Services Personnel in a leave/vacation status into the following three major categories:

1. Active Duty Uniformed Services personnel and their dependent family members who are visiting a country in a leave, or pass status.

2. Retired Uniformed Services personnel and their dependent family members who are visiting a country in an individual vacation status.

3. Active Status Reserve Component personnel and their dependent family members who are visiting a country in an individual vacation status. (Note: Most foreign countries treat this category as ordinary foreign visitors (tourist) who are not entitled to any benefits.)

We have limited our study to Uniformed Services personnel in a visiting status and not personnel who are in the process of Permanent Change of Station (PCS) assignment to or Temporary Duty/Temporary Detached Duty (TDY/TAD) in a foreign country. The support of forces assigned in each foreign country is outlined separately in a SOFA or other bilateral agreements.

CATEGORIES OF SUPPORT: The scope of support facilities and services range from very spartan at small installations, with limited U.S. Military forces, such as the Joint United States Military Assistance Group Thailand (JUSMAGTHAI), Bangkok, Thailand to very extensive support at installations with large numbers of U.S. Military personnel, such as Ramstein Air Base, Germany. The availability of support facilities and services is dependent upon the needs of the United States forces stationed in the country and the terms of the SOFA or other bilateral agreements.

We have grouped support facilities and services in the following four major groups:

1. Administrative Support
2. Logistical Support
3. Health and Welfare
4. Rest and Recreation

For each country listed in this book, we have detailed the support authorized by category of Uniformed Services personnel and their dependent family members, i.e. Active Duty, Retirees, and Active Status Reserve Component personnel. The items of support may be different for each foreign country based on both the availability of services and the terms of the agreements.

FOREIGN COUNTRY COVERAGE: We have selected the foreign countries to be covered in this book based on three key elements:

1. Countries where United States Military Combat, Combat Support, Combat Service Support and other U.S. units are permanently stationed.

2. Countries where a United States-Foreign Country Status of Forces Agreement (SOFA) or other bilateral agreement is in force.

3. Countries where there are United States military installations, facilities and services to which access has been granted to Uniformed Services personnel and their dependent families while visiting in a leave/vacation status.

RETIREE USE OF COMMISSARIES AND EXCHANGES: A recent Retiree Demographic Survey in Europe questioned the limitations of Retirees' use of commissaries and exchanges. The Retirees stated that they had earned a lifelong right to shop in commissaries and exchanges anywhere in the world. The answer, unfortunately, is that the NATO SOFA and other bilateral supplementary agreements between the United States and each host foreign country dictate the use of commissaries and exchanges by Retirees.

Another key element is that although Retirees are part of the "Total Force" from a United States government point of view, they are not part of "The Force" from a SOFA point of view. The SOFA makes the United States responsible for ensuring that duty free goods are distributed only to "The Forces." The access to commissaries and exchanges by Retirees varies from country to country because of bilateral supplementary agreements between the United States and host countries.

In the light of recent troop withdrawals and draw down of forces in foreign countries, it is not a good time, in the view of officials, to attempt to renegotiate the NATO SOFA. The U.S. Army Europè (USAREUR) Retirees Council concluded that Retirees should use currently authorized privileges discreetly, observing the restrictions and respecting the procedures.

AUSTRALIA

Active Duty personnel and their dependent family members are entitled to use all of the very limited U.S. military support services in Australia as follows: Space-A air, personnel administrative support (American Embassy only), and ambulance service.

Retirees and their dependent family members are entitled to use the same services and facilities as Active Duty personnel.

Active Status Reserve Component personnel are considered by the Australian government to be tourists but are entitled to use personnel administrative support and ambulance service.

BAHRAIN

Active Duty personnel and their dependent family members are entitled to use all U.S. military logistical support facilities and services in Bahrain.

Retirees and their dependent family members are entitled to use all U.S. military logistical support facilities except Package Stores (Class VI), finance (military) and medical services which are on a Space-A basis.

Active Status Reserve Component personnel and their dependent family members are considered by the government of Bahrain to be tourists but are entitled to: credit union, dry cleaning/laundry, ship store, telephone (C and DSN), and MWR facilities.

BELGIUM

Active Duty personnel and their dependent family members, assigned in other NATO countries, visiting Belgium are entitled to use all U.S. military facilities. Active Duty members, not assigned in NATO countries, are entitled to use all of the facilities and services except items which have restricted distribution (rationed) such as tobacco, coffee, tea, and hard alcohol.

Retirees and their dependent family members, as a result of the SOFA in Belgium, are not entitled to use any retail facilities or services such as commissary and exchange. Retirees may use clubs, messes, Space-A air, lodging (TML), and MWR facilities. Lastly, Retirees are entitled to use legal and medical services on a Space-A basis.

Active Status Reserve Component personnel are considered under the SOFA to be tourists and are not entitled to U.S. military support, except MWR facilities, on a Space-A basis.

CUBA

All of the facilities and services of the Guantanamo Naval Station are available to Active Duty, Retired, and Reservist personnel and their dependent family members, who with the Commander's permission are allowed to visit the installation. No one may enter Cuba from the military installation (Guantanamo Naval Station).

DENMARK (GREENLAND)

All of the facilities and services of the Thule Air Base are available to Active Duty personnel who are allowed to visit the installation.

Retired personnel, if they are allowed to visit the installation, may use lodging (TML), mess and medical (on a Space-A basis).

Reservists are not allowed to visit the installation except when on Active Duty for training, and in that status will be treated as Active Duty. Dependent family members of all categories of personnel are not allowed to visit the installation (except as the result of an aircraft emergency stop).

DIEGO GARCIA ATOLL (UK)

All of the U.S. military facilities and services located on the Diego Garcia Atoll are available to all Active Duty and Contractor personnel who are assigned permanently or on temporary duty to Diego Garcia. Advance clearance must be obtained. No other visitors to Diego Garcia are allowed at this time. Dependent and other family members are not allowed to visit. Space-A air passengers who are not permanently assigned or on TDY/TAD to Diego Garcia are not allowed to transit Diego Garcia. Only permanently assigned or temporary duty passengers may debark or embark aircraft at Diego Garcia. This travel restriction is contained in the DoD Foreign Clearance Guides and a SECDEF message.

GERMANY

Active Duty personnel and their families residing in Germany are entitled to use all U.S. military facilities and bases in Germany. Active Duty personnel and their families who are assigned to the USEUCOM area (NATO) outside of Germany are entitled to use all U.S. military facilities and benefits in Germany except retail (non-concession) exchanges and commissaries. Active Duty personnel and their dependent family members stationed outside of USEUCOM who are visiting Germany are considered by the German government (under the joint SOFA agreement) as tourists. The use of medical, dental, Space-A air, and MWR facilities such as TML, AFRC, gyms, legal and medical services are authorized on a Space-A basis.

Retiree personnel, their dependent family members and survivors of deceased retirees, who are visiting for a period of less than 30 days, are considered by the German government as tourists and therefore are not authorized logistical support from U.S. military facilities under the SOFA. Space-A air, Morale, Welfare and Recreation (MWR) facilities (libraries, recreation centers, including AFRC-E, TML, campgrounds, etc.) are authorized for use by those classified as tourists.

Retired personnel, their family members and survivors of deceased retirees who reside in Germany for 30 days or more, may be granted resident alien status and can be authorized access to commissary, exchange and Class VI facilities, provided they have registered with the nearest 42nd Military Police Group (Customs) and local German customs authorities to obtain a German Customs Certificate. All purchases are subject to a monthly payment of a 20 percent tax (rate subject to change) levied by German customs. Purchase of rationed items (coffee, tea, hard liquor, tobacco products and petroleum) is not authorized.

The use of Space-A air and other installation facilities, such as fitness centers, clubs, post theaters, is subject to availability. Use of medical and dental facilities by retirees in Germany is on a Space-A basis only.

Active Status Reserve Component personnel and their dependent family members who are visiting Germany are considered under the SOFA to be tourist and not entitled to support. They are entitled to use MWR facilities on a Space-A basis.

GREECE

Active Duty personnel and their dependent family members are entitled to use all U.S. military logistical support facilities and services in Greece.

Limited logistical support privileges are extended to retired U.S. military personnel, 100 percent disabled veterans and their family members who are living in Greece. By the phrase living in Greece we mean someone who is an ordinarily resident. Tourists or persons staying only a few months or less DO NOT qualify for this support. Medical care is on a Space-A basis.

Active Status Reserve Component personnel and their dependent family members are considered under the SOFA to be tourists and therefore are not entitled to logistical support.

HONDURAS

We know of no United States-Honduras bilateral agreement(s) which detail the support authorized to each category of U.S. Uniformed Services personnel in Honduras. Therefore, the U.S. military facilities and services at Soto Cano Air Base, HN can be used by all U.S. Uniformed Services personnel and their dependent family members, subject to approval of the U.S. base commander.

There are Honduran legal provisions which grant generous tax and related benefits to Retirees who are permanent residents of Honduras.

HONG KONG

We do not have any United States forces permanently and regularly stationed in Hong Kong and therefore there is not a SOFA or other stationing agreement. The limited U.S. military facilities located at Fenwick Pier and the Mariners' Club in Hong Kong are available to all categories of U.S. and Allied forces.

ICELAND

Active Duty personnel and their dependent family members are entitled to use all U.S. military logistical support, services and facilities in Iceland. There is a strictly enforced limit on the removal of retail purchased items from the base.

Retirees and their dependent family members may only use Space-A air, TML, MWR facilities and concession retail (i. e., Wendy's).

Active Status Reserve Component Personnel and their family members are considered under the joint SOFA to be tourists and are not entitled to U.S. military support. They may use MWR facilities on a Space-A basis.

ITALY

Active Duty personnel and their dependent family members are entitled to use all U.S. military logistical support, services and facilities in Italy.

Retirees and their dependent family members, like Active Duty, may use all of the logistical support services and facilities in Italy with the following restrictions: May not purchase rationed items, i.e., coffee, tea, hard liquor, tobacco products, petroleum; postal services limited to one pound weight limit on parcel mail; and medical and TML on a Space-A basis.

Active Status Reserve Component personnel and their family members are considered under the SOFA to be tourist. They may use MWR facilities on a Space-A basis.

JAPAN

Active Duty personnel and their dependent family members are entitled to use all U.S. military logistical support, services and facilities in Japan.

Retirees are authorized the use of exchanges, commissaries and beverage sales outlets; medical and dental care, on a Space-A basis; use of local recreational facilities to include messes, clubs, theaters and libraries; purchase of petroleum products at military outlets and billeting (TML) on a Space-A basis. Retirees are not entitled to use military post offices, banking facilities or personal military transportation other than Space-A air. Retirees must have Japanese visas in their passports and clear Japanese customs, regardless of their port of entry into Japan.

Dependent family members of Retirees are not entitled to any U.S. military support under the SOFA. They are entitled to Space-A medical and dental care. They may visit, with their sponsor, military retail outlets but they may not make purchases.

Active Duty Status Reserve Component personnel are considered to be tourists and are not entitled to any U.S. military support. They may use MWR facilities on a Space-A basis.

KOREA

Active Duty personnel and their dependent family members are entitled to all U.S. military logistical support and services. There are certain buying restrictions on high value items, tobacco products, liquor and commissary items. Temporary ration cards may be obtained by visitors from the Ration Control Issuing Agency at each installation.

Retiree personnel and their dependent family members are entitled to the same support as Active Duty personnel indicated above.

Active Status Reserve Component personnel and their dependent family members are classified under the SOFA as tourists and may use only MWR support and facilities on a Space-A basis.

KUWAIT

We know of no United States-Kuwait bilateral agreement(s) which detail the support authorized to each category of U.S. Uniformed Services personnel in Kuwait. Therefore, the very limited U.S. military facilities and services in Kuwait (Kuwait International Airport) can be used by all U.S. Uniformed Services personnel and their dependent family members.

NETHERLANDS

Active Duty personnel and their dependent family members are entitled to all U.S. military logistical support and services in The Netherlands.

Retirees and their dependent family members are allowed on U.S. military installations and may use those facilities which do not involve direct sale of tax-free retail type merchandise, i. e., medical, billeting (TML), and MWR facilities on a Space-A basis. We have been informed that retirees in the Netherlands now can use commissaries and post exchanges in the southeast portion of the country near Maastricht and Brunssum. A customs tax must be paid at the checkout counter on all purchases. The use of the U.S. Post Office (APO) is not authorized.

Active Status Reserve Component personnel and their dependent family members are considered under the SOFA to be tourists and are not entitled to support. They may use MWR facilities on a Space-A basis.

NEW ZEALAND

Active Duty personnel and their dependent family members are entitled to all U.S. military logistical support and services in New Zealand except: exchange, postal services, and medical and dental services.

Retirees and their dependent family members are entitled to the same support as Active Duty personnel.

Active Status Reserve Component personnel are entitled to the same support as Active Duty except Space-A air.

NORWAY

Active Duty personnel and their dependent family members are entitled to all U.S. military logistical support and services in Norway.

Retirees and their dependent family members are not entitled to use U.S. military retail facilities. They may use administrative support, medical and dental support on a Space-A basis.

Active Status Reserve Component personnel and their dependent family members are considered to be tourists and are not entitled to U.S. military support. They may use MWR facilities on a Space-A basis.

PORTUGAL (AZORES)

Active Duty personnel, assigned in the NATO area, and their dependent family members may use all U.S. military logistical support and services in the Azores and mainland Portugal. Active Duty personnel (not assigned in the NATO area) may use all U.S. military support except rationed items, i.e., cofee, tea, tobacco products, hard liquor and petroleum products.

Retirees and their dependent family members are allowed on U.S. military installations and may use those facilities which do not involve direct sale of tax-free retail type merchandise, i. e., medical, billeting (TML), and MWR facilities on a Space-A basis.

Active Status Reserve Component personnel and their dependent family members are considered under the SOFA to be tourists and are not entitled to support. They may use MWR facilities on a Space-A basis.

SAUDI ARABIA

Saudi Arabia does not grant visas to personnel desiring to visit on leave unless they are attending the Hajj or unless they are DoD-sponsored personnel.

SINGAPORE

Active Duty personnel and their dependent family members may use all U.S. military support in Singapore.

Retirees, Active Status Reserve Component personnel and their dependent family members are entitled to use: bank/credit union, dry cleaning/laundry, exchange, finance, Space-A air (Retirees only), telephone access (DSN and C), and lodging (TML).

TURKEY

Active duty personnel and their dependent family members are entitled to use all U.S. military logistical support and services in Turkey.

Retirees and their dependent family members along with Active Status Reserve Component personnel and their dependent family members, who visit Turkey for short periods of time, are considered under the SOFA to be tourists and are not entitled to support. They may however use clubs, MWR facilities, Space-A air (Retirees only), and TML on a Space-A basis.

Retirees and their dependent family members (limited to spouse and children) or widows/widowers who are living in Turkey. By living in Turkey it is meant ordinarily resident. Tourists or persons staying only a few months do not qualify for this limited logistical support. A retiree must demonstrate an intent to stay indefinitely in Turkey (one year minimum). This may be done by signing a lease, purchasing a home, importing household goods, or similar acts. A Retiree can only apply after being in the country for 90 days and there is an annual review and revalidation of the residency status. With this residency status Retirees are granted the same benefits as Active Duty personnel.

UNITED KINGDOM

Active Duty personnel and their dependent family members, stationed in the NATO area, are entitled to all U.S. military logistical support and services in the United Kingdom. Active Duty personnel assigned outside of NATO are entitled to all benefits but are not entitled to purchase rationed items, i. e., coffee, tea, liquor, tobacco and petroleum products.

Retirees and their dependent family members are entitled to use clubs/messes, cafeterias, TML, MWR facilities and Space-A air. Transient Retirees are not authorized commissary, exchange, postal service, and other retail activities. Resident Retirees may be permitted use of the exchange, and commissary only after issue of USAFE Form 174 and purchase of Value Added Tax (VAT) coupons.

Active Status Reserve Component personnel and their families are considered to be tourists under the SOFA and are not entitled to U.S. military support in the United Kingdom. They may use MWR facilities on a Space-A basis.

Installation Index

CENTRAL ORDER COUPON

P.O. Box 2347, Falls Church, VA 22042-0347
TEL: (703) 237-0203 FAX: (703) 237-2233

www.militaryliving.com
E-mail: militaryliving@aol.com

Item #	Publications	ISBN/ISSN	Price		QTY	Extended Amount
1	**R&R Travel News™.** *The worldwide travel newsletter.* 6 issues/year by Standard Business Mail **1 yr/$23.00 2 yrs/$34.00** Save 26%* **3 yrs/$46.00** Save 33%* **5 yrs/$69.00** Save 40%* **PLUS FREE GIFT** *Off 1-yr. Reg. Subscription Rate. With every **5-Year R&R Subscription or Renewal** you will receive a **FREE GIFT** of Military Living's **Military Travel Guide U.S.A!** (a $17.45 Military Living mail order value!) This special offer ends 31 December 2003. Sorry, no substitution on gift.	0740-5073	❑ new ❑ renewal			
6	**Assignment Washington Military Road Atlas.**	0-914862-91-X	$12.45	AW		
15 15A	**COLLECTOR'S ITEM! Desert Shield Commemorative Maps.** (Folded) (2 unfolded wall maps in a hard tube)	0-914862-27-8 0-914862-27-8	$8.75 $19.30	MAP DS		
29	**European U.S. Military Road Atlas, Plus Near East Areas.**	0-914862-73-1	$24.45	ERA		
32	**Military Space-A Air Basic Training.**	0-914862-89-8	$15.95	BT		
33	**Military Space-A Air Opportunities Air Route Map.** (folded) (2 unfolded wall maps in a hard tube)	0-914862-88-X	$13.25 $26.50	MAP SA MAP SA		
36	**Temporary Military Lodging Around the World.**	0-914862-90-1	$19.95	TML		
38 38A 38B	**U.S. Military Installation Road Map.** (Folded) (1 unfolded laminated wall map in a hard tube) (2 unfolded laminated wall maps in a hard tube)	0-9314-24-01-2 0-9314-24-01-2 0-9314-24-01-2	$ 9.25 $20.75 $36.25	MAP US		
39	**Military Travel Guide U.S.A.**	0-931424-00-4	$17.45	TGA		
40	**United States Military Road Atlas.**	1-931424-02-0	$21.75	ATL		
41	**Military RV, Camping & Outdoor Recreation Around the World Including Golf Courses and Marinas.**	1-931424-04-7	$19.55	RVC		
42	**United States Military Road Map Plastic Folded Version**	1-931424-03-9	$12.75	MAP-US-P		
43	**Military Space-A Air Travel Guide**	1-931424-05-5	$23.45	SAB		
	Virginia Addresses add 4.5% sales tax (Books, Maps, & Atlases only)					
				TOTAL $		

Mail order prices are for non- APO/FPO addresses within the U.S. APO/FPO addresses must add $4.00 **per order** for insurance and return receipt. Shipments to Canadian addresses must add an additional $2.50 **per item ordered** for additional postage, shipping, insurance and processing. We do not ship to overseas/international addresses other than U.S. Military Post Offices. Sorry, no billing.   We're as close as your telephone...by using our Telephone Ordering Service. We honor American Express, MasterCard, Visa, and Discover. Call us at **703-237-0203** (Voice Mail after hours); FAX: 703-237-2233 or E-mail: milliving@aol.com and order today! Sorry, no collect calls. Or...fill out and mail the order coupon below. Order by internet on our secure web order. Web address – **www.militaryliving.com**

NAME:_____

STREET:_____

CITY/STATE/ZIP:_____

PHONE:_____ SIGNATURE:_____

Credit Card #_____Card Expiration Date_____

Name/Address as it appears on credit card/credit card statement _____

_____

The above credit card information is necessary for credit card verification and to obtain approval on your card. It will not be used for any other purpose.

Mail check/money order to Military Living Publications, P.O. Box 2347, Falls Church, VA 22042-0347
Save $$$s by purchasing any of our Books, Maps, and Atlases at your military exchange.
Prices are subject to change. **Please check here if we may ship and bill the difference** ❑

revised 3/27/03

This form may be duplicated

ALL ORDERS SHIPPED BY 1ST CLASS/PRIORITY MAIL or UPS